GPU Pro

GPU Pro

Advanced Rendering Techniques

Edited by Wolfgang Engel

A K Peters, Ltd.

Natick, Massachusetts

Editorial, Sales, and Customer Service Office

A K Peters, Ltd.
5 Commonwealth Road, Suite 2C
Natick, MA 01760
www.akpeters.com

Library of Congress Cataloging-in-Publication Data

GPU Pro : advanced rendering techniques / edited by Wolfgang Engel.
  p. cm.
Includes bibliographical references and index.
ISBN 978-1-56881-472-8 (alk. paper)
 1. Computer graphics. 2. Real-time data processing. I. Engel, Wolfgang F.

T385.G6885 2010
006.6–dc22

2009048241

Cover images are from Techland's *Call of Juarez: Bound in Blood*, courtesy of Pawel Rohleder and Maciej Jamrozik.

Printed in India
12 11 10 09 08   10 9 8 7 6 5 4 3 2 1

For my wife, Katja, and my kids, Anna, Emma, and Lena.

Contents

I Mathematics   1

Sam Martin, editor

1 GPU Color Quantization   3

Chi Sing Leung, Tze-Yui Ho, and Yi Xiao

2 Visualize Your Shadow Map Techniques   15

Fan Zhang, Chong Zhao, and Adrian Egli

II   Geometry Manipulation   31
Natalya Tatarchuk, editor

1   As Simple as Possible Tessellation for Interactive Applications   33
Tamy Boubekeur

2   Rule-Based Geometry Synthesis in Real-Time   41
Milán Magdics and Gergely Klár

3   GPU-Based NURBS Geometry Evaluation and Rendering   67
Graham Hemingway

4   Polygonal-Functional Hybrids for Computer Animation and Games   87
D. Kravtsov, O. Fryazinov, V. Adzhiev, A. Pasko, and P. Comninos

III   Rendering Techniques   115
Wessam Bahnassi, editor

4   Virtual Texture Mapping 101   185

Matthäus G. Chajdas, Christian Eisenacher, Marc Stamminger,
and Sylvain Lefebvre

IV   Global Illumination   197

Carsten Dachsbacher, editor

1   Fast, Stencil-Based Multiresolution Splatting for Indirect Illumination   199

Chris Wyman, Greg Nichols, and Jeremy Shopf

2   Screen-Space Directional Occlusion   215

Thorsten Grosch and Tobias Ritschel

Acknowledgments

The GPU Pro: Advanced Rendering Techniques book series covers ready-to-use ideas and procedures that can solve many of your daily graphics-programming challenges. The first book in the series wouldn't have been possible without the help of many people. First of all I would like to thank the section editors for the fantastic job they did. The work of Wessam Bahnassi, Sebastien St. Laurent, Natalya Tatarchuk, Carsten Dachsbacher, Matthias Wloka, Christopher Oat, and Sam Martin ensures that the quality of the series stands up to the expectations of our readers. The great cover screenshots were taken from *Call of Juarez: Bound in Blood.* I would like to thank Techland for allowing us to use those shots. You will also find a postmortem of this game in the book. The team at A K Peters made the whole project happen. I want to thank Alice and Klaus Peters, Charlotte Henderson, and the whole production team, who took the articles and made them into a book. Special thanks go out to our families and friends, who spent many evenings and weekends during the long book production cycle without us. I hope you have as much fun reading the book as we had creating it.

—Wolfgang Engel

P.S. Plans for an upcoming *GPU Pro 2* are already in progress. Any comments, proposals, or suggestions are highly welcome (wolfgang.engel@gmail.com).

Web Materials

Example programs and source code to accompany some of the chapters are available at http://www.akpeters.com/gpupro. The directory structure closely follows the book structure by using the chapter number as the name of the subdirectory. You will need to download the DirectX August 2009 SDK.

General System Requirements

To use all of the files, you will need:

- The DirectX August 2009 SDK

- OpenGL 1.5-compatible graphics card

- A DirectX 9.0 or 10-compatible graphics card

- Windows XP with the latest service pack; some require VISTA or Windows 7

- Visual C++ .NET 2008

- 2048 MB RAM

- The latest graphics card drivers

Updates

Updates of the example programs will be periodically posted.

Comments and Suggestions

Please send any comments or suggestions to wolf@shaderx.com.

Mathematics

In order to drive the limited capabilities of an early GPU, a programmer may have required knowledge of linear algebra, basic lighting and animation techniques, and the occasional Bézier spline. Modern GPUs are significantly more general purpose than their predecessors, yet the mathematical models they are able to run grow increasingly complex. As our techniques become less specialized, we benefit from studying generalized solutions; and it is these techniques that are the focus of the Mathematics section.

In this edition, Chi Sing Leung et al. present a unique approach to quantization in "GPU Color Quantization." They demonstrate how the high quality vector quantization algorithm, self-organizing maps (SOM), can be parallelized and run on a GPU. They show how the unique properties of SOM can provide a significant quality improvement over the more traditional octree algorithm. The quantization technique is very general and can be easily applied to other vector quantization problems.

Fan Zhang et al. explore the delicate nature of aliasing errors in "Visualize Your Shadow Map Techniques." They use a scene-independent model for measuring the all-too-familiar aliasing errors that can be expected from any shadow mapping technique. Their results provide insight into the behavior of several common shadowing techniques, and explain why warping techniques can sometimes produce unexpected results.

—Sam Martin

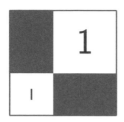

GPU Color Quantization

Chi Sing Leung, Tze-Yui Ho, and Yi Xiao

1.1 Introduction

Color quantization [Verevka 95, Kruger 94, Clark 96] is an example of the more general problem of vector quantization (VQ). It maps 24-bit or high dynamic range colors to a finite set of colors, which we call the color palette. The simplest way to quantize a color image is to pick a set of uniformly distributed colors for the pallet and replace each pixel by its nearest pallet entry. One such pallet is the well known set of "web safe" colors, and "nearest" is often measured by Euclidean distance. Although simple, this approach is known to produce poor quality results. Much better results can be obtained by carefully constructing the color pallet using information obtained from the image to the quantized.

There are several algorithms to create a useful color palette, including training-based methods such as *Self-Organizing Maps* (SOM) [Kohonen 01, Chang et al. 05], *Linde-Buzo-Gray* (LBG) [Verevka 95, Linde et al. 80], and the *octree method* [Clark 96]. In terms of mean square distortion, the training based methods usually give a much better quantization result. However, training based methods can also be time consuming. While the mean square distortion of LBG and SOM are similar [Leung and Chan 97], the SOM-generated pallet has a very interesting ordering property. To obtain the ordering property, we impose a neighborhood structure among the palette entries before training. After training, when two palette entries are neighbors of each other, they will have a similar color.

This article presents an efficient GPU implementation for the SOM training algorithm. We apply our approach to the problem of color quantization, and expect our results to be applicable to other vector quantization problems. Our implementation relies on the random write ability of the vertex shader and uses the GPU as the main computing processor. We review the training algorithm of SOM in Section 1.2. Color quantization through SOM is presented in

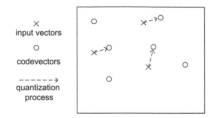

Figure 1.1. The quantization process in two-dimensional space.

Section 1.3. Section 1.4 presents our GPU implementation and the corresponding CG scripts. Section 1.5 discusses the results, the ordering property of SOM, and the applications of the ordering property. Section 1.6 presents our conclusions and summarizes the article.

1.2   The Self-Organizing Map

In vector quantization, we aim to map an input vector in a k-dimensional space to one of a finite set of codevectors in a codebook, $\mathcal{Y} = \{\vec{c}_1, \cdots, \vec{c}_M\}$. The codebook $\mathcal{Y}$ will be used to partition the k-D space into M regions $\Omega = \{\Omega_1, \cdots, \Omega_M\}$. To perform the quantization, we approximate each input vector by its nearest codevector as shown in Figure 1.1, thereby allowing us to store the index of the closest codevector in place of the original vector. In the SOM learning scheme [Leung and Chan 97], prior to training, a neighborhood structure represented by a graph $\mathcal{G} = \{\mathcal{V}, \mathcal{E}\}$, is imposed on the codebook, where $\mathcal{V} = \{v_1, \cdots, v_M\}$ is a set of vertices and $\mathcal{E}$ is the set of edges in this graph. In this representation, each vertex v_i is associated with a codevector $\vec{c}_i$. We will use the following definitions when we discuss the graph:

Definition 1.1. If the codevector $\vec{c}_i$ is defined to be a neighbor of codevector $\vec{c}_{i'}$, the two corresponding vertices, v_i and $v_{i'}$, in the graph are joined by an edge with a weighted value of 1.

Definition 1.2. The neighborhood distance between $\vec{c}_i$ and $\vec{c}_{i'}$ is the length of the shortest path between v_i and $v_{i'}$ in the graph $\mathcal{G}$.

Definition 1.3. A codevector $\vec{c}_i$ is a neighbor of $\vec{c}_{i'}$ in a u-sized neighborhood, if the neighborhood distance between the two codevectors is less than or equal to u.

Definition 1.4. For a codevector $\vec{c}_i$, the collection of indices of its neighbors in a neighborhood of size u is denoted as $I_i(u)$.

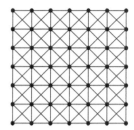

Figure 1.2. The regular grid neighborhood structure of the vertices in a two-dimensional SOM. Note that the graph does not reflect any geometric information of the codevectors in the data space.

Figure 1.2 shows the two-dimensional neighborhood structure used in our implementation of SOM. This structure can be used for mapping a high-dimensional data vector to two discrete indices. Since the sequential SOM learning algorithm [Kohonen 01] is not suitable for parallelization, this article considers the batch mode SOM [Kohonen 01]. Given a dataset $\mathcal{D} = \{\vec{x}_1, \cdots, \vec{x}_N\}$ and the initial codebook $\mathcal{Y}(0) = \{\vec{c}_1(0), \cdots, \vec{c}_M(0)\}$, the batch mode SOM is summarized as follows:[1]

1. A maximum number of iterations T is assigned, and the iteration index t is set to zero. The size of neighborhood u_t is a value decreasing along with t, which is given by

$$u_t = \begin{cases} 2, & \text{if } 0 \leq t < T/8, \\ 1, & \text{if } T/8 \leq t < T/2, \\ 0, & \text{otherwise.} \end{cases}$$

2. Create M empty sets, $\Psi_{i'}$, i.e., $\Psi_i = \varnothing$, for all $i = 1, \cdots, M$.

3. For each training vector $\vec{x}_j$, find its nearest codevector $\vec{c}_{i*}(t)$.

   Put $\vec{x}_j$ into the sets $\Psi_{i'}$'s, where $i' \in I_{i*}(u_t)$ as described in Definition 4. This will collect the training vectors to the sets whose corresponding codevectors have neighborhood distances to the nearest codevector less than u_t.

4. Update the codebook:

$$\vec{c}_i(t+1) = \frac{1}{|\Psi_i|} \sum_{\vec{x}_j \in \Psi_i} \vec{x}_j .$$

5. Set t=t+1 and go to Step 2 unless t has reached T.

---
[1]The initial codebook is initialized with random values.

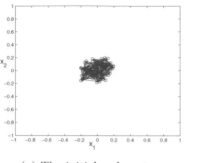
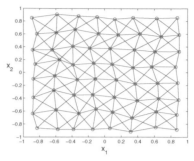

(a) The initial codevectors.   (b) The trained codevectors.

Figure 1.3. A typical run of a batch model SOM. The figure shows the codevectors in the data space. The neighborhood structure of the SOM is an 8×8 two-dimensional grid structure. To indicate the neighborhood structure of the SOM, we draw edges between codevectors if they are defined as neighbors to each other. In (a), the positions of the initial codevectors do not follow the layout of the neighborhood. However, as shown in (b), after training the codevectors are organized in the data space. Two trained codevectors are very close in the data space if they are neighbors to each other in the graph.

Due to the ordering property of the resulting codebook, the Euclidean distance between two trained codevectors is usually small if they are neighbors of each other in the graph $\mathcal{G}$. As demonstrated in Figure 1.3, while the initial codevectors do not form any ordering in the data space as shown in Figure 1.3(a), the trained codevectors form a helpful ordering as shown in Figure 1.3(b).

1.3   Color Quantization with SOM

In this application of vector quantization, we use a two-dimensional regular structured SOM to quantize a full color image. The training vectors, $\mathcal{X} = \{\vec{x}_1, \cdots, \vec{x}_N\}$, are the RGB values of the pixels in the image. Hence, the dimension k of the data space is 3. The codebook will become our image color pallet and is a finite set of RGB values $\mathcal{Y} = \{\vec{c}_1, \cdots, \vec{c}_M\}$. The neighborhood structure of the SOM is a two-dimensional regular grid structure as shown in Figure 1.2. With this arrangement, the trained color palette can be organized as a two-dimensional texture. After quantization, the color of each pixel $\vec{x}_j$ will be replaced by two ordered indices $i*$ whose corresponding palette entry $\vec{c}_{i*}$ is the closest palette entry to the original pixel $\vec{x}$. Note that the use of two indices, and the two-dimensional layout of the color pallet, provides additional structure at no extra cost that would be lost in an equivalent 1D color palette.

1.4   Implementation

We use the client server model to describe our implementation. In a training iteration, each pixel in the image can be considered as a client, and each palette entry can be considered as a service counter. Each pixel determines its nearest palette entry and generates a request to the nearest palette entry, as well as a number of requests to the palette entries neighborhood. When a pixel arrives at a palette entry, the palette entry performs an accumulation and records the number of arrived pixels. When all pixels are served, each entry holds the sum of the arrived pixel colors and the number of arrived pixels. Finally, we calculate the new color palette from the sums.

Suppose there are N training pixels and M colors in the color palette. All the training pixels are uploaded to GPU as a display list of points where pixels are represented by their vertex positions. The initial color palette is assigned with random values and then uploaded to GPU as uniform variables. A four-channel floating-point texture of resolution $\sqrt{M} \times \sqrt{M}$ is created to hold the accumulation of training pixel colors, as shown in Figure 1.4. We call this texture the accumulation color palette texture.

The user then needs to set an initial point size. In OpenGL, we can use `glPointsize()` to set the point size. For SOM, the point size should be set to $2u_t + 1$. If the point size is assigned to 1 for all training iterations, the resulting color palette would be a LBG color palette. In this case, the ordering property in the trained color palette would be lost. The flow diagram of our GPU implementation is shown in Figure 1.5. Within an iteration, for each training pixel, the vertex shader finds the texel position of the nearest palette entry. A point of size $2u_t + 1$ is rasterized at the texel position. Each vertex will generate a number of updates on the accumulation color palette texture as shown in Figure 1.6. In the

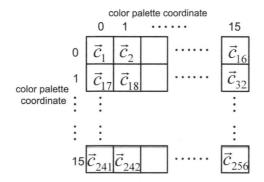

Figure 1.4. The accumulation color palette texture.

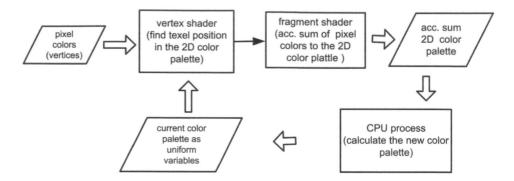

Figure 1.5. The flow of our shader implementation.

fragment shader, the training pixel and a constant "1" are passed to the graphics pipeline directly for accumulation. The constant "1" is there for counting the arrived pixels. This process generates all the accumulation data. Finally, we export the accumulation color palette texture to CPU for updating the color palette.

Our training is an iterative process. Prior to each iteration, the codebook texture is zero-initialized. The color palette is passed to the vertex shader as uniform variables. During an iteration, the training pixels are drawn as a set of points using the display list. In the vertex shader, shown in Listing 1.1, the pixel color is compared with all representative colors to find the index of the nearest representative color. We assign the output position of vertex shader depending on this index.

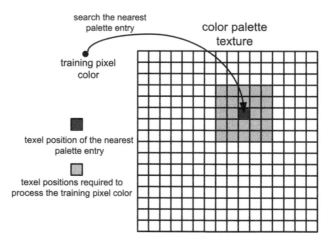

Figure 1.6. A training pixel will generate a number of updates on the accumulation color palette texture. In this example, the point size is 5.

```
void cgfl_vp_som (
  float3 ac : POSITION ,
  out float4 hPosition : POSITION ,
  out float3 bc : COLOR ,
  uniform float3 codebook [codebook_h][codebook_w]
){
  int i, j;
  int2 imin;
  float nd, dd;
  float3 dv;

  nd = FLT_MAX ;
  for ( i=0; i<codebook_h; i++ )
  for ( j=0; j<codebook_w; j++ )
  {
    dv = ac - codebook [i][j];
    dd = dot (dv,dv);
    if ( nd>dd )
    {
      nd=dd;
      imin=int2( j, i );
    }
  }

  hPosition = float4( float (2*imin.x)/codebook_w -1,
  float (2*imin.y)/codebook_h -1, 0,1);

  bc=ac;
}
```

Listing 1.1. The vertex shader of SOM training for locating the nearest representative color index.

```
  float3 bc     : COLOR ,
  out float4 color : COLOR
){
  color = float4 (bc,1);
}
```

Listing 1.2. The fragment shader of SOM training for the accumulation and the counting of training pixel colors.

Afterward, the output position along with the training pixel color are passed to fragment shader to perform the accumulation. By using the hardware blending functionality (available since Geforce 8 or equivalent), the implementation of the accumulation in the fragment shader is simple. This is shown in Listing 1.2.

1.5   Results and Discussion

We have tested various quantization schemes, including SOM, LBG, and Octree. The Octree implementation used was taken from [Priester 04]. The source image is a 24-bit color image of resolution 640×480 as shown in Figure 1.7(a). It is quantized to 8-bit color using the various schemes. The quantized images are shown in Figure 1.7(d)(e)(f). Table 1.1 summarizes their peak signal to noise ratios (PSNRs).

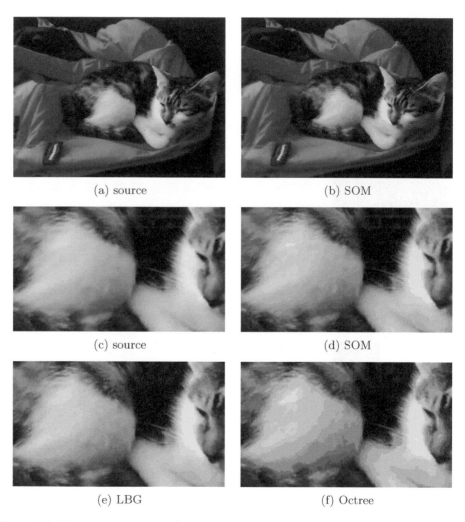

Figure 1.7. Visual comparisons of quantized images with different methods. The image resolution is 640×480.

	SOM	LBG	Octree
PSNR	37.09 dB	37.23 dB	33.0 dB

Table 1.1. The PSNR of quantized images.

As illustrated in Table 1.1, the LBG scheme and SOM scheme give a much better PSNR than the Octree scheme. The differences in PSNR can also be appreciated by comparing the quantized images in Figure 1.7. Note that, the image quantized using Octree scheme, Figure 1.7(f), has more contour artifacts than the others.

As mentioned earlier, the SOM color palette has an ordering property analogous to Figure 1.8. By considering this property, we can generate a "super color palette" based on a trained SOM color palette. As shown in Figure 1.9, given a

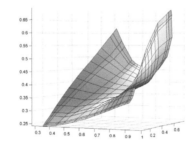

(a) SOM color palette.   (b) SOM color palette plotted in the three-dimensional space.

Figure 1.8. The SOM color palette. In (a) we plot the palette entries according to the two-dimensional SOM neighborhood structure.

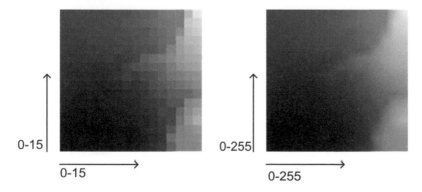

Figure 1.9. Create a high resolution color palette.

	SOM(GPU)	SOM(CPU)
Speed	10.38 ms	724.64 ms

Table 1.2. The speed is measured in time taken per iteration in milliseconds. The image is of dimension 640×480.

trained SOM color palette with 256 colors, we can plot the color palette according to the two-dimensional neighborhood structure and assign two indices, from 0 to 15, to the horizontal and vertical directions. To produce a higher resolution color palette, we can simply increase the resolution of the horizontal and vertical directions to 256×256. The entries of the higher resolution color palette are interpolated from the original color palette. Notice that in practice, we do not need to store the higher resolution color palette because it can be regenerated from the original color palette by interpolation.

We tested the speed of our implementation on a personal computer equipped with a Intel Core2 Duo 3.0 GHz CPU, 3.5GB RAM, and a NVIDIA GeForce 8800 GTX display card. The resulting performance is summarized in Table 1.2. As shown in Table 1.2, the SOM training speed accelerated by the GPU is significantly faster than that of the CPU.

1.6   Conclusion

This article describes a GPU implementation of the SOM training algorithm for color quantization. By using the vertex shader to search for the nearest palette entry and to perform random writes, the proposed scheme improves the training speed of the color palette significantly. With a slight modification, our approach can also perform the LBG training. The ordering property of SOM allows for several interesting extensions, including generation of "super color palettes" and reducing the dimension of input patterns [Togneri et al. 90]. Although our discussion focuses on the quantization of three-dimensional data, our implementation can be easily generalized to handle high-dimensional data.

Acknowledgments

The work was supported by a research grant from General Research Fund, HKSAR (Project No.: CityU 116508).

Bibliography

[Chang et al. 05] Chip-Hong Chang, Pengfei Xu, Rui Xiao, and T. Srikanthan. "New Adaptive Color Quantization Method Based on Self-Organizing Maps." *IEEE Transactions on Neural Networks*, pp. 237–249.

[Clark 96] D. Clark. "Color Quantization Using Octrees." *Dr. Dobb's Journal*, pp. 54–57.

[Kohonen 01] T. Kohonen. *Self-Organizing Maps*. Berlin: Springer, 2001.

[Kruger 94] A. Kruger. "Median-cut Color Quantization." *Dr. Dobb's Journal*, pp. 46–54.

[Leung and Chan 97] C.S. Leung and L.W. Chan. "Transmission of Vector Quantized Data over a Noisy Channel." *IEEE Transactions on Neural Networks* 8:1 (1997), 582–589.

[Linde et al. 80] Y. Linde, A. Buzo, and R.M. Gray. "An Algorithm for Vector Quantizer Design." *IEEE Transactions on Communications* 28:1 (1980), 84–95.

[Priester 04] Sjaak Priester. "Better GIFs with Octrees." Available online (http://www.codeguru.com/Cpp/G-M/gdi/gdi/print.php/c3677/).

[Togneri et al. 90] R. Togneri, E Lai, and Y. Attikiouzel. "Kohonen's Algorithm for the Numerical Parametrisation of Manifolds." *Pattern Recognition Letters* 11:5 (1990), 313–319.

[Verevka 95] Oleg Verevka. "Color Image Quantization in Windows Systems with Local K-means Algorithm." *Proceedings of the Western Computer Graphics Symposium '95*, pp. 74–79.

Visualize Your Shadow Map Techniques

Fan Zhang, Chong Zhao, and Adrian Egli

2.1 Introduction

Things that look simple on the outside may not be simple inside. *Shadow mapping* [Williams 78] is a very good example of this. One of the most popular real time shadowing techniques, shadow mapping has played a key role in realistic rendering in computer games. However, all shadowing solutions based on imperfect sampling suffer from aliasing. With the wide array of techniques available, it is not easy to compare their results. In this article, we present a quantitative analysis of several popular techniques using a novel mathematical model specifically designed for measuring the aliasing errors in shadow maps.

2.2 Article Overview

The quantitative analysis presented in this article is based on the mathematical model for measuring *aliasing errors* in shadow mapping presented in [Zhang et al. 09]. Given appropriate assumptions and simplifications, we are able to explicitly evaluate the aliasing error at an arbitrary frustum position for a general view light configuration. Our model can measure the expected aliasing error independently of scene geometry.

The remainder of this paper is organized as follows: First, we outline the problems that this article attempts to address in Section 2.3. The aliasing error in shadow mapping is discussed from a mathematical perspective in Section 2.4. In Section 2.5 we describe how we measure aliasing in our model. As a direct application of this model, Section 2.6 illustrates and analyzes the aliasing distributions in a few representative shadow map techniques. A corollary, Section 2.7, explains why a stronger *warping strength* may not always give an improved shadow quality.

2.3   Scope of Analysis

A full analysis of aliasing in shadow maps is beyond the scope of this article. Instead, we focus on providing a graphical illustration of the aliasing errors. This section describes the scope of our analysis.

The majority of our analysis establishes a quantitative comparison of different shadowing techniques (see Section 2.6). As illustrated in Figure 2.1, given a suitable example scene we can perceive the difference in visual quality produced by alternative shadowing techniques and varying lighting configurations. Our model gives a uniform description of the aliasing error independent of an example scene. We will use it to numerically quantify how "good" the shadow quality is at every position in the frustum, for a given technique and light configuration. This enables simpler comparisons of shadowing techniques.

As illustrated in Figure 2.2, the mathematical model described in Section 2.5 builds upon previous models of aliasing along the view direction only to

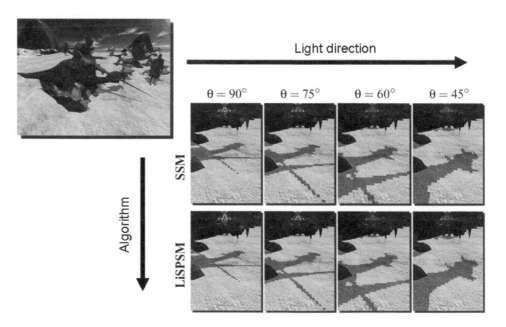

Figure 2.1. Shadowing techniques parameterized by light direction.

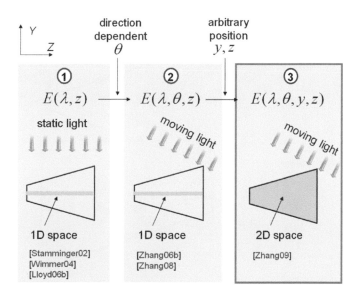

Figure 2.2. The evolution of mathematical models used for aliasing analysis. The first model [Stamminger and Drettakis 02, Wimmer et al. 04, Lloyd et al. 06b] is only valid for points along the view direction with an overhead directional light. The second model [Zhang et al. 06b] [Zhang et al. 08] extends the first to handle dynamic lights. Our model [Zhang et al. 09] works for both arbitrary light directions and frustum positions. Notice that we always consider the aliasing error in the YZ plane, so x does not appear.

include arbitrary light directions as a model parameter. Our model is applicable to most shadow mapping techniques, including *standard shadow maps* (SSM) [Williams 78], *perspective shadow maps* (PSM) [Stamminger02], *light space perspective shadow maps*(LISPSM) [Wimmer et al. 04], *trapezoidal shadow maps* (TSM) [Martin and Tan 04] and *cascaded shadow maps* (CSM) [Engel 06, Zhang et al. 06a].

The last issue we cover is an interesting corollary, which explains the unusual frustum warping behavior of TSM (see Section 2.7).

2.4   Aliasing Revisited

In this section, we review the aliasing error in shadow mapping from a mathematical perspective. The review will help us derive the aliasing representation in the next section.

As illustrated in Figure 2.3, consider a point $\mathbf{c}$ with eye-space coordinates (x, y, z), whose projections on the screen and shadow plane are $\mathbf{p}(p, q)$ and $\mathbf{s}(s, t)$,

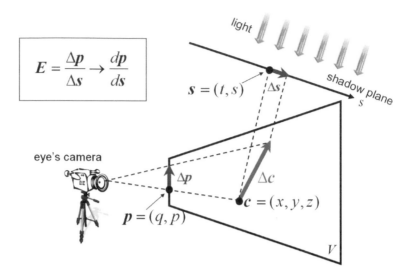

Figure 2.3. Measurement of aliasing in shadow mapping.

respectively. A small increment $d\mathbf{p} = (dx, dy, dz)$ in the view space will cause a
shift $d\mathbf{p} = (dq, dp)$ on the screen, and an offset $d\mathbf{s} = (ds, dt)$ on the shadow plane.
The aliasing error $\mathbf{E}$ at this position is measured as the ratio of the projected
lengths on the shadow plane and image plane: i.e.,

$$\mathbf{E} = (\mathrm{E}_q,\ \mathrm{E}_p) = \left(\left| \frac{\mathrm{d}q}{\mathrm{d}t} \right|,\ \left| \frac{\mathrm{d}p}{\mathrm{d}s} \right| \right).$$

We refer to E_q and E_p as the *aliasing functions* [Zhang et al. 09]. They are used
to quantify the aliasing in the vertical and horizontal dimensions of the screen,
respectively. When E_q or E_p becomes small, *under sampling* occurs and we can
expect shadow boundaries to appear jagged.

We can locate situations where aliasing occurs by understanding when the
aliasing functions become small. Figure 2.4 illustrates how the aliasing functions
can be defined on geometry. For a surface point $\mathbf{c}$, the local geometry is determined
by the frame $(\mathbf{c}; \mathbf{n}, \mathbf{l}, \mathbf{n} \times \mathbf{l})$, where $\mathbf{n}$ and $\mathbf{l}$ are the normal and tangent directions,
respectively. The angle between the light direction and view direction is denoted
by Θ. As shown in Figure 2.4, if we consider the aliasing problem on the two-
dimensional plane containing $\mathbf{l}$ and the light vector, then the aliasing functions
can be parameterized with respect to $\mathbf{c}, \Theta, \mathbf{l}$.

We do not wish to include knowledge of scene geometry, and by implication
the tangent direction $\vec{\mathbf{l}}$, in our model. To facilitate an *offline aliasing analysis*, we

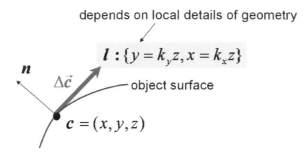

Figure 2.4. Defining aliasing functions at a surface point.

factorize the aliasing functions into two parts,

$$E(\mathbf{c}, \boldsymbol{\Theta}, \mathbf{l}) = E^{\mathrm{pers}}(\mathbf{c}, \boldsymbol{\Theta}) \times E^{\mathrm{proj}}(\mathbf{c}, \boldsymbol{\Theta}, \mathbf{l}). \qquad (2.1)$$

Equation (2.1) is a model for warping algorithms in which the aliasing is divided into *perspective aliasing* E^{pers} and *projection aliasing* E^{proj}, where $E \in \{E_q, E_p\}$. The term E^{proj} is scene dependent (i.e., depending on $\mathbf{l}$), but the term E^{pers} is independent of the scene geometry. Perspective aliasing comes from the perspective foreshortening effect and can be reduced by warping the distribution of shadow-map texels. In this article we examine E^{pers} in all well known warping and traditional shadow map algorithms.

2.5   A Representation of Aliasing Errors

In this section, we present a generalized representation of aliasing errors based on the simplified computational model shown in Figure 2.5. This representation is the essence of our aliasing theory, which will be used to visualize various techniques.

V and W	View frustum and warping frustum
θ	Angle between view and light directions
n and f	Near- and far-plane values for V
λ	Near-plane value for W
ϕ	Half field of view of V
$(O; X, Y, Z)$	Eye's coordinates frame
(q, p)	Normalized screen coordinates ($-1 \leq q,\ p \leq 1$)
(t, s)	Texture coordinates ($0 \leq s,\ t \leq 1$)
(E_q, E_p)	Aliasing functions

Table 2.1. Notations.

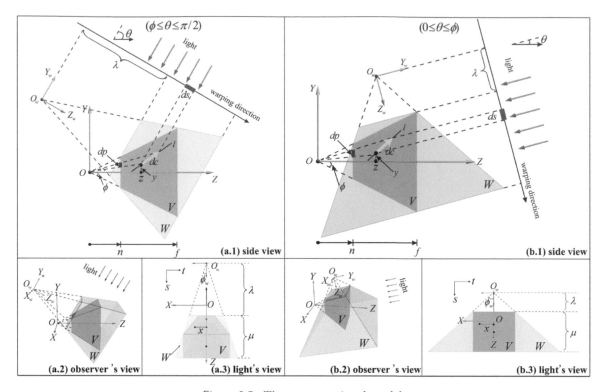

Figure 2.5. The computational model.

Frequently used notations may be found in Table 2.1. Please refer to the extra notes available at http://www.akpeters.com/gpupro for the full list of symbols used in our derivations.

Our model makes the following two simplifications:

1. *We assume directional light sources, confined to the YZ plane:* For point lights, the mapping from view coordinates (x, y, z) to texture coordinates (s, t) is not intuitive. Even though a preliminary result was presented for point lights [Lloyd et al. 06a], a comprehensive analysis in the general case remains challenging. Confining the movement of the light to the YZ plane allows us to restrict our study to the side view of the view frustum.

2. *We confine warping to be parallel to the shadow plane:* The choice of warping direction strongly influences the implementation complexity, because the type of light may switch between direction and point in the post-transformed space [Stamminger and Drettakis 02]. Wimmer et al. [Wimmer et al. 04] propose using a warping direction parallel with the shadow plane, and construct the warping frustum in the light space. An advantage is the direction

of the light source will not change in the post-transformed space, such that no mapping singularities result. Our computational model adopts the same parallel warping direction.

With the above simplifications, the warping frustum W is constructed as shown in Figure 2.5. Notice that we only need to consider the light directions $0 \leq \theta \leq \pi/2$ due to symmetry. In Equations (2.2) and (2.3), E_p and E_q quantify the aliasing in the vertical and horizontal dimensions of the screen independently. Here we simply state the result of our model. Detailed derivations for this model can be found in the extra notes available at http://www.akpeters.com/gpupro:

$$E_q \approx E_q^{\mathrm{pers}} = F_q(\lambda, \theta) \frac{z + G(y, \lambda, \theta)}{z} \tag{2.2}$$

$$E_p \approx E_p^{\mathrm{pers}} = F_p(\lambda, \theta) \frac{\left(z + G(y, \lambda, \theta)\right)^2}{z}. \tag{2.3}$$

We make use of an additional aliasing metric $E_{p \times q} = E_p \times E_q$ in this article. $E_{p \times q}$ is an aggregate measure of the aliasing errors in both dimensions. Remember that projection aliasing is ignored in all terms.

With the generalized representation of aliasing errors (Equations (2.2) and (2.3)), we are now ready to evaluate aliasing distributions in various techniques with respect to the metrics E_p, E_q and $E_{p \times q}$ in the next section.

2.6 Visualization

In this section, we perform three measurements to visually compare representative shadow map techniques.

The first measurement visualizes the λ distributions against θ for alternative techniques. For a fixed light view configuration, the main difference between the warping algorithms is the selection of the only free parameter, λ.

Given the λ distributions from the first measurement, the aliasing distributions within the view frustum can be directly visualized by using Equations (2.2) and (2.3). This gives us our second measurement.

Finally, we measure the aliasing distribution as it varies with view direction (i.e., $y = 0$).

2.6.1 Measurement 1: How the Warping Strength Varies as the Light Direction Changes

The purpose of this measurement is to plot λ against θ. This is shown in Figure 2.6, where we assume $n = 1$, $f = 400$ and $\phi = 30°$. For a detailed description of these λ values refer to the extra notes available at http://www.akpeters.com/gpupro.

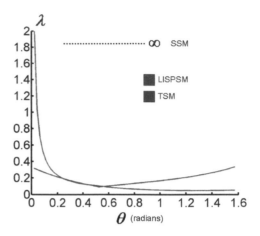

Figure 2.6. Warping strength varies as light direction changes.

Let λ_{SSM}, λ_{PSM}, $\lambda_{\mathrm{LISPSM}}$ and λ_{TSM} be the values in SSM, PSM, LISPSM, and TSM, respectively. We review the behavior of each algorithm in turn:

- λ_{SSM} does not employ any warping and therefore can be considered to have an infinite λ. The distribution of aliasing error in the camera frustum is inversely proportional to the view depth.

- λ_{PSM} produces a *linear* error distribution with respect to view depth [Wimmer et al. 04] [Zhang et al. 06b]. This linear behavior provides better shadow quality at the near camera frustum plane. Notice that typical PSM implementations in general cases $(\theta \neq \pi/2)$ do not use the computational model shown in Figure 2.5, thus we do not visualize PSM in this article.

- $\lambda_{\mathrm{LISPSM}}$ produces an error distribution that is minimal with respect to the L^{∞} *norm* [Wimmer et al. 04] [Zhang et al. 08], which empirically works better than PSM in both practice and theory.

- The *focus-driven* behavior of λ_{TSM} requires the user to specify the region for the majority of the shadow map resolution.

As we can tell from Figure 2.6, $\lambda_{\mathrm{LISPSM}} < \lambda_{\mathrm{TSM}} < \lambda_{\mathrm{SSM}}$ such that the warping strength becomes weaker from LISPSM to SSM. In the ideal case $\theta = \pi/2$, the stronger the warping strength is, the lower the aliasing errors are at the near region.

2.6.2 Measurement 2: How Aliasing Errors are Distributed Within the View Frustum

The purpose of this measurement is to visualize the distributions of aliasing error within the view frustum for different light directions across techniques. The result is shown in Figure 2.7.

For each combination of light direction and technique, alongside the colored error distributions, a simple scene comprised of 25 evenly spaced dragon models is used to illustrate the associated shadow map and shadow details.

In this article, the term *degenerate case* is used to describe the case when $\theta \leq \phi$. The term *dueling frusta* is often used to describe this case but in this article the term *dueling frusta* only refers to the extreme case $\theta = 0$.

To simplify our discussion further, we will mainly use the aggregate aliasing metric $E_{p \times q}$ to analyze Figure 2.7 in the following three cases:

1. *Ideal case.* $\theta = \pi/\mathbf{2}$ *(illustrated in the first column in Figure 2.7)*: In this case, the warping direction and the view direction are identical. The aliasing is constant in any vertical line for all techniques such that we only need to consider the aliasing distribution along the view direction. When examining SSM, we can see the aliasing errors in the near camera region are more intense (shown as red) than other warping algorithms. This illustrates why shadow quality can suffer on near objects in SSM. The algorithm places greater importance on the distant region which may not be as crucial to visual quality. Larger errors can be seen in LISPSM and TSM for distant regions, which are depicted in a yellow color. However, we see the aliasing for near objects is significantly alleviated in LISPSM and TSM due to warping rebalancing the sampling rate. This explains why shadow quality in warping algorithms can be significantly improved, especially in the ideal case.

2. *Normal case.* $\phi \leq \theta \leq \pi/\mathbf{2}$ *(illustrated in the second column in Figure 2.7)*: In theory, to minimize the maximum errors of $E_{p \times q}$ (also E_p and E_q), you need to choose an appropriate λ value to satisfy the condition $\min E_{p \times q} = \max E_{p \times q}$. The λ values satisfying this condition can be computed from Equations (2.2) and (2.3). Such λ values normally provide a very strong warping strength. It is possible to prove that it is not always possible to produce a positive (valid) λ value for some small θ values. Although stronger warping should provide higher quality at near regions, the warping direction is not identical with the view direction in normal cases (Figure 2.4). In this case the warping allocates more shadow map resolution to the region near the warping frustum's projection point (denoted by O_w in Figure 2.4), rather than the eye's position.

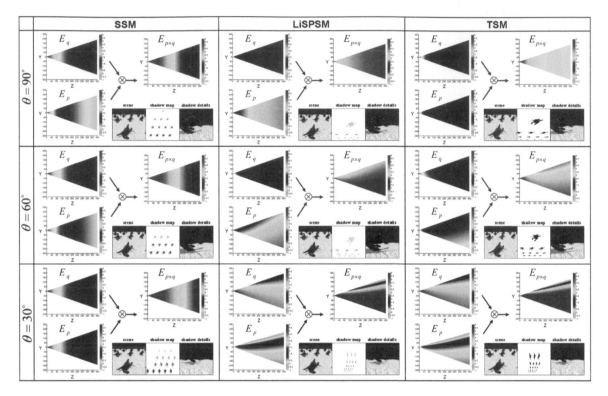

Figure 2.7. From left to right: the side views of aliasing distributions within the view frustum in SSM, LISPSM, and TSM, respectively. From top to bottom: the side views of aliasing distributions within the view frustum at different θ values. A sample scene is used to illustrate the corresponding shadow map and shadow quality for each. The values of the aliasing errors are colorized using the same color-bar in which the red color corresponds to the highest errors. The plots use a log_2 scale with $n = 1$, $f = 400$ and $\phi = \pi/6$.

3. *Degenerate case.* $\mathbf{0 \leq \theta \leq \phi}$ *(illustrated in the last column in Figure 2.7):* As we can see from Figure 2.4, in degenerate cases the view frustum is a quad from the light's point of view such that the warping is applied to the vertical direction. As we detailed earlier, perspective aliasing mainly results from the eye's projection transforming along the view direction (horizontal in the view space). Therefore, the effectiveness of redistributing perspective aliasing by using the warping transform decreases as θ goes to zero. For the dueling frusta case in particular, all warping algorithms fail to reduce E_p, and redistribute E_q and $E_{p \times q}$ in the vertical direction only. This is frequently undesirable because it will cause vertical stretch in shadow quality on the image plane from top to bottom. Therefore, all warping algorithms do not have an advantage over SSM in the degenerate case. As illustrated

by Figure 2.7, redistributing $E_{p \times q}$ is more effective in the vertical direction in both LISPSM and TSM. Subsequently, errors are smaller in the upper half frustum and larger in the lower half frustum. This phenomenon is particularly noticeable in $E_{p \times q}$ for TSM.

2.6.3 Measurement 3: How Aliasing Errors are Distributed along the View Direction

The purpose of this measurement is to visualize the aliasing distribution on the line $y = 0$ when the θ value changes. Figure 2.8 plots $E(z, \theta)$ for λ_{SSM}, λ_{LISPSM} and λ_{TSM} on this line at different θ values, where E stands for E_p, E_q and $E_{p \times q}$. We use the aggregated aliasing metric $E_{p \times q}$ to compare different techniques.

Our measurements are illustrative of how aliasing error in several techniques behaves in practice. However, it is a simplification and different shadowing techniques may suit different scenes. When implementing warping algorithms, there are no fixed criteria for determining an appropriate warping strength, because no criteria can suit all cases. The warping strength needs to be carefully tuned according to the scene model in practice.

2.7 Mismatch of View Direction and Warping Direction

In this section, we use our measurements to explain why a stronger warping strength does not always produce better shadow quality, due to the mismatch of the view direction and light direction in general cases.

In the general case $\theta \neq \pi/2$, the warping direction and view direction are not identical in the computational model (see Figure 2.5). As shown in Figure 2.9, due to the nature of the warping transform, a stronger warp will result in less resolution allocated to the "High Error" region. On the other hand, you can easily prove that the maximum errors of aliasing functions are located at the view frustum's left bottom or right bottom corners, which are covered by the "High Error" region. Therefore a strong warping strength will actually increase the maximum errors in the "High Error" region.

In many practical cases (e.g., a typical driving games), objects located in the lower half of the view frustum are the most important to a user's perception. However, the lower half of the view frustum receives less resolution from a typical sunlight as the warping strength increases. This phenomenon can be confusing as a weaker warp will produce a better shadow quality for objects in this region. Since different techniques produce different warping strengths this can make comparisons between techniques more complicated. For example, in Figure 2.7 we can see the errors in the lower half of the view frustum for TSM are lower than that for LISPSM.

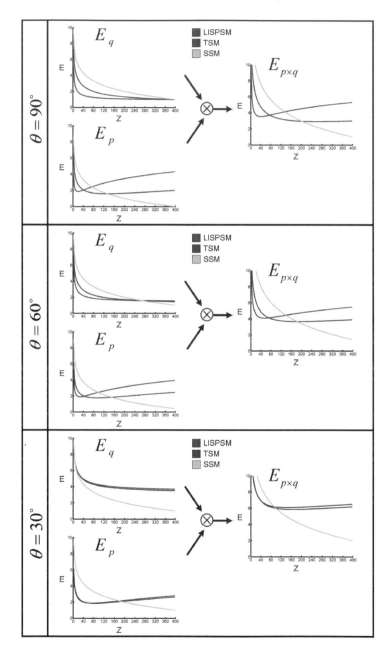

Figure 2.8. The aliasing distributions along the line $y = 0$ at different θ values. The plots use a log_2 scale with $n = 1$, $f = 400$ and $\phi = \pi/6$.

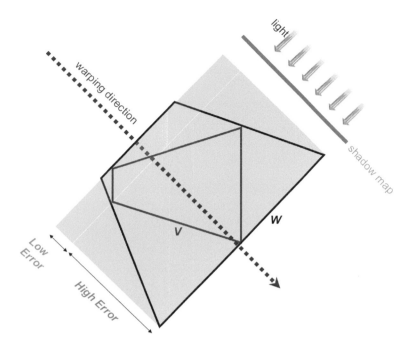

Figure 2.9. The mismatch of the warping direction and view direction.

2.8 Conclusion

In this article, we have used a model for measuring aliasing errors in shadow maps to examine the distribution of error independently of geometry. This has allowed us to visually compare the behavior of several popular techniques. We hope the results presented in this paper will help developers achieve a deeper understanding of shadow mapping techniques, and thus motivate further novel ideas in this field.

2.9 Supplementary Materials

The supplementary materials for this article include a set of videos and high quality pictures generated by Matlab that plot the aliasing functions in several techniques. An extra note is provided to provide a more detailed derivation of the underlying model.

2.10   Acknowledgments

Thanks to Sam Martin for his valuable review comments and patient proofreading. Thanks are also given to David Lam for his early review.

Bibliography

[Engel 06] Wolfgang Engel. "Cascaded Shadow Maps." In *ShaderX 5*, pp. 197–206. Charles River Media, 2006.

[Lloyd et al. 06a] Brandon Lloyd, Naga K. Govindaraju, David Tuft, Steve Molnar, and Dinesh Manocha. "Practical Logarithmic Shadow Maps." In *SIGGRAPH '06: ACM SIGGRAPH 2006 Sketches*, p. 103. New York: ACM Press, 2006.

[Lloyd et al. 06b] Brandon Lloyd, David Tuft, Sung-eui Yoon, and Dinesh Manocha. "Warping and Partitioning for Low Error Shadow Maps." In *Proceedings of the Eurographics Symposium on Rendering 2006*, pp. 215–226. Eurographics Association, 2006.

[Martin and Tan 04] Tobias Martin and Tiow-Seng Tan. "Anti-aliasing and Continuity with Trapezoidal Shadow Maps." In *The Eurographics Symposium on Rendering 2004*. Eurographics, Eurographics Association, 2004.

[Stamminger and Drettakis 02] Marc Stamminger and George Drettakis. "Perspective Shadow Maps." In *Proceedings of SIGGRAPH '02*, pp. 557–562. New York: ACM Press, 2002.

[Williams 78] Lance Williams. "Casting Curved Shadows on Curved Surfaces." In *Proceedings of SIGGRAPH '78*, pp. 270–274. New York: ACM Press, 1978.

[Wimmer et al. 04] Michael Wimmer, Daniel Scherzer, and Werner Purgathofer. "Light Space Perspective Shadow Maps." In *The Eurographics Symposium on Rendering 2004*. Eurographics, Eurographics Association, 2004.

[Zhang et al. 06a] Fan Zhang, Hanqiu Sun, Leilei Xu, and Lee Kit Lun. "Parallel-Split Shadow Maps for Large-Scale Virtual Environments." *Virtual Reality Continuum and Its Applications*, pp. 311–318.

[Zhang et al. 06b] Fan Zhang, Leilei Xu, Chenjun Tao, and Hanqiu Sun. "Generalized Linear Perspective Shadow Map Reparameterization." In *VRCIA '06: Proceedings of the 2006 ACM International Conference on Virtual Reality Continuum and its Applications*, pp. 339–342. New York: ACM Press, 2006.

[Zhang et al. 08] Fan Zhang, Hanqiu Sun, Chong Zhao, and Lifeng Wang. "Generalized Minimum-norm Perspective Shadow Maps." *Computer Animation and Virtual Worlds* 19:5 (2008), 553–567.

[Zhang et al. 09] Fan Zhang, Chong Zhao, and Hanqiu Sun. "An Aliasing Theory of Shadow Mapping." In *TPCG '09: Proceedings of the Seventh Theory and Practice of Computer Graphics 2009 Conference.* Eurographics Association, 2009.

Geometry Manipulation

The "Geometry Manipulation" section of the book focuses on the ability of *graphics processor units* (GPUs) to process and generate geometry in exciting and interesting ways.

Tamy Boubekeur covers Phong Tesselation in the article "As Simple as Possible Tessellation for Interactive Applications." This operator is simpler than GPU subdivision surfaces and their approximations but succeeds at hiding standard "polygonization" artifacts often encountered on mesh silhouettes and interior contours. P*hong Tessellation* can be implemented on today's GPU using either uniform or adaptive instanced tessellation (vertex shader), or on the geometry shader for low tessellation rates.

The article "Rule-Based Geometry Synthesis in Real-Time" by Milan Magdics and Gergely Klar presents a framework for synthesizing and rendering geometry described by a rule-based representation in real time. The representation is evaluated completely on the GPU; thus, the geometry synthesis can be very fast and there is no need to copy data between the CPU and the graphics card. By applying frustum culling and rule selection based on the distance from the camera during the synthesis, only what is required for rendering with dynamic level of detail is generated.

Graham Hemingway describes in the article "GPU-based NURBS Geometry Evaluation and Rendering" a method for using the GPU to calculate NURBS geometry. Compared to evaluation on the CPU, this method yields significant performance improvements without drawbacks in precision or flexibility.

The last article of the section "Polygonal-Functional Hybrids for Computer Animation and Games," by Denis Kravtsov et al., describes how to represent geometry with functions to overcome some of the challenges with polygons like produce animations involving dramatic change of the shape of the model and creating complex shapes with changing topology. They also cover the integration of existing polygonal models and functional representations.

—Natalya Tatarchuk

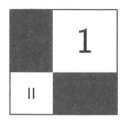

As Simple as Possible Tessellation for Interactive Applications

Tamy Boubekeur

A *tessellation operator* increases the number of nodes in a mesh and can be understood as an upsampling method for polygonal surfaces.

Using real-time tessellation allows the application developer to specify a coarse mesh at the application level, but dynamically add vertices as needed at GPU level. This high resolution mesh may then be used to sample a (visually) smoother surface, eventually displaced using scalar or vector maps.

We describe (Section 1.1) and extend (Section 1.2) *Phong tessellation*, a simple operator generating curved surfaces over piecewise linear surface meshes. This operator is simpler than GPU subdivision surfaces [Shiue et al. 05] and their approximations [Vlachos et al. 01] [Boubekeur and Schlick 07b] [Loop and Schaefer 08]. However, for a minimal computational cost, it succeeds at hiding standard "polygonization" artifacts often encountered on mesh silhouettes and interior contours (see Figure 1.1). This operator is purely local (per-polygon computation, without neighborhood queries) and reproduces quadratic geometry variations. It naturally completes Phong Normal Interpolation.

Phong tessellation can be implemented on today's GPU using either *uniform* or *adaptive instanced tessellation* (vertex shader), or on the geometry shader for low tessellation rates. Upcoming graphics hardware and APIs such as Microsoft Direct3D 11 [Gee 08] will feature a standard tessellator unit with two new programmable stages: the *Hull Shader*, which defines the control network of the polygon to tessellate (in our case, this is the polygon itself together with its normal vectors and without any additional control points), and the *Domain Shader*, which evaluates the curved geometry (in our case, a code similar to Listing 1.1).

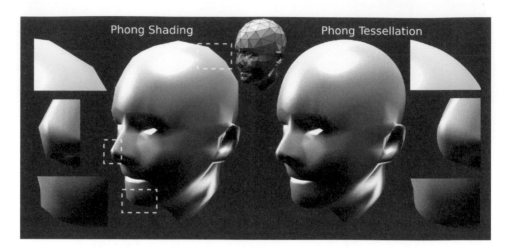

Figure 1.1. Phong tessellation (right) completes Phong shading (left).

1.1   Basic Phong Tessellation Operator

Consider a triangle $\mathbf{t}$ indexing three vertices $\{\mathbf{v}_i, \mathbf{v}_j, \mathbf{v}_k\}$, with $\mathbf{v} = \{\mathbf{p}, \mathbf{n}\}$, $\mathbf{p} \in \mathbb{R}^3$ the position and $\mathbf{n} \in S^2$ the normal vector. Generally, the tessellation of $\mathbf{t}$ generates a set of new vertices lying on a surface defined over $\mathbf{t}$. Linear tessellation simply generates vertices on the plane defined by $\mathbf{t}$. Each generated vertex $\mathbf{p}(u, v)$ in the linear tessellation corresponds to a barycentric coordinate $(u, v, w), u, v \in [0, 1], w = 1 - u - v$ defined by

$$\mathbf{p}(u, v) = (u, v, w)(\mathbf{p}_i, \mathbf{p}_j, \mathbf{p}_k)^{\mathsf{T}}.$$

Phong normal interpolation [Phong 75] uses the same process but normalizes the result in the end:

$$\mathbf{n}'(u, v) = (u, v, w)(\mathbf{n}_i, \mathbf{n}_j, \mathbf{n}_k)^{\mathsf{T}}, \quad \mathbf{n}(u, v) = \mathbf{n}'/\|\mathbf{n}'\|.$$

Phong tessellation [Boubekeur and Alexa 08] generalizes this idea to the generation of curved geometry (see Figure 1.2). Each vertex of the triangle defines a tangent plane (vertex position and normal), and the Phong tessellation interpolates between three points, which are the projections on each plane of a linear interpolation over $\mathbf{t}$:

$$\mathbf{p}^*{}_\alpha(u, v) = (1 - \alpha)\mathbf{p}(u, v) + \alpha(u, v, w) \begin{pmatrix} \pi_i(\mathbf{p}(u, v)) \\ \pi_j(\mathbf{p}(u, v)) \\ \pi_k(\mathbf{p}(u, v)) \end{pmatrix}.$$

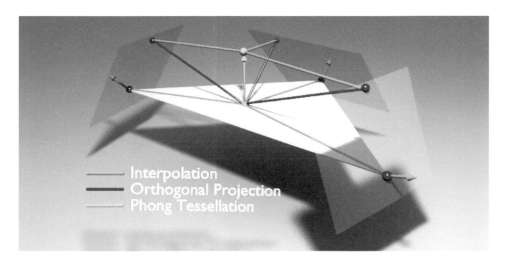

Figure 1.2. Phong tessellation performs in three steps: (1) Flat tessellation: vertices positions (red) are interpolated at a point (light blue); (2) Orthogonal projection: this point is orthogonally projected onto the three tangent planes defined at vertices (blue lines); and (3) Final displacement: these three points are interpolated again, defining the Phong tessellation displacement vector (in yellow). The initial interpolation (1) accounts for dynamic base mesh and standard tessellation methods, which starts from local coordinates expressed relatively to the current polygon.

Here $\pi_i(\mathbf{x})$ is the orthogonal projection of $\mathbf{x}$ on the plane defined by $\mathbf{v_i}$ and α acts as a simple shape factor interpolating between flat and curved triangle patch. We usually set it to $3/4$. Note that this operator defines a quadratic patch implicitly. The coarse mesh to tessellate can simply be set on the GPU using extra vertex attributes, textures or, for the sake of simplicity, *uniform* variables in the vertex shader (on a per-triangle basis):

```
uniform vec3 p0, p1, p2;
```

The Phong tessellation vertex shader is given in Listing 1.1. At rendering time, when a triangle has to be tessellated, we use *Instanced Tessellation* [Boubekeur and Schlick 05] for generating a large number of vertices for each triangle and evaluate the Phong tessellation vertex shader on each of them. The Phong normal interpolation already offers a visually smooth shading inside shapes, so there is no need to apply the Phong tessellation operator everywhere on the input mesh. It is needed only on locations where Phong normal interpolation cannot hide the lack of high order continuity of the geometry, namely, on contours and silhouettes. Therefore, we make use of *Adaptive Instanced Tessellation* [Boubekeur and Schlick 07a, Boubekeur and Schlick 08], where the adaptivity factor (i.e., level

```
vec3 p0, p1, p2; // Current coarse triangle vertex positions
vec3 n0, n1, n2; // Current coarse triangle vertex normals
float alpha = 3/4; // Shape factor
vec3 project (vec3 p, vec3 c, vec3 n) {
  return p - dot (p - c, n)*n;
}
// Curved geometry at p={w,u,v} (barycentric coord.).
vec3 PhongGeometry (float u, float v, float w) {
  vec3 p = w*p0 + u*p1 + v*p2;
  vec3 c0 = project (p, p0, n0);
  vec3 c1 = project (p, p1, n1);
  vec3 c2 = project (p, p2, n2);
  vec3 q = w*c0 + u*c1 + v*c2;
  vec3 r = mix (p, q, alpha);
  return r;
}
// Continuous normal field at p
vec3 PhongNormal (float u, float v, float w) {
  vec3 n = normalize (w*n0 + u*n1 + v*n2);
  return n;
}
```

Listing 1.1. Basic GLSL vertex shader for Phong Tessellation. The `PhongGeometry`
function defines the displacement to apply on any point of the tessellated polygon. Although watertight (C^0 continuity), we use a different function for interpolating normals
(`PhongNormal`) in order to prevent any visual continuity artifact.

of tessellation) is defined on the coarse mesh vertices and edges using a simple
silhouetteness measure based on vertex normals:

$$d_i = \left(1 - \left\| \mathbf{n}_i^\mathsf{T} \frac{\mathbf{c} - \mathbf{p}_i}{\|\mathbf{c} - \mathbf{p}_i\|} \right\| \right) m,$$

with $\mathbf{c}$ the position of the camera and m the maximum refinement depth. This
value can be mapped on the shape factor to modulate a progressive transition
between flat and curved geometry. We refer the reader to our paper [Boubekeur
and Alexa 08] for additional analysis on performances and visual quality. Note that
other tessellation environments may be used such as NVIDIA SDK's version of
Instanced Tessellation [NVIDIA 08] or the ADM Tessellation Library [Tatarchuk
et al. 09].

1.2   Extension to Quads

We extend Phong tessellation to quad and tri-quad meshes by redefining the
operator over a quadangular polygon $\mathbf{q} = \{\mathbf{v_i}, \mathbf{v_j}, \mathbf{v_k}, \mathbf{v_l}\}$, a primitive frequently

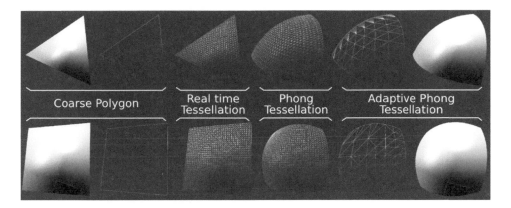

Figure 1.3. Phong tessellation for triangles and quads. Note that, while sampled with triangles, Phong geometry is defined at every point by the four vertices of the input quad.

used in production. We keep the basic idea of interpolation between tangent plane projections and simply replace the barycentric interpolation by a bilinear one (see Figure 1.3). This interpolation involves the four vertices of the quad and is substituted to the barycentric one wherever it appears in the triangle case, including the normal interpolation for shading:

$$\mathbf{p}^*{}_\alpha(u,v) = (1-\alpha)\mathbf{p}(u,v) + \begin{pmatrix} v(u\pi_i(\mathbf{p}(u,v)) + (1-u)\pi_i(\mathbf{p}(u,v))) + \\ (1-v)(u\pi_l(\mathbf{p}(u,v)) + (1-u)\pi_k(\mathbf{p}(u,v))) \end{pmatrix}.$$

Triangle and quad Phong tessellation reproduce the same geometry on polygon edges, as only edge vertices are involved on this parameter domain (linear interpolation of orthogonal projections in both cases). Therefore we obtain a

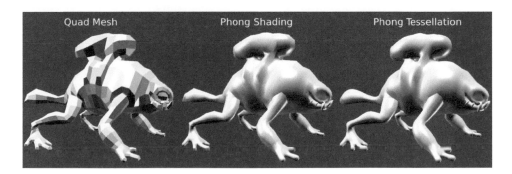

Figure 1.4. Phong tessellation extended to quad and tri-quad meshes.

crack-free tessellation scheme for triangle, tri-quad, and quad meshes. By doing this we avoid the typical trick consisting in triangulating quads, which often results in poor shape quality, even under (triangle) Phong tessellation. Note that while we define a curved geometry over a quad, this imposes no restriction on the way we sample the quad and triangle-based instanced tessellation can still be used safely with two triangular patches for sampling a single quad under quad Phong tessellation projection. Figure 1.4 illustrates the use of this extended operator.

1.3   Results and Discussion

Considering a typical scenario involving a dynamically deforming input coarse mesh (few thousands polygons) tessellated at level 6 (64×64)—a consistent 40% frame rate improvement is measured compared to Curved PN Triangle [Vlachos et al. 01] as well as a lower bandwidth usage for a similarly convincing rendering. Note that the aim of such an operator is to "fix" the strong polygonization artifacts appearing on silhouettes and interior contours, where Phong normal interpolation cannot hide the lack of continuity. Consequently, Phong tessellation differs significantly, for instance, from *subdivision surfaces approximations* [Boubekeur and Schlick 07b, Loop and Schaefer 08], which alterate significantly the perceived shapes in an attempt to generate globally smoother surfaces. Last, Phong tessellation is about 10% slower than flat tessellation when fragment shading is disabled. This number boils down to 2% when lighting and texturing are enabled and used, making it the cheapest way to generate visually smooth and curved geometry out of a dynamic polygonal mesh.

Bibliography

[Boubekeur and Alexa 08] Tamy Boubekeur and Marc Alexa. "Phong Tessellation." *ACM Transaction on Graphics - Special Issue on ACM SIGGRAPH Asia 2008* 27:5 (2008), 1–5.

[Boubekeur and Schlick 05] Tamy Boubekeur and Christophe Schlick. "Generic Mesh Refinement on GPU." In *Proceedings of ACM SIGGRAPH/Eurographics Graphics Hardware*, pp. 99–104, 2005.

[Boubekeur and Schlick 07a] Tamy Boubekeur and Christophe Schlick. *GPU Gems 3*, Chapter Generic Adaptive Mesh Refinement. Addison-Wesley, 2007.

[Boubekeur and Schlick 07b] Tamy Boubekeur and Christophe Schlick. "QAS: Real-time Quadratic Approximation of Subdivision Surfaces." In *Proceedings of Pacific Graphics 2007*, pp. 453–456, 2007.

[Boubekeur and Schlick 08] Tamy Boubekeur and Christophe Schlick. "A Flexible Kernel for Adaptive Mesh Refinement on GPU." *Computer Graphics Forum* 27:1 (2008), 102–114.

[Gee 08] K. Gee. "Direct3D 11 Tessellation." Presentation at Gamefest 2008, 2008.

[Loop and Schaefer 08] Charle Loop and Scott Schaefer. "Approximating Catmull-Clark Subdivision Surfaces with Bicubic Patches." *ACM Transaction on Graphics* 27:1 (2008), 1–8.

[NVIDIA 08] NVIDIA. "NVIDIA OpenGL SDK 10." Technical report, NVIDIA Corp., 2008.

[Phong 75] Bui Tuong Phong. "Illumination for Computer Generated Pictures." *Communications of the ACM* 18:6 (1975), 311–317.

[Shiue et al. 05] Le-Jeng Shiue, Ian Jones, and Jorg Peters. "A Realtime GPU Subdivision Kernel." In *Proceedings of ACM SIGGRAPH*, pp. 1010–1015, 2005.

[Tatarchuk et al. 09] Natalya Tatarchuk, Joshua Barczak, and Bill Bilodeau. "Programming for Real-Time Tessellation on GPU." Technical report, AMD Inc., 2009.

[Vlachos et al. 01] Alex Vlachos, Jorg Peters, Chas Boyd, and Jason Mitchell. "Curved PN Triangles." In *Proceedings of ACM Symposium on Interactive 3D*, pp. 159–166, 2001.

Rule-Based Geometry
Synthesis in Real-Time
Milán Magdics and Gergely Klár

2.1 Introduction

Procedural modeling is a very popular modeling technique, since it allows us to create complex models with a small amount of work. Furthermore, algorithmic scene and object representations are often very compact and have low storage costs. Using operations that repeat elements and add random variations, we can represent arbitrarily large and detailed scenes without increasing the storage needs, while the generated objects remain diverse.

Evaluating the algorithmic description on the fly or, in other words, generating only those objects that we see through the camera, results in a runtime storage cost proportional to the complexity of the potentially visible objects, allowing us to store and visualize potentially infinite virtual worlds.

Rule-based modeling, whether using different kinds of grammars like L-systems, or split grammars, is a good trade-off between simplicity, usability, expressiveness, and formalism and has been widely used to generate different kinds of objects such as plants, buildings, road systems, fractals, and subdivision surfaces. This article presents a framework for synthesizing and rendering geometry described by a rule-based representation in real time. The representation is evaluated completely on the GPU, thus, the geometry synthesis can be very fast, and there is no need to copy data between the CPU and the graphics card. By applying frustum culling and rule selection based on the distance from the camera during the synthesis, we can generate only what is required for rendering with dynamic level-of-detail.

Interaction with the procedural scene is also an important problem to solve. The article discusses a technique for discrete collision detection based on a very simple observation: if we use an object's bounding box instead of the viewing frustum for culling, we can get the intersection of the object with the procedural scene the same way as generating objects inside the camera frustum. Thus, the GPU can speed up the calculation of these intersections when the number of objects is large, which is useful for controlling a large number of AI players, having particle systems colliding with the procedural scene, or in physical simulations.

Synthesizing the geometry on the GPU requires shader programs that depend on the current rules. The article shows how to automate shader and client code generation from an arbitrary (but well-defined) grammar description that is easier to create and understand.

2.2   Building Up the Scene with Procedures

The model we use is built on *Procedural Geometric Instancing* (PGI), which was introduced by Hart in [Hart 92,Ebert et al. 02]. PGI is a scene graph model, where nodes are extended with a procedure that executes at the time of instantiation. This procedure can set the parameters of the node based on the parent node or global parameters, and it can create new nodes. The whole scene is built up by instantiating the root node(s).

Since the procedure of a node depends only on the parent node, if two nodes are not descendants of each other, they can be evaluated independently. For example, we can build up the scene graph level by level (which corresponds to the breadth-first traversal of the graph), and evaluate the nodes of a level in parallel, resulting in better performance. We use this kind of geometry generation in our work.

Another simple but important observation is that we get the same result if we start the generation from an interior node instead of the root nodes. This allows us to buffer some parts of the scene graph, and regenerate only a smaller part of the scene in subsequent frames.

2.3   L-systems and the PGI

An *L-system* [Prusinkiewicz and Lindenmayer 91] is a parallel rewriting system defined as a 4-tuple $L = (N, T, \omega, P)$, where T and N is the set of *terminal* and *nonterminal* symbols, ω is the *initial string*, or *axiom* of the system, and P is the set of *production rules*, defining the way nonterminal symbols can be *replaced* with combinations of terminals and other nonterminals. A rule consists of two strings: the *predecessor* and the *successor*. Similarly to formal grammars, the *production* of an L-system iteratively replaces a predecessor with a successor in the current string (this step is often called *applying* of the rule). In contrast to formal grammars, an L-system applies as many rules as possible in an iteration, thus, it is much more capable of describing the growth what we need for fast generation of procedural geometry. The *generated language* of an L-system is a set of symbol sequences (or *strings*) that can be generated by applying zero or more rules to the axiom.

To utilize L-systems in computer graphics we assign geometric meaning to each symbol: for example, a command that changes drawing position or draws a line. Additionally, to make the modeling easier and increase the expressiveness, we can assign parameters to symbols (the concept we get is usually called a *module*). For example, let symbol F denote drawing a line. In this case, the parametrized symbol $F(l)$ may denote drawing a line with length l. This way, any kind of mesh can be described as a sequence of symbols. The graphical objects that can be generated using a specific L-system L are the geometric interpretations of the strings in L's generated language.

The traditional method to evaluate the geometric interpretation of a string is the *turtle graphics model*. In turtle graphics, drawing commands and state modifier commands (i.e. those that change the current global rendering state) are assigned to the symbols. The string is processed sequentially, and every command is evaluated relative to the current rendering state. The main problem of this method is that the evaluation cannot be parallelized, since every command that changes the rendering state has effect on every following commands in the string.

In [Hart 92, Ebert et al. 02], Hart shows how a procedural scene description given in the PGI model can be translated to a context-free L-system (that is, an L-system in which every predecessor consists of exactly one symbol) and vice versa. Thus, in terms of geometric modeling PGI and context-free L-systems are equivalent. Figure 2.1 shows the correspondence of the two models. The most important consequence of the equivalence is that the geometric interpretation of an L-system generated string can be evaluated in parallel, or in other words, a string can be considered as a set of symbols. In our work, we extend Hart's scenegraph-based L-system model to give more flexibility. The details are described in Section 2.4.

Hart also showed how the rules used with the turtle graphics model should be transformed to allow parallel evaluation. Since the turtle graphics model is frequently used in rule-based geometry generation, we will discuss this transformation with respect to our model in Section 2.4.

Modeling objects with PGI requires writing programs, which can be difficult to modelers who are not familiar with programming. Although PGI and rule-based models are very similar, the formalism is different. According to other works [Parish and Müller 01, Wonka et al. 03, Müller et al. 06, Lipp et al. 08], modelers can easily learn and use rule-based modeling methods, which was our main reason to use rules for real-time geometry generation. Please note that when

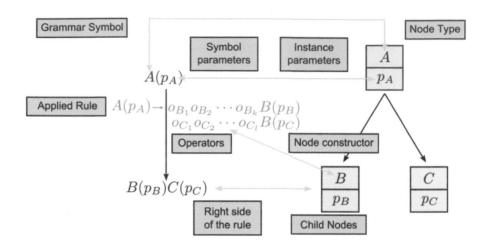

Figure 2.1. Equivalence of the PGI model with L-systems.

using only context-free rules, rules of a sequential grammar G can be evaluated in parallel. As a proof, consider the syntax tree of a string derived in G, the parallel breadth-first traversal of this tree corresponds to the L-system-style rule application. In terms of geometric modeling, when two procedural objects are independent they can always be refined independently, thus, in parallel.

Also note that this does not necessarily hold for context-sensitive rules (i.e., having more than one symbol in the predecessor), as context-sensitive rules are not allowed in our model. Thus, the expressibility of some complex conditions like connectivity and object dependency is very limited in our system.

2.4   Model Details and Implementation

In this section, we will give a detailed overview of the L-system-based model we used and we will describe its GPU implementation. Since our intention is to allow modelers to write rules instead of programs, we will also discuss automatic code generation from a grammar and describe what parts a grammar description should consist of to work with our model. The concrete, XML-based grammar descriptor format we used is included with the demo programs.

2.4.1   Symbols

Representing geometry. In the turtle graphics representation, geometry is created using symbols that represent drawing commands which are relative to the current rendering state. Here, these symbols represent the geometry (an arbitrary mesh) with their parameters and are called *instanced symbols*. Every instanced symbol stores every parameter needed for its drawing (*instancing*), thus, instanced symbols are independent. This enables parallel instancing, and a sequence of symbols becomes a set. In contrast to the turtle graphics model, instanced symbols cannot affect the rendering state in our model. Such symbols given in the turtle graphics model can be treated by splitting them into an instanced symbol and one or more operators (see the definition of operators below). For example, let module $F(l)$ mean drawing a line having length l and then moving the actual drawing position (a global rendering state) by l to the current direction. In the scene-graph-based representation this corresponds to $\overline{F}(l, o)m(\vec{v})$, where $\overline{F}(l, o)$ represents a line with length l and orientation o, and operator $m(\vec{v})$ represents translation, with vector $\vec{v}$ having the same effect as in $F(l)$. In this case, the operator has to follow the instanced symbol to get the same result. After these splitting transformations, the rules can be rewritten as described in Section 2.4.6.

Operators. Symbols representing a command that changes module parameters are called *operators*, we denote them with lower case letters. There is no global rendering state, as every operator modifies only the parameters of the next geometric object. In other words, every operator belongs to one specific instanced symbol in a string and modifies only that symbol's parameters. This way we can easily achieve equivalence with the PGI model, and these operators can hide the programs of the nodes that execute at the time of instantiation. Operators are relative to the left side of the rule, or in terms of PGI the parent node. For example, consider the rule

$$A \rightarrow hBhC$$

where operator h halves the size. The size parameter of both B and C will be the half of A's size.

Representation. In our model, each module is represented by a vertex, which allows us to implement rules and create new modules in the geometry shader. Section 2.4.2 will discuss the benefits of this decision.

Theoretically, different symbols can have different parameters. However, we found this impractical. Having multiple vertex types would result in more passes or additional branching in the shader code. Thus, our approach sacrifices storage space for efficiency and stores generic vertices that are capable of representing any type. The corresponding vertex type (a record in both the CPU and the GPU code) is created automatically as the union of all module data types and a symbol identifier. Thus, symbols appear as identifiers, mapped into integers between 1 and the number of symbols, which is also generated automatically from the grammar description, similarly to [Sowers 08]. To make the implementation of the code generation easier, we required the explicit specification of symbols in the grammar description, although they are implicitly given with the rules.

Since we merge all symbol types into one general record, the vertex type grows bigger. Therefore, it is easier to exceed the limit of the vertex size or the limit of the output size of the geometry shader. To overcome these problems we can use line or triangle primitives (instead of vertices) to represent modules or distribute module data between several primitives (vertex, line or triangle) and perform a single iteration step of the geometry generation in multiple passes. However, the first option alone does not solve the problem of the geometry shader's output limit, and splitting into multiple passes only works if rules do not depend on every attribute value at the same time. Fortunately, this holds in many cases; for example, position, size, and orientation are usually independent. We would like to note here that all our examples used a single vertex.

Modules are stored on the GPU in vertex buffers. In our experience 100 bytes is a reasonable upper bound for the storage requirement of one module (e.g., 25 float attributes can fit into it). Thus, the representation of one million vertices requires about 100 MB of storage, which can fit in a modern GPU's memory several times. Generating much more than one million modules with real-time rates exceeds the capabilities of our implementation, therefore, storage requirements of the algorithm should not cause any problems on high performance graphics cards.

2.4.2   Algorithm Overview

Figure 2.2 shows the overview of the complete algorithm. It consists of three main parts.

The first step is the generation of the procedural scene graph, called *generation step* (see Listing 2.1). This part is similar to the split grammar GPU implementation in [Sowers 08]. Starting with the axiom string, we perform iterations by applying rules of an L-system to generate instanced modules. These are only descriptors of different geometric objects stored as vertices, no concrete geometry is created here. Every operation is performed in the geometry shader, and modules are processed in parallel. The vertex shader simply passes its input without any modifications, and rasterization is disabled. We apply culling first for every module; this ensures that those objects that are not visible in the current frame are not generated. For modules that passed culling and were not terminated, we apply a rule. The left side of the rule is the symbol type of the module, which is stored in a symbol identifier. If there are multiple rules for that symbol, a *rule-selection algorithm* is applied to choose one of them. The chosen rule is applied by creating new modules and initializing them with the proper operators. As a last step,

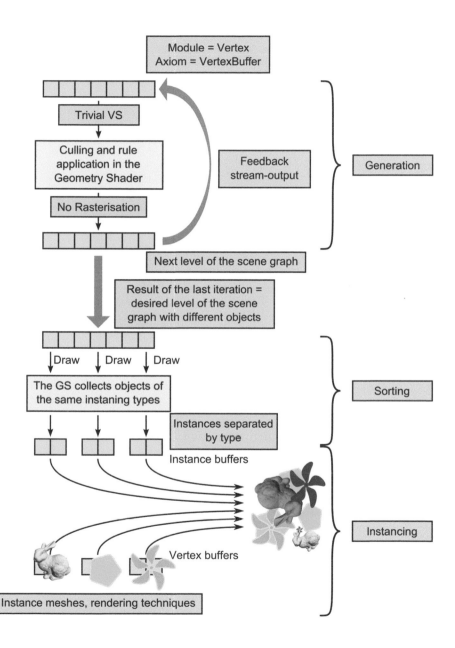

Figure 2.2. Overview of the implementation.

```
// The input of the first iteration is the axiom.
device->IASetVertexBuffers(0, 1, &axiomBuffer,
   &modulStrides, &zeroOffset);
// Apply generation shaders.
generationTechnique->GetPassByIndex(0)->Apply(0);
// Execute an iteration maxDepth times.
for (int depth = 0; depth < maxDepth; ++depth)
{
   // Set dstBuffer as stream output.
   device->SOSetTargets(1, &dstBuffer, &zeroOffset);
   // First draw call has to process the axiom.
   if (0 == depth)
      device->Draw(axiomLength, 0);
   else
      device->DrawAuto();
   // Ping pong
   ID3D10Buffer* nullBuffer = NULL;
   device->SOSetTargets(1, &nullBuffer, &zeroOffset);
   std::swap(dstBuffer, srcBuffer);

   // Set srcBuffer as input
   device->IASetVertexBuffers(0, 1, &srcBuffer,
      &modulStrides, &zeroOffset);
}
```

Listing 2.1. DX10 implementation of the CPU code of the generation step using fixed
iteration number.

the modules are inserted into the new set of modules (the stream output), which
is the input of the next iteration. Since we utilize the geometry shader for the
creation of new modules, only the desired number of output is generated. There
are no dummy symbols as in Hart's GPU L-system implementation using pixel
shaders [Lacz and Hart 04].

After the generation step, modules are sorted by instancing type; that is,
what kind of geometry they represent and what technique is used to render them.
Sorting is essential for the efficient instancing of the generated descriptors.

Finally, we render the scene using instancing.

2.4.3 Iteration and Termination

We build up the procedural scene graph using breadth-first traversal, generating
the subsequent level in every iteration step by performing a draw call and applying one rule for each non-terminated module. In most cases, the depth of the
generation can be exactly specified. The concrete depth depends on the grammar
as well as other conditions like dynamic level of detail. Thus, the most basic way

```
[maxvertexcount(MAX_SUCCESSOR_LENGTH)]
void gsGeneration(point Module input[1],
                  inout PointStream<Module> stream)
{
   // Perform culling here.

   // Checking termination
   if (input[0].terminated)
   {
      stream.Append(input[0]);
      return;
   }
   // Rule selection and application here.
}
```

Listing 2.2. The role of termination in the geometry shader.

to implement the CPU code is to execute the iteration maxDepth-times, where maxDepth is the desired level.

Objects usually do not need to be refined to the same level. For example, generating a building may need more iterations then a flower, or we add more details to a building closer to the camera then another building that is far away. To support this, we added a parameter (called **terminated**) to the module type that indicates whether the object is completed or not (see Listing 2.2). The ideal implementation would be to separate the completed objects from those that require further iterations, but the current shader model does not allow inserting different data into multiple stream outputs. We found it too inefficient to insert a sorting step that collects terminated modules and removes them from the working stream. Thus, we keep completed modules in the same buffer with the incomplete modules and simply pass them through the pipeline. Please note that if the shader model would allow dividing the data between multiple buffers, we could simply send the terminated modules into another stream.

Termination can be useful to implement another strategy to determine the generation depth. Sometimes it is better to perform iterations until there has been a change in the current modules. In other words, we can end the iterations if all modules are terminated. Unfortunately we cannot set any kind of global flag in the geometry shader to indicate that there is an incomplete module. However, we can extend the generation with a pixel shader stage, which discards pixels where the **terminated** parameter coming from the geometry shader is true. Thus, if any pixel is refreshed (this can be checked with a single occlusion query), that signals a change in the module set. To avoid writing the same pixels we can extend the Module struct with a module identifier. If M is the maximum number of symbols in successors, d is current generation level, and p denotes the position of the newly

```
[maxvertexcount(MAX_SUCCESSOR_LENGTH)]
void gsGeneration(point Module input[1],
                  inout PointStream<Module> stream)
{
    if ( cullModule( input[0] )
        return;
    // Check for termination. Select and apply rules.
}
```

Listing 2.3. Culling in the geometry shader.

created module in the applied rule, the following formula

$$\texttt{newModule.objectID} = M^d + \texttt{parent.objectID} * M + p$$

gives a unique identifier, which can be easily mapped to the pixels of the render target.

Note that with multiple different stream outputs this strategy is greatly simplified, the iteration has to be continued until the working buffer is not empty.

2.4.4   Culling

The goal of culling is to throw away those modules that do not effect the currently rendered frame. Formally, this corresponds to the application of the rule

$$A \to \epsilon$$

where ϵ is the empty string. However, adding this rule for every symbol would be too tedious; thus, it is not included in the grammar description. The implementation is simple—the geometry shader simply does not return anything for culled modules (see Listing 2.3).

The culling strategy can be very diverse depending on the procedural model; for example, culling based on size in pixels, alpha value, distance from the camera, or frustum culling.

We implemented spheres and *axis-aligned bounding boxes* (AABBs) as bounding geometries for frustum culling (we use it for interaction in Section 2.5 as well). These are resized to the module's size parameter (possibly three-dimensional) and centered to the module's position (see Listing 2.4). However, any kind of bounding volume can be stored or computed, possibly different for every symbol, and depending on the module parameters.

2.4.5   Rule Selection

Before applying a specific rule, we have to decide which rule to use. First, we have to identify the left side of the rule (the predecessor), which is simply the symbol

```
// Culling a sphere with a plane
bool isecPlaneSphere(float4 plane,float3 center,float radius)
{
    return dot( plane, float4(center,1) ) < -radius;
}

// Frustum culling of a bounding sphere
bool isecFrustumSphere( Module module )
{
    return isecPlaneSphere(p_near, module.pos, module.size)   ||
           isecPlaneSphere(p_far, module.pos, module.size)    ||
           isecPlaneSphere(p_left, module.pos, module.size)   ||
           isecPlaneSphere(p_right, module.pos, module.size)  ||
           isecPlaneSphere(p_top, module.pos, module.size)    ||
           isecPlaneSphere(p_bottom, module.pos, module.size);
}

// Main culling function
bool cullModule(Module module)
{
    if (enableModuleCulling)
       // Additional culling conditions can be or-ed
       return isecFrustumSphere(module);
    else
       return false;
}
```

Listing 2.4. An example of the culling function: frustum culling with a bounding sphere.

stored in the symbol ID of the module. These were mapped to numeric constants in compile time, so the selection between rules means a sequence of if-then-else statements as in [Sowers 08], or an equivalent switch-case statement.

We often assign multiple rules to a single symbol; thus, we have to select one. Allowing multiple rules for a symbol is important since this is the way we add variation to the generated geometry or describe different conditions. Traditionally, *stochastic* L-systems are used, where every rule has a probability, and they are chosen randomly. Additionally, we can assign conditions to rules; these are expressions of the module parameters of the predecessor. Thus, the most efficient way to select and apply rules is an if-then-else statement, where the conditions are the conjunction of the equality test with the symbol ID, the condition of the rule, and the test of the generated random value for handling probability, and the body of the if statement is the rule application, as in [Sowers 08] (see Listing 2.5).

In our model (see Listing 2.6), we use rule selection strategies to select between rules of a given predecessor (this is mostly a modification only in the terminology). The idea comes from [Parish and Müller 01], where the authors used the

```
[maxvertexcount(MAX_SUCCESSOR_LENGTH)]
void gsGeneration(point Module input[1],
                  inout PointStream<Module> stream)
{
   // Culling and termination check.

   // Any kind of one-dimensional GPU noise can be used here.
   float random = getRandomBetween_0_1();

   Module parent = input[0];
   if(parent.symbolID == ID_of_the_predecessor &&
      conditions_of_the_rule &&
      // Intervals of the allowed random values,
      // an_upper_bound-a_lower_bound is the
      // probability of the rule.
      a_lower_bound <= random &&
      random < an_upper_bound)
   {
      // Create and initialize successor modules here.
   }
   else if (/*...*/) {/*...*/}
   // Similar if statements for the remaining rules
}
```

Listing 2.5. Rule selection with if-then-else statements.

concepts *global goals* and *local constraints* to select rules and set module parameters. Identifiers are generated for rules in compile time (of the shader), and we obtain the length of each rule and store these as compile time constants. Rule selection strategies are functions that return a rule identifier and a rule length. The returned rule lengths are not necessarily constants, thus, we can simulate variable length rules like split or repeat in [Müller et al. 06]:

```
void selectRule_ModuleName(in Module parent,
                           out int rule_length,
                           out int ruleID);
```

Rule selection methods are discussed in more detail in Section 2.4.7.

Instead of the if-then-else statements described above, we used a different structure. It is only an insignificant technical detail, but we found it very comfortable to use. We made these changes to improve the quality and readability of the generated code by separating its main parts, however, it adds a small overhead to the generation. Code quality is not the most important goal in real-time computer graphics (unlike performance), but when the number of rules becomes larger and we would like to modify the code, it can help a lot. Although code generation is automated, nearly the same way as Sowers, we may want to modify

```
void selectRule (in Module module , out int rule_length ,
                 out int ruleID)
{
    switch (module.symbolID)
    {
        case a_symbol_ID :
            // Invokes the proper strategy assigned to the symbol
            // Such function is created for every symbol
            selectRule_symbolsName (module , rule_length , ruleID);
            break;
        // A case for other symbols
    };
}

[maxvertexcount (MAX_SUCCESSOR_LENGTH)]
void gsGeneration (point Module input [1],
                   inout PointStream <Module > stream)
{
    // Culling and termination check

    // Selecting a rule and getting its successor length
    // (number of modules in it)
    int rule_length , rule_id;
    selectRule ( input [0], rule_length , rule_id );

    // Getting the successor modules and streaming them out
    for ( int i = 1; i < rule_length; ++i )
    {
        stream.Append (getNextModule (input [0], rule_id , i));
    }
}
```

Listing 2.6. A less efficient, but more readable implementation of the rule selection and application.

the generated parts for debugging, optimize, or experiment with new rule selection strategies or operators.

To support automatic code generation, different rule selection strategies have to be implemented. These can be assigned to symbols by the modelers in the grammar description. Thus, the task of automatic code generation is simply the invocation of the proper pre-implemented function.

2.4.6 Rule Application

In our model a rule successor is a set of symbols, where operators can be assigned to every symbol. For example, the rules of the Sierpinski-triangle formally would

```
// Main module creation function
Module getNextModule(Module parent, // predecessor
                     int ruleID,    // ID of the selected rule
                     int index)     // position in the successor
{
    Module output;
    switch (ruleID)
    {
        // A case is created for every rule.
        case a_specific_ruleID:
            // A similar function is created for every ruleID.
            return getNextModule_a_RuleID( parent, index );
        // ...
    };
    return output;
}
// Module creation function for a rule
Module getNextModule_a_RuleID(Module parent, int index )
{
    Module output = parent;
    switch(index)
    {
        // The number of cases equals the number of
        // symbols in the successor.
        case i:
            output.symbolID = id_of_the_ith_symbol;
            // Invocation of the proper operators
        // ...
    };
}
```

Listing 2.7. Rule application functions, that return one module.

look like

$$T \rightarrow \{s(0.5)m(-0.5, -h/4)T, s(0.5)m(0.5, -h/4)T, s(0.5)m(0, h/4)T\},$$

where s multiplies the inherited size by the given parameter, $m(x, y)$ adds the vector $(x, y) * P.size$ to the parameter, and h denotes here the height of the unit triangle. In our XML-based grammar descriptor, this rule can be expressed as

```
<rule>
    <predecessor module="T" />
    <successor module="T">
        <operator name="resize" value="0.5" />
        <operator name="move_xy" x="-0.5" y="0.2165" />
    </successor>
```

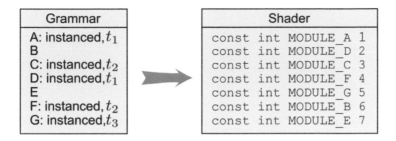

Figure 2.3. An example of the generated symbol IDs. Instancing types are denoted with t_i for simplicity.

```
...the remaining two modules are given similarly...
</rule>
```

If we have rules given in the turtle graphics style, we can easily rewrite them to get the same result. First, we have to split symbols representing drawing commands that change the rendering state as described in Section 2.4.1 (see Listing 2.7). Then, for each drawing command, we have to calculate the current rendering state at the point of its invocation, which is simply the concatenation of all operators before the symbol. For example, in the following rule

$$A \rightarrow \{o_1 B o_2 C o_3 o_4 D\},$$

the rendering state at C is the result of $o_1 o_2$. Thus, the rule is transformed to

$$A \rightarrow \{o_1 B, o_1 o_2 C, o_1 o_2 o_3 o_4 D\}.$$

Automatic code generation goes the same way as for rule selections. We have to pre-implement operators; the generated code will invoke these.

The performance of our system strongly depends on the number of different branches. Sorting the vertex buffer by symbol ID could greatly improve performance when there are many rules. However, adding a sorting step after each iteration would result in a significant performance loss (see Figure 2.3). Thus, performance issues of dynamic branching should be taken into account when designing the rules. Since the successor is a set (although theoretically there is no order between the symbols), it affects the order in which modules are inserted into the stream. For a very basic example, let us consider an L-system with the following three rules:

$$A \rightarrow BCBC$$
$$B \rightarrow BB$$
$$C \rightarrow CC$$

The first rule is theoretically equivalent to

$$A \rightarrow BBCC$$

If we compare a simple derivation using these rules, we can see that in the second case, the vertex buffer is sorted, therefore parallel threads will follow the same path except in one case. In contrast, using the unsorted vertex buffer, it is more likely that parallel threads always have to follow the path for two rules.

$$A \rightarrow BCBC \rightarrow BBCCBBCC \rightarrow BBBBCCCCBBBBCCCC$$
$$A \rightarrow BBCC \rightarrow BBBBCCCC \rightarrow BBBBBBBBCCCCCCCC$$

2.4.7   Expressiveness of the Model: Selection Strategies and Operators

As mentioned in the previous sections, automatic code generation becomes simple if we use predefined and implemented rule selection functions and operators. From the viewpoint of geometric modeling, these are the soul of the whole system, they determine usability and expressiveness, therefore, they should be well-designed.

The role of selection functions and operators is to hide programs from modelers. There is no restriction on the complexity of these programs, they can contain branching or even loops. Since in our knowledge, there are no standards of rule-based modeling, it is only a matter of taste what complex functions we allow. We would like to note here that branching in operators or selection functions can be replaced by using more rules and vice versa. Therefore, by allowing more complex operators, modeling of a specific scene can be represented with less rules in most cases, but makes it harder to learn and understand the operators. It is also important to note that the complexity of the shaders is about the same in both cases.

Many examples for both rule selection and operators can be found in the demo programs. To name a few, rule selection based on level-of-detail, stochastic selection, perturbation of a module attribute with a random value, changing its size or position or time dependent operators.

2.4.8   Sorting

Different types of objects may be rendered differently. For example, a window object and a trunk of a bonsai tree probably have different meshes and shaders. Thus, after the generation step we sort the created modules by instancing type. Any kind of sorting algorithm can be used here, we used bucket sort.

The symbol identifiers are sorted in compile time of the shader code such that the identifiers of the instanced symbols have smaller values and form a continuous interval. There is no reason to forbid assigning the same instancing type to two

```
[maxvertexcount(1)]
void gsSort(point Module input[1],
            inout PointStream<SortedModule> stream)
{
    // In every step minID and maxID are set by the CPU code.
    if (minID <= input[0].symbolID && input[0].symbolID <= maxID)
        // Unused attributes are removed; the rest are simply copied.
        stream.Append(convertToSorted(input[0]));
}
```

Listing 2.8. Geometry shader code of the sorting.

or more symbols. To handle this case, we sort the identifiers of the instanced symbols such that symbols with the same instancing type also form a continuous interval. Thus, modules with a specific instancing type can be collected using two arithmetic comparisons in the geometry shader. Modules with the current instancing type are emitted by the geometry shader, while others are pruned. As in the generation step, we use a trivial vertex shader and no rasterization. As an output of the geometry shader we use a different structure. To save space, those attributes that are not used in the instancing step (e.g., the symbol ID) are removed (see Listing 2.8).

The naive implementation of the bucket sort fills one bucket in every pass. If we denote the number of modules generated by the production step by N, this approach requires I passes, and N modules go through the pipeline in each pass (see Listing 2.9).

Since N is usually much larger than I, we should optimize the naive approach to reduce the size of the input of each pass. We can achieve this by using the same structure as a binary tree sorting: we recursively divide the modules into two parts, until each part corresponds to only one instancing type. Since only one stream output is allowed, we have to process each level of the binary tree sequentially. The leaves of this tree are the original buckets, thus the total number of passes needed is $2I - 1$, but the average size of the input of a pass will be approximately

$$N \frac{\log I}{(2I - 1)}$$

(assuming that instancing types have equal probability). Note that since all information we need for implementing the shader code that performs these passes is the value of I and the ID of the instanced symbols, this code can be generated automatically. Collecting more than one instancing type in a pass does not require modifications in the shader code, since the IDs are connected, continuous intervals.

```
const int moduleIDStart = grammarDescriptor ->getSymbolIDStart ();
// Query the number of emitted modules .
D3D10_QUERY_DESC queryDesc ;
queryDesc .Query = D3D10_QUERY_SO_STATISTICS ;
queryDesc .MiscFlags = 0;
ID3D10Query * pQuery ;
device ->CreateQuery (&queryDesc , &pQuery );
int offset = 0;
for(int i = 0;
    i < grammarDescriptor ->getInstancingTypeNumber (); ++i)
{
    pQuery ->Begin ();

    // Set interval borders .
    int minID = grammarDescriptor ->getInstancedIDInterval (i).min ;
    int maxID = grammarDescriptor ->getInstancedIDInterval (i).max ;
    minIDEffectVar ->AsScalar ()->SetInt (minID+moduleIDStart );
    maxIDEffectVar ->AsScalar ()->SetInt (maxID+moduleIDStart );
    sortingShader ->GetPassByIndex (0)->Apply (0);

    device ->SOSetTargets (1, &instancedModuleBuffer , &offset );
    device ->DrawAuto ();

    // Get the result of the query .
    pQuery ->End ();
    D3D10_QUERY_DATA_SO_STATISTICS queryData ;
    while(S_OK != pQuery ->GetData (&queryData ,
        sizeof (D3D10_QUERY_DATA_SO_STATISTICS ), 0))
    {}
    instancedModuleNumbers [i] = queryData .NumPrimitivesWritten ;
    offset += instancedModuleNumbers [i];
    instancedModuleOffsets [i] = offset ;
    pQuery ->Release ();
}
```

Listing 2.9. CPU code of the naive sorting.

Note that both sorting methods would gain a significant speedup in performance from the possibility to have multiple different stream outputs.

The buckets can be represented as a part of a single vertex buffer, or as separate vertex buffers. Separate vertex buffers can be wasteful if we do not assume anything about the distribution of the generated symbols, since we have to allocate a buffer having the same size as the result of the buffer used in the generation step to ensure that all modules fit into the buckets. Using a single buffer requires us to play with offsets and it needs only the same amount of memory as the buffer used in the generation step.

```
const unsigned int moduleStride = sizeof(SortedModule);
for(int i = 0;
    i < grammarDescriptor ->getInstancingTypeNumber(); ++i)
{
    // Set instance buffers.
    device ->IASetVertexBuffers(1, 1, &instancedModuleBuffer ,
                                &moduleStride ,
                                &instancedModuleOffsets [i]);
    // Set the proper rendering technique.
    setRenderingTechnique(i);
    // Rendering the mesh. This sets the vertex buffer as well.
    renderMesh(i,                          // instancing type ID
               instancedModuleNumbers [i]  // number of instances
}
```

Listing 2.10. Our CPU implementation of the instancing step in DX10.

2.4.9 Instancing

Now we have the generated object descriptors separated into buckets. Our last task is to render them. An *instancing type*, which is an ordered pair consisting of a mesh and a rendering technique, is assigned to every instanced symbol in the grammar description.

The rendering is performed using instancing; we bind the buckets as instance buffers and the corresponding meshes as vertex buffers (see Listing 2.10). Thus, the number of draw calls needed equals to the number of different instancing types used in the grammar description. Note that the geometry is fully synthesized on the GPU, no readback to the CPU is needed.

Using the instance information in the rendering code is straightforward. For example, assuming that every mesh is centered at the origin and normalized to have unit size, the world position of a vertex in an instance mesh can be calculated in the vertex shader as

```
output.pos.xyz = input.basic_pos;      // mesh coordinates
output.pos.xyz *= input.size;          // instance size
output.pos.xyz += input.inst_pos.xyz; // instance position
output.pos.w = 1;
```

2.5 Interaction with the Procedural Scene

Interaction with the environment is an important task in many applications (see Figure 2.4). To address this in our procedurally created scenes, we have to evaluate the intersection of an object with the procedural scene. We can use this information later to generate any kind of response. In the following, we refer the

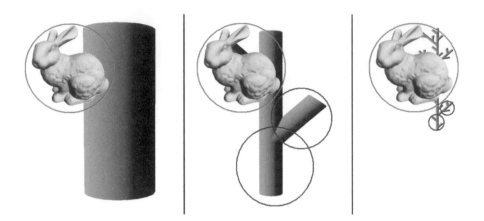

Figure 2.4. Intersection of an active object (the bunny) with a procedural fern. The orange circle shows the bounding sphere of the bunny, the red circles show the culled modules.

nodes of the procedural scene graph as *passive objects* and the objects that the procedural scene interacts with as *active objects*.

By assigning a bounding volume to every node in the procedural scene graph we can obtain a bounding volume hierarchy. This hierarchy is used as usual. During intersection tests, a node in the graph is thrown away, if it has no intersection with the current active object. Implementing this in our model can be achieved by creating a new module type and a new culling strategy. Naturally, it is designed for a large number of active objects (which is common in physical simulations, in games having AI-players, or particle systems), so we can utilize the parallel computing capabilities of the GPU. For only a few active objects, a CPU implementation would be sufficiently fast.

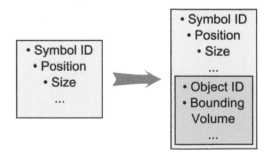

Figure 2.5. Extending the module type with information on an active object.

```
bool cullIntersect( Module module )
{
    float dist = length(module.pos-module.object_pos);
    return dist > module.size+module.object_radius;
}
```

Listing 2.11. HLSL implementation of the new culling strategy in the case of bounding spheres.

First, the original module type is extended with the parameters of the active object. Thus, instead of representing a single node of the procedural scene graph, now a module represents both the node (a passive object) and its intersection with an active object. Figure 2.5 shows the new module type.

If the represented node of the procedural scene does not intersect with the represented active object, the new culling strategy throws away a module. Listing 2.11 shows the HLSL implementation of the culling strategy in the case of bounding spheres.

The rest of the algorithm remains the same. Since we are not interested in rendering the intersections, we perform only the generation step. Every iteration generates the intersection of the active objects with the corresponding level of the procedural scene graph. Therefore, with the last iteration, we obtain the intersection with the leaf nodes.

Figure 2.6. A procedurally created labyrinth using recursive subdivisions and its intersection with balls.

After the GPU has finished the production, we can read back the results to the CPU and process it. The result is a vertex buffer in which, for each active object, there is a vertex for every procedural leaf node it intersects with. Each vertex stores the active object's ID (and its position and bounding volume information which are now irrelevant), and all information about the intersected procedural node. The appropriate collision response can be performed by processing this data sequentially on the CPU.

Figure 2.6 shows an example. The labyrinth is created procedurally using recursive subdivision rules (the exact rules are included with the demo programs). The balls are the (nonprocedural) active objects. The lower right picture shows the intersection of the balls with the scene, which is the result of the generation step.

2.6   Results

We implemented our model using C++, DirectX10, and HLSL. Tests were performed on a system with an ATI Radeon 4850 graphics card, a 3 GHz Intel Core 2 Duo CPU, and 4 GByte RAM.

As a performance test, we measured the times required to perform one iteration of the generation step and the perform the complete sorting steps. The input consisted of $100,000$ vertices in both cases. In our experience, the running times scaled approximately linearly with the size of the input for larger numbers, thus, we can estimate the values for different input size.

2.6.1   Performance of the Generation Step

In most cases, the successor of the rules consists of multiple symbols. This means that the size of the input is at least doubled in an iteration step. Therefore the performance of the whole generation is mostly affected by the last iteration. In other words, we can approximate the running time of the whole generation independently of the grammar and generation depth by measuring only one iteration.

The performance is mostly affected by dynamic branching. Thus we performed an iteration for up to 20 rules for a fixed input size of $100,000$ modules. For every symbol we had one rule, as the number of nonterminal symbols was equal to the number of rules. Rules created two new modules, and set one attribute. Culling and termination check was disabled.

We also tested the effect of the sortedness of the input buffer on the performance. Let us denote the nonterminal symbols with $A_1...A_n$. We initialized the vertex buffer as

$$A_1^k A_2^k ... A_n^k A_1^k A_2^k ... A_n^k ...$$

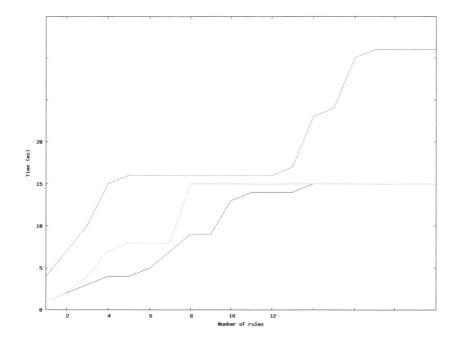

Figure 2.7. Time needed to perform an iteration for $100,000$ modules.

where A_i^k denotes repetition of A_i k-times. Thus, the sortedness of the buffer is increased with the value of k.

Figure 2.7 shows our results.

2.6.2 Performance of the Sorting Step

To test the performance of the sorting, we measured the running time of one pass (which collects modules with a specific instancing type or types), which was between 1 and 14 ms, depending on the sortedness. The times for a specific grammar can be approximated using the formulas described in Section 2.4.8.

2.6.3 Examples

To test the complete algorithm including rendering, we designed several simple examples; see Figures 2.8 and 2.9.

Collision detection was measured on the labyrinth example shown in Section 2.4.9. The average FPS rate was 25 for 1000 balls and labyrinth size of 128×128, including readback to the CPU and rendering the scene.

Figure 2.8. Rough model of a city generated from one vertex, using 22 rules, rendered at 22 FPS.

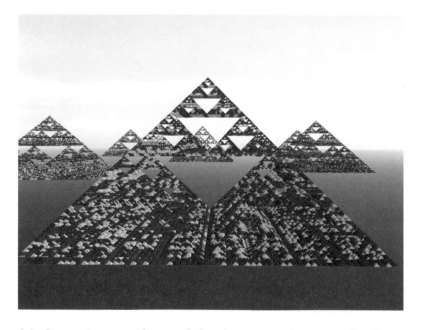

Figure 2.9. Sierpinski pyramids extended with random coloring, rendered at 55 FPS.

2.7   Conclusion

In this article, we proposed a framework for real-time generation of procedural geometry described by context-free L-systems or equivalent models. Our results showed that the system is capable of synthesizing complex geometry with real-time rates.

Additionally, we showed a simple modification to allow discrete collision detection with the procedural scene by calculating the intersection of any given objects with the procedurally generated environment. Our implementation worked well for a large number of objects.

Assuming the rule selection strategies and operators are fixed and previously implemented, every part of both the shader and the CPU code can be generated automatically. Thus, the modelers do not need to learn any programming.

Bibliography

[Ebert et al. 02] David S. Ebert, Kenton F. Musgrave, Darwyn Peachey, Ken Perlin, and Steven Worley. *Texturing and Modeling: A Procedural Approach.* Morgan Kaufmann, 2002.

[Hart 92] John C. Hart. "The Object Instancing Paradigm for Linear Fractal Modeling." In *Proceedings of the Conference on Graphics Interface '92*, pp. 224–231. San Francisco: Morgan Kaufmann Publishers, 1992.

[Lacz and Hart 04] P. Lacz and JC Hart. "Procedural Geometric Synthesis on the GPU." In *Proceedings of the ACM Workshop on General Purpose Computing on Graphics Processors*, 2, 2, pp. 23–23. New York: ACM, 2004. Available online (http://graphics.cs.uiuc.edu/~jch/papers/).

[Lipp et al. 08] Markus Lipp, Peter Wonka, and Michael Wimmer. "Interactive Visual Editing of Grammars for Procedural Architecture." 2008. Article no. 102. Available online (http://www.cg.tuwien.ac.at/research/publications/2008/LIPP-2008-IEV/).

[Müller et al. 06] Pascal Müller, Peter Wonka, Simon Haegler, Andreas Ulmer, and Luc Van Gool. "Procedural Modeling of Buildings." In *SIGGRAPH '06: ACM SIGGRAPH 2006 Papers*, pp. 614–623. New York: ACM, 2006.

[Parish and Müller 01] Yoav I. H. Parish and Pascal Müller. "Procedural Modeling of Cities." In *SIGGRAPH '01: Proceedings of the 28th Annual Conference on Computer Graphics and Interactive Techniques*, pp. 301–308. New York: ACM, 2001.

[Prusinkiewicz and Lindenmayer 91] Przemyslaw Prusinkiewicz and Aristid Lindenmayer. *The Algorithmic Beauty of Plants (The Virtual Laboratory)*. Springer, 1991. Available online (http://www.amazon.ca/exec/obidos/ redirect?tag=citeulike09-20&path=ASIN/0387972978).

[Sowers 08] B. Sowers. "Increasing the Performance and Realism of Procedurally Generated Buildings." Master's thesis, College of Engineering and Mineral Resources, West Virginia University, 2008.

[Wonka et al. 03] Peter Wonka, Michael Wimmer, François Sillion, and William Ribarsky. "Instant Architecture." *ACM Transactions on Graphics* 22:4 (2003), 669–677. Proceeding. Available online (http://artis.inrialpes.fr/ Publications/2003/WWSR03).

3

GPU-Based NURBS Geometry Evaluation and Rendering

Graham Hemingway

Non-uniform rational B-spline (NURBS) geometry is used in a wide range of three-dimensional applications. NURBS can represent nearly any curve or surface and require only a small set of values to precisely define every point within their domain. Their utility comes from their precise mathematical definition and their relative ease of use compared to other forms of mathematically-defined geometry, such as Bezier or Hermite curves. Increased precision comes at a cost though. NURBS geometry imposes a relatively heavy computational burden. Unlike simple geometry meshes, every NURBS vertex must be individually calculated using a parametric equation and a set of characteristic values. This computational cost has limited NURBS use to applications where the need for precision outweighs the increased computational overhead.

In this chapter we will demonstrate a method for using the GPU to calculate NURBS geometry and make the vertex data readily available for either rendering or further processing. Compared to evaluation on the CPU, this method yields significant performance improvements without drawbacks in precision or flexibility. We will also discuss an extension to the general NURBS evaluation method that allows for calculating trimmed NURBS surfaces. All of the methods discussed are applicable to a wide range of GPUs. Throughout our discussion we will use OpenGL and GLSL to illustrate our examples, but DirectX could just as easily be used.

3.1 A Bit of NURBS Background

Before discussing how to calculate NURBS on the GPU, it is important to have a good working understanding of the mathematics and terminology behind NURBS.

There are numerous approaches to representing curves and surface on computers. The most common in graphics is to use a free-form mesh of vertices. In a mesh, individual points are defined, but the geometry between two points is not fully defined. While this works well in many situations, some applications need to have geometry accurately specified throughout a curve or surface. For example, the process of designing mechanical parts demands extremely precise definition of all geometric entities since inaccuracies from the model can result in unexpected physical phenomenon, errors in manufacturing, and increased design cost.

The two methods most commonly used to mathematically express curves and surfaces are implicit and parametric functions. They provide a rigorous mathematical basis from which to construct geometry. An implicit function for a two-dimensional curve takes the form of $f(x, y) = 0$. The variables x and y vary in a coordinated way and yield a curve on the x, y plane. Similarly, a three-dimensional surface can be represented by an implicit function in the form $f(x, y, z) = 0$.

Parametric functions for two-dimensional curves take the following form:

$$C(u) = (x(u), y(u)) \quad a \leq u \leq b.$$

$C(u)$ is a vector-valued function of the independent variable u. a and b can be arbitrary, but in general it is assumed that the parametric value varies over the interval $[0, 1]$. The prototypical example of a parametric curve is the one for a unit circle centered at the origin:

$$
\begin{aligned}
x(t) &= \cos(t), \\
y(t) &= \sin(t).
\end{aligned}
$$

Parametric equations for surfaces are a simple extension from curves and have the form $S(u, v) = (x(u, v), y(u, v), z(u, v))$. Note that two independent variables, u and v, are now present. The use of two variables gives each surface a rectangular parametric space. This is important to keep in mind throughout the discussion of both NURBS surfaces and later, trimmed surfaces.

NURBS are a class of parametric equations that can represent either curves or surfaces depending on their formulation. As mentioned above, a NURBS curve has one parametric value, while a NURBS surface has two. Several pieces of information are needed to fully define NURBS geometry. Let us first consider what is needed to define a curve through three-dimensional space.

First, we require a set of characteristic points called the *control points*. These points define the general geometric shape of the curve, though the curve generally does not intersect them. In Figure 3.1 the blue dots represent the control points for the purple curve, which is the NURBS curve we are trying to define. The second piece of information is the *knot vector* and will be discussed further below. Finally, we need to specify the set of *control point weights*. These are used to "rationalize"

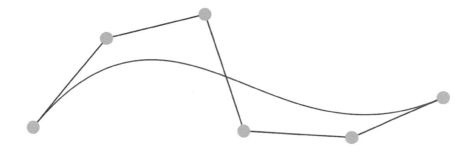

Figure 3.1. A simple NURBS curve

the curve and allow for certain shapes, such as circles or conic sections, to be modeled. With these pieces of information in hand, we can proceed to define the general equation for NURBS curves:

$$C(u) = \frac{\sum_{i=0}^{n-1} N_{i,p}(u) w_i \mathbf{P}_i}{\sum_{i=0}^{n-1} N_{i,p}(u) w_i} \qquad 0 \le u \le 1. \tag{3.1}$$

Given some parametric input, u, Equation (3.1) says that the result, $C(u)$, is a point in space with the same number of dimensions as the control points, $\mathbf{P}_i$. If three-dimensional control points are used, then the resulting point is also in three-dimensional space. The degree of the curve, p, determines the number of control points that are taken into account when calculating the result. The control point weights are w_i. The summation is done from 0 to $n-1$, which is the number of control points minus one. The final component of Equation (3.1) is the B-spline basis function, $N_{i,p}$. It is this basis function that gives NURBS geometry its special properties.

Before discussing the basis function we need to get a better understanding of the knot vector. The knot vector dictates how the control points relate to the NURBS curve. There are many different ways to construct a knot vector, but we are mostly concerned with non-periodic and non-uniform knot vectors. Knot vectors frequently take the following form:

$$U = \{\underbrace{a, \ldots, a}_{p}, u_p, \ldots, u_{m-p-1}, \underbrace{b, \ldots, b}_{p}\}. \tag{3.2}$$

The number of knot values, m, in a knot vector is determined by the degree of the curve, p, and the number of control points, n, with the relation $m = n + p + 1$. A curve with a knot vector in the form of Equation (3.2) will start and end exactly at the first and last control points. This is achieved through repeating a and b, typically 0 and 1, respectively, p times. The remainder of the knot values are non-decreasing and lie between a and b. An example knot vector for a third degree curve with five control points is $\{0, 0, 0, 0.25, 0.5, 0.75, 1, 1, 1\}$.

Now we are ready to consider the B-spline basis function itself:

$$N_{i,0}(u) = \{ \begin{array}{ll} 1 & \text{if } u_i \le u < u_{i+1} \\ 0 & \text{otherwise} \end{array}$$

$$N_{i,p} = \frac{u - u_i}{u_{i+p} - u_i} N_{i,p-1}(u) + \frac{u_{i+p+1} - u}{u_{i+p+1} - u_{i+1}} N_{i+1,p-1}(u). \tag{3.3}$$

Equation (3.3) defines the basis function for all NURBS geometry. The top portion of the equation determines if a particular control point will be included in calculating the output value based on the parametric value, u and its relationship to the values in the knot vector, called the *span*. The bottom portion of the equation calculates the actual basis function value, and is quite recursive. This recursiveness is, in large part, the source of the computational complexity involved in evaluating NURBS geometry. The top portion of the equation requires finding which knot values are closest to the parametric value, both above and below. This also causes a good deal of computation to search through the knot vector.

The construction of the B-spline basis function imparts many unique and valuable properties upon NURBS geometry. One of the most important is that the basis function provides local support. This means that if one control point is repositioned, the NURBS curve will only change shape in the area close to that control point. This property makes designing complex geometry with NURBS much easier than other representations that alter the entire curve if any of the control points are altered. There are numerous other interesting properties of NURBS but we leave the reader to explore those.

Equation (3.4) shows that the equation for a NURBS surface is just an extension of that for a NURBS curve. A second parametric value, v, is added which necessitates a second basis function and some additional summation. Once you have become familiar with calculating NURBS curves, moving to surfaces is straightforward:

$$S(u,v) = \frac{\displaystyle\sum_{i=0}^{n-1}\sum_{j=0}^{m-1} N_{i,p}(u)N_{j,q}(v)w_{i,j}\mathbf{P}_{i,j}}{\displaystyle\sum_{i=0}^{n-1}\sum_{j=0}^{m-1} N_{i,p}(u)N_{j,q}(v)w_{i,j}} \qquad 0 \le u, v \le 1. \tag{3.4}$$

Calculating trimmed NURBS surfaces is the next step beyond standard NURBS surfaces. Imagine projecting a circle onto a surface and then removing, or simply not rendering, the surface within the circle. This type of complex geometry is very difficult to realize with a single NURBS surface but can easily be created using a trimming profile created from NURBS curves and projected onto an underlying NURBS surface. We will discuss a method for evaluating and rendering trimmed NURBS surfaces later in this chapter.

This has been a very high-level overview of NURBS geometry. Hopefully you now posses the basic concepts and terminology necessary to understand the remainder of this chapter. NURBS are incredibly powerful and can do many things beyond simple curves and surfaces. For further information about NURBS we highly recommend reading [Piegl and Tiller 97] as it is an excellent reference for NURBS background and computation.

3.2 Related Work

There has been a great deal of work on computerized methods for evaluating and displaying NURBS geometry. All methods tend to build on the fundamental NURBS algorithms [Piegl and Tiller 97] to some extent. Algorithms for efficiently rendering NURBS [Abi-Ezzi and Subramanian 94] and for tessellating and rendering trimmed surfaces [Kumar and Manocha 95, Guthe et al. 02, Rockwood et al. 89] have been developed. Prior to the advent of suitable GPUs, most effort was focused on rapid evaluation of the geometry on a traditional CPU.

Once GPUs became sufficiently programmable, methods to exploit their processing power to evaluate NURBS were developed. Starting with [Guthe et al. 05], and expanded upon by [Krishnamurthy et al. 07] and [Kanai 07], there are now a range of approaches for evaluating NURBS geometry. These methods allow for generalized NURBS geometry to be evaluated and rendered using the GPU, thus greatly reducing the computation cost of using precise geometry. In this chapter we demonstrate a slightly modified version of these approaches.

Trimmed NURBS surfaces have specific additional requirements beyond basic NURBS. In [Guthe et al. 05] and [Guthe et al. 06], a fundamental insight was made by proposing to separate the evaluation of the underlying NURBS surface from the generation of a trim texture, which is blended onto the surface at render time. Due to a lack of general programming support in the available GPU APIs at that time, their proposed approach was limited in what could be accomplished on the GPU and significant portions of the algorithm executed on the CPU. In their approach, NURBS geometry is replaced with bi-cubic approximations calculated on the CPU. Since its original publication, additional research has extended this approach. [Krishnamurthy et al. 07] greatly reduces dependencies on CPU precalculation and uses an alpha blending approach for trim-texture generation that allows for non-view port parallel trimming profiles.

3.3   NURBS Surface and Curve Evaluation

Now that you have a working understanding of the mathematics behind NURBS we can move on to how we use the GPU to evaluate and render curves and surfaces. Our method closely follows the approaches in [Krishnamurthy et al. 07] and [Kanai 07]. At a high level, all necessary data is fed into one fragment shader via textures and uniform variables. The shader outputs into a framebuffer object (FBO) with an associated textures in `GL_RGBA32F_ARB` internal format. The 32-bit

```
void GenerateCurve(GLfloat start, GLfloat stop, int lod) {
    //Determine step size.
    GLfloat step = (stop - start) / (lod - 1);

    // Set up shader and uniform values.
    glUseProgram(this->_curveProgram);
    glUniform4i(this->_curveParam1, degree, numCP, lod, 1);
    glUniform2f(this->_curveParam2, start, step);

    // Generate the control points texture.
    this->GenerateControlPointsTexture();
    // Create a knotpoint texture.
    this->GenerateKnotPointsTexture();

    // Bind to framebuffer object.
    glBindFramebufferEXT(GL_FRAMEBUFFER_EXT, this->_framebuffer);
    // Set up the viewport and polygon mode.
    glPolygonMode(GL_FRONT_AND_BACK, GL_FILL);
    glViewport(0, 0, lod, 1);
    // Ready the input quad.
    GLfloat quad[] = { -1.0,-1.0,-1.0,1.0,1.0,1.0,1.0,-1.0 };
    glVertexPointer(2, GL_FLOAT, 0, quad);

    // Render the quad.
    glDrawArrays(GL_QUADS, 0, 4);
    // Bind to the PBO.
    glBindBuffer(GL_PIXEL_PACK_BUFFER, buffer);
    glBufferData(GL_PIXEL_PACK_BUFFER, sizeOfBuffer,
                         NULL, GL_DYNAMIC_DRAW);
    // Read the pixel data.
    glReadPixels(0, 0, lod, 1, GL_RGBA, GL_FLOAT, NULL);
}
```

Listing 3.1. NURBS curve evaluation.

```
void GenerateKnotPointsTexture(void) {
        // Set up Texture Parameters.
        glPixelStorei(GL_UNPACK_ALIGNMENT, 1);
        // Set up Texture.
        glActiveTexture(GL_TEXTURE2);
        glBindTexture(GL_TEXTURE_RECTANGLE_ARB, this->_knotTex);
        glTexSubImage2D(GL_TEXTURE_RECTANGLE_ARB, 0, 0, 0,
                        this->_numKnots, 1, GL_RGBA,
                        GL_FLOAT, this->_knotVector);
}
```

Listing 3.2. NURBS knot vector texture creation.

float texture provides an appropriate level of precision for mathematically defined geometry.

Our curve evaluation function is designed to allow all or part of a curve to be generated at any desired level of detail. We assume the parametric step between vertices is fixed. The primary C++ function, shown in Listing 3.1, takes a starting parametric value, an ending parametric value, and a level of detail value. From these we calculate the step size and what the dimensions of the rendering viewport must be. In order to limit CPU-bound precalculation we rely upon the normal rasterization process to calculate a portion of the parametric values for each vertex. The compiled shader is enabled, and several parameters and textures are passed to the shader via uniform variables. We will cover these variables shortly. Control points and knot vectors are loaded into textures (see Listing 3.2) for use in the shader. A centered unit quad is then rendered into a viewport that is sized to exactly the same dimensions as the desired output texture. This results in each rasterized pixel having a fragment coordinate corresponding to its relative parametric value. Listing 3.6 and its discussion will go into more detail on this point. The remainder of Listing 3.1 is the extraction of the evaluated NURBS curve data from the framebuffer via a pixel buffer object (PBO) that copies the vertex data from the output texture into a VBO buffer thus avoiding any client-side copies. The VBO is then ready to be rendered or used elsewhere.

Calculating NURBS geometry requires several inputs to the shader. As mentioned above, these are passed into the shader using uniform variables and textures. Each control point needs three float values to define it in space and also weight, making a total of four floats per control point that are packed into a 32-bit float texture. Listing 3.3 shows the NURBS curve evaluation fragment shader header which defines all of the global variables. Control points are passed them into a sampler2DRect. The *cp(index)* macro makes reading through the remainder of the code a bit easier. The knot vector is just a vector of floats so it too is passed into a sampler2DRect and has an access macro.

```
//extension GL_ARB_texture_rectangle : require

//Uniform textures
uniform sampler2DRect knotPoints;
#define kp(index) (texture2DRect(knotPoints, vec2(index)).r)
uniform sampler2DRect controlPoints;
#define cp(index) (texture2DRect(controlPoints, vec2(index)))

//Uniform inputs
uniform ivec4 numParams; // { degree, cp, texWidth, texHeight }
uniform vec2 fltParams;  // { start, step }
float bv[8];
```

Listing 3.3. NURBS curve shader globals.

The remaining variables are necessary to define the many parameters involved in calculating the curve. There is an integer vector of four values: curve degree, number of control points, width of the output texture and height of the output texture—which for curves is always 1. Additionally, there is a float vector of two values: parametric value start and parametric step. These are used to determine what the parametric value actually is and will become more evident in a moment.

In the NURBS background section we mentioned that a key step in calculating NURBS curves is to determine where a given parametric value falls in the knot vector. This value is called the *span* value. This value must be calculated for every parametric value, and therefore for each vertex being evaluated. Listing 3.4

```
int FindSpan(float u) {
   // Check the special case.
   if (u >= kp(numParams.y)) return numParams.y-1;

   // Set up search.
   ivec3 lmh = ivec3(numParams.x, 0, numParams.y);
   lmh.y = (lmh.x + lmh.z) / 2;
   // Start binary search.
   while ((u < kp(lmh.y)) || (u >= kp(lmh.y+1))) {
      if (u < kp(lmh.y)) lmh.z = lmh.y;
      else lmh.x = lmh.y;
      lmh.y = (lmh.x + lmh.z) / 2;
   }
   // Return the span value.
   return lmh.y;
}
```

Listing 3.4. NURBS curve shader span function.

```
void BasisValues(float u, int span) {
   ivec2 jr;
   vec2 tmp;
   vec4 left;
   vec4 right;

   //Basis[0] is always 1.0.
   bv[0] = 1.0;
   //Calculate basis values.
   for (jr.x=1; jr.x<=numParams.x; jr.x++) {
      left[jr.x] = u - kp(span+1-jr.x);
      right[jr.x] = kp(span+jr.x) - u;
      tmp.x = 0.0;
      for (jr.y=0; jr.y<jr.x; jr.y++) {
         tmp.y = bv[jr.y] / (right[jr.y+1] + left[jr.x-jr.y]);
         bv[jr.y] = tmp.x + right[jr.y+1] * tmp.y;
         tmp.x = left[jr.x-jr.y] * tmp.y;
      }
      bv[jr.x] = tmp.x;
   }
}
```

Listing 3.5. NURBS curve shader basis value function.

show the shader code that implements an efficient binary search through the knot vector to find the span value.

The function in Listing 3.5 is for calculating B-spline basis values. The parametric value and the span are passed and the array of basis values are calculated. It is important to note that in this implementation a global float vector, bv (defined in Listing 3.3), is used to store the basis values. This vector has eight components; therefore, this implementation is limited to seventh degree curves or lower. This was done because within our application we did not have a need for higher than seventh degree curves, but the implementation could be set arbitrarily high or low.

Finally, we come to the **main()** function of the curve evaluation shader in Listing 3.6. The first task of the shader is to determine this vertex's parametric value. Because the output texture is a rectangle, the **gl_FragCoord** values will be mostly whole numbers. We say *mostly* because some graphics card vendors will use 1.5 instead of 1.0, for example. The **floor()** function compensates for this fact. Using **fltParam.x** (initial parametric value) and **fltParam.y** (parametric step size) and **inPos.x** (number of vertices into the curve) we can calculate u, the actual parametric value for this vertex.

The remainder of the **main** function finds the span value, using the parametric value, then calculates the basis values and the final vertex x-, y-, and z-coordinates

```
void main(void) {
        int j, span, index;

        //Calculate u value.
        vec2 inPos = floor(gl_FragCoord.xy);
        float u = fltParams.x + inPos.x * fltParams.y;

        //Find the span for the vertex.
        span = FindSpan(u);
        BasisValues(u, span);

        //Make sure to zero the results.
        vec3 pos = vec3(0.0);
        float w = 0.0;
        //Loop through each basis value.
        for (j=0; j<=numParams.x; j++) {
                index = span - numParams.x + j;
                w = w + cp(index).a * bv[j];
                pos = pos + cp(index).rgb * cp(index).a * bv[j];
        }
        //Set the position (do the w divide) and write out.
        pos = pos / w;
        gl_FragColor = vec4(pos, 1.0);
}
```

Listing 3.6. NURBS curve shader main function.

implementing Equation (3.1). The final `vec4` value is written out to `gl_FragColor` which will be a pixel within the output texture. This value will then be converted from a pixel to a vertex using the PBO readback as seen in Listing 3.1. Figure 3.2 shows a sketch using a number of NURBS curves, including lines, circles, and arcs.

Evaluating NURBS surfaces is only slightly more complex. Knot vector textures for both u and v must be created and passed into the shader, as do more uniform variables for parametric start and step in the v direction. The only other major change is the need to calculate normals for each vertex. It turns out that the basis values already being calculated can be used to calculate the normals, so little additional computation is needed. Likewise the texture coordinates are the parametric values, u and v, so no additional computation is necessary. The NURBS surface fragment shader renders everything into an FBO with three associated textures, all in `GL_RGBA32F_ARB` internal format. Each piece of output data (vertex, normal, and texture coordinate) is rendered into a separate texture. As with curve evaluation, the textures are copied into separate VBOs using a PBO and `glReadPixels()`.

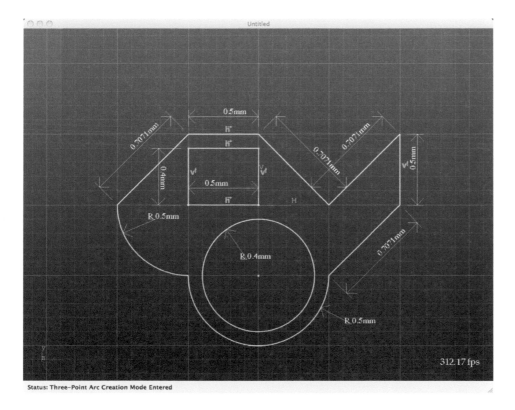

Figure 3.2. A sketch composed of NURBS curves.

3.4 Trimmed NURBS Surface Evaluation

Our approach for evaluating and rendering trimmed NURBS surfaces is comprised of five primary steps. As mentioned above, the separation of the underlying surface from that of the trimming texture is a key insight and our workflow for generating trimmed surfaces reflects this separation.

Figure 3.3 illustrates the steps and products of our approach. The five primary steps involved in our approach all execute fully on the GPU and the resulting outputs are stored as textures or are converted to VBOs. The steps are: generation of NURBS surface vertices, normals, and texture coordinates, generation of trimming profile vertices, inverse evaluation of profile vertices, rendering inverse profile vertices into the trim texture, and visually rendering the final trimmed surface. Each of these steps is covered in the following sections.

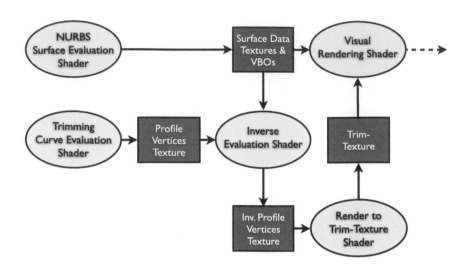

Figure 3.3. Trimmed NURBS surface workflow.

3.4.1   NURBS Surface and Curve Evaluation

The first step in evaluating a trimmed surface is to evaluate the underlying NURBS surface and all of the curves in the trimming profile. The evaluation process is exactly the same as discussed above, except that the final project is not read from the FBO into a VBO via a PBO, but is instead kept as textures. The reason for this is that the evaluated vertices are needed as input into the trim-texture generation process. Our implementation of this process requires that the data be formatted as textures and fed into a shader, so there is no need to copy the data into VBOs.

An additional important point regards the trim profiles. A profile can be composed of numerous different lines or curves and may contain one or more holes. Figure 3.2 is an excellent example as it demonstrates a reasonably complex trimming profile with several lines, curves, and two holes. Each curve in the profile must be individually evaluated at the appropriate level of detail, and all of this vertex information is then assembled into a single data texture. It is important to strictly order the trim profile vertices clockwise around the profile. The need for this will be discussed later.

3.4.2   Trimming Profile Projection

Once both the surface and the trimming profile have been evaluated, the next step is to project the profile vertices onto the surface. Profile projection serves two purposes: to map the trimming profile vertices into the parametric domain of the underlying surface, and to ensure that the trimming profile lies exactly on the surface. Without projecting the profile onto the surface the resulting trim texture can suffer from a inaccuracies and visual artifacts.

Many methods exist for point projection onto parametric geometry, also called *inverse evaluation*. Many of these algorithms use some form of iteration to search the parametric space for the correct value. [Piegl and Tiller 97] proposes a Newton interation-based method based on Equation (3.5) for inverse evaluation of a NURBS curve. In this equation $C(u_i)$ is the value of the curve evaluated at parametric value u_i, and P is the point to be projected:

$$u_{i+1} = u_i - \frac{f(u_i)}{f'(u_i)} = u_i - \frac{C'(u_i) \cdot (C(u) - P)}{C'' \cdot (C(u_i) - P) + |C'(u_i)^2|}. \tag{3.5}$$

Iteration continues until $|C - P| < tol$, $|u_i - u_{i+1}| < tol$, or another stopping tolerance is met. It is straightforward to extend this method to NURBS surfaces. [Krishnamurthy et al. 08] demonstrates a GPU-based approach for inverse evaluation. It uses an axis-aligned bounding box (AABB) algorithm instead of Newton Iteration.

Our approach is relatively simplistic in an attempt to yield an easier to implement, though still high performance, solution. Only one pass through the GPU is necessary to project all profile vertices onto the surface. The pass takes as input the outputs from the previous evaluation step, namely one texture filled with surface vertex data, and one texture filled with profile vertex data. The fragment shader is set up so that each fragment processed corresponds to a single profile vertex resulting in the primary input to the inversion fragment shader being a single profile vertex. While it would be possible to use the iterative Equation (3.5) to find the parametric value, it would require evaluating the surface several times instead of making use of the large set of evaluated surface vertex data already available. Instead of iteration, we use a simple brute force search through the existing surface vertex data.

The first step in the fragment shader is to find the surface vertex closest to the *profile* input vertex, called `pt`. A nested for-loop checks each vertex in the surface and reserves the index of the closest. We name this vertex the *prime* vertex, and its record its location with `markU` and `markV`.

The second step determines the two vertices closest to the *profile* and *prime* vertices, one each in the u and v directions of the surface, named `uPt` and `vPt`. This effectively determines in which quadrant from the *prime* vertex the profile vertex lies. A triangle is formed by *prime*, `uPt` and `vPt`.

The final step projects the *profile* vertex into this triangle and determines its barycentric coordinates. These coordinates are then easily translated into the parametric (u, v) values for the underlying surface which are written to the output texture.

The for-loop search through the entire texture of surface data is by far the most expensive portion of this algorithm. Obviously, the performance impact of inverse evaluation grows in direct proportion to the surface LOD, as a higher LOD demands a larger set of surface vertex data, which corresponds to slower inverse evaluation. On the positive side, through experimentation we have found the visual improvement from elevating surface LOD tends to plateau before performance is noticeably impacted by the inversion process.

One potential drawback of our approach relates to highly non-planar surfaces. In these situations the estimation approach employed by the inversion shader proves to be inadequate. Highly non-planar surfaces tend to have a higher occurrence of multiple surface points being equally close to the *profile* vertex. Imagine a point at the center of a sphere—all locations on the sphere are valid inversions. Our approach looks only for the single closest vertex on the surface, not for a set of such vertices. Accurately generating trimming profiles such that they lie as close to the surface as possible is a practical, though not perfect, remediation for this problem.

```
// Uniform Inputs
uniform sampler2DRect    verts;
uniform sampler2DRect    surfData;
#define sd(i,j)   (texture2DRect(surfData, vec2(i,j)))
uniform ivec2    params;    // { surfWidth, surfHeight }

void main(void) {
   // Variable setup etc.
   vec4 pt = texture2DRect(verts, floor(gl_FragCoord.xy));
   ...
   // Loop through all points on surface.
   for (v=0; v<params.y; v++) {
      for (u=0; u<params.x; u++) {
         // Determine distance from point to surface point.
         surfPt = sd(u,v);
         dist = distance(pt, surfPt);
         // Is this smaller than current smallest?
         if (dist <= minDist) {
            // Capture the location
            markU = u;
            markV = v;
            minDist = dist;
         }
      }
   }
   ...
   // Determine neighborhood points.
   if (markU > 0) {
      left = vec4( sd(markU-1, markV) );
      leftDist = distance(left, pt);
   }
```

```
    else leftDist = 10000.0;
    if (markU < params.x-1) {
        right = vec4( sd(markU+1, markV) );
        rightDist = distance(right, pt);
    }
    else rightDist = 10000.0;
    if (markV > 0) {
        bottom = vec4( sd(markU, markV-1) );
        bottomDist = distance(bottom, pt);
    }
    else bottomDist = 10000.0;
    if (markV < params.y-1) {
        top = vec4( sd(markU, markV+1) );
        topDist = distance(top, pt);
    }
    else topDist = 10000.0;
    ...
    // Find the quadrant and hPt and vPt.
    if (leftDist < rightDist) { hSign = -1.0; hPt = left; }
    else { hSign = 1.0; hPt = right; }
    if (bottomDist < topDist) { vSign = -1.0; vPt = bottom; }
    else { vSign = 1.0; vPt = top; }
    // Convert triangle values to [u,v] using hPt, vPt, and signs.
    ...
    // Record [u,v] value into output texture.
    gl_FragColor = vec4(uValue, vValue, 0.0, 1.0);
}
```

Listing 3.7. Trimmed surface point inversion fragment shader.

3.4.3 Trim Texture Generation

Finally, the trim texture itself can be generated. [Guthe et al. 05] and [Shreiner et al. 05] offer similar methods for rendering concave polygons properly, both using a stencil buffer-based approach. When rendering the trimming profile as a triangle fan, hence the strict clockwise ordering, pixels within the trimming profile will be covered by an odd number of triangles and pixels outside the profile will have an even coverage. Instead of counting coverage, the stencil buffer can flip single bits to track odd versus even coverage. The end result is a properly rendered texture.

After inverse evaluation, all of the profile vertices lie in the $[0, 1]$ range in both u and v, and the strictly clockwise ordering of the vertices around the profile has been maintained. A square viewport is set and an FBO is created with a stencil buffer and an attached texture sized according to the desired LOD for the trim texture. A single rendering pass, leveraging the stencil buffer but with no specialized shaders, generates the final trim texture.

```
// Trim texture
uniform sampler2DRect trimTexture;
// Texture size parameters
uniform vec2 texSize;

void main(void) {
    // Calculate trim texture lookup location.
    vec2 inPos = vec2(gl_TexCoord[0].s * texSize.x,
          gl_TexCoord[0].t * texSize.y);
    // Fetch trim texture value.
    vec4 texColor = texture2DRect(trimTexture, inPos);
    // Discard fragment if not present.
    if (texColor.x == 0.0) discard;
    gl_FragColor = gl_Color;
}
```

Listing 3.8. Trimmed surface visualization fragment shader.

3.4.4 Rendering Trimmed Surfaces

Once the vertices of the surface have been evaluated and the trim texture generated, rendering the trimmed surface may occur. For non-trimmed NURBS surfaces, rendering is simple. References to the surface's vertex—normal, index, and texture coordinate VBOs—are set in the GL state machine and a single call, with no specialized shaders, to `glDrawElements()` is made.

Only a slight adjustment to the pipeline is required in order to render a trimmed surface. A small fragment shader is inserted that checks the trim texture to see if the surface is present or not. Listing 3.8 shows the fragment shader necessary to properly display a trimmed surface using its trim texture.

In the shader, after the trim texture color is retrieved from the texture, a quick check is made to see if it is colored or not. If not, the *discard* command is used due to a lower computational cost as compared to setting the alpha value of the fragment to zero. Otherwise the fragment's color is set to the appropriate display color.

3.5 Results and Conclusion

The approach for evaluating and rendering NURBS geometry presented in this paper results in signification performance improvements compared to on the CPU. To evaluate our approach we performed all benchmarks on a MacBook Pro with a 2.53 GHz Intel Core 2 Duo processor, 4GB of RAM, and an NVIDIA GeForce 9600M GT graphics processor with 256MB of video memory at a 1440 × 900 screen resolution. Figure 3.4 shows our benchmark case. The model is composed

Figure 3.4. A three-dimensional object composed of NURBS geometry.

of twelve surfaces, some trimmed and some not, and every edge is outlined with a NURBS curve. Results from our experiments are summarized in Table 3.1.

In order to test regeneration speed the models were initially set to completely regenerate all data every frame. Using a strictly CPU-based implementation we achieved a frame rate of 8.2fps. Using GPU-based generation our approach resulted in a sustained throughput of roughly ten million vertices per second or a frame rate of 107.8fps. These results show that GPU-based geometry and trim-texture generation provide a significant performance increase. More interestingly, if we allowed the models to generate once and then render purely from stored data—being free to rotate and reorient randomly each frame as would be seen in

Algorithm	Benchmark Model
CPU-based with constant regen.	8.2fps
GPU w/ constant regen.	107.8fps
GPU w/ minimal regen.	752.4fps

Table 3.1. Performance benchmark results.

real-world usage—the frame rate jumped to 752.4fps. In other words, not having to regenerate each frame resulted in a further seven fold improvement in performance.

In this chapter we demonstrated how to evaluate and render mathematically well-defined NURBS geometry. Our approach is both flexible and provides much higher performance compared to evaluating the NURBS geometry on the CPU. The code for the work described in this paper is available for download at http://wildcat-cad.googlecode.com.

Bibliography

[Abi-Ezzi and Subramanian 94] S. S. Abi-Ezzi and S. Subramanian. "Fast Dynamic Tessellation of Trimmed NURBS Surfaces." *Computer Graphics Forum* 13:3 (1994), 107–126.

[Guthe et al. 02] Michael Guthe, J. Meseth, and Reinhard Klein. "Fast and Memory Efficient View-Dependent Trimmed NURBS Rendering." In *Pacific Graphis 2002*, 2002.

[Guthe et al. 05] Michael Guthe, Ákos Balázs, and Reinhard Klein. "GPU-based Trimming and Tessellation of NURBS and T-spline Surfaces." *ACM Transactions on Graphics* 24:3 (2005), 1016–1023.

[Guthe et al. 06] Michael Guthe, Ákos Balázs, and Reinhard Klein. "GPU-based Appearance Preserving Trimmed NURBS Rendering." *Journal of WSCG* 14.

[Kanai 07] Takashi Kanai. "Fragment-based Evaluation of Non-Uniform B-spline Surfaces on GPUs." *Computer-Aided Design and Applications* 4:3 (2007), 287–294.

[Krishnamurthy et al. 07] Adarsh Krishnamurthy, Rahul Khardekar, and Sara McMains. "Direct Evaluation of NURBS Curves and Surfaces on the GPU." In *SPM '07: Proceedings of the 2007 ACM symposium on Solid and Physical Modeling*, pp. 329 334, 2007.

[Krishnamurthy et al. 08] Adarsh Krishnamurthy, Rahul Khardekar, Sara McMains, Kirk Haller, and Gershon Elber. "Performing Efficient NURBS Modeling Operations on the GPU." In *SPM '08: Proceedings of the 2008 ACM Symposium on Solid and Physical Modeling*, pp. 257–268. ACM, 2008.

[Kumar and Manocha 95] S. Kumar and Dinesh Manocha. "Efficient Rendering of Trimmed NURBS Surfaces." *Computer-Aided Design* 27:7 (1995), 509–521.

[Piegl and Tiller 97] Les Piegl and Wayne Tiller. *The NURBS Book*, Second edition. Springer-Verlag, 1997.

[Rockwood et al. 89] A. Rockwood, K. Heaton, and T. Davis. "Real-Time Rendering of Trimmed Surfaces." *ACM Transactions on Graphics*, pp. 107–116.

[Shreiner et al. 05] Dave Shreiner, Mason Woo, Jackie Neider, and Tom Davis. *OpenGL Programming Guide*, Fifth edition. Addison Wesley, 2005.

4

Polygonal-Functional Hybrids for Computer Animation and Games

D. Kravtsov, O. Fryazinov, V. Adzhiev,
A. Pasko, and P. Comninos

4.1   Introduction

The modern world of computer graphics is mostly dominated by polygonal models. Due to their scalability and ease of rendering such models have various applications in a wide range of fields. Unfortunately some shape modeling and animation

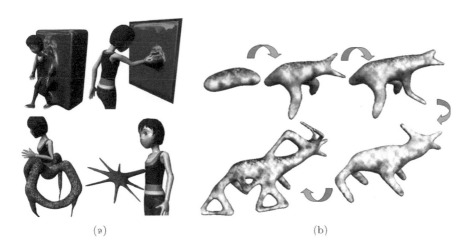

(a)   (b)

Figure 4.1. (a) Mimicked viscoelastic behavior and hybrid characters (Model "Andy" is courtesy of John Doublestein); (b) Iterations of character growth controlled by the user.

Figure 4.2. Variation of polygonization resolution.

problems can hardly be overcome using polygonal models alone. For example, dramatic changes of the shape (involving changes of topology) or metamorphosis between different shapes can not be performed easily. On the other hand, *function representation* (FRep) [Pasko et al. 95] allows us to overcome some of the problems and simplify the process of the major model modification. We propose to use a hybrid model, where we combine together both polygonal and FRep models. Hence we can take advantages of different model representations performing model evaluation entirely on the GPU. Our approach allows us to

- Produce animations involving dramatic changes of the shape (e.g., metamorphosis, viscoelastic behavior, character modifications, etc.) in short times (Figure 4.1(a)).

- Interactively create complex shapes with changing topology (Figure 4.1(b)) and specified LOD (Figure 4.2).

- Integrate existing animated polygonal models and FRep models within a single model.

4.2   Background

4.2.1   Implicit Surfaces and Function Representation (FRep)

FRep [Pasko et al. 95] incorporates implicit surfaces and more generic types of procedural objects. Any point in space can be classified to find out if it belongs to FRep object. FRep object can be defined by a scalar function and an inequality:

$$f(\mathbf{p}) : R^3 \rightarrow R \begin{cases} f(\mathbf{p}) > T, \mathbf{p} \text{ is inside the object,} \\ f(\mathbf{p}) = T, \mathbf{p} \text{ is on the object's boundary,} \\ f(\mathbf{p}) < T, \mathbf{p} \text{ is outside the object,} \end{cases}$$

where $\mathbf{p}$ is an arbitrary point in three-dimensional space and T is a threshold value (or isovalue). The subset $\{\mathbf{p} \in R^3 : f(\mathbf{p}) \geq T\}$ is called a solid object and

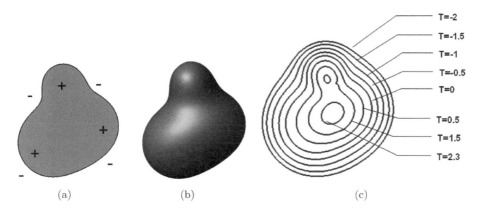

Figure 4.3. Scalar field (defining function): (a) the sign of a scalar field; (b) the extracted implicit surface ($T=0$); (c) different iso-surfaces for different values of T.

the subset $\{\mathbf{p} \in R^3 : f(\mathbf{p}) = T\}$ is called an iso-surface (see Figure 4.3). Function $f(\mathbf{p})$ can be a signed distance field or an arbitrary scalar field.

The first derivative of the function can be used to compute the gradient and the normal on the object's surface:

$$\nabla f(\mathbf{p}) = (\frac{\partial f(\mathbf{p})}{\partial x}, \frac{\partial f(\mathbf{p})}{\partial y}, \frac{\partial f(\mathbf{p})}{\partial z}); \nabla f, \mathbf{p} \in R^3,$$

$$\vec{n}(\mathbf{p}) = -\frac{\nabla f(\mathbf{p})}{\|\nabla f(\mathbf{p})\|}; \vec{n}(\mathbf{p}), \mathbf{p} \in R^3. \tag{4.1}$$

Unfortunately, only a small subset of these models is well known to a wider audience. One of the most popular types of implicit surfaces are blobs [Blinn 82], also known as metaballs or soft objects. Individual blobby objects defined by positions of their centers and radii can be smoothly blended with each other. Superposition of these simple primitives provides an opportunity to build more complex shapes with changing topology, which is usually hard to achieve with purely polygonal models.

Implicit objects are also known for easy definition of metamorphosis sequences (also known as morphing). One only needs to interpolate between values of two signed distance fields to retrieve an intermediate object (Figure 4.4):

$$f(\mathbf{p}, t) = f_\alpha(t) \cdot f_1(\mathbf{p}) + f_\beta(t) \cdot f_2(\mathbf{p}); \mathbf{p} \in R^3, t \in R,$$

where $f_\alpha(t)$ and $f_\beta(t)$ are continuous scalar functions. Parameter t is usually defined on the $[0; 1]$ interval and interpolating functions $f_\alpha(t)$, $f_\beta(t)$ are chosen to

Figure 4.4. Metamorphosis sequence.

satisfy the following constraints:

$$f(\mathbf{p}, 0) = f_1(\mathbf{p}); f(\mathbf{p}, 1) = f_2(\mathbf{p}).$$

Another known advantage of implicit surfaces is an easy implementation of constructive solid geometry (CSG) operations [Ricci 73]. Arbitrary objects can be combined together to produce shapes of high complexity. R-functions-based CSG operations preserving C^1-continuity were applied in FReps [Pasko et al. 95]:

$$S_1 \cup S_2 = f_1(\mathbf{p}) + f_2(\mathbf{p}) + \sqrt{f_1^2(\mathbf{p}) + f_2^2(\mathbf{p})},$$
$$S_1 \cap S_2 = f_1(\mathbf{p}) + f_2(\mathbf{p}) - \sqrt{f_1^2(\mathbf{p}) + f_2^2(\mathbf{p})}.$$

Preserving C^1 continuity of the resulting function may be especially important to overcome rendering artifacts when estimating gradient of the scalar field produced by the object. Another important operation available in FRep is *blending union*. This operation allows to perform smooth blending between two objects controlling the shape of the resulting object:

$$f_b(f_1, f_2) = f_1 + f_2 + \sqrt{f_1^2 + f_2^2} + \frac{a_0}{1 + \left(\dfrac{f_1}{a_1}\right)^2 + \left(\dfrac{f_2}{a_2}\right)^2},$$

where a_1 controls the contribution of the first object, a_2 controls the contribution of the second object and a_0 controls the overall "shift" from the resulting object. Blending set-theoretic operations allow us to dramatically change the resulting shape controlling the influence of each of the initial shapes being blended, as well as controlling the overall offset from the resulting shape (see Figure 4.5).

This is a small subset of FRep features that we will use to show a number of interesting applications later.

4.2.2 Convolution Surfaces

Aforementioned metaballs can be considered a subset of so called *convolution surfaces* [Bloomenthal and Shoemake 91]. These surfaces are defined by a lower-dimensional skeleton and a function-defining surface profile:

(a)   (b)   (c)   (d)

Figure 4.5. Changing blending parameters.

$$f(\mathbf{p}) = \int\limits_{R^3} g(\mathbf{r})h(\mathbf{p} - \mathbf{r})d\mathbf{r} = g \otimes h,$$

where $g(\mathbf{r})$ defines the geometry of the primitive (i.e., the skeleton function), $h(\mathbf{p})$ is a kernel function (similar to various potential functions used for metaballs), and $g(\mathbf{r})$ equals to "1," if point r belongs to the skeleton and equals to "0" everywhere else. Resulting convolution surface $f(\mathbf{p}) = T$ also depends on the threshold value T.

Convolution surfaces exhibit an important superposition property:

$$(g_1 + g_2) \otimes h = (g_1 \otimes h) + (g_2 \otimes h). \tag{4.2}$$

This means that the field produced by two independent skeletons is the same as the field produced by the combination of these skeletons, i.e., fields produced

(a)   (b)

Figure 4.6. Convolution surfaces: (a) underlying skeleton; (b) produced convolution surface.

by different skeletal elements blend together resulting in a smooth surface. Convolution surfaces can be defined by points, line segments, arcs, and triangles. Analytical solutions were obtained for a number of kernel functions [McCormack and Sherstyuk 98]. We will refer to Cauchy kernel:

$$h(d) = \frac{1}{(1 + s^2 d^2)^2}; d > 0,$$

where d specifies the Euclidean distance from a point of interest in space and s is a scalar value controlling the radius of the convolution surface. Let us write an equation for a convolution surface produced by a line segment. Given a line segment

$$\mathbf{r}(t) = \mathbf{b} + t\mathbf{a}; 0 \leq t \leq l,$$

where $\mathbf{b}$ is the segment base (position vector), $\mathbf{a}$ is the segment axis (direction vector), and l is the segment length. For an arbitrary point, $\mathbf{p} \in R^3$, the squared distance between $\mathbf{r}(t)$ and $\mathbf{p}$ is defined as

$$d^2(t) = |\mathbf{p} - \mathbf{b}|^2 + t^2 - 2t((\mathbf{p} - \mathbf{b}) \cdot \mathbf{a}).$$

A field function for an arbitrary point $\mathbf{p}$ is then defined as

$$f(\mathbf{p}) = \int_0^l \frac{dt}{(1 + s^2 d^2(t))^2}$$

$$= \frac{x}{2m^2 (m^2 + s^2 x^2)} + \frac{l - x}{2m^2 n^2} + \frac{1}{2sm^3} \left(\arctan \left[\frac{sx}{m} \right] + \arctan \left[\frac{s(l - x)}{m} \right] \right),$$

where x is the coordinate on the segment's axis,

$$x = (\mathbf{p} - \mathbf{b}) \cdot \mathbf{a},$$

$$m^2 = 1 + s^2(q^2 - x^2),$$

$$n^2 = 1 + s^2(q^2 + l^2 - 2lx).$$

According to Equation (4.2) the field produced by N line segments is defined as follows

$$F(\mathbf{p}) = \sum_{i=1}^N f_i(\mathbf{p})$$

where $f_i(\mathbf{p})$ is the field produced by the i-th line segment. An improved version of Cauchy kernel can be used to vary the radius along the line segment [Jin et al. 01].

A few other kernels can be used as well. But polynomial kernels require windowing (i.e., limiting function values within particular intervals), resulting in less smooth convolution surfaces. Besides, evaluation procedure requires more branching instructions, which is often undesirable when performing computations on the GPU. Some other kernels with infinite support are either more computationally expensive or provide less control over the resulting shape. In this article we will only refer to convolution surfaces produced by the line segments using Cauchy kernel.

4.2.3 Rendering FRep Models

Even though FReps have a lot of advantages, visualizing them is not as straightforward as visualizing polygonal models. It is often desirable to convert an FRep object to a polygonal mesh for efficient rendering. One of the well-known methods used for the extraction of isosurfaces from a scalar field is called Marching Cubes [Lorensen and Cline 87]. There are a number of other methods solving the same problem, but Marching Cubes is still popular due to its high speed and ease of implementation.[1] Texturing of isosurfaces requires additional attention as well. Traditional UV-unwrapping is not suitable for complex dynamic models. Known parameterization methods can be applied to calculate UV-coordinates of the extracted surface in real time (for instance, spherical or cubic projection often used for rendering of liquid substances; see Figure 4.7). Triplanar texturing [Geiss 07] provides a better way of texturing of complex functional objects. Another option could be the usage of procedural solid textures implemented in a shader [Ebert et al. 02]. Though pure procedural textures are not always well suited for rendering of arbitrary objects.

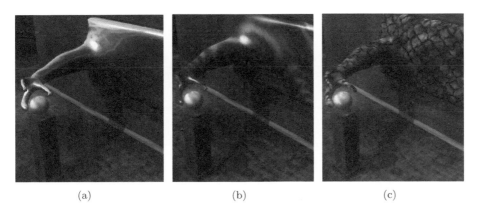

| (a) | (b) | (c) |

Figure 4.7. Texturing: (a) cubemap; (b) procedural shader; (c) triplanar texturing.

---

[1]Original Marching Cubes is known to have a number of ambiguous cases, though.

4.3   Working with FRep Models Using the GPU

Modern GPUs allow evaluation and rendering of certain types of FRep models entirely on the GPU in real time. Three main steps need to be performed:

1. Sample distance function values in the volume and save the results to a temporary buffer.

2. Extract isosurface and its normals from discretized data set.

3. Render extracted isosurface.

Sampling of distance functions can be performed in a vertex shader [Uralsky 06] or a fragment shader. In the latter case, the volume can be sliced with a set of two-dimensional planes or directly rendered to a volume texture. Isosurface extraction from discretized data set can be performed with the help of geometry shaders [Geiss 07, Tatarchuk et al. 07]. All of the above steps can be performed on any DirectX 10 compatible hardware. The code accompanying this article, available at http://www.akpeters.com/gpupro, is based on NVIDIA CUDA SDK [NVIDIA 09], which allows performing generic computations on the GPU without the necessity to overcome limitations of the existing graphics APIs. Moreover, CUDA SDK already includes an illustrative example of Marching Cubes running on the GPU. We used this code as a starting point for the implementation of our approach running on the GPU.

In the following sections we will describe each of the aforementioned steps in detail.

4.3.1   Function Evaluation

First of all, model parameters need to be updated and uploaded to the GPU. These parameters are stored in the constant memory and need to be modified

```
// Parameters of the segments defining convolution surface
__constant__
CONVOLUTION_SEGMENT segmentsOnDevice[segmentsNumMax];
// Other parameters of the model
...
// Copy segments from CPU to constant GPU memory.
cudaMemcpyToSymbol( segmentsOnDevice , segmentsOnHost ,
                    sizeof(CONVOLUTION_SEGMENT));
// Copy other parameters.
...
```

Listing 4.1. Update parameters.

before model evaluation. The `cudaMemcpyToSymbol` function can be used for this purpose, as shown in Listing 4.1.

The volume where the defining function will be evaluated needs to be defined. This volume is uniformly divided in a number of cells according to required resolution. Values of the function at the corners of each cell are evaluated in parallel threads, one thread per value.

We need to save the sampled function values to a temporary buffer in order to avoid function re-evaluations in the future. Writing to global memory is a relatively slow operation and should only be performed if computationally expensive functions are evaluated. Otherwise, the time required to save and load the results may appear to be significantly higher than the time needed for function evaluation (see Section 4.3.2). Depending on the computational complexity of the function being evaluated it may be beneficial to perform more than one evaluation in a kernel and store temporary results in a shared memory. After this, temporary results need to be copied from shared memory to global memory in one instruction, thus achieving coalescing.

In many circumstances high-precision function evaluation is not required, and faster math intrinsics available in CUDA can be used. They can either be called directly or automatically enabled via `use_fast_math` CUDA compiler option (refer to CUDA documentation for more details on the topic).

4.3.2 Isosurface Extraction

We have already mentioned that the Marching Cubes (MC) algorithm is commonly used to extract an isosurface from the scalar field. The MC algorithm works with individual cells uniformly distributed in the volume. The size and the number of the cells is determined by the required quality of the resulting isosurface. The algorithm allows us to find a set of polygons representing a surface patch of the functional object enclosed in each individual cell. Each cell is handled by an independent thread. Here are a number of steps required to efficiently extract an isosurface on the GPU:

1. For each cell,

    (a) Write out the number of vertices it contains.

    (b) Write out the flag indicating whether it contains any geometry.

2. Find the number of nonempty cells.

3. Create a group of all nonempty cells using the flags information from Step 1(b).

4. Generate the table of vertex buffer offsets for nonempty cells.

5. For each nonempty cell,

   (a) Find the number of vertices it outputs.

   (b) Generate vertices of the triangles being output from the cell.

   (c) Generate normal for each vertex being output.

   (d) Save vertices and normals using offset generated at Step 4.

This may look complicated at first, because a number of additional issues arise when performing polygonization on parallel computing devices. First of all, we want to find a set of cells that actually contain geometry in them. Usually the majority of the cells do not contain any geometry, as they are situated completely inside or outside the object, thus having no intersections with the surface of the object. It is important to discard such cells early in order to avoid redundant computations (Step 3). Secondly, each nonempty cell outputs from one to five triangles. For each cell we need to know the offset in the vertex buffer where the vertices will be output. But this offset depends on the number of vertices output from preceding cells. In the case of sequential MC this offset can be iteratively increased, while processing each cell one after another. But it gets more complicated when the cells are processed in parallel. This problem is solved at Step 4 using CUDA Data Parallel Primitives Library [Sengupta et al. 08]:

Step 1. In order to find out whether a cell is empty or not, its MC case index needs to be determined. To do so, we need to retrieve function values at eight corners of each cell and determine its MC case index. At this point we use the data sampled before (see Section 4.3.1), as shown in Listing 4.2.

```
// Based on original source code provided by NVIDIA Corporation

// Get MC case index depending on function values.
__device__ uint getMCIndex(const float* field,float threshold)
{
   uint indexMC;
   indexMC =  uint(field[0] < threshold);
   indexMC |= uint(field[1] < threshold) << 1;
   indexMC |= uint(field[2] < threshold) << 2;
   indexMC |= uint(field[3] < threshold) << 3;
   indexMC |= uint(field[4] < threshold) << 4;
   indexMC |= uint(field[5] < threshold) << 5;
   indexMC |= uint(field[6] < threshold) << 6;
   indexMC |= uint(field[7] < threshold) << 7;

   return cubeindex;
}

// Sample volume data set at the specified point.
```

```
__device__ float sampleVolume(uint3 point, uint3 gridSize)
{
   p.x = min(point.x, gridSize.x - 1);
   p.y = min(point.y, gridSize.y - 1);
   p.z = min(point.z, gridSize.z - 1);
   uint i = (point.z * gridSize.x * gridSize.y) +
            (point.y * gridSize.x) + point.x;
   return tex1Dfetch(volumeTex, i);
}

// Output number of vertices that need to be generated for
// current cell and output flag indicating whether current
// cell contains any triangles at all.
__global__ void
preprocessCell(...)
{
   ...
   float field[8];

   // Retrieve function values at eight corners of a cube.
   field[0]= sampleVolume(gridPos, gridSize);
   field[1]= sampleVolume(gridPos + make_uint3(1,0,0),gridSize);
   field[2]= sampleVolume(gridPos + make_uint3(1,1,0),gridSize);
   field[3]= sampleVolume(gridPos + make_uint3(0,1,0),gridSize);
   field[4]= sampleVolume(gridPos + make_uint3(0,0,1),gridSize);
   field[5]= sampleVolume(gridPos + make_uint3(1,0,1),gridSize);
   field[6]= sampleVolume(gridPos + make_uint3(1,1,1),gridSize);
   field[7]= sampleVolume(gridPos + make_uint3(0,1,1),gridSize);

   // Find out case index in the MC table.
   uint indexMC =  getMCIndex(field, threshold);

   // Read number of vertices produced by this case.
   uint numVerts = tex1Dfetch(numVertsTex, indexMC);
   if (cellIndex < numCells) {
      // Save the number of vertices for later usage.
      cellVerts[cellIndex] = numVerts;
      // Flag indicating whether this cell outputs any triangles
      cells[cellIndex] = (numVerts > 0);
   }
}
```

Listing 4.2. Step 1 of isosurface extraction.

In this case, **numVertsTex** is a table containing the number of triangle vertices contained in a cell corresponding to a certain MC case and **volumeTex** is the sampled volume data that was earlier bound to a one-dimensional texture, as shown in Listing 4.3. It is preferable to fetch data from textures rather than from global device memory as in this case texture cache can be utilized to reduce memory access times.

```
struct cudaChannelFormatDesc channelDesc =
   cudaCreateChannelDesc( 32,0,0,0,cudaChannelFormatKindFloat );

   cudaBindTexture(0, volumeTex, d_volume, channelDesc);
```

Listing 4.3. Fetching data from textures to utilize texture cache.

Step 2. Once output vertex information for each cell has been retrieved, the scan algorithm (also known as "Parallel Prefix Sum," see Listing 4.4) can be used. This operation allows to generate an array, in which each element contains the sum of all preceding values of the input array (see Figure 4.8) [Sengupta et al. 07].

In our case input array d_cells contains either "0" (empty cell) or "1" (non-empty cell). Hence each element of the array generated by an exclusive scan operation (d_cellsScan) applied to the input array contains the number of nonempty cells preceding it. The values of such elements can be interpreted as sequential indices of nonempty cell. The last element of the generated array is equal to the total number of all nonempty cells except the last one.

```
// Scan array of nonempty cells.
cudppScan( scanPlanExclusive , d_cellsScan ,
         d_cells , numCells );
// Copy the value of the last element from the GPU.
uint CellNumber , lastCellIsEmpty;
cudaMemcpy((void *) &CellNumber ,
         (void *) (d_cellsScan + numCells - 1),
         sizeof(uint), cudaMemcpyDeviceToHost );
// Add the value from the last cell as it may be nonempty too.
cudaMemcpy((void *) &lastCellIsEmpty ,
         (void *) (d_cells + numCells - 1),
         sizeof(uint), cudaMemcpyDeviceToHost );

// Final number of nonempty cells
CellNumber += lastCellIsEmpty;
```

Listing 4.4. Parallel Prefix Sum.

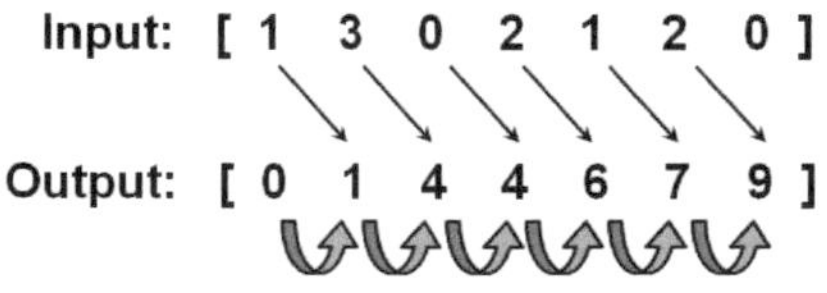

Input: [1 3 0 2 1 2 0]

Output: [0 1 4 4 6 7 9]

Figure 4.8. Exclusive scan.

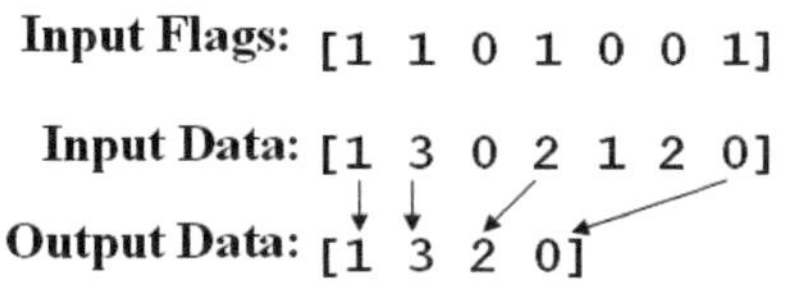

Input Flags: [1 1 0 1 0 0 1]

Input Data: [1 3 0 2 1 2 0]

Output Data: [1 3 2 0]

Figure 4.9. Compact algorithm.

Step 3. Stream compaction (a.k.a. *enumerate operation*) is used to generate an array containing indices of only nonempty cells. "Stream compaction" operation requires two input arrays. First array contains boolean values indicating whether respective elements from the second array need to be copied to the output array. Example input data sets and output generated by this operation are shown in Figure 4.9. In our case we provide an array of flags d_cells and a "scanned" array of nonempty cell indices d_cellsScan:

```
cudppCompact(compactPlan, d_compactedCells,d_CellNumber,
             d_cellsScan, d_cells, numCells);
```

After this step, d_compactedCells contains the set of indices of all nonempty cells.

Step 4. As was mentioned earlier, the generation of vertex buffer offsets (see Listing 4.5) for each cell is performed using scan operation (similar to Step 2). We apply an exclusive scan again, as we need each element in the array to contain the sum of previous elements excluding the current element. The first element in the array of offsets should be equal to "0." After the application of the scan operation each element of d_cellVBOffsets contains the total number of vertices contained in preceding cells (i.e. offset in the vertex buffer that can be used to output the vertices from the cell):

```
cudppScan( scanPlanExclusive, d_cellVBOffsets,
           d_cellVerts, numCells);
```

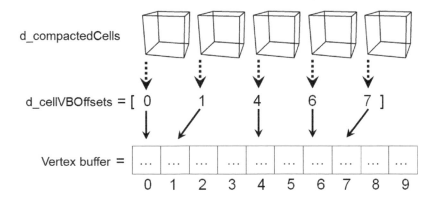

Figure 4.10. Offsets in the vertex buffer for each cell.

```
__device__
float3 interpolatePosition(float threshold,
                           float3 cellVertex1,float3 cellVertex2,
                           float funcValue1, float funcValue2)
{
   float t = (threshold - funcValue1) /
             (funcValue2 - funcValue1);
   return lerp(cellVertex1, cellVertex2, t);
}

// Write out vertices and normals.
__global__ void generateTriangles(...)
{
   ...
   // Vertices placed at the corners of current cell
   float3 cellVertices[8];
   ...
   // Field values at the eight corners of current cell
   float field[8];
   field[0] = sampleVolume(gridPos, gridSize);
   ...
   // Array of vertices placed along 12 edges of the cell
   // shared between different threads
   __shared__ float3 vertices[12 * NTHREADS];

   // Find positions of 12 vertices along all edges:
   vertices[threadIdx.x] = interpolatePosition(threshold,
                           cellVertices[0], cellVertices[1],
                           field[0], field[1]);

   vertices[NTHREADS+threadIdx.x] =
           interpolatePosition(threshold,
                           cellVertices[1], cellVertices[2],
                           field[1], field[2]);
   ...
   // Last vertex
   vertlist[(NTHREADS*11)+threadIdx.x] =
           interpolatePosition(threshold,
                           cellVertices[3], cellVertices[7],
                           field[3], field[7]);
   // Wait while threads are filling ''vertices'' buffer.
   __syncthreads();
   ...
```

Listing 4.5. Generation of vertex buffer offsets.

Step 5. Finally, we can start generating triangles and writing them to the specified vertex buffer. Each vertex being generated is placed along one of the 12 edges of the cell. The function value at each generated vertex is expected to be equal to the **threshold** value (in this case vertex is placed on the extracted isosurface)

```
...
// Get the number of triangles that need to be output
// in this MC case.
uint indexMC = getMCIndex(field, threshold);
uint numVerts = tex1Dfetch(numVertsTex, indexMC);

for(int i=0; i < numVerts; i++) {
   // Find the offset of this vertex in the vertex buffer.
   uint vertexOffset = cellVBOffsets[cellIndex] + i;
   if (vertexOffset >= maxVerts) {
      continue;
   }

   // Will get the vertex from the appropriate
   // edge of the cell
   uint edge = tex1Dfetch(triTex, (indexMC << 4) + i);

   // Write out vertex position to VB.
   float3 p = vertlist[(edge*NTHREADS)+threadIdx.x];
   positions[vertexOffset] = make_float4(p, 1.0f);
   // Evaluate normal at this point.
   normals[vertexOffset] = calcNormal(p);
}
```

Listing 4.6. Generating triangles.

Thus we can linearly interpolate function values along each edge in order to find locations where vertices have to be placed.[2]

You can see that the **vertices** array is placed in shared memory. This is done to decrease the amount of local storage required to run the kernel. Additionally, this memory is accessed in a special way. Each vertex of the cell is placed with a stride of **NTHREADS** elements, thus helping to avoid bank conflicts between the threads; i.e., consecutive threads access consecutive memory addresses and such memory requests can be serialized.[3] These are well-known optimization techniques often used in CUDA applications.

Once all output vertex positions have been retrieved, they need to be connected to form a set of triangles. We need to find the MC case index again, which is used to read the set of vertex indices from the MC triangles table. After this step a set of vertices and normals can be output to a vertex buffer as shown in Listing 4.6. In this case, the MC triangles table was earlier mapped to a one-dimensional texture **triTex** (in a fashion similar to the mapping of volume texture performed in Step 1).

---

[2]Non-linear interpolation schemes can be used to improve the quality of the resulting mesh. [Tatarchuk et al. 07].

[3]This need not be done for devices with CUDA Compute Capability 1.2 and above.

```
__device__
float4 calcNormal(float3 p)
{
    float f = fieldFunc(p.x, p.y, p.z);
    const float delta = 0.01f;
    // Approximate derivative:
    float dx = fieldFunc(p.x + delta, p.y, p.z) - f;
    float dy = fieldFunc(p.x, p.y + delta, p.z) - f;
    float dz = fieldFunc(p.x, p.y, p.z + delta) - f;
    return make_float4(dx, dy, dz, 0.f);
}
```

Listing 4.7. Generate normals.

Per-vertex analytic normals (see Equation (4.1)) are retrieved using forward differences approximation as shown in Listing 4.7.

It is important to note that polygonization does not have to be performed for each frame. Depending on the available processing power, mesh extraction can be performed only once for a number of frames. Alpha blending between the extracted meshes can be applied to perform smoother transition between them. *Note*: An issue of loading from and saving to global memory was mentioned in Section 4.3.1. From the code provided in this section it can be seen, that in case function values are not stored in the memory, eight function evaluations need to be performed for each cell (see `sampleVolume()` function). For instance, on a $64 \times 64 \times 64$ grid one would need to perform at least two million function evaluations (that is eight evaluations for each of 262,144 cells) only to find out the MC case index for each cell. Add about 10–20% of this number to get the total number of all required function evaluations. This includes actual vertex position and normal calculations for nonempty cells. For a number of example applications that will follow, saving to global memory results in better performance as memory latency is hidden by the expensive function evaluations.

4.3.3   Rendering

Once the vertex buffer has been filled with the geometry information it can be rendered as any conventional polygonal model. We only need to enable a shader making the extracted isosurface look more visually interesting (see Section 4.2.3).

It is worth noting that FRep models can be rendered using ray-casting [Fryazinov et al. 08], thus avoiding the necessity to perform the complex isosurface extraction procedure. At the moment, however, only relatively simple models can be rendered at high resolution in real time [Kravtsov et al. 08].

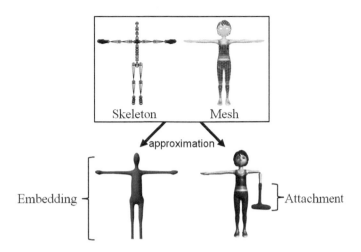

Figure 4.11. Possible approximations.

4.4 Applications

In Section 4.2 we have briefly described a small subset of FReps. In this section we will demonstrate a number of applications (see Figure 4.1) that can be implemented using the combination of FRep objects and polygonal meshes.

4.4.1 Approach Outline

A rigging skeleton is commonly used to animate polygonal meshes. Convolution surfaces described in Section 4.2.2, as well as a number of other implicit surfaces, can also be animated using similar skeletons.[4] We will use a skeleton as a base for the integration of FReps and polygonal models. The cases we will refer to can be generally classified as follows:

1. Embedding an FRep object inside a mesh object or coating mesh objects with FRep objects (Figure 4.11).

2. Attaching an FRep object to the mesh (Figure 4.11).

3. Attaching a polygonal object to the FRep object (Figure 4.19).

We will provide detailed descriptions of each case.

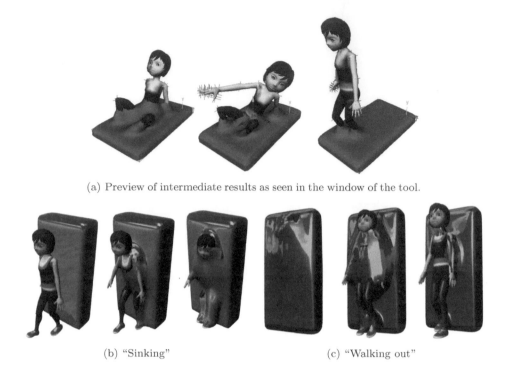

(a) Preview of intermediate results as seen in the window of the tool.

        (b) "Sinking"   (c) "Walking out"

Figure 4.12.   The interaction of an animated object with viscous liquid.

4.4.2   Embedding an FRep Object inside a Mesh Object

The embedding of an FRep object allows us to mimic the interaction of a viscous object with an animated character (Figure 4.12) as well as "supra-natural" behavior of the liquid material (Figure 4.16).

In this case we approximate an animated mesh with a convolution surface using the rigging skeleton. The resulting convolution surface is expected to be completely hidden inside the mesh. In most cases the approximation needs to be performed only once for the character's bind pose. We can estimate the parameters of the embedded convolution surface using the available information. For the initial approximation we use the rigging skeleton. Given the set of bones of the rigging skeleton, where each bone is a line segment in three-dimensional space, we use the set of these segments as the basis for an initial convolution

---

[4]We have chosen convolution surfaces mainly because of their relatively simple defining function and an absence of bulges and other unwanted artifacts.

Figure 4.13. Synchronization of polygonal and functional objects.

skeleton.[5] To calculate the radius of the convolution surface for each segment, we calculate the minimal distance between each line segment. For the set of rigging skeletal bones $s_i \in \mathbf{S}$ (where $\mathbf{S}$ is a set of skeletal bones) the radius of the ith convolution surface associated with the ith bone is

$$r_i = \min_{p_j \in \mathbf{P}}(\text{dist}(s_i, p_j)),$$

where p_j is the jth face of the polygonal mesh, $\mathbf{P}$ is a connected set of faces and $\text{dist}(s_i, p_j)$ is the distance between the bone s_i and the face p_j. Thus each individual convolution surface is fitted inside the mesh in its initial position.

After the initial approximation, a global optimization is usually required to achieve a better approximation of the given polygonal mesh using the embedded convolution surface (more details are provided in [Kravtsov et al. 08]). An additional embedding optimization step is usually necessary because only individual convolution surfaces are considered at the initial approximation step. In fact, the fields produced by all convolution surfaces sum up, which is equivalent to the increase of the radius of the individual convolution surfaces. This is especially noticeable in the locations near the skeleton branches. Alternatively, instead of global non-linear optimization, an artist can manipulate radius values of individual convolutions to achieve better embedding. Note that, if we wish to apply the blending union operation described in Section 4.2.1, the quality of the initial approximation does not play a significant part in this process.

After the approximation step, the segments of the convolution skeleton are transformed relative to the transformation of the rigging skeleton. Hence, the motion of the convolution surface is synchronized with the motion of the animated mesh (see Figure 4.13). Once the approximation of the animated mesh has been retrieved, we can apply FRep operations to achieve a number of effects (see Figure 4.14).

As the first application of our technique, we mimic the interaction of a viscous object with an animated object using the blending union of two implicit surfaces.

---

[5]A convolution skeleton does not need to have the same configuration as the original rigging skeleton. For instance, it can have different number of bones or positions of the bones can differ. The only requirement is that the convolution skeleton be defined relative to the rigging skeleton.

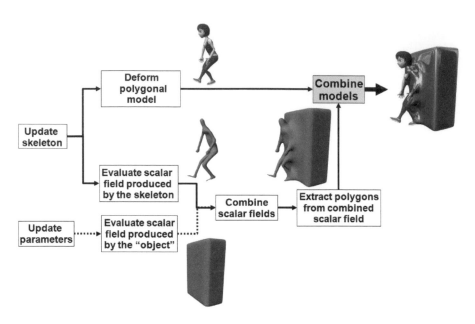

Figure 4.14. Approach outline.

As we mentioned above, the FRep object corresponding to the initial mesh is an embedded convolution surface. The second FRep object, representing the viscous object, can be modeled using a set of implicit primitives. If the defining functions of both objects have distance properties, the shape of the surface resulting from the blending operation depends on the distance between the original objects. The further the objects are from each other the less they are deformed (see Figure 4.15). The behavior of the blended shape visually resembles adhesion, stretching, and breach of the viscous material. If the blended shape is rendered together with the

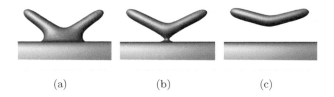

(a)   (b)   (c)

Figure 4.15. Phases of interaction between animated blended objects: (a) two objects and a single blend shape during blending; (b) the boundary case before two shapes separate; (c) two separate shapes with some deformation showing the objects' reciprocal attraction.

polygonal mesh, a part of the convolution surface embedded within the mesh becomes visible due to the deformation, thus contributing to the material interacting with the mesh (see Figure 4.12). Therefore, the quality of the initial approximation of the mesh by the convolution surface does not play a significant part in this application. It is more important just to fully embed the convolution surface into the mesh when no deformation is applied. Surely, such an approach is aimed at achieving verisimilitude rather than physically correct results.

The aforementioned approach can be used to model "supra-natural" behavior of the liquid material. In such an animation effect the convolution surface radii are increased over time, which creates the effect of the liquid flowing up the mesh and gradually engulfing it. It is possible to automatically generate this sort of

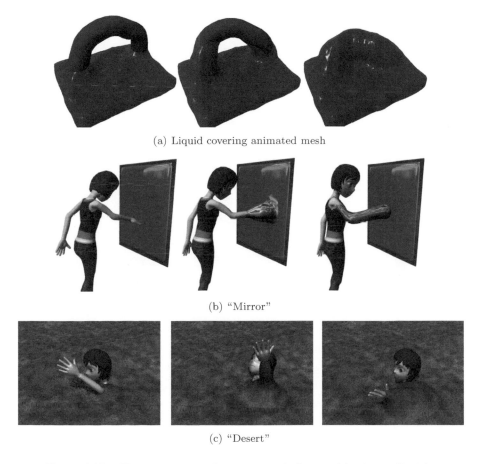

(a) Liquid covering animated mesh

(b) "Mirror"

(c) "Desert"

Figure 4.16. The interaction of an animated object with viscous liquid.

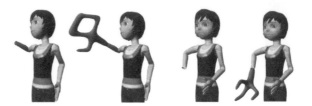

Figure 4.17. Attachment of functional object.

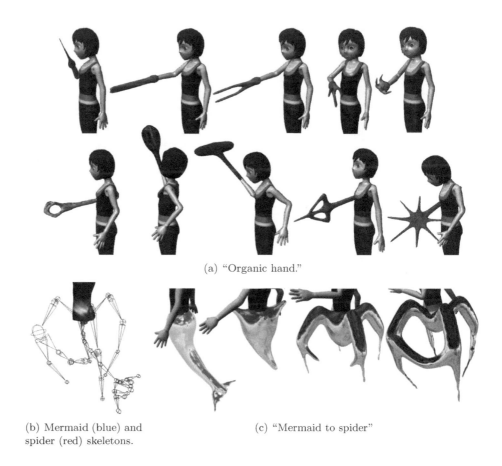

(a) "Organic hand."

(b) Mermaid (blue) and
spider (red) skeletons.

(c) "Mermaid to spider"

Figure 4.18.   Controlled metamorphosis sequences.

animation. The artist only needs to specify the first and last joint of the skeletal chain as well as the final "thickness" of the liquid flowing over the mesh (see Figure 4.16).

4.4.3 Attaching an FRep Object to the Mesh

In this case we attach an implicit surface to the mesh. To do so, we attach a skeleton defining convolution surface to the rigging skeleton that is animated in a usual way (Figure 4.17). Optionally the implicit surface can be fitted at its boundary attachment to the polygonal mesh. Animation of the skeleton defining the convolution surface leads to the automatic changes of the attached functional object, which means the resulting shape can be dramatically changed. No additional blending is required as convolution surfaces are automatically blended with each other. This approach can be used for the creation of easily metamorphosing parts of animated characters (Figure 4.18(a)). It is also possible to perform metamorphosis between implicit limbs with quite different geometry and topology. The user just needs to specify two skeletons (Figure 4.18(b)) and the time needed to morph from one to another. The intermediate meshes are generated automatically (Figure 4.18(c)).

4.4.4 Attaching a Polygonal Object to the FRep Object

In this case, the skeleton controlling the functional object is defined independently. The FRep object can be placed in the virtual environment as a self-contained entity. Various special effects can be implemented for this entity. The interaction

Figure 4.19. Attachment of polygonal object to the functional object.

Grid resolution for polygonization	"Supra-natural" (11 segments)	Andy (45 segments)	Hybrid Andy (10 segments)
32x32x32	3 ms	9 ms	2 ms
64x64x64	7 ms	22 ms	3 ms
128x128x128	30 ms	95 ms	14 ms

Table 4.1. Average times for mesh generation (milliseconds/frame) on an NVIDIA GeForce 8800 Ultra, 768 MB of RAM. Andy is a mesh model with an embedded convolution surface (Figure 4.12). Hybrid Andy is shown in Figure 4.18(a).

with polygonal objects can be performed using the "implicit skeleton." The polygonal objects can be attached to this skeleton and follow its motion (see Figure 4.19). Collision detection with an FRep object can also be implemented in a relatively simple way, as the scalar field produced by such an object has distance properties.

One can notice that implicit surfaces are a great tool in defining complex dynamic shapes with arbitrary topology. They can also be used for the creation and modification of the user-generated content (similar to EA's "Spore"). The user can define the skeleton and tweak its parameters seeing the resulting shape in real time (see Figure 4.1(b)). After the extraction of the convolution surface, it can be assigned skinning weights and later used in the virtual environment. LODs for such a mesh can be generated automatically via variation of the polygonization grid resolution (Figure 4.2).

We show the times required to evaluate the field and extract the mesh in Table 4.1.

4.5 Tools

Any technique loses its value if no appropriate tools are available for people who are actually producing the contentWe wanted to demonstrate that the proposed approach can be employed in a conventional animation pipeline with near real-time

Grid resolution for polygonization	"Supra-natural" (11 segments)	Andy (45 segments)	Hybrid Andy (10 segments)
20x20x20	25 ms	80 ms	30 ms
30x30x30	80 ms	220 ms	60 ms
50x50x50	310 ms	930 ms	260 ms
70x70x70	810 ms	2580 ms	670 ms

Table 4.2. Average times for mesh generation (milliseconds/frame) on a PC with a Dual Core Intel Xeon (2.66 GHz), 2 GB of RAM.

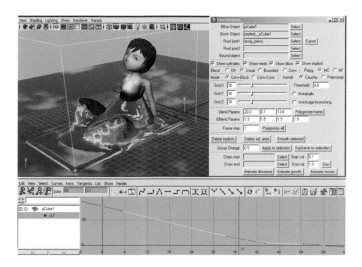

Figure 4.20. A screenshot of the working environment.

preview without a significant effort. Thus we have implemented our approach
as a plug-in for Maya. We have chosen Maya as it is a popular tool for modeling and animation used by a lot of professional artists. Our plug-in performs
polygonization on the CPU and feeds the extracted mesh back to the modeling
package. All the scenes illustrating the aforementioned ases were defined using a
set of developed plug-ins. Even though all calculations are performed on the CPU,
intermediate results can be seen in the editor in near real time (Figure 4.20). The
actual times for a number of models are shown in Table 4.2. Alternatively, the
mesh extracted on the GPU could be copied to RAM and provided to Maya for
further manipulation and rendering.

Integration of our technique into an existing animation package can decrease
the learning curve for the user. Users are free to produce an animation sequence
in a way that they are accustomed to within the familiar software environment,
while having an opportunity to see the results of his actions in near real time.
Thus, the incorporation of the plug-in in a general-purpose animation software
package allows the user to easily integrate the produced animation into complex
scenes developed using this package.

4.6 Limitations

The applied blending operation is based on the distance properties of the functions
defining the initial geometric objects being blended. The scalar fields produced by
known convolution surface kernels significantly decrease as the distance from the

line segment increases. At a particular distance from the line segment, the values
of such a field are almost equal to zero, and no blend shape is generated at these
distances by the blending operation. Thus it is hard to model the interaction
between the mesh and the viscous object at large distances. In such cases, an
approximation of the mesh with a set of blended quadric surfaces could provide
better results. Additionally as the distance between the two blended objects
increases, the deformation of the convolution surfaces decreases until these surfaces
are again embedded into the polygonal mesh and are no longer visible. The
proposed method does not allow us to easily model the separation of droplets
of the viscous liquid from the mesh. If this effect is desired, some additional
particles modeling this effect could be attached to the mesh. It is also possible to
introduce particles to the viscous object. These can improve the visual quality and
dynamism of the resulting animation sequence. Simplified particle-based physical
models can be applied to the implicit model to improve the default behavior of
the viscous object. A metaball representation of the particles is frequently used
to integrate these particles into the implicit model. Particle positions retrieved
after the physical simulation could be used to add metaballs to the final model.
This would allow for partial modeling of physically correct behavior within the
existing geometric model.

Also, the proposed approximation for polygonal meshes can only provide good
results for typical skeletal characters with axial symmetry. Other types of meshes
may require additional efforts in order to achieve better approximation.

4.7   Conclusion

We have outlined a number of advantages of function representation (FRep)
and demonstrated a number of applications suitable for computer animation and
games. This representation has low memory requirements. Natural resolution independence of the original model allows us to adjust rendering quality according
to available hardware specs. The discretization of the model can be performed
in parallel, so that it is well suited for modern GPUs and CPUs with an ever
increasing number of internal cores.

We believe that FReps have many more useful applications in the fields of
computer animation and games.

4.8   Source Code

At http://www.akpeters.com/gpupro you can find source code implementing the
proposed approach based on NVIDIA CUDA SDK release 2.1.

Bibliography

[Blinn 82] James F. Blinn. "A Generalization of Algebraic Surface Drawing." *ACM Transactions on Graphics* 1:3 (1982), 235–256.

[Bloomenthal and Shoemake 91] Jules Bloomenthal and Ken Shoemake. "Convolution Surfaces." *SIGGRAPH Computer Graphics* 25:4 (1991), 251–256.

[Ebert et al. 02] David S. Ebert, Kenton F. Musgrave, Darwyn Peachey, Ken Perlin, and Steven Worley. *Texturing & Modeling: A Procedural Approach*, Third edition. The Morgan Kaufmann Series in Computer Graphics, Morgan Kaufmann, 2002.

[Fryazinov et al. 08] O. Fryazinov, A. Pasko, and Adzhiev V. "An Exact Representation of Polygonal Objects by C^1-continuous Scalar Fields Based on Binary Space Partitioning." Technical Report TR-NCCA-2008-03, The National Centre for Computer Animation, Bournemouth University, UK, 2008.

[Geiss 07] Ryan Geiss. *GPU GEMS 3*, Chapter Generating Complex Procedural Terrains Using the GPU, pp. 7–38. Addison-Wesley Professional, 2007.

[Jin et al. 01] Xiaogang Jin, Chiew-Lan Tai, Jieging Feng, and Qunsheng Peng. "Convolution Surfaces for Line Skeletons with Polynomial Weight Distributions." *Journal of Graphics Tools* 6:3 (2001), 17–28.

[Kravtsov et al. 08] D. Kravtsov, O. Fryazinov, V. Adzhiev, A. Pasko, and P. Comninos. "Embedded Implicit Stand-ins for Animated Meshes: A Case of Hybrid Modelling." Technical Report "TR-NCCA-2008-01", The National Centre for Computer Animation, Bournemouth University, UK, 2008.

[Lorensen and Cline 87] William E. Lorensen and Harvey E. Cline. "Marching Cubes: A High Resolution 3D Surface Construction Algorithm." In *SIGGRAPH '87: Proceedings of the 14th Annual Conference on Computer Graphics and Interactive Techniques*, 21, 21, pp. 163–169. ACM Press, 1987.

[McCormack and Sherstyuk 98] Jon McCormack and Andrei Sherstyuk. "Creating and Rendering Convolution Surfaces." *Computer Graphics Forum* 17:2 (1998), 113–120.

[NVIDIA 09] NVIDIA. Compute Unified Device Architecture (CUDA). 2009.

[Pasko et al. 95] A. Pasko, V. Adzhiev, A. Sourin, and V. Savchenko. "Function Representation in Geometric Modeling: Concepts, Implementation and Applications." *The Visual Computer* 11:8 (1995), 429–446.

[Ricci 73] A. Ricci. "A Constructive Geometry for Computer Graphics." *The Computer Journal* 16 (1973), 157–160.

[Sengupta et al. 07] Shubhabrata Sengupta, Mark Harris, Yao Zhang, and John D. Owens. "Scan Primitives for GPU Computing." In *Graphics Hardware 2007*, pp. 97–106, 2007.

[Sengupta et al. 08] Shubhabrata Sengupta, Mark Harris, and Michael Garland. "Efficient Parallel Scan Algorithms for GPUs." Technical Report NVR-2008-003, NVIDIA Corporation, 2008.

[Tatarchuk et al. 07] Natalya Tatarchuk, Jeremy Shopf, and Christopher DeCoro. "Real-Time Isosurface Extraction Using the GPU Programmable Geometry Pipeline." In *SIGGRAPH '07: ACM SIGGRAPH 2007 courses*, pp. 122–137. New York: ACM, 2007.

[Uralsky 06] Y. Uralsky. "DX10: Practical Metaballs and Implicit Surfaces." Technical report, NVIDIA Corporation, 2006.

Rendering Techniques

Welcome to the *Rendering Techniques* section. This section is a reflection of some of the latest developments in the field of real-time rendering. Thanks to the flexibility of today's GPUs, we have witnessed an explosion in the number of methods and techniques used to sample real-world phenomenon or to model special effects from our own minds. It is great to see that almost every new game today holds a number of rendering recipes that gives it its unique look and feel. But it is even much greater that the makers of those products actually share their work with the entire community.

The articles in this section cover a wide selection of topics, from surface rendering to stylization to post-processing to rendering systems.

We start with the article, "Quadtree Displacement Mapping with Height Blending," by Michal Drobot. This is a complete production-proof surface rendering solution with a multitude of powerful capabilities. The technique provides an accelerated approach to render displaced surfaces via smart use of a quad-tree structure during height-field ray tracing. Michal covers the details of rendering dynamic displaced surfaces with multiple layers, soft-shadowing, ambient occlusion, and LOD support. This entire combination is achievable on current-generation hardware and consoles with a small memory footprint in comparison to basic normal mapping.

The next article in the section is "NPR Effects Using the Geometry Shader," by Pedro Hermosilla and Pere-Pau Vázquez. This is a new real-time implementation of non-photorealistic rendering effects by relying on the geometry shader stage in recent GPUs. The authors show how to calculate proper textured silhouettes which gives the capability to specify stylized outline ink types. A special discussion on pencil shading is also included.

The article, "Alpha Blending as a Post-Process," by Benjamin Hathaway introduces a novel and inspiring technique to render correct alpha-blended geometry without the need for depth sorting. It is a multi-pass approach that relies on a separate buffer for alpha-blending accumulation, which is then combined with the scene's render target in a single post-processing step.

The fourth article in the section is "Virtual Texture Mapping 101," written by Matthäus G. Chajdas, Christian Eisenacher, Marc Stamminger, and Sylvain Lefebvre. In this introductory article, the authors show the basics of a rendering system that supports rendering with a virtually unlimited set of textures while still utilizing a fixed amount of texture memory on the graphics card. The system manages streaming and paging textures into the GPU based on visible scene contents. The article discusses the system's implementation details, including texture filtering issues and other important considerations.

We conclude the section with Emil Persson's article, "Volume Decals." This is a practical technique to render surface decals without the need to generate special geometry for every decal. Instead, the GPU performs the entire projection operation. The author shows how to use volume textures to render decals on arbitrary surfaces while avoiding texture stretching and shearing artifacts.

It was a pleasure to edit these articles. I hope you enjoy reading them and making use of them in your projects.

—Wessam Bahnassi

Quadtree Displacement Mapping
with Height Blending
Michal Drobot

1.1 Overview

This article presents an overview and comparison of current surface rendering techniques, and introduces a novel approach outperforming existing solutions in terms of performance, memory usage, and multilayer blending. Algorithms and ideas researched during *Two Worlds 2* development are shared, and the article proposes strategies for tackling problems of realistic terrain, surface and decal visualization considering limited memory, and computational power on current-generation consoles. Moreover, problems of functionality, performance, and aesthetics are discussed, providing guidelines for choosing the proper technique, content creation, and authoring pipeline.

We focus on various view and light-dependant visual clues important for correct surface rendering such as displacement mapping, self-shadowing with approximate penumbra shadows, ambient occlusion, and surface correct texture blending, while allowing real-time surface changes. Moreover, all presented techniques are valid for high quality real-time rendering on current generation hardware as well as consoles (as Xbox 360 was the main target platform during research).

First, existing parallax mapping techniques are compared and contrasted with real-life demands and possibilities. Then we present a state-of-the-art algorithm yielding higher accuracy with very good performance, scaling well with large height fields. It makes use of empty space skipping techniques and utilizes texture MIP levels for height quadtree storage, which can be prepared at render time. Second, a soft shadows computation method is proposed, which takes advantage of the quadtree. We expand upon this to calculate an ambient-occlusion term. Next, we introduce an LOD technique which allows higher performance and

Figure 1.1. Normal mapped environment.

Figure 1.2. Fully featured surface rendering using the methods proposed in this article.

quality for minification. Then we focus on surface blending methods, proposing a new method that exhibits better resemblance to real life and allows aggressive optimization during blended height-field displacement mapping. The proposed methods—depending on combinations and implementation—guarantee fast, scalable, and accurate displacement mapping of blended surfaces, including visually pleasing ambient occlusion and soft penumbra soft shadowing (compare Figures 1.1 and 1.2). Specific attention will be given to the various implementations and the proper choice of rendering method and asset authoring pipeline.

1.2 Introduction

During the last change of console generation we have seen a dramatic improvement in graphics rendering quality. With modern GPUs pushing millions of triangles per second, we are looking for more fidelity in areas that are still being impractical for performance reasons. One of those is surface rendering, which is one of the most fundamental building blocks of believable virtual world.

Each surface at its geometric level has a number of complex properties such as volume, depth, and various frequency details that together model further visual clues like depth parallax, self-shadowing, self-occlusion, and light reactivity. The topic of light interactions depending on surface microstructure is well researched and so many widely used solutions are provided (such as Cook-Torrance's lighting model and its optimizations). However, correct geometry rendering is still problematic. The brute force approach of rendering every geometry detail as a triangle mesh is still impractical because it would have to consist of millions of vertices, thus requiring too much memory and computations. Moreover, surface blending such as widely seen on terrain (i.e., sand mixing with rocks) only complicate the situation in terms of blend quality and additional performance impact. Last but not least, we would like to manipulate surface geometric properties at render time (i.e., dynamic water erosion simulation, craters forming after meteor strike).

To sum up, we would like our surface rendering method to support:

- accurate depth at all angles (depth parallax effect);

- self-shadowing;

- ambient occlusion;

- fast blending;

- dynamic geometric properties;

- current-generation hardware (taking console performance into account);

- minimal memory footprint compared to common normal mapping.

Common normal mapping techniques (those which create the illusion of detailed surface by performing light computation on precalculated normal data set) fail to meet our demands, as they do not model visual geometry clues. However, we still find it useful in light interaction calculations, thus complementing more sophisticated rendering solutions.

The only rendering method class that is able to suit all our needs are height-field-based ray-tracing algorithms. The idea behind those algorithms is to walk along a ray that entered the surface volume, finding the correct intersection of the ray with the surface. They operate on grayscale images representing height values of surfaces, thus exchanging vertex for pixel transformations, which suits our hardware better in terms of performance and memory usage. Moreover, they mix well with existing normal mapping and are performing better as GPUs become more general processing units. However, none of them are aimed at high performance surface blending or ambient occlusion calculation.

During our research we were seeking for the best possible rendering method meeting our demands, being robust, functional and fast as we were aiming for Xbox360-class hardware. As our scenario involved fully-featured rendering of outdoor terrain with many objects and indoor cave systems, we were forced to take special care for an automatic LOD system. Several methods were compared and evaluated, finally ending with the introduction of a new solution that proved to be suiting all our needs. We describe our research and the motivation behind it, going in detail with each building block of the quadtree Displacement Mapping with Height Blending technique.

1.3   Overview of Ray-Tracing Algorithms

Every height-field-based ray-tracing algorithm is working with additional displacement data, commonly encoded in height map format (grayscale image scaled to [0; 1] range). Calculations are done in tangent space to allow computations for arbitrary surfaces. Correct surface depth is calculated by finding the intersection between viewing ray and height field. That ensures correct parallax offset for further color and lighting calculations.

Figure 1.3 illustrates the depth parallax effect and presents the general intersection calculation.

General height-field ray-tracing algorithms can be summarized as follows:

1. Calculate tangent-space normalized view vector V per-vertex, and interpolate for pixel shader.

2. Ray cast the view ray to compute intersection with the height field, acquiring the texture coordinate offset required for arriving at the correct surface

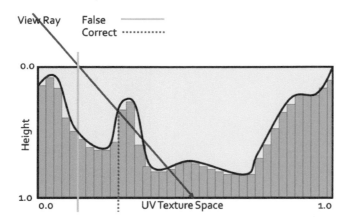

Figure 1.3. Height-field ray-trace scheme.

point. We start at texture input T1 coordinates, sampling along the surface's profile, finally computing new texture coordinates T2.

3. Compute the normal lighting equation using surface attributes sampled at the new texture coordinates T2.

The following algorithms implement various methods for intersection computation, varying in speed, accuracy and use of additional precomputed data.

1.3.1 Online Algorithms

Relief mapping. Relief mapping [Policarpo 2005] performs intersection calculation by linear search in two-dimensional height-field space followed by binary search.

We want to find the intersection point (p, r). We start by calculating point (u, v), which is the two-dimensional texture coordinate of the surface point where the viewing ray reaches a depth $= 1.0$. The point (u, v) is computed based on initial texture coordinates (x, y) on the transformed view direction with scaling factor applied. Then we search for (p, r) by sampling the height field between (x, y) and (u, v). We check for intersections by comparing ray depth with the stored depth at the current sampling point. When the latter is smaller, we have found the intersection and we can refine it using binary search. Figure 1.4 illustrates the process.

Binary search is taking advantage of texture filtering and operates in minimized space around the found intersection point. That ensures fast convergence and high accuracy. However, using that kind of search utilizes dependant reads on the GPU, thus vastly affecting performance. While a linear- and binary-search combo

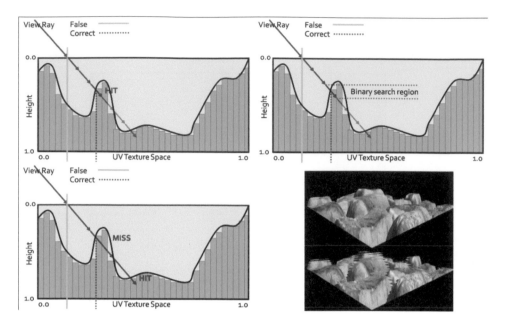

Figure 1.4. Relief Mapping. Top left: linear search. Top right: binary search around point found in linear search. Bottom left: possible miss of linear search. Bottom right: resulting aliasing artifacts as opposed to correct rendering.

is a known and proven solution, its linear part is prone to aliasing due to under sampling. During the search, when there are not enough search steps (step length is too big), we might miss important surface features as shown in Figure 1.4. Increasing search steps potentially minimizes the problem but severely affects performance, making this algorithm highly unreliable when sampling large height fields or surfaces exhibiting very large displacement scales. Nonetheless, it is still very effective in simple scenarios that do not require high sampling count, as the performance is saved on ALU instructions.

Parallax occlusion mapping. Several researchers tried to optimize this algorithm by omitting the expensive binary search. *Parallax occlusion mapping* [Tatarchuk 2006] relies on accurate high-precision intersection calculation (see Figure 1.5). A normal linear search is performed finding point (p, r) and last step point (k, l). Then the ray is tested against a line made of (p, r) and (k, l), effectively approximating the height profile as a piecewise linear curve. Moreover, solutions for additional LOD and soft shadows were proposed. POM, while being accurate enough and faster than relief mapping, is still prone to aliasing and so exhibits the same negative traits of linear search (Listing 1.1).

```
float Size = 1.0 / LinearSearchSteps;
float Depth = 1.0;
int StepIndex = 0;
float CurrD = 0.0;
float PrevD = 1.0;
float2 p1 = 0.0;
float2 p2 = 0.0;

while(StepIndex < LinearSearchSteps)
{
    Depth -= Size; //move the ray
    float4 TCoord = float2(p+(v*Depth)); // new sampling pos
    CurrD = tex2D(texSMP, TCoord).a; //new height
    if (CurrD > Depth) //check for intersection
    {
        p1 = float2(Depth, CurrD);
        p2 = float2(Depth + Size, PrevD); //store last step
        StepIndex = LinearSearchSteps; //break the loop
    }
    StepIndex++;
    PrevD = CurrD;
}

//Linear approximation using current and last step
//instead of binary search, opposed to relief mapping.
float d2 = p2.x - p2.y;
float d1 = p1.x - p1.y;

return (p1.x * d2 - p2.x * d1) / (d2 - d1);
```

Listing 1.1. POM code.

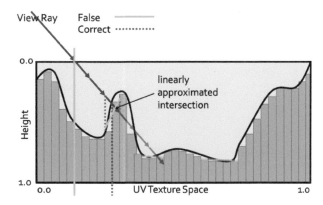

Figure 1.5. POM.

1.3.2   Algorithms Using Precomputed Data

In response to the arising problem of performance and accuracy, several solutions were proposed that make use of additional data to ensure skipping of empty space and prohibit missing surface features. However, additional memory footprint or preprocessing computation time limits their usefulness.

Per-pixel displacement with distance function. *Per-pixel displacement with distance function* [Donelly 2005] uses precalculated three-dimensional texture representation of the surface's profile. Each texel represents a sphere whose radius is equal to the nearest surface point. We are exchanging the well-known linear search for sphere tracing. With each sample taken we know how far we can march our ray without missing any possible intersection. Traversing that kind of structure allows skipping large space areas and ensures that we will not miss the intersection point. Moreover, the intersection search part is very efficient. However, memory requirements and precomputation time for this method make it impractical for real-time game environments. As stated in [Donelly 2005], even simple surfaces may require a three-dimensional texture size of $256 \times 256 \times 16$ with dimensions rising fast for more complex and accurate rendering. That increase in memory footprint is unacceptable for the limited memory of current consoles and PC hardware, not to mention the prohibitive preprocessing time.

Cone step mapping (CSM). CSM [Dummer 2006] is based on a similar idea. It uses a cone map that associates a circular cone with each texel of the height-field texture. The cone angle is calculated so that the cone is the largest one not intersecting the height field (see Figure 1.6). This information allows us

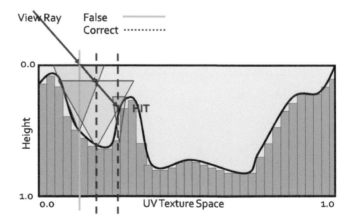

Figure 1.6. CSM. Ray traversal by cone radius distance.

to calculate a safe distance during sampling, as in per-pixel displacement with distance function. Consequently, the ray may skip empty spaces and never miss the correct intersection. Due to its conservative nature, the algorithm may require too many steps to actually converge. For performance reasons, it is required to set a maximum number of steps, which often results in stopping the ray trace too early and returning incorrect texture coordinates for further rendering.

Cone step mapping performance varies widely depending on the spatial coherency of the height field. Generally, it outperforms linear search algorithms while guaranteeing less noticeable errors. Its memory footprint is quite bearable as it requires only one additional 8-bit texture for cone maps. However, its preprocessing time makes it impossible to alter the height field at render time, as this would require recompilation of the cone map with every change. The precomputation algorithm is of complexity $O(n^2)$, where n denotes number of height-field texels, making it impractical on current GPUs. Moreover, properties of the cone map prohibit correct and easy surface blending.

Relaxed cone step mapping (RCSM). RCSM [Policarpo 2007] takes CSM one step further, making it less conservative. The idea is to use larger cones that intersect the height field only once. The search is performed the same way as in CSM. When the intersection is found, the correct point is searched, using binary search in space restricted by the last cone radius, therefore converging very quickly. The combination leads to more efficient space leaping, while remaining accurate, due to final refinement. Furthermore, an LOD scheme is proposed which, while it lacks accuracy, provides performance gains. In practice, RCSM is currently the fastest ray-tracing algorithm available, making it very useful in scenarios where neither long preprocessing times, disability of efficient blending, and dynamic height-field alteration are irrelevant.

1.4 Quadtree Displacement Mapping

We introduce a GPU-optimized version of the classic [Cohen and Shaked 1993] hierarchical ray-tracing algorithm for terrain rendering on CPU, using height-field pyramid, with bounding information stored in mipmap chain. It was presented on recent hardware by [OH 2006], yielding good accuracy and performance, but at the same time was less adequate for game scenario use. We describe our implementation, optimized for current GPUs, with an automatic LOD solution and accurate filtering. Moreover, we expand it for optimized surface blending, soft shadowing and ambient occlusion calculation.

QDM uses the mipmap structure for resembling a dense quadtree, storing maximum heights above the base plane of the height field (it is worth noting that our implementation is actually using depth maps as 0 value representing maximum displacement, as we are storing depth measured under the reference plane. In consequence, maximum heights are minimum depths, stored in our data structure). We traverse it to skip empty space and not to miss any detail. During traversal we are moving the ray from cell boundary to cell boundary, until level 0 is reached—hence valid intersection region. While moving through the hierarchy, we compute the proper hierarchy level change. Finally, we use refinement search in the region of intersection to find the accurate solution when needed.

Gf 8800	256^2	512^2	1024^2	2048^2
Quad tree	0.15ms	0.25ms	1.15ms	2.09ms
CSM	< 2min	< 14min	< 8h	/

Table 1.1. Data preprocessing time.

1.4.1   Quadtree Construction

The quadtree is represented by a hierarchical collection of images in a mipmap. The construction is simple, as it requires generating mipmaps with the min operator instead of average as during normal mipmapping. As a result, MIP level 0 (2^n) represents the original height field with the following levels 1 (2^{n-1}), 2 (2^{n-2}), ... containing the minimum value of the four nearest texels from levels above. The entire process can be run on the GPU. Due to hardware optimization, quadtree construction is very fast. The timings in Table 1.1 were obtained on a PC equipped with Intel Core 2 Duo 2.4 GHz and GeForce 8800. For comparison, timings for RCSM are given. The quadtree was computed on the GPU, while the cone map was on the CPU due to algorithm requirements.

Figure 1.7. Generated QDM on mipmaps.

As we can see, quadtree computation time is negligible, even for on-the-fly generation, whereas cone maps could even be problematic for off-line rendering during texture authoring (see Figure 1.7).

1.4.2 Quadtree Traversal

The general steps of intersection search are shown by the pseudocode in Listing 1.2. We start the computation at the highest mipmap level. The stopping condition of the main loop is to reach the lowest hierarchy level, which effectively means finding the intersection region where the linear approximation can be performed. At each step, we determine if we can move the ray further or if there is a need for further refinement. We algebraically perform the intersection test between the ray and the cell bounding planes and the minimum depth plane.

In case the ray does not intersect the minimum plane, then the current cell is blocking our trace. We have to refine the search by descending in the hierarchy by one level. In the other case, we have to find the first intersection of the ray with the minimum plane or the cell boundary. When the right intersection is computed, we move the ray to the newly acquired point. In case we have to cross the cell boundary, then we choose the next cell via the nearest-neighbor method, thus minimizing error. At this point, we perform hierarchy level update for optimization (see the optimization section).

Figure 1.8 presents step-by-step ray traversal in QDM: Step (a) shows a ray coming from the initial geometry plane and stopping at the maximum level or minimum plane. Steps (b) and (c) illustrate further refinement while the search descends to lower hierarchy levels. Step (d) presents where the ray must cross the cell in order to progress. While the minimum plane of the current cell is not blocking the way, we have to move the ray to the nearest cell boundary. Steps (e) and (f) show further ray traversal while refining the search while (g) presents the main loop's stopping condition, as the ray has reached level 0. Therefore, we can proceed to linear interpolation between the nearest texels in Step (h).

```
While (hierarchy_level > 0)
    depth=get_maximum_depth(position, hierarchy level)
    If(ray_depth < depth)
        move_ray_to_cell_boundry_or_minimum_depth_plane
    else
        descend_one_hierarchy_level
    end
    find_intersection_using_linear_interpolation
```

Listing 1.2. General QDM search steps.

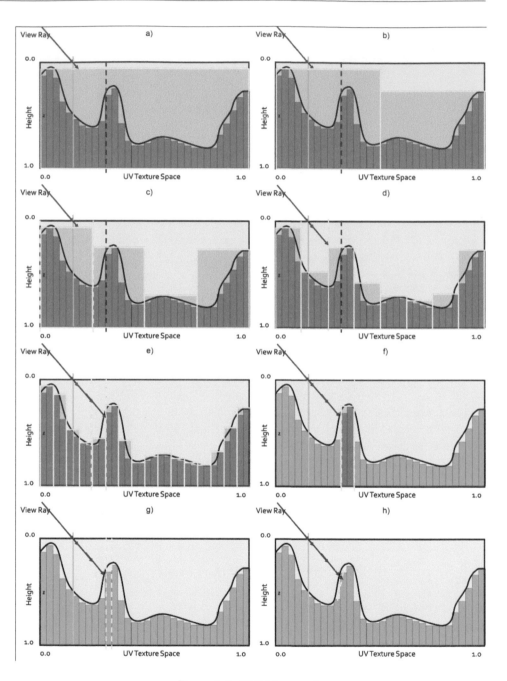

Figure 1.8. QDM traversal.

It is important to correctly calculate sampling positions since we are working with a discrete data structure. For correct results, we should use point-filtering on the GPU and integer math. However, if we cannot afford an additional sampler for the same texture using POINT and LINEAR, it is possible to use linear filtering with enough care taken for correct calculations. As SM 3.0 only emulates integer operations, we have to account for possible errors in calculations (using SM 4.0 is preferable, due to the presence of real integer math).

Listing 1.3 is heavily commented to explain the algorithm's steps in detail.

```
const int MaxLevel = MaxMipLvl;
const int NodeCount = pow(2.0, MaxLevel);
const float HalfTexel = 1.0 / NodeCount / 2.0;
float d;
float3 p2 = p;
int Level = MaxLevel;

//We calculate ray movement vector in inter-cell numbers.
int2 DirSign = sign(v.xy);

//Main loop
while (Level >= 0)
{
    //We get current cell minimum plane using tex2Dlod.
    d = tex2Dlod(HeightTexture, float4(p2.xy, 0.0 , Level)).w;

    //If we are not blocked by the cell we move the ray.
    if (d > p2.z)
    {
        //We calculate predictive new ray position.
        float3 tmpP2 = p + v * d;

        //We compute current and predictive position.
        //Calculations are performed in cell integer numbers.
        int NodeCount = pow(2, (MaxLevel - Level));
        int4 NodeID = int4((p2.xy , tmpP2.xy) * NodeCount);

        //We test if both positions are still in the same cell.
        //If not, we have to move the ray to nearest cell boundary.
        if (NodeID.x != NodeID.z || NodeID.y != NodeID.w)
        {
            //We compute the distance to current cell boundary.
            //We perform the calculations in continuous space.
            float2 a = (p2.xy - p.xy);
            float2 p3 = (NodeID.xy + DirSign) / NodeCount;
            float2 b = (p3.xy - p.xy);
```

```
        //We are choosing the nearest cell
        //by choosing smaller distance.
        float2 dNC = abs(p2.z * b / a);
        d = min(d, min(dNC.x, dNC.y));

        //During cell crossing we ascend in hierarchy.
        Level+=2;

        //Predictive refinement
        tmpP2 = p + v * d;
    }

    //Final ray movement
    p2 = tmpP2;
  }

  //Default descent in hierarchy
  //nullified by ascend in case of cell crossing
  Level--;
}
return p2;
```

Listing 1.3. QDM search steps.

1.4.3   Optimizations

Convergence speed-up. It is worth noting that during traversal, the ray can only descend in the hierarchy. Therefore, we are not taking full advantage of the quadtree. The worst-case scenario occurs when the ray descends to lower levels and passes by an obstacle really close, consequently degenerating further traversal to the linear search. To avoid that problem, we should optimally compute the correct level higher in the hierarchy during cell crossing. However, current hardware is not optimized for such dynamic flow. A simple one step up move in the hierarchy should be enough. For more complicated surfaces which require many iterations, we discovered that this optimization increases performance by 30% (tested on a case requiring >64 iterations).

Fixed search step count. While the algorithm tends to converge really quickly, it may considerably slow down at grazing angles on complex high-resolution height fields. Therefore, an upper bound on iterations speeds up rendering without very noticeable artifacts. The number of iterations should be exposed to technical artists to find optimal values.

Linear filtering step. Depending on surface magnification and the need for accurate results, final refinement may be used. One can utilize the well-know binary search which would converge quickly (five sampling points is enough for most purposes) due to the tight search range. However, we propose linear interpolation for piece-wise surface approximation, similar to the one proposed in POM. This approach proves to be accurate on par with binary search (considering limited search range), while being optimal for current hardware.

After finding the correct cell of intersection (at hierarchy level 0), we sample the height field in direction of the ray cast, one texel before and one texel after the cell. Then we find the intersection point between the ray and linearly approximated curve created by sampled points.

LOD scheme. Here we propose a mixed automatic level of detail scheme. First, we dynamically compute the number of iterations based on the simple observation that parallax is larger at grazing angles, thus requiring more samples, so we can express the correct value as a function of the angle between the view vector and the geometric normal. Notice that the minimum sampling number should not be less than the total number of hierarchy levels, otherwise the algorithm will not be able to finish traversal even without any cell crossing. Moreover, we observed that with diminishing pixel size on screen, parallax depth details become less visible. Thus, we can stop our quadtree traversal at a fixed hierarchy level without significant loss of detail. We determine the right level by computing the mipmap level per pixel scaled by an artist-directed factor. For correct blending between levels, we linearly interpolate between depth values from the nearest hierarchy level by the fractional part of the calculated mipmap level. After an artist-specified distance we blend parallax mapping to normal mapping.

This combined solution guarantees high accuracy via a dynamic sampling rate, and it guarantees high performance due to quadtree pruning, thus giving a stable solution overall. For performance and quality comparisons, see the results section.

Storage. For precision reasons, it is required that the stored quadtree is accurate. A problem arises when we want to store it with textures. Generally, textures compressed with DXT compression result in a significant speedup and memory footprint reduction. DXT is a lossy compression scheme; thus it is not recommended for accurate data storage (as opposed to, e.g., diffuse textures). However, we noticed that in the general case, storing the quadtree in the alpha channel of a DXT5-compressed texture results in minor artifacts (it highly depends on the surface's profile, so it must be done with care). Still, the preferable solution is to take the memory hit and store the additional data in 1-channel 8-bit lossless textures.

Comparison. Performance tests were conducted on a test machine equipped with Intel quad core 2.8Ghz CPU and GeForce 260 GTX in full HD, using three various levels from early beta of TW2. The results can be seen in Tables 1.2, 1.3, and 1.4.

Scenarios contained fully featured levels, using various height fields of resolution 512^2 to 1024^2. Each scene pushed around one million triangles, with the parallax displacement method of choice, covering the entire screen. Depth scale

Depth Scale	POM	QDM
1.0	5ms	5.7ms
1.5	6.65ms	6.7ms
5.0	18.9ms	9ms

Relief	CSM	QDM
$\sqrt{n}$	$\leq \sqrt{n}$	$\log n$

Table 1.2. Analytical performance.   Table 1.3. General scenario performance.

POM	QDM
73ms	14ms

Table 1.4. Extreme high detail performance.

dependence was measured, and iteration count was set for close quality match between methods. Table 1.4 shows the timing for ultra-high resolution and complexity case of the height field. Figures 1.9 and 1.10 show results for various implementations of ray- and height-field-intersection algorithms.

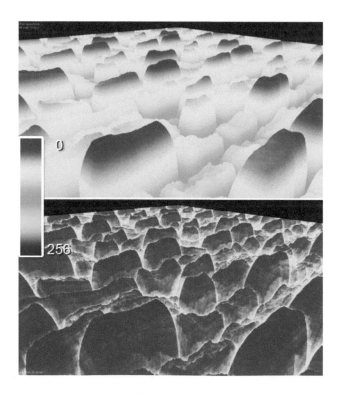

Figure 1.9. Convergence comparison.

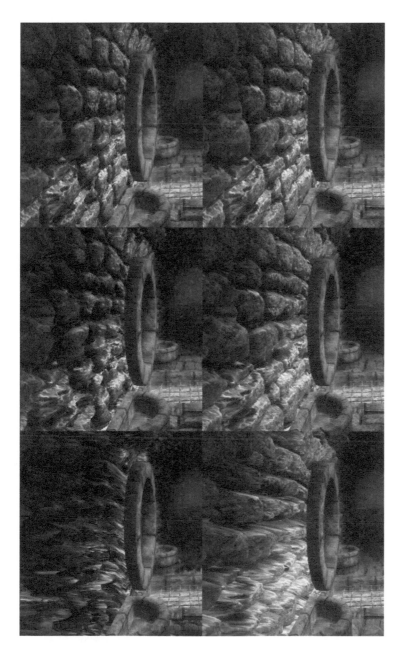

Figure 1.10. Quality comparison. Left POM. Right QDM. Depth Scale: 1.0, 1.5, 5.0. From depth scale 1.5 and above artifacts are visible while using POM.

As we can see, QDM is converging in a pace similar to RCSM, but results in worse performance due to higher ALU cost and less efficient texture cache usage (as many dependant samples, from various MIP levels tend to cause cache misses). However, it is still comparably fast compared to linear search algorithms, outperforming them when the height-field's complexity, depth, or resolution increases. After further research we discovered that QDM is a faster solution onwards from 512×512 high-complexity textures or for any 1024×1024 and larger sizes. Moreover, an additional advantage is visible with depth scale increase. We do not take into consideration RCSM for resolutions higher than 1024×1024 as the preprocessing time becomes impractical.

1.5   Self-Shadowing

1.5.1   General Self-Shadowing

The general algorithm for self-shadowing [Policarpo 2005] involves ray tracing along the vector from L (light source) to P (calculated parallax offset position), then finding its intersection PL with the height field. Then we simply compare PL with P to determine whether the light is visible from P or not. If not, then that means we are in shadow. See Figure 1.11 for illustration.

This method generates hard shadows using any intersection search method, thus suffering from the same disadvantages as the chosen algorithm (i.e., aliasing with linear search). Moreover, the cost is the same as view and height-field

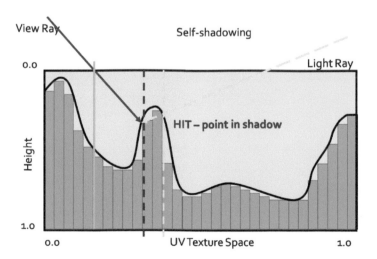

Figure 1.11. Shadow test.

intersection computations. When we are looking for soft shadows, we would have to perform several ray casts of the light vector, which is impractical for performance reasons.

A good approximation for soft shadow calculation was proposed in POM. We can cast a ray towards the light source from point P and perform horizon visibility queries of the height profile along the light direction. We sample the height profile at a fixed number of steps to determine the occlusion coefficient by subtracting sampled depth from original point P depth. This allows us to determine the penumbra coefficient by calculating blocker-to-receiver ratio (the closer the blocker is to the surface, the smaller the resulting penumbra). We scale each sample's contribution by the distance from P and use the maximum value, then we use the visibility coefficient in the lighting equation for smooth shadow generation. The algorithm makes use of linear sampling and produces well-behaving soft shadows. However, the alias-free shadow range is limited by the fixed sampling rate, so real shadows cannot be generated without searching through the entire height field, which effectively degenerates the algorithm to a linear search.

1.5.2 Quadtree Soft Shadowing

Fast horizon approximation. We propose a new algorithm based on POM soft shadowing. This algorithm makes use of the quadtree used in QDM.

First we introduce the algorithm for fast horizon visibility approximation. We use a method similar to POM by performing horizon visibility queries along a

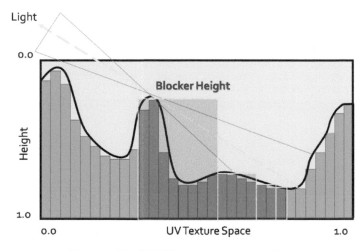

Figure 1.12. QDM horizon approximation.

given direction. The maximum height is taken from the calculated samples and is subtracted from the initial starting point P, thus giving the horizon visibility coefficient. See Figure 1.12 for illustration.

We use the observation that small scale details at distance have negligible impact on the result (especially during any lighting calculations). Thus we can approximate further lying profile features by using the maximum height data from higher levels of the quadtree. That way we can calculate the approximated horizon angle with a minimized number of queries. The full profile can be obtained in $\log n$ steps as opposed to n steps in POM, where n is the number of height-field texels along a given direction D. In all further solutions, we are using a slightly modified version of this algorithm, which is weighting each sample by a distance function. That makes it more suitable for penumbra light calculation as samples far away from P are less important.

QDM shadowing. For shadowing, we use a fast horizon visibility approximation using the parallax offset point P and the normalized light vector L. Accuracy and performance is fine-tuned by technical artists setting the plausible number of iterations ($\log n$ is the maximum number, where n is the height-field's largest dimension) and light vector scale coefficient as shown in Listing 1.4.

```
//Light direction
float2 lDir = (float2(l.x, -l.y)) * dScale;

//Initial displaced point
float h0 = tex2Dlod(heightTexture, float4(P,0,0)).w;
float h = h0;

//Horizon visibility samples
//w1..w5---distance weights
h = min(1,w1 * tex2Dlod(height, float4(P + 1.0 * lDir,0,3.66)).w);
h = min(h,w2 * tex2Dlod(height, float4(P + 0.8 * lDir,0,3.00)).w);
h = min(h,w3 * tex2Dlod(height, float4(P + 0.6 * lDir,0,2.33)).w);
h = min(h,w4 * tex2Dlod(height, float4(P + 0.4 * lDir,0,1.66)).w);
h = min(h,w5 * tex2Dlod(height, float4(P + 0.2 * lDir,0,1.00)).w);

//Visibility approximation
float shadow = 1.0 - saturate((h0 - h) * selfShadowStrength);

return shadow;
```

Listing 1.4. QDM soft shadows, fast, hard-coded solution.

Results. As we can see in Table 1.5, plausible soft shadows using the quadtree are significantly faster than traditional methods while still delivering similar quality

POM Shadows	QDM Shadows
1.6ms	0.5ms

Table 1.5. One light shadows calculation time for the test scene.

(see Figure 1.13). For further optimization we are calculating shadows only when $N \cdot L \geq 0$.

Figure 1.13. Soft shadows ON/OFF.

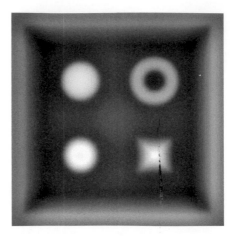

Figure 1.14. Generated high quality AO.

1.6   Ambient Occlusion

Ambient occlusion is computed by integrating the visibility function over the hemisphere H with respect to a projected solid angle:

$$A_0 = \frac{1}{\pi} \sum_H V_{p,\omega}(N \cdot \omega)d\omega,$$

where $V_{p,\omega}$ is the visibility function at p, such as $V_{p,\omega}$ is 0 when occluded in direction ω and 1 otherwise.

Ambient occlusion adds a great deal of lighting detail to rendered images (see Figure 1.14). It is especially useful for large-scale terrain scenarios, where objects can take the occlusion value from the terrain (i.e., darkening buildings lying in a valley).

1.6.1   QDM Ambient Occlusion

Dynamically calculating ambient occlusion for surfaces was thought to be impractical for performance reasons, as the visibility function and the integration were too slow to be useful. Now with fast horizon visibility approximation we can tackle that problem in a better way.

We approximate the true integral by integrating the visibility function in several fixed directions. We discovered that for performance reasons integration in four to eight directions lying in the same angle intervals yields acceptable results. Moreover, we can increase quality by jittering and/or rotating the directions by a random value for every pixel.

Accuracy	AO
4 directions	2.1ms
8 directions	6.3ms
4 jittered	2.6ms

Table 1.6. AO calculation time

1.6.2 Performance

As we can see from Table 1.6, the algorithm requires substantial processing power, being even less efficient with randomized directions (as it is hurting GPU parallelism, but it is still faster than integrating more directions). However, it is used only when the surface height field is changing. Moreover, it can be accumulated throughout several frames, amortizing the cost.

1.7 Surface Blending

1.7.1 Alpha Blending

Blending is commonly used for surface composites, such as terrain, where several varied textures have to mix together (e.g., rocky coast with sand).

Typically, surface blends are done using the alpha-blending algorithm given by the following equation:

$$\text{Blend} = \frac{(v_1, \ldots, v_n) \cdot (w_1, \ldots, w_n)}{(1, \ldots, 1) \cdot (w_1, \ldots, w_n)},$$

where $(w_1, \ldots, w_n)$ is the blend weight vector and $(v_1, \ldots, v_n)$ denotes the value vector.

Commonly, the blend vector for a given texel is supplied by vertex interpolation, stored at vertex attributes (thus being low frequency). During pixel shading, interpolated values are used to perform the blending.

1.7.2 Raytracing Blended Surfaces

Any height-field intersection algorithm can be used in such a scenario. We should compute the parallax offset for each surface and finally blend them together using the blend vector. However, it is worth noting that the computational cost for such blending would be n-times higher than one surface, where n is the total number of surfaces. Moreover, using vertex-interpolated values results in view-dependant surfaces floating near blend zones. Figure 1.15 illustrates the problem. However,

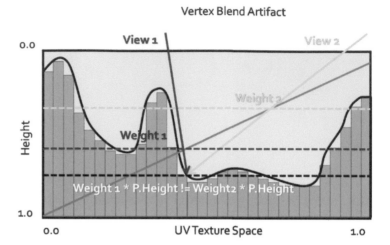

Figure 1.15. Depth floating artifact using vertex blend.

with enough care taken to minimize depth scale near blend zones, it should not be too distracting.

One possible solution is to use per-pixel blend weights that would modify the surface on-the-fly during intersection search. However, this would require sampling an additional weight texture with every iteration, thus doubling the sample count.

Let us consider four surface blends. Optimally, we can encode up to four blend weights in one RGBA 32-bit texture, so with each sample we get four weights. The blend texture can be fairly low-resolution, as generally it should resemble per-vertex blending (it can be even generated on the fly from vertex weights). Having a four-scalar blend vector, we can perform the intersection search on the dynamically modified height field simply by sampling all four height fields with each step and blending them by the blend vector. Moreover, we can compose all four height fields into one RGBA 32-bit texture, thus finally optimizing the blend intersection search.

The pseudocode in Listing 1.5 shows the modification for the intersection search method of choice.

```
d = tex2D(HeightTexture ,p.xy).xyzw;
b = tex2D(BlendTexture ,p.xy).xyzw;
d = dot(d,b);
```

Listing 1.5. Height profile blend code.

Modification requires only one additional sample and one dot product. However, we are sampling four channels twice instead of one channel (as in the single surface algorithm).

This solution is therefore very fast but lacks robustness, as it would require us to preprocess height-field composites, creating possibly dozens of new textures containing all possible height profiles composites. We can of course try sampling the data without composites, but that would result in additional sampling cost and cache misses (as four samplers would have to be used simultaneously, which would most probably result in a bandwidth bottleneck).

Another problem is that we cannot use this method for algorithms using precomputed distance data, as it would require us to recompute the distance fields (i.e., cone maps) for blend modified height fields, which effectively prohibits using advanced ray-casting algorithms.

1.7.3 Height Blending

To overcome the aforementioned problems, we introduce a new method for surface blending, which seems to fit the task more naturally, and it guarantees faster convergence.

First, let us consider typical alpha blending for surface mixing. In real life, surfaces do not blend. What we see is actually the highest material (the material on the top of the surface).

Therefore, we propose to use height information as an additional blend coefficient, thus adding more variety to blend regions and a more natural look as shown in Listing 1.6.

This method is not computationally expensive, and it can add much more detail as opposed to vertex-blended surfaces (as can be seen in Figure 1.16).

The most important feature is that we pick the highest surface, so during the intersection search phase, we need only to find the highest point.

Therefore, the new height field is produced by the new blend equation:

$$\text{Blend} = \max(h_1, \ldots, h_n).$$

Using this blend equation we are interested only in finding the intersection point with the highest surface profile modified by its blend weight. That effectively means taking a minimal number of steps, as we will stop the ray cast at the

Relief Mapping	POM	POM with HB
3ms	2.5ms	1.25ms

Table 1.7. Surface blend performance comparison

Figure 1.16. Vertex blend and height blend comparison.

```
float4 FinalH;
float4 f1, f2, f3, f4;

//Get surface sample.
f1 = tex2D(Tex0Sampler,TEXUV.xy).rgba;

//Get height weight.
FinalH.a = 1.0 - f1.a;
f2 = tex2D(Tex1Sampler,TEXUV.xy).rgba;
FinalH.b = 1.0 - f2.a;
f3 = tex2D(Tex2Sampler,TEXUV.xy).rgba;
FinalH.g = 1.0 - f3.a;
f4 = tex2D(Tex3Sampler,TEXUV.xy).rgba;
FinalH.r = 1.0 - f4.a;

//Modify height weights by blend weights.
//Per-vertex blend weights stored in IN.AlphaBlends
FinalH*= IN.AlphaBlends;

//Normalize.
float Blend = dot(FinalH, 1.0) + epsilon;
FinalH /= Blend;

//Get final blend.
FinalTex = FinalH.a * f1 + FinalH.b * f2 + FinalH.g * f3 +
           FinalH.r * f4;
```

Listing 1.6. Surface blend code.

first intersection with highest blend weight modified height profile, which—by definition—is the first one to be pierced by the ray.

With each intersection search step, we reconstruct the height-field profile using the new blend operator as shown in Listing 1.7.

As can be seen in Table 1.7, this method proved to minimize the convergence rate by 25% on average in our scenario without sacrificing visual quality (see Figure 1.17, and is more plausible for our new height blend solution. It can be used with blend textures or vertex blending, as well as every intersection search algorithm.

```
d = tex2D(HeightTexture,p.xy).xyzw;
b = tex2D(BlendTexture,p.xy) xyzw;
d *= b;
d = max(d.x,max(d.y,max(d.z,d.w)));}
```

Listing 1.7. Surface height blend code.

Figure 1.17. Surface blend quality comparison. Top: relief. Bottom: POM with height blending.

1.7.4   QDM with Height Blending

We still cannot use the height blend operator directly for algorithms based on precomputed data. However, QDM is based on depth data, so it is relatively easy to obtain new correct data structure. Note that

$$\max(x_1, x_2, \ldots, x_n) \cdot \max(w_1, w_2, \ldots, w_n) \geq$$
$$\max([(x_1, x_2, \ldots, x_n) \cdot (w_1, w_2, \ldots, w_n)]).$$

Thus multiplying one min/max quadtree by another gives us a conservative quadtree, and that is exactly what we need for correct surface blending. We can pack up to four blend quadtrees in one RGBA 32-bit texture with mipmaps containing blend vector quadtrees. Then in QDM, to reconstruct the blended surface quadtree, we simply sample and blend it at the correct position and level, and compute the dot product between it and the height-field vector sampled from the height-field composite.

The blend texture should map quadtree texels as close as possible. However, we discovered that while using hardware linear sampling and accepting small artifacts we can use sizes as small as 32^2 (while blending 1024^2 height fields) when the weight gradients are close to linear. Such blended quadtrees can be constructed on the fly in negligible time, allowing dynamic surface alterations.

Effectively, we can use QDM with all its benefits while blending surfaces for artifact-free rendering (see Figure 1.18). Convergence will be slower, due to the conservative quadtree, and more iterations may be needed depending on the height-field's complexity. In practice, the conservative approach needs <10% more iterations than what should be really used. This method proves to be the fastest method for dynamic accurate surface rendering of high complexity height fields.

In our implementation we decided to use vertex blending to avoid high texture cache misses. However, we were forced to accept small depth-floating artifacts.

As QDM is converging really fast in empty space regions, the algorithm can make the best use of faster convergence, due to height blending.

1.7.5 Self-Shadowing and Ambient Occlusion for Blended Surfaces

Self shadowing and ambient occlusion can be done while rendering blended surfaces. However, a naïve approach of calculating shadowing terms for each surface and blending the results is simply impractical for current generation hardware. We propose to use QDM and the height blend and perform computations for the highest modified height profile only. Proper height-field selection requires additional dynamic branching, further restricting GPU parallelism. Consequently, self shadowing and/or ambient occlusion are viable only for high-end hardware.

Figure 1.18. QDM height blend surface.

1.8   General Advice

In this article we proposed and discussed several battle-proven surface rendering methods, varying in ALU/Texture sampling performance, accuracy, and flexibility. Most solutions were introduced as general building blocks from which, depending on requirements, an optimal solution can be built.

1.8.1   Case Study

During *Two Worlds 2* production we decided to settle on several solutions used under specific circumstances. We present a case study of each method used:

General terrain blend. Our terrain exhibits small-scale height features such as cracks, small rocks, etc. The maximum number of blending surfaces was capped at four to allow texture packing. We are using linear search with linear piece-wise approximation, automatic LOD, and height blend optimization. Blending is done on a per-vertex basis. Depending on texture configuration, parallax can be switched off for each surface individually. The specular term and normal vectors are generated on-the-fly due to the Xbox360's memory restrictions.

Special terrain features. Several extreme detail terrain paths were excluded as additional decal planes. We are rendering them at ultra-high quality (high resolution, high accuracy) and alpha-blending them with existing terrain. Decal planes may present roads, paths, muddy ponds, and craters, etc. For rendering, we are using

QDM with automatic LOD and soft shadows. Where needed, QDM per-pixel height blending is used. Blend-based decals are for PC only.

General object surface. For general surface rendering, we are using linear search with linear piecewise approximation and automatic LOD. Soft shadows are used at the artist's preference. Surfaces with extreme complexity, depth scale, or resolutions over 1024^2 are checked, and using QDM is optimal. The same method is used on Xbox360 and PC.

1.8.2 Surface Rendering Pipeline

During asset finalization, technical artists optimized height-field-based textures, checking whether high resolution or additional details (such as soft shadows) are really needed. It is worth noting that low frequency textures tend to converge faster during the intersection search, so blurring height fields when possible is better for performance and accuracy reasons when using linear search-based methods.

One important feature of our surface rendering pipeline is the preference for generation of additional surface properties on-the-fly, as it allows us to save memory and performance on texture-fetch-hungry shaders.

Texture-heavy locations (such as cities) are using mostly two 24-bit RGB compressed textures per object. The specular term is generated from the diffuse color and is modified by an artist on a per-material-specified function such as inversion, power, or scale. The generated coefficient generally exhibits high quality.

Data generation is taken to the extreme during terrain rendering as individual terrain texture is using only 32-bit RGBA DXT5 textures, from which per-pixel normal vectors, specular roughness, and intensities (as the default lighting model is a simplified Cook-Torrance BRDF) are generated.

1.9   Conclusion

We have discussed and presented various surface rendering techniques with several novel improvements for industry proven approaches. Combinations of parallax mapping, soft shadowing, ambient occlusion, and surface blending methods were proposed to be in specific scenarios aiming for maximum quality/performance/memory usage ratio. Furthermore, a novel solution—Quadtree Displacement Mapping with Height Blending—was presented. Our approach proves to be significantly faster for ultra-high quality surfaces that use complex, high resolution height fields. Moreover, we proposed solutions for efficient surface blending, soft shadowing, ambient occlusion, and automatic LOD schemes using the introduced quadtree structures. In practice, our techniques tend to produce higher quality results with less iterations and texture samples. This is an advantage, as we are trading iteration ALU cost for texture fetches, making it more useful for GPU generations to come, as computation performance scales faster than bandwidth.

Surface rendering techniques research allowed us to make vast graphic improvements in our next-gen engine, thus increasing quality and performance. We hope to see the techniques described herein being used in more upcoming titles.

Bibliography

[Cohen and Shaked 1993] D. Cohen and A. Shaked. "Photo-Realistic Imaging of Digital Terrains." *Computer Graphics Forum* 12:3 (1993), 363–373.

[Donelly 2005] W. Donelly. "Per-Pixel Displacement Mapping with Distance Functions." In *GPU Gems 2*, edited by Matt Pharr, pp. 123–36. Reading, MA: Addison-Wesley, 2005.

[Dummer 2006] J. Dummer. "Cone Step Mapping: An Iterative Ray-Heightfield Intersection Algorithm." 2006. Available at http://www.lonesock.net/files/ ConeStepMapping.pdf.

[OH 2006] K. Oh, H. Ki, and C. H. Lee. "Pyramidal Displacement Mapping: a GPU based Artifacts-Free Ray Tracing through Image Pyramid." *In VRST '06: Proceedings of the ACM symposium on Virtual Reality Software and Technology* (2006), 75–82.

[Policarpo 2005] F. Policarpo, M. M. Oliveira, and J. L. D. Comba. "Real Time Relief Mapping on Arbitrary Polygonal Surfaces." *In Proceedings of I3D'05* (2005), 155–162.

[Policarpo 2007] F. Policarpo and M. M. Oliveira. "Relaxed Cone Step Mapping for Relief Mapping." In *GPU Gems 3*, edited by Hubert Nguyen, pp. 409–428. Reading, MA: Addison-Wesley Professional, 2007.

[Tatarchuk 2006] N. Tatarchuk. "Practical Parallax Occlusion Mapping with Approximate Soft Shadow." In *ShaderX5*. Brookline, MA: Charles River Media, 2006.

2

NPR Effects Using the Geometry Shader

Pedro Hermosilla and Pere-Pau Vázquez

2.1 Introduction

Non-photorealistic rendering (NPR) techniques [Achorn et al. 03, Gooch and Gooch 01] have been here for quite a while [Saito and Takahashi 90]. In contrast to traditional rendering, these techniques deal with geometric entities such as silhouettes, which makes them not easily amenable to GPU algorithms, although some papers already address some NPR algorithms in hardware [Dietrich 00, Mitchell et al. 02, Everitt 02, Card and Mitchell 02]. With the arrival of more modern graphics hardware that includes the geometry shader stage, some of these techniques can be implemented in hardware, making them real time in many cases [McGuire and Hughes 04, Dyken et al. 08, Doss 08]. In this chapter we present a set of techniques that can be implemented using the GPU by taking advantage of the geometry shader pipeline stage. Concretely, we show how to make use of the geometry shader in order to render objects and their silhouettes in a single pass, and to imitate pencil drawing.

2.2 Previous Work

Silhouette rendering has been studied extensively. Two major groups of algorithms require the extraction of silhouettes in real time: shadow volume-based approaches and non-photorealistic rendering [Gooch and Gooch 01].

From the literature, we may extract two different approaches: object-space and image-space algorithms. However, most modern algorithms work in either image space or hybrid space. For the purposes of this chapter, we are interested in GPU-based algorithms, and these are the ones we will present. We refer the interested reader to the works of [Isenberg et al. 03] and [Hartner et al. 03] for overviews and deep comparisons on CPU-based silhouette extraction algorithms.

GPU-assisted algorithms may compute the silhouette either using multiple rendering passes [Mitchell et al. 02] or in a single pass. Single pass methods usually use some sort of precomputation in order to store adjacency information into the vertices [Card and Mitchell 02], or make use of the geometry shader feature [Doss 08], as this may query adjacency information. These algorithms generate the silhouette in a single rendering pass, though still a first geometry pass is required for the object itself.

One of the first attempts to extract silhouettes using hardware is due to [Raskar 01], where a new stage at the rendering pipeline is introduced: the primitive shader. At this stage, polygons are treated as single primitives, similar to the way actual geometric shaders do. Raskar's proposal also requires modification of the incoming geometry. For instance, extending back faces to render silhouettes, and adding polygons in order to render ridges and valleys.

[Card and Mitchell 02] pack adjacent normals into the texture coordinates of vertices and render edges as degenerated quads, which expand if they are detected to belong to a silhouette edge in the vertex processor. This is a single pass algorithm that requires rendering extra geometry for the silhouette extraction. This approach is also used by [Achorn et al. 03]. [McGuire and Hughes 04] extend this technique to store the four vertices of the two faces adjacent to each edge, instead of explicit face normals. This allows the authors to construct correct face normals under animation and add textures to generate artistic strokes.

In [Ashikhmin 04], silhouettes are generated without managing adjacency information through a multiple rendering passes algorithm that reads back the frame buffer in order to determine face visibility. More recently, [Dyken et al. 08] extract silhouettes from a triangle mesh and perform an adaptive tessellation in order to visualize the silhouette with smooth curvature. However, this system neither textures the silhouettes nor extrudes the silhouette geometry. [Doss 08] develops an algorithm similar to the one presented here: he extrudes the silhouettes, but with no guarantee of continuity between the extrusions generated from different edges; consequently, gaps are easily noticeable as the silhouette width grows.

A completely different approach is used by [Gooch et al. 99], as they note that environment maps can be used to darken the contour edges of a model but, as a result, the rendered lines have uncontrolled variable thickness. The same idea was refined by [Dietrich 00], who took advantage of the GPU hardware available at that moment (GeForce 256). [Everitt 02] used MIP-maps to achieve similar effects. In all of these cases, it is difficult to fine-tune an artistic style because there is no support geometry underlying the silhouette.

The approach presented here is conceptually similar to [Raskar 01], but takes advantage of modern hardware. We also borrow ideas from [Doss 08] and [McGuire and Hughes 04] for silhouette geometry generation. In contrast to these approaches, we generate both the silhouette and the object in a single pass, and we present an algorithm for correct texturing with coherent and continuous texture coordinates along the entire silhouette.

2.3 Silhouette Rendering

Silhouette rendering is a fundamental element in most NPR effects, as it plays an important role in object shape understanding. In this section we present a novel approach for the detection, generation, and texturing of a model in a single rendering pass. First we will present an overview of our algorithm, and then we will detail how each of the steps is implemented.

2.3.1 Algorithm Overview

In order to carry out the entire process in a single step, we will take advantage of some of the modern features of GPUs; concretely, we will make an extensive use of the geometry shader. This stage permits triangle operations, with knowledge of adjacent triangles, and the generation of new triangles to the geometry.

Our process for silhouette rendering performs the following steps at the different stages of the pipeline (Figure 2.1):

- *Vertex shader.* Vertices are transformed in the usual way to camera space.

- *Geometry shader.* In this stage, edges that belong to the silhouette are detected by using the information of the current triangle and its adjacency, and the corresponding geometry is generated.

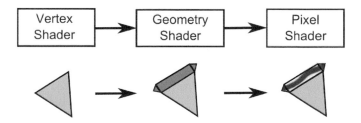

Figure 2.1. Pipeline overview: the vertex shader (left) transforms the vertex coordinates of the incoming geometry; the second step (geometry shader) generates new geometry for the silhouette of the object. Finally, the fragment shader generates correct texture coordinates.

- *Pixel shader.* For each rasterized fragment, its texture coordinates are generated and pixels are shaded according to the color obtained from the texture.

Before we may send a mesh throughout the pipeline, we first perform a special reordering of the indices of the triangles. This will make the adjacency information available at the geometry shader level. In order to access such information, we send six indices per triangle (instead of the normal three), ordered as depicted in Figure 2.2. The central triangle, identified by indices 0, 4, and 2 is the one to be analyzed. The remaining adjacent triangles are needed to show if any of the edges of the central triangle belong to the silhouette.

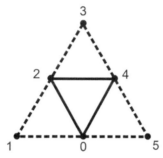

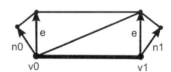

Figure 2.2. Index sort.   Figure 2.3. Edge geometry.

2.3.2   Silhouette Detection and Geometry Generation

We consider a closed triangle mesh with consistently oriented triangles. The set of triangles is denoted, $T_1 \ldots T_N$. The set of vertices is $v_1 \ldots v_n$ in $\Re^3$, and normals are given by triangles: n_t is the normal of a triangle $T_t = [v_i, v_j, v_k]$, using the notation by [Dyken et al. 08]. This triangle normal is defined as the normalization of the vector $(v_j - v_i) \times (v_k - v_i)$. Given an observer at position $x \in \Re^3$, we may say a triangle is *front facing* in v if $(v - x) \cdot n \leq 0$, otherwise it is *back facing*. The silhouette of a triangle mesh is the set of edges where one of the adjacent triangles is front facing while the other is back facing. In order to detect a silhouette in a triangulated mesh we need to process any triangle, together with the triangles that share an edge with it. This test is performed at the geometry shader level for each edge of the triangle being processed. In order to avoid duplicate silhouettes when processing both the front facing and the back facing triangles, we only generate silhouettes for the front-facing triangles. The code in Listing 2.1 shows how to detect a silhouette edge at the geometry shader level.

As shown in Figure 2.3, once an edge (indicated by $\overline{v0v1}$) has been determined as a silhouette one, we generate the geometry that will act as the silhouette by

```
[maxvertexcount(21)]
void main( triangleadj VERTEXin input[6],
         inout TriangleStream <VERTEXout > TriStream )
{

 //Calculate the triangle normal and view direction.
 float3 normalTrian = getNormal( input[0].Pos.xyz,
   input[2].Pos.xyz, input[4].Pos.xyz );
 float3 viewDirect = normalize(-input[0].Pos.xyz
   - input[2].Pos.xyz - input[4].Pos.xyz);

 //If the triangle is frontfacing
 [branch]if(dot(normalTrian,viewDirect) > 0.0f)
 {

  [loop]for(uint i = 0; i < 6; i+=2)
  {

   //Calculate the normal for this triangle.
   float auxIndex = (i+2)%6;
   float3 auxNormal = getNormal( input[i].Pos.xyz,
     input[i+1].Pos.xyz, input[auxIndex].Pos.xyz );
   float3 auxDirect = normalize(- input[i].Pos.xyz
     - input[i+1].Pos.xyz - input[auxIndex].Pos.xyz);

   //If the triangle is backfacing
   [branch]if(dot(auxNormal,auxDirect) <= 0.0f)
   {

    //Here we have a silhouette edge.

   }
  }
 }
}
```

Listing 2.1. Geometry shader silhouette detection code.

applying the algorithm in [McGuire and Hughes 04]. It consists of four triangles. The central triangles forming the quad are generated by extruding the edges' vertices using as the extrusion direction of a vector orthogonal to the edge and view directions. The remaining triangles are generated by extruding the vertices from the edge in the direction of the vertex normal as projected on screen. The generation of such geometry can be done either in world space or in screen space. We usually use screen space because this way is easier to obtain a silhouette geometry of constant size in screen. The code needed to generate this geometry appears in Listing 2.2.

```
//Transform the positions to screen space.
float4 transPos1 = mul(input[i].Pos,projMatrix);
transPos1 = transPos1/transPos1.w;
float4 transPos2 = mul(input[auxIndex].Pos,projMatrix);
transPos2 = transPos2/transPos2.w;

//Calculate the edge direction in screen space.
float2 edgeDirection = normalize(transPos2.xy - transPos1.xy);

//Calculate the extrude vector in screen space.
float4 extrudeDirection = float4(normalize(
  float2(-edgeDirection.y,edgeDirection.x)),0.0f,0.0f);

//Calculate the extrude vector along the vertex
//normal in screen space.
float4 normExtrude1 = mul(input[i].Pos + input[i].Normal
  ,projMatrix);
normExtrude1 = normExtrude1 / normExtrude1.w;
normExtrude1 = normExtrude1 - transPos1;
normExtrude1 = float4(normalize(normExtrude1.xy),0.0f,0.0f);
float4 normExtrude2 = mul(input[auxIndex].Pos
  + input[auxIndex].Normal,projMatrix);
normExtrude2 = normExtrude2 / normExtrude2.w;
normExtrude2 = normExtrude2 - transPos2;
normExtrude2 = float4(normalize(normExtrude2.xy),0.0f,0.0f);

//Scale the extrude directions with the edge size.
normExtrude1 = normExtrude1 * edgeSize;
normExtrude2 = normExtrude2 * edgeSize;
extrudeDirection = extrudeDirection * edgeSize;

//Calculate the extruded vertices.
float4 normVertex1 = transPos1 + normExtrude1;
float4 extruVertex1 = transPos1 + extrudeDirection;
float4 normVertex2 = transPos2 + normExtrude2;
float4 extruVertex2 = transPos2 + extrudeDirection;

//Create the output polygons.
VERTEXout outVert;

outVert.Pos = float4(normVertex1.xyz,1.0f);
TriStream.Append(outVert);
outVert.Pos = float4(extruVertex1.xyz,1.0f);
TriStream.Append(outVert);
outVert.Pos = float4(transPos1.xyz,1.0f);
TriStream.Append(outVert);
outVert.Pos = float4(extruVertex2.xyz,1.0f);
TriStream.Append(outVert);
outVert.Pos = float4(transPos2.xyz,1.0f);
TriStream.Append(outVert);
```

```
outVert.Pos = float4(normVertex2.xyz,1.0f);
TriStream.Append(outVert);

TriStream.RestartStrip();
```

Listing 2.2. Geometry shader silhouette generation.

In some cases, this solution may produce an error when the extrusion direction has a different direction than the projected normal version. There are several ways to solve this. One of the simplest ones consists of changing the direction of the projected normal, as commented in [Hermosilla and Vázquez 09]. Some cases also might require different silhouette geometry (see [McGuire and Hughes 04] for more details).

2.3.3 Silhouette Texturing

Once the silhouette geometry has been generated, it becomes obvious that texturing this geometry will increase the number of effects that can be achieved. In order to properly texture the silhouette geometry, we need to generate texture coordinates. Texture coordinates generation is a bit tricky, as we need to generate continuous coordinates along the entire silhouette. Therefore we may not simply assign coordinates from 0 to 1 for each edge, as this would cause irregular coordinate distribution if the edges are not created all with the same length. Instead we need a global strategy for coordinate generation because each triangle of the silhouette will not be aware of the neighbor triangles' coordinates.

From the two texture coordinates u and v, coordinate v can be simply defined, because it changes from zero to one as long as we go away from the object, as depicted in Figure 2.4.

Coordinate u has to be generated in such a way that its value is continuous along the silhouette of the object. In order to make sure that two adjacent edges will generate coherent texture coordinates, we will build a function that depends on the position of the projection of the vertices on screen. As a consequence, the coordinates will be continuous because neighbor edges share a vertex. This is achieved when the geometry shader sends the x- and y-coordinates of the

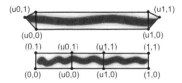

Figure 2.4. The v-coordinate has a value of 0 for the edge vertex and 1 for the extruded vertices.

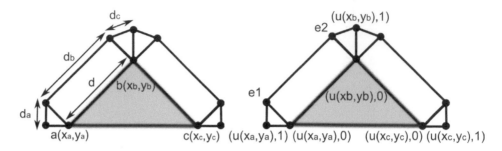

Figure 2.5. The u-coordinates are generated from the edge vertex coordinates in screen space. The first vertex of the edge and the vertex extruded from the first vertex normal gets the u-coordinate from the coordinates of the first vertex (a) The other edge endpoint, and the vertex extruded from the second vertex normal gets the u-coordinate from the coordinates of the second vertex (b) The vertices extruded from the extrusion vector ($e1$ & $e2$) obtain their u-coordinates by interpolation, as show in Equation (2.1).

generated vertices in screen, together with v-coordinate. The pixel shader will receive such coordinates as interpolated values, and will generate the corresponding u value. Figure 2.5 shows how this information is used.

Vertices e receive their coordinates from linear interpolation as shown in the following equations:

$$e1.ux = x_a + (|\vec{ab}| * ((d * d_a)/(d_a + d_b + d_c)))$$
$$e1.uy = y_a + (|\vec{ab}| * ((d * d_a)/(d_a + d_b + dc)))$$
$$e1.v = 0$$

$$e2.ux = x_b + (|\vec{ba}| * ((d * d_a)/(d_a + d_b + d_c)))$$
$$e2.uy = x_b + (|\vec{ba}| * ((d * d_a)/(d_a + d_b + d_c)))$$
$$e2.v = 0.$$

$$(2.1)$$

The pixel shader will receive those coordinates interpolated and will use them to compute the final texture coordinates.

In order to compute the final u component, we will transform components x and y into polar coordinates. The reference system will be the screen space position of the center of the bounding box of the object, and the x- and y- axes will be those of the viewport. Therefore, we will have polar coordinates computed as

- Polar angle: α will be the angle between the x-axis, and the vector with initial point at the origin of the coordinates system, and final point at (x, y).

- Distance: d is the distance from (x, y) to the origin of the coordinates system.

```
float4 main(PIXELin inPut):SV_Target
{
 //Initial texture coordinate.
 float2 coord = float2(0.0f,inPut.UV.z);

 //Vector from the projected center bounding box to
 //the location.
 float2 vect = inPut.UV.xy - aabbPos;

 //Calculate the polar coordinate.
 float angle = atan(vect.y/vect.x);
 angle = (vect.x < 0.0f)?angle+PI:
   (vect.y < 0.0f)?angle+(2*PI):angle;

 //Assign the angle plus distance to the u texture coordinate.
 coord.x = ((angle/(2*PI)) + (length(vect)*lengthPer))*scale;

 //Get the texture color.
 float4 col = texureDiff.Sample(samLinear,coord);

 //Alpha test.
 if(col.a < 0.1f)
  discard;

 //Return color.
 return col;
}
```

Listing 2.3. Silhouette Texturing.

Finally, we compute u as indicated in the following equation:

$$u = (\frac{\alpha}{2*\pi}) + (k*d).$$

As we may see, the polar angle is divided by 2π in order to transform it into a value in the [0..1] range. The distance is weighted by a factor k that may be changed interactively. For objects of a sphere-like shape, k value can be set to close to 0, but for objects with edges that roughly point to the origin of coordinates, the value k must be different from 0. Otherwise, texture coordinates at both ends of those edges would be similar. The code that implements this is shown in Listing 2.3.

This algorithm may produce small artifacts in edges that are projected on the screen close to the center of the bounding box. However, these are not visible in most of the models we tested.

2.3.4   Single Pass Geometry and Silhouette Rendering

Most silhouette rendering algorithms perform two passes, one for the geometry, and another one for the silhouettes. This means that the geometry is sent two times into the rendering pipeline. We can avoid this by taking further advantage of the geometry shader with little modifications to the original code. This is achieved by simply rendering the triangle being analyzed by the geometry shader, even if it does not have any edge belonging to the silhouette. This can be done thanks to the fact that the geometry shader may output more than a single triangle.

So far, the pixel shader code deals only with edges and textures them accordingly. In order to render the triangles belonging to the geometry in a single pass, we must inform the pixel shader of the sort of triangle that originated the rasterized fragment: silhouette or geometry. We encode this information in the texture coordinates. As we are passing three coordinates, we will use one of them—in this case the v-coordinate—to encode this information. For triangles belonging to this geometry, we assign the value 2. This way, the pixel shader can easily distinguish between both kinds of triangles, and shade them accordingly.

2.3.5   Results

We can see some results of our algorithm in Figure 2.6. The algorithm presented here achieves real-time performance, as can be seen in Table 2.1. These results were obtained on a 6 GB Quad Core PC equipped with a GeForce 9800 GX2 GPU. The viewport resolution (key for image space algorithms) was 1680×1050. Note that even complex objects (such as the Buddha model), with more than 1M polygons, achieve interactive framerates.

Models	Triangles	FPS
Buddha	1087716	8.50
Armadillo	345944	21.07
Asian Dragon	225588	25.75
Dragon	100000	60.07
Bunny	69666	110.78
Atenea	15014	337.59

Table 2.1. Framerates obtained with the textured silhouette algorithm on a GeForce 9800 GX2 GPU with a viewport resolution of 1680×1050.

Figure 2.6. Images showing the algorithm in action. Silhouettes have been generated and textured in real time.

2.4 Pencil Rendering

In this section we will present how to implement pencil rendering in the geometry shader. This is based on the technique presented by [Lee et al. 06].

2.4.1 Algorithm Overview

The original technique by [Lee et al. 06] works in the following way. First, the minimal curvature at each vertex is computed. Then, triangles are sent through the pipeline with this value as a texture coordinate for each vertex. In order to shade the interior of a triangle, the curvatures at the vertices are used to rotate a pencil texture in screen space. This texture is rotated three times in screen space, one for each curvature, and the result is combined with blending. Several textures with different tones are used at the same time, stored in an array of textures. The correct one is selected according to illumination.

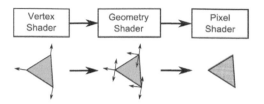

Figure 2.7. Pipeline overview: the vertex shader transforms the vertices to screen space; the geometry shader assigns the vertex curvatures of the triangle to the three vertices. Finally, the pixel shader generates texture coordinates for the three curvatures and calculates the final color.

We may implement this algorithm using the GPU pipeline in the following way (Figure 2.7):

- *Vertex shader.* Vertices are transformed to screen coordinates. Vertex curvature is transformed too, and only x- and y-components are passed through as a two-dimensional vector.

- *Geometry shader.* The curvature values are assigned to each vertex as texture coordinates.

- *Pixel shader.* Final color is computed.

2.4.2   Geometry Shader Optimization

This technique has an important shortcoming: It is necessary to make a copy of each vertex for each triangle that shares it. This is because each pixel receives the interpolated curvature by using each vertex, and the three curvatures are required unchanged. Each duplicated vertex is assigned the three curvatures of the vertices of the triangle in order to make each fragment get the three exact curvatures.

In order to avoid vertex duplication, we will use the geometry shader. At the geometry shader level, we receive the three vertices of a triangle, with its corresponding curvatures. These curvatures are assigned as three texture coordinates to the vertices of the output triangle in the same order. Thus, the fragment shader will receive the three values without interpolation. The code corresponding to the geometry shader appears in Listing 2.4.

2.4.3   Pixel Texturing

The final color composition is performed in the following way: the fragment shader receives the coordinates of the fragment, together with the curvatures. We will use components x and y of the fragment in screen space as texture coordinates. These coordinates are scaled to the range $[0..1]$.

```
[maxvertexcount(3)]
void main( triangle VERTEXin input[3],
    inout TriangleStream<VERTEXout> TriStream )
{
 //Assign triangle curvatures to the three vertices.
 VERTEXout outVert;
 outVert.Pos = input[0].Pos;
 outVert.norm = input[0].norm;
 outVert.curv1 = input[0].curv;
 outVert.curv2 = input[1].curv;
 outVert.curv3 = input[2].curv;
 TriStream.Append(outVert);

 outVert.Pos = input[1].Pos;
 outVert.norm = input[1].norm;
 outVert.curv1 = input[0].curv;
 outVert.curv2 = input[1].curv;
 outVert.curv3 = input[2].curv;
 TriStream.Append(outVert);

 outVert.Pos = input[2].Pos;
 outVert.norm = input[2].norm;
 outVert.curv1 = input[0].curv;
 outVert.curv2 = input[1].curv;
 outVert.curv3 = input[2].curv;
 TriStream.Append(outVert);

 TriStream.RestartStrip();
}
```

Listing 2.4. Pencil geometry shader.

In order to orient the texture according to the surface curvature, and to avoid deformations inside large triangles, the paper texture is oriented by using the three curvatures at the vertices, and blending them with equal weights. The implementation has three steps: First, the angles between curvatures and the x-axis are computed. Then, three two-dimensional rotation matrices are built using these angles. Finally, these matrices are used to transform the texture coordinates obtained from the fragment coordinates, and this yields three new texture coordinates. These are the ones used for final texturing.

The model may be shaded by using the dot product between the light direction and the surface normal in order to access a texture array of different tones. We use a single texture but modified with a function that changes brightness and contrast according to the incident illumination at each point. We use the following function:

```
p = 1.0 - {max}({dot}(light,normal),0.0)
colorDest = {pow}(colorSrc,p*S + 0).
```

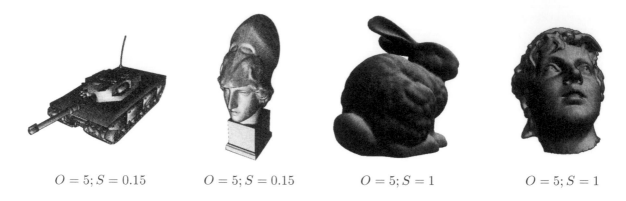

$O = 5; S = 0.15$ $\qquad$ $O = 5; S = 0.15$ $\qquad$ $O = 5; S = 1$ $\qquad$ $O = 5; S = 1$

Figure 2.8. Pencil rendering results.

The resulting color of texture mapping is powered to a value in the range $[O..S + O]$. This value is determined from the dot product between the light and normal vectors. This will darken dark regions and lighten lighter regions, as can be seen in Figure 2.8 where we show the comparison using different values of O and S. The code corresponding to the geometry shader is shown in Listing 2.5.

```
float4 main(PIXELin inPut):SV_Target
{
 float2 xdir = float2(1.0f,0.0f);
 float2x2 rotMat;
 //Calculate the pixel coordinates.
 float2 uv = float2(inPut.Pos.x/width,inPut.Pos.y/height);

 //Calculate the rotated coordinates.
 float2 uvDir = normalize(inPut.curv1);
 float angle = atan(uvDir.y/uvDir.x);
 angle = (uvDir.x < 0.0f)?angle+PI:
  (uvDir.y < 0.0f)?angle+(2*PI):angle;
 float cosVal = cos(angle);
 float sinVal = sin(angle);
 rotMat[0][0] = cosVal;
 rotMat[1][0] = -sinVal;
 rotMat[0][1] = sinVal;
 rotMat[1][1] = cosVal;
 float2 uv1 = mul(uv,rotMat);

 uvDir = normalize(inPut.curv2);
 angle = atan(uvDir.y/uvDir.x);
 angle = (uvDir.x < 0.0f)?angle+PI:
  (uvDir.y < 0.0f)?angle+(2*PI):angle;
 cosVal = cos(angle);
```

```
sinVal = sin(angle);
rotMat[0][0] = cosVal;
rotMat[1][0] = -sinVal;
rotMat[0][1] = sinVal;
rotMat[1][1] = cosVal;
float2 uv2 = mul(uv,rotMat);

uvDir = normalize(inPut.curv3);
angle = atan(uvDir.y/uvDir.x);
angle = (uvDir.x < 0.0f)?angle+PI:
 (uvDir.y < 0.0f)?angle+(2*PI):angle;
cosVal = cos(angle);
sinVal = sin(angle);
rotMat[0][0] = cosVal;
rotMat[1][0] = -sinVal;
rotMat[0][1] = sinVal;
rotMat[1][1] = cosVal;
float2 uv3 = mul(uv,rotMat);

//Calculate the light incident at this pixel.
float percen = 1.0f - max(dot(normalize(inPut.norm),
 lightDir),0.0);

//Combine the three colors.
float4 color = (texPencil.Sample(samLinear,uv1)*0.333f)
 +(texPencil.Sample(samLinear,uv2)*0.333f)
 +(texPencil.Sample(samLinear,uv3)*0.333f);

//Calculate the final color.
percen = (percen*S) + O;
color.xyz = pow(color.xyz,float3(percen,percen,percen));
return color;
}
```

Listing 2.5. Pencil pixel shader.

Models	Triangles	FPS
Buddha	1087716	87.71
Armadillo	345944	117.22
Asian Dragon	225588	199.20
Dragon	100000	344.28
Bunny	69666	422.20
Atenea	15014	553.55

Table 2.2. Framerates obtained with our implementation of the pencil rendering algorithm on a GeForce 9800 GX2 GPU graphics card and a viewport resolution of 1680×1050.

2.4.4   Results

Table 2.2 shows the framerates obtained with the pencil rendering technique. Note that we obtain high framerates because the implementation is relatively cheap, and that from the numbers we can deduce that the timings depend strongly on vertex count rather than rasterized fragments count.

2.5   Acknowledgments

The authors want to thank the reviewers for their valuable comments. This work has been supported by project TIN2007-67982-C02-01 of the Spanish Government.

Bibliography

[Achorn et al. 03] Brett Achorn, Daniel Teece, M. Sheelagh T. Carpendale, Mario Costa Sousa, David Ebert, Bruce Gooch, Victoria Interrante, Lisa M. Streit, and Oleg Veryovka. "Theory and Practice of Non-Photorealistic Graphics: Algorithms, Methods, and Production Systems." In *SIGGRAPH 2003*. ACM Press, 2003.

[Ashikhmin 04] Michael Ashikhmin. "Image-Space Silhouettes for Unprocessed Models." In *GI '04: Proceedings of Graphics Interface 2004*, pp. 195–202. School of Computer Science, University of Waterloo, Waterloo, Ontario, Canada: Canadian Human-Computer Communications Society, 2004.

[Card and Mitchell 02] Drew Card and Jason L. Mitchell. "Non-Photorealistic Rendering with Pixel and Vertex Shaders." In *Direct3D ShaderX: Vertex and Pixel Shader Tips and Tricks*, edited by Wolfgang Engel. Plano, Texas: Wordware, 2002.

[Dietrich 00] Sim Dietrich. "Cartoon Rendering and Advanced Texture Features of the GeForce 256 Texture Matrix, Projective Textures, Cube Maps, Texture Coordinate Generation and Dotproduct3 Texture Blending." Technical report, NVIDIA, 2000.

[Doss 08] Joshua Doss. "Inking the Cube: Edge Detection with Direct3D 10." http://www.gamasutra.com/visualcomputing/archive, 2008.

[Dyken et al. 08] Christopher Dyken, Martin Reimers, and Johan Seland. "Real-Time GPU Silhouette Refinement Using Adaptively Blended Bézier Patches." *Computer Graphics Forum* 27:1 (2008), 1–12.

[Everitt 02] Cass Everitt. "One-Pass Silhouette Rendering with GeForce and GeForce2." White paper, NVIDIA Corporation, 2002.

[Gooch and Gooch 01] Amy A. Gooch and Bruce Gooch. *Non-Photorealistic Rendering*. A K Peters, 2001. ISBN: 1568811330, 250 pages.

[Gooch et al. 99] Bruce Gooch, Peter-Pike J. Sloan, Amy A. Gooch, Peter Shirley, and Richard Riesenfeld. "Interactive Technical Illustration." In *1999 ACM Symposium on Interactive 3D Graphics*, pp. 31–38, 1999.

[Hartner et al. 03] Ashley Hartner, Mark Hartner, Elaine Cohen, and Bruce Gooch. "Object Space Silhouette Algorithms.", 2003. Unpublished.

[Hermosilla and Vázquez 09] Pedro Hermosilla and Pere-Pau Vázquez. "Single Pass GPU Stylized Edges." In *Proceedings of IV Iberoamerican Symposium in Computer Graphics*, pp. 47–54, 2009.

[Isenberg et al. 03] Tobias Isenberg, Bert Freudenberg, Nick Halper, Stefan Schlechtweg, and Thomas Strothotte. "A Developer's Guide to Silhouette Algorithms for Polygonal Models." *IEEE Comput. Graph. Appl.* 23:4 (2003), 28–37.

[Lee et al. 06] Hyunjun Lee, Sungtae Kwon, and Seungyong Lee. "Real-Time Pencil Rendering." In *NPAR '06: Proceedings of the 4th International Symposium on Non-photorealistic Animation and Rendering*, pp. 37–45. New York: ACM, 2006.

[McGuire and Hughes 04] Morgan McGuire and John F. Hughes. "Hardware-Determined Feature Edges." In *NPAR '04: Proceedings of the 3rd International Symposium on Non-photorealistic Animation and Rendering*, pp. 35–47. New York: ACM, 2004.

[Mitchell et al. 02] Jason L. Mitchell, Chris Brennan, and Drew Card. "Real-Time Image-Space Outlining for Non-Photorealistic Rendering." In *Siggraph 02*, 2002.

[Raskar 01] Ramesh Raskar. "Hardware Support for Non-photorealistic Rendering." In *2001 SIGGRAPH / Eurographics Workshop on Graphics Hardware*, pp. 41–46. ACM Press, 2001.

[Saito and Takahashi 90] Takafumi Saito and Tokiichiro Takahashi. "Comprehensible Rendering of 3-D Shapes." *SIGGRAPH90* 24:3 (1990), 197–206.

3

III

Alpha Blending as a Post-Process

Benjamin Hathaway

3.1 Introduction

In this article we will present a novel alpha-blending technique that was developed for the off-road racing game *Pure* (see Figure 3.1). *Pure* was released in the summer of 2008 for the Xbox360, PS3, and PC platforms and featured races that subjected the player to extreme elevations, revealing detailed vistas stretching out to a distance of over 30 kilometers. With the art direction set on a photo-realistic look and locations taken from around the globe—some would require a high degree of foliage cover to be at all believable, or even recognizable.

Figure 3.1. A typical scene from *Pure* (post tone mapping & bloom effects).

During development it became apparent that we were going to need alpha blending, and lots of it! Unfortunately, alpha blending is one aspect of computer graphics that is difficult to get right, and trade-offs between performance and visual quality are often made; indeed, reluctance to risk performance has led to some game titles avoiding the use of alpha blending altogether. For a thorough introduction to the issues posed by alpha blended rendering, the reader is referred to the [Thibieroz 08] paper on advanced rendering techniques and the seminal work [Porter and Duff 84].

3.2   The Alternatives

Pure was destined to run on several platforms, each being equipped with at least one Dx9 class GPU (supporting shader model 3). This immediately presented us with several (hardware assisted) options for rendering our foliage geometry.

Alpha blending. Alpha blending uses a scalar value output by the pixel shader (alpha-value) to blend a rendered fragment with the destination pixel data.

When rendering layers of foliage with alpha blending, z-buffering artifacts are common. This can largely be resolved if the rendered primitives are sorted to draw furthest from the camera first. Sorting primitives before rendering is usually a prohibitive CPU cost for game rendering, and in the case of intersecting primitives there may indeed be no single correct draw order.

Alpha testing. Alpha testing uses a binary value output by the pixel shader to determine if the output fragment is visible or not. Alpha testing is usually combined with z-buffering techniques, which can either negate the need for geometric depth sorting or provide fill-rate optimizations (by way of z-rejection) when the scene is sorted in a front-to-back order.

Alpha testing is one of the most commonly used solutions to date; however the technique is prone to aliasing at the alpha edges.

Alpha-to-coverage. Alpha-to-coverage converts the alpha value output by the pixel shader into a coverage mask. This coverage mask is combined with the standard multisample coverage mask to determine which samples should be updated.

When alpha-to-coverage is combined with alpha testing, softer edges can be rendered whilst maintaining all the technical benefits afforded by alpha test rendering, i.e., sort independence and z-rejection opportunities. Although this is an improvement on simple alpha testing, the resulting alpha gradients can be of a poor quality compared to those obtained in alpha blending. This is particularly true when using a low number of samples or on hardware that does not support flexible coverage masks.

3.3   The Source Artwork

To try and emulate the richness of natural foliage, each tree and bush was constructed from a multitude of polygonal planes. The planes were oriented as randomly as possible, thus increasing the perceived density of foliage.

As can be seen in Figure 3.2, this leads to a great deal of primitive intersection, which raises two issues:

1. How are we to correctly sort all the intersecting primitives?

2. How are we going to deal with the high degree of depth complexity present within a single foliage model?

Figure 3.2. Geometric structure of a typical tree model rendered in *Pure* (shown from the front and side).

To correctly depth sort the primitives would require that we split the primitives along all the intersections. However, this would have increased the vertex count substantially and put a heavy burden on our memory budget, while also increasing memory bandwidth usage.

These issues are further exacerbated when the foliage is allowed to react to dynamic influences such as the wind, or physical collisions. Such influences may even cause neighboring foliage models to overlap rather unpredictably, and would therefore be impossible to optimize off-line, instead requiring a more costly, real-time solution.

3.4   Initial Attempts

Due to the high levels of primitive interpenetration within the artwork, we initially implemented our foliage renderer in the simplest manner possible, by using a combination of z-buffering and alpha-test techniques. After auditioning a number of variations of the alpha-reference value, we managed to achieve some reasonable results, although the overall look of the foliage tended to appear a little harsh, or synthetic, at times.

The most objectionable effect occurred when the camera performed slow translational motions from side-to-side (for example, during the pre-race camera sequences). As the camera moved, the alpha-channeled holes & edges within the foliage would begin to *sparkle* (due to the binary nature of alpha testing) and would often be exaggerated by the high degree of depth complexity present within each foliage model.

Next, we turned our attention towards the alpha-to-coverage feature. Alpha-to-coverage rendering integrates alpha-testing techniques with multi-sample rendering; it produces softer edges while maintaining all the technical benefits of alpha-test rendering. While initial results were favorable and the sparkling artifacts were indeed attenuated, we struggled to reproduce consistent results across all of our platforms. We also suffered from the increased fill-rate and bandwidth costs incurred by rendering the foliage at MSAA resolutions.

Neither approach seemed to deliver a high enough visual quality and it seemed a shame to quantize all those beautiful alpha-textures so heavily. Something new was needed—and we felt the answer was hiding in the silhouette of the foliage.

3.5   The Screen-Space Alpha Mask

The solution we devised—screen-space alpha masking (SSAM)—is a multi-pass approach (see the overview in Figure 3.3) implemented with rendering techniques that negate the need for any depth sorting or geometry splitting. Our solution can

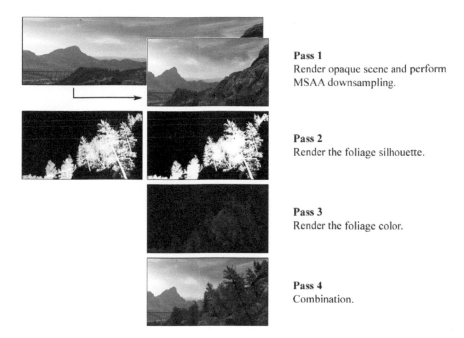

Pass 1
Render opaque scene and perform MSAA downsampling.

Pass 2
Render the foliage silhouette.

Pass 3
Render the foliage color.

Pass 4
Combination.

Figure 3.3. Diagram showing an overview of screen-space alpha masking.

yield results on par with alpha blending while correctly resolving internal overlaps (and depth intersections) on a per-pixel basis, using alpha-testing techniques.

We effectively performed *deferred alpha blending* using a full-screen post-process that resembles frame-buffer blending with the blend-operation set to ADD; the source and destination arguments are set to **SRCALPHA** and **INVSRCALPHA**, respectively. The inputs to the *blend* are rendered into three separate render targets and are then bound to texture samplers, referenced by the *final combination* post-process pixel shader (see Listing 3.2 in Section 3.11).

In terms of memory resources, we need at least three screen-resolution render-targets, two having at least three color channels (**rtOpaque** & **rtFoliage**), one with a minimum of two channels (**rtMask**), and a single depth buffer (**rtDepth**).

Note: this is *in addition* to any MSAA render-target memory requirements.

3.5.1 The Opaque Pass

During the first pass we rendered all our opaque scene elements into the color render target: **rtOpaque** (see Figure 3.4); the depth information generated was also kept and stored in the depth buffer: **rtDepth** (see Figure 3.5).

Figure 3.4. The opaque scene (color) written to rtOpaque.

For *Pure*, we rendered the opaque scene at 2× MSAA resolution and both the color and depth buffers were down sampled into screen-resolution render targets. Care had to be taken when down sampling the depth information, as incorrect samples were obtained when filtering was applied.

Figure 3.5. The opaque scene (depth) written to rtDepth.

Instead, we read a number of samples from the depth buffer (two, in the case of 2× MSAA), compared them, and simply retained the sample that was closest to the observer. For a more complete description of the solution adopted for *Pure*, the reader is referred to the work of [Iain Cantlay 04].

From this point onwards, we continued to render at non-MSAA resolutions, as it was observed that MSAA contributed little or nothing towards the quality of alpha generated edges—only those of a geometric nature. At this point, and depending on platform architecture, it may be necessary to copy the down sampled images back in to VRAM (repopulation) before further rendering can continue.

Additionally, at this point steps may need to be taken to update any hierarchical-z (hi-z) information that might be associated with `rtDepth`, and potentially optimize any subsequent draw calls that are depth occluded.

Note: Detailed information regarding the repopulation of depth information and restoration of Hi-Z can be obtained from the platform vendors and is unfortunately outside the scope of this article.

3.5.2   The Mask Generation Pass

In the second pass we generated a *silhouette*, or *mask*, of the foliage we wanted to render (see Figure 3.6). The silhouette image was rendered into our second render-target, `rtFoliage`, and we used the previously generated depth buffer, `rtDepth`, to correctly resolve any depth occlusions caused by the opaque scene.

Figure 3.6. Additively accumulated foliage alpha mask.

The mask is a monochromatic image of the alpha-channel values that would normally be used during regular alpha blending. The alpha-values are additively blended onto a black background, during which, we enabled depth testing, and disabled both back-face culling and depth writes.

As the additive blending of two primitives produces the same result regardless of the draw order, it seemed to be the ideal option for efficient mask generation. However, some artifacts were evident when the mask was used: *as-is*, (as the blend factor) due to the limited bit depth of the render-targets being used, during the *final combination* pass, the additively accumulated values would quickly saturate towards white—even at a modest depth complexity. The saturation was most evident when foliage close to the observer was expected to possess low-order opacity, but is rendered in an area of high foliage depth complexity.

To generate as high quality a mask as possible, we needed to obtain as much detail from our silhouette as we could; we therefore set the alpha-reference renderstate to zero during this pass, to avoid the rejection low opacity alpha-values.

A refinement on additive blending was the use of the max-blending mode. In this case we built up an image of the single highest alpha-value to have been written to each pixel, in effect acting as an *alpha-z-buffer*. As with additive blending, we set the source and destination blend arguments to `D3DBLEND_ONE`, but change the blend operation to `D3DBLENDOP_MAX`.

As can be seen in Figure 3.7, the max-blended mask contains a higher degree of structural information (than the additively blended mask) while still retaining the subtle alpha gradients located towards the outer edges of the foliage.

Figure 3.7. MAX blended foliage alpha mask.

Despite these attractive qualities, when the max-blended mask was used as the blend factor during the final combination pass, the foliage took on a wholly transparent look. We were left feeling that perhaps the solution lay somewhere in between the two approaches. And it did—quite literally.

The thought was that perhaps some linear combination of both masks would be the answer. Perhaps the saturation of the additive blending would compensate for the transparency of the max blending? And correspondingly, would the subtle alpha-gradients of the max-blended image reduce the saturation evident in the low-opacity, high-depth-complexity areas of the additive mask?

Fortunately the answer proved to be yes in both cases, and luckily for us all the platforms we were working with provided a method that could generate both of our masks in a single pass!

Separate alpha blend enable. Most DX9 class hardware supports the ability to specify separate blend operations and arguments for both the color *and* alpha channels, independently.

By enabling `D3DRS_SEPARATEALPHABLENDENABLE` and setting the correct series of operation and arguments, it is possible to simultaneously write the max-blended mask to the rgb channels (as a monochromatic image), and the additively-blended mask to the alpha channel (see Table 3.1).

Note: Both masks are combined at a later stage, prior to their use as the blend-factor in the final composition pass.

In order to send the alpha values to both blending units, we needed to replicate the alpha values across to all the color channels. This required a small modification to the end of the foliage shaders that resembled

```
Out.Color.xyzw = Out.Color.wwww;
```

Render State	Value
D3DRS_ALPHABLENDENABLE	TRUE
D3DRS_SEPERATEALPHABLENDENABLE	TRUE
D3DRS_BLENDOP	D3DBLENDOP_MAX
D3DRS_BLENDOPALPHA	D3DBLENDOP_ADD
D3DRS_SRCBLEND	D3DBLEND_ONE
D3DRS_SRCBLENDALPHA	D3DBLEND_ONE
D3DRS_DESTBLEND	D3DBLEND_ONE
D3DRS_DESTBLENDALPHA	D3DBLEND_ONE

Table 3.1. The blend-related render states used during mask generation.

The modification not only performed the replication, but also had the added benefit of optimizing the foliage-alpha rendering shader without us needing any prior knowledge of how the alpha value was generated. For example: to what sampler stage the alpha-texture-source was bound, etc.

All of the optimizing shader compilers we tested performed some form of *dead-code stripping*, see: ["Dead Code" 09]. This optimization removed any code that did not directly contribute to the output value, substantially increasing fill-rate efficiency, in this case, removing all of the color-related lighting equations and texture-fetch instructions that were not common to the generation of the alpha value.

HLSL source code for a typical mask rendering shader is provided in Listing 3.1 in Section 3.11.

3.5.3   The Color Pass

For the third rendering pass, we rendered an image of the foliage color into our final render-target: `rtFoliage` (see Figure 3.8), and again we use the depth buffer obtained during the opaque pass, stored in `rtDepth` (see Figure 3.9).

In order to maintain correct depth ordering (as is necessary in the case of the color image), we disabled both back-face culling and alpha blending, while enabling alpha test rendering, depth testing, and depth writes. Enabling depth writes during this pass also ensured that any subsequently rendered transparencies would be correctly depth sorted with the foliage.

When rendering the foliage color with alpha testing enabled, a suitable alpha reference value had to be chosen and we exposed the color-pass alpha reference value to the artists for tweaking.

The final value ended up being a trade-off between two values. First was a value high enough to produce visually pleasing alpha-test edges—for *Pure*, a value of $\approx$128. Second was a value low enough to minimize certain blending artifacts (that will be covered in Section 3.6), which for *Pure*, ended up being a value of $\approx$64.

3.5.4   The Final Composition Pass

In the fourth and final pass, we rendered a full screen post-process that essentially performed a linear interpolation of our opaque and foliage-color images, using the mask image as the blend-factor (see Figure 3.10).

The final composition blend equation resembled

```
finalColor = rtOpaque + (rtFoliage - rtOpaque) * rtMask;
```

Application of the post-process consisted of the rendering of an orthographically projected, quadrilateral polygon mapped over the entire screen onto which we

Figure 3.8. The foliage-color image written to `rtFoliage`.

Figure 3.9. The foliage-depth (alpha-tested) written into `rtDepth`.

Figure 3.10. The image produced by the final-combination pixel shader.

applied a pixel shader to actually perform the blending work. To ensure that we only sampled one texel per screen pixel, we took the platform's texture-sampling center into account and adjusted texture coordinates accordingly.

We now had two mask images to process, the max and additively blended masks, which needed to be combined in some way into a scalar blend-factor. For our implementation we chose to combine the masks using linear interpolation (or in HLSL, the *lerp* operation).

The final-composition blend equation, with linearly blended masks resembled

$$\texttt{mask = rtMask.a + (rtMask.r - rtMask.a) * maskLerp;}$$

$$\texttt{rtResult = rtOpaque + (rtFoliage - rtOpaque) * mask;}$$

The interpolation of the two masks introduced the value `maskLerp`, for which a value must be selected. Like the alpha-reference value, this is chosen on purely artistic grounds and was also exposed to the art team for experimentation. The final value for *Pure* was 0.85 (which produces a blend-factor composed of: 85% additive mask and 15% max-blended mask).

With `maskLerp` equal to 0.85, just enough max-blended mask is brought in to reduce the saturation artifacts without making the foliage too transparent.

In fact, it should be noted that some degree of transparency was found to be desirable. The slight transparency of the max contribution revealed distant structure (such as trunks and branches) belonging to foliage that would have otherwise have been completely occluded by near foliage (adding a certain richness to the forest scenes).

The full HLSL source for the final composition pixel shader is given in Listing 3.2 in Section 3.11.

3.6 Alpha Reference Issues

As alpha test rendering was employed during the foliage color pass, an alpha-reference value was chosen—one that was high enough to stop overlapping edges from appearing too chunky (as mentioned, for *Pure* a value was chosen somewhere between ≈64 and ≈128). As a consequence, halo-like blending artifacts are sometimes visible where the foliage blended into the opaque image (see Figure 3.11).

3.6.1 The Clear-Screen Color Fix

Due to the alpha-reference value being set to a higher value during the color pass than that set during the mask-generation pass (for which the alpha-reference value was actually zero), moving outwards along an alpha gradient (from a value of one to zero), you can actually run out of foliage-color pixels before the mask-intensity reaches zero. This would reveal a proportion of the color-pass background color in

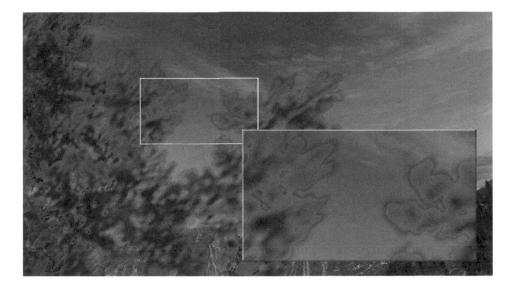

Figure 3.11. Image showing blending artifacts caused by a non-zero alpha reference value during the foliage-color pass.

Figure 3.12. The effect of different clear screen colors (from top to bottom): too dark, too light, and just right.

pixels whose mask intensity fell below the color-pass alpha reference value. The solution employed for *Pure* was to expose the foliage color passes' clear screen color to the artists, the idea being that by adjusting the color, you could lighten the artifact until it was hardly visible (see Figure 3.12).

The technique worked well but felt less than optimum, especially as the artists could only choose one color per level. The color also tended to affect the overall color balance of the scene and would have to work for foliage rendered in both the lightest and darkest of conditions—very much a compromise.

3.6.2   The Squared Alpha Trick

A small modification made to the last line of the final composition pixel shader substantially improved the quality of the blending, almost entirely compensating for the aforementioned alpha-reference artifacts (see Figure 3.13). If the final

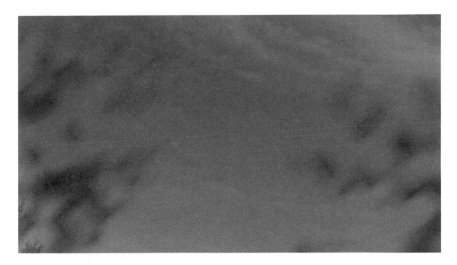

Figure 3.13. A close-up of the just-right clear screen color fix and the squared-alpha modification applied together.

mask value is numerically squared, the foliage alpha will roll off to black a little quicker while correctly maintaining areas of solid opacity.

```
return lerp(opaquePixel, foliagePixel, mask * mask);
```

It should be noted that while squaring the alpha channel does contract the foliage silhouette a little, a slight reduction in the foliage-color pass alpha-reference value should compensate for this.

3.7   Rendering Pipeline Integration

Foliage rendering is by no means the final step in rendering a game. There are many other alpha-blended elements to be integrated into the scene: grass, light shafts, and particle effects, to name but a few. Integration with these other stages is actually pretty straightforward, largely due to the fact that depth writing was enabled during the foliage-color pass.

This ensured that any subsequent depth testing would correctly resolve any depth-wise occlusions caused by the foliage (and/or opaque) scene elements.

3.8   Conclusion

In this article we have presented a novel (cross-platform) solution to the alpha blending of foliage, a solution that increases the quality of a wide range of alpha-test-class renderings, giving them the appearance of true alpha blending.

The use of SSAM within the game *Pure* had a profound effect on the overall perceived quality of the environments. The effect yielded a soft natural look without sacrificing any of the detail and contrast present in the source artwork. Below we list a few of the pros & cons to using SSAM:

Pros:

- Foliage edges are blended smoothly with the surrounding environment.

- Internally overlapping and interpenetrating primitives are sorted on a per-pixel basis using alpha testing techniques.

- The effect is implemented using simple, low-cost rendering techniques that do not require any geometric sorting or splitting (only consistency in primitive dispatch order is required).

- The final blending operations are performed at a linear cost (once per pixel) regardless of scene complexity and over-draw.

- The effect integrates well with other alpha-blending stages in the rendering pipeline (Particles, etc).

- When combined with other optimizations such as moving lighting to the vertex shader, and optimizing the shaders for each pass, overall performance can be higher than that of MSAA-based techniques.

Cons:

- The overhead of rendering the extra passes.

- Memory requirements are higher, as we need to store three images.

- The technique cannot be used to sort large collections of semi-transparent, glass-like surfaces (or soft alpha gradients that span large portions of the screen) without potentially exhibiting visual artifacts.[1]

3.9   Demo

A RenderMonkey scene, as well as several instructional .PSD files, are available at http://www.akpeters.com/gpupro.

---

[1]There are occasional opacity-related artifacts visible within overlapping alpha-gradients (when the alpha-foliage-mask is either: > 0 or, < 1). Fortunately, the foliage-color pass always yields the nearest, and therefore the most visually correct, surface color.

3.10   Acknowledgments

I would like to say a big thank you to everyone at Black Rock Studio who contributed to this article, particularly: Jeremy Moore and Tom Williams (for pushing me to write the article in the first place), and Damyan Pepper and James Callin for being there to bounce ideas off during the initial development.

An extra special thank you goes to Caroline Hathaway, Nicole Ancel, and Wessam Bahnassi for proofreading and editing the article.

3.11   Source Code

```
sampler2D foliageTexture : register(s0);

struct PS_INPUT
{
    half2 TexCoord : TEXCOORD0;
};

half4 main(PS_INPUT In) : COLOR
{
    return tex2D(foliageTexture, In.TexCoord).wwww;
}
```

Listing 3.1. HLSL source code for a typical mask rendering pixel shader.

```
sampler2D rtMask : register(s0);
sampler2D rtOpaque : register(s1);
sampler2D rtFoliage : register(s2);
half maskLerp : register(c0); // 0.85h

half4 main(float2 texCoord: TEXCOORD0) : COLOR
{
    half4 maskPixel = tex2D( rtMask, texCoord);
    half4 opaquePixel = tex2D( rtOpaque, texCoord);
    half4 foliagePixel = tex2D(rtFoliage, texCoord);
    half mask = lerp(maskPixel.x, maskPixel.w, maskLerp);

    return lerp(opaquePixel, foliagePixel, mask * mask);
}
```

Listing 3.2. HLSL source code for the final composition pixel shader.

Bibliography

["Dead Code" 09] "Dead Code Elimination." *Wikipedia.* Available at http://en.wikipedia.org/wiki/Dead_code_elimination, 2009.

[Iain Cantlay 04] Iain Cantlay. "High-Speed, Off-Screen Particles." In *GPU Gems 3*, edited by Hubert Nguyen. Reading, MA: Addison-Wesley Professional, 2007.

[Thibieroz 08] Nicolas Thibieroz. "Robust Order-Independent Transparency via Reverse Depth Peeling in DirectX10." In *ShaderX6: Advanced Rendering Techniques* (2008).

[Porter and Duff 84] Thomas Porter and Tom Duff. "Compositing Digital Images." *Computer Graphics* 18:3 (1984): 253–59.

4

Virtual Texture Mapping 101

Matthäus G. Chajdas, Christian Eisenacher,
Marc Stamminger, and Sylvain Lefebvre

4.1 Introduction

Modern games and applications use large amounts of texture data; the number
and the resolution of textures also continues to grow quickly. However, the amount
of available graphics memory is not growing at the same pace and, in addition
to textures, GPU memory is also used for complex post-processing effects and
lighting calculations. *Virtual texture mapping* (VTM) is a technique to reduce
the amount of graphics memory required for textures to a point where it is only
dependent on the screen resolution: for a given viewpoint we only keep the visible
parts of the textures in graphics memory, at the appropriate MIP map level (see
Figure 4.1).

In this chapter, we will investigate how to implement a fully functional VTM
system. Readers already familiar with VTM might want to skip right to Section 4.3, which covers several non-obvious implementation aspects. Our tutorial
implementation follows this article very closely, so we encourage you to look at
the relevant code for each section.

4.2 Virtual Texture Mapping

While early texture management schemes were designed for a single large texture [Tanner et al. 98], recent VTM systems are more flexible and mimic the
virtual memory management of the OS: textures are divided into small *tiles*, or
pages [Kraus and Ertl 02, Lefebvre et al. 04]. Those are automatically cached and
loaded onto the GPU as required for rendering the current viewpoint. However,
it is necessary to redirect accesses to missing data to a fallback texture. This

Figure 4.1. Uniquely textured terrain rendering using a single virtual texture.

prevents "holes" from appearing in the rendering, or blocking and waiting until the load request finishes.

Our implementation is inspired by the GDC talk of Sean Barrett [Barret 08] and we suggest watching the video of his presentation while reading this section. As illustrated in Figure 4.2, we begin each frame by determining which tiles are visible. We identify the ones not cached and request them from disk. After the tiles have been uploaded into the tile cache on the GPU, we update an *indirection texture*, or page table. Eventually, we render the scene, performing an initial lookup into the indirection texture to determine where to sample in the tile cache.

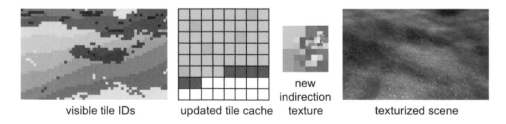

Figure 4.2. We render tile IDs, then identify and upload newly visible tiles into the tile cache (red), possibly overwriting ones that are no longer visible (blue). We update the indirection texture and render the texturized surfaces.

The indirection texture is a scaled down version of the complete virtual texture, where each texel points to a tile in the tile cache. In our case, the tile cache is simply one large texture on the GPU, containing small, square tiles of identical resolution. This means tiles from different MIP map levels cover differently sized areas of the virtual texture, but simplifies the management of the tile cache considerably.

4.2.1 Page Fault Generation

For each frame we determine the visible tiles, identify the ones not yet loaded onto the GPU, and request them from disk. Future hardware might simplify this with native page faults [Seiler et al. 08], but we still need to determine visible tiles, substitute data and redirect memory accesses.

A simple approach is to render the complete scene with a special shader that translates the virtual texture coordinates into a tile ID. By rendering the actual geometry of the scene, we trivially handle occlusion. The framebuffer is then read back and processed on the CPU along with other management tasks. As tiles typically cover several pixels, it is possible to render tile IDs at a lower resolution to reduce bandwidth and processing costs. Also, in order to pre-fetch tiles that will be visible "soon," the field of view can be slightly increased. The corresponding shader code can be found in Section 4.5.2.

4.2.2 Page Handler

The page handler loads requested tiles from disk, uploads them onto the GPU, and updates the indirection texture. Depending on disk latency and camera movement, loading the tiles might become a bottleneck. To illustrate this we fly over a large terrain covered by a single virtual texture and graph the time per frame in Figure 4.3. Given a reasonably large tile cache, very few tiles are requested and on average we need less than ten ms per frame for I/O and rendering. However, in frame 512 we turn the camera 180 degrees and continue backwards. This u-turn requests over 100 tiles, taking 350 ms to load.

To ensure smooth rendering we simply limit the number of updated tiles per frame. For requests not served in the same frame we adjust the indirection texture and redirect texture access to the finest parent tile available in the tile cache. The coarsest level is always present, and this distributes load spikes over several frames. If the update limit is larger than the average number of requested tiles, we are guaranteed to catch up with the requests eventually. For our example we request fewer than five tiles in 95% of the frames, and set the upload limit to a very conservative 20 tiles.

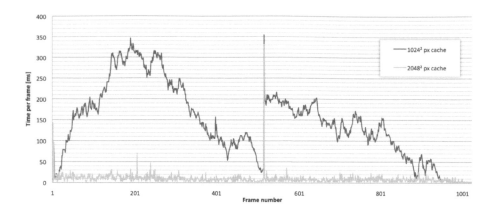

Figure 4.3. We fly over a terrain with one large virtual texture and record the time per frame. In frame 512 we turn the camera 180° and continue backwards. This turn is a worst case scenario for VTM: many new tiles—which are no longer in the cache—become visible and have to be loaded. While sufficiently large caches prevent thrashing, they help little in this challenging event.

Of course the missing tiles reduce visual quality. Therefore we upload the requested tiles with all their ancestors, prioritized from coarse to fine. This increases the total number of cache updates, but as Figure 4.4 shows, image quality is restored in a more balanced fashion—very similar to progressive JPEG. As more ancestors are present in the cache, this also improves quality in less challenging situations and reduces artifacts when rendering tile IDs with a very low resolution.

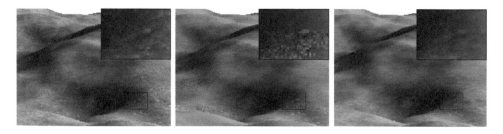

Figure 4.4. Half a second after the u-turn. Left: waiting for all tiles provides superior image quality but stalls for 330 ms. Middle: limiting the uploads per frame and using coarser MIP map levels as fallback provides smooth frame rates, but MIP levels vary strongly. Right: using prioritized loading of ancestors improves fallback, and image quality is much more balanced after the same time.

4.2.3 Rendering

When texturing the surface we perform a fast unfiltered lookup into the indirection texture, using the uv-coordinate of the fragment in virtual texture space. This provides the position of the target tile in the cache and the actual resolution of its MIP map level in the pyramid of the indirection texture. The latter might be different from the resolution computed from the fragment's MIP map level due to our tile upload limit. We add the offset inside the tile to the tile position and sample from the tile cache. The offset is simply the fractional part of the uv-coordinate scaled by the actual resolution:

$$\text{offset} := \text{frac}(uv \times \text{actualResolution}) = \text{frac}(uv \times 2^{\text{indTexEntry.z}}).$$

Note that storing the actual resolution as $\log_2(\text{actualResolution})$ allows us to use 8-bit textures. The complete shader code including the computation of correct texture gradients (see Section 4.3.3) can be found in Section 4.5.3.

4.3 Implementation Details

In this section we will investigate various implementation issues with a strong emphasis on texture filtering. Again we will follow the processing of one frame, from page fault generation over page handling to rendering.

4.3.1 Page Fault Generation

MIP map level. To compute the tile ID in the tile shader we need the virtual texture coordinates and the current MIP map level. The former are directly the interpolated uvs used for texturing, but on DX 9 and 10 hardware, we have to compute the latter manually using gradient instructions [Ewins et al. 98, Wu 98]: let $ddx = (\frac{\delta u}{\delta x}, \frac{\delta v}{\delta x})$ and $ddy = (\frac{\delta u}{\delta y}, \frac{\delta v}{\delta y})$ be the uv gradients in x- and y-direction. Using their maximal length we compute the MIP map level as

$$\text{MIP} = \log_2(\max(|ddx|, |ddy|)).$$

The corresponding shader code can be found in Section 4.5.1.

DX 10.1 provides the HLSL function `CalculateLevelOfDetail()`. Further DX 11 gives access to coarse gradients (`dd{x|y}_coarse()`) which might provide an even faster alternative to the level of detail function.

4.3.2 Page Handler

Compressed tiles. For efficient rendering it is desirable to have a DXTC compressed tile cache. It requires less memory on the GPU and reduces the upload and rendering bandwidth. However, as the compression ratio of DXTC is fixed and quite low, we store the tiles using JPEG and transcode them to DXTC before we upload them. This also allows us to reduce quality selectively and e.g., compress tiles of inaccessible areas stronger.

Disk I/O. For our tutorial implementation we store tiles as individual JPEG files for the sake of simplicity. However, reading many small files requires slow seeks and wastes bandwidth. Packing the tiles into a single file is thus very important, especially for slow devices with large sectors like DVDs.

It is possible to cut down the storage requirements by storing only every second MIP map level and computing two additional MIP maps for each tile: if an intermediate level is requested, we load the corresponding four pages from the finer level instead. More ideas about storage and loading can be found in [van Waveren 08].

Cache saturation. Unused tiles are overwritten with newly requested tiles using an LRU policy. However, the current working set might still not fit into the cache. In this case we remove tiles that promise low impact on visual quality. We replace the tiles with the finest resolution with their lower-resolution ancestors. This plays nicely with our progressive update strategy and quickly frees the tile cache. Other good candidates for removal are tiles with low variance or small screen space area.

Tile upload. Uploading the tiles to the GPU should be fast, with minimum stalling. Using DX 9, we create a managed texture and let the driver handle the upload to the GPU. Other approaches for DX 9 are described in detail by [Mittring 08]. For DX 10 and 11, we create a set of intermediate textures and update these in turn. The textures are copied individually into the tile cache [Thibieroz 08]. DX 11 adds the possibility to update the tiles concurrently, which further increases performance.

Indirection texture update. After the tiles have been uploaded, we update the indirection texture by recreating it from scratch. We start by initializing the top

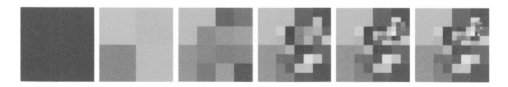

Figure 4.5. Creating the indirection texture for a camera looking over a large terrain: initializing the top level with the lowest resolution tile, we copy parent entries into the next finer level and add entries for tiles present in the cache.

of its MIP map pyramid with an entry for the tile with the lowest resolution, so each fragment has a valid fallback. For each finer level we copy the entries of the parent texels, but replace the copy with entries for tiles from that level, should they reside in the cache. We continue this process until the complete indirection texture pyramid is filled (see Figure 4.5).

If tiles are usually seen at a single resolution, we can upload only the finest level to the GPU. This reduces the required upload bandwidth, simplifies the lookup, and improves performance. This is sufficient when every object uses an unique texture, in particular for terrain rendering.

4.3.3 Rendering

While rendering with a virtual texture is straight forward, correct filtering, especially at tile edges, is less obvious. Neighboring tiles in texture space are very likely not adjacent to each other in the tile cache. Filtering is especially challenging if the hardware filtering units should be used, as those rely on having MIP maps and correct gradients available. The following paragraphs describe how to use HW filtering with an anisotropy of up to 4:1 as shown in Figure 4.6. The corresponding shader code can be found in Section 4.5.3.

Texture gradients. When two adjacent tiles in texture space are not adjacent in the tile cache, as shown in Figure 4.7, the *uv*-coordinates for the final texture lookup will vary a great deal between neighboring fragments. This results in large texture gradients and the graphics hardware will use a very wide filter for sampling, producing blurry seams. To address this, we manually compute the

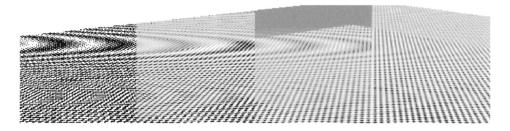

Figure 4.6. From left to right: Hardware point (175 fps), bilinear (170 fps), trilinear (170 fps), and 4:1 anisotropic filtering (165 fps) on an NVIDIA 9700M GT. The transition between tiles is especially pronounced with trilinear filtering. A single tile has to serve several MIP map levels in this example, but only one additional MIP map level is available for filtering per tile. All other methods seem to not use MIP maps at all with the tested driver version.

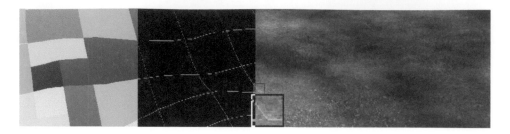

Figure 4.7. Even though the surface has a continuous mapping, the arrangement of the tiles in the cache causes discontinuities. From left to right: direct visualization of the lookup position into the tile cache; *uv* gradients, wrong across tile edges; blurry seams resulting from too wide filters when sampling. Manually scaled gradients fix this artifact.

gradients from the original virtual texture coordinates, scale them depending on the MIP map level of the tile and pass them on to the texture sampler.

Tile borders. Even with correct texture gradients, we still have to filter into neighboring pages, which very likely contain a completely different part of the virtual texture. To avoid the resulting color bleeding we need to add borders. Depending on what constraints we want to place on the size of the tile, we can use *inner* or *outer* borders.

We use the latter and surround our 128^2 tiles with a four-pixel border, making them 136^2. This keeps the resolution a multiple of four, allowing us to compress them using DXTC and perform 4:1 anisotropic filtering in hardware.

DXTC border blocks. As Figure 4.8 illustrates, adding a border to tiles might lead to different DXTC blocks at the edges of tiles. As the different blocks will be compressed differently, texels that represent the same points in virtual texture space will not have the same values in both tiles. This leads to color bleeding across tile edges, despite the border. By using a four-pixel outer border, these compression related artifacts vanish.

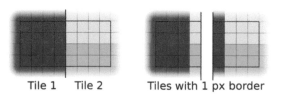

Tile 1   Tile 2   Tiles with 1 px border

Figure 4.8. Adding a one-pixel border around a tile creates different DXTC blocks for neighboring tiles. Depending on the texture they might be compressed differently, leading to visible seams in the virtual texture despite having borders.

4.4   Conclusion

In this chapter, we described a basic virtual texture mapping system. It is simple and fast, even on older hardware. We gave a few pointers on how to further improve performance, should your application or game require it. Even with newer hardware that might natively support page faults, strategies for loading, compressing and filtering textures will still be required. We hope this article and our tutorial implementation will help you to get started with VTM. You can integrate it into your own application or just play with different parameters and strategies.

4.5   Shader Code

4.5.1   MIP Map Calculation

```
float ComputeMipMapLevel(float2 UV_pixels, float scale)
{
    float2 x_deriv = ddx(UV_pixels);
    float2 y_deriv = ddy(UV_pixels);

    float d = max(length(x_deriv), length(y_deriv));

    return max(log2(d) - log2(scale), 0);
}
```

4.5.2   Tile ID Shader

```
float2 UV_pixels = In.UV * VTMResolution,

float mipLevel = ComputeMipMapLevel(UV_pixels, subSampleFactor);
mipLevel = floor(min (mipLevel, MaxMipMapLevel));

float4 tileID;
tileID.rg = floor(UV_pixels / (TileRes * exp2(mipLevel)));
tileID.b  = mipLevel;
tileID.a  = TextureID;

return tileID;
```

4.5.3   Virtual Texture Lookup

```
float3 tileEntry = IndTex.Sample(PointSampler, In.UV);
float actualResolution = exp2(tileEntry.z);

float2 offset = frac(In.UV * actualResolution) * TileRes;

float scale = actualResolution * TileRes;
float2 ddx_correct = ddx(In.UV) * scale;
float2 ddy_correct = ddy(In.UV) * scale;

return TileCache.SampleGrad(TextureSampler,
                           tileEntry.xy + offset,
                           ddx_correct,
                           ddy_correct);
```

4.6   Acknowledgments

We'd like to thank J.M.P van Waveren for generously sharing his insights on virtual texture mapping.

Bibliography

[Barret 08] Sean Barret. "Sparse Virtual Textures." 2008. http://silverspaceship. com/src/svt/.

[Ewins et al. 98] JP Ewins, MD Waller, M. White, and PF Lister. "MIP-Map Level Selection For Texture Mapping." *Visualization and Computer Graphics, IEEE Transactions on* 4:4 (1998), 317–329.

[Kraus and Ertl 02] Martin Kraus and Thomas Ertl. "Adaptive Texture Maps." In *HWWS '02: Proceedings of the ACM SIGGRAPH/EUROGRAPHICS Conference on Graphics Hardware*, pp. 7–15. Aire-la-Ville, Switzerland, Switzerland: Eurographics Association, 2002.

[Lefebvre et al. 04] Sylvain Lefebvre, Jerome Darbon, and Fabrice Neyret. "Unified Texture Management for Arbitrary Meshes." Technical Report RR5210, INRIA, 2004. Available online (http://www-evasion.imag.fr/Publications/ 2004/LDN04).

[Mittring 08] Martin Mittring. "Advanced Virtual Texture Topics." 2008. http://ati.amd.com/developer/SIGGRAPH08/Chapter02-Mittring -Advanced_Virtual_Texture_Topics.pdf.

[Seiler et al. 08] Larry Seiler, Doug Carmean, Eric Sprangle, Tom Forsyth, Michael Abrash, Pradeep Dubey, Stephen Junkins, Adam Lake, Jeremy Sugerman, Robert Cavin, Roger Espasa, Ed Grochowski, Toni Juan, and Pat Hanrahan. "Larrabee: A Many-Core x86 Architecture for Visual Computing." *ACM Trans. Graph.* 27:3 (2008), 1–15.

[Tanner et al. 98] C.C. Tanner, C.J. Migdal, and M.T. Jones. "The Clipmap: A Virtual Mipmap." In *Proceedings of the 25th Annual Conference on Computer Graphics and Interactive Techniques*, pp. 151–158. ACM New York, 1998.

[Thibieroz 08] Nicolas Thibieroz. "Ultimate Graphics Performance for DirectX 10 Hardware." GDC Presentation, 2008.

[van Waveren 08] J. M. P. van Waveren. "Geospatial Texture Streaming from Slow Storage Devices." 2008. http://software.intel.com/en-us/articles/geospatial-texture-streaming-from-slow-storage-devices/.

[Wu 98] Kevin Wu. "Direct Calculation of MIP-Map Level for Faster Texture Mapping." Hewlett-Packard Laboratories, 1998. http://www.hpl.hp.com/techreports/98/HPL-98-112.html.

Global Illumination

Full global illumination in complex scenes, as in current games, is still not possible in real time. But we are getting closer! Recent work has significantly improved the quality and the speed of the renderings, but trade-offs are still required when choosing the lighting technique for a game. In this section we have three articles pushing the limits towards our goal of full global illumination in real time, allowing for efficient indirect illumination, realistic shading, and reflections and refractions.

Chris Wyman, Greg Nichols, and Jeremy Shopf describe an interactive instant radiosity method, i.e., the indirect illumination in a scene is represented with a set of virtual point light sources, which significantly reduces fill-rate compared to previous work. They use a multiresolution splatting approach and demonstrate an efficient implementation using the stencil buffer. This technique does not require geometry shaders and thus fully utilizes GPU rasterization power. The hierarchical stencil culling ensures that illumination is rendered efficiently at appropriate resolutions.

In the "Screen-Space Directional Occlusion" article, Thorsten Grosch and Tobias Ritschel introduce their improvement on image space ambient occlusion techniques. With only little overhead, they sample environment light and visibility (in contrast to pure ambient occlusion, where both are computed separately). Their method displays oriented and colored shadows, and additionally computes one indirect bounce of light. As other image space methods, it is independent of the scene complexity and does not require precomputation.

Péter Dancsik and László Szécsi present their GPU real-time ray-tracing technique for rendering reflective and refractive objects, and their caustics. It exploits a representation of the geometry using geometry imposters, such as distance textures, height maps, and geometry images. This allows a fast intersection computation, and the separation of static and dynamic objects make interactive speed possible.

—Carsten Dachsbacher

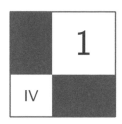

Fast, Stencil-Based Multiresolution Splatting for Indirect Illumination

Chris Wyman, Greg Nichols, and Jeremy Shopf

Realism has long been an important goal for both offline and interactive renderers. Global illumination provides visual richness not achievable with direct illumination models and plays a vital role in perceived realism. Unfortunately the cost of global effects generally precludes use in interactive applications and has led to the development of numerous approximations, including screen-space approximations [Ritschel et al. 09], fast ray tracing via intelligent shooting of select rays [McGuire and Luebke 09], and instant radiosity solutions [Dachsbacher and Stamminger 06].

Recent work significantly improves quality and speed, but important trade-offs must still be considered when selecting an interactive global illumination algorithm. Screen-space approximations, while easy to implement, generally achieve interactions only between adjacent geometry and exhibit problems near image discontinuities. Ray-tracing techniques have difficulties in fully dynamic scenes and require many rays to avoid undersampling. Instant radiosity solutions, typically based on reflective shadow maps [Dachsbacher and Stamminger 05], stress GPU fill-rate and scale linearly with the number of virtual point lights used to approximate lighting.

This chapter presents improvements to interactive instant radiosity solutions that significantly reduce fill rate by using *multiresolution* splats and demonstrates an efficient implementation using the stencil buffer. Unlike initial multiresolution splatting [Nichols and Wyman 09], this implementation does not perform amplification via geometry shaders and thus remains on the GPU fast path. Instead, we utilize the GPU's hierarchical stencil culling to efficiently render illumination at appropriate resolutions.

We first review the concepts of instant radiosity and reflective shadow maps before introducing multiresolution splatting and prior implementation techniques. Section 1.4 then describes our stencil-based splatting approach, provides pseudocode for the rendering algorithms, and details the mathematics of our splat refinement metrics.

1.1   Quick Review: Instant Radiosity

One way to quickly render complex lighting is *instant radiosity* [Keller 97], which is actually a bit of a misnomer. Instant radiosity can be thought of as a variant of bidirectional path tracing [Lafortune and Willems 93], where paths are traced from both the light source and the viewpoint and then combined to reduce variance in the computed illumination. Figure 1.1 depicts how instant radiosity's bidirectional approach works. First photons are emitted from the light. These photons may bounce a number of times, and each photon-surface intersection becomes a *virtual point light* (or VPL). In the second stage, paths from the eye are emitted and each intersection along the path gathers direct light from both the VPLs and original lights.

Graphics hardware can accelerate instant radiosity by rendering one shadow map per VPL and performing per-pixel shading computations using standard hardware lights to represent the VPLs. However, path emission usually occurs on the CPU and high quality illumination in dynamic scenes requires thousands of VPLs (and their shadow maps) each frame.

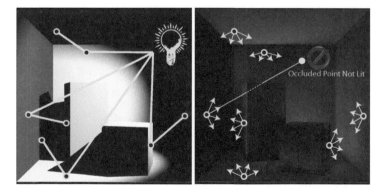

Figure 1.1. Instant radiosity emits photons probabilistically (left) and path intersections are stored as virtual point lights (VPLs). Each VPL acts as a point light (right), directly illuminating all unoccluded pixels. Combining direct light from the original source and the VPLs approximates a global illumination solution.

1.2   Quick Review: Reflective Shadow Maps

Reflective shadow maps improve instant radiosity's performance by adding assumptions that allow an efficient implementation entirely on the GPU. In particular, global illumination is limited to a single bounce. Additionally VPL visibility is ignored, allowing VPLs to illuminate all pixels despite occluders (see Figure 1.2). The basic algorithm [Dachsbacher and Stamminger 06] works as follows:

1. Render a shadow map augmented by position, normal, and color.

2. Select VPLs from this shadow map.

3. Render from the eye using only direct light.

4. For each VPL:

    (a) Draw a "splat" centered on the VPL in eye-space.

    (b) Each splat fragment illuminates one pixel from a single VPL.

    (c) Blend the fragments into the direct illumination buffer.

For a full solution each VPL must affect every pixel, requiring a full-screen splat for each VPL. Unfortunately, this consumes a lot of fillrate and quickly reduces performance with increasing resolution or VPL sampling (see Figure 1.3). Reducing the buffer resolution used during splatting improves performance at the cost of blurring illumination over discontinuities and high-frequency normal variations. Alternatively, smaller focused splats can be rendered around each VPL, but since every VPL cannot affect each pixel, the results can appear unnaturally dark.

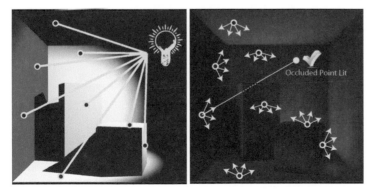

Figure 1.2. Reflective shadow maps select VPLs directly from the light's shadow map (left), limiting indirect light to a single bounce. Each VPL acts as a point light (right) that contributes direct illumination. Unlike instant radiosity, VPL visibility is ignored, allowing indirect illumination to travel through occluders.

Figure 1.3. Splatting illumination from each VPL onto the entire screen (left) consumes enormous fillrate. Reducing render buffer resolution (center) reduces fillrate in exchange for blurring illumination across discontinuities and normal variations. Focusing splats around their corresponding VPLs (right) artificially darkens illumination as only a subset of VPLs contribute to each pixel.

1.3 Multiresolution Splatting

Multiresolution splatting [Nichols and Wyman 09] addresses the fillrate problem by rendering splats into multiple buffers of varying resolution. This allows a full-screen splat for each VPL but allows adaptive selection of the splat resolution to reduce fill rate where illumination varies slowly. Where blurring is unacceptable, splats are rendered at high resolution. Elsewhere, splat resolution varies depending on the acceptable level amount of blur.

Using naive splatting techniques, each full-screen splat covers a million fragments (at 1024^2). Multiresolution splatting reduces this to around 60,000 multiresolution fragments, even in reasonably complex scenes such as in Figure 1.4. This fillrate reduction compares to naively splatting into a reduced resolution (256^2) buffer, without the resulting blur.

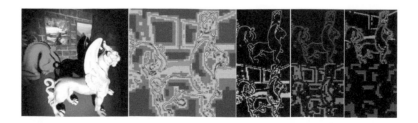

Figure 1.4. Multiresolution illumination splatting starts with a rendering of direct illumination (left). Each VPL spawns a full-screen splat, allowing each VPL to contribute light to every pixel. However, these splats are rendered at multiple resolutions depending on the speed of local illumination variations. A pseudocolor full-screen splat (center) shows the areas of varying resolution, which are rendered into distinct buffers (right).

1.3.1   Implementing Multiresolution Splatting

Implementing this multiresolution approach is quite similar to the prior technique from Section 1.2:

1. Render a shadow map augmented by position, normal, and color.

2. Select VPLs from this shadow map.

3. Render from the eye using only direct light.

4. For each VPL:

   (a) Draw a full-screen "splat."

   (b) Each splat fragment illuminates one texel (in one of the multiresolution buffers in Figure 1.4) from a single VPL, though this texel may ultimately affect multiple pixels.

   (c) Blend each fragment into the appropriate multiresolution buffer.

5. Combine, upsample and interpolate the multiresolution buffers.

6. Combine the interpolated illumination with the direct light.

This has two key algorithmic differences: splats are split into clusters of different resolution fragments (in step 4b) and the multiresolution buffer needs upsampling to final resolution (in step 6) prior to blending with the direct light. These are discussed in Sections 1.3.2 and 1.3.3.

1.3.2   Iterative Splat Refinement

Splitting splats into clusters of fragments at various resolutions proves quite time-consuming. Our prior work used the iterative refinement is depicted in Figure 1.5.

   For each VPL, this iterative approach spawns a full-screen splat at the coarsest possible illumination buffer resolution. At each fragment we determine if this coarse sampling blurs the illumination unacceptably, due to discontinuities inside the fragment (see Section 1.4.2 for details on discontinuity detection). Unacceptable blur results in a refinement of the fragment into four, finer resolution fragments. Otherwise the coarse sample is left alone. This process is repeated iteratively until no unacceptable blur remains or we refine to the final image resolution (see Listing 1.1).

   Our implementation uses a cheap preprocess to perform an initial coarse 16^2 sampling, stored into a small vertex buffer. The outer `for` loop is managed by the

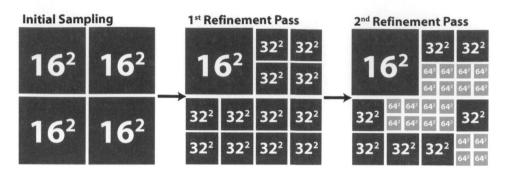

Figure 1.5. Iterative refinement of multiresolution splats starts with a uniform, coarse image sampling (e.g., 16^2 samples). Coarse fragments are processed, identifying those needing further refinement and creating four finer resolution fragments. Further iterations further refine fragments until some threshold is achieved, such as a maximal refinement level or exceeding a specified fragment count.

CPU, with each loop cycle invoking a render pass. A geometry shader processes each patch, checks for any image discontinuities, and selectively outputs either the original input patch or four refined patches. The output list of patches is either iteratively refined or rendered, as follows, as multiresolution fragments (see Listing 1.2).

Here, multiresolution fragments are rendered once per VPL. We found reversing the order of the loops, rendering the multiresolution splat just once, and gathering illumination from all VPLs generally gives better performance. Additionally, iterative patch refinement can either happen once per splat or once per frame. The second method leads to higher performance, in exchange for less flexible refinement metrics.

```
patches ← CoarseImageSampling();
for (i=1 to numRefinementPasses)  do
  for all (p ∈ patches)  do
    if ( NoDiscontinuity( p ) )  then
      continue;
    end if
    patches ← (patches − {p});
    patches ← (patches ∪ SubdivideIntoFour( p ) );
  end for
end for
```

Listing 1.1. Setting acceptable blur.

```
patches ← IterativelyRefinedPatches();
vpls ← SampledVirtualPointLights();
for all  ( v ∈ vpls )  do
  for all  ( p ∈ patches )  do
    TransformToFragmentInMultiresBuffer( p ); // In vertex shader
    IlluminateFragmentFromPointLight( p, v ); // In fragment shader
    BlendFragmentIntoMultiresBufferIllumination( p );
  end for
end for
```

Listing 1.2. Gathering illumination from VPLs for splatting.

1.3.3 Upsampling Multiresolution Illumination Buffers

Since our multiresolution illumination buffer contains fragments at various resolutions as well as large, empty regions, we need an upsampling stage to recreate a fully populated, high resolution buffer (see Listing 1.3). This upsampling basically uses a "pull" step from "push-pull" gap-filling algorithms (e.g., [Grossman and Dally 98]). The coarsest resolution buffer is upsampled by a factor of two with bilinear interpolation occurring only between valid texels (i.e., those covered by coarse splat fragments). Interpolated results are combined with the next finer resolution buffer and the upsample, interpolate, and combine process is iteratively repeated until a complete, full-resolution indirect illumination buffer is achieved.

```
coarserImage ← CoarseBlackImage();
for all  ( buffer resolutions j from coarse to fine )  do
  finerImage ← MultresBuffer( level j );
  for all  ( pixels p ∈ finerImage )  do
    if  ( InvalidTexel( p, coarserImage ) )  then
      continue; // Nothing to blend from lower resolution!
    end if
    p₁, p₂, p₃, p₄ ← FourNearestCoarseTexels( p, coarserImage );
    ω₁, ω₂, ω₃, ω₄ ← BilinearInterpolationWeights( p, p₁, p₂, p₃, p₄
    );
    for all  ( i ∈ [1..4] )  do
      ωᵢ = InvalidTexel( pᵢ, coarserImage ) ) ?  0 :  ωᵢ;
    end for
    finerImage[p] += (ω₁p₁ + ω₂p₂ + ω₃p₃ + ω₄p₄)/(ω₁ + ω₂ + ω₃ + ω₄)
  end for
  coarserImage ← finerImage;
end for
```

Listing 1.3. Unsampling the multiresolution illumination buffer.

Note that one ω_i must be nonzero (otherwise `InvalidTexel(` **p**, *coarserImage* `)` would be true).

1.4   Fast Stencil-Based Multiresolution Splatting

Sadly, splat refinement via iteratively applying a geometry shader causes most GPUs to fall off their "fast track," as the number of multiresolution fragments generated is not known in advance. This degrades performance significantly. It also initiates passes on the CPU, introducing synchronization points. Additionally, both a vertex *and* fragment shader process each multiresolution fragment.

We now introduce a significantly faster approach for multiresolution splatting that avoids these bottlenecks. Two key observations allow us to transform the problem. First, the iterative refinement steps have no dependencies (and can thus be parallelized) for most classes of discontinuity detectors. Second, we reformulate multiresolution splatting as a hierarchical culling problem utilizing the GPU's built-in hierarchical stencil culling.

1.4.1   Parallel Splat Refinement into a Stencil Buffer

Consider the depiction of a multiresolution splat shown in Figure 1.6. For a given fragment **F**, we can determine whether **F** belongs in the multiresolution splat by evaluating a discontinuity detector at **F** and the corresponding coarser fragment **F***. This suffices as long as a discontinuity in **F** implies that **F*** also contains a discontinuity. Given that most discontinuity detectors, including those outlined

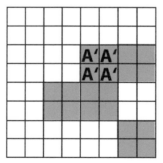

Figure 1.6. The multiresolution splat (left) depicted in Figure 1.5 can be computed in parallel rather than iteratively. All fragments in the multiresolution buffers (right) are processed in parallel. Fragment *A* still contains discontinuities, and is thus invalid (fragments *A'* are used instead). Fragment *B* is valid; it contains no discontinuities but fragment *B** does. Fragment *C* needs no refinement, but since *C** also has no discontinuities fragment *C* is unnecessary.

```
for all  (fragments f ∈ image)  do
  if  ( ∄j such that f ∈ MipmapLevel( j ) )  then
    continue; // Fragment not actually in multires buffer
  end if
  j ← GetMipmapLevel( f );
  if  ( IsDiscontinuity( f, j ) )  then
    continue; // Fragment needs further subdivision
  end if
  if  ( NoDiscontinuity( f, j + 1 ) )  then
    continue; // Coarser fragment did not need subdivision
  end if
  SetStencil( f );
end for
```

Listing 1.4. Parallel splat refinement.

in Section 1.4.2, satisfy this criteria, we can evaluate fragments in all levels of the multiresolution buffer in parallel (see Listing 1.4).

Note this refinement algorithm only has a single loop, instantiated by drawing a full-screen quad over the multiresolution buffer depicted in Figure 1.7. This multiresolution illumination buffer is actually stored as a single buffer containing all resolution buffers. Loop internals are performed in the fragment shader, simultaneously for all fragments.

Effectively, the shader splits fragments into four categories: those not in the multiresolution buffer (i.e., from the gray area of Figure 1.7), those that need additional refinement, those where a coarser fragment already suffices, and those

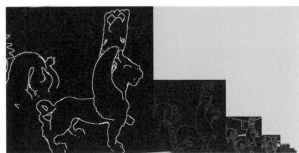

Figure 1.7. Conceptually, multiresolution rendering uses a "render-to-mipmap" approach (left). Our new stencil-based approach requires a flattened multiresolution buffer to instantiate a parallel refinement pass that sets fragment stencil bits (right).

that belong to the multiresolution splat. In the first three cases, the fragment is discarded. In the last case, we set a stencil bit to allow quick identification of appropriate fragments during splatting.

1.4.2   Discontinuity Detection

Discontinuity detection plays an important role in both performance and quality. Splatting relies on the observation that low resolution illumination suffices in smoothly changing areas, but finer resolution is necessary near discontinuities. Poor discontinuity detection either misses edges or refines excessively. Missing edges introduce blurring and excessive refinement requires additional splat fragments that add to the rendering cost.

We use a two-phase discontinuity detection. Most importantly, depth discontinuities around object silhouettes must be identified to avoid blur between background and foreground geometry. Secondly, large normal variations such as the creases on a cube also introduce high frequencies into the indirect illumination. While not necessarily apparent when combining with direct and indirect illumination, blur across large normal variations stands out in shadowed regions where only indirect light contributes.

Other factors may also influence the discontinuity detector. For instance, illumination discontinuities due to reflected Phong highlights may call for additional refinement. Similarly, the use of multiresolution splatting for screen space ambient occlusion may necessitate not only edge detection, but also proximity detection. However, for diffuse global illumination we found depth and normal tests suffice.

Detecting depth discontinuities. Silhouette edges exhibit large depth changes from one pixel to the next. The most space-efficient way to identify such discontinuities relies on a maximum mipmap, where each mipmap texel stores the maximal one-pixel depth discontinuity inside its screen-space area. We compute this max-mipmap by first applying a 3×3 filter to a linear-depth image. This filter computes a per-pixel derivative $\Delta \mathbf{D}_{x,y}$ as

$$\Delta \mathbf{D}_{x,y} = \frac{\max_{\forall s,t}(\mathbf{D}_{s,t}) - \min_{\forall s,t}(\mathbf{D}_{s,t})}{\mathbf{D}_{x,y}}.$$

Here $\mathbf{D}_{s,t}$ is the linear depth of the pixel (s,t), for $s \in [x-1...x+1]$ and $t \in [y-1...y+1]$. We then create a maximum mipmap, with each texel at level j storing the maximum of its four children at level $j-1$.

Computing $\Delta \mathbf{D}_{x,y}$ via a 3×3 filter (instead of in a 2×2 mipmap cluster) is vital to finding discontinuities occurring over power-of-two pixel boundaries.

The normalization by $\mathbf{D}_{x,y}$ chooses slightly smaller discontinuities nearer the viewer over larger, distant discontinuities. Blurring nearby edges is typically more noticeable than on smaller distant objects.

The function IsDiscontinuity($\mathbf{D}_{x,y}$, j) looks up $\Delta\mathbf{D}_{x,y}$ from mipmap level j and determines if it is larger than a specified depth threshold $\mathbb{T}_{depth}$. Larger values of $\mathbb{T}_{depth}$ results in fewer refined fragments, in exchange for additional blur across depth discontinuities. We found varying $\mathbb{T}_{depth}$ with mipmap level j can be helpful, starting with a lower value at coarse resolutions and increasing for finer levels. This avoids coarse splat fragments suddenly splitting into very fine fragments with small camera motions.

Detecting normal discontinuities. Strong illumination variations inside object silhouettes typically arise due to variations in surface orientation. To properly refine our multiresolution splats in these areas, we need a mipmap that identifies large normal variations. Ideally, we would create a normal cone for each mipmap texel and subdivide if the cone angle exceeds some threshold.

Unfortunately, we know no efficient approach for creating an image-space mipmap of normal cones. Instead we use a conservative approximation that gives similar results. Given a set of n unit length normals $\vec{\mathbf{N}}_0$, $\vec{\mathbf{N}}_1$, ..., $\vec{\mathbf{N}}_n$, we compute maximum and minimum vectors $\vec{\mathbf{N}}_{\max}$ and $\vec{\mathbf{N}}_{\min}$:

$$
\vec{\mathbf{N}}_{\max} = \begin{pmatrix} \max_{s\in[0..n]}(\vec{\mathbf{N}}_s.x) \\ \max_{s\in[0..n]}(\vec{\mathbf{N}}_s.y) \\ \max_{s\in[0..n]}(\vec{\mathbf{N}}_s.z) \end{pmatrix}, \quad \vec{\mathbf{N}}_{\min} = \begin{pmatrix} \min_{s\in[0..n]}(\vec{\mathbf{N}}_s.x) \\ \min_{s\in[0..n]}(\vec{\mathbf{N}}_s.y) \\ \min_{s\in[0..n]}(\vec{\mathbf{N}}_s.z) \end{pmatrix}.
$$

The angle between $\vec{\mathbf{N}}_{\max}$ and $\vec{\mathbf{N}}_{\min}$ then conservatively bounds the angle of a corresponding normal cone. Furthermore, these max and min operations can be efficiently performed during creation of a min-max mipmap (e.g., [Carr et al. 06]).

Simplifying further, we avoid computing the angle between $\vec{\mathbf{N}}_{\max}$ and $\vec{\mathbf{N}}_{\min}$ and instead compute $\Delta\vec{\mathbf{N}} = \vec{\mathbf{N}}_{\max} - \vec{\mathbf{N}}_{\min}$. Components of $\Delta\vec{\mathbf{N}}$ range from 0 for similar orientations to 2 for widely varying normals. We introduce a threshold $\mathbb{T}_{normal} \in [0..2]$ and detect a normal discontinuity whenever any component of $\Delta\vec{\mathbf{N}}$ exceeds $\mathbb{T}_{normal}$.

As image-space normals lie in a single z-hemisphere, we only store x-and y-components of $\vec{\mathbf{N}}_{\max}$ and $\vec{\mathbf{N}}_{\min}$ in a single, four-component mipmap. Our function IsDiscontinuity($\vec{\mathbf{N}}_{x,y}$, j) looks up the two-component vectors in the jth mipmap level and performs two threshold comparisons.

1.4.3   Rendering with Stenciled Multiresolution Splatting

After creating a stencil buffer containing the locations of our splat's multiresolution fragments, we must define how to render a splat. Standard splatting approaches render a single screen aligned quad per splat. However since many of our multiresolution fragments do not belong in our splats, we cannot expect good performance this way.

Instead, our approach relies on modern GPUs' hierarchical stencil and z culling. Naively drawing a full-screen multiresolution splat consumes significant fill rate. However, enabling the stencil test to draw only appropriate fragments (e.g., those shown in Figure 1.7) allows early stencil culling to cheaply eliminate nearly all extraneous fragments. Algorithmically, this works as shown in Listing 1.5.

```
pixels ←FullScreenQuad();
vpls ← SampledVirtualPointLights();
for all  ( v ∈ vpls )  do
  for all  ( p ∈ pixels )  do
    if  ( FailsEarlyStencilTest( p ) )  then
      continue; // Not part of multiresolution splat
    end if
    IlluminatePatchFromPointLight( p, v );
  end for
end for
```

Listing 1.5. Rendering.

Since this culling utilizes hierarchical rasterization hardware, it processes roughly the same number of splat fragments as the earlier implementation (from Section 1.3.2) without the overhead of running each fragment though an unnecessary vertex shader.

Stenciled splatting generates a multiresolution buffer *identical* to the slower implementation from Section 1.3.2. As before, this must be upsampled to a single full resolution buffer before combining indirect and direct illumination.

1.5   Results and Analysis

We implemented both the iterative and stencil refinement techniques in OpenGL using GLSL. Table 1.1 compares performance of the two techniques in four scenes of varying complexity. Timings were obtained on a dual-core 3GHz Pentium 4 with a GeForce GTX 280, with all results rendered at 1024^2. Both refinement and splatting techniques generate identical images, compared in Figure 1.8 to renderings without indirect illumination.

Rendering Steps for Iterative Refinement (Section 1.3)	Cornell Box	Feline Scene	Sponza Atrium	Indoor Garden
1) Render Direct Light	1.8 ms	5.8 ms	2.8 ms	2.8 ms
2) Render RSM	0.9 ms	2.3 ms	1.4 ms	1.6 ms
3) Create Min-Max Mipmap	0.7 ms	0.7 ms	0.7 ms	0.7 ms
4) Iterated Refinement	1.3 ms	1.7 ms	1.3 ms	1.6 ms
5) Splat All Fragments	45.8 ms	67.0 ms	58.1 ms	130.0 ms
6) Upsample Illumination	1.6 ms	1.7 ms	1.3 ms	1.3 ms
Total	52.1 ms	79.2 ms	65.6 ms	138.0 ms

Rendering Steps for Stenciled Refinement (Section 1.4)	Cornell Box	Feline Scene	Sponza Atrium	Indoor Garden
1) Render Direct Light	1.8 ms	5.8 ms	2.8 ms	2.8 ms
2) Render RSM	0.9 ms	2.3 ms	1.4 ms	1.6 ms
3) Create Min-Max Mipmap	0.7 ms	0.7 ms	0.7 ms	0.7 ms
4) Stenciled Refinement	0.7 ms	0.7 ms	0.7 ms	0.7 ms
5) Stencil Splatting	2.5 ms	3.5 ms	3.0 ms	6.6 ms
6) Upsample Illumination	1.6 ms	1.7 ms	1.3 ms	1.3 ms
Total	8.2 ms	14.7 ms	9.9 ms	13.7 ms

	Cornell Box	Feline Scene	Sponza Atrium	Indoor Garden
Total Frame Speedup	6.4×	5.4×	6.6×	10.1×
Step 4 and 5 Speedup	14.7×	16.4×	16.1×	18.0×

Table 1.1. Rendering costs for iterative refinement and splatting (discussed in Section 1.3) compared to stencil refinement and splatting (described in Section 1.4) for various scenes. Our fast stencil approach reduces per-frame rendering times 5–10×. Refinement and splatting costs alone decrease by more than 15×.

Key points to notice include that the variable cost iterative refinement is replaced by a constant cost stenciled refinement that does not depend on scene complexity. Costs for iterative refinement depend on the number of multiresolution fragments generated whereas costs for stenciled refinement depend only on image resolution. Additionally, stenciled refinement does not require Shader Model 3 hardware, allowing multiresolution splatting to run on older hardware.

The clear win with stenciled refinement, though, occurs during splatting. Each multiresolution fragment no longer needs to be instantiated as an individual point, properly positioned by a vertex shader, and rasterized into a single fragment. Instead a single full-screen quad eliminates all these extraneous vertex and rasterization steps and renders all fragments in parallel, utilizing hierarchical hardware culling to eliminate excess fragments.

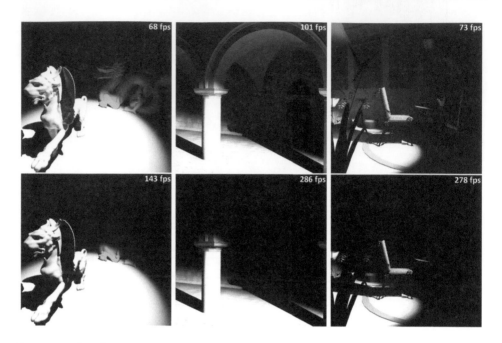

Figure 1.8. (Top) Renderings of the feline scene, Sponza atrium, and indoor garden using multiresolution splatting. (Bottom) The same renderings without one-bounce indirect lighting.

1.6 Conclusion

This article explored a new stencil-based formulation of multiresolution splatting. Multiresolution splatting significantly reduces the fillrate consumption used by GPU-based instant radiosity techniques for interactive diffuse global illumination. Our stenciled approach reduces the cost of approximate one-bounce indirect lighting to only a few milliseconds without introducing blur.

While presented in the context of interactive global illumination, we believe our stencil-based multiresolution technique applies to a variety of other problems. In particular, any problem decomposable into multiple independent frequencies may benefit from a similar approach.

1.7 Demo and Source

Available at http://www.cs.uiowa.edu/~cwyman/.

Bibliography

[Carr et al. 06] Nathan A. Carr, Jared Hoberock, Keenan Crane, and John C. Hart. "Fast GPU Ray Tracing of Dynamic Meshes Using Geometry Images." In *Graphics Interface*, 137, 137, pp. 203–209, 2006.

[Dachsbacher and Stamminger 05] Carsten Dachsbacher and Marc Stamminger. "Reflective Shadow Maps." In *Symposium on Interactive 3D Graphics and Games*, pp. 203–208, 2005.

[Dachsbacher and Stamminger 06] Carsten Dachsbacher and Marc Stamminger. "Splatting Indirect Illumination." In *Symposium on Interactive 3D Graphics and Games*, pp. 93–100, 2006.

[Grossman and Dally 98] J. Grossman and William Dally. "Point Sample Rendering." In *Eurographics Workshop on Rendering*, pp. 181–192, 1998.

[Keller 97] Alexander Keller. "Instant Radiosity." In *Proceedings of SIGGRAPH*, pp. 49–54, 1997.

[Lafortune and Willems 93] Eric Lafortune and Yves Willems. "Bi-Directional Path Tracing." In *Compugraphics*, pp. 145–153, 1993.

[McGuire and Luebke 09] Morgan McGuire and David Luebke. "Hardware-Accelerated Global Illumination by Image Space Photon Mapping." In *High Performance Graphics*, pp. 77–89, 2009.

[Nichols and Wyman 09] Greg Nichols and Chris Wyman. "Multiresolution Splatting for Indirect Illumination." In *Symposium on Interactive 3D Graphics and Games*, pp. 83–90, 2009.

[Ritschel et al. 09] Tobias Ritschel, Thorsten Grosch, and Hans-Peter Seidel. "Approximating Dynamic Global Illumination in Image Space." In *Symposium on Interactive 3D Graphics and Games*, pp. 75–82, 2009.

2

IV

Screen-Space Directional Occlusion

Thorsten Grosch and Tobias Ritschel

2.1 Introduction

Real-time global illumination is still an unsolved problem for large and dynamic scenes. Currently, real-time frame rates are only achieved through approximations. One such approximation is *ambient occlusion* (AO), which is often used in feature films and computer games, because of its good visual quality and simple implementation [Landis 02]. The basic idea is to pre-compute average visibility values at several places on the surface of the mesh. These values are then multiplied at runtime with the unoccluded illumination provided by the graphics hardware (see Figure 2.1). Typically, the visibility values are pre-computed and

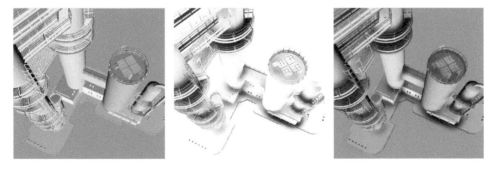

Figure 2.1. Ambient occlusion can be used to combine separately computed visibility values with the unoccluded illumination from the GPU. The left image shows the unoccluded illumination, the center image shows the ambient occlusion that darkens the cavities and contact regions only. If both are multiplied, a more realistic appearance can be obtained, as shown on the right.

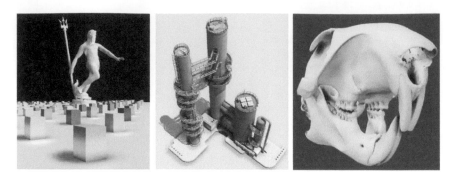

Figure 2.2. Screen-space directional occlusion examples.

stored for each vertex or texel of the mesh. The average visibility is computed by shooting some rays in the upper hemisphere of the surface point and counting the number of blocked rays. Due to this separation of visibility and illumination, ambient occlusion is only a coarse approximation of the actual illumination, but the results are often visually plausible. In this article, we present an extension of ambient occlusion that displays *oriented* and *colored* shadows correctly and additionally computes one *indirect bounce* of light [Ritschel et al. 09] (see Figure 2.2). Since our method works in image space, it is independent of the scene complexity and any kind of dynamic scenes can be illuminated at real-time frame rates without any pre-computation.

2.2 Screen-Space Ambient Occlusion

One drawback of ambient occlusion is that it works only for static scenes. If visibility values are pre-computed for each vertex or texel, these values become invalid if the mesh is deformed. Some first ideas for dynamic scenes were presented by [Bunnell 06] and [Hoberock and Jia 07] by approximating the geometry with a hierarchy of discs. The easiest way to deal with dynamic scenes is to compute ambient occlusion based on the information in the frame buffer, so-called *screen-space ambient occlusion* (SSAO). Here the depth buffer is used to compute the average visibility values *on-the-fly* instead of a pre-computation. As shown in [Mittring 07], the computational power of recent GPUs is sufficient to compute SSAO in real time. Moreover, this approach does not require any special geometric representation of the scene, since only the information in the frame buffer is used to compute the occlusion values. It is not even necessary to use a three-dimensional model that consists of polygons, since we can compute occlusion from any rendering that produces a depth buffer.

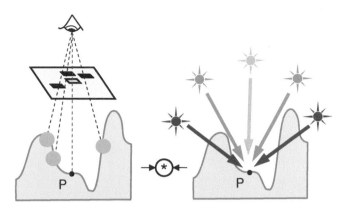

Figure 2.3. Screen-space ambient occlusion: for each pixel in the frame buffer, a set of neighboring pixels is inspected and a small sphere is placed at the corresponding three-dimensional position. An occlusion value is computed for each sphere and all these values are accumulated into one ambient occlusion value. Finally, this value is multiplied with the unoccluded illumination from all directions.

To explain the differences of our method (see Figure 2.3), let us have a look at the computation of standard SSAO [Shanmugam and Arikan 07] first: for each pixel in the frame buffer, we inspect some neighboring pixels and read their depth values. This allows us to compute the corresponding three-dimensional position and we can place a small sphere with a user-defined radius there. Now an occlusion value is computed for each sphere, which depends on the solid angle of the sphere with regard to the receiver point. These occlusion values are all accumulated into a single ambient occlusion value. Finally, the unoccluded illumination from all directions (e.g., from a set of point lights extracted from an environment map) is computed with the standard GPU pipeline and the AO value is multiplied with this unoccluded illumination.

2.2.1 SSAO Problems

Ambient occlusion typically displays darkening of cavities and contact shadows, but all *directional* information of the incoming light is ignored. This happens because only the geometry is used to compute ambient occlusion while the actual illumination is ignored. A typical problem case is shown in Figure 2.4: in case of directionally-varying incoming light, ambient occlusion will display a wrong color. Therefore we extend recent developments in screen-space AO towards a more realistic illumination we call *screen-space directional occlusion* (SSDO). Since we loop through a number of neighboring pixels in the fragment program, we can compute an *individual* visibility value for each of them instead of collapsing all

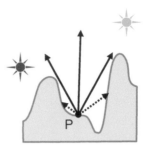

Figure 2.4. A typical problem case for ambient occlusion with a red and a green light. Since the red light is blocked and the green light illuminates the point **P**, we expect to see a green shadow here. But ambient occlusion computes the illumination from all directions first, so the point **P** is initially yellow and then scaled by some average occlusion value, resulting in a brown color.

the information into a single AO value. So the basic idea is to use the visibility information for the incoming light from each direction and illuminate *only* from the *visible* directions, resulting in a directional illumination. For the further description of SSDO we assume that we have a deep frame buffer that contains positions, normals, and reflectance values for each pixel.

2.3   Screen-Space Directional Occlusion

Since we can not directly shoot rays to test the visibility for a given direction, we need some kind of approximation for the visibility. Here we assume the local geometry around each point to be a height field. The test for visibility therefore reduces to a test whether a sample point is below or above the surface. All sampling points below the surface are treated as occluders while sampling points above the surface are classified as visible. Our algorithm is visualized in Figure 2.5 and can be summarized as follows: first, we place a hemisphere around the three-dimensional point of the pixel, which is oriented along the surface normal. The radius $r_{\max}$ of this hemisphere is a user parameter and determines the size of the local neighborhood where we search for blockers. Then, some three-dimensional sampling points are uniformly distributed inside the hemisphere. Again, the number of sampling points N is a user parameter for time-quality trade-off. Now we test if the illumination from each sampling direction is blocked or visible. Therefore, we back-project each sampling point into the deep frame buffer. At the pixel position we can read the three-dimensional position on the surface, and move each point onto the surface. If the sampling point moves towards the viewer, it was initially below the surface and it is classified as blocked. If it moves away from the

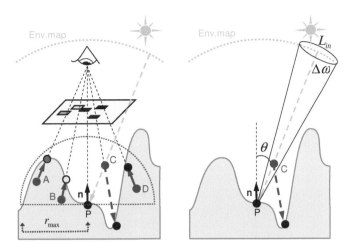

Figure 2.5. Screen-space directional occlusion. Left image: to compute the Directional Occlusion at point P, we create some uniformly distributed sampling points in a hemisphere and back-project them into the deep frame buffer. Each point which is (initially) below the surface is treated as an occluder. Right image: the illumination is only computed from the visible points. Here we assume a solid angle for each sampling direction and use the incoming radiance from a blurred environment map.

viewer, it was initially above the surface and it is classified as visible. In the example in Figure 2.5, the points **A**, **B** and **D** are below the surface and classified as blockers. Only sample **C** is visible, because it is above the surface. Consequently, the illumination is computed from direction **C** only. We found this to be a good approximation for the visibility. For details about misclassifications see [Ritschel et al. 09].

2.3.1 Direct Illumination

For natural illumination we use an environment map. Since we try to keep the number of samples low, we blur the environment map in a preprocess. The filter kernel is thereby adjusted to the solid angle of one sample. In this way we compute the average radiance over the solid angle of one sampling direction and we avoid flickering artifacts, e.g., when the environment map is rotated. Figure 2.6 shows an example of an environment map and the blurred version. Since the solid angle is different for each pixel in the environment map, a spatially-varying filter would be required. However, we found the visible error to be small and use a Gaussian filter with a fixed kernel size. Finally, the direct illumination can be

Figure 2.6. We use a blurred environment map for illumination since the number of samples is low; this image already contains the average of the incoming radiance inside the solid angle for each incoming direction. In this example we use a Lat/Long representation of the Kitchen Environment Map by Paul Debevec.

computed as follows:

$$L_{\mathrm{dir}}(P) = \sum_{i=1}^{N} \frac{\rho}{\pi} \cdot L_{\mathrm{in}}(\omega_i) \cdot V(\omega_i) \cdot \cos\theta_i \cdot \Delta\omega,$$

where L_{in} is the blurred radiance from the environment map in direction ω, V is our approximated visibility and $\frac{\rho}{\pi}$ is the diffuse BRDF of the surface. The $\Delta\omega$ is the solid angle for each direction and can be computed as $\Delta\omega = \frac{2\pi}{N}$. For a given resolution $w \times h$ of the environment map, the pixel width of the filter kernel can be approximated as $\sqrt{(w \cdot h/2)/N}$

Note that the environment map that we use in Figure 2.6 contains two main sources of light: an orange lamp on the ceiling and the light blue illumination which is coming in through the windows. Ambient occlusion does not correctly display the resulting shadows since the incoming illumination is ignored and only average visibility values are used. So the resulting ambient occlusion basically consists of static, grey contact shadows. But in fact, this illumination results in two colored, oriented shadows which are correctly reproduced with directional occlusion. Figure 2.7 shows the visual difference between directional occlusion and ambient occlusion, rendered at similar frame rates.

Listing 2.1 shows the main part of the GLSL fragment program that computes SSDO. We use a deep frame buffer that contains the position and normal in world coordinates for each pixel (`positionTexture` and `normalTexture`). Furthermore, we use pre-computed, random sampling points which are uniformly distributed in a unit hemisphere. These sampling points are stored in a two-dimensional texture (`seedTexture`), where each line contains N different sampling points. Each pixel then selects a different line, depending on the pixel position (see Section 2.4). Then, a local frame around the pixel normal is computed and the

Figure 2.7. Difference between ambient occlusion and directional occlusion. Note how ambient occlusion just displays grey contact shadows whereas directional occlusion can reconstruct the correct orientation and color for shadows of small-scale details.

sampling points are scaled by the hemisphere radius (`sampleRadius`) and rotated into the local frame. This world-space sample position is then projected into the current frame buffer and the corresponding texture coordinate is computed (`occluderTexCoord`). Next, we read the position buffer at this texture coordinate and compute the z-coordinate in camera coordinates of both the world space sample position and the position in the position buffer (`depth` and `sampleDepth`). Since we look along the negative z-axis, all depth values will be negative. If `-sampleDepth` is smaller that `-depth`, the sampling point moved towards the viewer and we found an occluder. For practical reasons, we ignore all occluders with a projected sample position which is outside the hemisphere (`distanceTerm`). Otherwise, the silhouette edges of all objects would be darkened. Instead of using 0 and 1 for visibility, we add another user-controlled parameter to adjust the SSDO strength (`strength`). Therefore, the sum of radiances `directRadianceSum` might become negative and we have to clamp to zero after the loop.

```glsl
// Read position and normal of the pixel from deep framebuffer.
vec4 position = texelFetch2D(positionTexture ,
                ivec2(gl_FragCoord.xy), 0);
vec3 normal = texelFetch2D(normalTexture ,
                ivec2(gl_FragCoord.xy), 0);

// Skip pixels without geometry.
if(position.a > 0.0) {

    vec3 directRadianceSum = vec3(0.0);
    vec3 occluderRadianceSum = vec3(0.0);
```

```glsl
vec3 ambientRadianceSum = vec3(0.0);
float ambientOcclusion = 0.0;

// Compute a matrix that transform from the unit hemisphere.
// along z = -1 to the local frame along this normal
mat3 localMatrix = computeTripodMatrix(normal);

// Compute the index of the current pattern.
// We use one out of patternSize * patternSize
// pre-defined unit hemisphere patterns (seedTexture).
// The i'th pixel in every sub-rectangle uses always
// the same i'th sub-pattern.
int patternIndex = int(gl_FragCoord.x) % patternSize +
                   (int(gl_FragCoord.y) % patternSize) *
                   patternSize;

// Loop over all samples from the current pattern.
for(int i = 0; i < sampleCount; i++) {

    // Get the i'th sample direction from the row at
    // patternIndex and transfrom it to local space.
    vec3 sample = localMatrix * texelFetch2D(seedTexture,
                  ivec2(i, patternIndex), 0).rgb;
    vec3 normalizedSample = normalize(sample);

    // Go sample-radius steps along the sample direction,
    // starting at the current pixel world space location.
    vec4 worldSampleOccluderPosition = position +
    sampleRadius * vec4(sample.x, sample.y, sample.z, 0);

    // Project this world occluder position in the current
    // eye space using the modelview-projection matrix.
    // Due to the deferred shading, the standard OpenGL
    // matrix can not be used.
    vec4 occluderSamplePosition = (projectionMatrix *
    modelviewMatrix) * worldSampleOccluderPosition;

    // Compute the pixel position of the occluder:
    // Do a division by w first (perspective projection),
    // then scale/bias by 0.5 to transform [-1,1] -> [0,1].
    // Finally scale by the texture resolution.
    vec2 occluderTexCoord = textureSize2D(positionTexture,0)
    * (vec2(0.5) + 0.5 * (occluderSamplePosition.xy /
    occluderSamplePosition.w));

    // Read the occluder position and the occluder normal
    // at the occluder texture coordinate.
    vec4 occluderPosition = texelFetch2D(positionTexture,
                            ivec2(occluderTexCoord), 0);
    vec3 occluderNormal = texelFetch2D(normalTexture,
                          ivec2(occluderTexCoord), 0);
```

```
// Compute depth of current sample pos. in eye space.
float depth = (modelviewMatrix *
worldSampleOccluderPosition).z;

// Compute depth of corresponding (proj.) pixel position.
float sampleDepth = (modelviewMatrix *
occluderPosition).z + depthBias;

// Ignore samples that move more than a
// certain distance due to the projection
// (typically singularity is set to hemisphere radius).
float distanceTerm = abs(depth - sampleDepth) <
singularity ? 1.0 : 0.0;

// Compute visibility when sample moves towards viewer.
// We look along the -z axis, so sampleDepth is
// larger than depth in this case.
float visibility = 1.0 - strength *
(sampleDepth > depth ? 1.0 : 0.0) * distanceTerm;

// Geometric term of the current pixel towards the
// current sample direction
float receiverGeometricTerm = max(0.0,
dot(normalizedSample, normal));

// Compute spherical coordinates (theta, phi)
// of current sample direction.
float theta = acos(normalizedSample.y);
float phi = atan(normalizedSample.z,normalizedSample.x);
if (phi < 0) phi += 2*PI;

// Get environment radiance of this direction from
// blurred lat/long environment map.
vec3 senderRadiance = texture2D(envmapTexture,
vec2( phi / (2.0*PI), 1.0 - theta / PI ) ).rgb;

// Compute radiance as the usual triple product
// of visibility, radiance, and BRDF.
// For practical reasons, we post-multiply
// with the diffuse reflectance color.
vec3 radiance = visibility * receiverGeometricTerm *
                senderRadiance;

// Accumulate the radiance from all samples.
directRadianceSum += radiance;

// Indirect light can be computed here
// (see Indirect Light Listing)
// The sum of the indirect light is stored
// in occluderRadianceSum
```

```
    }

    // In case of a large value of-strength, the summed
    // radiance can become negative, so we clamp to zero here.
    directRadianceSum = max(vec3(0), directRadianceSum);
    occluderRadianceSum = max(vec3(0), occluderRadianceSum);

    // Add direct and indirect radiance.
    vec3 radianceSum = directRadianceSum + occluderRadianceSum;

    // Multiply by solid angle and output result.
    radianceSum *= 2.0 * PI / sampleCount;
    gl_FragColor = vec4(radianceSum, 1.0);

} else {

    // In case we came across an invalid deferred pixel
    gl_FragColor = vec4(0.0);
}
```

Listing 2.1. SSDO source code.

2.3.2   Indirect Bounces of Light

SSDO can correctly handle directionally varying, incoming light. However, up to now we have described only direct light, which is arriving from an environment map. Additionally, some light is reflected from the surface, resulting in indirect light. Several offline techniques, like Radiosity or Path Tracing can compute such indirect light, but not at real-time frame rates for dynamic scenes. In contrast to this, we work in image space again and use the direct light stored in the frame buffer as a source of indirect light. The work by Mendez et al. [Mendez et al. 06] already mentions such an option: here, an average reflectance color is used to approximate the color bleeding. In contrast to this, we can include the *sender direction* and the actual *sender radiance*. In the previous section, we already classified each sampling point as visible or occluded. If a sampling point is occluded, we assumed that no light is arriving from this direction. But in fact, it is only the direct light which is blocked. Instead, some indirect light is reflected from the blocker position towards the receiver point. To compute this indirect light, we use the pixel color L_{pixel} of each sampling point which was classified as occluded and place a small, colored patch on the surface (an example is shown in Figure 2.8). The pixel normal is used to orient the patch on the surface. Now we compute the fraction of light that is arriving from this sender patch to our receiver point $\mathbf{P}$ using a *form factor*.

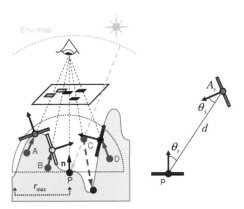

Figure 2.8. For indirect light, a small patch is placed on the surface for each occluder and the direct light stored in the frame buffer is used as sender radiance. To compute the fraction of light arriving at the receiver, we use a simple form factor approximation.

Finally, the indirect light at point $\mathbf{P}$ can be approximated as

$$L_{\text{ind}}(P) = \sum_{i=1}^{N} \frac{\rho}{\pi} \cdot L_{\text{pixel,i}}(\omega_i) \cdot (1 - V(\omega_i)) \cdot F_{rs},$$

where

$$F_{rs} = \frac{A_s \cdot \cos\theta_{s,i} \cdot \cos\theta_{r,i}}{\pi \cdot d_i^2}$$

is a simple form factor approximation that computes the fraction of light, which is transferred from sender s to receiver r. Angles $\theta_{s,i}$ and $\theta_{r,i}$ are the angles between the transmission direction and the sender / receiver normal, and d_i is the distance between sender and receiver. This distance should be clamped to avoid singularity problems. Alternatively, a constant can be added in the denominator. The area of the sender patch is A_s. Since we take the information from a single pixel, we do not know the actual shape of the sender, so we set this value to $A_s = \pi \cdot r_{\text{max}}^2 / N$. If we assume a flat, circular area around $\mathbf{P}$ and use N uniformly distributed samples, each sample will cover this area. Depending on the slope distribution inside the hemisphere, the actual value for can be higher, so we can use this parameter to control the strength of the color bleeding manually. In the example in Figure 2.8, no indirect light is calculated for patch $\mathbf{A}$, because it is back-facing. Patch $\mathbf{C}$ is in the negative half-space of $\mathbf{P}$, so it does not contribute, too. Patches $\mathbf{B}$ and $\mathbf{D}$ are both senders of indirect light. Figure 2.9 shows the visual effect if indirect light is included. Listing 2.2 shows an excerpt of the fragment program that computes the indirect light.

Figure 2.9. Difference between SSAO and SSDO with an additional indirect bounce. Note how the colored cubes reflect colored light onto the ground if they are directly illuminated.

```
// Read the (sender) radiance of the occluder.
vec3 directRadiance = texelFetch2D(directRadianceTexture,
                      ivec2(occluderTexCoord), 0);

// At this point we already know the occluder position and
// normal from the SSDO computation. Now we compute the distance
// vector between sender and receiver.
vec3 delta = position.xyz - occluderPosition.xyz;
vec3 normalizedDelta = normalize(delta);

// Compute the geometric term (the formfactor).
float unclampedBounceGeometricTerm =
    max(0.0, dot(normalizedDelta, -normal)) *
    max(0.0, dot(normalizedDelta, occluderNormal)) /
    dot(delta, delta);

// Clamp geometric term to avoid problems with close occluders.
float bounceGeometricTerm = min(unclampedBounceGeometricTerm,
                  bounceSingularity);

// Compute the radiance at the receiver.
vec3 occluderRadiance = bounceStrength * directRadiance *
                  bounceGeometricTerm;

// Finally, add the indirect light to the sum of indirect light.
occluderRadianceSum += occluderRadiance;
```

Listing 2.2. Source code for indirect light computation. At this point the pixel position and the occluder position / texture coordinate are known from the SSDO computation. This code can be included at the end of the loop in Listing 2.1

2.4   Interleaved Sampling

To reduce the number of samples per pixel we use *interleaved sampling*, as suggested by [Segovia et al. 06] and already used for ambient occlusion, e.g. in [Mittring 07]. Therefore, we pre-compute $M \times M$ sets of N low-discrepancy samples. At runtime, each pixel inside a block of $M \times M$ pixels selects one of the sets. The low-discrepancy sampling ensures that each set contains well-distributed, uniform samples, without a preferred direction. Consequently, a similar illumination is computed for each pixel. However, since we use a quite low number of samples, the repeating $M \times M$ pattern is often visible in the image, and the whole image looks noisy. To remove this noise, a geometry-sensitive blur is finally used. Figure 2.10 shows the original and the blurred image. For the geometry-aware blur, a kernel size of approximately $M \times M$ removes most of the noise. The filter we use inspects all values inside the filter kernel, but the average is computed only for those pixels with a position and normal which is similar to the position and normal of the center pixel. To avoid blurring over material edges, we apply this filter to irradiance values and multiply with the (colored) pixel reflectance after blurring. To further improve the rendering speed, a separated filter can be used: first, a vertical filter $(1 \times M)$ is used and then the output is passed to a horizonal filter $(M \times 1)$. Although this concatenation of two one-dimensional filters is not perfectly identical to the original two-dimensional filter [Pham and van Vliet 05], this is a useful approximation in many practical cases. Please have a look at the demo, available at http://www.akpeters.com/gpupro, to see the strong similarity of both filters and the difference in rendering speed.

Figure 2.10. Interleaved sampling. By using a different set of sampling points for each pixel, the original image looks noisy and the repeating $M \times M$ pattern is visible (left). This noise can be removed with a geometry-sensitive blur filter of approximately the pattern size (right).

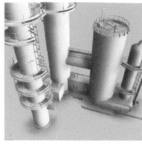

Figure 2.11. Varying the number of samples per pixel (from left to right: 4, 8, 16, and 32).

2.5   Discussion

Our method is an approximation of global illumination that correctly displays oriented and colored shadows as well as approximated indirect light, which is entirely computed in image space. The time and quality depends on several parameters: first of all, the number of samples N determines the quality of the resulting shadows, as shown in Figure 2.11. The corresponding timings are listed in Table 2.1. When increasing the search radius, more blockers can be found, but the sampling density is reduced if N is kept fixed. Figure 2.12 shows the effect of this. Increasing the radius of the hemisphere results in larger shadows, but shadows of small details start to disappear. A higher number of samples can be used to bring these shadows back.

Although we achieve plausible illumination, such an approach has several limitations. First of all, we can only simulate occlusion or indirect light which is visible in the frame buffer. If a blocker is not visible it will never throw a shadow.

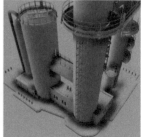

Figure 2.12. When varying the radius of the hemisphere, different types of shadows become visible. Using a small radius shows the shadows of the ladder and the small sticks on the ground. When increasing the radius (and keeping the number of samples fixed), these shadows disappear; shadows of larger structures, like the contact shadows of the tower, start to appear. Further increasing the radius results in larger shadows.

Resolution	N	SSDO	Indirect Light
512×512	4	2.1	1.0
512×512	8	3.4	3.8
512×512	16	9.4	5.0
512×512	32	16.4	8.9
1024×1024	4	9.2	2.9
1024×1024	8	18.2	8.4
1024×1024	16	32.1	17.9
1024×1024	32	60.2	37.0

Table 2.1. SSDO and indirect light timing values for different frame buffer resolutions and varying number of samples. All timing values are in milliseconds, measured on a NVIDIA GeForce GTX 280 graphics card.

This can happen for two reasons: the blocker is occluded by some other object from the current viewpoint or the blocker is outside the viewing frustum. For a moving camera, this can result in shadows that disappear and reappear later. The same can happen for sources of indirect light: anything which is not visible in the camera image will not create indirect light. Both cases can be solved by depth peeling and additional cameras, as shown in [Ritschel et al. 09]. However, the frame rate drops since we have to render the scene several times from several viewpoints. The use of a voxel model seems to be a promising alternative, as recently shown by [Reinbothe et al. 09].

2.6 Conclusion

In this article, we presented screen-space directional occlusion (SSDO). This technique is an improvement over ambient occlusion and allows fast computation of directional occlusion and indirect light, both entirely computed in image space. Due to the plausible results we think that SSDO can make its way into upcoming computer games for approximate real-time global illumination of large and dynamic scenes.

Bibliography

[Bunnell 06] M Bunnell. "Dynamic Ambient Occlusion and Indirect Lighting." In *GPU Gems 2*, edited by W. Engel, pp. 223–233. Addison-Wesley, 2006.

[Hoberock and Jia 07] Jared Hoberock and Yuntao Jia. "High-Quality Ambient Occlusion." In *GPU Gems 3*, Chapter 12. Reading, MA: Addison-Wesley, 2007.

[Landis 02] H. Landis. "RenderMan in Production." In *ACM SIGGRAPH 2002 Course 16*, 2002.

[Mendez et al. 06] A. Mendez, M. Sbert, J. Cata, N. Sunyer, and S. Funtane. "Realtime Obscurances with Color Bleeding." In *ShaderX4: Advanced Rendering Techniques*, pp. 121–133. Charles River Media, 2006.

[Mittring 07] Martin Mittring. "Finding Next-Gen: CryEngine 2." In *SIGGRAPH '07: ACM SIGGRAPH 2007 courses*, pp. 97–121. New York: ACM, 2007.

[Pham and van Vliet 05] T.Q. Pham and L.J. van Vliet. "Separable Bilateral Filtering for Fast Video Preprocessing." *IEEE International Conference on Multimedia and Expo.*

[Reinbothe et al. 09] Christoph Reinbothe, Tamy Boubekeur, and Marc Alexa. "Hybrid Ambient Occlusion." *EUROGRAPHICS 2009 Areas Papers.*

[Ritschel et al. 09] Tobias Ritschel, Thorsten Grosch, and Hans-Peter Seidel. "Approximating Dynamic Global Illumination in Image Space." In *Proceedings ACM SIGGRAPH Symposium on Interactive 3D Graphics and Games (I3D) 2009*, pp. 75–82, 2009.

[Segovia et al. 06] Benjamin Segovia, Jean-Claude Iehl, Richard Mitanchey, and Bernard Péroche. "Non-interleaved Deferred Shading of Interleaved Sample Patterns." In *SIGGRAPH/Eurographics Graphics Hardware*, 2006.

[Shanmugam and Arikan 07] Perumaal Shanmugam and Okan Arikan. "Hardware Accelerated Ambient Occlusion Techniques on GPUs." In *Proceedings of the ACM SIGGRAPH Symposium on Interactive 3D Graphics and Games*, pp. 73–80. ACM, 2007.

Real-Time Multi-Bounce Ray-Tracing with Geometry Impostors

Péter Dancsik and László Szécsi

Rendering reflective and refractive objects or their caustics is a challenging problem in real-time applications. It requires non-local shading, which is intricate with the incremental rendering pipeline, where a fragment shader can only work with local, interpolated vertex data and textures to find the color of a surface point. The above effects are usually associated with ray-tracing, which does not offer the same performance as incremental rendering. Typically, ray-tracing effects are added into real-time scenes using specialized tricks based on texturing. These usually assume that there is only one reflective or refractive object in the scene, and that it is enough to consider only one or two bounces of light. In this article, we follow a similar practical philosophy, but remove these limitations in order to be able to render scenes like a complete chessboard full of glass pieces, or even refractive objects submerged into animated liquids.

We extend previous approximate ray-tracing techniques that were based on environment distance impostors [Szirmay-Kalos et al. 05] in order to handle scenes with multiple reflective and refractive objects in real time. There are two key ideas that allow this. First we turn around the distance impostor approach not to intersect internal rays with enclosing environmental geometry, but external rays with an object. We show how the secondary reflected and refracted rays can be traced efficiently. We also examine how other types of geometry impostors—namely geometry images [Carr et al. 06] and height fields [Oliveira et al. 00, Policarpo et al. 05]—can be adapted to the same task.

The second idea is the separation of static and dynamic objects. Classic distance impostors can be used for the static environment, and only the environment impostors of moving objects need to be updated in every frame. Light paths passing through moving objects can be found by searching their geometry impostors.

The proposed rendering method maintains impostors of object meshes as well as impostors for the environment of reflective or refractive objects. When such an object is rendered, the shader uses both the environment impostor and impostors of other objects to find intersections of secondary rays. In the following article we first examine what impostor representations we can use and how they can be used for intersection. We then deal with strategies to organize static and dynamic geometry into the environment and object impostors to facilitate real-time rendering.

3.1   Geometry Impostors

Ray-tracing requires the intersection of a light ray with scene geometry. In order to make this feasible in real-time applications, instead of intersecting a ray with actual geometry primitives, approximate representations are used. Typically, the scene is rendered into a texture from a cleverly selected reference point, and this texture is queried for intersections. When the origin of the ray is not the same as the reference point, then finding the intersection becomes a search process using consecutive dependant texture fetches. There are several approaches on how to render the geometry into textures, and how to search for the intersections using these representations. All of them use a texture as a stand-in for the actual geometry. We refer to these textures as geometry impostors.

When a ray intersects the geometry, the next step is shading the intersected surface point, meaning that we have to find the radiance emitted towards the ray origin. Therefore, a texel of an impostor has to store shading information in addition to the location of the surface point. Typically, this means that the radiance emitted towards the reference point is evaluated and stored when creating the impostor, hoping that the ray origin will not be very far from the reference point, or that the surfaces are diffuse, and the direction we look at them from does not matter. In case of highly specular surfaces, however, we need to store the surface normal vector so that we can evaluate the shading formula exactly.

In case of mirror-like or glassy objects, the color of the surface is usually uniform and does not need to be stored in every texel, but the surface normal is important as it is necessary for the computation of secondary rays.

3.1.1   Distance Impostors

Distance impostors are very much like environment maps, but they also contain the distance between a reference point and the surface points visible in the texels. This can be stored in the alpha channel conveniently. They are usually cube maps,

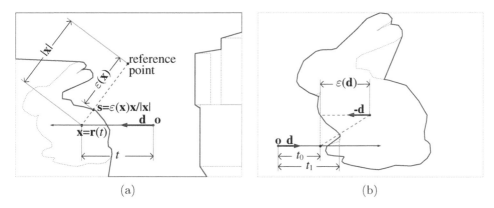

(a)   (b)

Figure 3.1. (a) Environment distance impostor nomenclature. (b) Object distance impostor with the first two steps of projection search.

addressable with the direction from the reference point. In case of reflective and refractive objects, the cube map contains the distance and the surface normal, and is called a *distance-normal impostor*.

If not all points of the geometry are visible from the reference point, the nonvisible parts will be missing in the impostor. Therefore, this representation works best with star-convex objects.

In this article, we use two distinct types of distance impostors. One of them is the *environment distance impostor* (Figure 3.1(a)). This is a cube map that contains the surrounding geometry of an object, and thus typically has multiple objects rendered onto it. We can assume that all ray origins are inside the environment, but the bounding box of included geometry is unknown. The other type of distance impostor contains a single object (Figure 3.1(b)). Rays to be traced might arrive from the outside, and the bounding box of the object is known. The objects handled this way are typically mirror or glass objects, which means these are usually distance-normal impostors.

3.1.2 Height Maps

Height maps are a classic and straightforward way of encoding 2.5-dimensional geometry in two-dimensional texture maps. The most prominent example is bump mapping, used mostly to add detail to triangle mesh models. To get a height map, the geometry is rendered onto a reference plane using an orthogonal projection, and every texel contains the distance of the surface point from the plane. There are numerous displacement mapping techniques [Szirmay-Kalos and Umenhoffer 08], ranging from bump mapping to relaxed cone tracing, that solve the ray–height map intersection problem with varying accuracy. Out of those, binary search is a simple-to-implement, solid and effective technique, even though it does not guarantee to find the first intersection.

Typically two height maps, storing displacements on the two sides of the reference plane, are needed to approximate a solid object. This representation requires a dimension along which the depth structure of the solid is simple, but arbitrary concavities are allowed in the other two dimensions.

If the solid is symmetric to the reference plane, a single height map is enough. If it has some rotational symmetry, then the reference plane can be rotated around the axis of symmetry without changing the geometry or the height map. When searching for an intersection, we can rotate the plane like a billboard to get optimal results. All intersection search algorithms perform best when the incoming rays arrive perpendicular to the reference plane.

3.1.3   Geometry Images

Geometry images [Carr et al. 06] also map surface points to a texture, but do so without projection to an image plane, using the classic UV-mapping instead. Thus finding an intersection with a ray cannot be done using a search that exploits the relation of texel coordinates and surface point locations. Instead, a bounding-volume hierarchy is built over the texels and stored in mipmap levels. The intersection algorithm is thus similar to that of ray-tracing with bounding volume hierarchies. The upside is that geometry of any complexity can be stored, but the intersection is more expensive to compute.

3.2   Intersection Computation with an Environment Distance Impostor

We can think of the environment visible from the reference point as the surface of a single, manifold object, as shown in Figure 3.1. To handle directions where nothing is visible, we can assume a skybox at a large but finite distance. The ray origin is always within the environment surface, and there always is an intersection. The ray equation is $\mathbf{r}(t) = \mathbf{o} + t\mathbf{d}$, where $\mathbf{o}$ is the ray origin, $\mathbf{d}$ is the ray direction, and t is the ray parameter. Let us use a coordinate system that has the reference point at its origin. Querying the environment with a point $\mathbf{x}$ returns $\varepsilon(\mathbf{x})$, which is the distance of the environment surface point $\mathbf{s}$ that is visible towards $\mathbf{x}$. We can compute $\mathbf{s}$ as $\varepsilon(\mathbf{x})\mathbf{x}/|\mathbf{x}|$.

At the intersection point, $\varepsilon(\mathbf{x}) = |\mathbf{x}|$, and the ratio $|\mathbf{x}|/\varepsilon(\mathbf{x})$ is one. Let $\delta(t)$ be $|\mathbf{r}(t)|/\varepsilon(\mathbf{r}(t))$, a function that computes this ratio for a point at a given ray parameter t. We call a ray parameter t' an undershooting if $\delta(t') < 1$, and an overshooting if $\delta(t') > 1$.

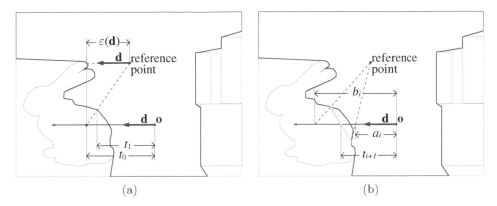

Figure 3.2. Projection and false position search in environment impostors.

We have to find the ray parameter $t^\star$ of the intersection. We use the iterative process proposed by Szirmay-Kalos [Szirmay-Kalos et al. 05], constructing a sequence of values $t_0, t_1, \ldots$ that converges to $t^\star$. Figure 3.2 shows how the values are generated. We start the first phase, which we call projection search, with classic environment mapping, querying the distance map for the ray direction, yielding distance $\varepsilon(\mathbf{d})$. This gives us an environment surface point at $\mathbf{d}\varepsilon(\mathbf{d})$. We look for the point on the ray which is the closest to this surface point. Its ray parameter t_0 can be computed as

$$t_0 = \varepsilon(\mathbf{d}) - \mathbf{o} \cdot \mathbf{d}.$$

The ray point can again be used to query the environment distance map, restarting the process. In general, the iteration can be written as

$$t_{i+1} = t_i + \varepsilon(\mathbf{d})(1 - \delta(t_i)).$$

Note that this sequence is not mathematically guaranteed to converge to the intersection, but it is easy to compute and works for practical scenes. A case that we still need to avoid is that the sequence oscillates and does not converge to the actual solution. Therefore we keep track of the largest undershooting (a_i denotes its value at the ith iteration) and the smallest overshooting (b_i at the ith iteration). As soon as we have one of both, we can switch to the false position root-finding method, depicted in Figure 3.2. We get the new guess for the ray parameter as

$$t_{i+1} = \frac{[\delta(b_i) - 1]\, a_i - [\delta(a_i) - 1]\, b_i}{\delta(b_i) - \delta(a_i)}.$$

We also update the undershooting or the overshooting value

$$a_{i+1} = \begin{cases} a_i & \text{if } \delta(t_{i+1}) > 1, \\ t_{i+1} & \text{if } \delta(t_{i+1}) < 1, \end{cases}$$

$$b_{i+1} = \begin{cases} t_{i+1} & \text{if } \delta(t_{i+1}) > 1, \\ b_i & \text{if } \delta(t_{i+1}) < 1. \end{cases}$$

Note that it is possible to use the false position root-finding method exclusively, with $a_0 = 0$, which is always an undershooting, and a sufficiently large b_0 to guarantee an overshooting.

3.3   Ray-Object Intersection Using Distance Impostors

First we calculate the intersections with the bounding box of the object. If there are none, then neither will there be any intersection with the object.

The most important difference between the ray–environment intersection and the ray–object intersection is that the ray origin is not within the surface, and an intersection is not guaranteed. However, if there is an intersection, then we can compute it as the intersection of a new ray started along the original one, from within the object, and in the opposing direction. The resulting search process is depicted in Figure 3.1. If there is no intersection, the algorithm returns a bogus result, but it is easy to check whether the δ value is near one, which holds true only for real intersections.

3.4   Ray-Object Intersection Using Height Maps

The two halves of the object are approximated by two height map impostors. When looking for an intersection with a ray, we call them the near half and the far half, depending on the ray direction and irrespective of the actual position of the ray origin. The solution of the ray–height map intersection problem is very similar to the search we performed in distance impostors. Let $z(\mathbf{x})$ be the distance of point $\mathbf{x}$ from the reference plane, and $h(\mathbf{x})$ the geometry height at the orthogonal projection of $\mathbf{x}$ onto the plane. We call a ray parameter a an undershooting if $z(\mathbf{r}(a)) > h(\mathbf{r}(a))$, and call b an overshooting if $z(\mathbf{r}(b)) < h(\mathbf{r}(b))$. Starting with an initial search range of (a_0, b_0), we iterate to get a convergent sequence just like we did with the false position method. However, now we use binary search (see [Oliveira et al. 00], [Policarpo et al. 05]). The next element is always computed as

$$t_{i+1} = \frac{a_i + b_i}{2}.$$

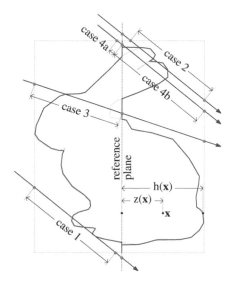

Figure 3.3. Height impostor.

The undershooting or the overshooting value is updated just like in the false position method. Note that binary search does not actually require us to query $h(a_0)$ or $h(b_0)$. Thus, if an adequate search range has already been obtained, it is preferable to the false position method. Furthermore, if both endpoints of the search range happen to be undershootings, binary search still has a decent chance to hit an actual overshooting, delivering a correct result. The false position method would instantly step out of the search range in such a situation.

With binary search, we need to identify the initial search ranges in the near and far height maps. First, we calculate the intersection ray parameters with the reference plane and with the bounding box of the object (see Figure 3.3). The ray crosses the plane at t_{plane}, enters the bounding box at t_{enter}, and leaves at t_{exit}. If the ray does not intersect the bounding box, then there will be no intersection with the object either. If $t_{\text{exit}} < t_{\text{plane}}$ (case 1 in Figure 3.3), we only need to search the height map of the near half between t_{enter} and t_{exit}. Likewise, if $t_{\text{plane}} < t_{\text{enter}}$ (case 2), we only have to search the height map of the far half between the entrance and exit points. Otherwise we first search the height map of the near half between t_{enter} and t_{plane} (case 3 and 4a). If no intersection has been found, we also search the far half between t_{plane} and t_{exit} (case 4b).

Note that binary search is not guaranteed to find the first intersection, and in cases 1 and 2 it can happen that both endpoints of the search range are undershootings. However, a tightly fitting bounding box minimizes those cases, and binary search often performs flawlessly in practice.

3.5   Tracing Multiple Refractions within a Single Object

Using any of the above impostors—or even geometry images—we can store surface
normals and use the surface normal at the found intersection point to spawn
refraction or reflection rays. Tracing these against the geometry can again be done
with the previously discussed methods, continuing up to an arbitrary number of
bounces. Two refractions within an object are typically sufficient to get plausible
results. When objects are rendered incrementally, we still can use the impostor
to trace secondary rays in the pixel shader.

3.6   Multiple Ray Bounces with Object Impostors Only

Rigid bodies like glass objects can have their impostors computed only once, when
loading the model geometry, and the impostors of dynamic geometries like fluids
must be rendered in every frame. Identical objects can share impostors. It is
straightforward to construct a ray tracer once all the objects in the scene have
their own object impostors. Simply, all objects must be intersected with all rays,
always keeping the smallest positive intersection. Exceptions can be made for
rays started within objects, where it is sufficient to only search the impostor of
the containing object itself. The first intersection with the eye rays can easily be
found by rasterization, and then the pixel shader operating on these first bounce
points can perform the rest of the ray-tracing.

However, for a reasonably populated scene, this approach is prohibitively expensive. One way to attack the problem would be to use spatial subdivision
schemes like regular grids or bounding volume hierarchies to decrease the number
of intersection computations. We found that maintaining and traversing these
structures carries an overhead that is in a higher order of magnitude than intersection searches themselves. Thus, they start to pay off at high object counts, and
less so in typical real-time rendering scenes. That said, a complete ray-tracing solution could be built on impostors and bounding volume hierarchies, without the
need to make assumptions on the dynamism of objects in the scene. In this article,
we discard this option in favor of real-time rendering of more typical scenes.

3.7   Multiple Ray Bounces with Environment Distance
Impostors Only

Every reflective or refractive object in the scene can have its own environment
distance impostor, storing the incoming radiance in every pixel. If there is any
kind of dynamism in the scene, then the environment impostors have to be
re-rendered in every frame. In the final to-screen pass, diffuse objects can be

rendered normally. The pixel shader of refractive or reflective objects has to perform a simple intersection search with the environment to obtain reflected colors.

Note that we can use the very same rendering algorithm also when creating the environment impostors, meaning that proper reflections will appear in the environment map itself. Of course, in the very first frame, the environment maps will only contain the diffuse color information. In the second frame, we can use the maps of the first frame when creating the new impostors, which will already contain reflections of a single bounce. In later frames, impostors will contain more and more bounces, even if somewhat delayed. Thus, multi-bounce rendering is fairly automatic. However, updating all cube maps requires a large number of rendering passes, which is not feasible in every frame. Applications mostly get around this by allowing only a single reflective object or by reflecting a static environment only.

3.8   Combination of Environment and Object Impostors

The object impostor method works great as long as we only have few objects, and environment impostors are effective if the environment is static. In a typical scene, only few objects are moving. Thus, it is possible to use environment impostors that do not need to be updated in every frame for the static environment, and add the moving objects back by using object impostors.

First, every refractive or reflective object should have an impostor of its own static environment, and only these have to be updated regularly (though not necessarily in every frame that belongs to moving objects). We also need object impostors for all meshes used by specular objects, for both multiple refraction and intersection with external rays.

Whenever a reflective or refractive object is rendered, the secondary rays are traced against the static environment using the environment impostor of the rendered object, and against all of the moving objects using their object impostors; this keeps the nearest result. The rendered object itself—if it happens to be a moving object—is excluded from intersections with the secondary rays. Figure 3.4 illustrates this process. At the shaded surface point (1), the reflection and refraction rays are generated, and the refraction ray is tested against the object impostor to get the exit point (2) and the second refraction. Then both exiting rays are tested against the environment (3 and 4) and the object impostors of moving objects. In the depicted example, the reflection ray hits such an object (5). There the process starts from the beginning, using the object impostor (6) and environment impostor (7 and 8) of the moving object. However, we do not test the exiting reflection and refraction rays for intersection with other moving objects anymore, as those would be hardly noticeable in the rendered image.

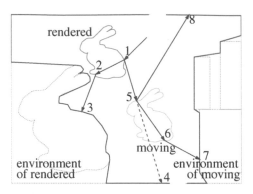

Figure 3.4. Combination of environment and object impostors.

3.9   Caustics and Shadows

As described by Wyman [Wyman and Davis 06], caustics can be rendered effectively using approximate geometry representations by tracing light paths from light sources. The geometry impostors can also be used this way. We render the scene placing a camera at the light source, with a shader that outputs the texture coordinates of diffuse surfaces hit after multiple bounces. Then these photon hits are splatted into the caustic light maps as small billboards, as described in [Szirmay-Kalos et al. 05]. The caustic light maps are used to modulate the diffuse color when rendering the objects. To add shadows, we used conventional shadow mapping.

Caustics or shadows due to moving objects can cause changing lighting conditions on static objects as well. This would invalidate the environment impostors of static objects, forcing us to update them in every frame, jeopardizing real-time performance and undermining the concept of separation of static and moving objects. There are two solutions to this problem. First, if we can identify potential caustics and shadow receivers, we can handle them as moving objects when tracing reflection and refraction rays. These objects are diffuse, so we can stop the process depicted in Figure 3.4 at hit 5. Second, we can avoid invalidating the static environment impostors by storing the texture coordinates instead of diffuse colors. When an intersection with the environment is found, the diffuse texture and the caustics light map can be accessed to determine the surface color. This requires a uniformly addressable texture mapping covering the complete static geometry, which can be a single UV-atlas or a texture array of individual UV-atlases, where supported.

3.10 Example Application: Glass Chess

A diffuse chessboard with a complete set of glass pieces—only one of them moving at any time—is an ideal scenario for the presented method. There are only seven meshes used (the board and the six chess piece types); thus only seven object impostors are required. All objects are symmetrical, accurately represented by height maps. Apart from the knight, all pieces exhibit cylindrical symmetry, allowing us to rotate the reference plane freely around the vertical axis. The chessboard itself is diffuse, and it is the only caustics and shadow receiver. It is handled as a moving object because of its dynamic lighting.

In every frame the shadow map, the caustics light map, and the environment impostor of the moving piece are updated. The object impostors and the environment impostors of stationary pieces remain unchanged. When rendering an object, the pixel shader intersects the reflected and refracted rays with the environment impostor, the chessboard, and the moving piece. When a new piece starts moving, the previously moving piece becomes stationary. All environment impostors must be updated to exclude the new moving piece and include the old one.

The chessboard scene with 33 glass pieces (a full chess set plus a sphere of glass) was rendered at a 640×480 resolution (see Figure 3.5 for screenshots). The height map impostors had 512×512 resolution, while the environment and object impostors had $6 \times 256 \times 256$ and $6 \times 512 \times 512$ texels, respectively. We

Figure 3.5. Left: the whole test scene. Right: double refraction using height map impostors.

	Height Map	Distance Impostor
No moving objects	102	188
Classic	2.5	3.5
Combined	22	35

Table 3.1. Frames per second rates achieved with different rendering algorithms and impostor representations.

used an NVIDIA GeForce 8800GTX graphics card for measurements. Table 3.1 summarizes the results. We compared three algorithms. In the first case, no objects were moving, and therefore it was not necessary to update any of the impostors in any frame. In the second case, we used the classic method described in Section 3.7, where environment impostors have to be updated in every frame. The last line of the table shows frame rates for our proposed method combining environment and object impostors. All cases were measured with both height map and distance cube map object impostors. As these impostors are used in all three algorithms for computing multiple refractions within objects, this choice impacts frame rates in all the three cases. The proposed method was ten times faster than the classic approach with both impostor representations.

3.11   Example Application: Alien Pool

The second application demonstrates how dynamic surfaces and intersecting refractive objects can be handled by placing an ice object into a pool of fluid. The static but caustics-receiving environment consists of the diffuse walls of the room. The container walls themselves form a reflective, transparent cylinder. Within the container, the liquid and the floating object are reflective and refractive moving objects.

The motion of the liquid is synthetized using ripple height maps, and the resulting surface can also be represented by a height map impostor. The floating object is star-convex and well approximated by an object distance impostor.

Even though the static environment is a caustics receiver, we avoid re-rendering the static environment impostor in every frame by storing the texture coordinates instead of diffuse colors, as described in Section 3.9. This map has a resolution of $6 \times 512 \times 512$ texels. Otherwise the settings were identical to those listed in Section 3.10. Figure 3.6 shows reflected and refracted light forming dynamic caustics patterns in the test scene. We measured 50 frames per second using both a geometry image for the floating solid and a distance object impostor.

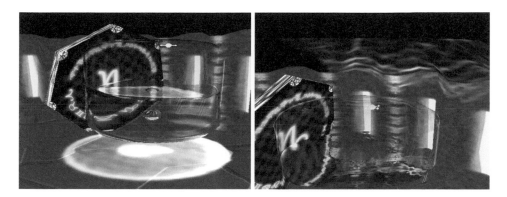

Figure 3.6. Left: refracted caustics under the pool. Right: reflected caustics above the pool.

3.12   Conclusion

With the use of geometry impostors, we can render convincing, complex ray-tracing effects in real-time applications. The two key points are: choosing a good representation for our geometry that avoids losing detail, but allows for fast intersection tests; and separating the static and dynamic aspects of the scene, so that we have to update only a few impostors in every frame. In our experience, cube map distance impostors are good approximations for even strongly concave environment geometries, with the relatively high construction cost amortized if we store only the static environment in such maps. Height map impostors proved to be surprisingly versatile and also well applicable to animated meshes. Finally, the separation of moving objects and handling them with object impostors made it possible to render multi-bounce effects in real time, in scenes densely populated with mirror-like and glass objects.

Bibliography

[Carr et al. 06] N.A. Carr, J. Hoberock, K. Crane, and J.C. Hart. "Fast GPU Ray Tracing of Dynamic Meshes Using Geometry Images." In *Proceedings of Graphics Interface 2006*, pp. 203–209. Toronto: Canadian Information Processing Society, 2006.

[Oliveira et al. 00] Manuel M. Oliveira, Gary Bishop, and David McAllister. "Relief Texture Mapping." *Proceedings of SIGGRAPH 2000*.

[Policarpo et al. 05] Fabio Policarpo, Manuel M. Oliveira, and J. L. D. Comba. "Real-Time Relief Mapping on Arbitrary Poligonal Surfaces." *ACM SIGGRAPH 2005 Symposium on Interactice 3D Graphics and Games.*

[Szirmay-Kalos and Umenhoffer 08] L. Szirmay-Kalos and T. Umenhoffer. "Displacement Mapping on the GPU-State of the Art." In *Computer Graphics Forum*, 27, 27, pp. 1567–1592. Citeseer, 2008.

[Szirmay-Kalos et al. 05] Laszlo Szirmay-Kalos, Barnabas Aszodi, Istvan Lazanyi, and Matyas Premecz. "Approximate Ray-Tracing on the GPU with Distance Impostors." *Computer Graphics Forum 24.*

[Wyman and Davis 06] Chris Wyman and Scott Davis. "Interactive Image-Space Techniques for Approximating Caustics." In *I3D '06: Proceedings of the 2006 Symposium on Interactive 3D Graphics and Games*, pp. 153–160. New York: ACM, 2006.

Image Space

In this section we will cover various algorithms that operate primarily in image space. Graphics programmers chose to work in image space for a number of reasons. Some techniques naturally map this space while others seek to exploit screen space because it offers an implicit LOD and visibility is handled automatically. The variety of algorithms in this section, drawing from several subfields of computer graphics, speaks to the power and convenience of working in screen space.

The first article in the image space section, "Anisotropic Kuwahara Filtering on the GPU," by Jan Eric Kyprianidis, Henry Kang, and Jürgen Döllner, describes a very interesting method for creating abstracted, non-photorealistic images by applying an anisotropic Kuwahara filter. The authors demonstrate a GPU implementation of the filter, which can be used for post-processing pre-rendered images to make them more artful. It could also be used in real time for creating stylized games.

Our next article tackles the challenge of anti-aliasing geometric edges in rendered scenes. As Hugh Malan discusses in his articles, "Edge Anti-aliasing by Post-Processing," standard multi-sampled anti-aliasing has a number of downfalls, one of which is that it is difficult to incorporate into a deferred renderer. This article provides a screen-space solution for anti-aliasing and is compatible with rendering engines that make use of deferred shading.

In "Environment Mapping with Floyd-Steinberg Halftoning," written by László Szirmay-Kalos, László Szécsi, and Anton Penzov, an algorithm is presented for computing importance samples using the GPU. This algorithm uses a clever application of a classic halftoning technique and is useful for accelerating the importance-sampling step in high quality environment mapped lighting.

Next, Thomas Engelhardt and Carsten Dachsbacher cover an algorithm for computing occluded sets in their article "Hierarchical Item Buffers for Granular Occlusion Culling." This technique demonstrates a method for computing sets of visible and occluded objects entirely on the GPU, thus allowing a renderer to skip objects that will not be visible in the final image.

In a more traditional screen space approach, "Real-Time Screen Space Cloud Lighting," Kaori Kubota discusses an efficient but visually compelling method for simulating lit clouds. Physically based cloud lighting algorithms are very computationally demanding. This article takes the approach of recreating the look of cloud lighting without depending on expensive, physically based simulation.

Depth of field is a very important visual element in many games and feature films. Artists can use depth of field to direct the viewer's eyes to a certain part of the screen or to provide a dramatic transition. In "Realistic Depth of Field in Postproduction," by David Illes and Peter Horvath, a high quality depth of field implementation suitable for GPU acceleration is described.

The final article in this section is "Screen-Space Subsurface Scattering," by Jorge Jimenez and Diego Gutierrez. The authors present an interesting twist on subsurface scattering; they describe a way to compute it in screen space. Some of the benefits of computing subsurface scattering in screen space are that it provides an implicit level of detail (objects farther from the viewer appear smaller on screen), and it dramatically decreases the number of draw calls and number of render targets necessary with more traditional texture-space algorithms.

The diversity of the methods discussed in this section demonstrates the growing popularity of image space algorithms. This popularity is due in part to the convenience of working with pixel buffers in their natural space on the GPU, but also because of the various other properties inherent in screen space.

—Christopher Oat

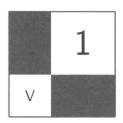

Anisotropic Kuwahara Filtering on the GPU

Jan Eric Kyprianidis, Henry Kang, and Jürgen Döllner

1.1   Introduction

Photorealistic depictions often contain more information than necessary to communicate the intended information. Artists therefore typically remove detail and use abstraction for effective visual communication. A typical approach to

Figure 1.1. Original image (left). Output of the anisotropic Kuwahara filter (right). A painting-like flattening effect is generated along the local feature directions, while preserving shape boundaries.

automatically create stylized abstractions from images or videos is the use of an *edge-preserving* filter. Popular examples *of* edge-preserving filters used for image abstraction are the *bilateral* filter [Tomasi and Manduchi 98] and *mean shift* [Comaniciu and Meer 02]. Both smooth low-contrast regions while preserving high-contrast edges. Therefore they may fail for high-contrast images, where either no abstraction is performed or relevant information is removed because of the thresholds used. They also often fail for low-contrast images, where typically too much information is removed.

An edge-preserving filter that overcomes this limitation is the *Kuwahara filter* [Kuwahara et al. 76]. Based on local area flattening, the Kuwahara filter properly removes details even in a high-contrast region, and protects shape boundaries even in low-contrast regions. Hence it helps to maintain a roughly uniform level of abstraction across the image, while providing an overall painting-style look. Unfortunately the Kuwahara filter is unstable in the presence of noise and suffers from block artifacts. Several extensions and modifications have been proposed to improve the original Kuwahara filter. A discussion can be found in [Papari et al. 07].

In this chapter we present an implementation of the anisotropic Kuwahara filter [Kyprianidis et al. 09]. The anisotropic Kuwahara filter is a generalization of the Kuwahara filter that avoids artifacts by adapting shape, scale, and orientation of the filter to the local structure of the input. Due to this adaption, directional image features are better preserved and emphasized. This results in overall sharper edges and a more feature-abiding painterly effect.

1.2   Kuwahara Filtering

The general idea behind the Kuwahara filter is to divide the filter kernel into four rectangular subregions which overlap by one pixel. The filter response is then defined by the mean of a subregion with minimum variance (Figure 1.2).

Let $f\colon \mathbb{Z}^2 \longrightarrow \mathbb{R}^3$ denote the input image, let $r > 0$ be the radius of the filter and let $(x_0, y_0) \in \mathbb{Z}^2$ be a point. The rectangular subregions are then given by

$$
\begin{aligned}
W_0 &= [x_0 - r, x_0] \times [y_0, y_0 + r], \\
W_1 &= [x_0, x_0 + r] \times [y_0, y_0 + r], \\
W_2 &= [x_0, x_0 + r] \times [y_0 - r, y_0], \\
W_3 &= [x_0 - r, x_0] \times [y_0 - r, y_0].
\end{aligned}
$$

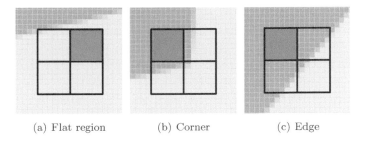

(a) Flat region   (b) Corner   (c) Edge

Figure 1.2. The Kuwahara filter divides the filter kernel into four rectangular subregions. The filter response is then defined by the mean of a subregion with minimum variance.

Let $|W_k| = (r+1)^2$ be the number of pixel in each subregion. The mean (average) of a subregion W_k is then defined as:

$$m_k = \frac{1}{|W_k|} \sum_{(x,y) \in W_k} f(x,y).$$

The variance is defined as the average of the square of the distance of each pixel to the mean:

$$s_k^2 = \frac{1}{|W_k|} \sum_{(x,y) \in W_k} \left(f(x,y) - m_k \right)^2$$

$$= \frac{1}{|W_k|} \sum_{(x,y) \in W_k} f^2(x,y) - m_k.$$

Assuming that the variances of the color channels do not correlate, we define the variance of the subregion W_k to be the sum of the squared variances of

Figure 1.3. Output of the Kuwahara filter.

```
uniform sampler2D src;
uniform int radius;

void main (void) {
  vec2 src_size = textureSize2D(src, 0);
  vec2 uv = gl_FragCoord.xy / src_size;
  float n = float((radius + 1) * (radius + 1));

  vec3 m[4];
  vec3 s[4];
  for (int k = 0; k < 4; ++k) {
    m[k] = vec3(0.0);
    s[k] = vec3(0.0);
  }

  struct Window { int x1, y1, x2, y2; };
  Window W[4] = Window[4](
    Window( -radius, -radius,       0,        0 ),
    Window(       0, -radius, radius,        0 ),
    Window(       0,       0, radius, radius ),
    Window( -radius,       0,       0, radius )
  );

  for (int k = 0; k < 4; ++k) {
    for (int j = W[k].y1; j <= W[k].y2; ++j) {
      for (int i = W[k].x1; i <= W[k].x2; ++i) {
        vec3 c = texture2D(src, uv + vec2(i,j) / src_size).rgb;
        m[k] += c;
        s[k] += c * c;
      }
    }
  }

  float min_sigma2 = 1e+2;
  for (int k = 0; k < 4; ++k) {
    m[k] /= n;
    s[k] = abs(s[k] / n - m[k] * m[k]);

    float sigma2 = s[k].r + s[k].g + s[k].b;
    if (sigma2 < min_sigma2) {
      min_sigma2 = sigma2;
      gl_FragColor = vec4(m[k], 1.0);
    }
  }
}
```

Listing 1.1. Fragment shader implementation of the Kuwahara filter.

the color channels:

$$\sigma_k^2 = s_{k,r}^2 + s_{k,g}^2 + s_{k,b}^2. \tag{1.1}$$

Now, the output of the Kuwahara filter is defined as the mean of a subregion with minimum variance:

$$F(x_0, y_0) := m_i, \quad i = \mathrm{argmin}_k \, \sigma_k.$$

In Figure 1.3 the output of an image processed with the Kuwahara filter is shown. Clearly noticeable are the artifacts in the output. These are due to the use of rectangular subregions. In addition, the subregion selection process is unstable if noise is present or subregions have the same variance. This results in randomly chosen subregions and corresponding artifacts. A more detailed discussion of limitations of the Kuwahara filter can be found in [Papari et al. 07]. An implementation of the Kuwahara filter is shown in Listing 1.1.

1.3   Generalized Kuwahara Filtering

Several attempts have been made to address the limitations of the Kuwahara filter. In this section we present an implementation of the generalized Kuwahara filter, which was first proposed in [Papari et al. 07]. To overcome the limitations of the unstable subregion selection process, a new criterion is defined. Instead of selecting a single subregion, the result is defined as the weighted sum of the means of the subregions. The weights are defined based on the variances of the subregions. This results in smoother region boundaries and fewer artifacts. To improve this further, the rectangular subregions are replaced by smooth weighting functions over sectors of a disc (Figure 1.4). As can be seen in Figure 1.5, this significantly improves the quality of the output.

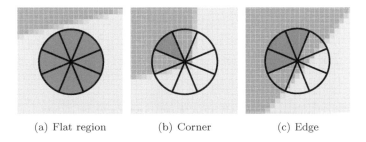

(a) Flat region   (b) Corner   (c) Edge

Figure 1.4.   The generalized Kuwahara filter uses weighting functions defined over sectors of a disc. The filter response is defined as a weighed sum of the local averages, where more weight is given to those averages with low standard deviation.

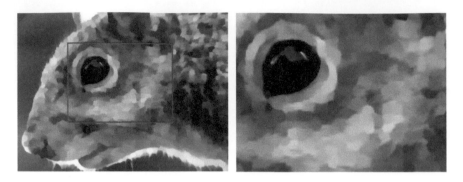

Figure 1.5. Output of the generalized Kuwahara filter.

We begin with the construction of the weighting functions. We divide the plane into N equal sectors by defining characteristic functions which are 1 over the sector and 0 otherwise:

$$\chi_k(x, y) = \begin{cases} 1 & \frac{(2k-1)\pi}{N} < \arg(x, y) \le \frac{(2k+1)\pi}{N} \\ 0 & \text{otherwise} \end{cases} \qquad k = 0, \dots, N-1.$$

Let

$$G_\sigma(x, y) = \frac{1}{2\pi\sigma^2} \exp\left(-\frac{x^2 + y^2}{2\sigma^2}\right)$$

be the Gaussian with standard deviation σ. To define smooth weighting functions, the characteristic functions of the different sectors χ_k are first convolved and then multiplied with a Gaussian:

$$w_k = \left(\chi_k \star G_{\sigma_s}\right) \cdot G_{\sigma_r} \tag{1.2}$$

The convolution smooths the characteristic functions such that they slightly overlap. The multiplication achieves a decay with increasing radius. Since $\sum_k w_k(x, y) = G_{\sigma_r}(x, y)$ for $(x, y) \in \mathbb{Z}^2$ the sum of the w_k is equivalent to a Gaussian filter.

Let f denote the input image. The weighted mean at a point $(x_0, y_0) \in \mathbb{Z}^2$ is then defined by

$$m_k = \sum_{(x,y)\in\mathbb{Z}^2} f(x, y)\, w_k(x - x_0, y - y_0),$$

and the weighted variance is given by

$$s_k^2 = \sum_{(x,y)\in\mathbb{Z}^2} \left(f(x, y) - m_k\right)^2 w_k(x - x_0, y - y_0)$$

$$= \sum_{(x,y)\in\mathbb{Z}^2} f^2(x, y)\, w_k(x - x_0, y - y_0) - m_k.$$

```
uniform sampler2D src;
uniform sampler2D K0;
uniform int N;
uniform int radius;
uniform float q;

const float PI = 3.14159265358979323846;

void main (void) {
  vec2 src_size = textureSize2D(src, 0);
  vec2 uv = gl_FragCoord.xy / src_size;

  vec4 m[8];
  vec3 s[8];
  for (int k = 0; k < N; ++k) {
    m[k] = vec4(0.0);
    s[k] = vec3(0.0);
  }

  float piN = 2.0 * PI / float(N);
  mat2 X = mat2(cos(piN), sin(piN), -sin(piN), cos(piN));

  for ( int j = -radius; j <= radius; ++j ) {
    for ( int i = -radius; i <= radius; ++i ) {
      vec2 v = 0.5 * vec2(i,j) / float(radius);
      if (dot(v,v) <= 0.25) {
        vec3 c = texture2D(src, uv + vec2(i,j) / src_size).rgb;
        for (int k = 0; k < N; ++k) {
          float w = texture2D(K0, vec2(0.5, 0.5) + v).x;

          m[k] += vec4(c * w, w);
          s[k] += c * c * w;

          v *= X;
        }
      }
    }
  }

  vec4 o = vec4(0.0);
  for (int k = 0; k < N; ++k) {
    m[k].rgb /= m[k].w;
    s[k] = abs(s[k] / m[k].w - m[k].rgb * m[k].rgb);

    float sigma2 = s[k].r + s[k].g + s[k].b;
    float w = 1.0 / (1.0 + pow(255.0 * sigma2, 0.5 * q));

    o += vec4(m[k].rgb * w, w);
  }
  gl_FragColor = vec4(o.rgb / o.w, 1.0);
}
```

Listing 1.2. Fragment shader implementation of the generalized Kuwahara filter.

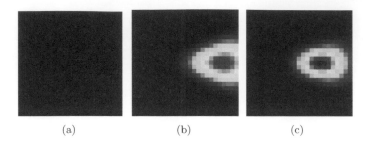

(a)   (b)   (c)

Figure 1.6. Approximation of the weighting function w_0 for $N = 8$: (a) characteristic function χ_0; (b) characteristic function χ_0 convolved with Gaussian function G_{σ_s}; (c) finally, multiplication with Gaussian function G_{σ_r}.

Let σ be defined as in Equation (1.1). We set

$$\alpha_k = \frac{1}{1 + \left(255 \cdot \sigma_k^2 \right)^{q/2}},$$

and define the output of the filter by

$$F(x_0, y_0) := \frac{\sum_k \alpha_k \, m_k}{\sum_k \alpha_k}. \tag{1.3}$$

The definition of the weighting factors α_k ensures that more weight is given to sectors with low standard deviation, i.e., those that are more homogeneous. This is similar to the approach of [Papari et al. 07], but avoids the indetermination, when some of the s_k are zero. The parameter q controls the sharpness of the output. We use $q = 8$ in our examples.

The weighting functions w_k are difficult to compute, because their computation requires convolution. A closed form solution is currently not known. Since the w_k do not depend on the pixel location, a straight forward approach would be to precompute them. We use a slightly different approach in our implementation, where all w_k are derived by bilinear sampling a texture map. We use this approach because it will easily generalize to anisotropic filtering which will be discussed in the next section. Let

$$R_\varphi = \begin{pmatrix} \cos\varphi & -\sin\varphi \\ \sin\varphi & \cos\varphi \end{pmatrix}.$$

be the rotation matrix that performs a rotation by the angle φ in counter-clockwise order. Since $\chi_k = \chi_0 \circ R_{-2\pi k/N}$, and since Gaussian functions are rotational invariant, we have

$$w_k = \left((\chi_0 \star G_{\sigma_s}) \cdot G_{\sigma_r} \right) \circ R_{-2\pi k/N}$$
$$= w_0 \circ R_{-2\pi k/N}.$$

Here, ∘ denotes composition of functions. For our implementation (Listing 1.2) we sample w_0 into a texture map K_0 of size 32×32. The sampling is performed using Equation (1.2) with

$$\sigma_r = \frac{1}{2} \cdot \frac{K_{\text{size}} - 1}{2} = 7.75,$$
$$\sigma_s = 0.33 \cdot \sigma_r,$$

and the origin moved to the center of the texture map. Figure 1.6 illustrates the different steps of the computation. Now suppose that $r > 0$ denotes the desired filter radius. Then the weighting functions w_k can be approximated by

$$w_k(x, y) = K_0 \left(\begin{pmatrix} 0.5 \\ 0.5 \end{pmatrix} + \frac{R_{-2\pi k/N}(x, y)}{2r} \right).$$

1.4 Anisotropic Kuwahara Filtering

The generalized Kuwahara filter fails to capture directional features and results in clustering artifacts. The anisotropic Kuwahara filter addresses these limitations by adapting the filter to the local structure of the input. In homogeneous regions the shape of the filter should be a circle, while in anisotropic regions the filter should become an ellipse whose major axis is aligned with the principal direction of image features (Figure 1.7). As can be seen in Figure 1.8, this avoids clustering and moreover creates a painterly look for directional image features (Figure 1.1).

Figure 1.9 shows an overview of the algorithm. We begin with calculating the structure tensor and smooth it with a Gaussian filter. Local orientation and a measure for the anisotropy are then derived from the eigenvalues and eigenvectors of the smoothed structure tensor. Finally, the actual filtering is performed.

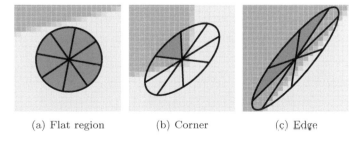

(a) Flat region   (b) Corner   (c) Edge

Figure 1.7. The anisotropic Kuwahara filter uses weighting functions defined over an ellipse, whose shape is based on the local orientation and anisotropy. The filter response is defined as a weighed sum of the local averages, where more weight is given to those averages with low standard deviation.

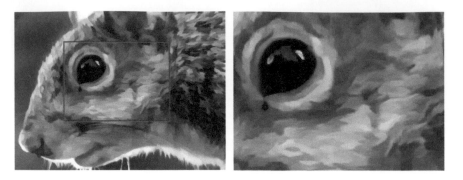

Figure 1.8. Output of the anisotropic Kuwahara filter.

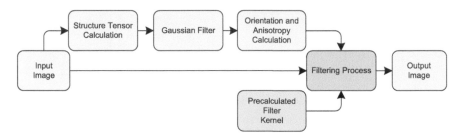

Figure 1.9. Schematic overview of the anisotropic Kuwahara filter.

1.4.1   Orientation and Anisotropy Estimation

The local orientation and anisotropy estimation is based on the *eigenvalues* and *eigenvectors* of the structure tensor [Brox et al. 06]. We calculate the structure tensor directly from the RGB values of the input [Kyprianidis and Döllner 08]. Let f be the input image and let

$$S_x = \frac{1}{4}\begin{pmatrix} +1 & 0 & -1 \\ +2 & 0 & -2 \\ +1 & 0 & -1 \end{pmatrix} \quad \text{and} \quad S_y = \frac{1}{4}\begin{pmatrix} +1 & +2 & +1 \\ 0 & 0 & 0 \\ -1 & -2 & -1 \end{pmatrix}$$

be the horizontal and vertical convolution masks of the Sobel filter. Then, approximations of the partial derivatives of f can be calculated by

$$f_x = S_x \star f \quad \text{and} \quad f_y = S_y \star f,$$

where $\star$ denotes convolution. The structure tensor of f is then defined by

$$(g_{ij}) = \begin{pmatrix} f_x \cdot f_x & f_x \cdot f_y \\ f_x \cdot f_y & f_y \cdot f_y \end{pmatrix} =: \begin{pmatrix} E & F \\ F & G \end{pmatrix}.$$

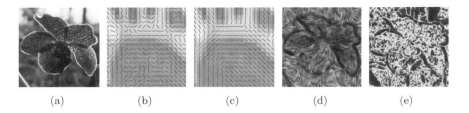

(a) (b) (c) (d) (e)

Figure 1.10. (a) Original image. (b) Eigenvectors of the structure tensor. (c) Eigenvectors of the smoothed structure tensor. (d) Visualization of the eigenvectors of the smoothed structure tensor using line integral convolution. (e) Anisotropy (blue=low, red=high).

Here, $\cdot$ denotes the scalar product. The eigenvalues of the structure tensor correspond to the squared minimum and maximum rate of change of f. The eigenvectors correspond to the respective directions. Selecting the eigenvector corresponding to the minimum rate of change gives a vector field. As shown in Figure 1.10(b) this vector field has discontinuities. In order to smooth the vector field, smoothing of the structure tensor is performed. The result of applying a Gaussian filter is shown in Figure 1.10(c). Smoothing the structure tensor is a linear operation on the tensor, but the effect on the eigenvectors is highly nonlinear and corresponds geometrically to principal component analysis. In our examples, we use a Gaussian filter with standard deviation $\sigma = 2.0$. Note that we do not normalize the tensor. Therefore, structure tensors corresponding to edges with large gradient magnitude get more weight during smoothing. Hence, orientation information of edges is distributed into the neighborhood of the edges (Figure 1.10(d)).

The eigenvalues of the structure tensor are non-negative real numbers and are given by

$$\lambda_{1,2} = \frac{E + G \pm \sqrt{(E - G)^2 + 4F^2}}{2}.$$

The eigenvector oriented in direction of the minimum rate of change is given by

$$t = \begin{pmatrix} \lambda_1 - E \\ -F \end{pmatrix}.$$

We define local orientation by

$$\varphi = \arg t.$$

To measure the amount of anisotropy, we use the approach proposed in [Yang et al. 96]:

$$A = \frac{\lambda_1 - \lambda_2}{\lambda_1 + \lambda_2}.$$

The anisotropy A ranges from 0 to 1, where 0 corresponds to isotropic and 1 corresponds to entirely anisotropic regions (Figure 1.10(e)).

```
uniform sampler2D src;

void main (void) {
  vec2 src_size = textureSize2D(src, 0);
  vec2 uv = gl_FragCoord.xy / src_size;
  vec2 d = 1.0 / src_size;

  vec3 c = texture2D(src, uv).xyz;
  vec3 u = (
            -1.0 * texture2D(src, uv + vec2(-d.x, -d.y)).xyz +
            -2.0 * texture2D(src, uv + vec2(-d.x,  0.0)).xyz +
            -1.0 * texture2D(src, uv + vec2(-d.x,  d.y)).xyz +
            +1.0 * texture2D(src, uv + vec2( d.x, -d.y)).xyz +
            +2.0 * texture2D(src, uv + vec2( d.x,  0.0)).xyz +
            +1.0 * texture2D(src, uv + vec2( d.x,  d.y)).xyz
          ) / 4.0;

  vec3 v = (
            -1.0 * texture2D(src, uv + vec2(-d.x, -d.y)).xyz +
            -2.0 * texture2D(src, uv + vec2( 0.0, -d.y)).xyz +
            -1.0 * texture2D(src, uv + vec2( d.x, -d.y)).xyz +
            +1.0 * texture2D(src, uv + vec2(-d.x,  d.y)).xyz +
            +2.0 * texture2D(src, uv + vec2( 0.0,  d.y)).xyz +
            +1.0 * texture2D(src, uv + vec2( d.x,  d.y)).xyz
          ) / 4.0;

  gl_FragColor = vec4(dot(u, u), dot(v, v), dot(u, v), 1.0);
}
```

Listing 1.3. Fragment shader for calculating the structure tensor.

1.4.2   Filtering Process

The filtering is performed using the ideas from the previous section, but with redefined weighting functions.

We begin with calculating the bounding rectangle of an ellipse. An axis-aligned ellipse with major axis a and minor axis b is defined by

$$\frac{x^2}{a^2} + \frac{y^2}{b^2} = 1.$$

By rotating x and y by an angle φ we get the equation of a rotated ellipse:

$$\frac{(x\cos\varphi - y\sin\varphi)^2}{a^2} + \frac{(x\sin\varphi + y\cos\varphi)^2}{b^2} = 1.$$

This is a quadratic polynomial in two variables and by expanding and collecting terms it can be rewritten in normalized form:

$$P(x,y) = Ax^2 + By^2 + Cx + Dy + Exy + F = 0, \tag{1.4}$$

```
uniform sampler2D src;

void main (void) {
  vec2 uv = gl_FragCoord.xy / textureSize2D(src, 0);
  vec3 g = texture2D(src, uv).xyz;

  float lambda1 = 0.5 * (g.y + g.x +
      sqrt(g.y*g.y - 2.0*g.x*g.y + g.x*g.x + 4.0*g.z*g.z));
  float lambda2 = 0.5 * (g.y + g.x -
      sqrt(g.y*g.y - 2.0*g.x*g.y + g.x*g.x + 4.0*g.z*g.z));

  vec2 v = vec2(lambda1 - g.x, -g.z);
  vec2 t;
  if (length(v) > 0.0) {
    t = normalize(v);
  } else {
    t = vec2(0.0, 1.0);
  }

  float phi = atan(t.y, t.x);

  float A = (lambda1 + lambda2 > 0.0)?
    (lambda1 - lambda2) / (lambda1 + lambda2) : 0.0;

  gl_FragColor = vec4(t, phi, A);
}
```

Listing 1.4. Fragment shader for calculating the local orientation and anisotropy.

with

$$A = a^2 \sin^2 \varphi + b^2 \cos^2 \varphi,$$
$$B = a^2 \cos^2 \varphi + b^2 \sin^2 \varphi,$$
$$C = 0,$$
$$D = 0,$$
$$E = 2(a^2 - b^2) \sin \varphi \cos \varphi,$$
$$F = -a^2 b^2.$$

The horizontal extrema are located where the partial derivative in the y-direction vanishes:

$$\frac{\partial P}{\partial y} = 2By + Ex = 0 \quad \Leftrightarrow \quad y = \frac{-Ex}{2B}.$$

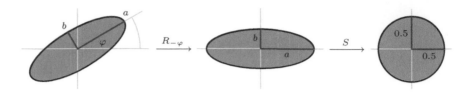

Figure 1.11. The mapping $SR_{-\varphi}$ defines a linear coordinate transform that maps an ellipse defined by major axis a, minor axis b and angle φ to a disc with radius 0.5.

```
vec4 t = texture2D(tfm, uv);
float a = radius * clamp((alpha + t.w) / alpha, 0.1, 2.0);
float b = radius * clamp(alpha / (alpha + t.w), 0.1, 2.0);

float cos_phi = cos(t.z);
float sin_phi = sin(t.z);

mat2 R = mat2(cos_phi, -sin_phi, sin_phi, cos_phi);
mat2 S = mat2(0.5/a, 0.0, 0.0, 0.5/b);
mat2 SR = S * R;

int max_x = int(sqrt(a*a * cos_phi*cos_phi +
                     b*b * sin_phi*sin_phi));
int max_y = int(sqrt(a*a * sin_phi*sin_phi +
                     b*b * cos_phi*cos_phi));

for (int j = -max_y; j <= max_y; ++j) {
  for (int i = -max_x; i <= max_x; ++i) {
    vec2 v = SR * vec2(i,j);
    if (dot(v,v) <= 0.25) {
      vec3 c = texture2D(src, uv + vec2(i,j) / src_size).rgb;
      for (int k = 0; k < N; ++k) {
        float w = texture2D(K0, vec2(0.5, 0.5) + v).x;

        m[k] += vec4(c * w, w);
        s[k] += c * c * w;

        v *= X;
      }
    }
  }
}.
```

Listing 1.5. Fragment shader implementation of the variance computation of the anisotropic Kuwahara filter.

Substituting y into Equation (1.4) yields

$$\left(A - \frac{E^2}{4B}\right)x^2 + F = 0.$$

The horizontal extrema of the ellipse are therefore given by

$$x = \pm\sqrt{\frac{F}{\frac{E^2}{4B} - A}} = \pm\sqrt{a^2\cos^2\varphi + b^2\sin^2\varphi}.$$

A similar calculation gives the vertical extrema:

$$y = \pm\sqrt{a^2\sin^2\varphi + b^2\cos^2\varphi}.$$

Suppose $r > 0$ is the desired filter radius. Let φ be the local orientation and let A be the anisotropy as defined in the previous section. We use the method proposed in [Pham 06] to define an elliptical filter shape. To adjust the eccentricity depending on the amount of anisotropy, we set

$$a = \frac{\alpha + A}{\alpha}r \quad \text{and} \quad b = \frac{\alpha}{\alpha + A}r.$$

The parameter $\alpha > 0$ is a tuning parameter. For $\alpha \to \infty$ the major axis a and the minor axis b converge to 1. We use $\alpha = 1$ in all examples, which results in a maximum eccentricity of 4. The ellipse defined by a, b and φ has its major axis aligned to the local image orientation. It has high eccentricity in anisotropic regions and becomes a circle in isotropic regions.

Now let

$$S = \begin{pmatrix} \frac{1}{2a} & 0 \\ 0 & \frac{1}{2b} \end{pmatrix},$$

then the mapping $SR_{-\varphi}$ maps points from the ellipse to a disc of radius 0.5 (Figure 1.11). Hence, the weighting functions over the ellipse can be defined by:

$$w_k(x, y) = K_0\left(\begin{pmatrix} 0.5 \\ 0.5 \end{pmatrix} + R_{-2\pi k/N}SR_{-\varphi}(x, y)\right).$$

The filter response is defined as in the case of the generalized Kuwahara filter by Equation (1.3).

The implementation of the anisotropic Kuwahara filter is very similar to the implementation of the generalized Kuwahara filter (Listing 1.2). Therefore, only the variance computation of the anisotropic Kuwahara filter is shown in Listing 1.5. In Listing 1.6 an optimized variance computation for $N = 8$ is shown.

```
{
  vec3 c = texture2D(src, uv).rgb;
  float w = texture2D(K0123, vec2(0.5, 0.5)).x;
  for (int k = 0; k < N; ++k) {
    m[k] += vec4(c * w, w);
    s[k] += c * c * w;
  }
}

for (int j = 0; j <= max_y; ++j) {
  for (int i = -max_x; i <= max_x; ++i) {

    if ((j !=0) || (i > 0)) {
      vec2 v = SR * vec2(i,j);

      if (dot(v,v) <= 0.25) {
        vec3 c0 = texture2D(src,uv + vec2(i,j)/src_size).rgb;
        vec3 c1 = texture2D(src,uv - vec2(i,j)/src_size).rgb;

        vec3 cc0 = c0 * c0;
        vec3 cc1 = c1 * c1;

        vec4 w0123 = texture2D(K0123, vec2(0.5, 0.5) + v);
        for (int k = 0; k < 4; ++k) {
          m[k] += vec4(c0 * w0123[k], w0123[k]);
          s[k] += cc0 * w0123[k];

          m[k+4] += vec4(c1 * w0123[k], w0123[k]);
          s[k+4] += cc1 * w0123[k];
        }

        vec4 w4567 = texture2D(K0123, vec2(0.5, 0.5) - v);
        for (int k = 0; k < 4; ++k) {
          m[k+4] += vec4(c0 * w4567[k], w4567[k]);
          s[k+4] += cc0 * w4567[k];

          m[k] += vec4(c1 * w4567[k], w4567[k]);
          s[k] += cc1 * w4567[k];
        }
      }
    }

  }
}
}
```

Listing 1.6.   Fragment shader implementation of the variance computation of the anisotropic Kuwahara filter (optimized for $N = 8$).

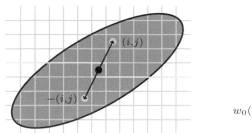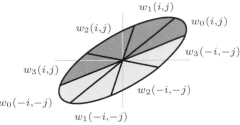

Figure 1.12. Symmetry about the origin of an ellipse (left). For $N = 8$ the values of the weighting functions can be fetched using two RGBA texture lookups (right).

In order to reduce the number of texture lookups, four weights are packed into a RGBA texture map. This texture map is constructed by sampling the weighting functions $w_0,...,w_3$ from section 1.3 as explained. Furthermore, the property of the ellipse being symmetric about the origin is used (Figure 1.12). Note that for $N = 8$ and $k = 0, \ldots, 3$ we have

$$w_{k+4}(x, y) = w_k(-x, -y).$$

1.5 Conclusion

In this chapter we have presented a GPU implementation of the anisotropic Kuwahara filter. Guided by the smoothed structure tensor, the anisotropic Kuwahara filter generates a feature-preserving, direction-enhancing look.

Unlike existing nonlinear smoothing filters, the anisotropic Kuwahara filter is robust against high-contrast noise and avoids overblurring in low-contrast areas, providing a consistent level of abstraction across the image. It also ensures outstanding temporal coherence when applied to video, even with per-frame filtering.

Acknowledgments

This work was supported by the German Research Foundation (DFG), Grant DO 697/5-1.

Original photographs from flickr.com kindly provided under Creative Commons license by Keven Law (Figure 1.3, 1.5, 1.8) and Tambako the Jaguar (Figure 1.1).

Bibliography

[Brox et al. 06] T. Brox, R. Boomgaard, F. Lauze, J. Weijer, J. Weickert, P. Mrázek, and P. Kornprobst. "Adaptive Structure Tensors and Their Applications." In *Visualization and Processing of Tensor Fields*, pp. 17–47. Springer, 2006.

[Comaniciu and Meer 02] D. Comaniciu and P. Meer. "Mean Shift: A Robust Approach Toward Feature Space Analysis." *IEEE Transactions on Pattern Analysis and Machine Intelligence* 24:5 (2002), 603–619.

[Kuwahara et al. 76] M. Kuwahara, K. Hachimura, S. Eiho, and M. Kinoshita. *Digital Processing of Biomedical Images*, pp. 187–203. Plenum Press, 1976.

[Kyprianidis and Döllner 08] J. E. Kyprianidis and J. Döllner. "Image Abstraction by Structure Adaptive Filtering." In *Proc. EG UK Theory and Practice of Computer Graphics*, pp. 51–58. Eurographics Association, 2008.

[Kyprianidis et al. 09] J. E. Kyprianidis, H. Kang, and J. Döllner. "Image and Video Abstraction by Anisotropic Kuwahara Filtering." *Computer Graphics Forum* 28:7. Special Issue on Pacific Graphics 2009.

[Papari et al. 07] G. Papari, N. Petkov, and P. Campisi. "Artistic Edge and Corner Enhancing Smoothing." *IEEE Transactions on Image Processing* 16:10 (2007), 2449–2462.

[Pham 06] T. Q. Pham. "Spatiotonal Adaptivity in Super-Resolution of Undersampled Image Sequences." Ph.D. thesis, Quantitative Imaging Group, Delft University of Technology, 2006.

[Tomasi and Manduchi 98] C. Tomasi and R. Manduchi. "Bilateral Filtering for Gray and Color Images." In *Proceedings International Conference on Computer Vision (ICCV)*, pp. 839–846, 1998.

[Yang et al. 96] G. Z. Yang, P. Burger, D. N. Firmin, and S. R. Underwood. "Structure Adaptive Anisotropic Image Filtering." *Image and Vision Computing* 14:2 (1996), 135–145.

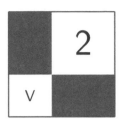

Edge Anti-aliasing by Post-Processing

Hugh Malan

2.1 Introduction

Anti-aliasing is critical for high quality rendering. For instance, high quality CG prioritizes anti-aliasing quality, and game "screenshots" produced for print and PR purposes are usually rendered with artificially high levels of super-sampling to improve image quality.

Hardware multi-sampled anti-aliasing (MSAA) [Kirkland 99] support is the standard way to implement anti-aliasing, but it is a very expensive way to achieve high quality anti-aliasing and offers little assistance for anti-aliasing deferred effects. This chapter introduces a new method for anti-aliasing edges by selective pixel blending. It requires a fraction of the space needed for MSAA, and is compatible with deferred effects.

2.1.1 Problems

Using deferred shading for shadows, localized lighting and decals is a very attractive option, but it will introduce aliasing problems if these effects are computed using a single depth or position value per pixel. For example, deferred effects that are partly occluded by geometry will introduce aliasing along the silhouette edge. Since deferred effects have a large per-sample cost, super-sampling them is often prohibitively expensive. Killzone 2 uses 2× super-sampling [Valient 07]; many titles apply deferred effects with no super-sampling (e.g., many Unreal Engine 3 titles).

Hardware support for MSAA is now standard. Modern GPUs offer a variety of MSAA options such as quincunx [Kilgard 01, Young 07]. The downside

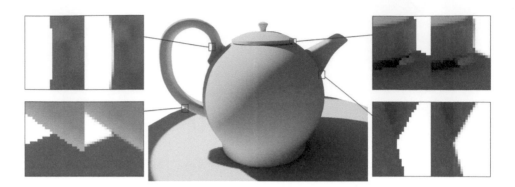

Figure 2.1. Example image, anti-aliased using our method, with close-ups.

to MSAA is that the frame buffer memory and bandwidth requirements scale in proportion to the number of samples, so high sample numbers are very costly. Recent graphics hardware can support up to $16\times$MSAA [NVIDIA 08] but $16\times$ the frame buffer memory and fill rate is a very high price, implying a correspondingly high opportunity cost. The requirements also scale with the per-pixel size, so a multi-sampled fat frame buffer can be extraordinarily expensive. Tabula Rasa quoted a size of 50MB for a 1024×768 frame buffer with no super-sampling [Koonce 07]; Killzone 2's frame buffer is 1280×720 with $2\times$MSAA and requires 37MB [Valient 07]. So using MSAA to achieve high quality anti-aliasing is extremely expensive in terms of memory size and bandwidth.

On current console hardware, frame buffer size limitations mean that there is a substantial cost for implementing even 1280×720 at $2\times$MSAA, so many games run at a lower resolution (*Call of Duty* series) or with MSAA disabled (*Halo 3*) [Beyond3D 09].

This chapter describes a new approach that can efficiently provide high-quality edge anti-aliasing for real-time three-dimensional applications. It applies to deferred effects and allows MSAA to be disabled. The technique duplicates the subtle pixel-wide gradients on edges due to varying coverage that appear in high quality anti-aliased renderings. It requires no additional geometry or additional passes.

Our method is executed in two stages. First, the image is rendered without any kind of multisampling or super-sampling. As part of the render hints about proximity to the silhouette edge are written out to the frame buffer. A post-processing pass is then applied, which uses these hints to update the edge pixels to provide anti-aliasing. Applying the post-process after rendering deferred effects means they will receive edge anti-aliasing. Figure 2.1 shows the method in action.

The central component of this approach provides pixel shaders with an efficient method for computing the location of the nearest silhouette edge. This technique can also applied to shadow map magnification, and provides a method for upscaling that preserves sharp edges.

2.1.2 Related Work

One strategy for minimizing edge anti-aliasing problems with deferred effects is to use forward rendering with MSAA enabled to render the majority of the objects and lighting, and use the bare minimum set of deferred effects so the majority of edges will be anti-aliased.

In cases where deferred effects affect the majority of pixels, this strategy offers no advantage. [Shishkovtso 05] presents a method for selective edge blurring (employed in S.T.A.L.K.E.R.), where the depth and normal buffers are searched for discontinuities and the relevant pixels blurred. This method softens edges but leaves all other pixels untouched so the image as a whole is not softened.

However, without sub-pixel-accurate coverage information, high quality anti-aliasing effects are impossible. Along the edge of an object in a highly super-sampled image, the pixels will be a combination of the background (occluded object) color and foreground (occluding object) color; the degree of blend between the two colors depends on how much the polygon covers the square corresponding to that pixel. Hence the requirement for coverage information.

DirectX 10.1 allows deferred effects to read from the individual samples of the multi-sampled depth buffer, so the code applying a deferred effect can detect edge pixels and enable super-sampling for those cases only [Huddy 08].

The solution outlined in the introduction requires the pixel shader to accurately calculate the location of the nearest silhouette edge. There are no good ways to efficiently find the mathematically correct answer; we take a different approach (i.e., cheat) to avoid this problem, and create robust silhouettes without the need for any new geometry.

A second problem is due to the hardware rasterizer. Given a triangle, rasterizers write to only the pixels whose centers are within that triangle. In the ideal anti-aliased image, any pixels that overlap the triangle will be affected by it. In Figure 2.2, three pixels that have their centers outside the triangle still overlap it. If we render them in the usual way, the three pixels will not be affected. In general, half the pixels affected by MSAA will have centers outside the triangle, and if they are ignored it will substantially degrade anti-aliasing quality.

In Section 2.2, we present a method that addresses both these problems, and in Section 2.3 we describe the post-process stage. After covering the role it provides, we work back to its data requirements, and then discuss how shaders can encode this information in the frame buffer. In Section 2.4 we list the known problems

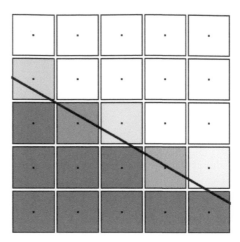

Figure 2.2.   The diagonal black line marks the edge of a triangle. The area covered by each pixel is represented by squares, with black dots indicating their centers. They are shaded to indicate coverage: the darker the color, the greater the fraction of its area covered by the triangle. Several pixels have centers outside the triangle but still overlap it; they should be affected by the triangle but the rasterizer will not write to them.

with the basic method, and provide some solutions. In Section 2.5 we cover implementation details.

2.2   Finding the Nearest Silhouette Edge

It is helpful to define some terms before describing the details of the solution. Let the *outward vector* of a vertex be the normalized, weighted average of the surface normals of all the triangles that meet at that point [Thürmer 98]. A *silhouette edge* is an edge shared by a back-facing and front-facing triangle.

The two problems described in the introduction were that the silhouette edge may be topologically distant from the current triangle, and that the rasterizer will not write to pixels that overlap the triangle, but have centers outside it.

Our solution to both these problems is to offset any vertex that has at least one back-facing triangle adjoining it outward, far enough to render at least an additional k-pixel border around the object. (Of course, the adjoining-back-face test result and offset vector must be the same for all coincident vertices to prevent the model splitting apart.)

Figure 2.3 shows how the vertex offset works in cross-section, with a one-pixel offset. This operation addresses both the problems described above. First, by

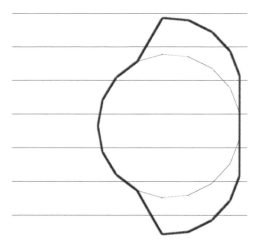

Figure 2.3. All vertices that adjoin a back-facing triangle are offset by one pixel. The regular horizontal lines indicate the view direction: the eye is some distance to the left, looking right. The original geometry is indicated by the thin black lines. After the vertices have been extruded, the geometry forms the shape indicated by the thick black lines.

offsetting vertices in this manner we render an additional set of pixels bordering the original geometry; if k>= $\sqrt{1/2}$ then the additional pixels will include all those that overlap the original geometry. Second, if we render the geometry with back-face culling enabled we can be confident that any rendered pixel closer than k pixels to the silhouette will be within a triangle with at least one vertex on the silhouette edge. To put it another way, the problem of finding the silhouette edge is avoided by explicitly forming the silhouette through this geometry change.

The per-vertex offset that meets these requirements could be found by finding the silhouette edges that meet at the vertex (which may be >2), express them in screen space, translate them outwards by k pixels, and find the appropriate intersection.

However, if the geometry can be assumed to never have creases sharper than 90 degrees, then simply offsetting by a distance of k$\sqrt{2}$ pixels is acceptable. In this case, the per-vertex offset may be found by projecting the outward vector defined above into screen space, setting Z=0 (to project to the screen plane), normalizing it, scaling it to account for screen resolution, and then scaling by the required pixel count of k$\sqrt{2}$. We will set k>=1 for reasons described in the next section.

One extremely useful benefit of the explicitly formed silhouette is that it allows the test determining whether to offset the vertex to be inaccurate without the silhouette shape being damaged. In Figure 2.3, imagine that a vertex closer to the viewer incorrectly passed the adjoining-back-face test, or that the silhouette vertices incorrectly failed that test. In both cases, a slightly reduced silhouette is still present.

In comparison, offsetting only the vertices adjoining a silhouette edge is fragile: missing a single silhouette vertex will noticeably damage the silhouette shape.

The vertex program outputs the variable `silhouetteParameter`: 0 if the vertex has been offset, and 1 if it has not. If back-face culling is enabled, the only time the interpolated value will be other than 1 is if the pixel is within a triangle with at least one vertex on the silhouette edge.

The interpolated value of `silhouetteParameter` bears some resemblance to distance: it will be 0.0 on the silhouette edge and increases towards the interior. However, the interior vertex or vertices of the triangle may be just outside the border region or quite some distance away, so the distance from the border is not a function of `silhouetteParameter`.

However, it is possible to compute the partial derivatives of `silhouetteParameter` in screen space using the `ddx/ddy` or `dFdx/dFdy` instructions in DirectX and OpenGL, respectively. With this information we can estimate the number of pixels to the silhouette edge horizontally and vertically. If `ddx(silhouetteParameter)` and `ddy(silhouetteParameter)` are the screen-space partial derivatives of `silhouetteParameter` then the estimated number of pixels to the silhouette edge horizontally is:

$$\texttt{hdist = -silhouetteParameter/ddx(silhouetteParameter)}$$

and vertically is:

$$\texttt{vdist = -silhouetteParameter/ddy(silhouetteParameter)}.[1]$$

From these two values we can compute an approximation of the position of or vector to the nearest point on the silhouette edge, and write it to the frame buffer if required. At this point we will consider the post-process step, and return to the issue of what data should be written into the frame buffer later.

---

[1] Since `silhouetteParameter` will be interpolated across the triangle accounting for perspective correction, its value will not be a linear function of screen-space position and so using the formula above will not give a precisely correct result. Also, for triangles with only one vertex on the silhouette edge, the formula will imply that the silhouette edge is parallel to the line connecting the two non-silhouette vertices of the triangle, which can be a completely incorrect assumption. So this method will not provide the mathematically correct result, but it is adequate for our needs.

2.3 The Post-Process

The overall goal for this technique is for geometry edges to appear to be super-sampled. Pixels that overlap a silhouette edge should be a blend of the colors of the relevant objects, weighted by coverage.

For now, we will only consider the simplest case where a pixel has a single silhouette edge passing through it. Since we have rendered the frame buffer without any kind of super-sampling or multisampling, the color of a pixel is completely due to a single object: this will be called the *foreground color*. If the contributing triangle were not rendered, the pixel would be shaded differently; this new color is called the *background color*.

If we are restricting ourselves to a standard frame buffer holding only a single color per pixel, as opposed to some kind of deep frame buffer, there is no way to know the actual foreground and background color at a pixel. We can approximate the background color by sampling one of those pixels' neighbors. The further away the chosen neighbor is, the lower the correlation between the neighbor's color and actual background color.

From the method described in Section 2.2, for each pixel we have sub-pixel-accurate values for the number of horizontal and vertical pixels to the silhouette edge. With this information we can infer the location and direction of the (estimated) silhouette edge.[2]

If we are to restrict sampling to an immediate neighbor (N, NE, E, SE, etc.), the post-process can only affect pixels on the very border of the object (see Figure 2.4: the hatched pixels are the only ones that can be affected).

The relevant pixels are those for which the horizontal or vertical distance to the edge is less than one pixel, i.e., `min(abs(hdist), abs(vdist))<1.0`, if `hdist` and `vdist` are the horizontal and vertical distances defined above. Given this restriction, it is natural to let the blend factor between foreground and background colors be given by the same equation:

```
blendfactor=min(abs(hdist), abs(vdist)).
```

This choice means the minimum value for k is 1 in the vertex offset discussion in Section 2.2; values any greater than this will simply grow the object without affecting the edge quality.

Pixels approaching the edge will be progressively more affected by the background color; pixels whose centers are only just inside the triangle will have a color very close to the background color. As can be seen in the example images, the blur turns jagged stair-stepped edges into a series of smooth pixel-wide gradients.

---

[2]Actually we get the location of the edge produced by the vertex offset operation, which is k pixels outwards from the silhouette edge that would have been rendered with the original geometry.

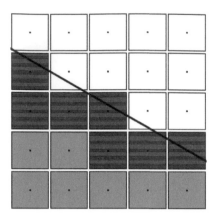

Figure 2.4.   Hatched squares correspond to pixels that have an immediate neighbor over the edge. This image is based on Figure 2.2; the black line indicates the new the triangle edge after the vertex offset operation.

Given a blend factor less than one, the next question is which neighbour pixel should be sampled to find the approximate background color (see Figure 2.4: there are many places where the only option is a diagonally adjacent neighbour. Therefore, one easy option is to choose the neighbour at (sign(hdist), sign(vdist)). This will sample diagonally unless the edge is precisely parallel to the X or Y-axis).

In principle we could calculate the (estimated) location and direction of the silhouette edge for the original geometry, and proceed to calculate an estimate of the coverage value with an arbitrary pixel filter function, to use for blending the foreground and background color. We will ignore this for two reasons. First, the background color is being approximated by sampling one of its neighbors, and the quality of that approximation dramatically degrades with distance. Restricting the sample to an immediate neighbor is the safest option. Second, the post-process operation is speed-critical, so long calculations will directly impact frame rate.

Given **hdist** and **vdist**, pseudocode for the post-process step is as follows:

```
colbase=sourceImage[pixelPos.x, pixelPos.y];
colneb=sourceImage[pixelPos.x+sign(hdist),
                    pixelPos.y+sign(vdist)];
blendfactor=min(abs(hdist), abs(vdist));
colfinal=lerp(colneb, colbase, blendfactor);
```

The **lerp** will output **colneb** if **blendfactor=0**; it blends to **colbase** as blendfactor increases, and will implicitly clamp blendfactor values >1. Then **colfinal** is written out to the target image.

Now that the post-process requirements are known, we will move to the question of what is stored in the frame buffer. Since any additional per-pixel data will make proportionate demands on memory bandwidth, additional or higher bit-depth render targets are an expensive choice, so minimizing the size of the hint data stored in the frame buffer is extremely important.

The post-process is required to compute the sample offset and blend factor; it has no other need for `hdist` and `vdist`. If we restrict the sample offset to the four diagonal corners, then it can be stored with two bits. The blend factor can take any number of bits: for example two bits would mean four levels, which is inferior to 4×MSAA (which has five). For our implementation we chose six bits, allowing 64 different blend levels. With the two bits required to specify the sample offset we make full use of the 8-bit alpha channel.

This choice moves some additional work from the post-process to the shader: it must now also find which of the four diagonal neighbors is the appropriate choice, calculate the blend factor, and encode all that information in the alpha channel.

2.4 Refinements

The method described in Sections 2.2 and 2.3 correctly provides anti-aliasing in the majority of cases, but there are some situations where it fails. When the anti-aliasing method fails for an edge, the edge is treated incorrectly by the post-process pass—i.e., either it remains unaffected by the post-process when it should become anti-aliased or it becomes blurred when it should have been left as is. Super-sampling and MSAA will implicitly handle some situations for which edge blurring requires explicit support.

In this section we'll cover the list of problem cases, and describe their solutions.

Edges with no neighboring triangle ("open edges"). This class of edge should always be classed as a silhouette edge and receive edge blurring. Therefore the solution is to flag any vertices that are on an open edge so they automatically pass adjoining-back-face test. For these vertices the outward direction must be defined differently: each open edge meeting at the vertex in question contributes a vector at right angles to the open edge and triangle normal; the final outward direction should be the weighted average of those vectors.

Edges with discontinuous shading. This includes material boundaries, discontinuous normals, discontinuous shading parameters including discontinuous UVs. Edge-blur should be always enabled for this class of edge. If the adjoining-back-face test passes then operate as usual, but if it fails scale the blend value so the blend between foreground and background is 50% on the edge instead of 0%.

The reason is because the edge-blur will be applied to pixels on both sides of the edge. If side A is red and side B is blue, then the blur applied to the pixels on each side needs to provide a soft transition to a 50% combination of red and blue on the edge. In comparison, the behavior on a silhouette edge is for the blend factor to be 0% on the edge, so the background color dominates. If this were applied at the red-blue transition, then the pixels on side A would smoothly transition to blue, the color would abruptly change to red across the edge, and on side B the color would then smoothly transition back to blue.

Triangles where all three vertices pass the adjoining-back-face test. See Figure 2.5. Imagine a cube viewed down one axis so only one face is visible. In that situation all four vertices of that face would adjoin back-facing triangles; `silhouette Parameter` would be 0.0 everywhere and the derivative method's prediction for edge distance would fail. One solution to this problem is to subdivide the geometry so the faces with potential problems have a center vertex, but this is not always possible.

Pixel-sized triangles. In comparison to $n \times$MSAA we have only one sample per pixel instead of n, so the Nyquist limit scales correspondingly. Triangles at this scale will suffer from under-sampling.

Pixel-sized gaps. Due to the vertex offset described in Section 2.2, a thin gap between geometry (such as the gap between extended fingers) will close. Like pixel-scale triangles, a pixel-scale gap will also suffer from under-sampling problems.

Alpha blending. Alpha-blended billboard textures need no anti-aliasing if their shape is provided by alpha from a texture rather than geometry. Similarly, windows in a frame would have their edges anti-aliased by the opaque geometry they share vertices with. When rendering these cases, updates to the edge-blur hints in the frame buffer should be disabled, so edges seen through the window will still be softened by the post-process.

A second case is alpha-blended geometry that isn't bounded by an opaque edge, such as an object faded to 50% opacity or a glass tabletop. In these cases it would be best if the edge-blend hints would only be written to pixels at the very edge of the object, where they were required. If the transparent object writes hints everywhere, it will disable anti-aliasing on the edges of the objects seen through it. If the edge hints are stored in the alpha channel, this cannot be done efficiently on standard GPUs. One option when rendering constant-alpha objects is to set up the hint bit packing so the blend factor is packed into the most significant six bits, with the sample direction is packed into the low two bits. Render using a separate alpha channel blend function, with the blend function set to max; color is combined with a constant blend factor. Alternatively, disabling writes to the alpha channel when rendering the object and adds the hints by re-rendering it, writing only to the alpha channel and using `clip()` to disable updates to any pixels not at the edge.

Surfaces intersecting in the depth buffer. Our method does not provide anti-aliasing in this case.

2.5 GPU Implementation and Results

Each stage of the anti-aliasing process will be considered in turn.

2.5.1 Offset Vertices

The vertex program implements this operation. The outward vector is required, but since the main restriction is that it be the same for all coincident vertices, it is often possible to reuse the existing per-vertex normal. For shapes with discontinuous normals such as a cube, this is not possible. If the number of edges with discontinuous normals is low it may be cheaper to insert a quad for each such edge to join the discontinuous vertices together, rather than increasing vertex size by adding another channel.

Example code to adjust the final projected vertex position (hPos) in homogeneous space is as follows:

```
hPos.xy+=normalize(screenNormal.xy)*hPos.w*2.0*
            aaExtrudeDistPixel()/screenSizePixel();
```

- `screenNormal` is the vertex normal, projected into screen space.
- `aaExtrudeDistPixel()` returns "k," the extrusion distance in pixels, e.g., 1.5.
- `screenSizePixel()` returns the screen size, e.g., `float2(1280, 720)`.

Implementing an exact adjoining-back-face test in the vertex program is complex and costly, especially for skinned characters. However, the silhouette construction is robust enough to survive an inexact test. Here are three basic options representing a trade-off between amount of vertex data, complexity, and accuracy:

```
dot(eye_vertex_vector, outward_vector)>=0
```

The most basic test, adequate for surfaces with low curvature.

```
dot(normalize(eye_vertex_vector), outward_vector)>threshold
```

This approximates the set of adjoining triangles with a cone. The `threshold` parameter is equal to -cos(half_cone_angle) and can be pre-computed and stored in the vertex stream. This test is more useful, but it fails at saddle points.

```
(dot(normalize(eye_vertex_vector), plane_normal[0])>0) ||
(dot(normalize(eye_vertex_vector), plane_normal[1])>0) ||
(dot(normalize(eye_vertex_vector), plane_normal[2])>0) ||
(dot(normalize(eye_vertex_vector), plane_normal[3])>0)
```

Figure 2.5.   Triangles where all three vertices have passed the (low-fidelity) adjoining-back-face test have been colored white.

With each vertex, store four surface normals chosen from the triangles meeting at that vertex. This is the most accurate method but will require the most vertex data and program time.

When the test is inaccurate, the question is whether the silhouette is formed in front of or behind the ideal silhouette edge. If it is behind, then there is a danger that the vertices are not offset far enough to be visible over the silhouette edge provided by the non-offset geometry, which will be aliased. Increasing k to compensate may help—either globally, on a per-object basis, or even as a per-vertex setting. However, every unit that k is increased will noticeably grow the object onscreen so improving the quality of the test may well be a better option.

If the silhouette edge is in front, then there will be visible triangles for which all vertices passed the adjoining-back-face test and so `silhouetteParameter` will be constantly 0 on them. This case will be covered in the next section.

Of course, an inadequate adjoining-back-face test just means that an aliased edge will appear—perhaps not a show-stopping problem!

2.5.2   Sample Offset and Blend Values

The calculations follow the text very closely, as shown in Listing 2.1.

Some care must be taken to avoid quantization problems when the GPU writes the final floating-point color to the 8-bit per channel frame buffer. Because 0.0 maps to 0 and 1.0 maps to 255, the best solution is to encode the desired value as an integer in $[0, 255]$ and divide by 255 so the 8-bit quantization has no effect.

```
float derivX=dFdx(silhouetteParameter);
float derivY=dFdy(silhouetteParameter);
vec2 approxEdgeDist=vec2(
      -silhouetteParameter/derivX,
      -silhouetteParameter/derivY);
// hdist and vdist, packed into a vector
float coverage=min(abs(approxEdgeDist.x),
                   abs(approxEdgeDist.y));
vec2 postStep=vec2(
sign(approxEdgeDist.x), sign(approxEdgeDist.y));
// Encode the postprocess step and coverage,
// to be written out to
// the 8-bit alpha channel
float encodedPostStepX=(postStep.x>=0) ? 128 : 0;
float encodedPostStepY=(postStep.y>=0) ? 64 : 0;
float encodedValInt=encodedPostStepX + encodedPostStepY +
                    (saturate(coverage)*63);
finalColor.a=encodedValInt/255.0;
```

Listing 2.1. Pixel shader code given `silhouetteParameter`.

One change that slightly improves the quality is to pass the variable `screenNormal` described in Section 2.5.1 into the pixel shader and to use it to determine the post-process sample offset. The occasional pixel has problems with the `ddx`/`ddy` method, and this change improves them:

```
float2 postStep=float2(sign(screenNormal.x), sign(-screenNormal.y));
```

The `-y` accounts for the texture coordinates being vertically flipped in comparison to screen space.

It is possible for all three vertices of a triangle to pass the adjoining-back-face test. There are two main ways that this might happen. First, when the adjoining-back-face test is inaccurately greedy and passes vertices of a front facing triangle near the silhouette. Secondly, for a triangle in the interior of the object, where the test failed perhaps because of saddle points.

If all three vertices of a triangle pass the adjoining-back-face test, `silhouette Parameter` will be a constant 0, and so the derivative calculations fail. In this case, the best option is to set coverage to 0 and set the post-process sample offset based on `screenNormal` as described above.

This will erase one-pixel-wide triangles on silhouette edges due to adjoining-back-face test inaccuracies, which are the most common problem case. On large triangles all pixels will be shifted diagonally by one step, but this is unlikely to cause visible problems beyond a possible aliased edge.

```
float encodedAAVal=sourceColor.a*255;
vec3 unpackedAAVal=frac(float3(encodedAAVal/256, encodedAAVal/128,
                               encodedAAVal/64) );
vec2 postStep;
postStep.x=(unpackedAAVal.x>=0.5) ? +1.0 :  -1.0;
postStep.y=(unpackedAAVal.y>=0.5) ? +1.0 :  -1.0;
float  coverage=unpackedAAVal.z;
```

Listing 2.2. Unpacking a number in floating point.

2.5.3   Blend Edge Pixels

Since we are working in floating-point rather than integers, unpacking the number is slightly more complex, as shown in Listing 2.2.

Then sample the texture at the requested offset, blend, and write out.

2.5.4   Implementation Costs

In likely order of cost, the requirements of the approach presented here are space for the additional (4–8) bits in the frame buffer, the additional post-process work, any additional vertex properties for the adjoining-back-face test, the additional pixel shader code, the additional vertex shader code, and the additional one or three interpolators. However, no changes to draw order, tessellation, or geometry are required: even a depth-prepass is supported.

2.6   Results

Interaction with a complex background is shown in Figure 2.6, including a 4×MSAA render for comparison. The magnified regions show the effect of sampling a neighboring pixel to approximate the background color: some lines in the background which approach the edge indirectly can be seen to be offset by one pixel in the blend region. This image was rendered using the four-plane adjoining-back-face test described in Section 2.5.1.

Skinned characters are much more difficult to support than static geometry. Saddle points are common, which means many triangles have all three vertices pass the adjoining-back-face test. Thin gaps (e.g., between fingers) will close up with every increase in k. Lastly, skinning complicates the adjoining-back-face test: implementing the four-plane test for a skinned character would be difficult, and would require quite a bit of extra vertex data.

For this reason, we used a simple and less accurate test for the skinned character shown in Figure 2.7. Here, we used the cone test described in 5.1b with a threshold value of -0.2 and k value of 1.5 pixels for all vertices. The cone test

Figure 2.6. Demonstration of interaction with a complex background. The left-hand image in each magnified section shows the 4×MSAA render; the right-hand image shows the edge-blur render. Interaction with straight lines in the background (top left). The post-process method provides more subtle sub-pixel detail than 4×MSAA (top right). The worst case situation for the post-process method—the diagonal sampling means the row of pixels in the blend area is noticeably shifted one step to the left (bottom right). Another example of strong parallel features, but since the lines approach the edge from roughly the same direction as the diagonal sample, no artifacts are visible (bottom left). As is apparent in the top left section, artifacts are much less noticeable without the regular parallel spacing.

Figure 2.7. Demonstration of the technique applied to a skinned character. A simpler and less exact adjoining-back-face test was used, meaning that a few edges did not become anti-aliased (see text for details).

is not exact and some silhouette edges don't receive the anti-aliasing blur. (All lighting including shadows and AO was baked into the textures for the character; the only change between poses is vertex position and normal.)

2.6.1   Performance

The most useful measure of cost is the increase in cycle count for the vertex and pixel shader, with the additional code required by our method. Timings are for an Xbox 360 at a screen resolution of 1280×720; cycle counts are comparable to DX9.

Vertex program.

- Cone test version (5.1b): 25 cycles per vertex.

- Four-plane test version (see 5.1c): 29 cycles per vertex.

Pixel shader.

- 14 cycles per pixel; ~ 0.67ms to fill the screen.

Post-process.

- 0.33ms to resolve the rendered image to a texture.

- 0.60ms for the full-screen post-process. This time is constant, as it is independent of scene content.

2.7   Other Applications

2.7.1   Shadow Mapping

Enabling pixel shaders to estimate the silhouette edge location with sub-pixel precision opens up some interesting possibilities. One application is shadow maps: if hints about the location of the shadow edge are encoded as well as depth, the magnification code can use that information to provide a sharp edge with sub-pixel accuracy (see Figure 2.8).

One way to do this is for each pixel, write out the parameters of the equation expressing distance to the nearest edge as a function of onscreen position.

When sampling the shadow map, a custom magnification function is used instead of bilinear filtering. Given a position on the shadow map texture, the four surrounding texels are sampled. The distance-to-edge equation provided by each of these four texels is evaluated, and the depth value associated with the texel corresponding to the highest distance-to-edge value is used for the shadow test.

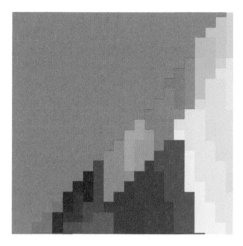

Figure 2.8. Example shadow map edge. A reasonably clean, anti-aliased edge is produced even though the triangles only cover a handful of pixels. The first image shows the resulting shadow map edge; the second image colors each pixel according to triangle index.

This means the shadow edge will run outside the group of texels that the shape rasterized to (without this property, clean intersections of silhouette edges are not possible).

The fragments of pixel shader code in Listing 2.3 implement this. Given silhouetteParameter, this code will encode the plane equation as a color to

```
float  derivX=dFdx(silhouetteParameter);
float  derivY=dFdy(silhouetteParameter);

vec2  vecToEncode=vec2(0.0, 0.0);
float  encWeight =0.0;
if(silhouetteParameter <1.0)
{
        float  d=sqrt((derivX*derivX)+(derivY*derivY))*1.0;
        vecToEncode.x=derivX/d;
        vecToEncode.y=derivY/d;
        encWeight =silhouetteParameter/d;
}
destColor.r=saturate(0.5 + vecToEncode.x*0.5);
destColor.g=saturate(0.5 + vecToEncode.y*0.5);
destColor.b=encWeight ;
```

Listing 2.3. Sampling the shadow map.

```
// Sample shadow edge hints for the relevant four texels/points
vec4 colAA=texture2D(shadowEdgeHintMap, baseUV +
        (vec2(0,0)*singleUVStep) );
vec4 colBA=texture2D(shadowEdgeHintMap, baseUV +
        (vec2(1,0)*singleUVStep) );
vec4 colAB=texture2D(shadowEdgeHintMap, baseUV +
        (vec2(0,1)*singleUVStep) );
vec4 colBB=texture2D(shadowEdgeHintMap, baseUV +
        (vec2(1,1)*singleUVStep) );

// Sample shadowmap depths for the relevant four texels/points
float depthAA=texture2D(shadowDepthMap, baseUV +
        (vec2(0,0)*singleUVStep) ).r;
float depthBA=texture2D(shadowDepthMap, baseUV +
        (vec2(1,0)*singleUVStep) ).r;
float depthAB=texture2D(shadowDepthMap, baseUV +
        (vec2(0,1)*singleUVStep) ).r;
float depthBB=texture2D(shadowDepthMap, baseUV +
        (vec2(1,1)*singleUVStep) ).r;
// Calculate the distance-to-edge function for the four points
vec3 weightFuncAA=CalcWeightFunction(vec2(0,0), colAA);
vec3 weightFuncBA=CalcWeightFunction(vec2(1,0), colBA);
vec3 weightFuncAB=CalcWeightFunction(vec2(0,1), colAB);
vec3 weightFuncBB=CalcWeightFunction(vec2(1,1), colBB);

// Evaluate the distance-to-edge function for the four points
vec3 fracPosH=vec3(fracUV.x, fracUV.y, 1.0);
float weightAA=dot(weightFuncAA, fracPosH);
float weightBA=dot(weightFuncBA, fracPosH);
float weightAB=dot(weightFuncAB, fracPosH);
float weightBB=dot(weightFuncBB, fracPosH);

// Find the least distance-to-edge value, and use the corresponding
// depth for the shadow test.
float leastDistToEdge=-10.0;
float depthForTest=0.0;
if(weightAA>leastDistToEdge)
        { leastDistToEdge=weightAA; depthForTest=depthAA; }
if(weightBA>leastDistToEdge)
{ leastDistToEdge=weightBA; depthForTest=depthBA; }
if(weightAB>leastDistToEdge)
{ leastDistToEdge=weightAB; depthForTest=depthAB; }
if(weightBB>leastDistToEdge)
{ leastDistToEdge=weightBB; depthForTest=depthBB; }
// depthForTest contains the depth to be used for the shadowmap test.
```

Listing 2.4. Shadowmap magnification.

```
vec3 CalcWeightFunction(vec2 samplePt, vec3 sampleCol)
{
   vec2 unpackedDist=(sampleCol.rg-0.5)*2.0;
   float baseWeight=sampleCol.b;
   vec3 rc=0;
   rc.x=unpackedDist.x;
   rc.y=unpackedDist.y;
   rc.z=baseWeight;
   // Skew the function slightly to artificially increase the
   // distance-to-edge value as the queried point gets further
   // from the key corner. This provides a clearly defined
   // nearest corner in cases where the distance-to-edge value is
   // a constant 1, because there is no nearby edge.
   vec2 fallVec=vec2(1,1)-(samplePt*2);
   rc.xy+=fallVec*-0.02;
   rc.z-=(rc.x*samplePt.x)+(rc.y*samplePt.y);
   return rc;
}
```

Listing 2.5. Unpacking the parameters of the distance-to-edge equation.

be written out to a 32bpp RGBA frame buffer. Further packing is undoubtedly possible!

The next step is shadowmap magnification, which is shown in Listing 2.4. The colors of the four texels surrounding the sample point are `colAA`, `colAB`, `colBA` and `colBB`; `depthAA`, etc., are the four corresponding depths. `baseUV` holds the sample point UV rounded down to the nearest texel. `fracUV` contains the fractional part of the UV-coordinate, i.e., $(0,0)$ is coincident with texel AA and $(1,1)$ is coincident with texel BB.

The `CalcWeightFunction()` function (see Listing 2.5) unpacks the parameters of the distance-to-edge equation. It is evaluated by taking the dot product of the returned vector with a homogeneous two-dimensional coordinate. (For example, see `weightAA` in Listing 2.4.)

Alternatively, the shadow map test could be applied to the corner points (e.g., take the value 0 if shadowed, 1 if not) and the four resulting values blended to produce a softer edge. This can be extended to produce an anti-aliased shadow edge.

This method works well when the triangles cover a reasonably large area, but the edge quality breaks down with small, under-sampled triangles. (See Figure 2.9. The left-hand image shows the shape of the resulting edge; the texel size is indicated. For the right-hand image, the shadow map texels are colored according to triangle index. Despite the small triangles, a clean edge still resulted.)

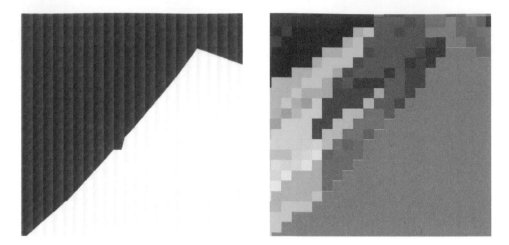

Figure 2.9.   Extrapolation problem due to an under-sampled triangle.

2.7.2   Upscaling

One of the most visible problems with upscaling images using bilinear interpolation (or similar) is that the original resolution is betrayed by the steps along edges. If an edge in the original image has three steps, then it will still have three steps when up-scaled (there are other telltale signs of upscaling such as artifacts from bilinear filtering of high-contrast edges and under-sampling artifacts, which we'll ignore for now).

If we have access to sub-pixel accurate information about the edge, an up-scaler could use that information to deliver an edge that's pixel-accurate at the target resolution. The method described in 7.1 can be used to provide a sub-pixel accurate edge at the target resolution. The edge-blur method described can provide anti-aliasing; Figure 2.10 shows the result of a $2\times$ up-scale demonstrating the technique in action.

Two possible uses for this idea are to render an image at (say) 720p, and then up-scale each frame to 1080p or, alternatively, to up-scale a low-res render target (e.g., for particles or transparencies) to the target frame buffer size. Since we are rendering to a smaller frame buffer, we save pixel shader time and bandwidth, but the low internal resolution does not reveal itself in the usual ways because the silhouette edges of the up-scaled result are still sharp.

One implementation of this idea suitable for small-scale factors is as follows. Each pixel of the source, low-res image has a color, distance to edge value, and partial derivatives of the distance-to-edge value. To find the color of a point on the destination image, begin by sampling the four containing samples in the

Figure 2.10. Close-up of a 2× up-scale using edge hints. The edge is pixel-accurate at the target resolution.

source image. Each of the four samples provides a distance-to-edge function. Depending on the distance-to-edge functions, one of two magnification modes will be used. If no silhouette edges run through the current quad, then simple bilinear interpolation will be used.

But if a silhouette edge runs through the current quad, then reproducing it in the destination (with anti-aliasing) requires more complex interpolation. Figure 2.11 shows an example situation.

For the situation in Figure 2.11, corners AA and BA are outside the silhouette, so they will hold the (default) function, which is a constant function returning the maximum value. Corners AB and BB are inside the silhouette and have a well-defined distance-to-edge function that will take the value 0 on the silhouette edge.

Corners AA/BA and AB/BB define distance-to-edge functions that are identical to the limit of precision. For reasons that will become clear shortly, we'll

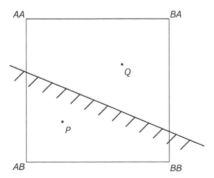

Figure 2.11. Upscaling when an edge passes through the quad. Points AA, AB, BA, and BB are the relevant four sample points in the source low-res image. Points P and Q are example points for consideration.

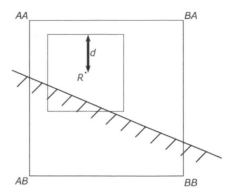

Figure 2.12.   Calculation of blend value for anti-aliasing an edge during upscaling. When shading the point R, the smaller square represents the area covered by the destination pixel. The value d measures half the edge length.

adjust these functions slightly so the returned value gradually increases with distance from their base corner.

When evaluating the functions at a particular point in the square, one function will now unambiguously return the lowest non-negative value. Using the color associated with that corner is one basic way to up-scale: it will provide a variation on nearest-neighbor sampling, but the border between the colors on one side of the edge (AA/BA) and the other (AB/BB) will precisely follow the silhouette edge.

The next step is to extend this approach to provide anti-aliasing, by blending the colors on either side of the edge based on coverage.

The two requirements are to find the two colors to blend between, and to define the blend parameter.

The requirements for the blend parameter are very similar to those for the original edge-blur: the blend parameter indicates coverage so it must approximate the coverage value in a plausible way, and it needs to be cheap.

A reasonable value for the coverage/blend parameter can be derived from the distance-to-edge value in the same way as the edge-blur. Set up the distance-to-edge function so it is defined using the Manhattan metric, as before. Calculate the blend parameter by linearly remapping the distance-to-edge value from $[-d, +d]$ to $[0, 1]$, where d is half the size of the sample region (see Figure 2.12). Instead of searching for the lowest nonnegative distance-to-edge value, we now search for the lowest value greater than $-d$.

Finding the colors to blend requires picking colors from opposite sides of the edge. Take the first color to be the one described above (i.e., belonging to the corner whose function yielded the lowest value). Find the direction of the rate of

Figure 2.13. Demonstration of a 200% up-scale with edge hints.

greatest decrease of that function; round to +1 or -1, and step in that direction
from the first corner. For point P in Figure 2.11, this would yield the colors from
corners AB and BA, respectively.

This method may sound overly complex, but there are cases where other methods can break down, e.g., choosing the diagonally opposite corner can fail if the
silhouette edge contains three corners.

This method is a very simple upscaling effect, so ugly artifacts start to appear
if it is pushed too far, but it produces acceptable results for low scaling factors.
This is enough to support the 150% up-scale from 720p to 1080p, for instance
Figure 2.13 shows an example image up-scaled by 200% using this technique.

While this method will preserve sharp edges, there are other standard upscaling problems that are still relevant. Geometry under-sampling is a danger:
in comparison to 4×MSAA, pixels might be four to eight times the area so the
Nyquist limit is raised proportionally.

Also, since bilinear filtering is used for all pixel quads not straddling an edge, high-contrast features will lead to the usual artifacts. One possibility is to encode edge hints in the texture, transform the hint to screen space and write out to the frame buffer so a sharp border due to a texture is preserved by the up-scale, but this is far from trivial. Another option is to move high-frequency shading to the up-scale: encode UVs and other parameters in the "frame buffer," and during the up-scale extrapolate these parameters and calculated the final color procedurally.

The filtering will also tend to smooth out detail. One option is that during render to the low-res buffer, extrapolate the UVs, take four samples of a detail map (with one level of LOD bias), and pack their values into the buffer. During the up-scale, these values can be used to tweak the replicated color to add detail back. Since the source is an MIP-mapped texture this will not add noise.

The two previous approaches could be generalized and combined: shade four pixels at once, with the resulting four colors packed into a single (fat) pixel of the low-res target (this would provide something like a software version of MSAA). Performance gains are possible by calculating low-frequency effects once for all four pixels; high-frequency effects are calculated for each of the four pixels individually so detail is not lost.

In closing, this approach offers a third option for increasing resolution, between simply paying a proportionally higher price for more samples and suffering the normal upscaling artifacts. It is not cheap: it is quite possible that the additional render time required or other costs means it can not offer a net gain. Also, it will magnify any quality problems, so shader aliasing will be even more apparent. But in some contexts (e.g., little high-frequency detail and a high per-pixel cost), it can offer high resolution and anti-aliasing at a fraction of the cost of other options.

2.8   Conclusion

This chapter describes a method for anti-aliasing edges for real-time applications that also applies to deferred effects and avoids the need for a super-sampled/multi-sampled frame buffer. Applications to static geometry and skinned characters are shown, and the results are often comparable to high-sample MSAA.

Enabling pixel shaders to robustly find the nearest silhouette edge with sub-pixel precision opens up some interesting possibilities; the shadow map magnification and upscaling described here are only two.

Future work includes finding better approximations for the background color. One layer of depth peeling would be ideal, but since it requires a full re-render it may well be prohibitively costly. A cheaper, more specialized alternative related to the stencil-routed A-buffer described in [Myers 07] may well exist. This would also allow more sophisticated pixel filter functions than the one suggested in Section 2.3.

Future work would also require looking into other possibilities for the adjoining-back-face test. We only tried a few tests beyond the three described in Section 2.5. It would be useful to have more options, representing different trade-offs between accuracy and expense.

Bibliography

[Beyond3D 09] "List of Rendering Resolutions and Basics on Hardware Scaling, MSAA, Framebuffers." *Beyond3D*. Available at http://forum.beyond3d.com/showthread.php?t=46241, 14 Sept. 2009.

[Huddy 08] Richard Huddy. *DirectX 10.1*. Game Developer's Conference, 2008.

[Kilgard 01] Mark J. Kilgard. "OpenGL Extension Registry: NV_vertex_array_range." *OpenGL Extension Registry*. Available at http://oss.sgi.com/projects/ogl-sample/registry/NV/vertex_array_range.txt, April 2001.

[Kirkland 99] Dale Kirkland, Bill Armstrong, Michael Gold, Jon Leech, and Paula Womack. "GL_ARB_multisample." *OpenGL Extension Registry*. Available at http://www.opengl.org/registry/specs/ARB/multisample.txt, 1999.

[Koonce 07] Rusty Koonce. "Deferred Shading in Tabula Rasa." In *GPU Gems 3*, edited by Hubert Nguyen, pp. 429–457. Boston: Addison-Wesley, 2008.

[Myers 07] Kevin Myers and Louis Bavoil. 2007. "Stencil Routed A-Buffer." *ACM SIGGRAPH 2007 Sketches* (2007).

[NVIDIA 08] NVIDIA. *NVIDIA GeForce GTX 200 GPU Datasheet*. 2008.

[Shishkovtso 05] Oles Shishkovtso. "Deferred Rendering in S.T.A.L.K.E.R." In *GPU Gems 2*, edited by Matt Pharr and Randima Fernando. Boston: Addison-Wesley, 2005.

[Thürmer 98] Grit Thürmer and Charles A. Wüthrich. "Computing Vertex Normals from Polygonal Facets." *Journal of Graphics Tools* 3:1 (Mar. 1998), 43–46.

[Valient 07] Michal Valient. "Deferred Rendering in Killzone 2." Develop Conference, Brighton, UK, July 2007.

[Young 07] Peter Young. "CSAA (Coverage Sampling Anti-Aliasing)." Technical Report, NVIDIA Corporation, 2007.

3

V

Environment Mapping with Floyd-Steinberg Halftoning

László Szirmay-Kalos, László Szécsi, and Anton Penzov

In many computer graphics applications we wish to augment virtual objects with images representing a real environment (sky, city, etc.). In order to provide the illusion that the virtual objects are parts of the real scene, the illumination of the environment should be taken into account when rendering the virtual objects [Debevec 98, Kollig and Keller 03]. Since the images representing the environment lack depth information, we usually assume that the illumination stored in these images comes from far surfaces. This means that the illumination of the environment is similar to directional lights, it has only directional characteristics, but its intensity is independent of the location of the illuminated point.

Environment mapping may be used to compute the reflected radiance of a *shaded point* $\vec{x}$ in *viewing direction* $\vec{\omega}$ as a directional integral

$$L(\vec{x}, \vec{\omega}) = \int_{\Omega} L^{\mathrm{env}}(\vec{\omega}') f_r(\vec{\omega}', \vec{x}, \vec{\omega}) \cos \theta'_{\vec{x}} V(\vec{x}, \vec{\omega}') \mathrm{d}\omega',$$

where Ω is the set of all incident directions, $L^{\mathrm{env}}(\vec{\omega}')$ is the radiance of the environment map at *illumination direction* $\vec{\omega}'$, f_r is the BRDF, $\theta'_{\vec{x}}$ is the angle between illumination direction $\vec{\omega}'$ and the surface normal at $\vec{x}$, and $V(\vec{x}, \vec{\omega}')$ is the indicator function checking whether environment illumination can take effect in shaded point $\vec{x}$ at direction $\vec{\omega}'$, i.e., no virtual object occludes the environment in this direction (Figure 3.1).

This integral is usually estimated by Monte Carlo quadrature, which generates M number of samples $\vec{\omega}'_1, \ldots, \vec{\omega}'_M$ with probability density $p(\vec{\omega}')$ and computes the

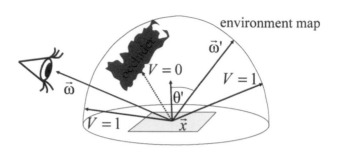

Figure 3.1.   The concept of environment mapping stored in a cube map.

estimate as an average:

$$L(\vec{x}, \vec{\omega}) \approx \frac{1}{M} \sum_{i=1}^{M} \frac{L^{\mathrm{env}}(\vec{\omega}_i') f_r(\vec{\omega}_i', \vec{x}, \vec{\omega}) \cos \theta_{\vec{x},i}' V(\vec{x}, \vec{\omega}_i')}{p(\vec{\omega}_i)}.$$

The most time consuming part of the evaluation of a sample is the computation of visibility factor V, i.e., the determination whether or not the environment is occluded. Real-time environment mapping algorithms usually ignore this factor and consequently the shadowing of environment lighting. However, for rendering photorealistic images, this simplification is unacceptable. Thus in this article we examine environment mapping approaches that correctly evaluate the occlusion of the illuminating environment.

The calculation of the visibility factor requires tracing a ray originating at shaded point $\vec{x}$ and having direction $\vec{\omega}_i'$. In order to improve the speed of environment mapping with shadow computation, the number of samples—that is, the number of traced rays—should be minimized.

For a given number of samples, the error of the quadrature depends on two factors:

1. *Importance sampling*: How well does density p mimic the integrand?

2. *Stratification*: How well does the empirical distribution of the finite number of samples follow the theoretical distribution defined by p?

This means that we should do a good job in both mimicking the integrand with the sample density and producing well stratified samples.

3.1   Parametrization of the Environment Map

The environment illumination is defined by a texture map $T(u, v)$ addressed by texture coordinates $u, v \in [0, 1]$. Thus we need a mapping or a parametrization that defines the correspondence between a texture coordinate pair and illuminating direction $\vec{\omega}'$.

A possible parametrization expresses direction $\vec{\omega}'$ by spherical angles θ', ϕ', where $\phi' \in [0, 2\pi]$ and $\theta' \in [0, \pi/2]$ in the case of hemispherical lighting and $\theta' \in [0, \pi]$ in the case of spherical lighting. Then texture coordinates (u, v) are scaled from the unit interval to these ranges. For example, in the case of spherical lighting, a direction is parameterized as

$$\vec{\omega}'(u, v) = (\cos 2\pi u \sin \pi v, \ \sin 2\pi u \sin \pi v, \ \cos \pi v),$$

where $u, v \in [0, 1]$.

A texture map is a two-dimensional image containing $R_u \times R_v$ texels where R_u and R_v are the horizontal and vertical resolutions, respectively. Note that the discussed parametrization is not uniform since different texels correspond to the same $\Delta u \Delta v = (1/R_u)(1/R_v)$ area in texture space, but different solid angles $\Delta \omega$ depending on texture coordinate v:

$$\Delta \omega = \sin \pi v \Delta u \Delta v = \frac{\sin \pi v}{R_u R_v}.$$

The integral of the reflected radiance can also be evaluated in texture space:

$$L(\vec{x}, \vec{\omega}) = \int_{u=0}^{1} \int_{v=0}^{1} E(u, v) R(u, v, \vec{x}, \omega) \mathbf{V}(u, v, \vec{x}) \mathrm{d}v \mathrm{d}v \approx$$

$$\frac{1}{R_u R_v} \sum_{i=1}^{R_u} \sum_{j=1}^{R_v} E\left(\frac{i}{R_u}, \frac{j}{R_v}\right) R\left(\frac{i}{R_u}, \frac{j}{R_v}, \vec{x}, \vec{\omega}\right) \mathbf{V}\left(\frac{i}{R_u}, \frac{j}{R_v}, \vec{x}\right),$$

where we used the following shorthand notations for the three main factors of the integrand:

$$E(u, v) = L^{\mathrm{env}}(\vec{\omega}'(u, v)) \sin \pi v = T(u, v) \sin \pi v$$

is the intensity of the *environment lighting* taking into account the distortion of the parametrization,

$$R(u, v, \vec{x}, \omega) = f_r(\vec{\omega}'(u, v), \vec{x}, \vec{\omega}) \cos \theta'_{\vec{x}}(u, v)$$

is the *reflection factor*, and

$$\mathbf{V}(u, v, \vec{x}) = V(\vec{x}, \vec{\omega}'(u, v))$$

is the *visibility factor*.

The evaluation of the reflected radiance by adding the contribution of all texels would be too time consuming. Therefore, we apply Monte Carlo methods, which approximate it from just a few sample directions, i.e., a few texels.

3.2   Importance Sampling

Monte Carlo methods use a probability density to select the sample points. According to the concept of importance sampling, we should find a density p that mimics the product form integrand. To define an appropriate density, we usually execute the following three main steps:

1. First we decide which factors of the product form integrand will be mimicked and find a scalar approximation of the usually vector valued integrand factor. In our case, environment lighting E and reflection factor R are vector valued since they assign different values for the wavelengths of the red, green, and blue light. Spectrum L can be converted to a scalar by obtaining the *luminance* of the spectrum $\mathbf{L}(L)$, which is a weighted sum of the red, green, and blue intensities. The resulting scalar approximation of the integrand is called the *importance function* and is denoted by I. Note that as the environment illumination is defined by a texture, the importance function is also represented by a two-dimensional image. When we want to emphasize this property, we refer to the importance function as the *importance map*.

   There are several options to define the importance function, as there are different alternatives of selecting those factors of the integrand that are mimicked. The simplest way is *BRDF sampling*, which mimics the luminance of the reflection factor. *Light-source sampling*, on the other hand, sets the importance function to be the luminance of the environment lighting. Finally, *product sampling* includes more than one factor of the integrand into the importance function. For example, the importance function can be the luminance of the product of the environment lighting and the reflection factor (double product sampling), or it can even incorporate a cheap visibility factor approximated by some simple proxy geometry included in the object (triple product sampling).

2. As the density should be normalized, the integral of the importance function needs to be computed for the whole domain. This computation can take advantage of the fact that the importance function is defined also as a two-dimensional array or a texture, similar to the texture map of the environment illumination:

$$\int_{u=0}^{1} \int_{v=0}^{1} I(u,v)\mathrm{d}v\mathrm{d}u \approx \frac{S}{R_u R_v},$$

   where

$$S = \sum_{u=1}^{R_u} \sum_{j=1}^{R_v} I\left(\frac{i}{R_u}, \frac{j}{R_v}\right)$$

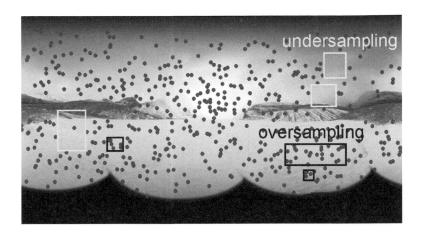

Figure 3.2. Environment map with random light-source sampling.

is the sum of all values in the importance map. Note that the importance function should be integrated as one step of the importance sampling. It means that the importance function must be much cheaper to evaluate and integrate than the original integrand.

3. Finally, the density is defined as the ratio of the importance function and the normalization constant:

$$p(u, v) = \frac{I(u, v)}{\int\limits_{u=0}^{1} \int\limits_{v=0}^{1} I(u, v) \mathrm{d}v \mathrm{d}u} = \frac{I(u, v) R_u R_v}{S}.$$

Having constructed the importance map and computed sum S, samples can be drawn with probability density p using the following simple method. We generate M statistically independent random numbers $r_1, \ldots, r_M$ that are uniformly distributed in the unit interval. Then for each random number, the two-dimensional array of the importance map is scanned, and the importance values are added together. This running sum is compared to $r_i S$. When the running sum gets larger, the scanning is stopped and the current texel (i.e., the direction corresponding to this texel) is considered as a sample. As can be easily shown, the process will select a texel with a probability proportional to its value.

Unfortunately, the application of statistically independent random samples provides poor results in many cases. To demonstrate the problem, we used light-source sampling to find directional samples on an environment map (Figure 3.2). The results are disappointing since making independent random texel selections, with probability in proportion to its luminance, does not guarantee that groups of samples will be well stratified. We still have large empty regions in important parts of the map (*undersampling*) and groups of samples needlessly concentrating to a small unimportant region (*oversampling*). We note that this problem has also been addressed by Kollig who proposed the relaxation of the samples [Kollig and Keller 03] and by Ostromoukhov who applied sophisticated tiling [Ostromoukhov et al. 04]. The method proposed in the next section provides similar results as these methods, but is much simpler and has practically no overhead with respect to the simple random approach.

3.3   Proposed Solution

The method proposed in this article has the goal of producing well stratified samples mimicking an *importance map*. It is effective, simple to implement, and is even faster than random sampling.

The proposed method is based on the recognition that importance sampling is equivalent to *digital halftoning* [Szirmay-Kalos et al. 09]. Halftoning is a technique used to render grayscale images on a black and white display (see Figure 3.3). The idea is to put more white points at brighter areas and fewer points at darker areas. The spatial density of white points in a region around a pixel is expected to be proportional to the gray level of that particular pixel. If we consider the gray level of the original image to be an importance function and the white pixels of the resulting image to be sample locations, then we can see that halftoning is equivalent to a deterministic importance sampling algorithm. The equivalence of importance sampling and halftoning stems from the fact that both of them are *frequency modulators* [Szirmay-Kalos and Szécsi 09]. The input of the frequency modulator is the upscal image or the importance map, respectively, and the output is a collection of discrete samples with a frequency specified by the input.

grayscale image   random halftoning   Floyd-Steinberg halftoning

Figure 3.3.   A grayscale image and its halftoned versions obtained with random halftoning and with the Floyd-Steinberg algorithm.

This equivalence holds for an arbitrary halftoning algorithm, including the random and ordered halftoning methods that add random noise or a periodic pattern to the original image before quantization, or, for example, error diffusion halftoning methods from which the Floyd-Steinberg algorithm is the most famous [Floyd and Steinberg 75]. Error diffusion halftoning provides better results than random or ordered halftoning because it does not simply make independent local decisions but gathers and distributes information to neighboring pixels as well. Because it takes gray levels in a neighborhood into account, the sample positions are stratified, making the resulting image smoother and reducing the noise compared to random or dithered approaches.

Because of these nice properties, we developed our sampler based on the Floyd-Steinberg method. Random dithering was implemented for comparison. We expected the same improvement in importance sampling as provided by the Floyd-Steinberg halftoning over random dithering.

3.3.1 Floyd-Steinberg Sampler

The sampling algorithm takes the importance map and computes the sum S of all texels. Then, the sampling is simply the execution of a Floyd-Steinberg halftoning on the map setting the threshold at $S/(2M)$ where M is the number of expected samples. In Figure 3.4 the threshold and the error are depicted by a red line and a white bar, respectively. The halftoning algorithm initializes an error value to 0 and scans the map row-by-row, changing the scanning order at the end of the rows. At each texel, the comparison of the error value to the threshold may have two outcomes. If the error is not greater than the threshold, then no sample is generated here (the texel becomes black) and the error is left unchanged. If the error is greater than the threshold, then this texel is a sample. The error value is decreased by S/M, i.e., we compute the negative complementer of the error represented by the black part of the bar in Figure 3.4.

In both cases, before stepping onto the next texel, the remaining error of the texel is distributed to its unvisited neighbors. The method continues similarly until all texels have been visited.

Listing 3.1 shows the implementation of this algorithm optimized to work as a geometry shader. Every time the shader is invoked, it processes the importance map of size $R.x \times R.y$, the values of which are queried using the `getImportance` function. It emits 32 directional samples, with the probability of sample selection stored in the alpha channel. The function `getSampleDir` returns the direction associated with a texel of the importance map. We avoid maintaining an actual array of importance values by storing only the importance that has been carried to the next row. Variable `cPixel` contains the importance to be transferred to the next pixel, `cDiagonal` must be added to the pixel below the next, and `cRow` is an

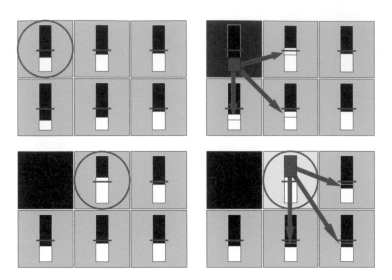

Figure 3.4. The Floyd-Steinberg sampling. The error (white bar) of the upper-left texel is smaller than the threshold (red line), so it is not selected (the texel will be black). Its error is distributed to the neighbors increasing their error levels. The next texel will have a larger error than the threshold, so it is selected (the texel will be white). The negative complementer error (black bar) is added to the neighbors, reducing their error value.

array, packed into `float4` vectors, that contains the importances to be added to pixels in the next row. Every row is processed in runs of four pixels, after which the four values gathered in variable `acc` can be packed into the `cRow` array. The size of `cRow` is `RX4`, which is the width of the importance map divided by four. Every time the importance map is read, the original importance value is loaded into variable `I`, and importance carried over from the neighbors is added to get the modified importance in variable `Ip`.

In addition to Floyd-Steinberg halftoning, the family of error diffusion methods has many other members that differ in the error distribution neighborhood and weights, as well as in the order of processing the texels [Kang 99]. These sophisticated techniques are also worth using as importance sampling methods. The weights need special care when the number of expected samples M is very small with respect to the number of texels. Multidimensional error diffusion methods perform well when they are in a stationary state, but need to warm up, i.e., they start producing samples later than expected. If very few samples are generated with the method, this delay becomes noticeable. To solve this problem, the weight of the faster running coordinate should be increased. In the extreme case, the algorithm should act as a one-dimensional error diffusion filter.

```
[maxvertexcount(32)]
void gsSampler( inout PointStream<float4> samples ) {
  uint M = 32; float S = 0;
  [loop]for(uint v = 0; v < R.y; v++)
    [loop]for(uint u = 0; u < R.x; u++)
      S += getImportance(uint2(u, v));
  float threshold = S / 2 / M;
  float4 cRow[RX4]={{0,0,0,0},{0,0,0,0},{0,0,0,0},{0,0,0,0}};
  float cPixel = 0, cDiagonal = 0, acc[4];
  [loop]for(uint j = 0; j < R.y; j++)  {
    uint kper4 = 0;
    [loop]for(uint k = 0; k < R.x; k += 4) {
      for(uint xi = 0; xi < 4; xi++) {
        float I = getImportance(uint2(k+xi, j));
        float Ip = I + cRow[kper4][xi] + cPixel;
        if(Ip > threshold) {
          float3 dir = getSampleDir(uint2(k+xi, j));
          samples.Append( float4(dir, I / S) );
          Ip -= threshold * 2;
        }
        acc[xi] = Ip * 0.375 + cDiagonal;
        cPixel = Ip * 0.375;
        cDiagonal = Ip * 0.25;
      }
      cRow[kper4++] = float4(acc[0], acc[1], acc[2], acc[3]);
    }
    j++; kper4--;
    [loop]for(int k = R.x-5; k >= 0; k -= 4) {
      for(int xi = 3; xi >= 0; xi--) {
        float I = getImportance(uint2(k+xi, j));
        float Ip = I + cRow[kper4][xi] + cPixel;
        if(Ip > threshold ) {
          float3 dir = getSampleDir(uint2(k+xi, j));
          samples.Append( float4(dir, I / S) );
          Ip -= threshold * 2;
        }
        acc[xi] = Ip * 0.375 + cDiagonal;
        cPixel = Ip * 0.375;
        cDiagonal = Ip * 0.25;
      }
      cRow[kper4--] = float4(acc[0], acc[1], acc[2], acc[3]);
    }
  }
}
```

Listing 3.1. The Floyd-Steinberg sampler implemented as a geometry shader.

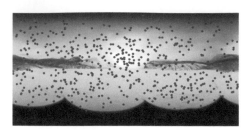 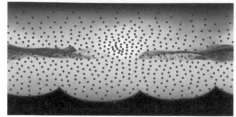

Figure 3.5.   Sampling weighted environment maps with random sampling (left) and Floyd-Steinberg halftoning (right).

3.3.2   Application to Light-Source Sampling

In light-source sampling the importance function is based on the environment illumination and we also take into account that different texels correspond to different solid angles:

$$I(u, v) = \mathbf{L}(E(u, v)).$$

Random sampling   Floyd-Steinberg   Reference

Figure 3.6.   Results of light-source sampling. Diffuse and specular bunnies illuminated by directional lights sampled randomly and with Floyd-Steinberg halftoning.

Ignoring the cosine weighted BRDF and the visibility degrades importance sampling. But since the importance function depends just on the illumination direction and is independent of the point being shaded, $\vec{x}$, sampling should be executed only once for all shaded points.

In this case, the proposed scheme is as simple as the Floyd-Steinberg halftoning of the environment map weighted by solid angle scaling $\sin \pi v$. Figures 3.5 and 3.6 compare the distribution of samples and the resulting images of the illuminated object for random sampling and for the Floyd-Steinberg sampler. As the Floyd-Steinberg sampler scans the map only once and obtains samples directly, it is not slower than random sampling. Sampling the 1024×512 resolution environment map of Figure 3.5 takes 47 msec on an NVIDIA GeForce 8800 GFX GPU.

3.3.3 Application to Product Sampling

Product sampling includes more than one factor of the integrand into the importance function. Note that the inclusion of all factors is not feasible since the computation of the importance must be cheaper than that of the integrand. In environment mapping, the expensive part is the visibility test, so we either ignore occlusions in the importance or replace it with some cheaper approximation. The importance function is defined as

$$I(u,v) = E(u,v)R(u,v,\vec{x},\vec{\omega})\tilde{\mathbf{V}}(u,v,\vec{x}).$$

where $\tilde{\mathbf{V}}$ is the approximation of the visibility factor. *Double product sampling* sets $\tilde{\mathbf{V}} = 1$ assuming that the environment is always visible when generating important directions. Alternatively, we can approximate visibility by computing intersections with a contained proxy geometry, for example, spheres inside the object. In this case, we talk about *triple product sampling*. We have to emphasize that the approximate visibility factor and the proxy geometry is used only in the definition of the importance map and for generating important directions. When the ray is traced, the original geometry is intersected, that is, the original visibility indicator is included into the integral quadrature. Triple product sampling helps to reduce the number of those rays that surely intersect some object, and thus their contribution is zero. Unfortunately, it is not always easy to find a simple proxy geometry that is inside the object. For example, in Figure 3.7 it is straightforward to put a sphere into the Ming head, but the definition of a proxy geometry for the wheel is difficult.

Unlike light-source sampling, now the importance function also depends on shaded point $\vec{x}$ and indirectly on the normal vector at $\vec{x}$. This means that we cannot process the environment map once globally for all shaded points, but the sampling process including the Floyd-Steinberg halftoning should be repeated

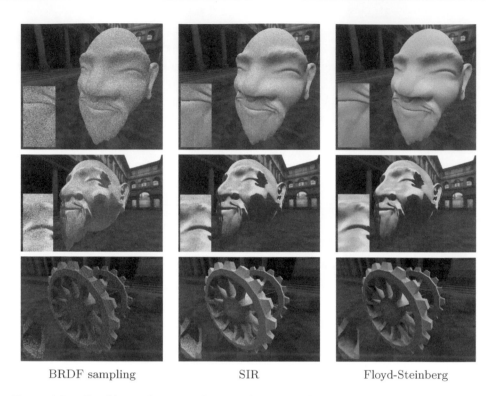

BRDF sampling   SIR   Floyd-Steinberg

Figure 3.7.   Double product sampling results. Note that the Floyd-Steinberg sampler
eliminated the noise at fully visible surfaces both for the diffuse and specular cases. The
lower row of images show a wheel having a lot of occlusions, which are not mimicked by
the double product importance.

for every single shaded point. Thus, while in light-source sampling the Floyd-
Steinberg sampler has no overhead, product sampling pays off if ray tracing is
more costly than the generation and processing of the importance map.

In order to test the approach, we have compared three techniques: BRDF
sampling, random halftoning, which is similar to *sampling-importance resampling*
(SIR) [Burke et al. 04, Talbot et al. 05] in the case of product sampling, and the new
Floyd-Steinberg scheme. All three were implemented as GPU algorithms, which
run on NVIDIA GeForce 8800 GFX graphics hardware. All methods traced $M =
32$ rays per pixel. Both sampling-importance resampling and the Floyd-Steinberg
sampler obtained the real samples from 32×32 local importance maps generated
separately for every shaded point $\vec{x}$. The results are shown by Figure 3.7. Note
that the Floyd-Steinberg sampler completely eliminated the noise at fully visible
surfaces, and some noise remained only at partially occluded regions.

3.4   Conclusion

The most important message of this article is that halftoning and importance sampling are equivalent, thus we can exploit the sophisticated halftoning algorithms in importance sampling. We investigated the application of the Floyd-Steinberg halftoning method in environment mapping and concluded that this approach produces samples with better distribution than random sampling. Thanks to this, the integrals evaluated with these samples are more accurate.

Bibliography

[Burke et al. 04] David Burke, Abhijeet Ghosh, and Wolfgang Heidrich. "Bidirectional Importance Sampling for Illumination from Environment Maps." In *ACM SIGGRAPH 2004 Sketches*, p. 112, 2004.

[Debevec 98] Paul Debevec. "Rendering Synthetic Objects Into Real Scenes: Bridging Traditional and Image-Based Graphics with Global Illumination and High Dynamic Range Photography." In *SIGGRAPH '98*, pp. 189–198, 1998.

[Floyd and Steinberg 75] Robert W. Floyd and Louis Steinberg. "An Adaptive Algorithm for Spatial Gray Scale." In *Society for Information Display 1975 Symposium Digest of Tecnical Papers*, p. 36, 1975.

[Kang 99] Henry R. Kang. *Digital Color Halftoning.* Bellingham, WA: SPIE Press, 1999.

[Kollig and Keller 03] Thomas Kollig and Alexander. Keller. "Efficient Illumination by High Dynamic Range Images." In *Eurographics Symposium on Rendering*, pp. 45–51, 2003.

[Ostromoukhov et al. 04] Victor Ostromoukhov, Charles Donohue, and Pierre-Marc Jodoin. "Fast Hierarchical Importance Sampling with Blue Noise Properties." *ACM Transactions on Graphics* 23:3 (2004), 488–498.

[Szirmay-Kalos and Szécsi 09] László Szirmay-Kalos and László Szécsi. "Deterministic Importance Sampling with Error Diffusion." *Computer Graphics Forum (EG Symposium on Rendering)* 28:4 (2009), 1056–1064.

[Szirmay-Kalos et al. 09] László Szirmay-Kalos, László Szécsi, and Anton Penzov. "Importance Sampling with Floyd-Steinberg Halftoning." In *Eurographics 09, Short Papers*, pp. 69–72, 2009.

[Talbot et al. 05] Justin Talbot, David Cline, and Parris K. Egbert. "Importance Resampling for Global Illumination." In *Rendering Techniques*, pp. 139–146, 2005.

4

Hierarchical Item Buffers for Granular Occlusion Culling

Thomas Engelhardt and Carsten Dachsbacher

4.1 Introduction

Culling algorithms are key to many efficient, interactive rendering techniques. Their common goal is to reduce workload from virtually all stages of the rendering pipeline. Although they have been studied by many researchers, thus spanning a large spectrum of variety and complexity, they often build upon the integral building block of visibility determination.

The most common algorithms employ frustum and portal culling in the application stage to exclude invisible geometry, often organized in a hierarchical data structure. More sophisticated algorithms precompute entire visibility sets in an expensive offline pre-process for efficient online visibility evaluation.

Recent advancements in the field of (occlusion) culling [Bittner et al. 04] employ hardware occlusion queries as a mechanism for efficient from-point visibility determination, provided by commodity graphics hardware. Geometry is rasterized against an existing depth buffer and pixels that pass the depth test are counted. The query result, however, has to be read back to the application and thus conservative visibility-based culling inherently synchronizes the otherwise asynchronous execution of CPU and GPU; a problem, the recently introduced occlusion predicates try to avoid.

Beyond that, GPUs exploit the built-in early-z optimization to autonomously discard pixels that fail the depth test before the pixel shader is executed. This optimization, however, becomes disabled in certain scenarios, e.g., in case that the pixel shader writes a depth value.

In [Engelhardt and Dachsbacher 09] we described a method that computes from point visibility in an output-sensitive way. It is designed to complement the early-z optimization and to extend the repertoire of existing GPU-based culling methods, in particular for rendering techniques that involve costly shaders. It is flexible in terms of adapting to varying user and shader demands by computing visibility of configurable granularity. That is, it is capable of computing visibility for different entities, i.e., individual primitives, batches of primitives or entire (batches of) objects. This is achieved by using a variant of an item buffer. Entities are assigned an identifier and rendered into the item buffer. Afterwards the occurrence of each entity in the item buffer is counted exploiting GPU-based scattering. Because the method executes entirely on the GPU, it is easy to implement and does not require any application feedback. This, for instance, enables visibility-based culling and LOD control in the geometry shader as well as in the upcoming tesselation shaders, and further enables culling in scenarios where the early-z optimization is disabled.

4.2   Hierarchical Item Buffers

The foundation of our method is the well-known item buffer [Weghorst et al. 84]. Similar to the original approach, we store a unique identifier (ID) for each rasterized entity that passed the depth test. An entity, for example, may be an individual triangle, a cluster of triangles, an individual instance within an instanced draw call, or in the simplest case, an object. Thus the type of an entity defines the granularity of the query. Afterwards, as illustrated in Figure 4.1 we employ a histogram algorithm to count the occurrence of each ID and thus compute an entity's visibility.

To compute the histogram, we use a scattering algorithm on the GPU similar to [Scheuermann and Hensley 07]. The item buffer is reinterpreted as a point list and the vertex shader computes a bin index from the ID. Each bin stores a counter and by rendering point primitives, we increment the counters in the histogram render target using additive blending (Figure 4.2). Afterwards an entity's visibility

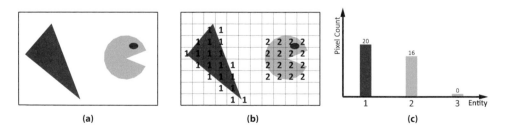

(a)   (b)   (c)

Figure 4.1. (a) Entities to determine visibility of; (b) the item buffer after rasterization; (c) histogram of the item buffer. No occurrences were counted for entity 3; hence it is invisible.

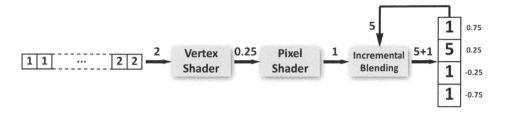

Figure 4.2. The histogram algorithm: a point with ID 2 is rendered and the vertex shader computes pixel address 0.25. Using additive blending, the value in the histogram bin is incremented.

can be queried in any shader stage accessing its bin (texel) in the histogram texture.

4.2.1 ID Assignment

Obviously, the assignment of IDs to entities plays an integral part in the algorithm. In the simplest case a single ID can be assigned per object. Such an ID may be a user-specified attribute, but system generated semantics like the primitive or instance ID are also possible. However, more sophisticated assignment schemes can be used that enable visibility queries for subregions in screen-space. Therefore we subdivide the screen space into $2^t \times 2^t$ tiles and compute the final ID as follows:

$$ID = 2^{2t}ID_{\text{base}} + 2^t y_{\text{tile}} + x_{\text{tile}}.$$

Not only does such an assignment scheme allow querying the visibility of an entity in particular regions of the screen, but also enables queries in a hierarchical fashion building a quad-tree type structure. For instance, consider Figure 4.3(b). The

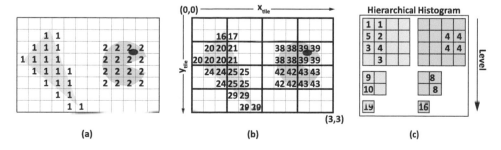

Figure 4.3. (a) The item buffer stores one base identifier per entity; (b) item buffer with 4×4 screen tiling; (c) histogram hierarchy obtained from (b).

visibility of the triangle in tiles $[0, 1] \times [2, 3]$ can be queried with a single access to the hierarchy(Figure 4.3(c)).

4.2.2   Direct3D 10 Implementation

To integrate the hierarchical item buffer into the Direct3D 10 rendering pipeline, the following steps have to be implemented: creating the item buffer and scattering.

Creating the item buffer. Creating the item buffer is performed in two steps. First we render all occluders into the depth buffer (see Listing 4.1). In a second pass we render all entities while leaving depth testing, as well as writing to the depth buffer enabled. The pixel shader then computes the entity's ID and, to decouple histogram coordinate computation from scattering, the according bin index, i.e., a texture coordinate within the histogram texture.

```
cbuffer cbHistogramDimensions
{
  float2 hDim;        // Width & height of histogram
  float2 tDim;        // Width & height of a tile in pixels
  float3 idScaling;   // = float3(2^(2t), 2^t, 1)
};

struct PS_ID {
  float4 Position  : SV_POSITION;
  float BaseID     : TEXCOORD0;
};

float2 psRenderItemBuffer( in PS_ID vsIn ) : SV_TARGET0 {

  // Base ID and tile IDs
  float3 ID = float3( vsIn.BaseID,
    floor(vsIn.Position.xy) / tDim );

  // Composed ID
  float  itemID = dot( idScaling, ID );

  // Relative histogram texture coordinates [0,1]^2
  float tmp = itemID / hDim.x;
  float x   = frac( tmp );
  float y   = floor( tmp ) / hDim.y;

  // Relative viewport coordinates [-1;1]^2
  return (-1 + 2 * float2(x,y) + 1 / hDim);
}
```

Listing 4.1. HLSL pixel shader for rendering into an item buffer.

```
Texture2D <float2 > tItemBuffer ;

float4 vsScatter ( in uint VertexID : SV_VERTEXID ) : SV_POSITION {
  uint w,h;
  tItemBuffer .GetDimensions ( w, h );

  uint x = VertexID % w;
  uint y = VertexID / w;

  return float4 ( tItemBuffer .Load (int3 (x,y,0)), 0, 1 );
}
```

Listing 4.2. HLSL vertex shader for scattering.

Scattering. Scattering is the second pass of the algorithm (see Listing 4.2). The histogram render target is bound to the output merger stage and the blending stage is configured to perform additive blending. The item buffer obtained in the previous pass is bound as an input resource to the vertex shader and a point list as large as the item buffer's pixel count is rendered. From the system generated vertex ID a lookup coordinate into the item buffer is computed to load the histogram bin's coordinate computed in the previous pass, which then is directly sent to the rasterization stage.

As a final and optional step, the natively supported mipmap generation scheme may be used to construct the hierarchy on the histogram. Please note that due to the inherent filtering in this creation scheme, the counters in the histogram bins have to be incremented by 2^{2t} in order to ensure correct results in the coarsest hierarchy level.

A potential performance bottleneck regarding scattering should be considered when implementing the algorithm. Scattering may trigger many successive increments by sending point primitives to the same bin and hence generates a lot of overdraw which degenerates the overall scattering performance. This is especially the case when screen tiling is kept low and the entity covers a large area in the item buffer.

Another cause for degraded performance are pixels that are not covered by an entity after they have been rasterized. Unfortunately, these pixels cannot be discarded before scattering, and reserving an additional bin to count the occurance of uncovered pixels may cause massive overdraw. Fortunately those pixels can be removed in the scattering process by initializing the item buffer with a bin index or histogram coordinate that does not fall into the histogram viewport. Hence we can rely on the rasterization stage to automatically cull those point primitives when scattered.

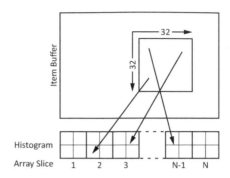

Figure 4.4. The compute shader operates on 32×32 blocks of the item buffer. For each ID in the item buffer, address (array slice, pixel coordinates) in the histogram is computed.

```
RWTexture2DArray <uint> Histogram : register ( u0 );
Texture2D <uint> ItemBuffer        : register ( t0 );

[numthreads (32,32,1)]
void CSMain (
  uint3 GID   : SV_GROUPID ,
  uint3 DTID  : SV_DISPATCHTHREADID ,
  uint3 GTID  : SV_GROUPTHREADID ,
  uint  GI    : SV_GROUPINDEX )
{
  // Input dimensions
  uint w0,h0,s0;
  uint w1, h1;
  Histogram . GetDimensions ( w0, h0, s0 );
  ItemBuffer . GetDimensions ( w1, h1 );

  // xy pixel coordinate in the item buffer
  int2 pixelIndex = DTID . xy;

  // Entity ID
  uint entityID   = ItemBuffer [pixelIndex ];

  // xy pixel coordinate in the histogram
  uint2 tileIndex = pixelIndex *
    uint2 ( w0, h0 ) / uint2 ( w1, h1 );

  // Interlocked increment
  InterlockedAdd ( itemHistogram [int3(tileIndex ,entityID)], 1 );
}
```

Listing 4.3. The scattering compute shader for generating the entity histogram.

4.2.3 Direct3D 11 Implementation

One of the new features of Direct3D 11 is the direct support for scattering in pixel and compute shaders. This greatly simplifies and extends the implementation of the hierarchical item buffer. Instead of exploiting the conventional graphics pipeline, a compute shader can be used to transform the item buffer into an entity histogram. As illustrated in Figure 4.4 our implementation of the compute shader operates on blocks of 32×32 item buffer pixels. Each pixel in the block is associated with a thread. Each thread reads the ID or histogram bin index from the item buffer and computes the target address, depending on the format or layout of the histogram texture. For simplicity we allocated a histogram texture array, where each array slice corresponds to one entity and each pixel in the slice corresponds to one screen tile. After the address of the histogram bin has been computed, an interlocked operation (as can be seen in Figure 4.3), is performed to increment the counter in the bin.

Rendering into an item buffer may limit certain applications since only one entity can appear in a pixel of the item buffer, i.e., mutual occlusion of entities has to be resolved in the item buffer creation pass. This limitation, inherent in our Direct3D 10 implementation, can be circumvented with Direct3D 11. Instead of rendering into an item buffer and scattering afterwards, the scattering can be directly exploited in the pixel shader to build the entity histogram. Care must be taken to ensure that the depth test against the previously rendered depth buffer is performed. By disabling depth writes, the early-z optimization ensures that an entity's visibility is correctly resolved before the pixel shader is executed.

4.3 Application

In the demo available at http://www.akpeters.com/gpupro, we demonstrate the granularity and efficiency of our algorithm by means of a small example. We applied the item buffer visibility determination algorithm to speed up the shadow volume rendering technique for instanced shadow casters. Instancing greatly reduces the draw call overhead for many instances of the same object and shadow volumes are capable of producing highly accurate shadows, but are quite costly to render. Since the introduction of the geometry, shader shadow volumes can be created directly on the GPU. Hence this algorithm is now capable of handling dynamic scenes as gracefully as purely static ones. Unfortunately, the shadow volume extrusion can be quite costly, especially for many or complex objects. Besides that, the extruded shadow volumes have to be rasterized which consumes a lot of fill rate. Our solution is inspired by the algorithm described in [Lloyd et al. 04]. We refrain from extruding a shadow volume if the shadow caster lies within the shadow volume of another caster. This case is easily detected by applying a visibility pass from the light source's point of view.

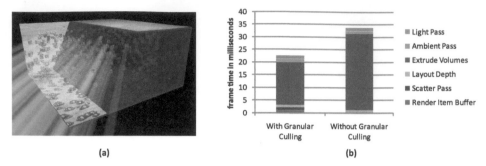

(a)   **(b)**

Figure 4.5. (a) Our application rendering 400 shadow casters. We do not extrude shadow volumes for casters contained in the shadow of the box. (b) Statistics for the frame seen in (a) obtained on a GeForce 8800 GTX. Creating a 512×512 item buffer and scattering into the histogram took about two milliseconds. Scattering alone took about one millisecond.

In our example, shadow casters are rendered with instancing and the on-the-fly generated instance ID is used to identify each individual instance in the item buffer. The volume extrusion pass then queries the visibility directly on the GPU and only creates a shadow volume, if the instance is visible from the light source. For more details on the implementation, please refer to the source code available at http://www.akpeters.com/gpupro.

4.4   Results

We have analyzed several aspects of our algorithm. Our results are restricted to Direct3D 10 level hardware, because the succeding generation of graphics cards is not yet available at the time this article is written. Figure 4.5 shows an in-depth analysis of the rendering time for a particular frame rendered on a Geforce 8800

(a)   **(b)**   **(c)**

Figure 4.6. Three different stages of culling. From left to right, an increased number of shadow volumes are extruded.

Configuration	100 objects			250 objects			500 objects		
	A	B	C	A	B	C	A	B	C
NC+NI	85	85	85	36	36	36	14	14	14
NC+I	102	102	102	45	45	45	22	22	22
PC+NI	72	72	72	30	30	30	15	15	15
IB+I	188	125	107	93	60	52	51	32	27

Table 4.1. Rendering performance on a Geforce 8800 GTX. **NC:** No Culling, **NI:** No Instancing, **I:** Instancing, **PC:** Predicated Culling, **IB:** Item Buffer.

GTX gaphics card. The application renders 400 shadow casters with a single instanced draw call. As can be seen, the shadow volume extrusion pass takes a significant amount of the entire frame time. In this example, an item buffer of 512×512 pixels was used while the final image was rendered at a resolution of 1280×720 pixels. Both item buffer creation and scattering took about two milliseconds. Scattering alone took about one millisecond in this example. Please note, that the frame time for the scattering pass does not depend on the number of entities, but on the resolution of the item buffer.

Further, we compared our method to occlusion predicates. In this case, we cannot exploit instanced rendering because hardware occlusion queries operate on a per draw call granularity, i.e., visibility for individual entities, like individual instances, cannot be resolved. Thus each shadow caster is individually rendered and tested for visibility. In our predicated render path, we create a Direct3D 10 query object for each caster at application startup, set the occlusion predication flag and use a depth buffer of 512×512 pixels in the visibility pass. As illustrated in Figure 4.6, we have measured rendering performance for an increasing amount of objects for which shadow volumes have to be extruded. Results are shown in Table 4.1 and Table 4.2. Like in the previous example the rendering resolution was 1280×720 pixels and the resolution of the item buffer was 512×512 pixels. For completeness we included performance measurements for scenarios that did not exploit any kind of culling.

Configuration	100 objects			250 objects			500 objects		
	A	B	C	A	B	C	A	B	C
NC+NI	153	153	153	66	65	65	26	28	32
NC+I	193	199	280	85	92	130	45	49	71
PC+NI	85	58	51	35	25	20	16	10	9
IB+I	405	263	326	244	146	177	137	79	99

Table 4.2. Rendering performance on a Radeon 4890. **NC:** No Culling, **NI:** No Instancing, **I:** Instancing, **PC:** Predicated Culling, **IB:** Item Buffer.

As can be seen, our culling approach outperformed all other rendering paths in the application by large margins. Due to the costly geometry shader, culling is quite beneficial and rendering performance increases significantly. Interestingly, occlusion-predicated rendering exposes rather subpar performance in our scenarios, even for a small number of objects.

4.5   Conclusion

We have presented a culling method that operates directly on the GPU, which is entirely transparent to the application and very simple to implement, especially on the next generation of hardware and graphics APIs. We have shown that with very little overhead, rendering time per frame can be reduced significantly, especially for costly shaders or costly rendering techniques. It is especially targeted at early shader stages like the geometry shader and we believe that its target applications are manifold. For example, [Engelhardt and Dachsbacher 09] have shown an application of this technique to accelerate per pixel displacement mapping, but it also opens the possibility for visibility-based LOD control and culling in tesselation shaders.

Bibliography

[Bittner et al. 04] Jiří Bittner, Michael Wimmer, Harald Piringer, and Werner Purgathofer. "Coherent Hierarchical Culling: Hardware Occlusion Queries Made Useful." *Computer Graphics Forum* 23:3 (2004), 615–624. Proceedings EUROGRAPHICS 2004.

[Engelhardt and Dachsbacher 09] Thomas Engelhardt and Carsten Dachsbacher. "Granular Visibility Queries on the GPU." In *I3D '09: Proceedings of the 2009 Symposium on Interactive 3D Graphics and Games*, pp. 161–167. New York: ACM, 2009.

[Lloyd et al. 04] Brandon Lloyd, Jeremy Wend, Naga K. Govindaraju, and Dinesh Manocha. "CC Shadow Volumes." In *Rendering Techniques*, pp. 197–206, 2004.

[Scheuermann and Hensley 07] Thorsten Scheuermann and Justin Hensley. "Efficient Histogram Generation Using Scattering on GPUs." In *I3D '07: Proceedings of the 2007 Symposium on Interactive 3D Graphics and Games*, pp. 33–37. New York: ACM, 2007.

[Weghorst et al. 84] Hank Weghorst, Gary Hooper, and Donald P. Greenberg. "Improved Computational Methods for Ray Tracing." *ACM Transactions on Graphics* 3:1 (1984), 52–69.

Realistic Depth of Field in Postproduction

David Illes and Peter Horvath

Depth of field (DOF) is an effect, typical in photography, which results in regions of varying focus based on their distance from the camera. In computer-generated special effects, artists try to mimic the effects of DOF to produce more realistic images [Demers 04]. When integrating computer-generated effects, which are rendered in perfect focus, with real captured images, DOF must be applied during the compositing phase. Mixing real and synthetic images requires a realistic defocus effect that can mimic the behavior of the original camera.

In this article we present an interactive GPU-accelerated DOF implementation that extends the capabilities of the existing methods with automatic edge improvements and physically based parameters. Defocus effects are usually controlled by blur radius, but can also be driven by physically based properties. Our technique supports postproduction defocus on images and sequences using a grayscale depth map image and parameters like focal length, f-stop values, subject magnitude, camera distance, and the real depth of the image.

5.1 Depth-of-Field Equations

Realistic depth of field is necessary compositing live action and CGI images. The quality of the results can be enhanced if depth of field is configured using real-world camera parameters.

Replace the far distance by an arbitrary distance D, the blur disk diameter b at that distance is

$$b = \frac{fm_s}{N}\frac{D-s}{D},$$

where f is the focal length, m_s is the subject magnification, N is the f-stop number, and s is the focus distance. F-stop number can be calculated using the following formula:

$$N = 2^{i/2},$$

where $i = 1(f/1.4)$, $i = 2(f/2)$, $i = 3(f/2.8)$, etc.

On a real-world camera, the *f-number* is usually adjusted in discrete steps called *f-stops*. Each value is marked with its corresponding *f-number*, and represents a halving of the light intensity from the previous stop. This corresponds to a decrease of the pupil and aperture diameters by a factor of $\sqrt{2}$ or about 1.414.

When the background is at the far limit of DOF, the blur disk diameter is equal to the circle of confusion c, and the blur is just imperceptible. The *circle of confusion* (CoC) is an optical spot caused by the effect of light rays from a lens not coming to a perfect focus when imaging a point source.

Based on the equations, the artist can set the camera *focal length, subject magnitude factor* and the *f-stop* value. An image sequence with depth maps typically does not contain real physical distance values. The user must provide the image range, which represents the foreground and background distance of the image, as well as the camera distance, which is the camera's distance from the image foreground (see Figure 5.1). The real physical distance between the camera and the focus point is computed as

$$s = d_{\text{camera}} + Im_r(Z_{\text{focus}}/Z_{\text{max}}),$$

where d_{camera} is the camera distance from the foreground, Im_r is the image range, Z_{focus} is the depth value of the focus point, Z_{max} is the maximum value of the Z-depth.

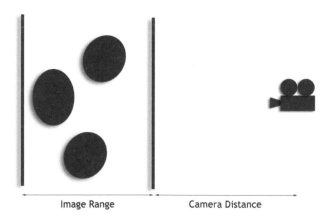

Figure 5.1. Camera position and image range.

Let x_d be the distance of the current pixel from the focus point. The distance is calculated based on the following equation:

$$x_d = Im_r|Z_{\text{focus}} - Z_{\text{current}}|/Z_{\text{max}}.$$

Using the above distances, the blur diameter b is defined as

$$b = \frac{fm_s}{N}\frac{x_d}{s}.$$

5.2 Camera Lens Simulation

Diaphragms are generally constructed with aperture blades that form an iris shape. Aperture shape (see Figure 5.2) affects the form of the light beams projected on the film. More blades result in more circular light beam shapes on the resulted image. Such aperture shapes can be constructed using curves or can be read as a custom bitmap image. A custom image aperture mask makes it possible to generate defocus effects based on real camera apertures. Instead of the advanced layered blurring in [Kraus and Strengert 07], our approach uses a local neighborhood search to approximate the final pixel color based on the depth properties of the image.

Our depth of field system uses several masks based on the depth value of the current pixel. For a seamless depth of field effect, the aperture kernel matrices need to have an odd width and height, and they must be interpolated. Smooth changes in depth of field require subpixel precision and floating-point values for the masks. The current kernel mask is calculated with the original adjacent kernels. For example if the new kernel size is 12.4×12.4 we generate the new mask from the 11×11 and from the 13×13 kernels with linear interpolation.

5.3 Exposure Simulation

During the exposure process, the film or the CCD unit records exposure values. The film is chemically processed and scanned, or the CCD matrix values are read

Figure 5.2. Examples for the shape of the aperture blade.

and converted to obtain a digital image. The final image I is transformed into pixel values without any additional physical properties. Exposure values are converted to pixel values using a non-linear mapping.

Also during the exposure process, each disk of light contributes to a neighborhood on the film. In theory, this results in a convolution of the pixel values similar to a Gaussian blur; however, simply performing a convolution on the pixel values would not generate the same visual result as a real world defocus.

We use the idea of [Cyril et al. 05] to simulate this phenomenon using an inverse mapping of the film. We also want to mix the effect of the contributing pixels in the exposure space.

5.3.1   Improvements by Local Neighborhood Blending

Current depth of field post processing implementations usually do not produce realistic results; edges are often blurred incorrectly, generating artifacts such as color bleeding, and darkened silhouettes. These artifacts result in images that are unrealistic. In the following sections we present a local neighborhood interpolation technique for eliminating these artifacts. Our approach uses an edge improvement algorithm for automatic and realistic depth of field calculation and is performed in three steps: pixel accumulation, pixel re-accumulation, and bloom.

Pixel Accumulation. The color of the current pixel is calculated from the color and luminance value of the adjacent pixels (Listing 5.1) based on the aperture mask (Figure 5.3).

The R,G,B, and luminance channels coming from the neighboring pixels are accumulated in different buffers. The number of neighbors which take part in the accumulation depends on the Z-depth. In an image where two objects with

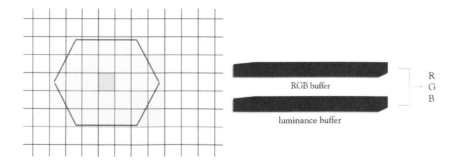

Figure 5.3. Marked pixels are processed during the accumulation phase. Pixel colors and luminance values are stored in the accumulation buffers. Final pixel is calculated based on the results of the two buffers.

```
for all neighboring pixels {
  // a.) Luminance:
  L = 0.3 * R + 0.59 * G + 0.11 * B;
  // b.) Multiply luminance with the aperture mask value
  multL = F(z) * L,
  // where F(z) scales the mask based on the pixel distance.
  // c.) Accumulate the resulting value with the RGB values.
  pixel->r += neighborColor->r * multL;
  pixel->g += neighborColor->g * multL;
  pixel->b += neighborColor->b * multL;
  // d.) Accumulate the luminance of the pixel.
  pixel->lum += multL;
}
// After accumulation, calculate the final color from
// the color and luminance buffers.
if (pixel->lum > 0) {
  pixel->r /= pixel->lum;
  pixel->g /= pixel->lum;
  pixel->b /= pixel->lum;
}
```

Listing 5.1. Pixel accumulation scheme.

different distances are close to each other the result can contain artifacts, since different mask sizes are used on the layers. Let us define an epsilon value as the minimum depth difference at which the two layers shall appear with different mask sizes, i.e., where there are edges in the image. Here the dominant pixel from the original image is always the one which is blurred the most. In order to get more realistic result, the sharper pixels have to be recalculated using the depth value associated with the more defocused pixel. The final color is a distance-based weighted average of the original color and the recalculated color. If the object in the background appears sharper, we ignore the pixels from the accumulation step which are outside a specified distance called samplingRadius.

Pixel Re-accumulation. The pixel recalculation phase is executed differently depending on where the focus point is. First case is when the focus point is between the foreground and the background. The other type is when the objects are all behind the focus point. In the first approach, if the foreground is more defocused than the background, then the pixels need to be recalculated with the kernel belonging to the foreground pixel weighted with the distance of the two pixels (Figure 5.4). Since the foreground pixel kernel is bigger, the values needed for recalculation *(depth, distance)* can be defined in the accumulation step of the foreground pixel (Listing 5.2). So the foreground recalculation can be processed only when all the pixel calculations are ready. Recalculation is based on the

Figure 5.4. The figure shows the original rendered image, the image with defocus applied without the re-accumulation phase, and the effect of the re-accumulation step.

```
float dist = (abs(imgX - neighX)*abs(imgX - neighX)
+ abs(imgY - neighY)*abs(imgY - neighY));
float distScale = 1.0f - dist / zKernel->r;
if (distScale > recalcDist[neighborIndex])
  recalcDist[neighborIndex] = distScale;
if (zValue > recalcZValue[neighborIndex]) {
  recalcZDepth[neighborIndex] = zDepth;
  recalcZValue[neighborIndex] = zValue;
}
```

Listing 5.2. Collecting parameters of foreground re-accumulation.

previous calculation technique using the new calculated kernel, but all the adjacent pixels take part in the computation.

In the second approach the background recalculation is based on layers where the image is divided into N range, and the adjacent pixels are grouped by their depth value (Listing 5.3).

The current pixel is recalculated based on each dominant layer. A layer is dominant if its distance and the number of contained pixels is above a specified threshold (Listing 5.4).

```
int group = neighborPixel->group;
pixelCategoriesNum[group]++;
if (distScale > pixelCategoriesDist[group])
  pixelCategoriesDist[group] = distScale;
if (neighborPixel->zDepth < pixelCategoriesZDepth[group]) {
  pixelCategoriesZDepth[group] = neighborPixel->zDepth;
  pixelCategoriesZValue[group] = neighborPixel->zValue;
}
```

Listing 5.3. Collecting parameters of background re-accumulation.

```
if (pixelCategoriesDist[i] > 0.05f
 && pixelCategoriesNum[i] > zKernel->size / 40) {
      reaccumulateBG(image,&kernel,pixelCategoriesZDepth[i],
             pixelCategoriesZValue[i],pixelCategoriesDist[i],
             pos,i);
}
```

Listing 5.4. Dominant layer filtering.

```
for all pixels {
 for all neighbors {
  float multiplicator = (1.0f - distance / zKernel->r)
   *(recalcZDepth[pos]?recalcZDepth[pos]:
   imagePixels[pos].zDepth);
  if (multiplicator > 0)
      bloomValues[neighborIndex] += multiplicator;
 }
}
float bloomScale = bloomValues[pos]*bloomAmount/1000.0f;
newColor = bloomScale*white + (1.0f - bloomScale)*pixelColor;
```

Listing 5.5. Bloom effect.

The per-pixel-based recalculation can be done right after the calculation step. During the recalculation phase, only those pixels that are in the current layer or behind it are taken into account. Pixels that come from a layer closer to the camera are skipped.

Blooming. For more realistic highlights during the accumulation and reaccumulation steps, a *multiplicator* value is defined for the adjacent pixels based on the distance and the aperture kernel. Using the external bloom amount parameter, which controls the strength of the bloom effect, the current pixel color is scaled into white (Listing 5.5).

5.4 CUDA-Accelerated Computation

This depth of field approach has been implemented on the GPU using NVIDIA's CUDA API. With the CUDA architecture, computation-intensive parts of the program can be offloaded to the GPU. Highly parallelizable portions of our technique can be isolated into functions that are executed on the GPU. A given function can be executed many times, in parallel, as many threads. The resulting program is called a *kernel*. In our implementation each thread computes a single pixel.

```
// Parameters
CUDA_SAFE_CALL(cudaMalloc((void**)&paramsGPU,
sizeof(float) * 20));
CUDA_SAFE_CALL(cudaMemcpy(paramsGPU, params,
sizeof(float) * 20, cudaMemcpyHostToDevice));

CUDA_SAFE_CALL(cudaMalloc((void**)&imageGPU,
sizeof(float) * 4 * image.getSize()));
CUDA_SAFE_CALL(cudaMalloc((void**)&zMapGPU,
sizeof(float) * zMap.getSize()));
CUDA_SAFE_CALL(cudaMalloc((void**)&kernelsGPU,
sizeof(float) * kernelBufferSize));
CUDA_SAFE_CALL(cudaMalloc((void**)&outputGPU,
sizeof(float) * 4 * image.getSize()));
CUDA_SAFE_CALL(cudaMalloc((void**)&recalcDistGPU,
sizeof(float) * image.getSize()));
CUDA_SAFE_CALL(cudaMalloc((void**)&recalcZDepthGPU,
sizeof(float) * image.getSize()));
CUDA_SAFE_CALL(cudaMalloc((void**)&bloomValuesGPU,
sizeof(float) * image.getSize()));

// Upload buffers to the GPU device.
CUDA_SAFE_CALL(cudaMemcpy(imageGPU, imageData,
sizeof(float) * 4 * image.getSize(), cudaMemcpyHostToDevice));
CUDA_SAFE_CALL(cudaMemcpy(zMapGPU, zMapData,
sizeof(float) * zMap.getSize(), cudaMemcpyHostToDevice));
CUDA_SAFE_CALL(cudaMemcpy(kernelsGPU, kernels,
sizeof(float) * kernelBufferSize, cudaMemcpyHostToDevice));
```

Listing 5.6. Allocating buffers and uploading data.

In the first step, the input data is offloaded to the GPU's global memory. The input data includes the source buffers with red, green, blue, and luminance values, and the Z-depth map with a scalar grayscale value (Listing 5.6).

Based on the depth, we place masks of every possible size above the pixels produced from the original kernel mask by linear transformation. The transformed main aperture kernels are precomputed by the CPU and are also offloaded to the

```
dim3 threadBlock(NUM_THREADS,NUM_THREADS);
int blockCount = (int)(numPixels /
      (NUM_THREADS*NUM_THREADS)) + 1;
accumulateGPU<<<blockCount, threadBlock>>>(imageGPU,zMapGPU,
      kernelsGPU,paramsGPU,outputGPU,
      recalcDistGPU,recalcZDepthGPU);
```

Listing 5.7. Computation step.

```
float* resultData = new float[4*size];
CUDA_SAFE_CALL(cudaMemcpy(resultData, outputGPU,
 sizeof(float) * 4 * size, cudaMemcpyDeviceToHost));

for(int i=0;i<numPixels;i++) {
    int pos = pixels[i];
    int index = 4*i;
    imagePixels[pos].r = resultData[index];
    imagePixels[pos].g = resultData[index+1];
    imagePixels[pos].b = resultData[index+2];
    imagePixels[pos].lum = resultData[index+3];
}
```

Listing 5.8. Downloading results.

device. The user parameters (like focal point, blur strength, edge improvements constans, threshold for highlighting pixels, amount of highlights etc.) are also collected and transferred.

Kernel interpolation is computed on the GPU (Listing 5.7) using the uploaded kernel matrices because interpolation is unique for all threads depending on the actual pixel parameters. Each thread calculates a pixel and accumulates the result of the defocus to the global buffer channels on the GPU. During accumulation the pixels which must take part in the additional recalculation step are marked. The information for recalculation is stored in different global buffers.

In the third stage, pixels requiring edge quality improvements are recalculated. Like the previous calculation, this process can be assigned to the GPU.

Finally, the calculated color and luminance values are downloaded (Listing 5.8) and the final image may be displayed on the screen or saved to a file.

5.5 Results

The technique has been implemented as a Spark plugin for Autodesk Flame 2009 (Figure 5.5). The spark extension has been successfully used in various commercial and short film projects.

In order to demonstrate the efficiency of our technique, we provide some performance results here (see Tables 5.1, 5.2, and 5.3). These results were measured on an AMD Athlon 6000+ (3GHz) workstation with 2 GB RAM and GeForce 9800 GT GPU.

The demo application can be initialized with two input clips (*image and depth map*). The DOF effect may be controlled interactively using the graphical user interface. Each parameter is animatable to allow artists to control DOF transitions. The focus may be changed by selecting a part of the image that should be

Figure 5.5. The rendered image and the image with defocus applied. (Image courtesy of GYAR Post Production.)

	CPU 100%	GPU 100%
Accumulation	13.469 sec	6.265 sec
Re-accumulation	2.969 sec	1.438 sec
Calculation	16.5 sec	7.776 sec

Table 5.1. Simulation speed using a 64×64 kernel.

fully in focus. The application is able to render the DOF effect using two modes: *artist* and *physically based*. In the artist mode, the amount of defocus is set by adjusting the kernel size. In the physically-based mode, real-world properties and camera parameters can be defined for the defocus effect. In this mode the amount of blur is computed based on the camera parameters.

Post-processing solutions for DOF are only approximations of the distributed ray tracing technique described by [Cook et al. 84]. These approximations are imperfect because there is typically insufficient information about partially occluded scene elements at post-processing time. Therefore, the proposed approach may be used to mimic real-world depth of field with some limitations.

Because the single input image (with depth map) does not contain information about transparent objects and disoccluded geometries, some artifacts may result. A possible extension to our post-processing technique might be to use multiple

	CPU 60%	GPU 60%
Accumulation	4.984 sec	2.468 sec
Re-accumulation	0.579 sec	0.469 sec
Calculation	5.625 sec	3.063 sec

Table 5.2. Simulation speed using a 64×64 kernel resized to 60%.

	CPU 20%	**GPU 20%**
Accumulation	0.766 sec	0.328 sec
Re-accumulation	0.015 sec	0.079 sec
Calculation	0.844 sec	0.531 sec

Table 5.3. Simulation speed using a 64×64 kernel resized to 20%.

images per-frame as suggested by [Kass et al. 06]. Using this extension, the input scene is rendered into separate foreground and background layers that are defocused into a single output image. Another possible algorithm is to render deep images (similar to deep shadows [Lokovic and Veach 00]) with multiple color and depth values.

The disadvantage of our algorithm is the usual $O(n^2)$ complexity of the defocus problem. With increasing kernel size and image size the computation can take minutes to complete. For this problem, [Kass et al. 06] suggested a diffusion based solution with linear complexity, but the aperture size is limited to a Gaussian one. Our implementation gives more control for the depth of field effect, and scalability is maintained by caching repeating kernel calculations together with proxy image calculation for faster feedback.

5.6 Conclusion

The additional edge quality improvements in our depth of field implementation result in more realistic and believable images. The disadvantage of the local neighborhood blending algorithm is the quadratic computational capacity, however this can be compensated by the GPU.

Bibliography

[Cook et al. 84] Robert L. Cook, Thomas Porter, and Loren Carpenter. "Distributed Ray Tracing." In *Proceedings of SIGGRAPH '84*, 26, 26, 1984.

[Cyril et al. 05] Pichard Cyril, Michelin Sylvain, and Tubach Olivier. "Photographic Depth of Field Blur Rendering." In *Proceedings of WSCG 2005*, 2005.

[Demers 04] Joe Demers. "Depth of Field: A Survey of Techniques." In *GPU Gems*, pp. 375–390. Boston: Addison-Wesley, 2004.

[Kass et al. 06] Michael Kass, Aaron Lefohn, and John Owen. "Interactive Depth of Field Using Simulated Diffusion on a GPU." *Technical Report*.

[Kraus and Strengert 07] M. Kraus and M. Strengert. "Depth-of-Field Rendering by Pyramidal Image Processing." In *Proceedings of Eurographics 2007*, pp. 584–599, 2007.

[Lokovic and Veach 00] Tom Lokovic and Eric Veach. "Deep Shadow Maps." In *Proceedings of SIGGRAPH 2000*, 2000.

6
V

Real-Time Screen Space Cloud Lighting
Kaori Kubota

6.1 Introduction

Clouds are an important visual element when creating realistic virtual environments. Without clouds, the scene would appear too simple and monotonous. However, rendering beautiful clouds in real time can be very challenging because clouds exhibit multiple scattering that is difficult to calculate while maintaining interactive frame rates. Unfortunately most games can not afford the computational cost of computing physically correct cloud lighting.

This chapter introduces an extremely simple screen space technique for rendering plausible clouds in real time. This technique has been implemented on the PLAYSTATION3 and was used in the game *Uncharted Waters Online*. This technique is not focused on strict physical accuracy but instead relies on recreating the empirical appearance of clouds. This technique is suitable for ground scenes where players stay on the ground and are only able to view the clouds from a distance.

Lighting is one of the most important aspects of creating beautiful and realistic clouds. When sun light passes through clouds, it is absorbed, scattered, and reflected by cloud particles. Figure 6.1 demonstrates a typical outdoor scene. As shown in the figure, when looking at clouds from the view point indicated in the diagram, the clouds nearest to the sun appear brightest. This phenomenon is due to the sun's light reaching the back portion of the cloud and then, through multiple scattering events, re-emerging on the front part of the cloud (nearest the viewer). This observation is a key part of the technique presented in this chapter. In order to recreate this visual cue, a simple point blur or directional blur in screen space is sufficient to mimic light scattering through clouds.

Figure 6.1. A typical outdoor scene. The clouds nearest the sun exhibit the most scattering and appear brightest.

6.2   Implementation

Our technique for rendering clouds is executed in three passes. First, cloud density is rendered to an off screen render target. Cloud density is a scalar value that can be painted by an artist. Next, the density map is blurred. Finally the blurred density map is used to render the clouds with the appearance of scattering.

6.2.1   Lighting

When light goes through clouds, it is attenuated and scattered by cloud particles. At a given point on the cloud, there is incoming light, which arrives directly from the sun, as well as scattered light, which has reached that point through one or more bounces. Some of the light that reaches a point on the cloud is absorbed and some is scattered deeper into the cloud before finally emerging on the other side (the side nearest the viewer). Lighting clouds involves computing the amount of light passing through the clouds along the lighting ray. [Mitchell 07] estimates the probability of occlusion of the light source at each pixel by summing samples along a ray from the viewer to the light source. We consider cloud particles as transparent occluders and take transparency into account.

During the lighting pass, we compute the amount of light that passes through cloud particles at each pixel on the cloud plane. The cloud plane will be described in Section 6.2.2. We use a density map which represents the density of clouds at each pixel. The density map rendered in the first pass is blurred toward the sun's position.

The sun's position is given by perspective-transforming the sun's light direction vector at each pixel. Note that the blur becomes directional if the light ray is perpendicular to the view ray, and the blur direction should be inverted when the sun is behind the view position. Refer to [Kozlov 04] for a detailed discussion of perspective-transforming a directional vector.

```
// Pixel shader input
struct SPSInput {
    float2 vUV        : TEXCOORD0 ;
    float3 vWorldDir  : TEXCOORD1 ;
    float2 vScreenPos : VPOS;
};
// Pixel shader
float4 main( SPSInput Input ) {
    // compute direction of blur.
    float2 vUVMove = Input.vScreenPos * SCALE + OFFSET ;

    // Scale blur vector considering distance from camera.
    float3 vcDir = normalize ( Input.vWorldDir );
    float  fDistance = GetDistanceFromDir( vcDir );
    vUVMove *= UV_SCALE / fDistance ;

    // Limit blur vector length.
    float2 fRatio = abs ( vUVMove / MAX_LENGTH );
    float fMaxLen = max ( fRatio.x, fRatio.y );
    vUVMove *= fMaxLen > 1.0f ? 1.0f / fMaxLen : 1.0f;

    // Compute offset for weight.
    // FALLOFF must be negative so that far pixels affect less.
    float fExpScale = dot ( vUVMove , vUVMove ) * FALLOFF ;

    // Blur density toward the light.
    float fShadow = tex2D ( sDensity, Input.vUV ).a;
    float fWeightSum = 1.0f;
    for ( int i = 1; i < FILTER_RADIUS; ++i ) {
        float fWeight = exp ( fExpScale * i );
        fShadow +=
            fWeight * tex2D(sDensity, Input.vUV+vUVMove*i).a;
        fWeightSum += fWeight ;
    }
    fShadow /= fWeightSum ;

    // 0 means no shadow and 1 means all shadowed pixel.
    return fShadow ;
}
```

Listing 6.1. A pixel shader code snippet; constants are capitalized. This shader can provide either parallel or point blurring by setting the SCALE and OFFSET constants appropriately.

There are several requirements of the blur. The blur weights fall off according to distance from the sun because particles at a far distance are affected less by in-scattering. Also, the blur length or strength should be tweaked according to distance in world space. Sample code is shown in Listing 6.1.

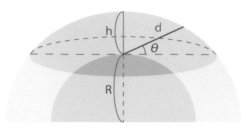

Figure 6.2. The earth and atmosphere. The deep blue regions is recognized as sky by a player.

6.2.2 Distance to the Sky and Clouds

We render sky as a screen quad in the final pass. In the pixel shader, the screen position is back projected to the world direction and is used to compute the distance light passes through the atmosphere. This distance is used to approximate the amount of scattering.

When the player stands on the ground, the atmospheric volume is represented as a spherical cap; you can visualize this as a piece of a sphere that is cut by a plane. Figure 6.2 demonstrates the shape of the volume. Clearly, when the sun is on the horizon, light must travel further to reach the viewer than when the sun is directly overhead. The distance light pass through the atmosphere d is

$$d(\theta) = -R \sin \theta + \sqrt{R^2 \sin^2 \theta + h^2 + 2h}.$$

Where R is the radius of the earth, h is the thickness of the atmosphere and θ is the vertical angle between a ground plane and the direction vector. We also compute the distance to the clouds using this equation with h' in the final pass (h' is the height of clouds and $h' < h$).

6.2.3 Scattering

In the final pass, sky, clouds and all other geometry are rendered with daylight scattering using [Hoffman and Preetham 02]. Here is the equation:

$$L(s, \theta) = e^{-s\beta_{ex}} L_0 + \left(\frac{\beta_{sc}(\theta)}{\beta_{ex}} E_{\text{sun}} \right) (1 - e^{-s\beta_{ex}}),$$

where s is the distance from the view position, β_{ex} is an extinction parameter, $\beta_{sc}(\theta)$ is in-scattering phase function, E_{sun} is the sun light, and L_0 is light from surfaces. For the sky, L_0 is zero. For the clouds, the blurred density map is used to compute L_0. We compute L_0 by scaling and adding an ambient term. The density map is also used as transparency.

To make the scene more natural, we extended the equation as follows:

$$L(s, \theta) = e^{-s\beta_{ex}} L_0 + (\frac{\beta_{sc}(\theta)}{\beta_{ex}} E_{\text{sun}} * \text{shadow} + C)(1 - e^{-s\beta_{ex}}),$$

where "shadow" is a shadow term. The shadow term represents the shadows cast by clouds. It is calculated in the second pass using a different falloff parameter and stored in another channel of the blurred map. Although we render a shadow map to cast shadows from clouds, there could be a lit part of terrain under dark clouds, which spoils the natural appearance. Therefore this shadow term is effective to darken the ground under clouds. The term C is a constant that can be used as a standard fog parameter which is useful for artists.

6.3   Results

Figure 6.3 contains screen shots of our technique. In the demo, the clouds are rendered as a uniform grid. A cloud texture includes four density textures in each channel. Each channel represents different layers of clouds and are blended in the pixel shader according to the weather in the first pass. It is also animated by scrolling the texture coordinates.

Figure 6.3. Screen shots that demonstrate our technique.

Figure 6.4. The density map (left) and result (right) without layering.

The size of render target used for blurring is a quarter of the screen resolution, which is sufficient because clouds tend to be somewhat nebulous and low frequency.

6.4   Extensions

Since lighting is performed as a two-dimensional blur, when the clouds become thick, clouds near the sun cast shadow to neighboring area. This phenomenon is acceptable in sunset or sunrise because it is happen in real environment. However, when the sun is above, clouds should not cast shadow to others otherwise it spoils lighting effect and results in poor toned and too darkened clouds.

To solve this, layering the density would be useful. When rendering to the density map, store neighboring clouds to different channels. Figure 6.4 and 6.5 render the same cloud density, but Figure 6.5 divides density as alternate stripes and stores them to R and G channels, respectively. Blur is also applied to both

Figure 6.5. The density map (left) and result (right) with layering.

channels, and these results are combined in the final pass. This approach is suitable for stratocumulus.

6.5 Conclusion

We discussed a technique for rendering a convincing sky in real time. Since the shape of clouds is decoupled from the lighting, procedural cloud generation and animation are possible.

We ignore certain physical properties of the atmosphere in order to create a more efficient technique. For example, no consideration for the density of the atmosphere is made. This property would be necessary in order to create realistic looking sunsets and sunrises. We also ignore the color of the light which goes into the clouds. In a scene with a sunset or sunrise, only the area close to the sun should be lit brightly and colorfully. It is necessary to take a more physically based approach to simulating the scattering between the sun and clouds to get more natural result.

Bibliography

[Hoffman and Preetham 02] Naty Hoffman and Arcot J Preetham. "Rendering Outdoor Light Scattering in Real Time." Available online (http://ati.amd .com/developer/dx9/ATI-LightScattering.pdf).

[Kozlov 04] Simon Kozlov. "Perspective Shadow Maps: Care and Feeding." In *GPU Gems*, edited by Randima Fernando. Boston: Addison-Wesley, 2004. Available online (http://http.developer.nvidia.com/GPUGems/gpugems_ch14.html).

[Mitchell 07] Kenny Mitchell. "Volumetric Light Scattering as a Post-Process." In *GPU Gems 3*, edited by Hubert Nguyen. Boston: Addison-Wesley, 2007. Available online (http://http.developer.nvidia.com/GPUGems3/gpugems3_ ch13.html).

Screen-Space Subsurface Scattering

Jorge Jimenez and Diego Gutierrez

7.1 Introduction

Many materials exhibit a certain degree of translucency, by which light falling onto an object enters its body at one point, scatters within it, then exits the object at some other point. This process is known as *subsurface scattering*. We observe many translucent objects in our daily lives, such as skin, marble, paper, tree leaves, soap, candles, and fruit. In order to render these materials in a realistic way, we must recreate the effects of subsurface scattering in the rendering pipeline.

Skin is one of the most important materials that demonstrates a significant degree of subsurface scattering. Many video games are very character and story driven. These kinds of games seek to create believable, realistic characters so that the player becomes fully immersed in the game. Adding accurate subsurface scattering to human skin, especially on faces, can dramatically improve the overall impression of realism.

There has been an emerging trend towards applying computationally expensive three-dimensional methods (such as ambient occlusion or global illumination) in screen space. We present an algorithm capable of simulating subsurface scattering in screen space as a post-process (see Figure 7.1), which takes as inputs the depth-stencil and color buffer of a rendered frame.

In this article we will describe a very efficient screen-space implementation of subsurface scattering. We will measure the cost of our technique against other common screen-space effects such as depth of field or bloom, in order to motivate its implementation in current game engines. As we will see, our method maintains the quality of the best texture-space algorithms but scales better as the number of objects increases (see Figure 7.2).

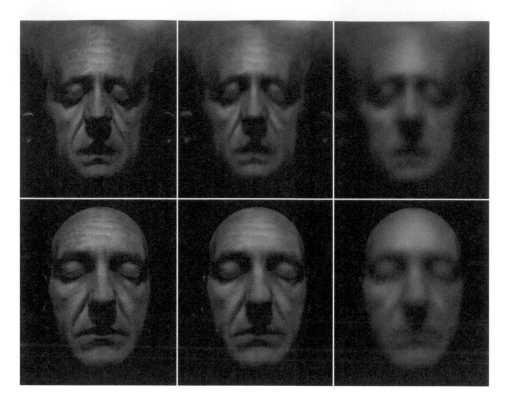

Figure 7.1. Blurring performed in texture space, as done by current real time subsurface scattering algorithms (top). Blurring done directly in screen space (bottom).

7.2   The Texture-Space Approach

7.2.1   Subsurface Scattering and Diffusion Profiles

Homogeneous subsurface scattering can be approximated by using one-dimensional functions called diffusion profiles. A diffusion profile defines how the light attenuates as it travels beneath the surface of an object, or in other words, it describes how light intensity ($R(r)$) decays as a function of the radial distance to the incidence point (r). As shown in Figure 7.3, a majority of the light intensity occurs close to the point of incidence, and quickly decays as it interacts with the inner structure of the object before escaping through the surface.

7.2.2   Irradiance Texture

Applying a diffusion profile implies calculating the irradiance at incident and adjacent points for each point of the surface, which leads to wasted calculations.

Figure 7.2. Examples of our screen-space approach. Unlike the texture-space approach, our method scales well with the number of objects in the scene (top). Rendering marble without taking subsurface scattering into account leads to a stone-like appearance (bottom left); our subsurface scattering technique is used to create a softer appearance, more indicative of subsurface scattering (bottom right).

In order to perform an efficient profile evaluation, an irradiance map—also known as light map—is created which stores the incoming light at each point of the surface, and serves as light *cache*, in the sense that it enables you to calculate the lighting at each point once but use that value many times. Figure 7.1 (top left) shows an example of an irradiance texture.

7.2.3 Gaussians and the Jittered Kernel

Once an irradiance map is calculated, applying a diffusion profile consists of no more than applying a two-dimensional convolution over this map. There are a few previous works that provide detailed insights into how to perform this convolution in an efficient way, all for the specific case of skin rendering.

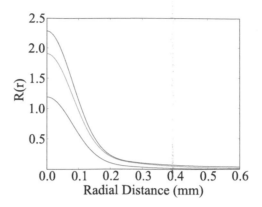

Figure 7.3. Diffusion profile of the three-layer skin model described in [d'Eon and Lue-bke 07].

The approach followed by d'Eon and Luebke [d'Eon and Luebke 07], consists of approximating this lengthy two-dimensional convolution by a sum of Gaussians, which can be separated into faster 1D convolutions. To summarize, rendering subsurface scattering using this sum-of-Gaussians consists of the following steps:

1. Render the irradiance map.

2. Blur the irradiance map with six Gaussians.

3. Render the scene, calculating a weighted sum of the six Gaussians, which will approximate the original diffusion profile.

While rendering an irradiance map (and in the following blurs), two optimizations that would otherwise be implicitly performed by the GPU are lost, namely backface culling and view frustum clipping. Jimenez and Gutierrez [Jimenez and Gutierrez 08] reintroduce those two optimizations in the rendering pipeline proposed in [d'Eon and Luebke 07]. They also perform an optimal, per-object modulation of the irradiance map size based on a simple, depth-based method.

Hable et al [Hable et al. 09], using a 13-sample jittered kernel, together with a small 512×512 irradiance map and a similar culling optimization, managed to improve the performance over the 6-Gaussian implementation [d'Eon and Luebke 07], at the cost of a loss of *fleshiness*, as the authors noticed.

7.2.4   Texture-Space Diffusion Problems

Current real-time subsurface scattering algorithms rely on texture-space diffusion, which has some intrinsic problems that can be easily solved by working in screen space instead. We outline the most important ones:

- It requires special measures to bring back typical GPU optimizations (back-face culling and viewport clipping), and to compute an irradiance map proportional to the size of the subject on the screen. In screen space, these optimizations are straightforward.

- Each subject to be rendered requires her own irradiance map (thus forcing as many render passes as subjects). In image space, *all subjects* of the same material are processed at the same time.

- Furthermore, rendering large amounts of objects with subsurface scattering is not efficient as either you have to use an irradiance map for each object, in order to be able to use instancing (which would be especially useful for rendering tree leaves for example), or you have to reuse the same irradiance map, and render each object sequentially.

- The irradiance map forces the transformation of the model vertices twice: during the irradiance map calculation, and to transform the final geometry at the end. In screen-space, only this second transformation is required.

- In texture space, for materials like skin that directly reflect a significant amount of light, lighting is usually calculated twice (once for the irradiance map and again for the sharpest of the Gaussian blurs since this Gaussian blur is usually replaced by the unblurred lighting in the final compositing pass). In screen-space, lighting must be calculated only once.

- Modern GPUs can perform an early-Z rejection operation to avoid overdraw and useless execution of pixel shaders on certain pixels. In texture space, it is unclear how to leverage this and optimize the convolution processes according to the final visibility in the image. In screen space, a depth pass can simply discard occluded fragments before sending them to the pixel shader.

- Adjacent points in three-dimensional world space may not be adjacent in texture space. Obviously this will introduce errors in texture-space diffusion that are naturally avoided in screen space. This implies that special care must be taken when preparing the UV map of the models, in order to reduce the number of seams as much as possible.

7.3 The Screen-Space Approach

7.3.1 The Big Picture

Our algorithm translates the evaluation of the diffusion approximation from texture- to screen-space. Instead of calculating an irradiance map and convolving

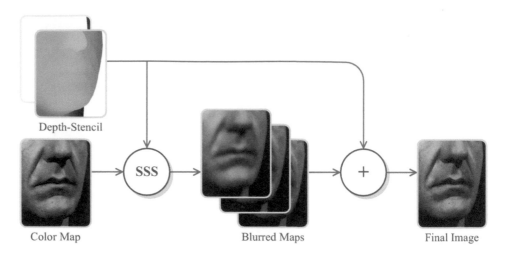

Figure 7.4. Conceptual interpretation of our algorithm (see text in the article for actual implementation details).

it with the diffusion profile, we apply the convolution directly to the final rendered image. Figure 7.4 shows an overview of our algorithm. As we have said, to perform this task in screen-space we need as input the depth-stencil and color buffer of a rendered frame.

As subsurface scattering should only be applied to the diffuse component of the lighting function, we could store the diffuse and specular components separately, for which we could use multiple render targets or the alpha channel of the main render target. However, we have found that applying subsurface scattering to both the diffuse and specular components of the lighting yields very appealing results, because a) the specular component is softened creating a more natural look, with less apparent aliasing artifacts, and b) it creates a nice bloom effect for the specular highlights.

In order to efficiently mask out pixels that do not need to be processed we use the stencil buffer. This vastly improves the performance when the object is far away from the camera, and thus occupies a small area in screen space. We also tried to use dynamic branching in our pixel shaders but we found the stencil method to be more efficient particularly when a large percentage of the screen must be rejected.

Our algorithm also requires linear depth information [Gillham 06] which we render into an additional render target. We use this depth together with the original depth-stencil map, which serves to perform the stenciling and to implement a depth-based Gaussians level of detail, as we will see in the next section. It is possible to access the depth buffer directly, but we are not able to simultaneously use the same depth buffer both as an input texture and as depth stencil buffer, so we must create a copy.

With the depth-stencil information as input, we apply the diffusion profile directly to the final rendered image, instead of applying it to a previously calculated irradiance map. For skin rendering, we use our own four-Gaussian fit of the three-layer skin model defined in [d'Eon and Luebke 07] (see Section 7.3.3 for details), and, as done in this work, perform each of them as two separated one-dimensional convolutions (horizontal and vertical blurs). The results obtained using our four-Gaussian fit are visually indistinguishable from the original six-Gaussian fit. For marble we calculated the profile using the parameters given by [Jensen et al. 01], for which we obtained a four-Gaussian fit (see [d'Eon and Luebke 07] for details on how to perform this fitting).

In screen space we need to take into account the following considerations:

- Pixels that are far from the camera need narrower kernel widths than pixels that are close to the camera.

- Pixels representing surfaces that are at steep angles with respect to the camera also need narrower kernels.

These considerations translate into the following *stretch factors*:

$$s_x = \frac{\text{ssslevel}}{d(x,y) + \text{correction} \cdot \min(abs(ddx(d(x,y), \text{maxdd})}},$$
$$s_y = \frac{\text{ssslevel}}{d(x,y) + \text{correction} \cdot \min(abs(ddy(d(x,y), \text{maxdd})}},$$

where $d(x,y)$ is the depth of the pixel in the depth map, "ssslevel" indicates the global subsurface scattering level in the image, "correction" modulates how this subsurface scattering varies with the depth gradient, and "maxdd" limits the effects of the derivative. This derivative limitation is required for very soft materials (like marble), as subtle artifacts may arise at depth discontinuities under very specific lighting conditions. These artifacts are caused by the huge derivatives found at those locations, that locally nullify the effect of subsurface scattering. The first and second terms in the denominators account for the first and second considerations listed above. This stretching is similar in spirit to the UV stretching performed in texture space algorithms.

The *stretch factors* are then multiplied by each Gaussian width in order to obtain the final kernel width:

$$\text{finalwidth}_x = s_x \cdot \text{width},$$
$$\text{finalwidth}_y = s_y \cdot \text{width}.$$

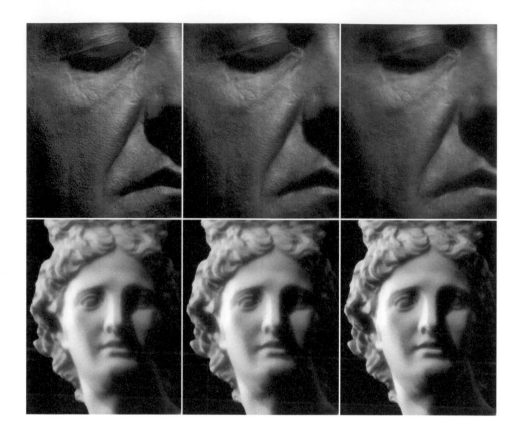

Figure 7.5. The influence of the ssslevel and correction parameters. Fixed correction = 800, maxdd = 0.001 and varying ssslevel of 0, 15.75 and 31.5, respectively (top). Note how the global level of subsurface scattering increases. Fixed ssslevel = 31.5, maxdd = 0.001 and varying correction of 0, 1200 and 4000, respectively (bottom). Note how the gray-to-black gradient on the nose gets readjusted according to the depth derivatives of the underlying geometry (the range of the correction parameter has been extended for visualization purposes; it usually is limited to [0..1200] because of the limited precision of the derivatives).

In the silhouette of the object, the derivatives will be very large, which means that the kernel will be very narrow, thus limiting the bleeding of background pixels into object's pixels. The value of ssslevel is influenced by the size of the object in three-dimensional space, the field-of-view used to render the scene and the viewport size (as these parameters determine the projected size of the object), whereas maxdd only depends on the size of the object. The images included in this article use fixed values of ssslevel = 31.5, correction = 800 and maxdd = 0.001;

```
float width;
float sssLevel, correction, maxdd;
float2 pixelSize;
Texture2D colorTex, depthTex;

float4 BlurPS(PassV2P input) : SV_TARGET {
  float w[7] = { 0.006, 0.061, 0.242, 0.382,
                 0.242, 0.061, 0.006 };

  float depth = depthTex.Sample(PointSampler,
                                 input.texcoord).r;
  float2 s_x = sssLevel / (depth + correction *
                    min(abs(ddx(depth)), maxdd));
  float2 finalWidth = s_x * width * pixelSize *
                    float2(1.0, 0.0);

  float2 offset = input.texcoord - finalWidth;
  float4 color = float4(0.0, 0.0, 0.0, 1.0);
  for (int i = 0; i < 7; i++) {
    float3 tap = colorTex.Sample(LinearSampler, offset).rgb;
    color.rgb += w[i] * tap;
    offset += finalWidth / 3.0;
  }

  return color;
}
```

Listing 7.1. Pixel shader that performs the horizontal Gaussian blur.

these values were chosen empirically for a head 1.0 units tall, a field-of-view of $20°$, and a viewport height of 720 pixels. Figure 7.5 illustrates the influence of ssslevel and correction in the final images.

Listing 7.1 shows the implementation of previous equation for the case of the horizontal blur. Our subsurface scattering approach just requires two short shaders, one for the horizontal blur and a similar one for the vertical blur.

Certain areas of the character, such as hair or beard, should be excluded from these calculations; we could therefore want to locally disable subsurface scattering in such places. For this purpose, we could use the alpha channel of the diffuse texture to modulate this local subsurface scattering level. We would need to store the alpha channel of this texture into the alpha channel of the main render target during the main render pass. Then, in our post-processing pass we would use the following modified stretch factors:

$$s'_x = s_x \cdot \text{diffuse}(x, y).a$$
$$s'_y = s_y \cdot \text{diffuse}(x, y).a$$

In the following, we describe the two key optimizations that our algorithm performs.

7.3.2   Depth-Based Gaussians Level of Detail

Performing the diffusion in screen space allows us to disable Gaussians on a per-pixel basis as we fly away from the model. Narrow Gaussians are going to have little effect on pixels far away from the camera, as most of the samples are going to land on the same pixel. We can exploit this to save computations.

For this purpose we use the following inequality, based on the final kernel width equation from the previous section, where we are making the assumption of camera facing polygons which have zero-valued derivatives:

$$\frac{\text{width} \cdot \text{ssslevel}}{d(x, y)} > 0.5.$$

If the width of the kernel for the current pixel is less than 0.5—that is, a half a pixel—all samples are going to land on the same pixel and thus we can skip blurring at this pixel (Figure 7.6, left).

We can use depth testing to efficiently implement this optimization. If we solve the previous inequality for $d(x, y)$:

$$2 \cdot \text{width} \cdot \text{ssslevel} > d(x, y),$$

then we just need to render the quad used to perform the convolution at a depth value of $2 \cdot \text{width} \cdot \text{ssslevel}$ and configure the depth testing function to *greater than*. However, we have found that instead using a value of $0.5 \cdot \text{width} \cdot \text{ssslevel}$ allows us to disable them much faster without any noticeable popping.

Though we have a copy of the depth-stencil buffer in linear space, the original depth-stencil buffer is kept in non-linear space for precision issues. This means that we have to transform the left side of previous inequality into the same non-linear space [Gillham 06], and clamp the resulting non-linear depth values to [0..1].

7.3.3   Alpha Blending Workflow

Using n Gaussians to approximate a diffusion profile means we need n render targets for irradiance storage. In order to keep the memory footprint as low as possible, we accumulate the sum of the Gaussians on the fly, eliminating the need to sum them in a final pass.

In order to accomplish this task, we require two additional render targets. The first render target is used to store the widest Gaussian calculated thus far (RT1) and the second for the usual render target ping ponging (RT2).

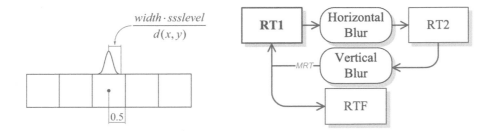

Figure 7.6. If a Gaussian is narrower than a pixel, the result of its application will be negligible (left). Alpha blending workflow used to enhance memory usage (right). Multiple Render Targets (MRT) is used to render to RT1 and RTF simultaneously.

Applying one of the Gaussians consists of two steps:

1. Perform the horizontal Gaussian blur into RT2.

2. Perform the vertical Gaussian blur by sampling from the horizontally blurred RT2 and outputting into both RT1 and RTF (the final render target) using multiple render targets. For RTF we use an alpha blending operation in order to mix the values accordingly. The exact weight required for the blending operation will be examined in the following paragraphs.

Figure 7.6 (right) shows the alpha blending workflow used by our algorithm. We need to sum the n Gaussians as follows:

$$R = \sum_{i=k}^{n} w_i G_i,$$

where w_i is the weight vector (different for each RGB channel) of each Gaussian G_i, and k is the first Gaussian that is wide enough to have a visible effect on the final image, as explained in the previous section.

As we may not calculate all Gaussians, we need to find a set of values w'_i that will produce a normalized result at each step i of the previous sum:

$$w'_i = \frac{w_i}{\sum_{j=1}^{i} w_i}.$$

Then we just need to configure alpha blending to use a blend factor as follows:

$$\text{color}_{\text{out}} = \text{color}_{\text{src}} \cdot \text{blendfactor} + \text{color}_{\text{dst}} \cdot (1 - \text{blendfactor}),$$

where blendfactor is assigned to w'_i. Listing 7.2 shows the FX syntax for the BlendingState that implements this equation.

```
BlendState BlendingAccum {
  BlendEnable[0] = FALSE; // RT2
  BlendEnable[1] = TRUE;  // RTF
  SrcBlend = BLEND_FACTOR;
  DestBlend = INV_BLEND_FACTOR;
};
```

Listing 7.2. Blending state used to blend a Gaussian with the final render target.

Table 7.1 shows the original weights of our skin and marble four-Gaussian fits (w_i), alongside with the modified weights used by our screen-space approach (w_i').

In the case of skin, the first Gaussian is too narrow to be noticeable. Thus the original unblurred image is used instead, saving the calculation of one Gaussian. Note that the weight of the first Gaussian for both fits is 1.0; the reason for this is that the first Gaussian does not need to be mixed with the previously blended Gaussians.

Note that as we are performing each Gaussian on top of the previous one, we have to subtract the variance of the previous Gaussian to get the actual variance. For example, for the widest Gaussian of the skin fit, we would have $2.0062 - 0.2719 = 1.7343$. Also keep in mind that the width that should be passed to the shader shown in the Listing 7.1 is the standard deviation, thus in this case it would be $\sqrt{1.7343}$.

Skin	w_i			w_i'		
Variance	**R**	**G**	**B**	**R**	**G**	**B**
0.0064	0.2405	0.4474	0.6157	1.0	1.0	1.0
0.0516	0.1158	0.3661	0.3439	0.3251	0.45	0.3583
0.2719	0.1836	0.1864	0.0	0.34	0.1864	0.0
2.0062	0.46	0.0	0.0402	0.46	0.0	0.0402

Marble	w_i			w_i'		
Variance	**R**	**G**	**B**	**R**	**G**	**B**
0.0362	0.0544	0.1245	0.2177	1.0	1.0	1.0
0.1144	0.2436	0.2435	0.1890	0.8173	0.6616	0.4647
0.4555	0.3105	0.3158	0.3742	0.5101	0.4617	0.4791
3.4833	0.3913	0.3161	0.2189	0.3913	0.3161	0.2189

Table 7.1. Gaussian variances and original weights (w_i) of our Gaussian fits that approximate the three-layer skin and marble diffusion profiles, alongside with the modified weights used by our algorithm (w_i').

7.3.4 Anti-aliasing and Depth-Stencil

For efficiency reasons, when using MSAA we might want to use the resolved render targets (downsampled to MSAA 1x) for performing all the post-processing, in order to save memory bandwidth. However this implies that we cannot use the original MSAA stencil buffer to perform the depth-based blur modulation or the stenciling.

We explored two approaches to solve this problem:

1. Use dynamic branching to perform the stenciling by hand.

2. Downsample the depth-stencil buffer to be able to use hardware stenciling.

Both methods rely on generating multi-sample render targets containing depth and stencil values during the main pass, for which multiple render targets can be used.[1]

We found that in our implementation using hardware stenciling outperforms the dynamic branching method.

7.4 Model Preparation

When using models with hand painted normals (as opposed to scanned models) there are some considerations that must be taken into account. As noticed in [Hable et al. 09], most artists paint normals trying to match the soft aspect of subsurface scattering, without being able to use algorithms that simulate this effect. Thus they usually resort to make the normals much softer than they are physically. However, when using subsurface scattering for rendering, the best results will be obtained using bumpier normals, as subsurface scattering will be in charge of softening the illumination.

7.5 Discussion of Results

Table 7.2 shows the performance of our screen space algorithm (SS) in the case of skin rendering, against the texture space algorithm proposed by Hable et al [Hable et al. 09] (TS). We have chosen [Hable et al. 09] because it outperforms the original [d'Eon and Luebke 07] algorithm for skin rendering. For other materials, for which there is no clear way of applying the approach by Hable et al, we resort to comparisons with [d'Eon and Luebke 07], which is much more flexible.

For skin simulation, the distances we have chosen have the following meaning: near is a close-up of the head, usually found on in-game cut scenes; medium is

---

[1]When using DirectX 10.1 we can sample from the MSAA depth-stencil buffer directly, with no need to output depth and stencil values using multiple render targets.

Heads	TS	SS	Lights	TS	SS	Distance	TS	SS
1	102/72	137/73	2	102/72	137/73	**Near**	60/52	50/40
3	47/33	67/52	4	63/56	90/64	**Medium**	102/72	137/73
5	29/21	50/38	6	54/43	69/54	**Far**	120/82	220/91

Table 7.2. Performance measurements (fps) of our algorithm (SS), using both $1\times/8\times$ MSAA, in comparison with the texture space approach proposed in Hable et al. [Hable et al. 09] (TS). For each test we fixed the following parameters: the number of heads, the number of lights and the distance were set to 1, 2, and medium, respectively.

the distance typically found for characters of first-person shooters; at far distance the head covers very little screen area, and the effects of subsurface scattering are negligible. In the following text we will quote the performance for $1\times$MSAA (see Table 7.2 for a more detailed report). We can see how our algorithm scales better as we increase the number of heads (from 29 to 50 fps for 5 heads), as the number of lights increases (from 54 to 69 fps for six lights) and as we fly away from the model (from 120 to 220 fps for far distance). In the case of 10 heads, two lights and far distance, we obtain a speedup factor of $3.6\times$. We performed an additional test to explore the impact of the early-z optimization on both algorithms, which shows that when rendering five heads behind a plane that hides them from the camera, our screen space algorithm manages to perform at $2\times$ with respect to the texture-space approach. Similar speed-ups could be found when the objects fall outside of the viewport.

As we have discussed, there is no clear extension to Hable et al.'s algorithm that would allow for other translucent materials. We present an example of such materials by simulating marble (see Figure 7.2) and compare it with the approach of d'Eon et al. In this example, we achieve a speedup factor of up to $2.8\times$ when rendering five Apollo busts with two lights at medium distance.

In general, the best speed ups are found when there are many objects (or very large objects that would require huge irradiance textures) at very different distances (for example, when rendering tree leaves). In this kind of situation, no single irradiance map size would be a perfect fit.

In the image shown in Figure 7.2 (top), where subsurface scattering is dominating the scene, the costs of the bloom, depth-of-field, and subsurface scattering effects are 2.7ms, 5.8ms, and 14ms, respectively. On the other hand, in a more typical scene with three heads at medium distance, the costs are 2.7ms, 5.8ms, and 4.6ms.

Our performance measurements were taken using a shadow map resolution of 512×512, diffuse and normal maps with a resolution of 1024×1024. The human head and Apollo bust models have 3904 and 14623 triangles, respectively,

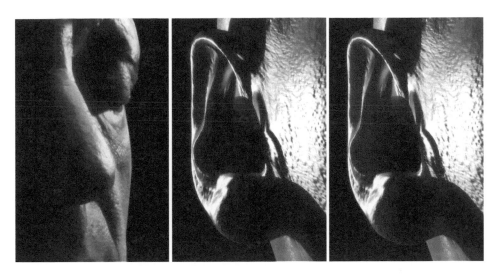

Figure 7.7. Screen space limitations and artifacts. Small haloes produced by incorrect diffusion from nose to cheek (left). Screen- vs. texture-space comparison where we can see how we cannot account for the diffusion produced in thin, high curvature features, as in screen space we do not have information from behind (Center and right).

both obtained from XYZRGB.[2] All renderings were performed on a machine equipped with a GeForce 8600M GS at a resolution of 1280×720. As recommended in [Gritz and d'Eon 07], we used sRGB render targets, which is crucial for multi-pass, physically based shaders like ours. For the specular highlights we used the Kelemen-Szirmay-Kalos approach [d'Eon and Luebke 07]. The rendered images shown in this article are filtered with a Gaussian bloom filter at the end of the rendering pipeline. Figure 7.2 (top) was rendered with an additional depth-of-field effect.

Quality-wise, the screen space approach manages to maintain the full *fleshiness* that the Hable et al. loses as result of using a small jittered kernel. Furthermore, it does not exhibit the stretching artifacts produced by texture space algorithms, especially by the Hable et al. approach [Hable et al. 09]. Finally, it is free from the seam problems imposed by the model's UV unwrapping (refer to the high resolution images available at http://www.akpeters.com/gpupro for examples).

Our algorithm can introduce its own artifacts however. In certain camera and light conditions, small haloes may appear at depth discontinuities, as shown in Figure 7.7 (left). In this situation, light incorrectly scatters from the nose to the cheek. This artifact could be seen as the screen-space counterpart of both

---

[2]See http://www.xyzrgb.com/.

the stretching and seam problems of the texture-space approach. However, these haloes are low frequency artifacts and thus they generally do not hamper the soft appearance of translucent materials. Also, as shown in Figure 7.7 (middle and right), our algorithm is unable to reproduce the scattering produced in high-curvature, thin features like the ears or nose, as we do not have information from the back facing surfaces. In the case of skin, these issues do not seem to damage its general appearance, as has been proven by our previous work [Jimenez et al. 09]. In addition, the usage of very blurry profiles (like the one required for marble) can lead to aliasing problems, as the MSAA resolve is performed before applying subsurface scattering.

Another important difference is that our shader uses pre-scatter texturing (which means that we applied subsurface scattering after the full diffuse color is applied), in contrast with the Hable et al. approach [Hable et al. 09] that uses post-scatter texturing because the usage of a small irradiance map would excessively blur the high frequency details of the diffuse map. We believe that what looks best is a matter of subjective preference.

From an ease-of-use perspective, our algorithm offers various advantages. Being a post-process, integrating our technique into an existing pipeline will not require major changes. It is composed of two short shaders that can be encapsulated in a small class. Additionally, it does not require special UV unwrapping nor does it require dealing with seams, which can account for significant artist time. As we have described, there is no need to take care of special situations such as the objects being out of the viewport, or too far away from the camera, etc., as they are implicitly taken into account by the algorithm.

7.6 Conclusion

We have presented an efficient algorithm capable of rendering realistic subsurface scattering in screen space. This approach reduces buffer management and artist effort. It offers similar performance to the Hable et al. approach [Hable et al. 09] when the object is at moderate distances and scales better as the number of objects increases. Our method generalizes better to other materials. At close-ups it does lose some performance in exchange for quality, but it is able to maintain the *fleshiness* of the original d'Eon approach [d'Eon and Luebke 07]. However, in such close-ups, there is a good chance that the player will be focusing closely on the character's face, so we believe it is worth spending the extra resources in order to render the character's skin with the best quality possible. We believe that our subsurface scattering algorithm has a very simple implementation, has few requirements, and makes a nice balance between performance, generality, and quality.

7.7 Acknowledgments

We would like to thank Luisa García for her endless support, Christopher Oat for his very detailed review and XYZRGB Inc. for the high-quality head scans. This research has been partially funded by the Spanish Ministry of Science and Technology (TIN2007-63025) and the Gobierno de Aragón (OTRI 2009/0411). Jorge Jimenez was funded by a research grant from the Instituto de Investigación en Ingeniería de Aragón.

Bibliography

[d'Eon and Luebke 07] Eugene d'Eon and David Luebke. "Advanced Techniques for Realistic Real-Time Skin Rendering." In *GPU Gems 3*, edited by Hubert Nguyen, Chapter 14, pp. 293–347. Addison Wesley, 2007.

[Gillham 06] David Gillham. "Real-time Depth-of-Field Implemented with a Postprocessing-Only Technique." In *ShaderX5*, edited by Wolfgang Engel, Chapter 3.1, pp. 163–175. Charles River Media, 2006.

[Gritz and d'Eon 07] Larry Gritz and Eugene d'Eon. "The Importance of Being Linear." In *GPU Gems 3*, edited by Hubert Nguyen, Chapter 24, pp. 529–542. Addison Wesley, 2007.

[Hable et al. 09] John Hable, George Borshukov, and Jim Hejl. "Fast Skin Shading." In *ShaderX7*, edited by Wolfgang Engel, Chapter 2.4, pp. 161–173. Charles River Media, 2009.

[Jensen et al. 01] Henrik Wann Jensen, Steve Marschner, Marc Levoy, and Pat Hanrahan. "A Practical Model for Subsurface Light Transport." In *Proceedings of ACM SIGGRAPH 2001*, pp. 511–518, 2001.

[Jimenez and Gutierrez 08] Jorge Jimenez and Diego Gutierrez. "Faster Rendering of Human Skin." In *CEIG*, pp. 21–28, 2008.

[Jimenez et al. 09] Jorge Jimenez, Veronica Sundstedt, and Diego Gutierrez. "Screen-Space Perceptual Rendering of Human Skin." *ACM Transactions on Applied Perception*. (to appear).

VI

Handheld Devices

The mobile device market is continuing its explosive growth, with advanced hardware graphics accelerated smartphone devices rapidly gaining in market share over more mainstream devices. Today several hundred million devices are available in the market with Imagination Technologies' POWERVR MBX or SGX technology alone, representing a massive opportunity for software developers. With great prospects in terms of installed user base, which already today exceeds the console market, and with a strong ramp-up, these devices will soon exceed the PC market volumes on a year-to-year basis.

The iconic devices of 2009, from the iPhone 3GS to the Samsung OmniaHD (i8910), the Sony Ericsson Satio, Nokia's N900, Palm's Pre, and Microsoft's Zune HD, all offer hardware accelerated OpenGL ES 2.0: shader-based graphics capabilities matching the console and PC market feature-sets of only a couple of years ago. The market has matured: this is no longer a Java software graphics market.

Kick-started by the Apple iPhone, graphics acceleration is now a mandatory feature for any embedded device, be it mobile, handheld, or for HDTV or set-top box. The consumer now expects an easy-to-use advanced smooth graphical user interface where usability is critical. But it is no longer just about the user interface either. The introduction of the Apple App Store, with tens of thousands of applications dependent on graphics hardware, has further extended the opportunities for visual creativity in this market segment. This is now solidly backed up by exciting new developments from all major developers, including ID Software and EA.

This part builds on the articles from previous ShaderX books. We concentrate on the evolution from OpenGL ES 1.1 to ES 2.0 shader-based graphics with two articles. The first article, "Migration to OpenGL ES 2.0," by Ken Catterall, provides an overall introduction to the possibilities and code changes required to take advantage of this next generation API. The second article, "iPhone 3GS Graphics Development and Optimization Strategies," by Andrew Senior, looks at the specific opportunities and capabilities of the iPhone 3GS by looking at the development environment and by providing specific recommendations for best performance and image quality results. Both these articles are backed up by software development kits and tools available at http://www.akpeters.com/gpupro, providing you with all the elements required to get started.

With many devices now becoming touch-driven and offering few physical keys, the effective usage of touch screens is critical. The third article, "Touchscreen-Based User Interaction," by Andrea Bizzotto, provides valuable insight into the complexities and solutions required to achieve the best possible user-interaction and experience through a touch-based interface.

Finally, "Optimizing a 3D UI Engine for Mobile Devices," by Hyunwoo Ki, offers detailed insights into optimizing a user interface for mobile devices, looking at the importance of font rendering engines and "dirty region"-based optimizations to avoid rendering more than is actually required.

With the combination of an ever growing installed user base, rapidly evolving hardware capabilities and performance, and the portability that enables gaming anywhere, the opportunity is yours to bring more advanced and impressive content into this highly lucrative market.

Here's looking forward to another year of exciting novel developments in the embedded market!

—Kristof Beets

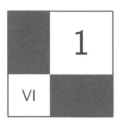

1

VI

Migration to OpenGL ES 2.0

Ken Catterall

1.1 Introduction

With the recent successes of three-dimensional-accelerated phones and mobile devices, we have seen an explosion in the development of mobile applications with three-dimensional capability accessible on these platforms through OpenGL ES. The latest generation of handsets, accelerated by POWERVR SGX, provides support for the 2.0 version of this API. Mindful of the powerful new features this

Figure 1.1. Digital Legends' *Kroll* for iPhone, OpenGL ES 1.1.

Figure 1.2. *Kroll*, OpenGL ES 2.0 version.

brings, many developers have already begun exploring its enhanced capabilities with their latest applications (see Figures 1.1 and 1.2); others are eager to migrate their existing applications to it.

This article will provide developers an overview of the transition from OpenGL ES 1.1 to 2.0 by explaining the key differences between the APIs; by showing the optimal implementation of the fixed-function pipeline under a fully shader-based framework; and by illustrating some of the new techniques made possible in ES 2.0.

1.2   Key API Differences

1.2.1   Programmable Pipeline

Those readers familiar with any 1.x version of OpenGL ES (1.1 and earlier) will know that it, like the desktop variation of OpenGL from which it is derived, consists of a vast state machine with a copious selection of user-controlled switches that control the various stages of the rendering pipeline (Figure 1.3). Vertex transformations, for example, are controlled by setting built-in model-view and projection matrices; textures are similarly scaled using the texture transformation matrix; lighting parameters are accessed via `glLights` and `glMaterials`. Blending and multi-texturing are configured with a complicated set of mode flags and

Existing Fixed Function Pipeline

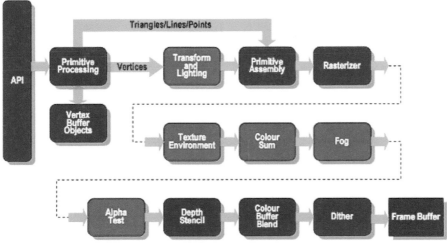

Figure 1.3. OpenGL ES 1.x, Fixed function rendering pipeline.

switches (**glBlendFunc**, **glTexEnv**, etc.). These flags notify the hardware of how to process vertex positions before assembly into triangles, and then how to color the post-rasterization primitive fragments.

Most of this is removed in OpenGL ES 2.0, and replaced by the vertex and fragment processors that run user-specified shader programs (Figure 1.4).

Vertex shader programs operate on one or more vertex attribute arrays (containing the vertex data, plus normals, colors, and any other per-vertex data). Within the program the vertex transformation is computed, typically using transformation matrices passed as *uniforms* (constants, which do not vary on a per-vertex basis), and the output of the program is a transformed vertex position.

Fragment shader programs process the rasterized primitives (e.g., triangles) on a per-fragment basis (a fragment is a portion of the triangle occupying exactly one pixel on the output framebuffer). An operation in the fragment shader is usually more expensive than the same operation in the vertex shader, simply because there are usually more fragments than vertices to process.

The fragment shader may be passed data from the vertex shader as *varyings*, such as calculated lighting values, which are then interpolated across the vertices. It may also be passed uniform variables (as with the vertex shader). The output of the fragment shader is the final color of the fragment being processed.

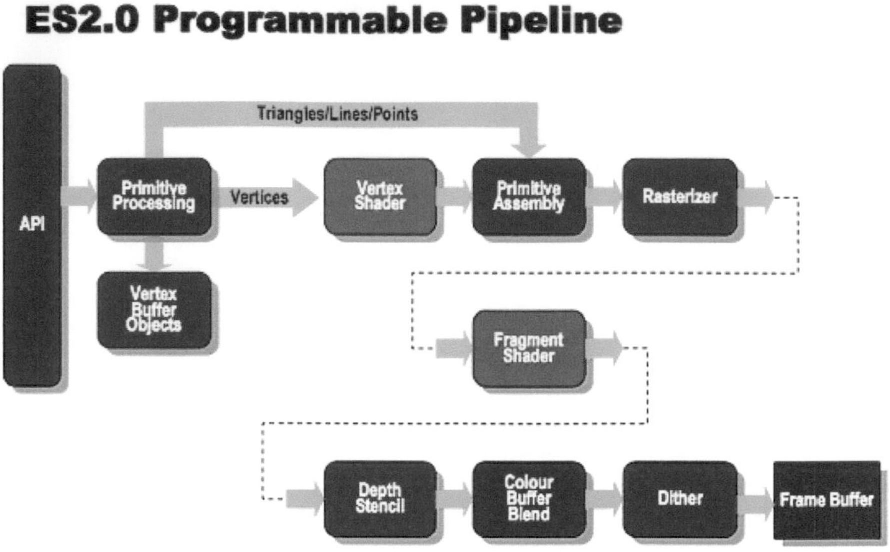

ES2.0 Programmable Pipeline

Figure 1.4. OpenGL ES 2.0 rendering pipeline.

Unlike OpenGL 2.0, OpenGL ES 2.0 does not maintain backwards compatibility, striving instead to remove superfluous or redundant elements of the API. Therefore the fixed-function pipeline of OpenGL ES 1.x has been removed, as it should be entirely possible to replicate it using shader programs. We will look at some examples of this later on.

As a consequence of this, many commonly used functions associated with fixed-function rendering have disappeared—along with the fixed model-view and projection matrices, the matrix stack (`glPushMatrix` / `glPopMatrix`), matrix transforms (`glScale`, `glRotate`, `glTranslate`), and predefined projections (`glOrtho` / `glFrustum`). Matrix calculations are left entirely to the user; the resultant matrices can be passed as uniforms to the vertex shader, which then uses them to transform the vertices.

Similarly, the built-in lighting model has been removed, as simple vertex lighting can be calculated in the vertex shader. Moreover, more complex per-fragment lighting models may be implemented. Bump mapping is an example of a technique easy to implement in shaders.

The shader language itself is discussed in more detail in the next section.

1.2.2 Vertex Attributes

Under OpenGL ES 1.x, vertex data was specified using `glVertexPointer` (the `gBegin` / `glEnd` paradigm having already been removed). Additional per-vertex data could then be specified with `glNormalPointer`, `glTexCoordPointer`, and `glColorPointer`.

In OpenGL ES 2.0 there is a similar approach. However, the generic `glVertexAttribPointer` is now used for all kinds of vertex data; the predefined types above are no longer supported. As with ES 1.x, we can improve performance by specifying vertex buffer objects to store vertex data in server memory. The example in Listing 1.1 is the simple case, without the use of buffer objects.

```
// On initialization , we define the attribute indices we will be using
// and associate them with attribute variables in the vertex shader.
// In this case , myVertex , myNormal , and myTexCoord.
#define VERTEX_ARRAY 0
#define NORMAL_ARRAY 1
#define TEXCOORD_ARRAY 2

glBindAttribLocation(uiProgramObject , VERTEX_ARRAY , "myVertex");
glBindAttribLocation(uiProgramObject , NORMAL_ARRAY , "myNormal");
glBindAttribLocation(uiProgramObject , TEXCOORD_ARRAY , "myTexCoord");

// The vertex data is then passed to the vertex shader for processing
// as follows :
GLsizei stride = ... // Get data stride

//These offsets are pointers to the beginning of the vertex , normal ,
// and texcoord data , respectively.
GLuint vertexOffset = ... // Get vertices offset
GLuint normalOffset = ... // Get normals offset
GLuint texcoordOffset = ... // Get texture coords offset

glEnableVertexAttribArray(VERTEX_ARRAY);
glVertexAttribPointer(VERTEX_ARRAY , 3, GL_FLOAT , GL_FALSE , stride ,
                      (void*)vertexOffset);
glEnableVertexAttribArray(NORMAL_ARRAY);
glVertexAttribPointer(NORMAL_ARRAY , 3, GL_FLOAT , GL_FALSE , stride ,
                      (void*)normalOffset);
glEnableVertexAttribArray(TEXCOORD_ARRAY);
glVertexAttribPointer(TEXCOORD_ARRAY , 2, GL_FLOAT , GL_FALSE ,
                      stride , (void*)texcoordOffset);
```

Listing 1.1. Simple example of defining and processing vertex data.

1.2.3 Other New Features

- *Cubemaps.* OpenGL ES 2.0 provides support for these, basically a texture unit with six faces of the cube loaded into it. These can be accessed in the shader as a `samplerCube` uniform, and the `textureCube` lookup function uses a directional vector from the centre of the cube outward to sample the texture. They are useful for providing environment-mapped reflections and specular highlights, for example.

- *Framebuffer objects (FBO).* An extension in desktop OpenGL, FBOs are a core feature of OpenGL ES 2.0. These allow the creation of off-screen renderable surfaces, independent of the system's display properties. A texture may be attached to an FBO, allowing efficient render-to-texture.

1.3 The Shader Language

The OpenGL ES Shading Language (GLSL ES) is a language, based on the C programming language, designed to be run on the graphics hardware. The per-vertex and per-fragment shader programs in the programmable pipeline are written in this language.

GLSL ES is based on the OpenGL Shading Language (GLSL). Programs are often directly compatible between the two languages with the exception of variable precision qualifiers which are a requirement for GLSL ES fragment shaders.

The full specification of GLSL ES can be found on the Khronos website: http://www.khronos.org/registry/gles/.

1.3.1 Vertex Programs

Listing 1.2 is a basic vertex shader. It uses only one attribute (`myVertex`), which would be passed to the shader as specified earlier. Because it does not use normals or texture coordinates, it cannot perform lighting or texturing. The variable

```
attribute highp vec4 myVertex;
uniform highp mat3 myMVPMatrix;

void main(void)
{
    gl_Position = myMVPMatrix * myVertex;
}
```

Listing 1.2. A fairly basic vertex shader, which simply transforms each incoming vertex by the model-view-projection matrix (as supplied by the main program).

```
const lowp vec4 red_color = vec4(1.0,0.0,0.0,1.0);
void main(void)
{
    gl_FragColor = red_color;
}
```

Listing 1.3. The simplest kind of fragment shader, simply assigning the color red to each fragment.

`myMVPMatrix` is declared uniform because it is invariant across the vertices of the primitive.

1.3.2 Fragment Programs

When coupled with the vertex shader in Listing 1.2, Listing 1.3 will render the geometry correctly transformed, but colored a uniform bright red.

1.3.3 Precision Modifiers

Precision modifiers or qualifiers are used to indicate the minimum accuracy required for a floating-point or integer variable (see Table 1.1). These qualifiers are used as the variable is declared.

Using lower-precision variables where appropriate can often lead to faster performance as less memory will be allocated for them and fewer cycles will be expended per operation on them. This is a trade-off between efficiency and precision: in some circumstances high precision will be necessary to ensure output quality (see the typical use cases in the table). Nor is there, in every case, a performance benefit from lower versus higher precision. Care should be taken, for instance, to avoid unnecessary overhead of converting variables' precisions. This can be

Precision	Size	Typical uses
highp	32-bit	Vertex position calculations, transformation matrices. Lighting and texture coordinate calculations in the vertex shader
mediump	16-bit	Texture coordinate varyings. HDR colors
lowp	10-bit	Colors. Normals from a normal map texture. Note that a lowp float can only represent values between -2.0 and +2.0.

Table 1.1. Precision modifiers.

unintentionally introduced with operations involving operands with different precision levels, which would force such a conversion.

Explicit precision modifiers are required for all float-type variables in the fragment shader (there is no default set). In the vertex shader, float variables declared without precision qualifiers will default to highp. On the other hand, sampler variables (textures) default to `lowp` in both vertex and fragment shaders. You can also set a custom default precision in the shader as with the following line:

```
precision highp float;
```

As noted above, however, for the sake of performance it is highly recommended to use the appropriate precision qualifiers, rather than opting for the "lazy" alternative of sticking to a default. It is also recommended to use a shader profiling tool, such as the PVRUniSCo Editor, a utility which is part of the publicly available POWERVR OpenGL ES 2.0 SDK. This utility allows the developer to see line-by-line cycle count costs of the shader programs. The SDK is available at http://www.akpeters.com/gpupro.

1.4   Initialization

We will precede our examples with a quick note on setting up the application. Before making OpenGL ES calls in the application it is necessary to create a rendering context so that OpenGL ES can draw to the native display. The aforementioned POWERVR SDK contains the example "Initialization," which shows how to set up the context with the open-standard EGL interface.

EGL is an API which provides a mechanism to bind to native windowing systems, so rendering surfaces can be created. There are a few minor differences with the initialization of EGL between OpenGL ES 1.x and OpenGL ES 2.0 (summarized in Table 1.2). These include differences in the naming of the header files and library which must be linked.

	OpenGL ES 1.1	**OpenGL ES 2.0**
Include files:	GLES/egl.h	EGL/egl.h
	GLES/gl.h	GLES2/gl2.h
Libraries:	libEGL	libEGL
	libGLES_CM or libGLES_CL	libGLESv2

Table 1.2. Initialization differences between OpenGL ES 1.1 and OpenGL ES 2.0.

The other main differences are that

1. When specifying configuration attributes, OpenGL ES 2.0 requires `EGL_RENDERABLE_TYPE` set to `EGL_OPENGL_ES2_BIT`.

2. When specifying context attributes, OpenGL ES 2.0 requires `EGL_CONTEXT_CLIENT_VERSION` set to 2, which is not required for OpenGL ES 1.0.

1.5 Basic Shaders: Implementing the Fixed-Function Pipeline

1.5.1 Implementing Matrix Transforms

The removal of built-in matrix management and transformation handling seems at first the most notable inconvenience in OpenGL ES 2.0. However, developers will soon find it is easy to manage their own matrices, given a well-implemented set of mathematical routines to handle the most common operations. The examples in this article use the PVRTools API from the POWERVR SDK. The basic 4×4 matrix structure in our tools is the `PVRTMat4` class.

User-defined transformations may even be preferable in OpenGL ES 1.x, giving a greater control over the transformation stack. See, for example, Listing 1.4, which may be replaced with Listing 1.5.

```
glMatrixMode(GL_MODELVIEW);
glLoadIdentity();
glRotatef(rot_value, 0,0,1);
glTranslatef(xtrans, ytrans, ztrans);
```

Listing 1.4. OpenGL ES 1.1 matrix code.

You may observe from this snippet that the static functions `RotationZ` and `Translation` each return an instance of the appropriate transformation matrix, and that the multiplication operator is properly overloaded for matrix multiplication. This intuitive approach mirrors that found in the OpenGL ES 2.0 shader language, where vector and matrix types are defined with corresponding operations.

```
PVRTMat4 mTransform = PVRTMat4::RotationZ(rot_val) *
                      PVRTMat4::Translation(xtrans, ytrans, ztrans);
glMatrixMode(GL_MODELVIEW);
glLoadMatrix(mTransform.f);
```

Listing 1.5. OpenGL ES 2.0 matrix code.

```
/* .. shader code .. */
gl_Position = myMVPMatrix * myVertex;

// The matrix is passed to the shader as a uniform, in the following
//  way:
PVRTMat4 mMVP = mTransform * mProjection;

// Here mTransform is used as model-view; mProjection has been set up
// earlier.
float *pointer = mMVP.f;

// API uses a float pointer to pass data to the shader.
int i32Location = glGetUniformLocation(m_uiProgramObject,
                                       "myMVPMatrix");
glUniformMatrix4fv(i32Location, 1, GL_FALSE, pointer);

/* Now set up vertex attrib arrays; Draw calls follow */
```

Listing 1.6. Simple matrix transformation.

The PVRTools can also create projection matrices with static Perspective and Ortho functions, similar to those API calls from OpenGL ES 1.x.

In addition, useful functions like inverse and transpose are defined. As we will see, these become vital tools in OpenGL ES 2.0 when calculating matrices for lighting, as well as for transformation.

1.5.2   Example 1: Simple Transform

Under OpenGL ES 2.0, the matrix **mTransform** may be passed as the model-view matrix. More commonly, however, this will be pre-multiplied with the projection matrix, rather than performing the multiplication in the vertex shader (and hence per-vertex, which is pointless). As shown in Listing 1.6, the resultant model-view projection matrix may be used in shaders such as Listing 1.2 to correctly transform the vertices.

1.5.3   Example 2: Basic Diffuse Lighting

In OpenGLES 1.x, the setup code for basic diffuse lighting will look something like that shown in Listing 1.7.

We can see here the main information required by the graphics hardware: an array of per-vertex normal data, a single light direction vector, and the material color. This is required in addition to the vertex transformation data from the previous example.

In OpenGL ES 2.0, the inverse transpose of the model-view matrix will be passed as an additional uniform. This model-view inverse-transpose (IT) matrix

```
glEnable(GL_LIGHTING);
glEnable(GL_LIGHT0);

//Specifies a parallel light along the vector (0,0,1)
float aLightDirection[] = {0.0f, 0.0f, 1.0f, 0.0f};

//Assigns the light direction to the light number 0
glLightv(GL_LIGHT0, GL_POSITION, aLightDirection);
glMaterial4f(GL_FRONT_AND_BACK, GL_AMBIENT, 1.0f, 1.0f, 1.0f, 1.0f);
glMaterial4f(GL_FRONT_AND_BACK, GL_DIFFUSE, 1.0f, 1.0f, 1.0f, 1.0f);
glEnableClientState(GL_NORMAL_ARRAY);
glNormalPointer(GL_FLOAT, stride, (void*)(offset));

//Draw
```

Listing 1.7. Setup code for basic diffuse lighting.

must be used to convert the normals rather than the model-view matrix, as any scaling would change the direction of the normal. Note that as the normals and light direction are directions, rather than positions, we only need three-component vectors to represent them. The normals themselves are passed as an additional vertex attribute, similarly to the vertices themselves.

The vertex shader then uses these values to calculate the intensity of the lighting at each vertex (varDot). It uses a simple dot product of the light direction in view space and vertex normal in view space. The value is then passed to the fragment shader as a varying.

Finally, the fragment shader multiplies the base color by this light intensity value to produce the color of the fragment (see Listing 1.8).

```
//Calculate the model-view inverse-transpose here as mat3.
PVRTMat3 mModelViewIT = PVRTMat3(mTransform.inverse().transpose());

//Bind the model-view inverse-transpose matrix to the shader.
i32Location = glGetUniformLocation(m_uiProgramObject,
                                   "myModelViewIT");
glUniformMatrix3fv( i32Location, 1, GL_FALSE, mModelViewIT.f );

//Bind the light direction vector to the shader.
i32Location = glGetUniformLocation(m_uiProgramObject,
                                   "myLightDirection");
glUniform3f( i32Location, 0, 0, 1 );

//Pass the normals data.
glEnableVertexAttribArray(NORMAL_ARRAY);
glVertexAttribPointer(NORMAL_ARRAY, 3, GL_FLOAT, GL_FALSE, stride,
                      (void*)(offset));
```

```
//Draw

//Vertex shader:
attribute highp vec4 myVertex;
attribute mediump vec3 myNormal;
uniform mediump mat4 myMVPMatrix;
uniform mediump mat3 myModelViewIT;
uniform mediump vec3 myLightDirection;
varying mediump float varDot;

void main(void)
{
    gl_Position = myMVPMatrix * myVertex;
    mediump vec3 transNormal = myModelViewIT * myNormal;
    varDot = max(dot(transNormal, myLightDirection), 0.0 );
}

//Fragment shader:
varying mediump float varDot;

void main (void)
{
    lowp vec3 baseColour = vec3(1.0, 1.0, 1.0);
    gl_FragColor = vec4(baseColour * varDot, 1.0);
}
```

Listing 1.8. Combining light intensity and base color to produce fragment color.

As a final note, the light direction in this example could have been declared a constant variable in the vertex shader, rather than a uniform. If however the value of the light direction comes from the main program (e.g., if it changes over time), it must obviously be passed as seen here. Conversely, the `baseColor` variable could have also been passed to the fragment shader as a uniform.

1.5.4   Example 3: Basic Texturing

Let us look at an example (see Listing 1.9) where a texture has been bound: in this case, to the first texture unit.

In OpenGL ES 2 the texture lookup must be performed explicitly in the shader. The handles to the texture and vertex texture coordinates are passed to the shader, as a uniform and an attribute, respectively. The vertex shader passes the texture coordinates straight through to the fragment shader. The fragment shader uses these texture coordinates to look up the color from the texture. This color is used as the fragment color.

The value passed as a uniform to the sampler variable is, in fact, the number of the texture unit to which the texture is bound. Thus, multiple textures may be passed by using different values (see Listing 1.10).

```
int nTextureUnit = 0;
glActiveTexture(GL_TEXTURE0 + nTextureUnit);
glBindTexture(GL_TEXTURE_2D, texturehandle);

// In OpenGL ES 1.x, we need only to enable texturing and submit the
// texture coordinates:

// Load the texture and set filtering parameters.
glEnable(GL_TEXTURE_2D);
glEnableClientState(GL_TEXTURE_COORD_ARRAY);
glTexCoordPointer(2, VERTTYPEENUM, stride, (void*)(offset));

// DRAW
```

Listing 1.9. Basic texturing.

```
// Load the texture and set filtering parameters as in ES 1.x.
// Sets the sampler2D variable to the correct texture unit
glUniform1i(glGetUniformLocation(uiProgramObject, "sampler2d"),
            nTextureUnit);

// Pass the texture co-ordinate data.
glEnableVertexAttribArray(TEXCOORD_ARRAY);
glVertexAttribPointer(TEXCOORD_ARRAY, 2, GL_FLOAT, GL_FALSE,
                      stride, (void*)(offset));

// Draw

// Vertex Shader:
attribute highp vec4 myVertex;
attribute mediump vec2 myUV;
uniform mediump mat4 myMVPMatrix;
varying mediump vec2 varCoord;

void main (void)
{
    gl_Position = myMVPMatrix * myVertex;
    varCoord = myUV.st;
}

// Fragment Shader:
uniform sampler2D sampler2d;
varying mediump vec2 varCoord;

void main (void)
{
    gl_FragColor = texture2D(sampler2d, varCoord);
}
```

Listing 1.10. Multiple textures.

Now it should be apparent how to combine this with the vertex lighting of the previous example, by setting all the additional instructions required and multiplying the final color (in the red, green, and blue channels) by the light intensity.

1.5.5 Shader Tools

As an additional note, there are some tools around that allow you to generate an equivalent shader for a given fixed-function rendering state. One such is the 3DLabs GLSL ShaderGen, which may be found at http://mew.cx/glsl/shadergen/. Such a tool may be a useful starting point in converting a fixed-function application, though bear in mind that the shader code generated would likely benefit from optimization and correct precision modifiers.

1.6 Advanced Effects Made Easy

The POWERVR OpenGL ES 2.0 SDK illustrates a number of basic techniques in its TrainingCourse section. The examples range from the re-implementation of fixed-function effects (as in the examples we have just seen; these may also be contrasted with examples from the corresponding OpenGL ES 1.1 SDK), to techniques which are more difficult under the fixed-function API (but can now form the basic building blocks of more advanced effects), up to effects which are impossible or completely impractical (without significant extensions to the API) under fixed-function.

The following selection of techniques mainly fall into the middle category (other useful techniques presented by the SDK but not covered here include skinned animation and shadow rendering).

1.6.1 Multi-texturing

It is the ability to freely manipulate the texture environment which may be the greatest asset of OpenGL ES 2.0 over its predecessors. The fixed-function pipeline provided a number of predefined functions for combining textures, which could be specified by setting the TEXTURE_ENV_MODE. This may be set to such values as GL_ADD, GL_MODULATE, GL_COMBINE, etc. To see the full horror of these function definitions, you may consult the OpenGL ES specification at http://www.khronos.org (for OpenGL ES 1.1, an HTML version is available). Correct use of these functions to achieve the effect you want typically involved a lot of trial and error for all but the most basic requirements.

Here the added flexibility of fragment shaders becomes self-evident. In OpenGL ES 2.0, the developer has full control over the texture lookup and combine function(s). The tasty example in Listing 1.11 shows how multiple samplers bound to different texture units can be easily mixed.

```
// An example: I want 30% pie and 70% spaghetti.
uniform lowp sampler2D pie_texture;
uniform lowp sampler2D spag_texture;
varying highp vec2 tex_coord;
const lowp float ratio = 0.3;

void main()
{
    lowp vec4 pie_color = texture2D(pie_texture, tex_coord);
    lowp vec4 spag_color = texture2D(spag_texture, tex_coord);
    gl_FragColor = mix(pie_color, spag_color, ratio);

    // Done! Try doing that with ES 1.x ...
}
```

Listing 1.11. Mixing samplers.

More complex mixing functions may be substituted at will, and the mixing ratio may be made non-constant. For example, if the ratio variable is provided as a uniform, it can be made time-dependent, so the texture can fade from one image to the other. Branching may also be used (if-else statements); so can step functions, used to create more abrupt cut-offs. More textures can be added, though it should be kept in mind that each additional texture lookup comes with a performance cost; therefore, they should be kept to no more than necessary.

1.6.2 Reflections with Cubemaps

The fixed-function pipeline allowed reflection effects using two-dimensional spherical mapping, and transforming the texture coordinates manually or else via extensions. This approach is of course straightforward to implement in shaders as well.

Cubemapping is however more intuitive, more 'correct,' and with support for cubemap textures in OpenGL ES 2.0, just as easy (if not easier) to implement. The cubemap itself is simply a collection of six faces of the cube, and the handle to it is used in a similar way to a two-dimensional texture except that API calls must specify the target **GL_TEXTURE_CUBE_MAP** rather than **GL_TEXTURE_2D**. The same map will often be used to texture the skybox for outdoor environments.

The texture lookup itself requires a direction vector, which in this case is the view vector reflected in the surface of the object being rendered. This reflection vector can be calculated in the vertex shader given the untransformed vertex normal and the eye position in model space (see Listing 1.12).

This can easily be modulated or combined with a base texture or color (see previous example) for a realistic reflection effect.

```
// Calculate eye direction in model space.
mediump vec3 eyeDir = normalize(inVertex - EyePosModel);

// Reflect eye direction over normal and
// transform to world space.
ReflectDir = ModelWorld * reflect(eyeDir, inNormal);

// The lookup can then be performed in the fragment shader as follows:
uniform samplerCube sCubeMap;
varying mediump vec3 ReflectDir;

void main()
{
    gl_FragColor = textureCube(sCubeMap, ReflectDir);
}
```

Listing 1.12. Reflection vector.

1.6.3   Proper Bump Mapping

There are numerous white papers on the topic of correct bump mapping in real time. For a practical example you may consult the POWERVR SDK. To briefly

Figure 1.5. Earth bump map applied to a smooth sphere, plus blue coloring for oceans.

```
highp vec3 bitangent = cross(inNormal, inTangent);
highp mat3 tangentSpaceXform = mat3(inTangent, inNormal, bitangent);
LightVec = lightDirection * tangentSpaceXform;
```

Listing 1.13. Transform for bump mapping.

summarize, it works by transforming the light direction in to the vertex's *tangent space*, that is, the space oriented so that the vertex normal is "up." The diffuse value is then calculated by taking the dot product of this vector and a per-pixel "normal" obtained by sampling a normal-map texture.

To transform the light vector to tangent space, the main program will need to supply a tangent vector, in addition to the usual normal vector, as an extra vertex attribute. The transform then looks like that shown in Listing 1.13.

Figure 1.5 shows an example of bump mapping on a sphere.

1.6.4 Vertex Texturing and Displacement Mapping

Just as it is possible to sample textures in the fragment shader, the same can be done in the vertex shader. The most obvious implication of this is that it is possible to transform vertices based on texture information.

Displacement mapping involves using a height-map texture, usually a greyscale image where the color intensity represents the height value. The sampled value shows how much the vertex should be displaced. This is done by moving the vertex from its original position along the direction of the vertex normal:

```
lowp float displacement_value = texture2D(heightsampler, texCoord.xy);

vertex_pos = vertex_pos + displacement_value * vertex_unit_normal;
```

This can be used, for instance, to transform a flat tessellated plane or a smooth sphere into a bumpy terrain (Figure 1.6). It may also be used in conjunction with either bump mapping or a static light texture to add more detail.

1.6.5 Post-Processing

FBOs provide a fast and easy way of performing render to texture, and when combined with fragment shaders this allows a variety of post-processing effects such as blurring, bloom effects, and color space conversions, to name but a few.

The Shader Views demo (Figure 1.7) displays a number of the post-processing effects made possible.

Figure 1.6. Earth model with displacement, bump mapping, and specular lighting

Figure 1.7. Post-processing effects on the Shader Views demo

1.7 Conclusion

We have seen that although the OpenGL ES 2.0 API is not a superset of its predecessors, it has retained their capabilities; that basic rendering techniques continue to be well-supported; and that with a bit of effort it is easy to migrate fixed-function applications to the programmable shader interface. Furthermore, the benefits gained from such a transition are well worth this effort.

The examples presented are just a beginning; the code samples here serve mainly to illustrate the concepts and more complete examples may be found in the SDK at http://www.akpeters.com/gpupro.

(The SDK examples will compile and run on an OpenGL 2.0 capable Windows PC; the OpenGL ES environment is created through a PC emulation library). The same SDK is also available via the POWERVR *Insider* website (http://www.powervrinsider.com) for both Windows and Linux PC emulation, as well as for various supported platforms including Symbian S60 and iPhone.

1.8 Acknowledgments

This article owes much to the document *Migration from OpenGL ES 1.x to OpenGL ES 2.0* by Stefan Senk and others of Imagination Technologies' Developer Technology group. The original document may be found in the POWERVR SDK under Documentation. The author would like to thank the whole DevTech team for their ongoing efforts on the SDKs, and in particular, Stefan, Gordon MacLachlan, and Georg Kolling; as well as Kristof Beets and Andrea Bizzotto, for their contribution and feedback. The author would also like to thank the team at Digital Legends including Nino Ceraolo and Xavier Costa for the images they have provided.

Touchscreen-Based
User Interaction
Andrea Bizzotto

2.1 Introduction

The touchscreen plays a major role in user interaction on mobile devices. Although some of these systems come with high-level APIs that could be used by the programmer to detect gestures, others provide just raw access to the samples read from the hardware. This article illustrates a mathematical framework that can be used to estimate the motion and position of the input pointer on screen (see Figure 2.1). An application for controlling the position of a camera in a three-dimensional spherical coordinate system is presented as an usage example.

2.2 Motion Estimation

Let us approach the problem of estimating the motion on screen, given a set of samples described by three values:

- The time when the sample was read.

- The position of the sample along the x axis.

- The position of the sample along the y axis.

The context of this problem is a main-loop based graphics application. With this respect, the platform-specific touchscreen implementation might provide one sample per-frame, or multiple samples (as it is the case if the touchscreen subsystem is independent from the main loop).

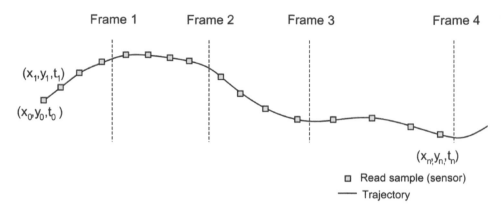

Figure 2.1. Touchscreen input: while the user drags the pointer on screen, the new samples become available and at the beginning of each frame they can be used to estimate the motion and position.

A very simple approach would be to calculate the motion as the velocity between two consecutive samples as in Equation (2.1), where t_i is the time of the sample i, $s(t_i)$ the corresponding position and $v(t_i)$ the velocity:

$$v(t_n) = \frac{s(t_n) - s(t_{n-1})}{t_n - t_{n-1}}. \qquad (2.1)$$

Given the small screen size of mobile devices and their relatively high resolution, reading consecutive samples can result in different x- and y-coordinates, even if the pointer is not moving on screen. This effect was observed on OMAP Zoom platforms, where a set of samples with slightly different positions was returned even when the input position was fixed.

We can take in account this behavior in our model by assuming that the samples are affected by Gaussian noise, whose variance is platform-dependent. If on a particular device this side effect does not exist, our model is still valid as it means that the variance of the noise is zero. Since we want our motion estimation algorithm to be virtually unaffected by the presence of noise, we introduce a method for noise reduction followed by a thresholding operation.

A very common technique for noise reduction is to apply an average filter on the set of available samples, therefore reducing the error by a factor of N (where N is the size of the set).

If the user drags the pointer on screen and we want to estimate the motion of such interaction, we can use a more effective approach that reduces the noise and makes use of all the samples in a given time interval:

1. Choose a "time window" that contains all the most recent samples. To do so, we store all the samples that we want to process in an circular queue. At each frame we update our queue by adding all the samples that were read since the previous frame, and discarding the ones that are too old. If no samples are read for some time, the queue will quickly empty and we can set the motion to 0.

2. Calculate all the velocities between consecutive samples in the queue.

3. Obtain the average on those velocities.

This method is much more reliable than the previous one and introduces a trade-off between accuracy and responsiveness of the filter:

Bigger window. More samples are stored: the accuracy increases but the responsiveness of the filter decreases. Since we are using a causal filter, if ΔT is the length of the window, we are introducing a delay equal to $\Delta T/2$.

Smaller window. Fewer samples are stored: the accuracy decreases but the responsiveness increases.

```
void update(Sample *pSamples, int num, float &mx, float &my) {
  //Add the samples read in the last frame.
  queue.add(pSamples, num);
  //Deletes old samples
  queue.remove(getTime() - timeWindow);
  if (queue.size() < 2) {
    mx = my = 0.0f;
    return;
  }
  int i = 0;
  Iterator iter = queue.begin();
  Sample curr, prev = iter.data();
  while (iter.next()) {
    curr = iter.data();
    //Motion is an array that stores motions of consecutive
    samples.
    motion[i].dx = (curr.x - prev.x) / (curr.t - prev.t);
    motion[i].dy = (curr.y - prev.y) / (curr.t - prev.t);
    prev = curr;
    i++;
  }
  CalculateAverage(motion, i, mx, my);
  //Apply thresholds
  if (mx < thresholdX) mx = 0.0f;
  if (my < thresholdY) my = 0.0f;
}
```

Listing 2.1. Motion estimation routine.

The method can be made even more robust: we can define a platform-dependent threshold that is proportional to the variance of the noise, and if the estimated motion is smaller than this threshold, we set it to zero. This will guarantee that no motion is detected if the input position does not change (taking noise into account).

The complete method for updating the motion is summarized in Listing 2.1.

Such an approach has been successfully tested on several platforms. For the purpose of motion estimation, choosing a time interval of 0.2 seconds gives good results on an OMAP Zoom platform, while on the Samsung Omnia the read input coordinates are constant if the pointer doesn't move on screen, and the time interval and threshold can be smaller as no noise needs to be removed. The same applies on Windows emulation, where the mouse is used as a pointing device to simulate the touchscreen.

2.3   Position Prediction

Position estimation seems to be an easy task as the position of the last sample can be used directly. Some considerations can be made nevertheless:

- The instant when the input is processed (beginning of the new frame) is not necessarily the same as the time of the last read sample.

- The graphics pipeline takes some time to render the frame and swap the buffers, so if the input position is used to draw a target on screen (for example a cursor), it might be worth to adjust this position according to the time when the frame will be actually rendered.

These two contributions are put together in Equation (2.2), where $\triangle_{\text{read}}$ is the difference between the current time and the time of the last sample, and $\triangle_{\text{frame}}$ is the time to render the current frame, equal to the time to render the previous frame (we can assume that the framerate is locally constant):

$$\triangle_{\text{total}} = \triangle_{\text{read}} + \triangle_{\text{frame}}. \tag{2.2}$$

The predicted position is then as in Equation (2.3), where $v(t_{\text{last}})$ is the motion estimated as described and t_{last} the time of the last read sample:

$$s(t_{\text{new}}) = s(t_{\text{last}}) + v(t_{\text{last}}) \cdot (t_{\text{last}} + \triangle_{\text{total}}). \tag{2.3}$$

2.4 Application: Controlling a Camera in a Spherical Coordinate System

A possible application is to use our new motion primitives to move a camera around an object in the center of the scene. The target of the camera is therefore fixed to the origin of the world coordinate system. If required, this constraint can be relaxed by setting the target on an arbitrary point in three-dimensional space, as with a simple translation this case can be included in the former one.

The position of the camera is determined by a vector (x, y, z) of coordinates, while only the motion in the x- and y-directions of the screen is available. As it is not intuitive to map these directions to a point in a cartesian coordinate system, we can use an alternative representation for the position of the camera:

Yaw. Rotation around the y-axis.

Pitch. Rotation around the x-axis.

Radius. Distance of the camera from the origin.

This allows us to use the x- and y-motion on the touchscreen to update the yaw and pitch angles of the camera, while leaving the radius fixed or adjustable through other input controls.

Figure 2.2 shows the concept. The camera position is initially set to $(0, 0, R)^{\mathrm{T}}$. At each frame the yaw and pitch angles are updated according to the motion on the touchscreen, and the position is updated.

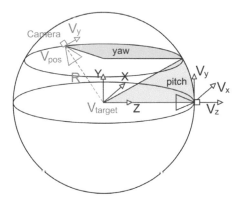

Figure 2.2. Three-dimensional spherical coordinate system: upon application of the yaw and pitch angles the camera moves from the initial position (marked in blue) to the final one (green). The camera defines a coordinate system defined by the position and the three orthonormal vectors (V_x, V_y, V_z).

To render our scene from the viewpoint of the camera we need to calculate the roto-translation matrix that transforms a point from world space coordinates to camera space coordinates. In OpenGL such a matrix is known as model-view matrix and can be computed once the position, target and up direction of the camera are known; therefore, we want to find these values first.

The spherical coordinate system is useful to update the yaw and pitch angles, but to find the model-view matrix the position needs to be expressed again in the canonical coordinate system. This is done by applying the rotation matrices that correspond to the two angles to the initial position, as in Equations (2.4), (2.5) and (2.6).

$$\mathbf{R_y}(\alpha) = \begin{pmatrix} \cos(\alpha) & 0 & -\sin(\alpha) \\ 0 & 1 & 0 \\ \sin(\alpha) & 0 & \cos(\alpha), \end{pmatrix} \mathbf{R_x}(\alpha) = \begin{pmatrix} 1 & 0 & 0 \\ 0 & \cos(\alpha) & -\sin(\alpha) \\ 0 & \sin(\alpha) & \cos(\alpha) \end{pmatrix}.$$

$$(2.4)$$

$$\mathbf{M_{rot}} = \mathbf{R_y}(\text{yaw}) \cdot \mathbf{R_x}(\text{pitch}). \tag{2.5}$$

$$\mathbf{V_{pos}} = \mathbf{M_{rot}} \cdot \begin{pmatrix} 0 \\ 0 \\ R \end{pmatrix}. \tag{2.6}$$

The target of our camera is fixed at the origin, as Equation (2.7) states, and the up direction (V_y) is determined by Equation (2.8).

$$\mathbf{V_{target}} = \mathbf{0^T}. \tag{2.7}$$

$$\mathbf{V_y} = \mathbf{M_{rot}} \cdot \begin{pmatrix} 0 \\ 1 \\ 0 \end{pmatrix}. \tag{2.8}$$

The model-view matrix is composed by a translation that shifts the coordinate system to the position of the camera and by a rotation that takes into account its relative orientation. Such rotation can be expressed as a matrix formed by three orthonormal vectors that can be immediately derived from the position, target and up direction of the camera. Equations (2.9), (2.10) and (2.11) illustrate the concept:

$$\mathbf{V_z} = -\frac{\mathbf{V_{target}} - \mathbf{V_{pos}}}{||\mathbf{V_{target}} - \mathbf{V_{pos}}||}. \tag{2.9}$$

$$\mathbf{V_x} = \mathbf{V_y} \times \mathbf{V_z}. \tag{2.10}$$

$$\mathbf{M_{view}} = \begin{pmatrix} \mathbf{V_x^T} & 0 \\ \mathbf{V_y^T} & 0 \\ \mathbf{V_z^T} & 0 \\ \mathbf{0^T} & 1 \end{pmatrix} \cdot \left(\begin{array}{c|c} \mathbf{0_{3x3}} & -\mathbf{V_{pos}} \\ \hline \mathbf{0^T} & 1 \end{array} \right). \tag{2.11}$$

It can be noticed that the vectors V_x, V_y, and V_z represent the axes of a right-handed reference frame. For this reason the direction of the camera is opposite of the vector V_z.

This mathematical framework allows the setup of an interactive system where the user can spin the camera around the observed object. The yaw and pitch angles can be updated at each frame by adding the motion on the x- and y-axes, but once the user releases the pointer, the camera movement immediately stops. It would be more realistic if the camera had a residual inertial motion, and the next section illustrates how to implement this.

2.4.1 Adding Inertia

The desired effect consists in letting the camera spin for a short amount of time, until the residual motion is zero. Such effect is best modeled by a decreasing exponential function like the one in Equation (2.12):

$$f(t) = \begin{cases} 0, & t < 0, \\ 1 - e^{-\tau t}, & t \geq 0. \end{cases} \tag{2.12}$$

If t_r is the time when the input is released and M_x the corresponding motion on the x-axis, the residual speed at any instant in time is given by $x(t) = M_x \cdot f(t - t_r)$.

This value can be integrated over time to update the yaw angle (the same procedure is valid for the y-axis / pitch angle). The integration is a discrete operation as it can be performed at each frame, and Equation (2.13) provides a method to update the angle frame by frame:

$$x(t_n) = \sum_{i=0}^{n} M_x \cdot f(t_i - t_r)(t_i - t_{i-1}) = x(t_{n-1}) + M_x \cdot f(t_n - t_r)(t_n - t_{n-1}). \tag{2.13}$$

2.5 Algorithm Overview

The general algorithm for updating the camera position within the main loop is illustrated in Listing 2.2.

The motion is estimated using the discussed technique and used to update the yaw and pitch angles. When the input is released the current time and the motion are saved and later used to add the inertial contribution to the angles

```
t = getTime();
touchscreen.GetMotion(motionX, motionY);
if (touchscreen.Released()) {
  releaseMotionX = motionX;
  releaseMotionY = motionY;
  tr = t;
}
yaw = yaw + motionX + releaseMotionX * f(t - tr);
pitch = pitch + motionY + releaseMotionY * f(t - tr);
MView = CalculateMatrix(yaw, pitch, radius);

RenderGeometry(MView);
```

Listing 2.2. Render loop.

(appropriate scaling factors can be used when updating the angles in order to calibrate the speed of the camera position as desired). Finally, the model-view matrix can be calculated with the techique previously described and the geometry can be rendered using that matrix.

Figure 2.3 illustrates how the presented techniques have been used in an OpenGL ES 2.0 demo developed at Imagination Technologies.

Figure 2.3. Flowers demo. This demo shows procedural plant growth with detailed flowers and makes use of the described touchscreen implementation to spin the camera around the growing plant.

2.6   Conclusion

This article showed how to approach motion estimation by means of a robust algorithm whose parameters can be adapted on different platforms to get optimal results. The length of the time window and the threshold can be tweaked as necessary according to the requirements of the final application.

A simple OpenGL ES 2.0 demo that allows to control the camera in the spherical coordinate system previously described is available at http://www.akpeters .com/gpupro, together with full source code for OMAP Zoom1, Zoom2 and Windows emulation, where the mouse is used to simulate the touchscreen interaction.

2.7   Acknowledgments

The author would like to thank Kristof Beets and the whole BizDev and DevTech teams for their work, contribution, and feedback.

iPhone 3GS Graphics Development and Optimization Strategies

Andrew Senior

The iPhone was first released in June 2007 and has since had two major revisions: the 3G and the 3GS. In early 2008, Apple released an official iPhone SDK which enabled developers to create native applications for the device. A physical device is not required for most of development as a software implemented iPhone Simulator is provided with the SDK. Only members of the paid developer program are able to test their creations on a physical device and subsequently submit them to the App Store for distribution.

All revisions of the iPhone have three-dimensional hardware acceleration enabled by POWERVR cores. The original iPhone, iPhone 3G and first two revisions of the iPod Touch are capable of running OpenGL ES 1.1. The newer and more powerful iPhone 3GS adds OpenGL ES 2.0 capability to this (as do the 32- and 64-GB versions of the third-generation iPod Touch). The iPhone 3GS also boasts a faster CPU and double the amount of memory seen in previous models. This makes it a perfect candidate for a major gaming development platform.

This document is intended to provide developers with the essential help required to start creating graphical demos for the iPhone 3GS using OpenGL ES 2.0. At the time of writing the current version of the official iPhone SDK is 3.0. Version 3.0 was released along side the iPhone 3GS and is the first version to support OpenGL ES 2.0.

3.1 Software Development Kits

Apple provides a free SDK for the iPhone available from the Apple Developer Connection (http://developer.apple.com/iphone/). The iPhone SDK provides the developer with all the tools, libraries, and documentation needed to create any native application for the iPhone or iPod Touch. Many different types of application can be created for the iPhone, utilising one or more of the several input and output features of the device. The SDK provides a wizard utility to create an OpenGL ES application, currently only an OpenGL ES 1.1 implementation. With the recent release of the iPhone 3GS, it is now possible to benefit from the programmable graphics pipeline of its POWERVR SGX core by utilizing its OpenGL ES 2.0 support.

It is essential for any iPhone development that the iPhone SDK is installed on an Intel based Mac running Mac OS X Leopard version 10.5.7 or later.

3.1.1   iPhone SDK

The first step towards starting iPhone development is to visit the iPhone Developer Connection and sign up for a free account. Once signed in you can download the iPhone SDK. Included within the rather large download is Xcode, Apple's IDE for creating, debugging and optimising iPhone applications. The installation process of the iPhone SDK will perform a full installation of Xcode; there is no need to install it independently.

The iPhone SDK is written in Objective-C, an object-oriented extension to the C language. This can be quite frustrating to first time iPhone developers wishing to use knowledge of C/C++ to write an OpenGL ES application. It is a requirement that the developer at least understands how the Objective-C language works; an Objective-C programming guide can be obtained from the Apple Developer Connection website [Apple 09] for reference. As Objective-C is an extension of the C language it is perfectly legal to include C code in your application. An Objective-C program can also include C++ code by signifying to the compiler that you wish to use Objective-C++. In a regular Objective-C application the header and source code files have the extension .h and .m. To enable Objective-C++ it is just a matter of renaming the source file from .m to .mm, this is the only change Xcode requires in order to compile Objective-C++.

The installation process of the SDK will extract all the libraries, tools and other files to /Developer and Xcode can be found in the Applications sub-directory (/Developer/Applications). It is probably a good idea to drag Xcode onto your dock as during development you will be using it quite a lot.

3.1.2   POWERVR SDK

The POWERVR SDK for iPhone is now available free to developers from the POWERVR Insider page at http://www.powervrinsider.com. Imagination Technologies provides a comprehensive SDK offering tutorials, source code, utility applications, documentation, and a valuable tools library. Available is an OpenGL

ES 1.1 SDK for iPhone and iPod Touch, and an OpenGL ES 2.0 SDK for iPhone 3GS.

As mentioned in the previous section, newcomers to iPhone development may be put off by the Objective-C language. The POWERVR SDK encapsulates all of the system code and provides the user with a C++ interface via PVRShell. PVRShell is a C++ class used to make programming for POWERVR platforms easier and more portable. PVRShell takes care of all API and OS initialization and handles viewport creation and clearing. The application interface inherits from PVRShell and comprises five derived functions: `InitApplication`, `InitView`, `ReleaseView`, `QuitApplication`, and `RenderScene`. These functions will be invoked by PVRShell; `InitApplication` will be called before the graphics context is created and just before exiting the program `QuitApplication` will be called. `InitView` will be called upon creation of the rendering context and `ReleaseView` will be called when finishing the application, before `QuitApplication`. The previous four functions will only be called once per application execution. The main rendering loop function of the program is `RenderScene`. This function must return false when the user wants to terminate the application. PVRShell will call this function every frame and will manage the relevant OS events. There are other PVRShell functions available to the user to get information, such as input back from the iPhone: these include `PVRShellGet()` and `PVRShellSet()`. `PVRShellSet()` is recommended to be used in `InitApplication()` so the user preferences are applied at the API initialization.

It is recommended to use the PVRShell interface to promote cross platform compatibility for all POWERVR SGX hardware on Symbian, Linux, Android and WinCE as well as Mac OS. Using the PVRShell interface it is also possible to develop using the WindowsPC or LinuxPC emulation SDKs, also found at the POWERVR Insider web page. All non-system specific code will transfer between platforms seamlessly.

The POWERVR SDK contains tools and utilities to export and load compressed textures and animated three-dimensional models. Located within the Training Course folder of the SDK are many small demos each outlining a specific task or problem. The utilities bundled with the SDK will be described in the next section.

3.1.3 Tools and Utilities

Apple. Xcode is Apple's official development suite for OS X. Xcode is free and the latest developer version is included with every iPhone SDK release. Xcode includes all the tools needed to create, debug, and optimize your iPhone applications. The Xcode toolset includes the Xcode IDE, Apple's integrated development environment comprising of a text editor, compiler, and debugger. The iPhone simulator is part of Xcode, which enables testing directly on the development machine under a software implemented emulator. Generally the simulator will produce the exact same output as the physical device. To judge performance you should never use the simulator, always test on a device. Performance analysis can be run using Instruments, a profiling tool to help dynamically track processes and examine their behavior. Instruments can help you optimize your application detailing CPU and memory usage and even OpenGL ES graphics performance. Instruments can be used on the iPhone and the simulator, some restrictions apply to both. Using Instruments on the simulator you can record your input and replay it several times emulating touch input exactly as you recorded it. This is handy for testing input without all the tedious clicking and dragging. It is only possible to monitor OpenGL ES performance while running an OpenGL ES application on an actual device.

POWERVR. Provided with the POWERVR SDK is a suite of utilities including PVRTexTool, PVRShaman and PVRUniSCoEditor. These utilities provide content (textures, three-dimensional models and shaders) that can quickly and easily be integrated into PVRTools for rapid development. PVRTools is a three-dimensional graphics utility library written in C++. It includes functions to load compressed textures, three-dimensional animated models, and POWERVR PFX shader effect files.

PVRTexTool has both a GUI and a command line utility. PVRTexTool can compress any standard bitmap file (e.g., BMP, JPG, PNG, TGA, etc) into a PVRTC texture, recognized by the iPhone as a compressed image format. PVRTC has many benefits as described in Section 3.2.2. PVRTexTool can generate mipmaps for POT (power of two) textures and can compress them into either four or two bits-per-pixel PVRTCs. PVRTexTool supports normal map and skybox generation as well as scale, rotate and flip transforms.

PVRShaman is an integrated shader development environment allowing rapid prototyping of new vertex and fragment shader programs. PVRShaman brings together geometry exported using PVRGeoPOD (or converted using Collada2POD), textures compressed using PVRTexTool, and on-the-fly editing of shader programs with editing functionality on the same level as the PVRUniSCo Editor. Shader effects can be saved as POWERVR FX files allowing easy integration with your base code.

PVRUniSCo Editor is the graphical front-end for the PVRUniSCo shader compiler. It allows easy creation and editing of OpenGL ES 2.0 shading language vertex and fragment shader programs, in addition to POWERVR FX (PFX) files.

3.2 General Optimization Strategies

This section will outline the most essential optimization techniques to speed up your OpenGL ES 2.0 applications on the iPhone 3GS. Although the shader optimization section is OpenGL ES 2.0-specific, the rest should apply to ES 1.1 developments as well.

By sticking to these golden rules you can expect your graphics applications to perform much better. Each rule will be explained in greater detail further in this chapter:

- *Do not access the framebuffer from the CPU.* Any access to the framebuffer will cause the driver to flush queued rendering commands and wait for rendering to finish, removing all parallelism between the CPU and the different modules in the graphics core.

- *Use vertex buffer objects and indexed geometry.* Vertex and index buffers will benefit from driver and hardware optimizations for fast memory transfers.

- *Batch your primitives to keep the number of draw calls low.* Try to minimize the number of calls used to render the scene, as these can be expensive. Using branching in your shaders may help to have better batching.

- *Perform rough object culling on the CPU.* Your application has more knowledge about the scene than the GPU. Whenever you have the opportunity to quickly detect that objects are invisible, do not render them!

- *Use texture compression and mipmapping.* Texture compression and mipmapping reduce memory page breaks, and will make better use of the texture cache.

- *Perform calculations per vertex instead of per fragment whenever possible.* The number of vertices processed is usually much lower than the total number of fragments, so operations per vertex are considerably cheaper than per fragment.

- *Avoid discard in the fragment shader.* POWERVR and other architectures offer performance advantages that are negated when discard is used.

3.2.1 Managing Vertex Data Efficiently

Vertex buffer objects. Geometry should be stored in a *vertex buffer object* (VBO) where possible. A VBO allows vertex array data to be stored in an optimal memory layout that drastically reduces data transfer to the GPU. You will see a noticeable increase in performance using vertex buffer objects on the iPhone 3GS.

This increase might not be as noticeable on the previous MBX enabled iPhone or iPod Touch devices but it will not degrade performance either. It is encouraged not to create a VBO for every mesh but to group meshes that are always rendered together in order to minimize buffer rebinding.

Interleaved attributes. There are several ways of storing data in memory. The two most common are interleaved and sequential arrays. Interleaved data stores all data for one vertex followed by all data for the next vertex. Storing the data in sequential arrays separates all vertex attributes into their own arrays, one array for position, one for normals, and so on. Interleaved attributes can be considered an array-of-structs while sequential arrays represent a struct-of-arrays.

Generally interleaved data provides better performance because all data for a vertex can be gathered in one sequential read which greatly improves cache efficiency. If a vertex attribute is shared across multiple meshes it can be faster to create a sequential array of its own rather than duplicating the data. The same is true if there is one attribute that needs frequent updating while other attributes remain unchanged.

Cull invisible objects. Although POWERVR SGX is very efficient in removing invisible objects, not submitting them at all is still faster. Your application has more knowledge of the scene contents and positions of objects than the GPU and OpenGL ES driver, and it can use that information to quickly cull objects based on occlusion or view direction. Especially when you're using complex vertex shaders it is important that you keep the amount of vertices submitted reasonably low.

To perform this culling it is important that your application uses efficient spatial data structures. Bounding volumes can help to quickly decided whether an object is completely outside the viewing frustum. If your application uses a static camera, perform view frustum culling offline.

Submitting geometry and rendering order. The order in which objects are submitted for rendering can have a huge impact on the number of state changes required and therefore on performance. This section outlines the fundamental rules to attain the desired result while achieving the best possible performance. As blended objects rely on the current value of the framebuffer, they would need to be rendered back-to-front.

Opaque objects are rendered without framebuffer blending or discarding pixels in the fragment shader. Always submit all opaque objects first, before transparent ones. To achieve the best possible results follow this order of object processing:

- Separate your objects into three groups: opaque, using discard, using blending.

- Render opaque objects sorted by render state.

```
#ifdef OPTIMIZED
for(int i = 0; i $<$ numParticles; i++)
{
    addParticleToInterleavedArray(particle[i]);
}
drawParticles();
#else
for(int i = 0; i $<$ numParticles; i++)
{
drawParticle(i);
}
#endif
```

Listing 3.1. Optimized batch rendering.

- Render objects using discard sorted by render state (avoid discard where possible).

- Render blended objects typically sorted back-to-front.

Sorting opaque objects by render state. Due to the advanced hidden surface removal (HSR) mechanism of POWERVR SGX opaque objects do not require to be sorted by depth. It would be considered a waste of CPU cycles sorting opaque objects front-to-back; instead objects should be sorted by render state. An example of this would be to render all objects using the same shader together. This will reduce the number of texture and uniform updates, as well as all other state changes.

Batching. Dynamically generated geometry such as a particle system should be rendered together in one *batch*. Batching reduces the number of draw calls per frame increasing performance. Opaque and transparent objects should be split up into separate batches. For best performance on POWERVR SGX you should always draw all geometry as a single indexed triangle list (see Listing 3.1).

3.2.2 Textures

A common misconception is that bigger textures always look better. Using a 1024×1024 texture for an object that never covers more than a small part of the screen just wastes storage space. Choose your textures' sizes based on the knowledge of how they will be used. Ideally you would choose the texture size so there is about one texel mapped to every pixel the object covers when it is viewed from the closest distance allowed.

NPOT textures. Non-power-of-two (NPOT) textures are supported by POWERVR SGX to the extent required by the OpenGL ES 2.0 core specification. This means

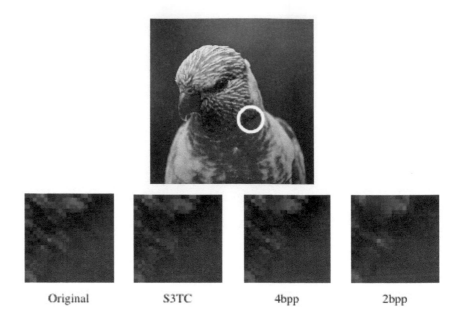

Figure 3.1. PVR texture compression comparison.

that mipmapping is not supported with NPOT textures, and the wrap mode must be set to `CLAMP_TO_EDGE`.

The main use of NPOT textures is for screen-sized render targets necessary for post-processing effects. Due to the mipmapping restriction it is not recommended to use NPOT textures for normal texture mapping of meshes due to memory access and cache inefficiency.

Texture formats and texture compression (PVRTC). POWERVR supports a proprietary texture compression format called PVRTC. It boasts very high quality for competitive compression ratios. As with S3TC, this compression is block based, but benefits from a higher image quality than S3TC as data from adjacent blocks are also used in the reconstruction of original texture data (See Figure 3.1). PVRTC supports opaque and translucent textures in both four bits-per-pixel and two bits-per-pixel modes. This reduced memory footprint is advantageous for embedded systems where memory is scarce, and also considerably minimizes the memory bandwidth requirements (while improving cache effectiveness). For more information about PVRTC please refer to [Fenney 03].

Mipmaps. Mipmaps are smaller, pre-filtered variants of a texture image, representing different levels of detail (LOD) of a texture. By using a minification filter mode that uses mipmaps, the hardware can be set up to automatically calculate which LOD comes closest to mapping one texel of a mipmap to one pixel in the render target, and use the according mipmap for texturing.

Using mipmaps has two important advantages. It increases performance by massively improving texture cache efficiency, especially in cases of strong minification. At the same time using pre-filtered textures improves image quality by countering aliasing that would be caused by severe under-filtering of the texture content. This aliasing usually shows itself as a strong shimmering noise on minified textures.

Mipmaps can be created offline with a utility such as PVRTexTool which can be found in the POWERVR SDK. Alternatively you can save the file storage space for mipmaps and generate them at runtime in your application. The OpenGL ES function `glGenerateMipmap` will perform this task for you, but it will not work with PVRTC textures. Those should always be offline generated. This function is also useful when you want to update mipmaps for render target textures.

In combination with certain texture content, especially with high contrast, the lack of filtering between mipmap levels can lead to visible seams at mipmap transitions. This is called mipmap banding. Trilinear filtering (`GL_LINEAR_MIPMAP_LINEAR`) can effectively eliminate these seams and thus achieve higher image quality. However, this quality comes at a cost, as whenever two mipmaps levels need to be blended together, the texture unit needs an additional cycle to fetch and filter the required data. In the worst case, trilinear achieves half the texturing performance compared to bilinear filtering. If you are using complex math-heavy shaders however, the texture unit may have cycles to spare and you can get trilinear filtering for a low bandwidth cost.

Rendering to a texture. The iPhone supports framebuffer objects (FBO) with textures as attachments; pbuffer surfaces are not supported on the iPhone. Creating an OpenGL ES view requires the generation of an FBO. The framebuffer generated should be treated as the back buffer for that view. All of the rendering on the iPhone is to an offscreen framebuffer object, this enables the OS to use fancy hardware driven transition and composition effects with high performance.

Texture atlases. By using texture atlases you can reduce the number of texture binds. Texture atlases consist of multiple texture images, usually the same size, arranged into a singular texture. If you can, use them to group texture images which are used interchangeably with the same shader program.

One issue with texture atlases you need to be aware of is that texture filtering, especially with mipmaps, may cause texels from neighbouring images to blend into each other. To avoid or reduce artifacts from this you need to either leave large enough borders around each image or place images with sufficiently similar edges next to each other. Using texture atlases also clashes with using texture repeat modes.

3.2.3 Shaders

Discard. The GLSL ES fragment shader operation `discard` can be used to stop fragment processing and prevent any buffer updates for this fragment. It provides the same functionality as the fixed function alpha test in a programmable fashion.

On mobile graphics architectures, discard is an expensive operation because it requires a fragment shader pass to accurately determine visibility of fragments. This reduces or removes any possible benefits from early depth rejection mechanisms.

The use of `discard` in shaders should be avoided wherever possible. Often the same visual effect can be achieved using the right blend mode and forcing the fragments alpha value to 0. If the use of `discard` is not avoidable, make sure the object that is using the shader is submitted after all opaque objects.

Placing a conditional branch around discard will not remove any performance issues explained earlier in this section. If discard is not needed, it should be removed from the shader entirely. A separate `discard` shader should be created if discard cannot be avoided.

Attribute data types. There are six different types of vertex attributes available in OpenGL ES2.0: `BYTE`, `UNSIGNED_BYTE`, `SHORT`, `UNSIGNED_SHORT`, `FLOAT` and `FIXED`.

Vertex shaders always expect attributes as type float, which means all types other than `FLOAT` require a conversion. The `FIXED` attribute type should be ignored when developing on the iPhone due to this. Moreover the iPhone has a dedicated FPU so there is unlikely to be a benefit from using fixed point arithmetic in general.

Attribute read times can be increased by ensuring that all attribute data is aligned to four-byte boundaries. For attributes that are less than 32 bits wide, one may have to add padding bytes to promote better attribute read times. It may be possible to pack different attribute vectors with fewer than four components together to minimize the space wasted.

Move calculations to the vertex shader. Try to move as much calculation from the fragment shader into the vertex shader as possible. There are generally a lot fewer vertices than there are fragments (pixels); by moving these calculations into the vertex shader you can drastically reduce shader cycles.

Often per-vertex equivalents can look just as good as costly per-pixel calculations. An example of this is lighting. Per-pixel lighting can look very nice, but for a real-time simulation, per-vertex is usually more than adequate.

Unrolling loops. If your application is still running slowly after you have tried the other strategies within this section, it might help to unroll any small loops in your shaders. It can help the compiler and possibly speed up the shader execution time.

3.3 Conclusion

This article addresses the main optimization strategies while developing for the iPhone and other POWERVR architectures. By following these optimization recommendations, it is possible to maximize performance of your OpenGL ES graphical demos and games.

For more support with the POWERVR SDK or PVRTools & Utilities visit the POWERVR Insider Forums at http://www.powervrinsider.com/forum/. The Khronos Group provides the OpenGL ES specification and reference manuals as well as hosting a developer support forum (http://www.khronos.org). Any questions relating to the Apple SDK, Xcode, or iPhone can be asked at the Apple Developer Connection forums at https://devforums.apple.com (paid membership required).

Bibliography

[POWERVR 09] Imagination Technologies. "POWERVR SGX OpenGL ES 2.0 Application Development Recommendations." 2009

[Apple 09] Apple Inc. "The Objective-C 2.0 Programming Guide." 2009. Available at http://developer.apple.com/iphone/library/documentation/Cocoa/Conceptual/ObjectiveC/ObjC.pdf

[Fenney 03] Simon Fenney. "Texture Compression using Low-Frequency Signal Modulation." *Graphics Hardware*. White paper, 2003. Available at http://www.imgtec.com/whitepapers/PVRTextureCompression.pdf.

Optimizing a 3D UI Engine for Mobile Devices

Hyunwoo Ki

A graphical user interface (GUI) is the preferred type of user interface (UI). It provides more intuitive visual components with images or animations, as opposed to a text-based interface. Such a GUI is essential for both graphics applications (for example, games) and non-graphics applications (for example, a phonebook). It should offer us convenience as well as beauty. With advancement of embedded systems, UI design shows a trend toward presenting three-dimensional graphical looks. Because the UI is a fundamental component for all applications, a UI engine should provide high performance and low memory consumption. The major mission of our UX development group at INNOACE Co., Ltd., is developing an optimized three-dimensional UI engine and an authoring tool for various mobile devices to maximize user experience. Our core engine supports two-dimensional and

Figure 4.1. Examples using a three-dimensional UI engine base on OpenGL ES 2.0.

three-dimensional widgets, scene management, resource management, TrueType font rendering, three-dimensional transition, visibility culling, occlusion culling, widget caching, partial rendering, etc. Based on this core engine, we migrated our UI engine to various platforms, for example LINUX, Windows Mobile, Android and GPOS. We developed a hardware renderer based on OpenGL ES 2.0 for high-end smartphones and PMPs, and a software renderer for common mobile phones. This article presents practical optimization methods for a three-dimensional UI engine based on OpenGL ES 2.0 with our development experience (see Figure 4.1). However, we expect some features of our core engine would be useful for OpenGL ES 1.1 or software renderers.

4.1   Overview

Optimization methods presented in this article include rendering pipeline optimization, TrueType font rendering, widget caches with partial update, and resource management.

1. *Rendering pipeline optimization.* We describe fundamental development guidelines of OpenGL ES 2.0 for a three-dimensional UI engine. We show our usage examples of render states, shaders, textures, draw calls, and etc.

2. *TrueType font rendering.* Texts are a very important component of the UI, and rendering texts requires higher costs than rendering other widgets. Particularly, processing Asian languages (e.g., Korean and Chinese) lower engine efficiency because it must handle many font glyphs. We present our text renderer's design and implementation issues to minimize draw calls and texture changes with low memory consumption.

3. *Widget caches with partial update.* We render a composite widget to a render texture, and consider this texture as a widget cache until a sub-widget of the composite widget is changed. This widget cache accelerates rendering a composite widget. Furthermore, according to interaction and logic, we partially update this widget cache to reduce update costs.

4. *Resource management.* We developed an efficient resource management system based on DirectX, one with resource garbage collectors. For example, if a managed texture has not been used for a long time, we dispose it on memory, and this texture is automatically restored from storage when we use it. We describe design and implementation issues of our resource management system.

4.2 Optimization Methods

4.2.1 Rendering Pipeline Optimization

We describe development guidelines for OpenGL ES 2.0 for a three-dimensional UI engine with our development experience.

Render states and shaders. A lot of changes of render states, textures and shaders in a single frame cause a UI engine to drop performance. Therefore these changes should be kept to a minimum. Fortunately, UI rendering does not require many changes. Most widgets use a texture which has an alpha channel, and there is no lighting or other color blending. If we render two-dimensional styled transparent widgets in back-to-front order, we do not need a depth test. Based on these properties, general render states are as follows:

- Shader: simple texture mapping shader.

- Texture: one color texture.

- Color: 1.0, 1.0, 1.0, 1.0 (RGBA).

- Alpha blend: enabled.

- Depth Test & Depth Mask: disabled.

Our renderer manages render states and shaders in a simple way. We save the current render states, textures and shader information. When we render a widget, we compare the current render states, textures and shader with the material property of the widget. If state changes are not required, we do not call OpenGL functions.

We minimize querying current state values by calling `glGet*` functions. Instead we get the values by calling our renderer's inline functions because our renderer always clones the values. We predefine important limits of our target devices such as the maximum texture before releasing our engine package. Validation checks using the `glGetError` function are very expensive. Thus, for a release build we use the `glGetError` function only for critical (but infrequent) APIs such as the `glTexImage2D` function. For resource generation functions such as `glGenTextures` and `glGenFramebuffers`, we compare the resultant values of the functions with zero without calling the `glGetError` function. If a value is zero, it means resource generation has failed and thus we do error handling.

Because our target resolution of WVGA (480 × 800) has many pixels, fragment shaders are very costly. Therefore we keep to a minimum the number of instructions for fragment shaders. If a conditional branch such as an if statement or a discard instruction to mimic an alpha test is added, the performance will drop. Using an alpha blend with a texture that has zero alpha values instead of using an alpha test, is enough to render alpha-tested widgets in many cases. We use a small set of predefined shaders and load precompiled shader binaries. The renderer maps hash keys to OpenGL uniform IDs for each shader to quickly write shader parameters without querying uniform IDs in rendering time.

Textures. Generally, in a UI design, a texture is designed with perfect one-to-one mapping of texture texels to screen pixels. Therefore we use mipmapping and linear filtering only for scaled or rotated widgets, or three-dimensional models if an application requires it. For most widgets, to save memory we recommend not using mipmaps, and using nearest-filtering. Our target LCD's color format is 16-bit R5G6B5, and we prefer 16-bit textures (R5G6B5 or R4G4B4A4) instead of 24-bit (R8G8B8) or 32-bit (R8G8B8A8) ones in order to improve performance for texture uploading and reading. Using 24- or 32-bit textures sometimes results in a banding artifact on the screen. Bit conversion with dithering and other preprocessing using a graphic tool are required for better image quality.

Using compressed textures greatly increases engine efficiency. DXT1 compression reduces memory usage to 1/6 for R8G8B8 textures. It also reduces a texture upload time. Image decoding is also removed unlike JPG and PNG formats. For some devices (e.g., FIMG 3D from Samsung Electronics), a format conversion to replace an original image format to a hardware internal format, for example from R8G8B8A8 to B8G8R8A8, is removed. Similarly, using hardware internal formats also reduces texture loading time by ignoring format conversion. For a 480×800 resolution texture, we saved a factor of ten in loading time, including texture uploading, compared with a JPG texture on a device based on FIMG 3D. Using compressed textures also improves rendering performance because it reduces memory bandwidth and increases cache hit rates.

If your target devices support non-power-of-two (NPOT) resolution textures, we recommend to use such textures to reduce memory usage by removing empty texels for padding. Because we do not prefer mipmaps generally, we do not have to be concerned about using NPOT textures. NPOT textures (but a multiple of four texels textures) with DXT compression were very useful for thumbnail images, animated images, etc. We provide a software DXT compressor for applications, and they compress thumbnail images for list widgets when original images are stored. Although DXT compression speed is not fast, it is acceptable because image size is small and compression is done at storage time with a progress widget. Most importantly, such compression improves loading and rendering speed, and reduces memory usage.

Miscellaneous. Reducing a vertex data size is an important strategy. We always use indexed vertex arrays to reduce vertex data by sharing. We also use interleaved vertex arrays (a.k.a. packed vertex arrays) instead of separated arrays to maximize memory access efficiency. An interleaved vertex array is structured by a single large array with each vertex attribute, using a structure of the C language. Because most widgets are rendered by a simple quad or a rounded quad with texturing, level of detail of vertex data is not necessary.

Visibility culling, occlusion culling, and scissor tests increase frame rates. Basically we set a scissor box and a visibility culling area to the full screen size. Some widgets need to clip child widgets or own text. For example, several list items of a list box are located in the outside of the list box. In this case, we do not have to render these list items (visibility culling). Another list item may be located in the boundary of the list box. In this case, parts of the list items are displayed and the other parts are not displayed by clipping. We can implement such clipping using a stencil test, but it increases rendering passes and rendering costs for accessing the stencil buffer. For example, an implementation using scissor tests was more than two times faster than using stencil tests for FIMG 3D. If an application needs only rectangular clipping, we recommended using scissor tests instead of stencil tests.

We implemented a simple, user-guided occlusion culling. If a widget is assigned as an occluder, we render occluder widgets first. Then we compare other widgets' bounding boxes with occluders' ones in screen coordinates. If a widget is completely occluded by an occluder, we skip rendering this widget. Such occlusion culling is useful for a fullscreen popup or a keypad. Our keypad covers half of fullscreen in top-most order.

4.2.2 TrueType Font Rendering

Text rendering is a very important feature to deliver information for users. This section describes design and implementation issues of our TrueType font renderer.

Figure 4.2 shows our TrueType font rendering algorithm. To render a text, we render each character-sized quad (Figure 4.2(a)) and do texture mapping using corresponding font textures with alpha blending (Figure 4.2(c)). Each font texture has bitmaps of characters and is grouped by a font size and font face (font name).

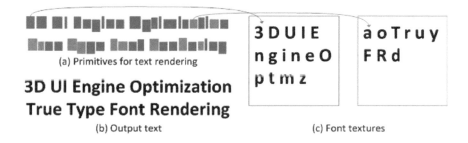

Figure 4.2. Our approach for TrueType font rendering.

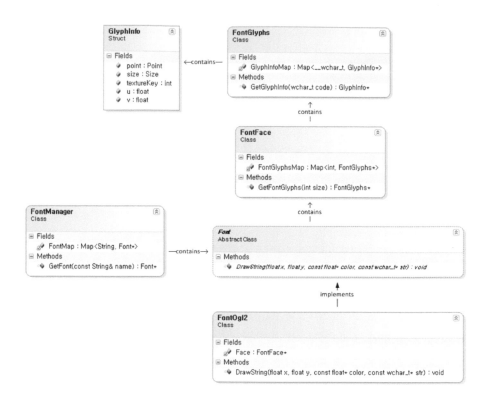

Figure 4.3. Simple class diagrams of our TrueType font renderer.

Each character's bitmap is written on a font texture when the character is used. If a character is already written on a font texture, we reuse it without rewriting to save memory and avoid writing.

We now describe the design of our TrueType font renderer. Figure 4.3 shows simple class diagrams. Every font and every text buffer is entirely managed by the font manager, which has containers for fonts and text buffers, and performs operations to create, destroy, and get fonts or text buffer instances. The Font class is an abstract class that has functionalities to render texts and calculate a text size. A derived class of the Font class for a certain target platform has a FontFace instance. The FontFace class has data loaded from a TTF file, and has a container for FontGlyphs instances grouped by font size. A FontGlyphs instance of a FontFace instance is added when a certain font size is first used. The FontGlyphs class has a container for GlyphInfo instances grouped by a character code. A GlyphInfo instance of a FontGlyphs instance is also added when a certain character code is first used. Therefore, we store only the information of used characters of used sizes of the specified font face. The GlyphInfo structure stores a position, a size, a texture's coordinates, and a texture key to render a character. The texture key is used to get a font texture instance quickly and safely. When we require a character for text rendering, a font texture stores the bitmap of the character. Bitmaps of characters are filled in consecutive order (see, e.g., Figure 4.2(c)).

To render a text, for each character in the text we expand work to compute world position of a quad and its texture coordinates corresponding to the bitmap of the character using information of a FontGlyphs instance. Usually there are many texts on the screen and doing such work causes a significant performance drop. We use pre-generated text buffers until a caption, an alignment, a size or other property is changed, to improve performance.

As described above, a text is rendered by drawing a quad per character and by mapping a corresponding font texture. Because a single font texture cannot store all character's bitmap data, we will often use several font textures for rendering a single text. Especially, Asian languages such as Korean and Chinese use many more unique characters than English, and as a result rendering a single text often needs many font textures. It increases the number of draw calls with texture changes and thus it significantly drops rendering efficiency, assuming each character is never overlapped by another. Rendering orders of characters are not important in text rendering. By exploiting this property, we design a text buffer by grouping vertex buffers by a same font texture. At rendering time, we set render states and shader parameters once and then we render each vertex buffer with changing font textures. Such an approach minimizes the number of draw calls and texture changes. As an example, we show the number of draw calls and texture changes for a text in Figure 4.2, before and after grouping in Figure 4.4.

Similarly, for rich text rendering, we group vertex buffers by same image texture, same line color, or same text background color (RGBA color is encoded by a 32-bit unsigned integer).

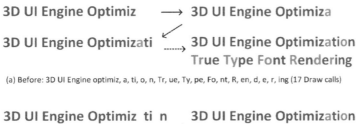

Figure 4.4. Reducing draw calls using a text buffer.

4.2.3 Widget Caches with Partial Update

There are various basic widgets such as a button, a label, and an image. Some widgets are composite widgets composed of several basic or (and) other composite widgets such as a keypad and a list box. Rendering a composite widget is slower because it has a high fill area and requires many draw calls. We introduce an algorithm to replace rendering a composite widget by rendering a single image. We first create a render texture covering a composite widget entirely. Then we render a composite widget onto this render texture instead of the frame buffer. We call this render texture a *widget cache* and use it for rendering the composite widget until the appearance of the composite widget is changed. Although quality inequality exists, it is useful for us because we do not need mipmaps generally and we ignore hardware anti-aliasing, dithering, etc.

Using a widget cache significantly improves rendering performance. However, if the appearance of a composite widget frequently changes, it causes a performance drop because it requires both updating a widget cache and rendering the composite widget using this cache. In order to solve this problem, we develop partial update rendering. Pseudocode for this is shown in Listing 4.1. We describe the algorithm in detail in the next paragraph.

When a sub-widget's property (e.g., position, color, texture, and caption) is changed, we set a flag to notify that a widget cache must be updated. At rendering time (Widget::Render), we find flagged subwidgets and merge all bounding boxes of them (Widget::UpdateDirtyRectRecursive). We also merge the bounding box of the previous frame with the current merged bounding box to update the dirty area of the previous frame. This prevents footprint-like artifacts due to an animation. Now we project the merged bounding box onto screen-space to compute a dirty rectangle in screen-space. We set a visibility culling area and a scissor box for this dirty rectangle (`Renderer::SetClipRect`) and then update the widget cache by rendering the flagged subwidgets including their child widgets without clearing the widget cache (`Renderer::RenderWidgetToTexture`). For example, if we press a single button of a keypad widget, a button image is highlighted by a texture change and the dirty rectangle is the same as the bounding box of the button in screen-space (see Figure 4.5). At the cache update time, only the background widget and the button pass visibility culling tests, and an area corresponding to the bounding box of the button in screen-space passes scissor tests. These tests greatly reduce costs to update a widget cache, and thus incredibly improve rendering performance. Although such a widget cache consumes large memory space, we selectively use widget caches and destroy them when we do not use them any longer.

```
void Widget::Render()
{
    if (HasCache())
        UpdateCache();
    if (IsValidCache())
    {
        Renderer->RenderCache(widget);
        return;
    }
    for (int i = 0; i < GetChildCound(); ++i)
        GetChildAt(i)->Render();
    Renderer->Render(this);
    SetDirty(false);
}

void Widget::UpdateCache()
{
    if (! UpdateDirtyRectRecursive())
        return;
    Renderer->PushClipRect();
    Renderer->RenderWidgetToTexture(this);
    Renderer->PopClipRect();
    SetValidCache(true);
}

void Widget::UpdateDirtyRectRecursive()
{
    ClearDirtyRect();
    for (int i = 0; i < GetChildCound(); ++i)
    {
        Widget *child = GetChildAt(i);
        if (child->IsDirty())
            MergeDirtyAABB(child->GetAABB());
        child->UpdateDirtyRectRecursive();
    }
    AABB curDirtyAABB = GetDirtyAABB();
    MergeDirtyAABB(GetPrevDirtyAABB());
    SetPrevDirtyAABB(curDirtyAABB);
    SetDirtyRect(TransformToScreen(GetDirtyAABB()));
}

void Renderer::RenderWidgetToTexture(Widget *widget)
{
    TransformWorldToFullScreen(widget);
    SetRenderTarget(widget->GetCache());
    SetClipRect(widget->GetDirtyRect());
    Widget->Render();
    SetRenderTarget(NULL);
}
```

Listing 4.1. Pseudo-code for widget cache update.

Figure 4.5. An example of partial update rendering: (a) original keypad; (b) and (c) partial update.

4.2.4   Resource Management

Imagine that during writing a multimedia mail using your cell phone, you can attach a photo from a photo-album application. Concurrently, you can hear a song and receive a message or phone call. In the described scenario, several applications need to cooperate on a small finite memory pool.

OpenGL gives most frequently used (MFU) textures high priority and assigns them as resident textures. The resident textures are placed in video memory for fast access, and the other textures are placed in system memory until these textures are used. A developer can set the priority of textures using the glPrioritizeTextures function. However, such a resource management system is not supported on OpenGL ES 2.0.

We implemented our resource management system similar to DirectX. All resources such as textures and render textures have a reference counter and a time stamp recorded when a resource is referenced. A resource has a unique key, priority, status, pool type, and memory usage. The priority is more preferential rather than the time stamp for resource sorting.

Our resource pool types are based on DirectX, but there are many differences. There are four types: *default, managed, semi-managed,* and *system.* A resource of a default type is never destroyed unless the resource manager or an application explicitly destroys it. A resource of a managed type can be disposed of at any time in order to gain available memory and can restore its memory and data. A resource of a semi-managed type can be also disposed at any time. However, it can only reallocate memory by itself and thus the renderer must restore its data before using it. A resource of a system type is similar to the default type but is always located in system memory.

For using such a resource management system, derived classes of the Resource class must implement **Dispose** and **Restore** methods. The **Dispose** method frees allocated memory and makes a resource status **LostMemory**, whereas the **Restore** method recovers a disposed resource according to its pool type. A resource of a managed type is completely restored and thus a status will be `Valid`, whereas a resource of a semi-managed type is only reallocated memory without restoring data and thus it makes a resource status `EmptyData`. The other types are never restored automatically.

Generally we use a managed type for textures loaded from image files. Our target device's memory system is a unified memory architecture (UMA) and the total memory space is insufficient to run many applications. Therefore, we restore a managed texture from an original image file instead of system memory unlike DirectX. We used nandflash storage and its access speed was sufficiently fast. Applications can use background loading using threading based on a simple user-guided prediction algorithm. UI design has a usage flow by scenarios and such flow is reflected at a structure of content. We preload the next possible components in the background. An application can customize loading methods by using texture buffer update instead of setting a texture filename. An image viewer application based on our engine used a small alternative image while an original image is loading. When we restore a texture we also restore an address mode, texture filtering, etc.

We use the semi-managed type for text buffers and widget caches. Text buffers and widget caches can be disposed and reallocated when we want. Typically we dispose of them when they disappear from the screen and reallocate them when they reappear. The data of a text buffer is restored by recomputing position and texture coordinates and rebuilding vertex buffers, and the data of a widget cache is restored by rendering widgets to a render texture when we use them. In the view of an application, the semi-managed type is the same as the managed type. However, in the view of the renderer, complex restoring—for example, processing events and business logic, traversing scenes, and rendering widgets—is needed as compared with simple file loading or memory copy for a managed type. This is the reason why we call it semi-managed rather than managed. A system type is a special type. We use it for mixing three-dimensional and two-dimensional rendering. For example, a texture of a system type is directly copied (or bit-blitting) to the frame buffer.

Our texture manager has a garbage collector and it disposes of managed textures when the textures is not used for a long time and its reference counter is less than two (see Listing 4.2). We consider total used memory, available memory space, frame time, and time stamp, and an application can control various settings for garbage collection.

All managed and semi-managed resources are managed by the resource manager. The resource manager compulsorily disposes of low prioritized resources if available memory space is insufficient to create a new resource (see Listing 4.2). It releases all resources including non-managed typed resources when an application is terminated to prevent memory leaks. An application can also control management conditions. Basically, we prepare a minimum of four times the memory rather than the required size because actual available memory space is less than a measured size due to memory fragmentation, and we also want to minimize the number of times of processing for supplying available memory.

A memory supplement process is as follows. First, the resource manager collects managed and semi-managed resources whose reference counter is less than two. Then we sort collected resources using a priority and a time stamp, and dispose of resources until available memory is sufficiently supplied (`ResourcePool::SupplyAvailableMemory`). If memory is still insufficient, we dispose of remained, managed, and semi-managed resources, ignoring their reference counter (`ResourcePool::EvictManagedResourcesAll`). We limit the maximum memory space for OpenGL.

If an application uses memory over this limit, our engine informs it of an out-of-memory error. Although memory usage does not go over the limit, if the `GL_OUT_OF_MEMORY` error happens from the `glTexImage2D` or the `glRenderBuffer Storage` function, we set available memory of our resource pool to zero and limit the maximum memory to the current memory usage (`ResourcePool::Zero AvailableMemory`). This error is due to memory fragmentation or usage by other applications.

Optionally, we also dispose of all managed and semi-managed resources when an application is hidden by other applications to supply available memory for other application and to reduce a memory fragmentation problem. At the end of the frame, we explicitly unbind all resources, such as textures, to decrease their reference counters. It helps our resource manager to release resources that are no longer in use.

```
bool Texture::Allocate()
{
    if (! ResourcePool.IsAvailable(requiredMemory))
        ResourcePool.SupplyAvailableMemory(requireMemory);
    Texture *texture = NULL;
    glTexImage2D(...);
    GLenum errorGL = glGetError();
    if (errorGL == GL_OUT_OF_MEMORY)
    {
        ResourcePool.ZeroAvailableMemory();
        ResourcePool.SupplyAvailableMemory(requireMemory);

        // retry
        glTexImage2D(...)
        errorGL = glGetError();
        if (errorGL == GL_OUT_OF_MEMORY)
```

```
        {
            ResourcePool.EvictManagedResourcesAll();

            // retry
            glTexImage2D(...)
            errorGL = glGetError();
            if (errorGL == GL_OUT_OF_MEMORY)
            {
                // TODO: error handling
                return false;
            }

            // TODO: other error handlings code
        }

        // TODO: other error handlings code
    }
    return true;
}

int ResourcePool::ZeroAvailableMemory()
{
    available = 0;
    limit = used;
    if (limit < MinLimit)
    {
        limit = MinLimit;
        EvictManagedResourcesAll();
    }
}

int ResourcePool::SupplyAvailableMemory(int required)
{
    int safe = required * 4;
    safe = MIN(safe, limit);
    if (safe < avaiable)
        return 0;
    Vector<Resource*> disposableResources;
    disposableResources.Reserve(resouces.Count());
    GatherManagedResources(disposableResources);
    disposableResources.Sort();
    int oldUsed = used;
    for (int i = 0; i < disposableResources.Count(); ++i)
    {
        Resource *resource = disposableResources[i];
        if (! resource || resource->GetRefCount() > 1)
            continue;
        resource->Dispose();
        if (safe < available)
            break;
    }
```

```
    if (safe > available)
        EvictManagedResourcesAll();
    return oldUsed - used;
}
```

Listing 4.2. Resource pool management.

4.3   Conclusion

We presented optimization methods to implement a three-dimensional UI engine for mobile devices. They play important roles to deploy our solution on a commercial scale and make many applications more efficient. We show captured images of applications based on our three-dimensional UI engine at http://www.akpeters .com/gpupro. We spared no efforts to generalize our solution to support other platforms. However, you must improve algorithms and develop additional optimizations for your target platforms. We have been extending our business to support various platforms and have been continuing to optimize our engine for various targets. For example, we use partial update rendering for all widgets on a set-top box. For this, we assume the current page that has all widgets in the current view is one of composite widgets. Such an approach greatly increases frame rates.

We believe this article supplies development guidelines for not only mobile three-dimensional UI engines but also all mobile three-dimensional applications.

Bibliography

[Munshi et al. 08] Aaftab Munshi, Dan Ginsburg, and Dave Shreiner. *OpenGL(R) ES 2.0 Programming Guide.* Boston: Addison-Wesley Professional, 2008.

[Pulli et al. 07] Kari Pulli, Jani Vaarala, Ville Miettinen, Tomi Aarnio, and Kimmo Roimela. *Mobile 3D Graphics: with OpenGL ES and M3G.* San Francisco: Morgan Kaufmann, 2007.

[Beets 09] Kristof Beets, Mikael Gustavsson, and Erik Olsson. "Optimizing your first OpenGL ES Applications." *ShaderX7: Advanced Rendering Techniques.* Boston: Charles River Media, 2009.

[Catterall 09] Ken Catterall. "Optimised Shaders for Advanced Graphical User Interfaces." *ShaderX7: Advanced Rendering Techniques.* Boston: Charles River Media, 2009.

[Khronos 09] Khronos OpenGL ES. 2009. Available at http://www.khronos.org/ opengles/.

[Imagination Technologies 09] Khronos OpenGL ES 2.0 SDKs for POW-ERVR SGX. 2009. Available at http://www.imgtec.com/powervr/insider/sdk/KhronosOpenGLES2xSGX.asp.

[Microsoft 09] Microsoft DirectX. 2009. Available at http://msdn.microsoft.com/en-us/directx/default.aspx.

VII   Shadows

In this section we will cover various algorithms that are used to generate shadow data. Shadows are the dark companion of lights and although both can exist on their own, they shouldn't exist without each other in games. Achieving good visual results in rendering shadows is still considered one of the particularly difficult tasks of graphics programmers.

There are three articles that deal with the softness of the shadow penumbra and one article that covers a fundamentally new projection and storage pattern.

The article "Fast Conventional Shadow Filtering," by Holger Gruen, covers an algorithm that can be used to reduce the number of necessary PCF texture operations roughly to a third. This allows the usage of larger filter kernels and therefore results in a softer penumbra that is necessary to reduce the perspective aliasing of shadow pixels along the view frustum.

Holger Gruen's second article has a similar target. In "Hybrid Min/Max Plane-Based Shadow Maps" he shows a way to derive a secondary texture from a normal depth-only shadow map that can be used to speed up expensive shadow filtering kernels. He stores a plane equation or min/max depth data for a block of pixels of the original shadow map. Both techniques are especially tailored to rendering shadows on the upcoming generation of graphics hardware.

Hung-Chien Liao demonstrates in his article "Shadow Mapping for Omnidirectional Light Using Tetrahedron Mapping" a new way to store shadow data. Instead of using a cube or dual-paraboloid map, he proposes using a tetrahedron projection and storing the data in a two-dimensional map. He also compares his method to cube and dual-paraboloid shadow mapping and concludes that it is faster than cube shadow maps and more accurate compared to dual-paraboloid shadow maps.

In the last article in the section "Screen Space Soft Shadows," Jesus Gumbau, Miguel Chover and Mateu Sbert describe a soft shadow map technique that is built on Randima Fernando's Percentage Closer Soft Shadows and improves on the original idea in speed and flexibility. They use a screen-aligned texture that contains the distance between the shadow and potential occluders and then use this to run an adjustable anisotropic Gauss filter kernel over the original shadow data. This method is quite efficient and has a robustness that makes it suitable for game usage.

—Wolfgang Engel

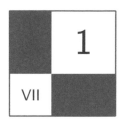

Fast Conventional Shadow Filtering

Holger Gruen

1.1 Overview

This chapter presents ideas on how to reduce the number of hardware-accelerated *percentage closer filtering* (PCF) texture operations for conventional shadow map filtering. A uniform 8×8 filter that would usually be carried out using 49 PCF textures operations can now be carried out with only 16 PCF operations. As the number of texture operations is usually the limiting factor for conventional shadow filtering, the speedup achieved is significant. The techniques described here reduce the number of necessary PCF texture operations from $(N-1) \times (N-1)$ to $(N/2) \times (N/2)$ for uniform(*) and separable shadow filters. Further on, an algorithm to implement box filters with nonseparable unique weights in only $(N-1) \times (N/2)$ instead of $(N-1) \times (N-1)$ PCF texture operations is explained. This algorithm can be used for advanced shadow filtering effects. Please note that the methods described here can also be carried over to filtering color textures.

1.2 Introduction

Conventional shadow filtering works by directly filtering binary visibility results (see [Williams 78]) obtained from a depth-only shadow map. Techniques like [Annen et al. 07], [Donnelly at al. 06], [Dmitriev at al. 07], [Gruen 08], or [Gumbau et al. 10] are not considered to be conventional shadow filtering techniques as they use data in addition to a depth-only shadow map.

Most games still make use of conventional uniform shadow filters. This means that the importance of all shadow map based visibility results (e.g., is the light visible) is equal. In order to achieve soft shadow to light transitions, as a minimal solution four visibility samples, e.g., a 2×2 neighborhood of shadow map samples, are taken into account. These four samples are bi-linearly weighted using sub-texel coordinates to generate a smooth result. This approach is called *percentage closer filtering* (PCF), and is supported by all Direct3D 10.0 class hardware and some Direct3D 9.x class hardware.

A naive way to compute the result of uniformly filtering an $N \times N$ block of shadow map texels is to perform $(N - 1) \times (N - 1)$ PCF shadow map lookups and to divide their sum by $(N - 1) \times (N - 1)$. It is possible though to reduce the number of PCF texture samples to $(N/2) \times (N/2)$. This reduction in texture operation count is achievable by computing shifted texture coordinates for the PCF shadow map lookups. Further the result of each PCF lookup needs to be multiplied by a post texturing weight.

Large uniform filters produce smooth shadows but can blur away fine details. This chapter further describes how to compute higher quality filters that e.g., use a separable Gaussian-like weight matrix to weight each PCF sample. The math behind shifted texture positions and post texturing weights can be used again to implement the separable filter with only $(N/2) \times (N/2)$ PCF samples.

Finally, in order to gain even higher control over the weights in the weights-matrix and to create fully customizable shadow filtering quality, similar math is used to reduce the number of texture operations for nonseparable unique weights from $(N - 1) \times (N - 1)$ to only $(N - 1) \times (N/2)$ for Direct3D.

Note. Since shadow mapping only uses the first data channel of a texture, Shader Model 4.1 or Shader Model 5.0 capable hardware can be used to reduce the number of texture operations to $(N/2) \times (N/2)$ for every conceivable filter for an $N \times N$ pixel block. The reason for this is that the `Gather()` texture operation delivers the values for four adjacent texels. If you are using Direct3D 10.1, Direct3D 11 or above, none of the tricks described below are necessary anymore.

The remainder of the chapter walks through the various conventional shadow filtering techniques. The chapter closes by presenting two exemplary techniques that use a filter matrix with nonseparable weights.

1.3   Uniform Shadow Filtering

As described above, most games still use uniform shadow filters. The naive way to implement these is to carry out $(N - 1) \times (N - 1)$ PCF samples. The following text describes how to get this down to the $(N/2) \times (N/2)$ PCF samples mentioned above.

Please consider the following 4×4 shadow map texel grid in Figure 1.1. Each v_{ij} is a binary visibility [0 or 1] sample derived from the corresponding shadow

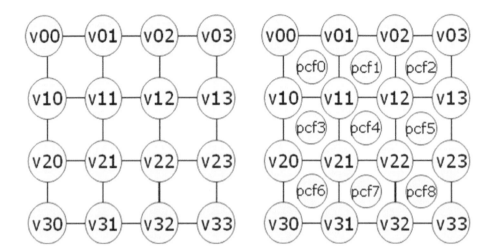

Figure 1.1. $N \times N$ binary visibility samples (0=shadow, 1=full light). A row of weights is applied horizontally first.

Figure 1.2. $N \times N$ binary visibility results are reduced to $(N - 1) \times (N - 1)$ PCF results—the same weights are now applied vertically as well.

map sample (e.g., by comparing each sample with the light space depth of the current pixel).

A uniform PCF sample based filter collapses each 2×2 visibility information block to a PCF filtered visibility result PCF_k by performing a PCF texture lookup as shown in Figure 1.2.

The final filtered result (for $N \times N$ shadow map pixels) is then obtained by computing the term in Equation (1.1):

$$\frac{\sum_{k=0}^{(N-1)\cdot(N-1)} PCF_k}{(N - 1) \cdot (N - 1)}. \tag{1.1}$$

As mentioned above, a naive way to implement this using only Shader Model 4.0 would involve doing $(N - 1) \times (N - 1)$ PCF texture samples. There is a better way though.

The term in Equation (1.1) can also be computed through some ALU shader instructions and only $(N/2) \times (N/2)$ PCF texture instructions as shown in Figure 1.3 for a 4×4 block of visibility results.

In order to understand how this works only one row of visibility samples v_k is considered initially. Assigning weights w_k to each one-dimensional PCF result in that row does produce the term shown in Equation (1.2). Here, x is the sub-texel

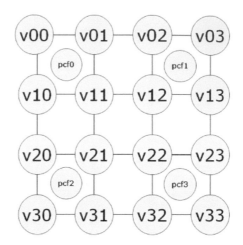

Figure 1.3. It is possible to evaluate the $(N - 1) \times (N - 1)$ PCF-based filter with just $(N/2) \times (N/2)$ PCF sample + some ALU—the unrolled weighted term for bi-linear filtering each 2×2 visibility block.

coordinate ranging from 0.0 to 1.0 (excluding 1.0):

$$\sum_{k=0}^{N-2} (1 - x) \cdot v_k + x \cdot v_{k+1}. \tag{1.2}$$

Equation (1.2) simplifies to Equation (1.3):

$$(1 - x) \cdot v_0 + \left(\sum_{k=1}^{N-2} v_k \right) + x \cdot v_{N-1}. \tag{1.3}$$

To compute shifted texture coordinates x' for PCF texture operations and post texturing weights wp, the following three cases have to be considered:

1. Left border of the filter row (the terms that refer to v01, v02, v11, and v12). The system of equations $(1 - x') \cdot wp \cdot v_0 = (1 - x) \cdot v_0$ and $x' \cdot wp \cdot v_1 = v_1$ is solved by $x' = -\frac{1}{x-2}$ and $wp = 2 - x$.

2. Right border of the filter row. ($N \times N$ binary visibility samples: 0=shadow, 1=full light).The system of equations $(1 - x') \cdot wp \cdot v_{N-2} = v_{N-2}$ and $x' \cdot wp \cdot v_{N-1} = x \cdot v_{N-1}$ is solved by $x' = \frac{x}{x+1}$ and $wp = x + 1$.

3. Central values of the filter row $N \times N$ binary visibility results are reduced to $(N-1) \times (N-1)$ PCF results. The system of equations $(1 - x') \cdot wp \cdot v_k = v_k$ and $x' \cdot wp \cdot v_{k+1} = v_{k+1}$ is solved by $x' = \frac{1}{2}$ and $wp = 2$.

Using these formulas, the filtering for one row can be carried out with only $(N/2)$ PCF samples. Since the filter is symmetric in the y direction, the full box filter can evaluated using only $(N-1) \times (N/2)$ PCF texture samples.

The shaders in Listing 1.1 demonstrate optimized implementations for Direct3D 10.0.

```
#define FILTER_SIZE 8 // 8x8 shadow map samples
#define GS2 ( (FILTER_SIZE -1)/2 )

float shadow_filter( float3 tc )
{
  tc.xyz /= tc.w;

  float  s   = 0.0;
  float2 stc = ( SMAP_size * tc.xy ) + float2( 0.5, 0.5 );
  float2 tcs = floor( stc );
  float2 fc;

  fc    = stc - tcs;
  tc.xy = tc.xy - ( fc * ( 1.0/SMAP_size ) );

  float2 pwAB = ( ( 2.0 ).xx - fc );
  float2 tcAB = ( 1.0/SMAP_size ).xx / pwAB;
  float2 tcM  = (0.5/SMAP_size ).xx;
  float2 pwGH = ( ( 1.0 ).xx + fc );
  float2 tcGH = (1.0/SMAP_size) * ( fc / pwGH );

  for( int row = -GS2; row <= GS2; row += 2 )
  {
    for( int col = -GS2; col <= GS2; col += 2 )
    {
if( row == -GS2 ) // Top row
{
    if( col == -GS2 ) // left
      s += ( pwAB.x * pwAB.y ) * s_smap.SampleCmpLevelZero(
              smp_smap, tc.xy + tcAB, tc.z,
              int2( col, row ) ).x;
    else if( col == GS2 ) // Right
      s += ( pwGH.x * pwAB.y )* s_smap.SampleCmpLevelZero(
              smp_smap, tc.xy + float2( tcGH.x, tcAB.y),
              tc.z, int2( col, row ) ).x;
    else // center
      s += (2.0 * pwAB.y )*s_smap.SampleCmpLevelZero(
              omp_smap, tc.xy + float2( tcM.x, tcAB.y),
              tc.z, int2( col, row ) ).x;
}
  else if( row == GS2 )  // Bottom row
  {
    if( col == -GS2 ) // Left
      s += ( pwAB.x * pwGH.y ) * s_smap.SampleCmpLevelZero(
```

```
                 smp_smap , tc.xy + float2 ( tcAB.x, tcGH.y ) ,
                 tc.z, int2( col , row ) ).x;
    else if( col == GS2 ) // Right
      s += ( pwGH.x * pwGH.y ) * s_smap.SampleCmpLevelZero(
                 smp_smap , tc.xy + tcGH, tc.z,
                 int2( col , row ) ).x;
    else // Center
      s += (    2.0 * pwGH.y ) * s_smap.SampleCmpLevelZero(
                 smp_smap , tc.xy + float2( tcM.x, tcGH.y ) ,
                 tc.z, int2( col , row ) ).x;
  }
  else // Center rows
  {
    if( col == -GS2 ) // Left
      s += ( pwAB.x * 2.0   ) * s_smap.SampleCmpLevelZero(
                 smp_smap , tc.xy + float2( tcAB.x, tcM.y ) ,
                 tc.z, int2( col , row ) ).x;
    else if( col == GS2 ) // Right
      s += ( pwGH.x * 2.0   ) * s_smap.SampleCmpLevelZero(
                 smp_smap , tc.xy + float2( tcGH.x, tcM.y),
                 tc.z, int2( col , row ) ).x;
    else // Center
      s += (    2.0 * 2.0   ) * s_smap.SampleCmpLevelZero(
                 smp_smap , tc.xy + tcM, tc.z,
                 int2( col , row ) ).x;
  }
    }
  }

  return s/((FILTERSIZE -1) * (FILTERSIZE -1));
}
```

Listing 1.1. Fast Shader Model 4.0 uniform shadow filter.

1.4   Separable Shadow Filters

Uniform box filters tend to blur out details that should better be preserved. One solution to this problem is to use a Gaussian filter. Gaussian filters are separable. This section therefore takes a closer look at separable shadow filters. Figure 1.4 shows how filter weights that define a separable filter are first used to weight each PCF result in a shadow filter.

The next step is to apply the filter weights vertically, as shown in Figure 1.5.

In order to understand if a separable filter can be implemented with less than the naive $(N-1) \times (N-1)$ PCF operations please consider the weighted bi-linearly filtered visibility results for each 2×2 visibility block as shown in Figure 1.6.

As an example now concentrate on the 2×2 block in orange as shown in Figure 1.7. In order to understand how to select shifted texture coordinates and

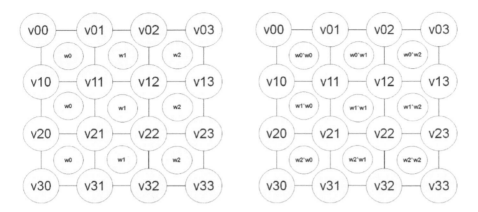

Figure 1.4. A weight is applied to each PCF result.

Figure 1.5. Shader Model 4.0 needs $(N/2) \times (N-1)$ PCF ops plus some ALU.

post texturing weights, one needs to look at all neighboring 2×2 blocks to find all terms that refer to the visibility block from Figure 1.7.

Assigning terms to each corner of the 2×2 visibility block creates a system of four equations (see Figure 1.8), which needs to satisfy the three unknowns x', y', and p_w.

For a filter that looks at $N \times N$ visibility samples, this means one needs to consider nine cases of equation systems.

For brevity's sake, just the solutions of these equations for the nine cases are presented here.

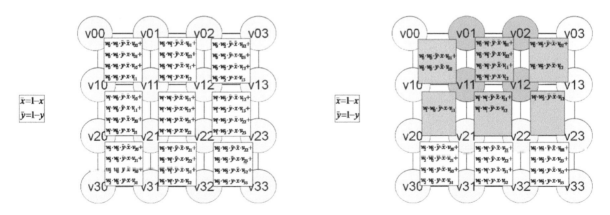

Figure 1.6. Shader Model 4.1 only needs to do $(N/2) \times (N/2)$ gathers plus some ALU.

Figure 1.7. Triangle-shaped filter kernel.

```
            *y    z/y   +{/y    z   y                        *3/ { € *3/ z € r z
    **y  y /y  +z/y   y +{   *y  /y   y +z  y   y            *3/ { € z Cr z
    **y  y /y  +z/y   y    y  +{/y   y   z  y   y            { c*3/ z € r z
**y /4 y   y    y  +z/y    y   y +{   *y   y /y  +z   y       { Cz Cr z
```

Figure 1.8. Half-moon-shaped kernel.

1. Top left:

$$x' = \frac{(w_1 - w_0) \cdot x - w_1}{w_1 \cdot x - w_1 - w_0},$$

$$y' = \frac{(w_1 - w_0) \cdot y - w_1}{w_1 \cdot y - w_1 - w_0},$$

$$p_w = \left(w_1^2 \cdot x - w_1^2 - w_0 \cdot w_1\right) \cdot y + \left(-w_1^2 - w_0 \cdot w_1\right) \cdot x + 2 \cdot w_0 \cdot w_1 + w_0^2.$$

2. Top center:

$$x' = \frac{(w_{kx+1} - w_{kx}) \cdot x - w_{kx+1}}{(w_{kx+1} - w_{kx-1}) \cdot x - w_{kx+1} - w_{kx}},$$

$$y' = \frac{(w_1 - w_0) \cdot y - w_1}{w_1 \cdot y - w_1 - w_0},$$

$$\begin{aligned}
p_w = &\left((w_1 \cdot w_{kx+1} - w_1 \cdot w_{kx-1}) \cdot x - w_1 \cdot w_{kx+1} - w_1 \cdot w_{kx}\right) \cdot y \\
&+ (w_1 + w_0) \cdot w_{kx} + \left((-w_1 - w_0) \cdot w_{kx+1} + (w_1 + w_0) \cdot w_{kx-1}\right) \cdot x \\
&+ (w_1 + w_0) \cdot w_{kx+1}.
\end{aligned}$$

3. Top right:

$$x' = \frac{w_{n-1} \cdot x}{w_{n-2} \cdot x - w_{n-1}},$$

$$y' = \frac{(w_1 - w_0) \cdot y - w_1}{w_1 \cdot y - w_1 - w_0},$$

$$\begin{aligned}
p_w = &\left(-w_1 \cdot w_{n-2} \cdot x - w_1 \cdot w_{n-1}\right) \cdot y + (w_0 + w_1) \cdot w_{n-2} \cdot x \\
&+ (w_1 + w_0) \cdot w_{n-1}.
\end{aligned}$$

4. Center left:

$$x' = \frac{(w_1 - w_0) \cdot x - w_1}{w_1 \cdot x - w_1 - w_0},$$

$$y' = \frac{(w_{ky+1} - w_{ky}) \cdot y - w_{ky+1}}{(w_{ky+1} - w_{ky-1}) \cdot y - w_{ky+1} - w_{ky}},$$

$$\begin{aligned}
p_w = &\left((w_1 \cdot w_{ky+1} - w_1 \cdot w_{ky-1}) \cdot x + (-w_1 - w_0) \cdot w_{ky+1}\right. \\
&\left.+ (w_1 + w_0) \cdot w_{ky-1}\right) \cdot y + (-w_1 \cdot w_{ky+1} - w_1 \cdot w_{ky}) \cdot x \\
&+ (w_1 + w_0) \cdot w_{ky+1} + (w_1 + w_0) \cdot w_{ky}.
\end{aligned}$$

5. Center center:

$$x' = \frac{(w_{kx+1} - w_{kx}) \cdot x - w_{kx+1}}{(w_{kx+1} - w_{kx-1}) \cdot x - w_{kx+1} - w_{kx}},$$

$$y' = \frac{(w_{ky+1} - w_{ky}) \cdot y - w_{ky+1}}{(w_{ky+1} - w_{ky-1}) \cdot y - w_{ky+1} - w_{ky}},$$

$$p_w = (((w_{kx+1} - w_{kx-1}) \cdot w_{ky+1} + (w_{kx-1} - w_{kx+1}) \cdot w_{ky-1}) \cdot x$$
$$+ (-w_{kx+1} - w_{kx}) \cdot w_{ky+1} + (w_{kx+1} + w_{kx}) \cdot w_{ky-1}) \cdot y$$
$$+ ((w_{kx-1} - w_{kx+1}) \cdot w_{ky+1} + (w_{kx-1} - w_{kx+1}) \cdot w_{ky}) \cdot x$$
$$+ (w_{kx+1} + w_{kx}) \cdot w_{ky+1} + (w_{kx+1} + w_{kx}) \cdot w_{ky}.$$

6. Center right:

$$x' = \frac{w_{n-1} \cdot x}{w_{n-2} \cdot x - w_{n-1}},$$

$$y' = \frac{(w_{ky+1} - w_{ky}) \cdot y - w_{ky+1}}{(w_{ky+1} - w_{ky-1}) \cdot y - w_{ky+1} - w_{ky}},$$

$$p_w = ((w_{n-2} \cdot w_{ky-1} - w_{n-2} \cdot w_{ky+1}) \cdot x - w_{n-1} \cdot w_{ky+1} + w_{n-1} \cdot w_{ky-1}) \cdot y$$
$$+ (w_{n-2} \cdot w_{ky+1} + w_{n-2} \cdot w_{ky}) \cdot x + w_{n-1} \cdot w_{ky+1} + w_{n-1} \cdot w_{ky}.$$

7. Bottom left:

$$x' = \frac{(w_1 - w_0) \cdot x - w_1}{w_1 \cdot x - w_1 - w_0},$$

$$y' = \frac{w_{n-1} y}{w_{n-2} \cdot y + w_{n-1}},$$

$$p_w = ((w_1 + w_0) \cdot w_{n-2} - w_1 \cdot w_{n-2} \cdot x) \cdot y - w_1 \cdot w_{n-1} \cdot x + (w_0 + w_1) \cdot w_{n-1}.$$

8. Bottom center:

$$x' = \frac{(w_{kx+1} - w_{kx}) \cdot x - w_{kx+1}}{(w_{kx+1} - w_{kx-1}) \cdot x - w_{kx+1} - w_{kx}},$$

$$y' = \frac{w_{n-1} \cdot y}{w_{n-2} \cdot y - w_{n-1}},$$

$$p_w = ((w_{kx-1} - w_{k+1}) \cdot w_{n-2} \cdot x + (w_{kx+1} + w_{kx}) \cdot w_{n-2}) \cdot y$$
$$+ (w_{kx-1} - w_{kx+1}) \cdot w_{n-1} \cdot x + (w_{kx+1} + w_{kx}) \cdot w_{n-1}.$$

9. Bottom right:

$$x' = \frac{w_{n-1} \cdot x}{w_{n-2} \cdot x + w_{n-1}},$$

$$y' = \frac{w_{n-1} \cdot y}{w_{n-2} \cdot y + w_{n-1}},$$

$$p_w = (w_{n-2} \cdot w_{n-2} \cdot x - w_{n-1} \cdot w_{n-2}) \cdot y + w_{n-2} \cdot w_{n-1} \cdot x + w_{n-1} \cdot w_{n-1}.$$

Using these formulas, the separable filter can now be evaluated using only $(N-1) \times (N/2)$ PCF texture samples using Shader Model 4.0.

The shader in Listing 1.2 demonstrates an optimized implementation for Direct3D 10.0. This shader compiles to binary code that is only slightly slower than the shader in Listing 1.1. There is no reason not to use a separable shadow filter if the additional quality is needed.

```
//#Define SMAP_SIZE 512.
#define INV_SCALE ( 1.0 / SMAP_SIZE )

#define FILTER_SIZE 9 // 8x8 shadow map samples
#define FSH ( FILTER_SIZE/2 )

#if PCF_FILTER_SIZE == 9
static const float SG[9] = { 2,4,6,8,9,8,6,4,2 };
#endif
#if PCF_FILTER_SIZE == 7
static const float SG[7] = { 2,4,6,7,6,4,2 };
#endif
#if PCF_FILTER_SIZE == 5
static const float SG[5] = { 2,4,5,4,2 };
#endif
#if PCF_FILTER_SIZE == 3
static const float SG[3] = { 2,3,2 };
#endif

float shadow_fast_separable( float3 tc )
{
   float   s   = 0.0;
   float   pw;
   float   w= 0.0;
   float2 st;
   float2 stc = ( SMAP_SIZE * tc.xy ) + float2( 0.5, 0.5 );
   float2 tcs = floor( stc );
   float2 fc;
   int    row, col;

   fc    = stc - tcs;
   tc.xy = tc - ( fc * INV_SCALE );

   for( row = 0; row < FILTER_SIZE -1; ++row )
   {
      for( col = 0; col < FILTER_SIZE -1; ++col )
         w += SG[row]*SG[col];
   }

   for( row = -(FSH-1); row <= (FSH-1); row += 2 )
   {
      for( col = -(FSH-1); col <= (FSH-1); col += 2 )
      {
```

```
     if( row == -(FSH-1) ) // Top row
{
  if( col == -(FSH-1) ) // Top left
  {
    pw=(SG[1]*SG[1]*fc.x-SG[1]*SG[1]-SG[0]*SG[1])*fc.y+
          (-SG[1]*SG[1]-SG[0]*SG[1])*fc.x+SG[1]*SG[1]+
          2*SG[0]*SG[1]+SG[0]*SG[1];
    st.x=((SG[1]-SG[0])*fc.x-SG[1])/(SG[1]*fc.x-
             SG[1]-SG[0]);
    st.y=((SG[1]-SG[0])*fc.y-SG[1])/(SG[1]*fc.y-
             SG[1]-SG[0]);
  }
  else if( col == (FSH-1) ) // Top right
  {
    pw=(-SG[1]*SG[FILTER_SIZE-2-1]*fc.x-
          SG[1]*SG[FILTER_SIZE-1-1])*fc.y+
          (SG[1]+SG[0])*SG[FILTER_SIZE-2-1]*fc.x+
          (SG[1]+SG[0])*SG[FILTER_SIZE-1-1];
    st.x=(SG[FILTER_SIZE-1-1]*fc.x)/
             (SG[FILTER_SIZE-2-1]*fc.x+SG[FILTER_SIZE-1-1]);
    st.y=((SG[1]-SG[0])*fc.y-SG[1])/
             (SG[1]*fc.y-SG[1]-SG[0]);
  }
  else // Top center
  {
    pw=((SG[1]*SG[col+(FSH-1)+1]-SG[1]*SG[col+
          (FSH-1)-1])*fc.x-SG[1]*
          SG[col+(FSH-1)+1]-SG[1]*SG[col+(FSH-1)])*
          fc.y+((-SG[1]-SG[0])*
          SG[col+(FSH-1)+1]+(SG[1]+SG[0])*SG[col+(FSH-1)
          -1])*fc.x+(SG[1]+SG[0])*SG[col+
          (FSH-1)+1]+(SG[1]+SG[0])*SG[col+(FSH-1)];
    st.x=((SG[col+(FSH-1)+1]-SG[col+(FSH-1)])*
             fc.x-SG[col+(FSH-1)+1])/
             ((SG[col+(FSH-1)+1]-SG[col+(FSH-1)-1])*
             fc.x-SG[col+(FSH-1)+1]-SG[col+(FSH-1)]);
    st.y=((SG[1]-SG[0])*fc.y-SG[1])/(SG[1]*
             fc.y-SG[1]-SG[0]);
  }
    }
    else if( row == (FSH-1) )  // Bottom row
{
  if( col == -(FSH-1) ) // Bottom left
  {
    pw=((SG[1]+SG[0])*SG[row+(FSH-1)-1]-
          SG[1]*SG[row+(FSH-1)-1]*fc.x)*fc.y-
          SG[1]*SG[row+(FSH-1)]*fc.x+
          (SG[1]+SG[0])*SG[row+(FSH-1)];
    st.x=((SG[1]-SG[0])*fc.x-SG[1])/(SG[1]*fc.x-SG[1]-
             SG[0]);
    st.y=(SG[row+(FSH-1)]*fc.y)/(SG[row+(FSH-1)-1]*
```

```
                          fc.y+SG[row+(FSH-1)]);
        }
      else if( col == (FSH-1) ) // Bottom right
      {
        pw=(SG[col+(FSH-1)-1]*SG[row+(FSH-1)-1]*
                fc.x+SG[col+(FSH-1)]*SG[row+(FSH-1)-1])*fc.y+
                SG[col+(FSH-1)-1]*SG[row+(FSH-1)]*fc.x+
                SG[col+(FSH-1)]*SG[row+(FSH-1)];
          st.x=(SG[col+(FSH-1)]*fc.x)/(SG[col+(FSH-1)-1]*fc.x+
                  SG[col+(FSH-1)]]);
          st.y=(SG[row+(FSH-1)]*fc.y)/(SG[row+(FSH-1)-1]*fc.y+
                  SG[row+(FSH-1)]]);
        }
      else // Bottom center
      {
        pw=((SG[col+(FSH-1)-1]-SG[col+(FSH-1)+1])*
                SG[row+(FSH-1)-1]*fc.x+(SG[col+(FSH-1)+1]+
                SG[col+(FSH-1)])*SG[row+(FSH-1)-1])*fc.y+
                (SG[col+(FSH-1)-1]-SG[col+(FSH-1)+1])*
                SG[row+(FSH-1)]*fc.x+(SG[col+(FSH-1)+1]+
                SG[col+(FSH-1)])*SG[row+(FSH-1)];
          st.x=((SG[col+(FSH-1)+1]-SG[col+(FSH-1)])*fc.x-
                  SG[col+(FSH-1)+1])/((SG[col+(FSH-1)+1]-
                  SG[col+(FSH-1)-1])*fc.x-SG[col+(FSH-1)+1]-
                  SG[col+(FSH-1)]);
          st.y=(SG[row+(FSH-1)]*fc.y)/
                  (SG[row+(FSH-1)-1]*fc.y+SG[row+(FSH-1)]]);
        }
      }
    else // Center rows
    {
      if( col == -(FSH-1) ) // Center left
      {
        pw=((SG[1]*SG[row+(FSH-1)+1]-SG[1]*
                SG[row+(FSH-1)-1])*fc.x+(-SG[1]-SG[0])*
                SG[row+(FSH-1)+1]+(SG[1]+SG[0])*
                SG[row+(FSH-1)-1])*fc.y+(-SG[1]*
                SG[row+(FSH-1)+1]-SG[1]*SG[row+(FSH-1)])*
                fc.x+(SG[1]+SG[0])*SG[row+(FSH-1)+1]+
                (SG[1]+SG[0])*SG[row+(FSH-1)];
          st.x=((SG[1]-SG[0])*fc.x-SG[1])/(SG[1]*
                  fc.x-SG[1]-SG[0]);
          st.y=((SG[row+(FSH-1)+1]-SG[row+(FSH-1)])*
                  fc.y-SG[row+(FSH-1)+1])/
                  ((SG[row+(FSH-1)+1]-SG[row+(FSH-1)-1])*
                  fc.y-SG[row+(FSH-1)+1]-SG[row+(FSH-1)]);
        }
      else if( col == (FSH-1) ) // Center right
      {
        pw=((SG[col+(FSH-1)-1]*SG[row+(FSH-1)-1]-
                SG[col+(FSH-1)-1]*SG[row+(FSH-1)+1])*
```

```
                   fc.x-SG[col+(FSH-1)]*SG[row+(FSH-1)+1]+
               SG[col+(FSH-1)]*SG[row+(FSH-1)-1])*fc.y+
               (SG[col+(FSH-1)-1]*SG[row+(FSH-1)+1]+
               SG[col+(FSH-1)-1]*SG[row+(FSH-1)])*fc.x+
               SG[col+(FSH-1)]*SG[row+(FSH-1)+1]+
               SG[col+(FSH-1)]*SG[row+(FSH-1)]);
    st.x=(SG[col+(FSH-1)]*fc.x)/
             (SG[col+(FSH-1)-1]*fc.x+SG[col+(FSH-1)]);
    st.y=((SG[row+(FSH-1)+1]-SG[row+(FSH-1)])*fc.y-
             SG[row+(FSH-1)+1])/((SG[row+(FSH-1)+1]-
             SG[row+(FSH-1)-1])*fc.y-SG[row+(FSH-1)+1]-
             SG[row+(FSH-1)]);
  }
  else // Center center
  {
    pw=(((SG[col+(FSH-1)+1]-SG[col+(FSH-1)-1])*
             SG[row+(FSH-1)+1]+(SG[col+(FSH-1)-1]-
             SG[col+(FSH-1)+1])*SG[row+(FSH-1)-1])*
             fc.x+(-SG[col+(FSH-1)+1]-
             SG[col+(FSH-1)])*SG[row+(FSH-1)+1]+
             (SG[col+(FSH-1)+1]+SG[col+(FSH-1)])*
             SG[row+(FSH-1)-1])*fc.y+((SG[col+(FSH-1)-1]-
             SG[col+(FSH-1)+1])*SG[row+(FSH-1)+1]+
             (SG[col+(FSH-1)-1]-SG[col+(FSH-1)+1])*
             SG[row+(FSH-1)])*fc.x+(SG[col+(FSH-1)+1]+
             SG[col+(FSH-1)])*SG[row+(FSH-1)+1]+
             (SG[col+(FSH-1)+1]+SG[col+(FSH-1)])*
             SG[row+(FSH-1)];
    st.x=((SG[col+(FSH-1)+1]-SG[col+(FSH-1)])*fc.x-
             SG[col+(FSH-1)+1])/((SG[col+(FSH-1)+1]-
             SG[col+(FSH-1)-1])*fc.x-SG[col+(FSH-1)+1]-
             SG[col+(FSH-1)]);
    st.y=((SG[row+(FSH-1)+1]-SG[row+(FSH-1)])*fc.y-
             SG[row+(FSH-1)+1])/((SG[row+(FSH-1)+1]-
             SG[row+(FSH-1)-1])*fc.y-SG[row+(FSH-1)+1]-
             SG[row+(FSH-1)]);
  }
}
s+=pw*g_txShadowMap.SampleCmpLevelZero(g_samShadowMap,
      tc.xy + INV_SCALE * st, tc.z, int2( col, row ) ).x;
  }
}
return s/w;
}
```

Listing 1.2. Fast Shader Model 4.0 uniform shadow filter.

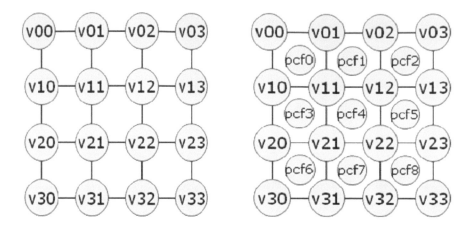

Figure 1.9. Uniformly smooth shadows.   Figure 1.10. Contact hardening shadows.

1.5   Nonseparable Unique Weights per PCF Result

Having covered uniform and separable shadow filters this section now looks at filters that are not separable. A nonseparable filter can be used in situations where the filter matrix is dynamic or is, e.g., used to embed the shape of the light source like in [Soler et al. 98].

Consider the 4×4 shadow map texel grid in Figure 1.9. Each v_{ij} is again a binary visibility [0 or 1] sample derived from the corresponding shadow map sample.

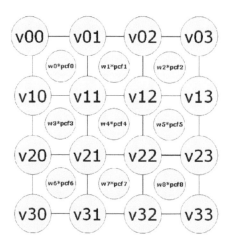

Figure 1.11. Weighted PCF.

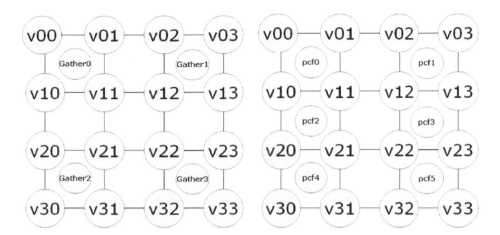

Figure 1.12. Shader Model 4.1/5.0 Implementation of filger shown in Figure 1.13.

Figure 1.13. Shifted Texture Coordinates and post PCF weights.

Now a uniform PCF filter collapses each 2×2 visibility information block to a PCF filtered visibility result PCF_k as shown in Figure 1.10.

A weights matrix now assigns a unique weight w_k to each PCF_k result so one arrives at the situation depicted in Figure 1.11.

The final filtered result (for $N \times N$ shadow map pixels) is then obtained by computing the term in Equation (1.4):

$$\frac{\sum_{k=0}^{(N-1)\cdot(N-1)} w_k \cdot PCF_k}{(N-1) \cdot (N-1)}. \tag{1.4}$$

Using Shader Model 4.1 or Shader Model 5.0 Equation (1.4) can be evaluated through some ALU work and $(N/2) \cdot (N/2)$ Gather() instructions as shown in Figure 1.12 for a 4×4 block of visibility results.

Again, the naive way to implement this using only Shader Model 4.0 would involve doing $(N-1) \cdot (N-1)$ PCF texture samples. There is a better way with again fewer PCF instructions as shown in Figure 1.13. Again, shifted texture coordinates and post PCF weights are used to achieve this.

To understand how this works, now consider only one row of visibility samples. v_k. Assigning weights w_k to each one-dimensional PCF result in that row produces the term shown in Equation (1.5). Here x is the sub-texel coordinate ranging from 0.0 to 1.0 (excluding 1.0):

$$\sum_{k=0}^{N-2} (1-x) \cdot v_k \cdot w_k + x \cdot v_{k+1} w_k. \tag{1.5}$$

Equation (1.5) simplifies to Equation (1.6):

$$(1 - x) \cdot v_0 \cdot w_0 + \left(\sum_{k=1}^{N-2} v_k \cdot ((w_{k-1} - w_k) \cdot x + w_k) \right) + x \cdot v_{N-1} \cdot w_{N-2}. \quad (1.6)$$

To compute the shifted texture coordinates x' for PCF texture operations and post texturing weights wp, the following three cases need to be considered:

1. *Left border of the filter row.* The system of equations $(1 - x') \cdot wp \cdot v_0 = (1 - x) \cdot w_0 \cdot v_0$ and $x' \cdot wp \cdot v_1 = v_1 \cdot (x \cdot (w_0 - w_1) + w_1)$ is solved by $x' = \frac{(w_1 - w_0) \cdot x - w_1}{w_1 \cdot x - w_1 - w_0}$ and $wp = -w_1 \cdot x + w_1 + w_0$.

2. *Right border of the filter row.* The system of equations $(1 - x') \cdot wp \cdot v_{N-2} = v_{N-2} \cdot (x \cdot (w_{N-2} - w_{N-1}) + w_{N-1})$ and $x' \cdot wp \cdot v_{N-1} = x \cdot w_{N-1} \cdot v_{N-1}$ is solved by $x' = \frac{w_{N-1} \cdot x}{w_{N-2} \cdot x + w_{N-1}}$ and $wp = w_{N-2} \cdot x + w_{N-1}$.

3. *Central values of the filter row.* The system of equations $(1 - x') \cdot wp \cdot v_k = v_k \cdot (x \cdot (w_{k-1} - w_k) + w_k)$ and $x' \cdot wp \cdot v_{k+1} = v_{k+1} \cdot (x \cdot (w_k - w_{k+1}) + w_{k+1})$ is solved by $x' = \frac{(w_{k+1} - w_k) \cdot x - w_{k+1}}{(w_{k+1} - w_{k-1}) \cdot x - w_{k+1} - w_k}$ and $wp = (w_{k-1} - w_{k+1}) \cdot x + w_{k+1} + w_k$.

Using these formulas the filter can now be evaluated using only $(N-1) \times (N/2)$ PCF texture samples using Shader Model 4.0. The PCF samples do only use a modified x-component of the texture coordinates for sampling the shadow map. The y-component stays as it is.

1.6   Advanced Shadow Filtering Techniques

1.6.1   Light Shape-Dependent Shadows for Directional Lights

[Soler et al. 98] describe that a shadow that depends on the shape of the light source can be generated by convoluting an image of the light source and a shadow map. If one assumes that the shape of a light source is rotationally invariant and that the projected size of the light source does not change, one can embed the shape of the light source in the weights matrix used for shadow filtering. Since this weights matrix usually doesn't present a separable filter, one needs to carry out $(N/2) \times (N - 1)$ PCF instructions to carry out the "convolution" of light source and shadow.

Please note that Shader Model 4.1 and Shader Model 5.0 can again get away with $(N/2) \times (N/2)$ `Gather()` texture instructions.

Figures 1.14 and 1.15 show screen shots of a scene renderer with different filter/light shapes.

Figure 1.14. Screen shots of a scene renderer.

Figure 1.15. Screen shots of a scene renderer.

The shader shown in Listing 1.3 contains an implementation of light shape-dependent shadows for a range of light shapes.

```
#define FILTER_SIZE 9
#define GS  ( FILTER_SIZE )
#define GS2 ( FILTER_SIZE / 2 )

// Weight matrices that contain a weight for each pcf
// Result of each 2x2
// pixel block of the shadow map.

#define SM_FILTER_DISC          1
#define SM_FILTER_TRIANGLE         2
#define SM_FILTER_HALFMOON         3

#if FILTER_SIZE == 9
#if FILTER == SM_FILTER_HALFMOON
static const float W[9][9] = {
{ 0.2,1.0,1.0,1.0,1.0,0.0,0.0,0.0,0.0 },
{ 0.0,0.1,1.0,1.0,1.0,1.0,1.0,0.0,0.0 },
{ 0.0,0.0,0.0,0.5,1.0,1.0,1.0,1.0,0.0 },
{ 0.0,0.0,0.0,0.0,1.0,1.0,1.0,1.0,0.0 },
{ 0.0,0.0,0.0,0.0,0.0,0.5,1.0,1.0,1.0,0.5 },
{ 0.0,0.0,0.0,0.0,0.0,1.0,1.0,1.0,1.0,0.0 },
{ 0.0,0.0,0.0,0.0,0.5,1.0,1.0,1.0,0.0,0.0 },
{ 0.0,0.1,1.0,1.0,1.0,1.0,0.0,0.0,0.0 },
{ 0.2,1.0,1.0,1.0,1.0,0.0,0.0,0.0,0.0 }
};
#endif

#if FILTER == SM_FILTER_TRIANGLE
static const float W[9][9] = {
{ 0.0,0.0,0.0,0.0,1.0,0.0,0.0,0.0,0.0 },
{ 0.0,0.0,0.0,0.5,1.0,0.5,0.0,0.0,0.0 },
{ 0.0,0.0,0.0,1.0,1.0,1.0,0.0,0.0,0.0 },
{ 0.0,0.0,0.5,1.0,1.0,1.0,0.5,0.0,0.0 },
{ 0.0,0.0,1.0,1.0,1.0,1.0,1.0,0.0,0.0 },
{ 0.0,0.5,1.0,1.0,1.0,1.0,1.0,0.5,0.0 },
{ 0.0,1.0,1.0,1.0,1.0,1.0,1.0,1.0,0.0 },
{ 0.5,1.0,1.0,1.0,1.0,1.0,1.0,1.0,0.5 },
{ 1.0,1.0,1.0,1.0,1.0,1.0,1.0,1.0,1.0 }
};
#endif

#if FILTER == SM_FILTER_DISC
static const float W[9][9] = {
{ 0.0,0.0,0.0,0.5,1.0,0.5,0.0,0.0,0.0 },
{ 0.0,0.0,1.0,1.0,1.0,1.0,1.0,0.0,0.0 },
{ 0.0,1.0,1.0,1.0,1.0,1.0,1.0,1.0,0.0 },
{ 0.5,1.0,1.0,1.0,1.0,1.0,1.0,1.0,0.5 },
{ 1.0,1.0,1.0,1.0,1.0,1.0,1.0,1.0,1.0 },
```

```
{ 0.5,1.0,1.0,1.0,1.0,1.0,1.0,1.0,0.5 },
{ 0.0,1.0,1.0,1.0,1.0,1.0,1.0,1.0,0.0 },
{ 0.0,0.0,1.0,1.0,1.0,1.0,1.0,0.0,0.0 },
{ 0.0,0.0,0.0,0.5,1.0,0.5,0.0,0.0,0.0 }
};
#endif

#ifdef DX10_1
// 10.1 shader for one unique weight per pcf sample.
// Since it uses Gather(), only (N/2)x(N/2) texture ops
// are necessary. This runs as fast as the uniform or
// separable filter under 10.0.
float shadow_dx10_1( float3 tc )
{
   float4 s = (0.0).xxxx;
   float2 stc = ( SMAP_SIZE * tc.xy ) + float2( 0.5, 0.5 );
   float2 tcs = floor( stc );
   float2 fc;
   int    row;
   int    col;
   float  w = 0.0;
   float4 v1[ GS2 + 1 ];
   float2 v0[ GS2 + 1 ];

   fc.xy = stc - tcs;
   tc.xy = tcs * INV_SCALE;

   for( row = 0; row < GS; ++row )
   {
      for( col = 0; col < GS; ++col )
         w += W[row][col];
   }

   // Loop over the rows.
   for( row = -GS2; row <= GS2; row += 2 )
   {
   [unroll]for( col = -GS2; col <= GS2; col += 2 )
   {
     float fSumOfWeights = W[row+GS2][col+GS2];

     if( col > -GS2 )
       fSumOfWeights += W[row+GS2][col+GS2-1];

     if( col < GS2 )
       fSumOfWeights += W[row+GS2][col+GS2+1];

     if( row > -GS2 )
     {
       fSumOfWeights += W[row+GS2-1][col+GS2];

       if( col < GS2 )
```

```
            fSumOfWeights += W[row+GS2-1][col+GS2+1];

        if( col > -GS2 )
          fSumOfWeights += W[row+GS2-1][col+GS2-1];

    }

    if( fSumOfWeights != 0.0 )
      v1[(col+GS2)/2]=( tc.zzzz <= g_txShadowMap.Gather(
                               g_samPoint, tc.xy,
                               int2( col, row ) ) ) ?
                              (1.0).xxxx : (0.0).xxxx;
    else
       v1[(col+GS2)/2] = (0.0f).xxxx;

       if( col == -GS2 )
       {
      s.x += ( 1 - fc.y ) * ( v1[0].w *
                    ( W[row+GS2][col+GS2] -
                    W[row+GS2][col+GS2] * fc.x ) +
              v1[0].z * ( fc.x * (
                    W[row+GS2][col+GS2] -
                    W[row+GS2][col+GS2+1] ) +
                    W[row+GS2][col+GS2+1] ) );
        s.y += (      fc.y ) * ( v1[0].x *
                    ( W[row+GS2][col+GS2] -
                    W[row+GS2][col+GS2] * fc.x ) +
               v1[0].y * ( fc.x * ( W[row+GS2][col+GS2] -
                    W[row+GS2][col+GS2+1] ) +
                    W[row+GS2][col+GS2+1] ) );
     if( row > -GS2 )
     {
       s.z += ( 1 - fc.y ) * ( v0[0].x *
                     ( W[row+GS2-1][col+GS2] -
                       W[row+GS2-1][col+GS2] * fc.x ) +
          v0[0].y * ( fc.x * ( W[row+GS2-1][col+GS2] -
                    W[row+GS2-1][col+GS2+1] ) +
                    W[row+GS2-1][col+GS2+1] ) );
       s.w += (      fc.y ) * ( v1[0].w *
                     ( W[row+GS2-1][col+GS2] -
                       W[row+GS2-1][col+GS2] * fc.x ) +
          v1[0].z * ( fc.x * ( W[row+GS2-1][col+GS2] -
                    W[row+GS2-1][col+GS2+1] ) +
                    W[row+GS2-1][col+GS2+1] ) );
     }
       }
       else if( col == GS2 )
       {
     s.x += ( 1 - fc.y ) * ( v1[GS2].w * ( fc.x *
                 ( W[row+GS2][col+GS2-1] -
                 W[row+GS2][col+GS2] ) +
```

```
                W[row+GS2][col+GS2] ) +
        v1[GS2].z * fc.x * W[row+GS2][col+GS2] );
  s.y += (       fc.y ) * ( v1[GS2].x * ( fc.x *
          ( W[row+GS2][col+GS2-1] -
            W[row+GS2][col+GS2] ) +
            W[row+GS2][col+GS2] ) +
        v1[GS2].y * fc.x * W[row+GS2][col+GS2] );

if( row > -GS2 )
{
  s.z += ( 1 - fc.y ) * ( v0[GS2].x * ( fc.x *
        ( W[row+GS2-1][col+GS2-1] -
          W[row+GS2-1][col+GS2] ) +
          W[row+GS2-1][col+GS2] ) +
     v0[GS2].y * fc.x * W[row+GS2-1][col+GS2] );
  s.w += (       fc.y ) * ( v1[GS2].w * ( fc.x *
            ( W[row+GS2-1][col+GS2-1] -
              W[row+GS2-1][col+GS2] ) +
              W[row+GS2-1][col+GS2] ) +
     v1[GS2].z * fc.x * W[row+GS2-1][col+GS2] );
}
    else
    {
  s.x += ( 1 - fc.y ) * ( v1[(col+GS2)/2].w *
            ( fc.x * ( W[row+GS2][col+GS2-1] -
              W[row+GS2][col+GS2+0] ) +
              W[row+GS2][col+GS2+0] ) +
            v1[(col+GS2)/2].z * ( fc.x *
            ( W[row+GS2][col+GS2-0] -
              W[row+GS2][col+GS2+1] ) +
              W[row+GS2][col+GS2+1] ) );
  s.y += (       fc.y ) * ( v1[(col+GS2)/2].x * ( fc.x *
            ( W[row+GS2][col+GS2-1] -
              W[row+GS2][col+GS2+0] ) +
              W[row+GS2][col+GS2+0] ) +
     v1[(col+GS2)/2].y * ( fc.x *
            ( W[row+GS2][col+GS2-0] -
              W[row+GS2][col+GS2+1] ) +
              W[row+GS2][col+GS2+1] ) );
if( row > -GS2 )
{
  s.z += ( 1 - fc.y ) * ( v0[(col+GS2)/2].x * ( fc.x *
            ( W[row+GS2-1][col+GS2-1] -
              W[row+GS2-1][col+GS2+0] ) +
              W[row+GS2-1][col+GS2+0] ) +
     v0[(col+GS2)/2].y * ( fc.x *
            ( W[row+GS2-1][col+GS2-0] -
              W[row+GS2-1][col+GS2+1] ) +
              W[row+GS2-1][col+GS2+1] ) );
  s.w += (       fc.y ) * ( v1[(col+GS2)/2].w * ( fc.x *
            ( W[row+GS2-1][col+GS2-1] -
```

```
                         W[row+GS2-1][col+GS2+0] ) +
                         W[row+GS2-1][col+GS2+0] ) +
             v1[(col+GS2)/2].z * ( fc.x *
                          ( W[row+GS2-1][col+GS2-0] -
                           W[row+GS2-1][col+GS2+1] ) +
                          W[row+GS2-1][col+GS2+1] ) );
       }
        }

   if( row != GS2 )
     v0[(col+GS2)/2] = v1[(col+GS2)/2].xy;
     }
   }

   return dot(s,(1.0).xxxx)/w;
}

#endif
// 10.0 shader for one unique weight per pcf sample.
// This shader makes use of
// shifted texture coords and post weights to reduce
// the texture op counts for dx10.0.
// Without this trick, a naive implementation would need
// (N-1)x(N-1) pcf samples.
// This shader only does (N/2)x(N-1) pcf samples instead.
float shadow_dx10_0( float3 tc )
{
   float   s   = 0.0;
   float2 stc = ( SMAP_SIZE * tc.xy ) + float2( 0.5, 0.5 );
   float2 tcs = floor( stc );
   float2 fc;
   int     row;
   int     col;
   float   w = 0.0;

   fc      = stc - tcs;
   tc.xy   = tc - ( fc * INV_SCALE );
   fc.y    *= INV_SCALE;

   for( row = 0; row < GS; ++row )
   {
      for( col = 0; col < GS; ++col )
         w += W[row][col];
   }

   for( row = 0; row < GS; ++row )
   {
     [unroll]for( col = -GS2; col <= GS2; col += 2 )
     {
if( col == -GS2 )
{
```

```
   if( W[row][col+GS2+1] != 0 ||  W[row][col+GS2] != 0 )
      {
    s += ( ( 1.0 - fc.x ) * W[row][col+GS2+1] +
            W[row][col+GS2] ) *
            g_txShadowMap.SampleCmpLevelZero(
            g_samShadowMap , tc.xy +
            float2( g_vShadowMapSize.z * ( (
            W[row][col+GS2+1] - fc.x * ( W[row][col+GS2+1]
            - W[row][col+GS2] ) ) / ( ( 1.0 - fc.x ) *
            W[row][col+GS2+1] + W[row][col+GS2] ) ),
            fc.y ), tc.z, int2( col, row - GS2 ) ).x;
   }
   else if( col == GS2 )
   {
      if( W[row][col+GS2-1] != 0 ||  W[row][col+GS2] != 0 )
   s += ( fc.x * W[row][col+GS2-1] +
            W[row][col+GS2] ) *
            g_txShadowMap.SampleCmpLevelZero(
            g_samShadowMap , tc.xy +
            float2( g_vShadowMapSize.z * ( ( fc.x *
            W[row][col+GS2] ) / ( fc.x  *
            W[row][col+GS2-1] + W[row][col+GS2] ) ),
            fc.y ), tc.z, int2( col, row - GS2 ) ).x;
   }
   else
   {
      if( ( W[row][col+GS2-1] - W[row][col+GS2+1] ) != 0
          || ( W[row][col+GS2] + W[row][col+GS2+1] ) != 0 )
   s += ( fc.x * ( W[row][col+GS2-1] -
            W[row][col+GS2+1] ) + W[row][col+GS2] +
            W[row][col+GS2+1] ) *
            g_txShadowMap.SampleCmpLevelZero(
            g_samShadowMap , tc.xy +
            float2( g_vShadowMapSize.z *
            ( ( W[row][col+GS2+1] - fc.x *
            ( W[row][col+GS2+1] - W[row][col+GS2] ) ) /
            ( fc.x * ( W[row][col+GS2-1] -
            W[row][col+GS2+1] ) + W[row][col+GS2] +
            W[row][col+GS2+1] ) ), fc.y ),
            tc.z, int2( col, row - GS2 ) ).x;
   }
  }
  }
  return s/w;
}
```

Listing 1.3. Light shape-dependent shadow filters.

1.6.2   Contact Hardening Shadows

In order to achieve physically plausible shadows, percentage closer soft shadows (PCSS) [Fernando 05] were introduced as a real-time method to achieve contact hardening shadows. Typical implementations of PCSS however suffer from noise and banding artifacts that result from the use of a poisson disk of samples. This book introduces a new technique [Gumbau et al. 10] that improves PCSS and removes the artifacts of the original algorithm. However, as previously stated, it is not considered a conventional shadow filtering technique as it adds additional rendering passes and cannot just be dropped into a game engine instead of a normal PCF-based filter.

The shader in Listing 1.4 now uses a large box (12×12) of shadow map samples in combination with a non-stationary filter weights matrix to achieve a transition from sharp to soft shadows. The sample accepts the fact that one needs to limit the size of the light source in order to achieve high quality results. Since the sun can usually be treated as a relatively small light source the technique works well for a directional light.

Figure 1.16. Screenshot of the example in the DirectX SDK with soft shadows.

The Shader Model 5.0 instructions `GatherRed()` and `GatherCmpRed()` are used to accelerate the computation of average-blocker-depth and to accelerate the non-stationary and nonseparable dynamic filter operation.

The screen shots in Figures 1.16 and 1.17 show the difference between shadows that are equally smooth everywhere and shadows that get harder at contact regions.

Blocker search. The search for blockers for an $N \times N$ shadow map filter footprint is carried out using only $(N/2) \times (N/2)$ `GatherRed()` operations. The shader performs 36 of these instructions. A Shader Model 4.0 implementation would need to perform 144 point samples in order to obtain the same information.

Filtering with a dynamic filter matrix. Based on the average blocker depth and the size of the light source, a factor between 0.0 (sharp) to 1.0 (completely blurry) is computed. This factor is used to compute a dynamic weight matrix that results from feeding four matrices into a cubic Bezier function. The math presented above is used to compute the filter, reducing the necessary ALU through the use of `Gat` of `GatherCmpRed()`. Note that the shader from Listing 1.4 can be modified to perform the dynamic filter under Shader Model 4.0 with a reduced set of texture ops.

Figure 1.17. Screenshot of the example in the DirectX SDK without soft shadows.

```
#define FILTER_SIZE     11
#define FS   FILTER_SIZE
#define FS2 ( FILTER_SIZE / 2 )

// Four control matrices for a dynamic cubic bezier filter
// weights matrix.

static const float C3[11][11] =
{ { 1.0,1.0,1.0,1.0,1.0,1.0,1.0,1.0,1.0,1.0,1.0 },
  { 1.0,1.0,1.0,1.0,1.0,1.0,1.0,1.0,1.0,1.0,1.0 },
  { 1.0,1.0,1.0,1.0,1.0,1.0,1.0,1.0,1.0,1.0,1.0 },
  { 1.0,1.0,1.0,1.0,1.0,1.0,1.0,1.0,1.0,1.0,1.0 },
  { 1.0,1.0,1.0,1.0,1.0,1.0,1.0,1.0,1.0,1.0,1.0 },
  { 1.0,1.0,1.0,1.0,1.0,1.0,1.0,1.0,1.0,1.0,1.0 },
  { 1.0,1.0,1.0,1.0,1.0,1.0,1.0,1.0,1.0,1.0,1.0 },
  { 1.0,1.0,1.0,1.0,1.0,1.0,1.0,1.0,1.0,1.0,1.0 },
  { 1.0,1.0,1.0,1.0,1.0,1.0,1.0,1.0,1.0,1.0,1.0 },
  { 1.0,1.0,1.0,1.0,1.0,1.0,1.0,1.0,1.0,1.0,1.0 },
  { 1.0,1.0,1.0,1.0,1.0,1.0,1.0,1.0,1.0,1.0,1.0 },
  };

static const float C2[11][11] =
{ { 0.0,0.0,0.0,0.0,0.0,0.0,0.0,0.0,0.0,0.0,0.0 },
  { 0.0,0.2,0.2,0.2,0.2,0.2,0.2,0.2,0.2,0.2,0.0 },
  { 0.0,0.2,1.0,1.0,1.0,1.0,1.0,1.0,1.0,0.2,0.0 },
  { 0.0,0.2,1.0,1.0,1.0,1.0,1.0,1.0,1.0,0.2,0.0 },
  { 0.0,0.2,1.0,1.0,1.0,1.0,1.0,1.0,1.0,0.2,0.0 },
  { 0.0,0.2,1.0,1.0,1.0,1.0,1.0,1.0,1.0,0.2,0.0 },
  { 0.0,0.2,1.0,1.0,1.0,1.0,1.0,1.0,1.0,0.2,0.0 },
  { 0.0,0.2,1.0,1.0,1.0,1.0,1.0,1.0,1.0,0.2,0.0 },
  { 0.0,0.2,1.0,1.0,1.0,1.0,1.0,1.0,1.0,0.2,0.0 },
  { 0.0,0.2,0.2,0.2,0.2,0.2,0.2,0.2,0.2,0.2,0.0 },
  { 0.0,0.0,0.0,0.0,0.0,0.0,0.0,0.0,0.0,0.0,0.0 },
  };

static const float C1[11][11] =
{ { 0.0,0.0,0.0,0.0,0.0,0.0,0.0,0.0,0.0,0.0,0.0 },
  { 0.0,0.0,0.0,0.0,0.0,0.0,0.0,0.0,0.0,0.0,0.0 },
  { 0.0,0.0,0.2,0.2,0.2,0.2,0.2,0.2,0.2,0.0,0.0 },
  { 0.0,0.0,0.2,1.0,1.0,1.0,1.0,1.0,0.2,0.0,0.0 },
  { 0.0,0.0,0.2,1.0,1.0,1.0,1.0,1.0,0.2,0.0,0.0 },
  { 0.0,0.0,0.2,1.0,1.0,1.0,1.0,1.0,0.2,0.0,0.0 },
  { 0.0,0.0,0.2,1.0,1.0,1.0,1.0,1.0,0.2,0.0,0.0 },
  { 0.0,0.0,0.2,1.0,1.0,1.0,1.0,1.0,0.2,0.0,0.0 },
  { 0.0,0.0,0.2,0.2,0.2,0.2,0.2,0.2,0.2,0.0,0.0 },
  { 0.0,0.0,0.0,0.0,0.0,0.0,0.0,0.0,0.0,0.0,0.0 },
  { 0.0,0.0,0.0,0.0,0.0,0.0,0.0,0.0,0.0,0.0,0.0 },
  };

static const float C0[11][11] =
```

```
{ { 0.0,0.0,0.0,0.0,0.0,0.0,0.0,0.0,0.0,0.0,0.0 },
  { 0.0,0.0,0.0,0.0,0.0,0.0,0.0,0.0,0.0,0.0,0.0 },
  { 0.0,0.0,0.0,0.0,0.0,0.0,0.0,0.0,0.0,0.0,0.0 },
  { 0.0,0.0,0.0,0.0,0.0,0.0,0.0,0.0,0.0,0.0,0.0 },
  { 0.0,0.0,0.0,0.0,0.8,0.8,0.8,0.0,0.0,0.0,0.0 },
  { 0.0,0.0,0.0,0.0,0.8,1.0,0.8,0.0,0.0,0.0,0.0 },
  { 0.0,0.0,0.0,0.0,0.8,0.8,0.8,0.0,0.0,0.0,0.0 },
  { 0.0,0.0,0.0,0.0,0.0,0.0,0.0,0.0,0.0,0.0,0.0 },
  { 0.0,0.0,0.0,0.0,0.0,0.0,0.0,0.0,0.0,0.0,0.0 },
  { 0.0,0.0,0.0,0.0,0.0,0.0,0.0,0.0,0.0,0.0,0.0 },
  { 0.0,0.0,0.0,0.0,0.0,0.0,0.0,0.0,0.0,0.0,0.0 },
  };

// Compute dynamic weight at a certain row, column of the matrix.
float Fw( int r, int c, float fL )
{
    return (1.0-fL)*(1.0-fL)*(1.0-fL) * C0[r][c] +
           fL*fL*fL * C3[r][c] +
           3.0f * (1.0-fL)*(1.0-fL)*fL * C1[r][c]+
           3.0f * fL*fL*(1.0-fL) * C2[r][c];
}


#define BLOCKER_FILTER_SIZE    11
#define BFS   BLOCKER_FILTER_SIZE
#define BFS2 ( BLOCKER_FILTER_SIZE / 2 )
#define SUN_WIDTH g_fSunWidth


//================================================================
// This shader computes the contact hardening shadow filter.
//================================================================
float shadow( float3 tc )
{
    float  s   = 0.0f;
    float2 stc = ( g_vShadowMapDimensions.xy * tc.xy ) +
                 float2( 0.5, 0.5 );
    float2 tcs = floor( stc );
    float2 fc;
    int    row;
    int    col;
    float  w = 0.0;
    float  avgBlockerDepth = 0;
    float  blockerCount = 0;
    float  fRatio;
    float4 v1[ FS2 + 1 ];
    float2 v0[ FS2 + 1 ];
    float2 off;

    fc    = stc - tcs;
    tc.xy = tc - ( fc * g_vShadowMapDimensions.zw );

    // Find number of blockers and sum up blocker depth.
```

```
for( row = -BFS2; row <= BFS2; row += 2 )
{
    for( col = -BFS2; col <= BFS2; col += 2 )
    {
        float4 d4 = g_txShadowMap.GatherRed( g_SamplePoint ,
                        tc.xy, int2( col, row ) );
        float4 b4= ( tc.zzzz <= d4 ) ?
                        (0.0).xxxx : (1.0).xxxx;

        blockerCount += dot( b4, (1.0).xxxx );
        avgBlockerDepth += dot( d4, b4 );
    }
}

// Compute ratio using formulas from PCSS.
if( blockerCount > 0.0 )
{
    avgBlockerDepth /= blockerCount;
    fRatio = saturate( ( ( tc.z - avgBlockerDepth ) *
            SUN_WIDTH ) / avgBlockerDepth );
    fRatio *= fRatio;
}
else
{
    fRatio = 0.0;
}

// Sum up weights of dynamic filter matrix.
for( row = 0; row < FS; ++row )
{
    for( col = 0; col < FS; ++col )
    {
        w += Fw(row,col,fRatio);
    }
}

// Filter shadow map samples using the dynamic weights.
[unroll(FILTER_SIZE)]for( row = -FS2; row <= FS2; row += 2 )
{
    for( col = -FS2; col <= FS2; col += 2 )
    {
        v1[(col+FS2)/2] = g_txShadowMap.GatherCmpRed(
                        g_SamplePointCmp , tc.xy, tc.z,
                        int2( col, row ) );

            if( col == -FS2 )
            {
                s += ( 1 - fc.y ) * ( v1[0].w *
                    ( Fw(row+FS2,0,fRatio) -
                        Fw(row+FS2,0,fRatio) * fc.x ) + v1[0].z *
                    ( fc.x * ( Fw(row+FS2,0,fRatio) -
```

```
                         Fw(row+FS2,1,fRatio) ) +
                         Fw(row+FS2,1,fRatio) ) );
              s += (       fc.y ) * ( v1[0].x * (
                    Fw(row+FS2,0,fRatio) -
                    Fw(row+FS2,0,fRatio) * fc.x ) +
                    v1[0].y * ( fc.x*( Fw(row+FS2,0,fRatio) -
                    Fw(row+FS2,1,fRatio) ) +
                    Fw(row+FS2,1,fRatio) ) );
           if( row > -FS2 )
           {
              s += ( 1 - fc.y ) * ( v0[0].x *
                    ( Fw(row+FS2-1,0,fRatio) -
                      Fw(row+FS2-1,0,fRatio) * fc.x ) +
                    v0[0].y *
                    ( fc.x * ( Fw(row+FS2-1,0,fRatio) -
                      Fw(row+FS2-1,1,fRatio) ) +
                      Fw(row+FS2-1,1,fRatio) ) );
                 s += (       fc.y ) * ( v1[0].w *
                    ( Fw(row+FS2-1,0,fRatio) -
                      Fw(row+FS2-1,0,fRatio) * fc.x ) +
                    v1[0].z *
                    ( fc.x * ( Fw(row+FS2-1,0,fRatio) -
                      Fw(row+FS2-1,1,fRatio) ) +
                      Fw(row+FS2-1,1,fRatio) ) );
           }
        }
        else if( col == FS2 )
        {
           s += ( 1 - fc.y ) * ( v1[FS2].w * ( fc.x *
                 ( Fw(row+FS2,FS-2,fRatio) -
                   Fw(row+FS2,FS-1,fRatio) ) +
                   Fw(row+FS2,FS-1,fRatio) ) + v1[FS2].z * fc.x *
                   Fw(row+FS2,FS-1,fRatio) );
           s += (       fc.y ) * ( v1[FS2].x * ( fc.x *
                 ( Fw(row+FS2,FS-2,fRatio) -
                   Fw(row+FS2,FS-1,fRatio) ) +
                   Fw(row+FS2,FS-1,fRatio) ) + v1[FS2].y *
                   fc.x*
                   Fw(row+FS2,FS-1,fRatio) );
           if( row > -FS2 )
           {
              s += ( 1 - fc.y ) * ( v0[FS2].x * ( fc.x *
                    ( Fw(row+FS2-1,FS-2,fRatio) -
                      Fw(row+FS2-1,FS-1,fRatio) ) +
                      Fw(row+FS2-1,FS-1,fRatio) ) +
                      v0[FS2].y*fc.x * Fw(row+FS2-1,FS-1,fRatio) );
              s += (       fc.y ) * ( v1[FS2].w * ( fc.x *
                    ( Fw(row+FS2-1,FS-2,fRatio) -
                      Fw(row+FS2-1,FS-1,fRatio) ) +
                      Fw(row+FS2-1,FS-1,fRatio) ) +
                      v1[FS2].z*fc.x*Fw(row+FS2-1,FS-1,fRatio) );
```

```
                                }
                        }
                        else
                        {
                          s += ( 1 - fc.y ) * ( v1[(col+FS2)/2].w * ( fc.x *
                                ( Fw(row+FS2,col+FS2-1,fRatio) -
                                  Fw(row+FS2,col+FS2+0,fRatio) ) +
                                  Fw(row+FS2,col+FS2+0,fRatio) ) +
                                  v1[(col+FS2)/2].z * ( fc.x *
                                ( Fw(row+FS2,col+FS2-0,fRatio) -
                                  Fw(row+FS2,col+FS2+1,fRatio) ) +
                                  Fw(row+FS2,col+FS2+1,fRatio) ) );
                          s += (     fc.y ) * ( v1[(col+FS2)/2].x * ( fc.x *
                                ( Fw(row+FS2,col+FS2-1,fRatio) -
                                  Fw(row+FS2,col+FS2+0,fRatio) ) +
                                  Fw(row+FS2,col+FS2+0,fRatio) ) +
                                  v1[(col+FS2)/2].y * ( fc.x *
                                ( Fw(row+FS2,col+FS2-0,fRatio) -
                                  Fw(row+FS2,col+FS2+1,fRatio) ) +
                                  Fw(row+FS2,col+FS2+1,fRatio) ) );
                      if( row > -FS2 )
                      {
                        s += ( 1 - fc.y ) * ( v0[(col+FS2)/2].x * ( fc.x *
                              ( Fw(row+FS2-1,col+FS2-1,fRatio) -
                                Fw(row+FS2-1,col+FS2+0,fRatio) ) +
                                Fw(row+FS2-1,col+FS2+0,fRatio) ) +
                                v0[(col+FS2)/2].y * ( fc.x *
                              ( Fw(row+FS2-1,col+FS2-0,fRatio) -
                                Fw(row+FS2-1,col+FS2+1,fRatio) ) +
                                Fw(row+FS2-1,col+FS2+1,fRatio) ) );
                        s += (     fc.y ) * ( v1[(col+FS2)/2].w * ( fc.x *
                              ( Fw(row+FS2-1,col+FS2-1,fRatio) -
                                Fw(row+FS2-1,col+FS2+0,fRatio) ) +
                                Fw(row+FS2-1,col+FS2+0,fRatio) ) +
                                v1[(col+FS2)/2].z * ( fc.x *
                              ( Fw(row+FS2-1,col+FS2-0,fRatio) -
                                Fw(row+FS2-1,col+FS2+1,fRatio) ) +
                                Fw(row+FS2-1,col+FS2+1,fRatio) ) );
                      }
                    }

                  if( row != FS2 )
                  {
                    v0[(col+FS2)/2] = v1[(col+FS2)/2].xy;
                  }
                }
            }
        }
    return s/w;
}
```

Listing 1.4. Smooth contact hardening shadows using a dynamic filter matrix.

Bibliography

[Annen et al. 07] Thomas Annen, Tom Mertens, Philippe Bekaert, Hans-Peter Seidel, and Jan Kautz. "Convolution Shadow Maps." *Eurographics Symposium on Rendering* 18 (2007).

[Donnelly et al. 06] William Donnelly and Andrew Lauritzen. "Variance Shadow Maps." *SI3D '06: Proceedings of the 2006 Symposium on Interactive 3D Graphics and Games* (2006), 161–165.

[Dmitriev et al. 07] Kirill Dmitriev and Yury Uralsky. "Soft Shadows Using Hierarchical Min-Max Shadow Maps." Presented at Game Developers Conference, San Francisco, March 5–9, 2007. Available at http://developer.download .nvidia.com/presentations/2007/gdc/SoftShadows.pdf.

[Fernando 05] Randima Fernando. "Percentage-Closer Soft Shadows." *International Conference on Computer Graphics and Interactive Techniques* 35 (2005). Available at http://download.nvidia.com/developer/presentations/ 2005/GDC/Sponsored_Day/Percentage_Closer_Soft_Shadows.pdf.

[Gruen 07] Holger Grün. "Approximate Cumulative Distribution Function Shadow Mapping." In *ShaderX6 Advanced Rendering Techniques*, edited by Wolfgang Engel. Boston: Charles River Media, 2007, 239–256.

[Gumbau et al. 10] Jesus Gumbau, Miguel Chover, and Mateu Sbert. "Screen-Space Soft Shadows." In *GPUPro Advanced Rendering Techniques*, edited by Wolfgang Engel. Natick, MA: A K Peters, 2010.

[Soler et al. 98] C. Solor and F. Sillion,. "Fast Calculation of Soft Shadow Textures Using Convolution." *Computer Graphics (SIGGRAPH '98 Proceedings)* (1998): 321–32.

[Williams 78] Lance Williams. "Casting curved shadows on curved surfaces." *Computer Graphics (SIGGRAPH '78 Proceedings)* 12 (1978): 270–274.

Hybrid Min/Max Plane-Based Shadow Maps

Holger Gruen

2.1 Overview

This chapter presents how to derive a secondary texture from a normal depth-only shadow map. This secondary texture can be used to heavily speed up expensive shadow filtering with big filter footprints. It stores hybrid data in the form of either a plane equation or min/max depth for a two-dimensional block of pixels in the original shadow map. The technique is specifically suited to speeding up shadow filtering in the context of big filter footprint and forward rendering, e.g., when the shadow filtering cost increases with the depth complexity of the scene.

2.2 Introduction

Hierarchical min/max shadow maps [Dmitriev at al. 07] were introduced in order to quickly (hierarchically) reject or accept sub-blocks in a shadow filter footprint that are in full light or in full shadow. For these sub-blocks no additional expensive texture lookup or filtering operations are necessary and this helps to greatly increase the speed of filtering.

Walking the min/max shadow hierarchy does add to the texturing cost. Ideally the texture operations count for quick rejections should be as low as possible. Also min/max shadow maps tend to not always quickly reject pixel blocks for flat features like floor polygons. This is especially true if one pixel in the min/max shadow map maps to a quadrangle of on-screen pixels. To be quickly rejected, one of these on-screen pixels has to either be in front of the minimum depth or behind the maximum depth. Without a big depth bias and all its associated problems

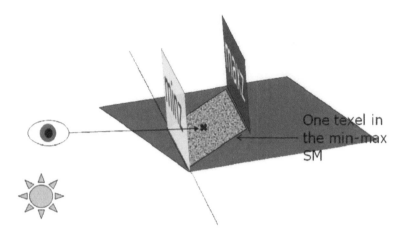

Figure 2.1. One min/max shadow map pixel (noisy quadrangle) can map to many on-screen pixels.

a pixel can usually only be rejected after a deep descent down the min/max hierarchy. This situation is depicted in Figure 2.1.

In order to remedy these shortcomings, this chapter first proposes flattening the min/max texture hierarchy from [Dmitriev at al. 07] to just one min/max texture T that contains the min/max depth data for a block of texels of the original shadow map. This block should be big enough to ideally allow for min/max rejections for all texels of the original shadow map that fall into the block with only one texture lookup.

To also get around losing the quick rejections for planar features, T is used to either store min/max depth data or a plane equation. The plane equation is stored if the block of shadow map pixels that is considered for constructing one min/max pixel lies within a plane. The plane equation allows to decide if a pixel is in front or behind a plane and does not suffer from the need for a high depth bias. Because T stores min/max depth or a plane equation it can be called a *hybrid min/max plane shadow map* (HPSM). A simple form of HPSM has been introduced in [Lobanchikov et al. 09].

The remainder of the text will discuss how to construct an HPSM, how to use the HPSM to quickly reject expensive filter operations, and other uses for HPSMs.

2.3   Construction of an HPSM

If one wants to construct an HPSM from a shadow map, the first thing to decide is what dimension to chose for the HPSM. A typical choice could be to make it 1/4 of the width and 1/4 of the height of the original shadow map.

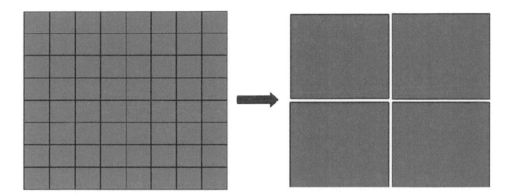

Figure 2.2. A shadow map (left) is converted into an HPSM that is 1/16 the size of the shadow map.

This means that a naive algorithm to construct the HPSM is to just collapse 4×4 texels of the shadow map into one pixel of the HPSM (see Figure 2.2).

Unfortunately, since the filter footprint of a shadow filter can also touch neighboring pixels this may not be enough to construct the most efficient HPSM for quickly rejecting pixels as fully lit or fully shadowed. Figure 2.3 shows that with a naive construction method several texture fetches are necessary to get the data for all HPSM texels that touch the shadow map filter.

The target is to get down to only one texture fetch for quick rejections. One solution to reach that target is to not only look at a 4×4 block of texels but extend this block on all sides (top, bottom, left and right) by half of the size of the shadow filtering kernel as depicted in Figure 2.4.

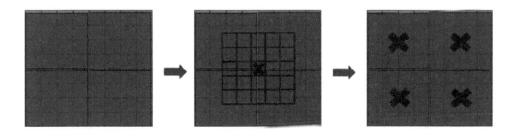

Figure 2.3. A shadow map (left) is converted into an HPSM. The filter footprint of the shadow filter touches more than just one HPSM texel (middle). Instead it can touch four or more neighboring HPSM texels (right).

Figure 2.4. One of the HPSM pixels covering 4×4 shadow pixels is highlighted (left). Extending the box from 4×4 to 10×10 (middle) makes sure that the shadow filter footprint always stays inside the support of the HPSM pixel (right).

It is obvious that one needs to consider quite a lot of shadow map texels to create an HPSM that can reject pixels with only one texture instruction. This can make HPSM construction expensive if only Shader Model 4.0 instructions are available. Direct3D 10.1 and Direct3D 11 support the `Gather()` instruction, which can speed up HPSM instruction enormously since one texture instruction can get four depth values from the shadow map. Further, using Compute Shaders under Direct3D 11 allows facilitating the thread shared memory that significantly speeds up HPSM construction for overlapping construction kernels.

Computing min/max depth of a box of pixels is trivial. How about detecting a plane equation? One way to do this is to convert each shadow map depth value of the construction texel block back to linear a three-dimensional space, e.g., light view camera space:

$$
\begin{aligned}
Q &= \frac{Z_f}{Z_f - Z_n}, w = \cot\left(\frac{\text{fov}_w}{2}\right), h = \cot\left(\frac{\text{fov}_h}{2}\right). \\
Z_{\text{cam}} &= \frac{-Q \cdot Z_n}{Z_{\text{sm}} - Q}.
\end{aligned}
\tag{2.1}
$$

Equation (2.1) shows how to convert from shadow map depth (Z_{sm}) back to linear light space depth Z_{cam} for a perspective light view used to draw the shadow map. Listing 2.1 now presents a shader function that converts a depth value from the shadow map back to a three-dimensional light space point.

Given Listing 2.1, the pixel shader code for creating an HPSM is presented in Listing 2.2. Please note that the length of the three-dimensional vector stored in the yzw part of the HPSM encodes if an HPSM pixels stores a plane or just min/max depth.

```
// Convert from camera space depth to light space 3d.
// f2ShadowMapCoord is the shadow map texture coordinate for
// fDepth.
float3 GetCameraXYZFromSMDepth(float fDepth,
                               float2 f2ShadowMapCoord )
{
  float3 f3CameraPos;

  // Compute camera Z: see Equation 2.1.
  f3CameraPos.z = -g_fQTimesZNear / ( fDepth - g_fQ );

  // Convert screen coords to projection space XY.
  f3CameraPos.xy = (f2ShadowMapCoord * g_f2ShadowMapSize ) -
                   float2( 1.0f, 1.0f );

  // Compute camera X.
  f3CameraPos.x = g_fTanH * f3CameraPos.x * f3CameraPos.z;

  // Compute camera Y.
  f3CameraPos.y = - g_fTanV * f3CameraPos.y * f3CameraPos.z;

  return f3CameraPos;
}
```

Listing 2.1. A function to convert from shadow map depth to a linear camera space three-dimensional point.

```
float4 main(float4 pos2d : SV_POSITION ) : SV_Target
{
  float2 tc      = pos2d.xy / (g_f2ShadowMapSize / 4 );
  float4 f4MinD = ( 10000.0).xxxx;
  float4 f4MaxD = (-10000.0).xxxx;
  float  fPlane = 1.0f;

  // Call function to gather four depth values from
  // the shadow map: for a Shader Model > 4.0
  // Gather() can be used; otherwise four point samples
  // need to be used.
  float4 f4D  = gather_depth( tc, int2( 0, 0 ) );
  float3 f3P0 = GetCameraXYZFromSMDepth(f4D.x, tc +
               float2( 0,1 ) * 1.0f / g_f2ShadowMapSize );
  float3 f3P1 = GetCameraXYZFromSMDepth(f4D.y, tc +
               float2( 1,1 ) * 1.0f / g_f2ShadowMapSize );
  float3 f3P2 = GetCameraXYZFromSMDepth(f4D.y, tc +
               float2( 1,0 ) * 1.0f / g_f2ShadowMapSize );

  float3 f3N0 = normalize( fP0 - fP1 );
  float3 f3N1 = normalize( fP0 - fP2 );

  // Construct plane normal at central point.
```

```
float3 f3N = cross( fN0, fN1 );

for( int row  = -SHADOW_FILTER_WIDTH/2;
         row  < 4 + SHADOW_FILTER_WIDTH/2;
         row += 2 )
{
  for( int col  = -SHADOW_FILTER_WIDTH/2;
           col  < 4 + SHADOW_FILTER_WIDTH/2;
           col += 2 )
  {
    // Gather four depth values from the shadow map.
    float4 f4D = gather_depth( tc, int2( row, col ) );

    // Min/max construction
    f4MinD = min( f4D, f4MinD );
    f4MaxD = max( f4D, f4MinD );

    // Look at each cam space point.
    float3 f3P = GetCameraXYZFromSMDepth(f4D.x, tc +
                ( float2( 0,1 ) * float2 ( row, col ) ) *
                1.0f / g_f2ShadowMapSize );

    // EPS is the maximum allowed distance from the plane
    // defined by f3P and f3N.
fPlane *= abs( dot( f3P - f3P0, f3N ) ) < EPS ?
                1.0f : 0.0f;

  }
}

// If this is a plane
if( fPlane != 0.0f )
{
  // res.x = distance of plane from origin.
  // res.yzw is normalized normal of plane.
  return float4( length( f3P0 ), f3N );
}
else
{
  // Make sure that length(yzw) is bigger than 1
  return float4( min( min( f4MinD.x, f4MinD.y ),
                      min( f4MinD.z, f4MinD.w ) ),
                 max( max( f4MaxD.x, f4MaxD.y ),
                      max( f4MaxD.z, f4MaxD.w ) ),
                 100.0f, 100.0f );
}
}
```

Listing 2.2. A pixel shader that constructs an HPSM from a normal shadow map.

2.4 Using an HPSM

Having constructed an HPSM, using it is straightforward and demonstrated by
the shader snippet in Listing 2.3.

```
// LSP is the light space position of the current pixel;
// tc.xy is the shadow map texture coordinate for the current
// pixel; tc.z is light space depth of the pixel.
// It is assumed that any necessary depth bias (e.g., to
// deal with the EPS for plane construction) has already been
// add to tc.z.
float shadow(float3 LSP, float3 tc, inout float fLight )
{
  float4 f4HPMS          = g_txHPSM.SampleLevel( s_point, tc.xy,
                                                 0 );
  float  fLenSqrNormal = dot( f4HPMS.yzw, f4HPMS.yzw );
  float  fReject = false;

  // Min/max
  if( fLenSqrNormal > 1.1 )
  {
    float fMin = f4HPMS.x;
    float fMax = f4HPMS.y;

    if( tc.z < fMin )
      fLight = 1.0f;
    else if( tc.z > fMax )
      fLight = 0.0f;
    else // call expensive filter
      fLight = filter_shadow( tc );
  }
  else // Plane
  {
    float3 f3P  = f4HPMS.x * f4HPMS.yzw;
    float fDist = dot( f3P - LSP, f4HPMS.yzw );

    if( fDist <= -EPS )
      fLight = 0.0f;
    else // Full light
      fLight = 1.0f;
  }
}
```

Listing 2.3. A pixel shader that uses the HPSM to reject pixels that are in full light or
in full shadow.

2.5   Other Uses for the HPSM

As pointed out in [Lobanchikov et al. 09], HPSM can be used to accelerate all sort of shadow map queries. [Lobanchikov et al. 09] uses a simple form HPSMs to accelerate not only normal shadow filtering but also the rendering of sun shafts. Basically, the shader in question integrates light along a ray from the scene towards the eye. For each point on the ray four PCF shadow map samples are necessary to generate smooth looking sun shafts. Using an HPSM to quickly reject points on a sun shaft ray generates a speedup of $\sim$12% at a resolution of 1600×1200 on an AMD HD4870 GPU versus doing all four PCF samples for every point on the ray.

Bibliography

[Dmitriev et al. 07] Kirill Dmitriev and Yury Uralsky. "Soft Shadows Using Hierarchical Min-Max Shadow Maps." Presented at Game Developers Conference, San Francisco, March 5–9, 2007. Available at http://developer.download .nvidia.com/presentations/2007/gdc/SoftShadows.pdf

[Lobanchikov et al. 09] I. Lobanchikov and H. Gruen, "Stalker: Clear Sky—A Showcase for Direct3D 10.0/1." Presented at Game Developers Conference, San Francisco, March 23–27, 2009. Available at http://www.gdconf.com/ conference/Tutorial.

Shadow Mapping for Omnidirectional Light Using Tetrahedron Mapping

Hung-Chien Liao

Shadow mapping is a popular method of rendering shadows for a three-dimensional scene. William's original Z-buffer shadow mapping algorithm [Williams 78] is for directional light. We need a different method to approach an omnidirectional light. There are two popular ways to approach omnidirectional light: one is cube mapping [Voorhies and Foran 94] and the other is dual-paraboloid mapping [Heidrich and Seidel 98]. In this paper I present a new shadow mapping technique for omnidirectional lights using tetrahedron mapping.

3.1 Shadow Mapping

The traditional Z-buffer shadow mapping algorithm [Williams 78] consists of two steps. In a first step from the point of view of the camera, the scene is rendered into a shadow map. The shadow map holds then the nearest depth value. In the second step, when the scene is rendered from the point of view of the player camera, the pixels are transformed to light space and compared to the depth values in the shadow map. If the current pixel depth value is larger than the shadow map depth value, then the current pixel is shadowed.

3.2 Tetrahedron Shadow Mapping

A *tetrahedron* is made by four equilateral triangular faces, as depicted in Figure 3.1.

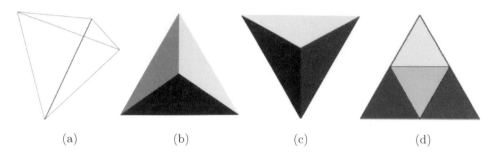

Figure 3.1. (a) Tetrahedron in a wire frame; (b) solid tetrahedron; (c) solid tetrahedron at a different angle; (d) unwrapped tetrahedron.

There are two main steps. The first is to use tetrahedron mapping to render all objects from the omnidirectional light position to each tetrahedron face and to store the nearest depth value into a two-dimensional texture. The second is to render the scene normally from the player's point of view. During the second step we transform the pixel into the correct light face space to get the depth value and a two-dimensional texture coordinate. Then we use the texture coordinate data to fetch the depth value and compare it with the current pixel depth value.

3.2.1　Step One: Generating Tetrahedron Shadow Map

There are four equilateral triangular faces in a tetrahedron. Consequently, from the center of the tetrahedron to each of its faces, we can get four different frustums that each contain an equilateral triangular face. As shown in Figure 3.2, we use the specific orientation of the tetrahedron in a local light space to generate tetrahedron shadow mapping. We can use any orientation of the tetrahedron to do the same thing, and I will explain why we use this specific orientation of the tetrahedron.

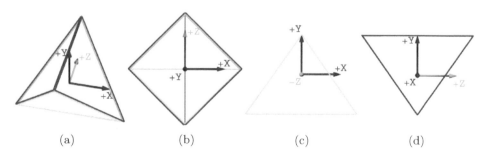

Figure 3.2. The center of tetrahedron is at the origin of the local light space: (a) perspective view; (b) top view; (c) front view; (d) right view.

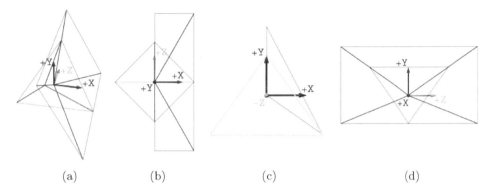

Figure 3.3. (a) Perspective view; (b) top view; (c) front view; (d) right view.

Figure 3.3 is a frustum made from the center of a tetrahedron to the red face and contains the whole red face.

We need to calculate the frustum field of view in the y- and x-directions, as depicted in Figure 3.4.

For the field of view in the y-direction, as depicted in Figure 3.5, Segment C is the distance from the origin to each vertex of the tetrahedron, and each Segment C is the same. Therefore angle α and angle β are the same, too.

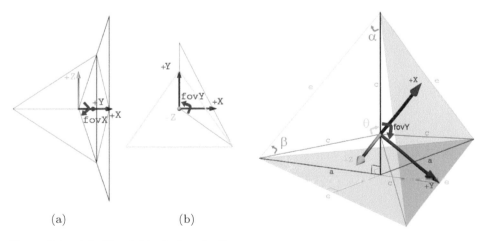

Figure 3.4. (a) The field of view in the x-direction; (b) the field of view in the y-direction.

Figure 3.5. Field of view in the y-direction.

We can compute

$$a = \frac{\left(\frac{e}{2}\right)}{\cos 30°},$$

$$\frac{a}{e} = \sin \alpha.$$

From these two equations we can get:

$$\angle a = \sin^{-1} \frac{1}{2 \times \cos 30°},$$

$$\angle \theta = 180° - 2 \times a.$$

From angle α and β we can get

$$\text{fov}Y = \frac{360° - \theta}{2} = 90° + \alpha \approx 125.26438968°.$$

Then, for the field of view in the x-direction (see Figure 3.6):

$$\frac{\left(\frac{e}{2}\right)}{d} = \tan \frac{\theta}{2}.$$

Therefore,

$$\frac{e}{2} = d \times \tan \frac{\theta}{2};$$

$$\frac{f}{d} = \cos \frac{\text{fov}Y}{2}.$$

Therefore,

$$f = d \times \cos \frac{\text{fov}Y}{2};$$

$$\frac{\left(\frac{e}{2}\right)}{f} = \tan \frac{\text{fov}X}{2}.$$

From these three equations we can get

$$\text{fov}X = 2 \times \tan^{-1} \left(\frac{\left(\frac{e}{2}\right)}{f} \right)$$

$$= 2 \times \tan^{-1} \left(\frac{d \times \tan \frac{\theta}{2}}{d \times \cos \frac{\text{fov}Y}{2}} \right)$$

$$\approx 143.98570868°.$$

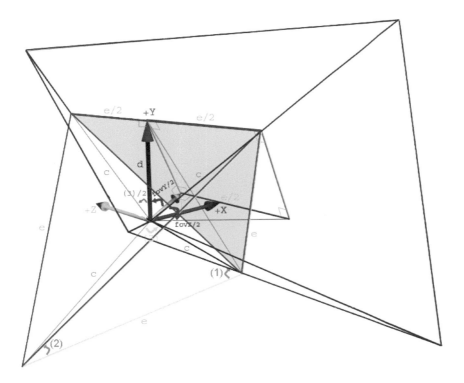

Figure 3.6. The field of view in the X direction.

After we get the field of view in the x- and y-directions, we can then create the frustum perspective matrix. We need to know how big the angle is between the +X-axis and the frustum direction for calculating the view matrix. The angle between +X and frustum direction $= 90° - (fovY/2) \approx 27.36780516°$. In Figure 3.7 you can see four different frustums that contain each equilateral triangular face.

The following is the procedure code for generating a tetrahedron shadow map:

1. Make a two-dimensional render target texture for a tetrahedron shadow map.

2. Set the tetrahedron shadow map as the render target.

3. Set up the field of view of the light face perspective matrix as $143.98570868°$ in the x-axis and $125.26438968°$ in the y-axis.

4. For the green face:

   (a) Set up the screen view port, from zero to half the width of the tetrahedron shadow map in the x-axis, and from zero to half height of the tetrahedron shadow map in the y-axis.

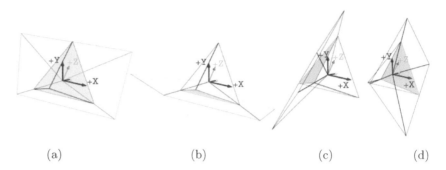

(a)   (b)   (c)   (d)

Figure 3.7. Four frustums that cover all tetrahedron faces: (a) green face; (b) yellow face; (c) blue face; (d) red face.

(b) Set up the local light view matrix so it corresponds to the green face, from the origin of the local light space to Roll 0.0°, Pitch 27.36780516°, and Yaw 0.0°.

(c) Render all shadow casting objects that correspond to the green face within light range and store depth value into the tetrahedron shadow map.

5. For the yellow face:

(a) Set up the screen view port, from half the width of the tetrahedron shadow map to one width of the tetrahedron shadow map in the x-axis, and from 0 to half the height of the tetrahedron shadow map in the y-axis.

(b) Set up the local light view matrix so it corresponds to the yellow face, from the origin of the local light space to Roll 0.0°, Pitch 27.36780516°, and Yaw 180.0°.

(c) Render all shadow casting objects that correspond to the yellow face within light range and store depth value into the tetrahedron shadow map.

6. For the blue face:

(a) Set up the screen view port, from 0 to half the width of the tetrahedron shadow map in the x-axis, and from half the height of the tetrahedron shadow map to one height of the tetrahedron shadow map in the y-axis.

(b) Set up the local light view matrix so that it corresponds to the blue face, from the origin of the local light space to Roll 0.0°, Pitch $-27.36780516°$, and Yaw $-90.0°$.

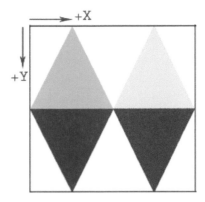

Figure 3.8. Tetrahedron shadow map.

    (c) Render all shadow casting objects that correspond to the blue face within light range and store depth value into the tetrahedron shadow map.

7. For the red face:

    (a) Set up the screen view port, from half the width of the tetrahedron shadow map to one width of the tetrahedron shadow map in the x-axis, and from half the height of the tetrahedron shadow map to one height of the tetrahedron shadow map in the y-axis.

    (b) Set up the local light view matrix so that it corresponds to the red face, from the origin of the local light space to Roll $0.0°$, Pitch $-27.36780516°$, and Yaw $90.0°$.

    (c) Render all shadow casting objects that correspond to the red face within light range and store depth value into the tetrahedron shadow map.

After the above steps, you should get a tetrahedron shadow map with depth value, which may look like Figure 3.8.

3.2.2 Step Two: Render the Scene

After we are done rendering the shadow casting object and get the tetrahedron shadow map, it is time to use it. First, we need to combine view, perspective, and texture scale matrix for each face:

$$\text{Offset}X = 0.5/\text{TetrahedronShadowMapWidth},$$
$$\text{Offset}Y = 0.5/\text{TetrahedronShadowMapHeight};$$

GreenfaceViewPerspectiveTexMatrix

$\qquad$ = GreenfaceViewMatrix × LightfacePerspectiveMatrix

$$\times \begin{bmatrix} 0.25 & 0.0 & 0.0 & 0.0 \\ 0.0 & -0.25 & 0.0 & 0.0 \\ 0.0 & 0.0 & 1.0 & 0.0 \\ 0.25 + \text{Offset}X & 0.25 + \text{Offset}Y & 0.0 & 1.0 \end{bmatrix},$$

YellowfaceViewPerspectiveTexMatrix

$\qquad$ = YellowfaceViewMatrix × LightfacePerspectiveMatrix

$$\times \begin{bmatrix} 0.25 & 0.0 & 0.0 & 0.0 \\ 0.0 & -0.25 & 0.0 & 0.0 \\ 0.0 & 0.0 & 1.0 & 0.0 \\ 0.75 + \text{Offset}X & 0.25 + \text{Offset}Y & 0.0 & 1.0 \end{bmatrix},$$

BluefaceViewPerspectiveTexMatrix

$\qquad$ = BluefaceViewMatrix × LightfacePerspectiveMatrix

$$\times \begin{bmatrix} 0.25 & 0.0 & 0.0 & 0.0 \\ 0.0 & -0.25 & 0.0 & 0.0 \\ 0.0 & 0.0 & 1.0 & 0.0 \\ 0.25 + \text{Offset}X & 0.75 + \text{Offset}Y & 0.0 & 1.0 \end{bmatrix},$$

RedfaceViewPerspectiveTexMatrix

$\qquad$ = RedfaceViewMatrix × LightfacePerspectiveMatrix

$$\times \begin{bmatrix} 0.25 & 0.0 & 0.0 & 0.0 \\ 0.0 & -0.25 & 0.0 & 0.0 \\ 0.0 & 0.0 & 1.0 & 0.0 \\ 0.75 + \text{Offset}X & 0.75 + \text{Offset}Y & 0.0 & 1.0 \end{bmatrix}.$$

Second, we can get four center face vectors, one from the center of each tetrahedron, as shown in Figure 3.9. These center vectors are different than the vector of each face view matrix. The green face center vector is $(0.0, -0.57735026, 0.81649661)$; the yellow face center vector is $(0.0, -0.57735026, -0.81649661)$; the blue face center vector is $(-0.81649661, 0.57735026, 0.0)$; and the red face center vector is $(0.81649661, 0.57735026, 0.0)$.

Third, we want to know the corresponding tetrahedron shadow map coordinate given a vertex in local light space. In pseudocode, this looks like Listing 3.1.

Finally, `vResult.x` and `vResult.y` is the (x, y) texture coordinate on the tetrahedron shadow map. We use this texture coordinate to fetch the depth value on the tetrahedron shadow map and compare it with `vResult.z`. If `vResult.z` is bigger this vertex is shadowed; otherwise this vertex is lit.

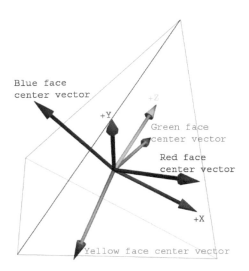

Figure 3.9. Four face center vectors.

```
vector4 vPosition (x, y, z, 1.0);
vector4 vResult;
float g = dot product(vPosition.xyz, green face center vector);
float y = dot product(vPosition.xyz, yellow face center vector);
float b = dot product(vPosition.xyz, blue face center vector);
float r = dot product (vPosition.xyz, red face center vector);
float maximum = max ( max (g, y), max (b, r) );
if (maximum == g)
    vResult = vPosition * green face ViewPerspectiveTexMatrix;
else if (maximum == y)
    vResult = vPosition * yellow face ViewPerspectiveTexMatrix;
else if (maximum == b)
    vResult = vPosition * blue face ViewPerspectiveTexMatrix;
else
    vResult = vPosition * red face ViewPerspectiveTexMatrix;
vResult.x = vResult.x / vResult.w;
vResult.y = vResult.y / vResult.w;
vResult.z = vResult.z / vResult.w;
```

Listing 3.1. Calculate vertex texture coordinate on tetrahedron shadow map and vertex depth to the light.

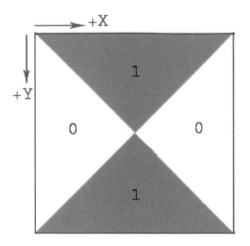

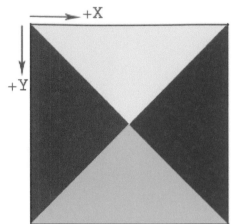

Figure 3.10. Stencil buffer.

Figure 3.11. Tetrahedron shadow map with stencil buffer.

3.3   Optimization

There are some optimizations we can do to further improve tetrahedron mapping. One is using a stencil buffer to improve the quality of the tetrahedron shadow map. In Figure 3.8, we only use half of a tetrahedron shadow map to store the depth value. In order to use a full tetrahedron shadow map to store the depth value, we need to use a stencil buffer. First, we need to initialize the stencil buffer (as shown in Figure 3.10) when we create a depth buffer and stencil buffer. We initialize the gray area to be one, and other area remains zero.

Remember, we do not modify the stencil buffer after we initialize it. After that, we need to roll the view matrix and use a different screen view port when we generate the tetrahedron shadow map. Then we can generate a tetrahedron shadow map like Figure 3.11. In this way, we can use the full tetrahedron shadow map and lose just a little performance.

Another way to optimize is using frustum culling when generating a tetrahedron shadow map for each face. But it is slightly different than the original frustum culling because for each face we project the depth value into a triangle, not a quad. I will use the green face as an example here. First, we test to see if the shadow caster is inside the lighting range or not. Then we use the origin with every two vertices of the green face to generate three planes. After that, we use a plane to a bounding sphere or bounding box collision detection to see if the shadow caster will project into the green face or not. This way we can also reduce the number of draw calls.

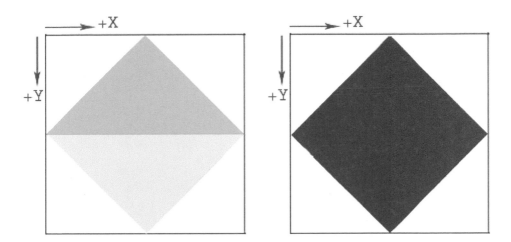

Figure 3.12. Texture Coordinate Group 1.   Figure 3.13. Texture Coordinate Group 2.

3.4 Lookup Map

The hardware does not support sampling from a tetrahedron map, but a cube map does. Therefore, we can create a lookup texture by projecting a tetrahedron map into a cube map in order to save some instructions. But it is difficult to linear sample between tetrahedron face boundaries from the lookup cube map. In order to solve this problem, we need to project into two separate sets of texture coordinates as in Figures 3.12 and 3.13.

In Texture Coordinate Group 1, the texture coordinate can be linear sampled correctly between the green and yellow face. It is the same with Group 2. Listing 3.2 shows the actual functions to create the lookup map by using C++ and DirectX 9.

```
void ConvertToViewMatrix(D3DXMATRIX& mOutView,
                         const D3DXMATRIX& mIn)
{
    D3DXMATRIX mTemp(mIn);
    // Right vector for view matrix
    mOutView.m[0][0] = mTemp.m[0][0];
    mOutView.m[1][0] = mTemp.m[0][1];
    mOutView.m[2][0] = mTemp.m[0][2];
    // Up vector for view matrix
    mOutView.m[0][1] = mTemp.m[1][0];
    mOutView.m[1][1] = mTemp.m[1][1];
    mOutView.m[2][1] = mTemp.m[1][2];
    // Look at vector for view matrix
    mOutView.m[0][2] = mTemp.m[2][0];
    mOutView.m[1][2] = mTemp.m[2][1];
```

```
    mOutView.m[2][2] = mTemp.m[2][2];
    // Position for view matrix
    mOutView.m[3][0] = -D3DXVec3Dot( (D3DXVECTOR3 *)mTemp.m[0],
        (D3DXVECTOR3 *)mTemp.m[3] );
    mOutView.m[3][1] = -D3DXVec3Dot( (D3DXVECTOR3 *)mTemp.m[1],
        (D3DXVECTOR3 *)mTemp.m[3] );
    mOutView.m[3][2] = -D3DXVec3Dot( (D3DXVECTOR3 *)mTemp.m[2],
        (D3DXVECTOR3 *)mTemp.m[3] );

    mOutView.m[0][3] = 0.0f;
    mOutView.m[1][3] = 0.0f;
    mOutView.m[2][3] = 0.0f;
    mOutView.m[3][3] = 1.0f;
}

void CreateCubeToTSMCoord(LPDIRECT3DDEVICE9 lpD3DDevice)
{
    const float TSMFaceFOVX = 143.985709f;
    const float TSMFaceFOVY = 125.264389f;
    const float TSMFaceFOVXR = D3DXToRadian(TSMFaceFOVX);
    const float TSMFaceFOVYR = D3DXToRadian(TSMFaceFOVY);
    D3DXMATRIX mTSMFaceViewProj0, mTSMFaceViewProj1,
        mTSMFaceViewProj2, mTSMFaceViewProj3;

    D3DXMATRIX mTexScaleBias(0.5f, 0.0f, 0.0f, 0.0f,
                             0.0f, -0.25f, 0.0f, 0.0f,
                             0.0f, 0.0f, 1.0f, 0.0f,
                             0.5f, 0.25f, 0.0f, 1.0f);

    D3DXMATRIX mLightProjVert, mLightProjHorz;
    D3DXMATRIX mLightView;
    // Calculate all four face direction light-view-projection
    //   matrix for Tetrahedron.
    D3DXMatrixPerspectiveFovLH(&mLightProjHorz, TSMFaceFOVYR,
        tanf(TSMFaceFOVXR * 0.5f) / tanf(TSMFaceFOVYR * 0.5f),
        0.1f, 1000.0f);
    D3DXMatrixPerspectiveFovLH(&mLightProjVert, TSMFaceFOVXR,
        tanf(TSMFaceFOVYR * 0.5f) / tanf(TSMFaceFOVXR * 0.5f),
        0.1f, 1000.0f);

    // ...Calculate the first face light-view-projection matrix.
    D3DXMatrixRotationYawPitchRoll(&mLightView, 0.0f,
        D3DXToRadian(27.3678055f), 0.0f);
    ConvertToViewMatrix(mTSMFaceViewProj0, mLightView);
    D3DXMatrixMultiply(&mTSMFaceViewProj0, &mTSMFaceViewProj0,
        &mLightProjHorz);
    D3DXMatrixMultiply(&mTSMFaceViewProj0, &mTSMFaceViewProj0,
    &mTexScaleBias);
    // ...Calculate the second face light-view-projection matrix.
    D3DXMatrixRotationYawPitchRoll(&mLightView, D3DX_PI,
        D3DXToRadian(27.3678055f), D3DX_PI);
```

```
ConvertToViewMatrix(mTSMFaceViewProj1 , mLightView );
D3DXMatrixMultiply(&mTSMFaceViewProj1 , &mTSMFaceViewProj1 ,
    &mLightProjHorz );
mTexScaleBias.m[3][1] = 0.75f;
D3DXMatrixMultiply(&mTSMFaceViewProj1 , &mTSMFaceViewProj1 ,
    &mTexScaleBias );
// ...Calculate the third face light -view-projection matrix.
D3DXMatrixRotationYawPitchRoll(&mLightView , -D3DX_PI * 0.5f,
    -D3DXToRadian(27.3678055f), D3DX_PI * 0.5f);
ConvertToViewMatrix(mTSMFaceViewProj2 , mLightView );
D3DXMatrixMultiply(&mTSMFaceViewProj2 , &mTSMFaceViewProj2 ,
    &mLightProjVert );
mTexScaleBias.m[0][0] = 0.25f;
mTexScaleBias.m[1][1] = -0.5f;
mTexScaleBias.m[3][0] = 0.25f;
mTexScaleBias.m[3][1] = 0.5f;
D3DXMatrixMultiply(&mTSMFaceViewProj2 , &mTSMFaceViewProj2 ,
    &mTexScaleBias );
// ...Calculate the fourth face light -view-projection matrix.
D3DXMatrixRotationYawPitchRoll(&mLightView , D3DX_PI * 0.5f,
    -D3DXToRadian(27.3678055f), -D3DX_PI * 0.5f);
ConvertToViewMatrix(mTSMFaceViewProj3 , mLightView );
D3DXMatrixMultiply(&mTSMFaceViewProj3 , &mTSMFaceViewProj3 ,
    &mLightProjVert );
mTexScaleBias.m[3][0] = 0.75f;
D3DXMatrixMultiply(&mTSMFaceViewProj3 , &mTSMFaceViewProj3 ,
    &mTexScaleBias );

LPDIRECT3DCUBETEXTURE9 lpCubeToTSM = NULL;
const int CUBE_SIZE = 128;
lpD3DDevice ->CreateCubeTexture(CUBE_SIZE , 1, 0,
    D3DFMT_A16B16G16R16F , D3DPOOL_SYSTEMMEM , &lpCubeToTSM ,
    NULL);
D3DLOCKED_RECT data;
D3DXVECTOR4 vVertexPos ;
for (int iFace = 0; iFace < 6; ++iFace)
{
    lpCubeToTSM ->LockRect((D3DCUBEMAP_FACES)iFace , 0, &data,
        NULL, 0);
    LPBYTE lpBits = (LPBYTE)data.pBits;
    for (float fCoordY = CUBE_SIZE * -0.5f + 0.5f;
        fCoordY < CUBE_SIZE * 0.5f; ++fCoordY)
    {
        D3DXFLOAT16 *pTexels = (D3DXFLOAT16 *)lpBits;
        lpBits += data.Pitch;

        for (float fCoordX = CUBE_SIZE * -0.5f + 0.5f;
            fCoordX < CUBE_SIZE * 0.5f;
            ++fCoordX , pTexels += 4)
        {
            switch(iFace)
```

```
{
case D3DCUBEMAP_FACE_POSITIVE_X:
    vVertexPos = D3DXVECTOR4(CUBE_SIZE * 0.5f -
        0.5f, -fCoordY, -fCoordX, 1.0f);
    break;
case D3DCUBEMAP_FACE_NEGATIVE_X:
    vVertexPos = D3DXVECTOR4(CUBE_SIZE * -0.5f +
        0.5f, -fCoordY, fCoordX, 1.0f);
    break;
case D3DCUBEMAP_FACE_POSITIVE_Y:
    vVertexPos = D3DXVECTOR4(fCoordX,
        CUBE_SIZE * 0.5f - 0.5f, fCoordY, 1.0f);
    break;
case D3DCUBEMAP_FACE_NEGATIVE_Y:
    vVertexPos = D3DXVECTOR4(fCoordX,
        CUBE_SIZE * -0.5f + 0.5f, -fCoordY,
        1.0f);
    break;
case D3DCUBEMAP_FACE_POSITIVE_Z:
    vVertexPos = D3DXVECTOR4(fCoordX, -fCoordY,
        CUBE_SIZE * 0.5f - 0.5f, 1.0f);
    break;
case D3DCUBEMAP_FACE_NEGATIVE_Z:
    vVertexPos = D3DXVECTOR4(-fCoordX, -fCoordY,
        CUBE_SIZE * -0.5f + 0.5f, 1.0f);
    break;
}
D3DXVECTOR4 vResult1, vResult2;
// In group 1, we only need to differentiate
//   face 1 and 2.
if (vVertexPos.z > 0.0f)
{
    D3DXVec4Transform(&vResult1, &vVertexPos,
        &mTSMFaceViewProj0);
}
else
{
    D3DXVec4Transform(&vResult1, &vVertexPos,
        &mTSMFaceViewProj1);
}
// In group 2, we only need to differentiate
//   face 3 and 4.
if (vVertexPos.x > 0.0f)
{
    D3DXVec4Transform(&vResult2, &vVertexPos,
        &mTSMFaceViewProj3);
}
else
{
    D3DXVec4Transform(&vResult2, &vVertexPos,
        &mTSMFaceViewProj2);
```

```
                  }
                  vResult1.x /= vResult1.w;
                  vResult1.y /= vResult1.w;
                  vResult2.x /= vResult2.w;
                  vResult2.y /= vResult2.w;
                  // Save group 1 texture coordinate info in Red
                  //  and Green channel.
                  D3DXFloat32To16Array(&pTexels[0],
                      &vResult1.x, 1);
                  D3DXFloat32To16Array(&pTexels[1],
                      &vResult1.y, 1);
                  // Save group 2 texture coordinate info in Blue
                  //  and Alpha channel.
                  D3DXFloat32To16Array(&pTexels[2],
                      &vResult2.x, 1);
                  D3DXFloat32To16Array(&pTexels[3],
                      &vResult2.y, 1);
              }
          }
          lpCubeToTSM->UnlockRect((D3DCUBEMAP_FACES)iFace, 0);
      }
      D3DXSaveTextureToFile("Textures/CubeToTSMCoord2.dds",
          D3DXIFF_DDS, lpCubeToTSM, NULL);
      SAFE_RELEASE(lpCubeToTSM);
}
```

Listing 3.2. Create lookup map.

After we create the lookup map, we can move forward to use it. Because of the way we align the tetrahedron map, we can calculate the current rendering pixel depth if we are using hardware shadow (see the pseudocode in Listing 3.3).

We can calculate the shadow map coordinate by using the lookup map (see the pseudocode in Listing 3.4).

```
vector3 vPosition (x, y, z);
vector3 vAbsPosition = abs(vPosition);
vector4 vTestPosition(vAbsPosition.x, vPosition.y,
    vAbsPosition.z, 1.0f);
vector4 vResult;
float g = dot product (vTestPosition, green face center vector);
float r = dot product (vTestPosition, red face center vector);
if (g > r)
    vResult=vTestPosition * green face ViewPerspectiveTexMatrix;
else
    vResult = vTestPosition * red face ViewPerspectiveTexMatrix;
vResult.z = vResult.z / vResult.w;
```

Listing 3.3. Rendering pixel depth from the light.

```
vector3 vPosition (x, y, z);
vector3 vAbsPosition = abs(vPosition);
vector4 vTestPosition(vAbsPosition.x, vPosition.y,
    vAbsPosition.z, 1.0f);
vector2 vShadowMapCoord;
float g = dot product (vTestPosition, green face center vector);
float r = dot product (vTestPosition, red face center vector);
if (g > r)
{
    vShadowMapCoord = texCUBE(LookupMap, vPosition).xy;
    vShadowMapCoord.y += 0.5f;
}
else
{
    vShadowMapCoord = texCUBE(LookupMap, vPosition).zw;
    vShadowMapCoord.x += 0.5f;
}
```

Listing 3.4. Rendering pixel texture coordinate on tetrahedron shadow map.

3.5   Conclusion

Table 3.1 is a comparison of dual-paraboloid mapping, cube mapping, and tetrahedron mapping.

Tetrahedron mapping can be used not only on shadow maps but also on environment maps. Prior to the development of tetrahedron mapping, one had to create an extra cube texture or one more two-dimensional texture for an omnidirectional shadow map. Thanks to tetrahedron mapping, one can now save video memory and just use the same two-dimensional texture that is used by the directional and spotlights.

	Dual-Paraboloid Mapping	Cube Mapping	Tetrahedron Mapping
Render Scene	2 times	6 times	4 times
Switch Render Target	2 times	6 times	1 time
Hardware Shadow Map Support (NVIDIA Geforce3 +)	Yes	No	Yes
Accuracy	Not 100% accurate: depends on polygon count.	100%	100%

Table 3.1. Comparison between dual-paraboloid mapping, cube mapping, and tetrahedron mapping.

Figure 3.14. One point light and use dual-paraboloid shadow mapping with two 1024 × 1024 two-dimensional textures.

Figure 3.15. One point light and use cube shadow mapping with one 512 cube texture.

Figure 3.16. One point light and use tetrahedron shadow mapping with one 1024×1024 two-dimensional texture.

Figure 3.17. One point light and use tetrahedron shadow mapping with stencil buffer. The two-dimensional depth texture size is 1024×1024.

Figure 3.18. One point light and use tetrahedron shadow mapping with hardware shadow mapping. The two-dimensional depth texture size is 1024×1024.

Figure 3.19. One point light and use tetrahedron shadow mapping with stencil buffer and hardware shadow mapping. The two-dimensional depth texture size is 1024×1024.

Figure 3.20. Four point lights and use cube shadow mapping with one 512 cube texture.

Figure 3.21. Four point lights and use tetrahedron shadow mapping with stencil buffer and hardware shadow mapping. The two-dimensional depth texture size is 1024×1024.

Performance can improve by twenty percent or more by switching from cube mapping to tetrahedron mapping—even more if you use NVIDIA hardware shadow map and get an extra percentage of closest filtering. Figures 3.14, 3.15, 3.16, 3.17, 3.18, 3.19, 3.20, and 3.21 are screen shots from a test scene.

Bibliography

[Williams 78] Lance Williams. "Casting Curved Shadows on Curved Surfaces." *Computer Graphics (SIGGRAPH '78 Proceedings)* 12.3 (1978): 270–274.

[Voorhies and Foran 94] Douglas Voorhies and Jim Foran. "Reflection Vector Shading Hardware." *Proceedings of SIGGRAPH '94* (1994): 163–166.

[Heidrich and Seidel 98] Wolfgang Heidrich and Hans-Peter Seidel. "View-Independent Environment Maps." *1998 SIGGRAPH / Eurographics Workshop on Graphics Hardware* (1998): 39–46.

Screen Space Soft Shadows

Jesus Gumbau, Miguel Chover, and Mateu Sbert

This work presents a new technique for the real-time rendering of shadows with penumbrae based on shadow mapping. The method uses a screen-aligned texture that contains the distance between the shadow and its potential occluder. This information is used to set up the size of an anisotropic Gaussian filter kernel applied in screen space, which smoothens the standard shadows to create the penumbra. Given that a Gaussian filter is separable, the number of samples required to create the penumbra is much lower than in other soft shadowing approaches. In consequence, higher performance is obtained while also allowing perceptually correct penumbrae to be represented.

4.1 Introduction

Shadows are a very important element in synthetic scenes because they greatly contribute to enhance the realism of the rendered images (see Figure 4.1). Shadow mapping is the most used technique in real-time applications nowadays, because it can be implemented efficiently on the graphics hardware and its performance scales very well. It is also the most active field on shadowing research in the last years.

Unfortunately the standard shadow mapping algorithm is unable to generate shadows with penumbrae (see Figure 4.2 for an example of real-world penumbrae), or soft shadows, as it can not handle area light sources (see Figure 4.3).

In order to generate physically correct penumbrae, we need to determine the amount of light visible from the point being shaded, which is proportional to the size of the penumbra.

A common idea used for representing shadows with penumbrae is to approximate area lights by a set of point light sources, and then to combine the contributions of each single shadow. With this method, the softness of the penumbra is

Figure 4.1. Scene rendered using our method with an 11×11 Gaussian anisotropic kernel in screen space. The image shows how the soft shadow becomes sharper as it approaches the occluder.

proportional to the number of virtual light sources used. In practice this method is very expensive, because the shadow casters need to be rendered many times, introducing a huge overhead in geometry-limited scenes. Therefore, more practical solutions are needed in order to be used in real-time applications.

The aim of this work is to introduce a new soft shadow mapping algorithm for generating variable-sized penumbrae that minimizes texture lookups in order to maximize performance. Our technique generates shadows with penumbrae using an anisotropic Gaussian blur filter in screen space with variable size. The idea

Figure 4.2. Example of real-world penumbrae. Shadows become sharper as they approach the occluder.

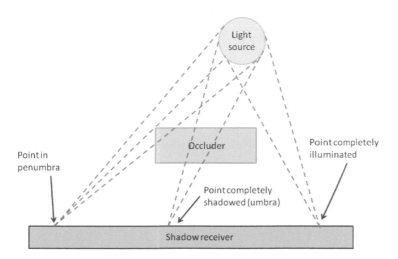

Figure 4.3. The size of the penumbra is determined by the amount of light rays reaching the point being rendered.

behind this work is simple: as a Gaussian filter is separable, it requires far fewer texture accesses than other kernel-based sampling approaches, thus improving performance.

4.2 Previous Work

This paper is an improvement of the traditional shadow mapping technique, which was developed by Williams in 1978 [Williams 78]. It is based on capturing the depth of the shadow casters from the light source. This information is stored into a depth texture that is projected over the scene in order to determine whether a certain pixel is in shadow or not, with a single depth comparison in light space.

In 1987, Reeves [Reeves et al. 87] presented a technique called *percentage closer filtering* (PCF), which makes it possible to reduce the aliasing and to simulate an artificial penumbra of uniform size. The technique was based on performing multiple fetches over the shadow map to determine the amount of light over a given surface.

To allow the rendering of visually pleasant penumbrae, F. Randima [Fernando 05] introduces percentage closer soft shadows (PCSS) which is able to represent soft shadows with variable-sized penumbrae. This technique is usually combined with a filtering technique like [Donnelly and Lauritzen 06] or [Salvi 07] to reduce the noise. Working source code of this technique can be found at NVIDIA's webpage [Bavoil 08b].

For more information, refer to Hasenfratz et al. [Hasenfratz et al. 03] who presented a survey of techniques for the rendering of penumbrae, which was updated in 2008 by other authors [Bavoil 08a].

4.3   Screen Space Soft Shadows

This work proposes a new method for calculating soft shadows with variable penumbrae in real time. The method is based on blurring the shadows from the observer's point of view by using an anisotropic Gaussian filter of variable size. The aspect ratio of the anisotropic Gaussian filter is determined by using the normal at the point being rendered. The size of the area affected by the filter, which generates softer or sharper penumbrae, varies per pixel and depends on the amount of light potentially received from the area light source. This factor is determined by the visibility of the area light from the point being rendered. The formula used to estimate how much light is received was proposed by [Fernando 05] (see Equation (4.1)).

$$w_{\text{penumbra}} = \frac{(d_{\text{receiver}} - d_{\text{blocker}}) \cdot w_{\text{light}}}{d_{\text{blocker}}}, \tag{4.1}$$

where w_{penumbra} is the final width of the penumbra, d_{receiver}; d_{blocker} are the distances of the receiver and the blocker to the light; and w_{light} is the size of the area light.

Observation reveals that shadows produced by area lights (including the penumbra) are larger than shadows produced by point lights, because the area affected by the penumbra increases with the size of the light source (see Figure 4.4). Therefore our method generates a "dilated" version of the shadow map in order to evaluate the Gaussian filter for those pixels potentially belonging to the area affected by the penumbra. This process is detailed in Section 4.3.1. Without this "dilated" shadow map, we only would be able to render the so-called inner penumbrae.

As a result, this method is able to generate soft shadows with perceptually correct penumbrae, which softens as their distance to the occluder as well as the size of the light source increases (see Figure 4.1).

The following steps describe the process to be performed, for each light source, in order to generate shadow penumbrae with our method:

1. Calculate the standard shadow map (S_{map}) and a "dilated" version (S'_{map}) of the shadow map (see Section 4.3.1 for details).

2. Render the scene from the observer's point of view and calculate the following elements in the same rendering pass: the shadows without penumbrae (or hard shadows), the depth buffer, a normal buffer and the shading of

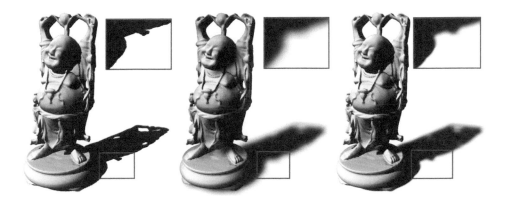

Figure 4.4. Importance of perceptually correct shadows: shadows with no penumbra (left), with uniform penumbra (middle) and with variable penumbra rendered with our method (right). Notice how the penumbra becomes sharper as the shadow approaches the occluder. Notice also the quality of self-shadows compared to uniform penumbra methods.

the scene (without shadows). The distances map is also calculated in the same rendering pass. This map contains the distance from the point being evaluated (P) to the first light occluder, as well as the linear distance to the observer. See Section 4.3.2 for details.

3. Deferred shadowing: render a full screen quad with our custom anisotropic Gaussian blur filter to blur the hard-edged shadows in screen space and to combine them with the shaded scene. The per-pixel size of the area affected by the blurring kernel is calculated using the data in the distances map.

The following are the configuration of the multiple render targets, used to calculate all needed buffers in one rendering pass (step 2):

- MRT0. Diffuse color without shadows.

- MRT1. Normal-depth buffer (RGB: normal's XYZ. Depth is stored in the alpha channel).

- MRT2. Shadow buffer.

- MRT3. Distances map, which contains the following information in the first three channels:

    - R: distance of the shadow caster to the point being rendered (D).

    - G: distance of the observer to the point being rendered (Z).

Figure 4.5. Different intermediate steps of our algorithm. From left to right: the model with hard shadows, the standard shadow map, the dilated shadow map and the final result of blurring the shadows with the anisotropic Gaussian filter.

— B: mask value determining whether the point is inside the penumbra or not.

4.3.1   Calculating the Shadow Maps

First of all, the standard shadow map is calculated from the light source. It is important to note that this information is insufficient to directly determine the distance to the occluder in order to represent the outter penumbrae.

To solve this problem, we create a coarser version of the shadow map by preprocessing it in the following way: each pixel of the coarse shadow map will approximate a block of pixels of the standard shadow map. The criterion used for this approximation is the minimum value (closest to the light). Take into account that the contents of the coarse shadow map are used as a depth estimation to calculate the distance map, not to generate the shadow itself. We use this criterion because, performing the average of samples of the shadow map without taking into account the shadow receiver, would compute incorrect z-values, and thus incorrect penumbrae.

The dilation is performed in light space, by applying an isotropic min-filter to the original shadow map, after it is computed. Given that this filter is separable, it is computed efficiently as two one-dimensional filters.

The amount of dilation is proportional to the size of the area light source because the size of the penumbra is also proportional to the size of the light source. This is implemented by increasing the radius of the "minimum-value" filter kernel. However, as we are performing the dilation of the shadow map in image space, the shadow receiver cannot be taken into account to calculate the size of the penumbra. As a consequence, the user has to apply a constant factor to the amount of dilation, because the size of the penumbra is also proportional to the distance between the shadow caster and the shadow receiver. This factor is interpreted as the maximum distance to the occluder possible in the scene. If this parameter is too small, penumbrae will not be completely smooth. On the other hand, if the parameter is too large, the resulting penumbrae will be less accurate. In practice, it is not difficult to visually set up this value for a given scene.

Once calculated, the filtered shadow map will allow us to calculate the distances map (see Section 4.3.2) for every point of the penumbrae (including the outer penumbra) in screen space.

4.3.2 Calculating the Distances Map

The distances map is a screen-aligned texture that contains, per pixel, the distance of the shadow to its potential occluder and its distance to the observer. This is computed by rendering a full screen quad so that every pixel in the screen is evaluated. Distances to the occluder are computed by transforming the point being evaluated to the light space. This way, its depth value can be compared directly with the depth of the coarse occluder.

For optimization purposes, the distances map also stores a mask determining which pixels will never receive neither a shadow nor a penumbra. The shadow mask is useful to reduce texture lookups and improve performance.

4.3.3 Applying the Gaussian Filter

Determining the size of the penumbrae. This step generates the penumbra by applying an anisotropic Gaussian blur filter in screen space. The size of the region affected by the kernel varies per pixel depending on:

- The distance of the shadow to the occluder.

- The distance of the light source to the occluder.

- The size of the light source.

To take these factors into account, F. Randima [Fernando 05] introduced a formula (see Equation (4.1)) that estimates the size of the penumbra by using the parallel planes approach. This assumes that the occluder, shadow receiver, and light sources are parallel. However, in practice it works very well and provides a formula which is not expensive to evaluate.

We derive Equation (4.1) by adding the distance of the pixel to the observer to the computations, because our filter is applied in screen-space and the area affected by the filter diminishes as its distance from the observer increases. Equation (4.2) shows how the previously calculated buffers are now combined in order to determine the size of the area affected by the filter in screen space:

$$w_{\text{penumbra}} = \frac{(d_{\text{receiver}} - d_{\text{blocker}}) \cdot w_{\text{light}}}{d_{\text{blocker}} \cdot d_{\text{observer}}}. \tag{4.2}$$

In Equation (4.2), the size of the penumbra (w_{penumbra}) depends on the following members: ($d_{\text{receiver}} - d_{\text{blocker}}$) represents the distance between the shadow receiver and the shadow caster; d_{observer} is the distance to the observer. These parameters are stored in the distances map; w_{light} is the size of the light source; and d_{blocker} represents the contents of the "coarse" shadow map and stores the distance to the blocker in light space.

Anisotropic filtering. The anisotropic Gaussian filter is a separable filter. One two-dimensional blurring can be performed in two sequential one-dimensional blurring passes: one horizontal and one vertical. This is the key to our method, because applying a Gaussian filter to create the penumbra requires far fewer texture accesses compared to the PCSS approach, which is not separable, allowing the cost of our method to be $O(n + n)$ instead of $O(n^2)$.

For each sample accessed to perform the Gaussian filter, their distance to the observer is taken into account to discard samples whose distance to the current pixel is greater than a certain threshold. This is used to prevent the filter kernel from taking into account parts of the scene that are close in eye space but are far away in world space. It also avoids having to filter the shadows with the contents of the background. The number of samples taken by the Gaussian filter determines both the quality of the shadows and the performance. Therefore this trade-off decision is left to the user as a customizable parameter. An interesting optimization, in order to reduce the number of texture accesses, is to decrease the number of samples as the area affected by the blurring kernel decreases.

To determine the shape of the anisotropic filtering, the normal of the current pixel is fetched from the normal buffer (generated previously using `Multiple RenderTargets`). Using this normal, the local tangent space is calculated and used to determine the local x-, y- and z-axes. Projecting these axes to eye space allows us to determine the shape and orientation of the ellipse which defines the anisotropic filter.

To perform the anisotropic filtering in an efficient way, we use the method presented by [Geusebroek and Smeulders 03]. This work derives the anisotropic Gauss filtering and proposes to apply it as a separable kernel, which can be evaluated efficiently.

Finally, after the vertical blurring pass is performed, the penumbra has already been calculated so the pixel shader combines it with the unshadowed scene C to create the final image, with complete shadows with penumbrae.

4.3.4 Using Average Instead of Minimum Depth

Our technique provides a simplification that allows us to rapidly generate penumbrae, minimizing the number of texture accesses per pixel as based on the minimum depth texture approach. However, while this technique is able to generate plausible soft shadows in most scenes, it may not be completely accurate for some scenes with very complex shadow casters and receivers.

Fernando [Fernando 05] shows how the average depth of the potential occluders is a valid measure to determine the size of the penumbra at a given point. This process, called the *blocker search* step, is accomplished by performing a number of samples over the shadow map in order to determine the average distance of potential occluders. The size of the sampling area is proportional to the size of the light source. On typical scenes, performing 5×5 samples over the shadow map is sufficient to provide accurate results. However, as the size of the light source increases, more samples may be needed for detailed objects to avoid artifacts due to the spacing of the samples in texture space.

Annen et al [Annen et al. 08] introduce an optimization to the blocker search step by performing it as a convolution filter. This way, this step can be done efficiently on the graphics hardware.

Therefore, if desired, a traditional approach based on the blocker search can be implemented to use the average depth instead of the minimum depth, as used in percentage closer soft shadows, while still being able to use our screen-based anisotropic Gaussian filtering to generate the penumbrae.

Obviously the minimum depth texture is not longer necessary when computing the size of the penumbra. Therefore, the step of generating that texture can be safely skipped.

4.4 Results

This section presents performance and quality tests performed using our method with different scene configurations. All tests were run on an Athlon +3500 processor with 3GB of RAM memory and a GeForce 8800GT graphics card. In order to best show the quality of the shadows, quality comparative images were rendered using a black ambient light over untextured surface. This way, shadows can be studied easily.

4.4.1 Quality Tests

The number of samples used by the Gaussian kernel greatly affects the final quality of the penumbra, especially when large light sources are used and large penumbrae must be generated. Figure 4.6 shows a set of shadows generated with different

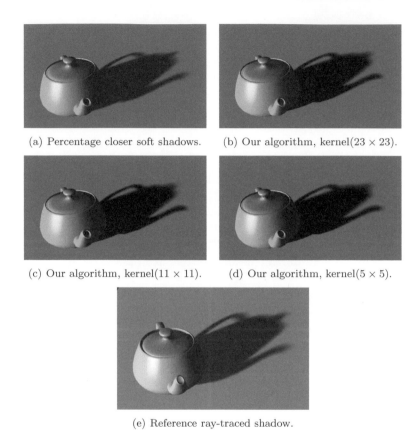

(a) Percentage closer soft shadows.   (b) Our algorithm, kernel(23×23).

(c) Our algorithm, kernel(11×11).   (d) Our algorithm, kernel(5×5).

(e) Reference ray-traced shadow.

Figure 4.6. Visual quality comparison between our algorithm (with three different kernel sizes, shown in (b), (c), and (d)) and other approaches: (e) a ray-traced shadow and (a) an implementation of PCSS.

kernel sizes in order to show penumbrae quality with different configurations. Three kernel sizes were used: 5×5, 11×11 and 23×23. The image shows how the small 5×5 kernel produces some discretization artifacts in the penumbra. The 11×11 kernel is useful for the majority of cases, but it can be insufficient when the camera comes close to the penumbra. In these cases a 23×23 kernel is more than enough for obtaining good quality.

Figure 4.7 shows the effects of increasing the size of the area light. This figure shows how the size of the penumbra grows proportionally to the size of the light source. Figure 4.7(c) shows that, even with a huge area light, the algorithm is able to represent visually pleasant shadows with perceptually correct penumbrae.

Figure 4.8 shows a complex scene using our soft shadowing technique.

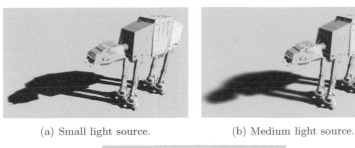

(a) Small light source. (b) Medium light source.

(c) Large light source.

Figure 4.7. Effects of changing the size of the light source; the size of the penumbra is proportional to the size of the light source.

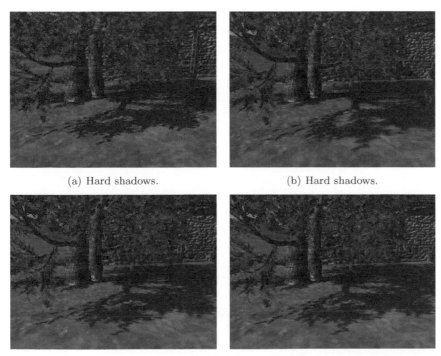

(a) Hard shadows. (b) Hard shadows.

(c) Our algorithm with a 5×5 blur kernel. (d) Our algorithm with a 23×23 blur kernel.

Figure 4.8. Shadows quality in a complex scene with complex shadow casters.

Method	Kernel setup	800×600	1280×1024	1600×1200
standard	*None*	942 fps	595 fps	245 fps
PCF	$PCF(3 \times 3)$	462 fps	230 fps	175 fps
SSSS	$K(5 \times 5)$	553 fps	278 fps	213 fps
	$K(11 \times 11)$	513 fps	256 fps	181 fps
	$K(23 \times 23)$	441 fps	221 fps	155 fps
PCSS	$B_s(5 \times 5) + PCF(5 \times 5)$	504 fps	239 fps	183 fps
	$B_s(5 \times 5) + PCF(11 \times 11)$	251 fps	106 fps	78 fps
	$B_s(5 \times 5) + PCF(23 \times 23)$	122 fps	49 fps	37 fps

Table 4.1. Performance results measured in frames per second (FPS) on the AT-AT scene (200K triangles). SSSS stands for our method (Screen Space Soft Shadows). K refers to the kernel sizes used with each technique. B_s stands for *blocker search*, used in the PCF algorithm.

4.4.2   Performance Tests

Table 4.1 compares performance in the AT-AT scene, using different configurations and techniques. The first and second columns indicate the methods and configurations used, while the rest of the columns show performance (measured in frames per second) for each configuration in both scenes. Standard shadow mapping is used to provide the time needed to calculate shadows without penumbra. In the second row, the time needed to calculate a uniform-sized penumbra is provided. This penumbra is calculated using a percentage closer filter combined with a screen space blur filter that removes artifacts and softens penumbrae. Next, many timings are taken using our method with some different kernel configurations under different screen resolutions. It can be seen that our method performs very well, being that its costs are similar to the uniform-sized penumbrae cost. Finally, percentage closer soft shadows are used in order to provide performance measurements for comparing our technique with a well known soft shadowing method.

As shown in the table, our technique is able to perform very well even at high screen resolutions, outperforming PCSS with similar kernel sizes and screen resolutions. Moreover, it can be seen how performance drops when using PCSS while incrementing the screen resolution and kernel sizes, while performance remains more stable with our algorithm.

4.5   Conclusion

This work presents a new approach for calculating soft shadows with variable-sized penumbrae in real time (see Figure 4.9). To optimize this task, we introduce the concept of distance map, which stores the distance from a pixel potentially affected

Figure 4.9. Example of penumbrae with different light sizes and different light colors.

by the penumbra to the occluder that produces that shadow. This distance is used to generate penumbrae in screen space using an anisotropic Gaussian blurring kernel.

The bottleneck of the PCSS approach is the number of texture accesses required to achieve smooth penumbrae. First, it has to perform a blocker search to determine the overall distance of the shadow to the occluder. Although this step requires at least 3×3 texture reads, it is advisable to use at least 5×5 or even 7×7 to completely avoid artifacts on complex shadow casters. Our method performs the blocker search by just accessing the distances map, which can be generated from a low-resolution coarse shadow map. In addition, PCSS needs to take multiple samples of the shadow map in order to generate the penumbrae. In practice, 13×13 is a good kernel size to achieve smooth shadows with PCSS. Thus, the number of samples required to generate the penumbra with this method is: 5×5 (blocker search) $+ 13 \times 13$ (PCF) $= 194$ texture reads.

On the other hand, since our algorithm uses a separable filter, the cost of computing the penumbra is $O(n + n)$ instead of $O(n^2)$, as in the PCSS approach. As an example, using an 11×11 kernel with PCSS would require $11 \times 11 = 121$ texture accesses, while by using a separable Gaussian blur it can be performed with only $11+11=22$ texture lookups. This method also proves to be very scalable because increasing the kernel to 17×17 requires only 34 samples with our method and 289 samples with PCSS. This means that even using a massive 50×50 Gaussian filter ($50+50 = 100$ texture lookups), our method would offer better performance compared to PCSS while generating extremely smooth penumbrae.

Moreover, the use of an anisotropic filtering allows our method to take into account the orientation of the surface being shadowed. This way, the screen space filtering is able to deliver precise penumbrae even at grazing angles.

Another advantage of using our method is that it complies with the concept of deferred shading. This shading scheme, which is commonly used in films and postproduction, is becoming popular in the field of real-time graphics. Deferred lighting (see [Engel 08]) uses a similar approach for rendering efficiently a high amount of lights in real time. Our technique is easily integrable in a deferred shading pipeline, performing all the calculations in screen space, taking as input the same buffers used in the deferred shading (except for the distances map). The direct benefits of our approach are that no superfluous calculations are wasted on invisible pixels, as it is applied in screen space over the computed shadow buffer.

On the other hand, this technique presents some limitations. The first limitation is that we are simplifying the blocker search by using a minimum depth filter, which selects the minimum depth from the light source instead of an average depth of the blockers. Another issue is that the coarse shadow map can not take into account the distance of the shadow to the receiver in order to dilate the shadow map, which forces the user to set a fixed safe distance by hand.

However, despite its limitations, our technique is able to deliver perceptually correct penumbrae on controlled scenes, with a performance boost compared with PCSS, almost multiplying by three the performance obtained with large kernels.

Acknowledgments

This work was supported by Ministerio Español de Ciencia y Tecnología (grant TSI-2004-02940 and projects TIN2007-68066-C04-01 and TIN2007-68066-C04-02) and by Bancaja (P1 1B2007-56).

Bibliography

[Annen et al. 08] Thomas Annen, Zhao Dong, Tom Mertens, Philippe Bekaert, Hans-Peter Seidel, and Jan Kautz. "Real-Time, All-Frequency Shadows in Dynamic Scenes." *Proceedings of SIGGRAPH* 3 (2008), 1–8.

[Bavoil 08a] Louis Bavoil. "Advanced Soft Shadow Mapping Techniques." *Game Developers Conference.*

[Bavoil 08b] Louis Bavoil. "Percentage-Closer Soft Shadows." *NVIDIA.* Available online (http://developer.download.nvidia.com/SDK/10.5/direct3d/samples .html).

[Donnelly and Lauritzen 06] William Donnelly and Andrew Lauritzen. "Variance Shadow Maps." In *Proceedings of the 2006 Symposium on Interactive 3D Graphics and Games*, pp. 161–165, 2006.

[Engel 08] Wolfgang Engel. "Designing a Renderer for Multiple Lights: The Light Pre-Pass Renderer." *ShaderX7 : Advanced rendering techniques.*

[Fernando 05] Randima Fernando. "Percentage-Closer Soft Shadows." In *SIGGRAPH '05: ACM SIGGRAPH 2005 Sketches*, p. 35, 2005.

[Geusebroek and Smeulders 03] Jan M. Geusebroek and Arnold W. M. Smeulders. "Fast Anisotropic Gauss Filtering." *IEEE Transactions on Image Processing* 12:8 (2003), 99–112.

[Hasenfratz et al. 03] Jean-Marc Hasenfratz, Marc Lapierre, Nicolas Holzschuch, and François Sillion. "A Survey of Real-Time Soft Shadows Algorithms." *Computer Graphics Forum* 22:4 (2003), 753–774.

[Reeves et al. 87] William T. Reeves, David H. Salesin, and Robert L. Cook. "Rendering Antialiased Shadows with Depth Maps." *SIGGRAPH '87* 21:4 (1987), 283–291.

[Salvi 07] Marco Salvi. "Rendering Filtered Shadows with Exponential Shadow Maps." *ShaderX6 : Advanced rendering techniques.*

[Williams 78] Lance Williams. "Casting Curved Shadows on Curved Surfaces." In *SIGGRAPH '78*, 12, 12, pp. 270–274, 1978.

VIII   3D Engine Design

The topics in this section target the design of a renderer. A renderer is a very complex software module that requires attention to a lot of details. The requirements and attention also vary greatly on different hardware platforms. This section spans topics that cover rendering of transparent data, rendering a huge number of lights on the PS3, design of a cross-API renderer, and a simple way to achieve multi-threaded rendering while utilizing the DirectX 9 API.

The article "Multi-Fragment Effects on the GPU Using Bucket Sort" covers a technique on how to render order-independent transparency by utilizing a bucket sort system. Traditionally, pixels or fragments are processed in depth order rather than rasterization order and modern GPUs are optimized to capture the nearest and furthest fragment per pixel in each geometry pass. Depth peeling offers a simple and robust solution by peeling of one layer per pass, but rasterizing depth data multiple times leads to performance bottlenecks. Newer approaches like the K-Buffer approach capture fragments in a single pass but suffer from read-modify-write (RMW hazards). This article presents a method that utilizes a bucket array per pixel that is allocated using MRT as the storage. It is more efficient than classical depth peeling while offering good visual results.

The next article, "Parallelized Light Pre-Pass Rendering with the Cell Broadband Engine," demonstrates the efficient implementation of a light pre-pass / deferred lighting engine on the PS3 platform. Distributing the workload of rendering many lights over the SPE and GPU requires some intricate knowledge of the platform and software engineering skills that are covered in the article.

The article "Porting Code between Direct3D9 and OpenGL 2.0," by Wojciech Sterna, is an introduction to cross-API renderer design. Keeping an engine portable between platforms is a fundamental requirement for reusing data on several platforms.

The last article in the section, "Practical Thread Rendering for DirectX 9," covers a trick on how to make a DirectX 9 based engine cross-platform. It covers the usage of double buffered command buffers with dedicated rendering threads to execute those command buffers.

—Wolfgang Engel

Multi-Fragment Effects on the GPU Using Bucket Sort

Meng-Cheng Huang, Fang Liu, Xue-Hui Liu, and En-Hua Wu

1.1 Introduction

Efficient rendering of multi-fragment effects has long been a great challenge in computer graphics, which always require to process fragments in depth order rather than rasterization order. The major problem is that modern GPUs are optimized only to capture the nearest or furthest fragment per pixel each geometry pass. The classical depth peeling algorithm [Mammen 89, Everitt 01] provides a simple but robust solution by peeling off one layer per pass, but multi-rasterizations will lead to performance bottleneck for large-scale scene with high complexity. The k-buffer [Bavoil et al. 07, Liu et al. 06] captures k fragments in a single pass but suffers from serious read-modify-write(RMW) hazards.

This article presents a fast approximation method for efficient rendering of multi-fragment effects via bucket sort on GPU. In particular, a bucket array of size K is allocated per pixel location using MRT as storage, and the depth range of each pixel is consequently divided into K subintervals. During rasterization, fragments within the kth ($k = 0, 1, \cdots, K - 1$) subinterval will be routed to the kth bucket by a bucket sort. Collisions will happen when multiple fragments are routed to the same bucket, which can be alleviated by multi-pass approach or an adaptive scheme. Our algorithm shows great speedup to the classical depth peeling with visually faithful results, especially for large scenes with high complexity.

1.2   Design of Bucket Array

The bucket array can be constructed as a fixed size buffer per pixel location in GPU memory, thus the MRT buffers turn out to be a natural candidate. Since modern GPUs can afford at most eight MRTs with internal pixel format of `GL_RGBA32F_ARB`, the size of our bucket array can reach up to 32, which is often enough for most common applications.

The default `REPLACE` blending of the MRTs will introduce two problems. First, when multiple fragments are trying to update the bucket array on the same pixel location concurrently, the number of the operations on that location and the order in which they occur is undefined, and only one of them is guaranteed to succeed. Thus they will produce unpredictable results under concurrent writes. Second, modern GPUs have not yet supported independent update of arbitrary channels of MRT buffers. The update of a specific channel of the MRT buffers will result in all the remaining channels being overwritten by the default value zero simultaneously. As a result, the whole bucket array will hold at most one depth value at any time.

Fortunately, these problems can be solved via the 32-bit floating-point MAX/MIN blending operation, which is available on recent commodity NVIDIA GeForce 8 or its ATI equivalents. Take the MAX blending operation as an example, which performs a comparison between the source and the destination values of each channel of MRTs, and keeps the greater one of each pair. This atomic operation guarantees all the read, modify, write operations to the same pixel location will be serialized and performed without interference from each other, thus completely avoiding the first problem of RMW hazards.

The second problem can be solved by initializing each bucket of the bucket array to zero. When updating a certain bucket, if the original value in the bucket is zero, the update will always succeed since the normalized depth values are always greater than or equal to zero; otherwise, the greater one will survive the comparison. As for other buckets, we implicitly update them simultaneously by the default value zero so that their original values are always greater and can be kept unchanged. When multiple fragments are routed to the same bucket, i.e., a collision happens, the MAX blending operation assures that the maximum depth value will win all the tests and finally stay in the bucket. MIN blending is performed in a similar way except initializing each bucket and explicitly updating the other buckets by one. The MAX/MIN blending operation enables us to update a specific bucket independently, and guarantees correct results free of RMW hazards. Since the default update value for each channel of the MRT is zero, we prefer to utilize MAX blending in our implementation for simplicity.

1.3   The Algorithm

The depth value of each fragment is normalized into a range $[0,1]$, but for most pixels, the geometry only occupies a small subrange. Thus a bounding box or a coarse visual hull can be first rendered to approximate the depth range $[z\mathrm{Near}, z\mathrm{Far}]$ per pixel in the same way as dual depth peeling [Bavoil and Myers 08]. During rasterization, the consecutive buckets per pixel are bind into 16 pairs and the depth range are divided into 16 corresponding subintervals uniformly. We then perform the dual depth peeling within each subinterval concurrently. For a fragment with depth value d_f, the corresponding bucket pair index k can be computed as follows:

$$k = \mathrm{floor}(\frac{16 \times (d_f - z\mathrm{Near})}{z\mathrm{Far} - z\mathrm{Near}}).$$

Then the kth pair of buckets will be updated by $(1 - d_f, d_f)$ and the rest pairs by $(0,0)$. When the first geometry pass is over, the minimum and maximum depth values within the kth subinterval can be obtained from the kth pair of buckets, i.e.,

$$\mathrm{dmin}_k^1 = 1 - \max_{d_f \in [d_k, d_{k+1})}(1 - d_f), \quad \mathrm{dmax}_k^1 = \max_{d_f \in [d_k, d_{k+1})}(d_f).$$

It is obvious that these fragments in the consecutive depth intervals are in correct depth ordering:

$$\mathrm{dmin}_0^1 \leq \mathrm{dmax}_0^1 \leq \mathrm{dmin}_1^1 \leq \mathrm{dmax}_1^1 \leq \cdots \leq \mathrm{dmin}_{15}^1 \leq \mathrm{dmax}_{15}^1.$$

If there is no fragment within the kth subinterval, both dmax_k^1 and dmin_k^1 will remain the initial value 0 and can be omitted. While if there is only one fragment within the kth subinterval, dmax_k^1 and dmin_k^1 will be equal and one of them can be eliminated. In a following fullscreen pass, the bucket array will be sequentially accessed as eight input textures to retrieve the sorted fragments for post-processing.

For applications that need other fragment attributes, taking order independent transparency as an example, we can pack the RGBA8 color into a 32-bit positive floating-point using the Cg function *pack_4ubyte*. The alpha channel will be halved and mapped to the highest byte to ensure the positivity of the packed floating-point. We then divide the depth range into 32 subintervals corresponding to the 32 buckets and capture the packed colors instead of the depth values in a similar way. In post-processing, we can unpack the floating-point colors to RGBA8 and double the alpha channel for blending.

1.4   Multi-pass Approach

The algorithm turns out to be a good approximation for uniformly distributed scenes with few collisions. But for non-uniform ones, collisions will happen more frequently especially on the silhouette or details of the model with noticeable artifacts. The algorithm can be extended to a multi-pass approach for better results. In the second geometry pass, we allocate a new bucket array for each pixel and the bucket array captured in the first pass will be taken as eight input textures. For a fragment within the kth subinterval, if its depth value d_f satisfies condition $d_f \geq \mathrm{dmax}_k^1$ or $d_f \leq \mathrm{dmin}_k^1$, it must have been captured in the previous pass, thus can be simply discarded. When the second pass is over, the second minimal and maximum depth values dmin_k^2 and dmax_k^2 in the kth subinterval can be retrieved from the kth pair of buckets similarly. The depth values captured in these two passes are naturally in correct ordering:

$$\mathrm{dmin}_0^1 \leq \mathrm{dmin}_0^2 \leq \mathrm{dmax}_0^2 \leq \mathrm{dmax}_0^1 \leq \mathrm{dmin}_1^1 \leq \mathrm{dmin}_1^2 \leq \mathrm{dmax}_1^2,$$

$$\leq \mathrm{dmax}_1^1 \leq \cdots \leq \mathrm{dmin}_{15}^1 \leq \mathrm{dmin}_{15}^2 \leq \mathrm{dmax}_{15}^2 \leq \mathrm{dmax}_{15}^1.$$

During post-processing, both bucket arrays can be passed to the pixel shader as input textures and accessed for rendering of multi-fragment effects.

Theoretically, we can obtain accurate results by enabling the occlusion query and looping in the same way until all the fragments have been captured. However, the sparse layout of depth values in the bucket arrays will lead to memory exhaustion especially for non-uniform scenes and high screen resolutions. Artifacts may also arise due to the inconsistency between the packed attribute ordering and the correct depth ordering. We instead propose a more robust scheme to alleviate these problems at the cost of an additional geometry pass, namely adaptive bucket depth peeling. The details will be described as follows.

1.5   The Adaptive Scheme

The uniform division of the depth range may result in some buckets overloaded while the rest idle for non-uniform scenes. Ideally, we prefer to adapt the division of subintervals to the distribution of the fragments per pixel, so that there is only one fragment falling into each subinterval. The one-to-one correspondence between fragments and subintervals will assure only one fragment for each bucket, thus can avoid the collisions.

Inspired by the image histogram equalization, we define a depth histogram as an auxiliary array with each entry indicating the number of fragments falling into the corresponding depth subinterval, thus is a probability distribution of the geometry. We allocate eight MRT buffers with pixel format `GL_RGBA32UI_EXT` as our depth histogram. Considering each channel of the MRT as a vector of 32 bits, the depth histogram can be cast to a bit array of size 4*8*32=1024, with each bit as a binary counter for fragments. Meanwhile, the depth range is divided into 1024 corresponding subintervals: $[d_k, d_{k+1}), d_k = z\mathrm{Near} + \frac{k}{1024}(z\mathrm{Far} - z\mathrm{Near}), k = 0, 1, \cdots, 1023$. The depth range is always on a magnitude of 10^{-1}, so the subintervals will be on a magnitude of 10^{-4}, which are often small enough to distinguish almost any two close layers. As a result, there is at most one fragment within each subinterval on most occasions, thus a binary counter for each entry of the depth histogram will be sufficient most of the time.

Similarly, we begin by approximating the depth range per pixel by rendering the bounding box of the scene in an initial pass. In the first geometry pass, an incoming fragment within the kth subinterval will set the kth bit of the depth histogram to one using the OpenGL's 32-bit logic operation GR_OR. After the first pass, each bit of the histogram will indicate the presence of fragments in that subinterval or not. A simplified example with depth complexity $N = 8$ (the maximum number of layers of the scene at all viewing angles) is

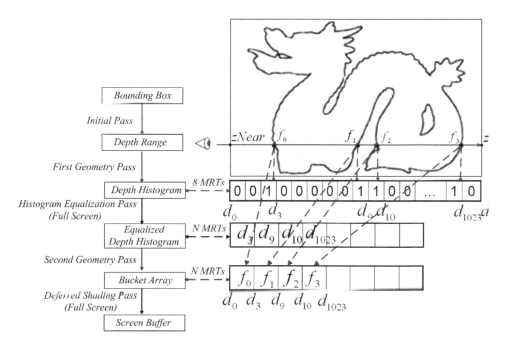

Figure 1.1. An example of adaptive bucket depth peeling. The red arrows indicate the operations in the first geometry pass and the blue arrows indicate the operations in the second geometry pass.

```
void main(   float4   wpos : WPOS,
             uniform samplerRECT depthRange,

             //Output histogram as eight MRTs.
             out unsigned int4   color0 : COLOR0,
             out unsigned int4   color1 : COLOR1,
             ......
             out unsigned int4   color7 : COLOR7 )
{
  float z = wpos.z;
  float4 range = texRECT(depthRange, wpos.xy);

  float zNear = 1 - range.x;
  float zFar = range.y;

  int k = floor( 1024 * ( z-zNear)/(zFar-zNear) );
  int i = k >> 5;
  int j = k & 0x1F;

  unsigned int SetBit = 0x80000000 >> j;

  if(i==0) color0 = unsigned int4(SetBit,0,0,0);
  else if(i==1) color0 = unsigned int4(0,SetBit,0,0);
  else if(i==2) color0 = unsigned int4(0,0,SetBit,0);
  ......
  else if(i==30) color7 = unsigned int4(0,0,SetBit,0);
  else color7 = unsigned int4(0,0,0,SetBit);
}
```

Listing 1.1. The pixel shader in the first geometry pass.

shown in Figure 1.1. Suppose at a certain pixel location, the eye ray intersects the scene generating four fragments $f_0 - f_3$ within four different subintervals $[d_2, d_3], [d_8, d_9], [d_9, d_{10}], [d_{1022}, d_{1023}]$. They will set the 3rd, 9th, 10th, and the 1023rd bit of the depth histogram to 1 in the first geometry pass. The code snippet Listing 1.1 shows the pixel shader in the first geometry pass.

The depth histogram is equalized in a following fullscreen pass. For scenes with depth complexity N less than 32, the histogram is passed into the pixel shader as eight input textures, and new floating-point MRT buffers with N channels will be allocated as an equalized histogram for output. We can consecutively obtain the jth bit of the ith $(i, j = 0, 1, 2, \cdots, 31)$ channel of the input depth histogram. If the bit is zero, it means that there is no fragment falling into the kth $(k = i*32+j)$ depth subinterval, thus can be simply skipped over; otherwise, there is at least one fragment within that subinterval, so we store the corresponding upper bound d_{k+1} consecutively into the equalized histogram for output. As for the example in Figure 1.1, two MRT buffers with eight channels will be allocated as the equalized histogram, and the upper bounds d_3, d_9, d_{10}, and d_{1023} will be stored into it in the equalization pass. The code snippet Listing 1.2 shows the pixel shader in the histogram equalization pass.

```
void main(  float4  wpos  : WPOS,
            uniform samplerRECT depthRange,
            //Input histogram as eight textures.
            usamplerRECT fbcolor0,
            usamplerRECT fbcolor1,
            ......
            usamplerRECT fbcolor7,
            //Output equalized histogram as eight MRTs.
            out float4 color0 : COLOR0,
            out float4 color1 : COLOR1,
            ......
            out float4 color7 : COLOR7 )
{
  float4 range = texRECT(depthRange, wpos.xy);
  float zFar = range.y;  if( zFar == 0 ) discard;
  float zNear = 1 - range.x;

  unsigned int4 fb0 =   texRECT(fbcolor0, wpos.xy);
  unsigned int4 fb1 =   texRECT(fbcolor0, wpos.xy);
  ......
  unsigned int4 fb7 =   texRECT(fbcolor7, wpos.xy);

  // Discard pixels that are not rendered.
  if( any( fb0|fb1|fb2|fb3|fb4|fb5|fb6|fb7 ) == 0 ) discard;

  unsigned int Histogram[32];
  Histogram[0]=fb0.x; Histogram[1]=fb0.y;
  Histogram[2]=fb0.z; Histogram[3]=fb0.w;
  ......
  Histogram[30]=fb7.z; Histogram[31]=fb7.w;

  float EquHis[32]; // Equalized histogram
  float coeff = (zFar - zNear) / 1024.0;
  int HisIndex = 1, EquHisIndex = 0;

  for(int i = 0; i < 32; i++, HisIndex += 32)
  {
    unsigned int remainded = Histogram[i];
    // End the inner loop when the remained bits are all zero
    for(int k = HisIndex; remainded != 0; k++, remainded <<= 1)
    {
      if(remainded >= 0x80000000)
      {
        // The $k$th bit of the histogram has been set to one,
        // so store the upper bound of the $k$th subinterval.
        EquHis[EquHisIndex++] = k * coeff + zNear;
```

```
        }
      }
    }
    color0 = float4(EquHis[0],EquHis[1],EquHis[2],EquHis[3]);
    color1 = float4(EquHis[4],EquHis[5],EquHis[6],EquHis[7]);
    ......
    color7 = float4(EquHis[28],EquHis[29],EquHis[30],EquHis[31]);
}
```

Listing 1.2. The pixel shader of the histogram equalization pass.

We perform the bucket sort in the second geometry pass. The equalized histogram is passed to the pixel shader as input textures and a new bucket array of the same size N is allocated as output for each pixel. The upper bounds in the input equalized histogram will redivide the depth range into non-uniform subintervals with almost one-to-one correspondence between fragments and subintervals. As a result, there will be only one fragment falling into each bucket on most occasions; thus collisions can be reduced substantially. During rasterization, each incoming fragment with a depth value d_f will search the input equalized histogram (denoted as EquHis for short). If it belongs to the kth subinterval, i.e., it satisfies conditions $d_f \geq$ EquHis$[k-1]$ and $d_f <$ EquHis$[k]$, it will be routed to the kth bucket. In the end, the fragments are consecutively stored in the output bucket array, so our adaptive scheme will be memory efficient. The bucket array will then be passed to the fragment shader of a fullscreen deferred shading pass as textures for post-processing. As for our example in Figure 1.1, the upper bounds in the equalized histogram redivide the depth range into 4 subintervals: $[0, d_3), [d_3, d_9), [d_9, d_{10}), [d_{10}, d_{1023}]$. Fragment f_0 is within the first subinterval $[0, d_3)$, so it is routed to the first bucket. Fragment f_1 is within the second subinterval $[d_3, d_9)$, and is routed to the second bucket, and so on. After the second geometry pass, all of the four fragments are stored in the bucket array for further applications.

This adaptive scheme can reduce the collisions substantially, but collisions might still happen when two close layers of the model generate two fragments with a distance less than 10^{-4}, especially on the silhouette or details of the model. These fragments are routed to the same bucket and merged into one layer, thus resulting in artifacts. In practice, we can further reduce collisions by binding the buckets into pairs and performing dual depth peeling within each non-empty subinterval. Theoretically, the multi-pass approach can be resorted to for better results.

For applications that need multiple fragment attributes, the one-to-one correspondence between fragments and subintervals can assure the attributes consistency, so we can bind consecutive buckets into groups and update each group by the attributes simultaneously.

For scenes with more than 32 layers, we can handle the remaining layers by scanning over the remaining part of the histogram in a new fullscreen pass to get another batch of 32 nonzero bits. We then equalize it and pass the equalized histogram to the next geometry pass to route the fragments between layer 32 and 64 into corresponding buckets in the same way, and so on, until all the fragments have been captured.

1.6 Applications

Many multi-fragment effects can benefit from our algorithm and gain high performance in comparison to the previous methods. To demonstrate the results, we took several typical ones as examples. Frame rates are measured at 512×512 resolution on an NVIDIA 8800 GTX graphics card with driver 175.16 and Intel Duo Core 2.4G Hz with 3GB memory.

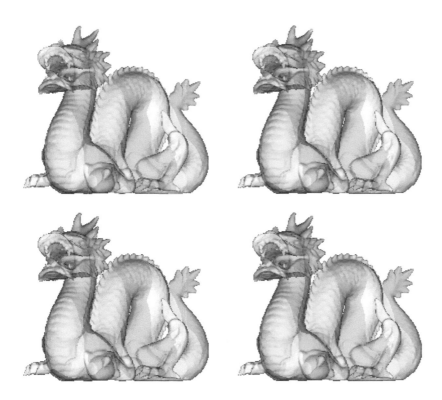

Figure 1.2. Transparent effect on Stanford Dragon (871K triangles). The left top is rendered by BDP (256fps); the right top is by BDP2 (128fps); the left bottom is by ADP (106fps); and the right bottom is the ground truth generated by DP (24fps).

1.6.1   Transparent Effect

Figure 1.2 shows the order independent transparent effect on Stanford Dragon rendered by our bucket depth peeling with a single pass (BDP) and its two-pass extension (BDP2) and the adaptive bucket depth peeling (ADP) in comparison to the classical depth peeling (DP). The differences between the results of our algorithm and the ground truth genertated by DP are visually unnoticeable, so one pass would be a good approximation when performance is more crucial.

1.6.2   Translucent Effect

The translucent effect can be rendered accounting only for absorption and ignoring reflection [NVIDIA 05]. The ambient term I_a can be computed using

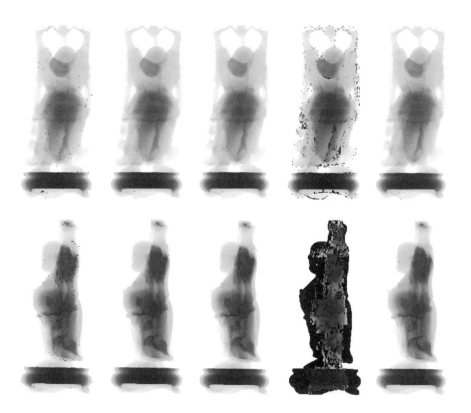

Figure 1.3. Translucent effect on the Buddha model (1,087K triangles). The first column is rendered by BDP (212fps); the second and third are by BDP2 and ADP (106fps); the third is by the k-buffer of 16 layers without modifications (183fps); and the last one is the ground truth generated by DP (20fps).

Beer-Lambert's law: $I_a = \exp(-\sigma_t l)$, where σ is the absorption coefficient and l is the accumulated distance that light travels through the material, which can be approximated by accumulating the thickness between every two successive layers of the model per pixel. As a result, the translucent effect is quite sensitive to errors. Figure 1.3 shows the translucent effect on the Buddha model using different methods. Experimental results show that for k-buffer the RMW hazards are more severe on the side views with more layers, while in contrast, the single pass BDP provides a good approximation and the two-pass approach or the adaptive scheme is preferred for better visual quality.

1.6.3   Fresnel's Effect

Taking into account the attenuation of rays, Schlick's approximation can be used for fast calculation of Fresnel's transmittance of each fragment: $Ft = 1 - (1 - \cos(\theta))^5$. Figure 1.4 shows the results of Fresnel's effect rendered by ADP. In the second geometry pass, we transform the normal into eye space and pack it into a positive floating-point using the Cg function `pack_4byte`. The buckets are bind into pairs and each pair will be updated by the packed normal and the depth value simultaneously. In the deferred shading pass, the ambient term of each pixel can be obtained using Beer-Lambert's law. For a certain pixel, the eye direction can be restored by transforming the fragment position from the screen space back to the the eye space. We then unpack the normal of each fragment and perform a dot product with the eye direction to get the incident angle θ on that surface. In

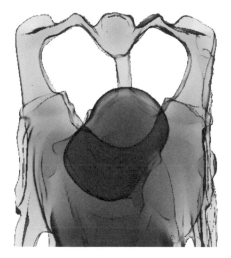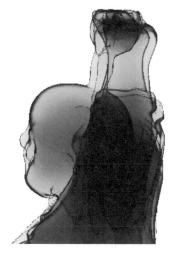

Figure 1.4. Fresnel's effect on the Buddha model (1,087K triangles) rendered by ADP.

the end, Fresnel's transmittance of each fragment can be computed and multiplied together as the final attenuating factor to the ambient term on that pixel location. The code snippet Listing 1.3 shows the pixel shader for the deferred shading of the Fresnel's effect.

More applications such as constructive solid geometry (CSG), depth of field, shadow maps, refraction, and volume rendering will also benefit from our algorithms greatly in a similar way.

```
// Restore the eye-space position of the fragment from the depth
//  value.
float3 TexToEye(float2 pixelCoord, float eye_z,float2 focusLen)
{
    pixelCoord.xy -= float2(0.5, 0.5);
    pixelCoord.xy /= float2(0.5, 0.5);
    float2 eye_xy = (pixelCoord.xy / focusLen) * eye_z;
    return float3(eye_xy, eye_z);
}


void main(   float4 pixleCoordinate : TEXCOORD0,
             float4 wpos            : WPOS,
             uniform float2 focusLength,//Focus length of camera
             //Input bucket array as eight textures.
             uniform samplerRECT fbcolor0,
             uniform samplerRECT fbcolor1,
             ......
             uniform samplerRECT fbcolor7,
             out float4 color : COLOR)
{
  float4 fb0 = texRECT(fbcolor0, wpos.xy);
  float4 fb1 = texRECT(fbcolor1, wpos.xy);
  ......
  float4 fb7 = texRECT(fbcolor7, wpos.xy);

  unsigned int DepthNormal[32]; //Depth value and packed normal
  DepthNormal[0]=fb0.x; DepthNormal[1]=fb0.y;
  DepthNormal[2]=fb0.z; DepthNormal[3]=fb0.w;
  ......
  DepthNormal[30]=fb7.z; DepthNormal[31]=fb7.w;

  float thickness = 0;
  float x = -1;
  float coeff = 1.0; //The final attenuating factor

  for(int i=0;i<32;i+=2)
  {
    if( DepthNormal[i] > 0 )
    {
      float z = DepthNormal[i];
      thickness += x*z; //Accumulating the thickness
      x = -x;
```

```
    //Unpack eye-space normal N.
    float3 N = normalize(unpack_4byte(DepthNormal[i+1]).xyz);
    //Compute eye-space position P and incident direction I.
    float3 P = TexToEye(pixleCoordinate.xy,z,focusLength);
    float3 I = normalize(P);
    float cosTheta = abs(dot(I,N));   //Incident angle
    coeff *= (1-pow(1.0-cosTheta,5));//Fresnel's transmittance
  }
}
if( thickness == 0 ) discard;
float4 jade = float4(0.14,0.8,0.11,1.0) * 8;
color = exp(-30*thickness) * jade * coeff;
}
```

Listing 1.3. The pixel shader for rendering of Fresnel's effect.

1.7 Conclusions

This article presents a novel framework of bucket depth peeling, the first linear algorithm for rendering multi-fragment effects via bucket sort on GPU. Experiment results show great speedup to classical depth peeling with faithful results, especially for large-scale scenes with high depth complexity.

The main disadvantages are the approximate nature of the algorithm and the large memory overhead. In the future, we are interested in forming more efficient schemes to reduce collisions further more. In addition, the memory problem might be alleviated by composing the fragments within each bucket per pass, and finally composing all the buckets after done.

Bibliography

[Bavoil and Myers 08] Louis Bavoil and Kevin Myers. "Order Independent Transparency with Dual Depth Peeling." Technical report, NVIDIA Corporation, 2008.

[Bavoil et al. 07] Louis Bavoil, Steven P. Callahan, Aaron Lefohn, Jo ao L. D. Comba, and Cláudio T. Silva. "Multi-Fragment Effects on the GPU Using the k-Buffer." In *Proceedings of the 2007 Symposium on Interactive 3D Graphics and Games*, pp. 97–104, 2007.

[Everitt 01] Cass Everitt. "Interactive Order-Independent Transparency." Technical report, NVIDIA Corporation, 2001. Available at http://developer.nvidia.com/object/Interactive_Order_Transparency.html.

[Liu et al. 06] Bao-Quan Liu, Li-Yi Wei, and Ying-Qing Xu. "Multi-Layer Depth Peeling via Fragment Sort." Technical report, Microsoft Research Asia, 2006.

[Mammen 89] Abraham Mammen. "Transparency and Antialiasing Algorithms Implemented with the Virtual Pixel Maps Technique." *IEEE Computer Graphics and Applications* 9:4 (1989), 43–55.

[NVIDIA 05] NVIDIA. "GPU Programming Exposed: the Naked Truth Behind NVIDIA's Demos." Technical report, NVIDIA Corporation, 2005.

Parallelized Light Pre-Pass Rendering with the Cell Broadband Engine

Steven Tovey and Stephen McAuley

The light pre-pass renderer [Engel 08, Engel 09, Engel 09a] is becoming an ever more popular choice of rendering architecture for modern real-time applications that have extensive dynamic lighting requirements. In this article we introduce and describe techniques that can be used to accelerate the real-time lighting of an arbitrary three-dimensional scene on the Cell Broadband Engine without adding any additional frames of latency to the target application. The techniques described in this article were developed for the forthcoming PLAYSTATION3 version of *Blur* (see Figure 2.1), slated for release in 2010.[1]

2.1 Introduction

As GPUs have become more powerful, people have sought to use them for purposes other than graphics. This has opened an area of research called GPGPU (General Purpose GPU), which even major graphics card manufacturers are embracing. For example, all NVIDIA GeForce GPUs now support PhysX technology, which enables physics calculations to be performed on the GPU.

However, much less has been made of the opposite phenomenon—with the increase in speed and number of CPUs in a system, it is becoming feasible on some architectures to move certain graphics calculations from the GPU back onto the

---

[1] "PlayStation," "PLAYSTATION," and the "PS" family logo are registered trademarks, and "Cell Broadband Engine" is a trademark of Sony Computer Entertainment Inc. The "Blu-ray Disc" and "Blu-ray Disc" logos are trademarks. Screenshots of *Blur* appear courtesy of Activision Blizzard Inc. and Bizarre Creations Ltd.

CPU. Forthcoming hardware such as Intel's Larrabee even combines both components [Seiler 08], which will certainly lead to CPU-based approaches to previously GPU-only problems becoming more popular. Today, one such architecture is the PLAYSTATION3 where the powerful Cell Broadband Engine was designed from the outset to support the GPU in its processing activities [Shippy 09].

This paper expands upon the work of Swoboda in [Swoboda 09] and explains how the Cell Broadband Engine can be used to calculate lighting within the context of a light pre-pass rendering engine.

2.2   Light Pre-Pass Rendering

A recent problem in computer graphics has been how to construct a renderer that can handle many dynamic lights in a scene. Traditional forward rendering does not perform well with multiple lights. For example, if a pixel shader is written for up to four point lights, then only four point lights can be drawn (and no spotlights). We could either increase the number of pixel shader combinations to handle as many cases as possible, or we could render the geometry multiple times, once more for each additional light. Neither of these solutions is desirable as they increase the number of state changes and draw calls to uncontrollable levels.

A popular solution to this problem is to use a deferred renderer, which uses an idea first introduced in [Deering 88]. Instead of writing out fully lit pixels from the pixel shader, we instead write out information about the surface into a *G-Buffer*, which would include depth, normal, and material information. An example G-buffer format is shown in Figure 2.2.

Figure 2.1. A screenshot from the forthcoming *Blur*.

R (8bit)	G (8bit)	B (8bit)	α (8bit)	
Depth 24bpp			Stencil	**DS**
Lighting Accumulation RGB			Intensity	**RT0**
Normal X (fp16)		Normal Y (fp16)		**RT1**
Motion Vectors XY		Spec Power	Spec Inten	**RT2**
Diffuse Albedo RGB			Sun Occ.	**RT3**

Figure 2.2. An example G-Buffer format from a deferred rendering engine (after [Valient 07]).

We then additively blend the lights into the scene, using the information provided in the G-Buffer. Thus many lights can be rendered, without additional geometry cost or shader permutations. In addition, by rendering closed volumes for each light, we can ensure that only calculations for pixels directly affected by a light are carried out. However, with deferred rendering, all materials must use the same lighting equation, and can only vary by the properties stored in the G-Buffer. There are also huge memory bandwidth costs to rendering to (and reading from) so many buffers, which increases with MSAA.

In order to solve these problems, Engel suggested the light pre-pass renderer, first online in [Engel 08] and then later published in [Engel 09], although a similar idea had been recently used in games such as *Uncharted: Drake's Fortune* [Balestra 08]. Instead of rendering out the entire G-Buffer, the light pre-pass renderer stores depth and normals in one or two render targets. The lighting phase is then performed, with the properties of all lights accumulated into a lighting buffer. The scene is then rendered for a second time, sampling the lighting buffer to determine the lighting on that pixel.

Using a *Blinn-Phong lighting model* means that the red, green, and blue channels of the lighting buffer store the diffuse calculation, while we can fit a specular term in the alpha channel, the details of which are described in [Engel 09]. This means that unlike a deferred renderer, different materials can handle the lighting values differently. This increased flexibility, combined with reduced memory bandwidth costs, has seen the light pre-pass renderer quickly increase in popularity and is now in use in many recent games on a variety of hardware platforms.

Yet the deferred renderer and light pre-pass renderer share the fact that lighting is performed in image space, and as such requires little to no rasterization. This makes the lighting pass an ideal candidate to move from the GPU back onto the CPU. Swoboda first demonstrated this method with a deferred renderer on the PLAYSTATION3 and Cell Broadband Engine in [Swoboda 09], and now we expand upon his work and apply similar techniques to the light pre-pass renderer.

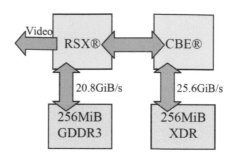

Figure 2.3.   The PLAYSTATION3 architecture.   (Illustration after [Möller 08, Perthuis 06]).

2.3   The PLAYSTATION3 and the CBE

Sony Computer Entertainment released the PLAYSTATION3 in 2006. It contains the Cell Broadband Engine, which was developed jointly by Sony Computer Entertainment, Toshiba Inc., and IBM Corp. [Shippy 09, Möller 08, IBM 08]. The cell is the central processing unit (CPU) of the PLAYSTATION3. In addition to the cell chip, the PLAYSTATION3 also has a GPU, the reality synthesizer (RSX). The RSX was developed by NVIDIA Corporation and is essentially a modified GeForce7800 [Möller 08]. A high-level view of the architecture can be found in Figure 2.3.

Inside the Cell chip one can find two distinctly different types of processor. There is the PowerPC Processing Element (PPE) and eight[2] pure SIMD processors [Möller 08] known as Synergistic Processing Elements (SPEs) all of which are connected by a high speed, token-ring bus known as the *element interconnect bus* (EIB; see Figure 2.4). The techniques introduced and described in this paper are chiefly concerned with the usage of the SPEs and as such further discussion of the PPE has been omitted.

One interesting quirk of the SPE is that it does not directly have access to the main address space, and instead has its own internal memory known as the *local store*. The local store on current implementations of the CBE is 256KB in size. The memory is unified, untranslatable, and unprotected [Bader 07, IBM 08] and must contain the SPE's program code, call stack, and any data that it may happen to be processing. To load or store data from or to the main address space a programmer must explicitly use the memory flow controller (MFC). Each SPE has its own MFC which is capable of queuing up to sixteen Direct Memory Accesses (DMAs) [IBM 08].

---

[2]One of the eight SPEs is locked out to increase chip yield and another is reserved by the Sony's Cell OS. Applications running on the PLAYSTATION3 actually have six SPEs to take advantage of.

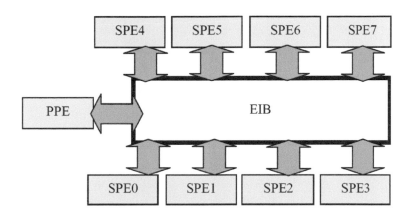

Figure 2.4. The Cell Broadband Engine (after [IBM 08]).

As the SPU ISA operates primarily on SIMD vector operands, both fixed-point and floating-point [IBM 09], it is very well equipped to process large quantities of vectorised data. It has a very large register file (4KB) which is helpful to hide the latencies of pipelined and unrolled loops, and while the local store is relatively small in capacity, it is usually sufficient to allow a programmer is able to hide the large latency of main memory accesses[3] through effective multi-buffering. Code that is to efficiently execute on the SPE should be written to play to the SPE's strengths.

A more in-depth discussion of the PLAYSTATION3 and the Cell Broadband Engine is out of the scope of this paper, interested readers can refer to IBM's website for more in depth details about the Cell chip [IBM 09], and Möller, Haines and Hoffman describe some of the PLAYSTATION3 architecture in [Möller 08].

2.4 GPU/SPE Synchronization

As the number of processors in our target platforms becomes ever greater, the need to automate the scheduling of work being carried out by these processing elements also becomes greater. This has continued to the point where game development teams now build their games and technology around the concept of the job scheduler [Capcom 06]. Our engine is no exception to this trend and the solution we propose for GPU/SPE interprocessor communication relies on close integration with such technology. It is for this reason we believe our solution to be a robust and viable solution to the problem of RSX/SPE communication that many others can easily foster into their existing scheduling frameworks.

---

[3]As one might expect, linear access patterns fair significantly better than random access.

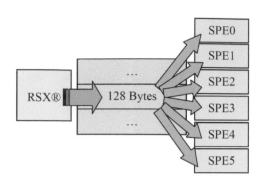

Figure 2.5. The RSX and SPE communication. The RSX writes a 128 byte value when the normal/depth buffer is available for processing. The SPEs poll the same location to know when to begin their work.

In order to perform fragment shading on the SPE without introducing unwanted latency into the rendering pipeline there needs to be a certain amount of interprocessor communication between the GPU and SPEs. This section discusses the approach we used in achieving this synchronization.

Each SPE has several memory mapped I/O (MMIO) registers it can use for interprocessor communication with other SPEs or the PPU. However, these are unfortunately not trivially writable from the RSX. An alternative approach is required in order to have the RSX signal the SPEs that the rendering of the normal/depth buffer is complete and that they can now begin their work, without having the desired SPE programs spinning on all six of the available SPEs wasting valuable processing time.

When adding a job to our job scheduler it is optionally given an address in RSX-mapped memory upon which the job is dependent. When the scheduler is pulling the next job from the job queue it polls this address to ensure that it is written to a known value by the RSX. If this is not the case, the job is skipped and the next one fetched from the queue and processed, if the location in memory is written however, then our job is free to run. This dependency is visualized in Figure 2.5.

The problem of ensuring that the GPU waits for the light buffer to be available from the SPEs is solved by a technique that is well-known to PLAYSTATION3 developers, but unfortunately we cannot disclose it here; interested developers can consult Sony's official development support website.

It is desirable for the RSX to continue doing useful work in parallel with the SPEs performing the lighting calculations. In *Blur* we are fortunate in that we have a number of additional views that are rendered which do not rely on the lighting buffer, for example, planar reflections and a rear-view mirror (in

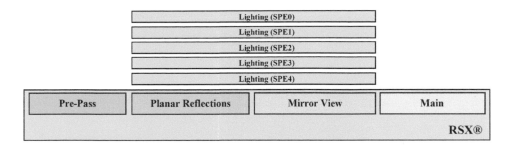

Figure 2.6. The RSX continues to do useful work as the SPEs calculate the dynamic lighting for our scene.

other applications these might also include the rendering of a shadow buffer). This is shown in Figure 2.6. If no useful work can be performed on the RSX, it may be possible (depending on your memory budget and the requirements of your application) to perform the lighting calculations one frame latent as in [Swoboda 09], this approach also has the added benefit of reducing the likelihood of stalling the RSX.

2.5 The Pre-pass

To begin the lighting pre-pass we must first construct the normal and depth buffers. We store view space normals in an 8:8:8:8 format, and since we are able to read from the depth buffer on our chosen hardware, we have no need for a separate target for the depth. We chose to perform our lighting in view space as we find it faster compared with world space.

Next we render the relevant solid and alpha-test geometry into the buffers. We only render the geometry affected by the lights—we cull all draw calls against the bounding spheres of the lights and also bring in the far clip plane (note that a simple sphere test is not sufficient, since we also need to render near objects that occlude the light spheres). These methods of culling reduce the cost of drawing the pre-pass geometry by approximately half.

When rendering the scene, we enable stencil writes with a reference value of 0xFF. The stencil buffer is cleared to 0x00 beforehand, which gives us the relevant region of the screen masked out in the stencil buffer. Whether rendering lights on the RSX or the SPE, this enables us to use the early stencil to ensure that we only light relevant pixels.

We do not currently render the pre-pass or the light buffers with MSAA. This has a number of disadvantages, including some lighting artifacts around the edges of objects, and the loss of the ability to use the depth buffer as a depth pre-pass with the main scene (which we render with MSAA). However, we found the artifacts minimal, and the extra cost of rendering the light pre-pass MSAA outweighed the saving from having a depth pre-pass. This is still an area we wish to return to in the future.

Once we have the normal and depth buffers, we are able to perform the lighting. Currently, we use the Lambert diffuse model for our lights, and render the lights into an 8:8:8:8 buffer. This is for simplicity and performance reasons, but with the cost of no specular and limited lighting range. This also means that the alpha channel of the lighting buffer is unused. Some ideas for its use are explained in Section 2.9.

We maintain a GPU implementation of our lighting model for reference and for other platforms. First, the stencil test is set to "equals" with a reference value of `0xFF`, so we only render to pixels marked in the stencil buffer. Then, the lights are rendered, with point lights and spot lights using two very different methods.

Point lights are rendered as in [Balestra 08]: the frame buffer is split into tiles, and we gather lists of lights (up to a maximum of eight) that affect each tile. We then render each tile using a shader corresponding to its number of lights. This method saves on fill rate, enabling us to perform the reconstruction of view space position and normal from our normal and depth buffers only once per pixel, no matter the number of point lights.

Spot lights use the more standard method of rendering bounding volumes of the lights: in this case, cones. We render front faces, unless we are inside the volume, in which case we render back faces.

We further optimize the lighting code by making use of the depth bounds test, when it is available on the target hardware. The depth bounds test compares the depth buffer value at the current fragment's coordinates to a given minimum and maximum depth value. If the stored depth value is outside the given range, then the fragment is discarded. When drawing either a tile of point lights, or a spot light volume, we set the depth bounds range to be the minimum and maximum depth extents of the light (or lights, in case of the point lights).

This gives us a fast, optimized GPU implementation of our lighting model. However, it is still a significant percentage of our frame rendering time, and its image space nature makes it a perfect candidate to offload from the GPU onto the SPEs.

2.6   The Lighting SPE Program

This section describes in detail the SPE program that performs our lighting calculations. In order to try to contextualize each subsection, we have included Figure 2.7, which shows the high-level structure of the SPE program as a whole.

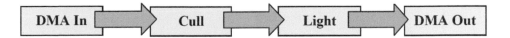

Figure 2.7. The high-level flow of our SPE lighting program.

2.6.1 The Atomic Tile Arbiter

Due to the relatively large memory footprint of a 720p frame buffer; the limitations imposed by the size of an SPE's local store; and the internal format of a surface created by **PLAYSTATION3**'s RSX, our lighting SPE program works on *tiles* of the frame buffer, 64×64 pixels in size, as shown in Figure 2.8. Thus, there is a need to keep track of which tile is free to bring in to local store for processing. The simplest and most concurrent way we found of achieving this was by way of an atomically incremented tile index which resides in main memory. It should be noted that the SPE and RSX are only able to *efficiently* cooperate on the processing of resources that are placed into correctly mapped main memory.

For efficiency (and to avoid contention for the cache line) the tile index is aligned to a 128 byte boundary and padded to 128 bytes in size to exactly match the cache line width of the SPEs atomic unit (ATO) [IBM 08, IBM07]. The effective address (EA) of the tile is given by the product of the tile index and the total size of a single tile summed with the address of the beginning of the frame buffer, as in Equation (2.1). For our chosen tile size, the resulting effective address always falls on a 16 byte boundary since our tile size is itself a 16 byte multiple.

$$\text{tile}_{\text{address}_i} = \text{tile}_{\text{index}_i} \times \text{tile}_{\text{size}} + \text{tile}_{\text{address}_0}. \tag{2.1}$$

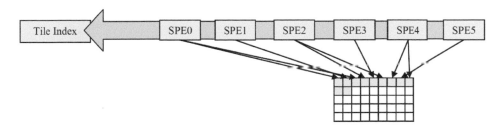

Figure 2.8. Each SPE assigns itself a task by atomically incrementing a tile index held in main memory.

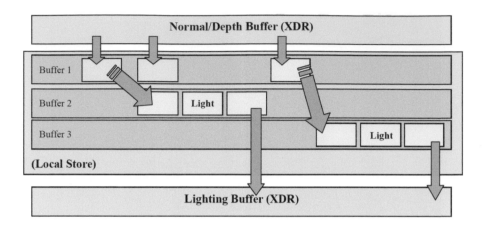

Figure 2.9. The triple-buffering strategy in our lighting SPE program.

2.6.2   Multi-Buffering

Multi-buffering is a must for almost all SPE programs that process any significant volume of data [Bader 07] and our lighting program is no exception. In our implementation we use triple buffering to minimize the latency of accesses to the normal/depth buffer in main memory. Each buffer in the triple buffer has enough space to support a single unit of work (i.e., a single tile of the frame buffer). The first of the buffers in our triple buffer is used as the target for inbound DMA, it utilizes its own tag group and DMA into this buffer are initiated as soon as the tile decoding process[4] on the previous tile has completed. The second and third buffers are used as the output targets for the decoding process. In addition to this, they act as scratch memory for the lighting calculations and are the source of the outgoing DMA from the running SPE program back to the light buffer in main memory.[5] This is achieved by using the two buffers alternately in order to allow outgoing DMA to complete, asynchronously, the tile decoding and lighting of the next tile. A high level view of our multi-buffering strategy is depicted in Figure 2.9.

The multi-buffering system described here works so effectively that our SPE program spends an average of $2\mu s$ per frame waiting for data to be transferred to and from main memory, with the bulk of this delay being introduced early in the program's execution as one should expect.

---

[4]For information on how to decode, Sony PLAYSTATION3 developers can consult the RSX User's Manual.

[5]We do not currently encode the lighting results; please see further work for more information.

2.6.3 Light Gathering and Culling

When the incoming DMAs for the normal buffer and depth-stencil buffer tiles have completed, we can begin processing. Before we light, we first gather the lights that affect a given tile. We do this by constructing a view frustum for each tile and culling the bounding spheres of the lights against the frustum. In addition, we also cull against the stencil buffer. This is a vital optimization as it minimizes the work done in the expensive lighting phase.

In order to perform the culling and the lighting, we actually work on *sub-tiles* of the frame buffer tile, 32×16 pixels in size. Culling over a smaller region is more effective, and we found sub-tiles of the above size to be optimal in our case.

Next we iterate over the depth-stencil tile to collect the minimum and maximum depth values and the minimum and maximum stencil values for each sub-tile. The depth values will form the near and far clip planes of our sub-tile's view frustum and the stencil values allow us to do a stencil test akin to the early-stencil hardware on a GPU.

In Section 2.5 we described how we write `0xFF` into the stencil buffer when rendering the pre-pass buffers: hence any pixels with a stencil of `0x00` we do not wish to light. However, we do not stencil on a per-pixel basis, but instead skip the lighting on a sub-tile if the maximum stencil value is equal to `0x00` (hence it is `0x00` across the entire sub-tile).

Once a sub-tile has passed the stencil test, we construct its view frustum. Knowing the screen-space position of the corners of the sub-tile, using values from the projection matrix we can construct its position in view-space space, at a fixed distance of one meter from the camera (see Equation (2.5)). Multiplication by the minimum and maximum view-space depth values then gives us the eight vertices of the frustum, from which we can construct the frustum's six planes (see Equation (2.4) for how to construct view-space z from a depth buffer value).

We then construct separate lists of point lights and spot lights that intersect this view frustum. The bounding sphere of each light is tested against each frustum plane, with successful point lights added to a point light list, and successful spot lights added to a spot light list: see Equation (2.2).

$$p_x l_x + p_y + p_z l_z \leq l_{\text{radius}}. \tag{2.2}$$

If no lights are gathered, then the sub-tile follows the same path as one which fails the stencil test the lighting is skipped and we output zero to the frame buffer. However, if at least one light does affect the sub-tile, then the lists of point lights and spot lights are passed into our lighting function to perform the most important part of the work.

2.6.4   Point Lights

The SPE program used for lighting is written in C and makes heavy use of SPE-specific language extensions. We made the choice early on to favor the si-style of intrinsic over the higher-level spu-style. This is due to a closer mapping to the underlying opcodes generated by the compiler [Acton08].

Lighting code is an excellent candidate for both software pipelining and loop unrolling; our lighting is performed on batches of 16 pixels at a time. We found that 16 pixels gave us a very small number of wasted cycles per iteration of our lighting loops while still allowing us to fit everything we needed into the 4KB (128 × 16 byte) register file.[6] The large numbers of independent instructions that result from lighting a relatively large set of pixels mean that the latency caused by dependent instructions closely following one another is almost completely eliminated and overall performance is massively increased (limited only by the number of issued instructions). Non-dependent instructions are interleaved with one another. The results are used some time later when they are available: this well-known optimization technique also has the side effect of improving the balance of instructions over the odd and even execution pipelines because there are a greater number of suitable, non-dependent instructions that can occupy a single fetch group in the synergistic execute unit (SXU). We found that we were able to achieve approximately three times the pixel throughput from batching pixels into groups of 16 over our earlier attempts, which loosely mimicked RSX quads by lighting smaller groups of four pixels:

$$[(\text{point})] \downarrow \text{value} = \text{sat}(\hat{n} \cdot \hat{l}) \times \text{sat}(1 - \frac{[(\|l\|)]^\top 2}{r^\top 2}). \qquad (2.3)$$

Before any lighting can begin it is important to reconstruct the correct input to our lighting equation expressed in Equation (2.3). Equation (2.4) demonstrates how to reconstruct the z component of the view-space position of a pixel given its depth buffer value and the near and far planes of the view frustum:

$$Z_{\text{view}} = \left(Z_{\text{val}} \times \left(Z_{\text{far}}^{-1} - Z_{\text{near}}^{-1} \right) + Z_{\text{near}}^{-1} \right)^{-1}. \qquad (2.4)$$

Calculating the x- and y-components of the view-space position is equally trivial when given the x- and y-coordinates of the pixel in screen-space and the view projection matrix. This is shown by Equation (2.5).

$$xy_{\text{view}} = \left(xy_{\text{screen}} \times \left(\frac{1}{[\text{width, height}]} \times [2, -2] \right) + [-1, 1] \right) \times$$
$$[vp_{0,0}^{-1}, vp_{1,1}^{-1}] \times z_{\text{view}}. \quad (2.5)$$

---

[6]Any more pixels in a single loop in our implementation would risk causing registers to be spilled.

```
// HLSL saturate, clamp to [0..1].
qword x = si_cfltu(q, 0x20);
qword y = si_cuflt(x, 0x20);
```

Listing 2.1. Saturate a `qword` in two odd pipeline instructions.

In HLSL/Cg shaders it is quite common to use the saturate intrinsic function to clamp values to a [0..1] range. To achieve this on the SPE, there is a clever trick that we feel is certainly worthy of mention here. Day et al. introduced the fast saturate/clamp technique, which uses the SPU's floating-point conversion instructions in order to achieve clamping of a floating-point value to a variety of different ranges. This depends on the combination of scale bias operands issued with the instructions [Day 08]. In a pipelined loop, such as our lighting loop, instruction count is oftentimes the overriding determinant of the code's execution speed and as such we are able to employ this trick to great effect. Listing 2.1 demonstrates this technique.

One interesting difference between the GPU implementation of our lighting and the SPE implementation is the switch from the default *array of structures* (AoS) data layout on the GPU, to the transposed, SIMD-friendly *structure of arrays* (SoA)[7] data layout on the SPE. The difference in format of the data is illustrated below in Figure 2.10. By storing, loading and shuffling data into a SoA layout we are able to perform our lighting calculations much more optimally on the SPEs. A pleasant side effect of the switch is that the resulting C code becomes much more scalar-like in appearance, making it easier for other programmers to follow [Bader 07].

The SPE is only equipped to deal with 16 byte aligned writes and reads to and from its local store [Bader 07, IBM 08, IBM 08a]. The targets from all load and store operations first undergo a logical "and" with the LSLR register (set to `0x3ffff` for current implementations of the CBE) before the SPU Store and Load unit (SLS) fetches or writes the address [IBM 08, IBM 08a]. Writing scalar values is achieved by way of a load-shuffle-store pattern. It is therefore desirable to

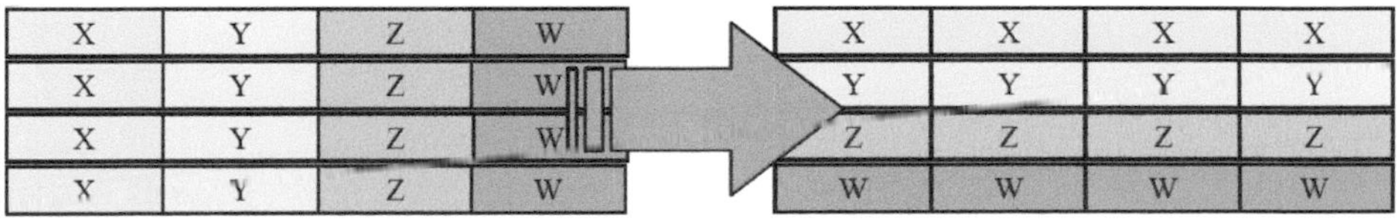

Figure 2.10. Shuffling an AoS into a SoA.

_____

[7]SOA organization is also known as "parallel-array."

```
qword  c0          = si_cfltu(dif0, 0x20);
qword  c1          = si_cfltu(dif1, 0x20);
qword  c2          = si_cfltu(dif2, 0x20);
qword  c3          = si_cfltu(dif3, 0x20);
       dif         = si_ila(0x8000);
qword  scale       = si_ilh(0xff00);
       dif0        = si_mpyhhau(c0, scale, dif);
       dif1        = si_mpyhhau(c1, scale, dif);
       dif2        = si_mpyhhau(c2, scale, dif);
       dif3        = si_mpyhhau(c3, scale, dif);
const vector unsigned char _shuf_uint =
  { 0xc0, 0x00, 0x04, 0x08,
    0xc0, 0x10, 0x14, 0x18,
    0xc0, 0x00, 0x04, 0x08,
    0xc0, 0x10, 0x14, 0x18 };
qword  s_uint      = (const qword)_shuf_uint;
qword  base_addr   = si_from_ptr(result);
qword  p0_01       = si_shufb(dif0, dif1, s_uint);
qword  p0_02       = si_shufb(dif2, dif3, s_uint);
qword  p0          = si_selb(p0_01, p0_02, m_00ff);
                     si_stqd(pixel0, base_addr, 0x00);
```

Listing 2.2. Pixels are converted from their floating-point representations into 32 bit values, batched into 16 byte chunks, and stored.

perform loads and stores on 16 byte boundaries only. As our program required a lot of four byte loads from our normal/depth buffer and a lot of similarly sized writes to our light buffer we ended up batching these loads and stores into 16 byte chunks in order to eliminate the overhead of the additional code that would be required if we were to perform these operations on a pixel-by-pixel basis. This proved to deliver a significant performance increase, especially in the case of storing where nearly all pipeline bubbles were eliminated. We present a portion of our pixel writing code in Listing 2.2 for a single four pixel block.

2.6.5 Spot Lights

In the interest of completeness we present the mathematics used for our, regular spotlights in Equation (2.6).

$$\text{spot}_{\text{value}} = \text{sat}\left(\hat{n} \cdot \hat{l}\right) \times \text{sat}\left(1 - \frac{\|l\|^z}{r^z}\right) \times \text{sat}\left(\frac{\hat{d} \cdot \hat{l} - \cos\frac{\phi}{2}}{\cos\frac{\theta}{2} - \cos\frac{\phi}{2}}\right). \quad (2.6)$$

Note that this is the same as the equation for the point lights, with an additional term at the end. The direction of the light is d (as opposed to l, which is the direction from the light to the point), θ is the angle of the inner cone and φ

is the angle of the outer cone. However, we store their cosines on the light rather than calculating them every time. All lighting values for both point and spot lights are summed for each pixel, yielding Equation (2.7).

$$\text{pixel}_{\text{final}} = \text{sat} \left(\begin{array}{l} \displaystyle\sum_{i=0}^{\text{point}_{\text{count}}} \left[\text{point}_{\text{value}_i} \times \text{point}_{\text{color}_i} \right] + \\ \displaystyle\sum_{i=0}^{\text{spot}_{\text{count}}} \left[\text{spot}_{\text{value}_i} \times \text{spot}_{\text{color}_i} \right] \end{array} \right) \qquad (2.7)$$

2.7 The Main Pass

When the SPEs have finished calculating the light buffer, they then signal to the RSX that the main pass can be rendered. As mentioned above, the synchronization at this stage is very important—we do not want to be reading from an incomplete light buffer. To composite the light buffer with the main scene, we read it as a texture in the pixel shaders. However, as not every pixel in our scene receives light from our pre-pass (see above, we only render geometry into the pre-pass that receives light), we use two shader techniques in the scene: one which samples from the light buffer, and one which does not. For the former technique, each pixel looks up its lighting in the light buffer using its screen-space coordinate, and then composites the light value as a diffuse light, as shown in Equation (2.8).

$$\text{light}_{\text{diffuse}} = \text{surface}_{\text{albedo}} \times \text{light}_{\text{buffer}}. \qquad (2.8)$$

It might be tempting to simply additively or multiplicatively blend the lighting buffer over the scene, but as can be seen above, that method will result in incorrect lighting. This is due to the presence of additional static lighting in our scene.

It is also possible to read from the normal buffer in the main pass. This means that reading from normal maps and converting from tangent space to view (or world) space only happens once. However, this also means that the low precision of the normals stored in the pre-pass becomes more noticeable (only eight bits per component). For this reason and others we did not use this option.

At the end of rendering we have a scene with many dynamic lights rendered using the Cell Broadband Engine. Not only does this open up exciting new possibilities for our rendering engine, but it does so with minimal GPU cost, with a large amount of work performed on the CPU.

2.8   Conclusion

We have presented a method which splits the work of light pre-pass rendering between the RSX and the SPEs on the Cell Broadband Engine. We use the strengths of both components to our advantage: the rasterization performance of the RSX to render the pre-pass geometry, and the vector maths performance of the SPEs to calculate the lighting buffer. By parallelizing the lighting calculation on the SPEs with some other rendering on the RSX (for instance, a dynamic cube map), the lighting becomes *free* and thus this can be a major GPU optimization. Even without the added bonus of parallelization, we found that in some cases, five SPEs running carefully crafted programs could outperform the RSX when performing lighting calculations.

As new architectures emerge we believe there will be increasing opportunities to take processing load off the GPU and place it back onto the CPU. It remains to be seen how things will pan out when the two are combined in Intel's Larrabee [Seiler 08], but on the Cell Broadband Engine we offer that the GPU can be massively accelerated in cases such as deferred lighting or light pre-pass rendering by writing a custom CPU implementation that executes on the SPEs.

2.9   Further Work

There are many improvements that could be done to techniques we describe. Firstly, we currently omit specular from our lighting model. We propose either writing out specular to a separate lighting buffer or placing a monochrome specular term in the alpha channel of the lighting buffer as in [Engel 09]. Material properties could be controlled by adding a specular power in the alpha channel of the normal buffer. Another problem is that our lighting is currently LDR, as it is stored in an 8:8:8:8 integer format. One option is moving to a 16:16:16:16 float, but Wilson suggests instead using the CIE Luv color space [Wilson 09]. Using this method, we can still use an 8:8:8:8 buffer, but with the luminance part of the color using 16 bits. This technique has problems on the GPU, as additive blending of lights on top of each other no longer works. But in the SPE program we have no such problem and thus this becomes more feasible; if one wished to implement a more GPU-friendly technique, then diffuse light intensity could also be stored in the alpha channel as in [Valient 07].

Both of the previous suggestions involve making use of the currently unused alpha channel in the lighting buffer. While there are certainly many possible uses for this byte, one idea we are currently investigating is storing the amount of fog for each pixel. We believe this could be especially beneficial for more expensive fogging equations, for instance, if height fog is being used. This is an example of *adding value* to the SPE program [Swoboda 09a].

Figure 2.11. Another screenshot from *Blur*.

Given the amount of work already being done, including processing the entire normal and depth buffers, there is extra rendering work that could be done in the SPE program. One simple example is performing a down-sample of the depth buffer to a quarter resolution—this could be output asynchronously through the MFC, adding little overhead to the SPE program, and would be useful for many reduced resolution effects such as motion blur, soft particles, occlusion culling, and even screen-space ambient occlusion. It would be possible to reduce the amount of processing on the normal depth buffers by combining the view-space normals and depth into a single 32-bit buffer. By encoding the x- and y-components of the normal into the first two channels (or by converting them to spherical coordinates), and packing linear view-space depth into the remaining 16 bits. This halves the amount of data needed by our SPE program. In fact, this approach is the method we chose for the final version of *Blur* (see Figure 2.11).

Finally, it is our intention to remove the decoding of the buffers altogether and perform lighting on encoded normal/depth buffers, this has several advantages. The decoding process can be replaced with a simple pass over all the pixels in the frame buffer tile, which should yield a minor increase in overall lighting performance together with saving the memory required for the lighting buffer. However, this extra performance and improved memory footprint come at the cost of added mathematical complexity, as deriving the view-space position of pixels becomes non-trivial. This is due to the need to take into account the effects of the encoded buffer's format on the final view-space position of the pixel.

2.10 Acknowledgments

First and foremost we would like to extend our unending thanks to Matt Swoboda of SCEE R&D for laying the groundwork for our continuing efforts and for his suggestions for our implementation. We would also like to thank Colin Hughes of SCEE R&D for his help and suggestions with optimizations.

We also extend our thanks to all the supremely talented individuals that form the Core Technologies Team at Bizarre Creations Ltd., especially to Ian Wilson, Paul Malin, Lloyd Wright, Ed Clay, Jose Sanchez, Charlie Birtwistle, Jan van Valburg, Kier Storey, Fengyun Lu, Jason Denton, Dave Hampson, Chris Cookson and Richard Thomas.

Bibliography

[Acton 08] M. Acton and E. Christensen. "Insomniac's SPU Best Practices." Game Developers Conference, 2008. Available at http://www.insomniacgames.com/tech/articles/0208/files/insomniac_spu_programming_gdc08.ppt.

[Bader 07] D. A. Bader. "Cell Programming Tips & Techniques." Available at http://www.cc.gatech.edu/~bader/CellProgramming.html, 2007.

[Balestra 08] C. Balestra and P. Engstad. "The Technology of Uncharted: Drake's Fortune." Game Developers Conference, 2008. Available at http://www.naughtydog.com.

[Capcom 06] Capcom Inc. "The MT Framework." Available at http://game.watch.impress.co.jp/docs/20070131/3dlp.htm, 2006.

[Day 08] M. Day and J. Garrett. "Faster SPU Clamp." http://www.insomniacgames.com/tech/articles/0308/faster_spu_clamp.php, 2008.

[Deering 88] M. Deering. "The Triangle Processor and Normal Vector Shader: A VLSI System for High Performance Graphics." ACM SIGGRAPH Computer Graphics 22:4 (1988), 21–30.

[Engel 08] W. Engel. "Light Pre-Pass Renderer." *Diary of a Graphics Programmer*. http://diaryofagraphicsprogrammer.blogspot.com/2008/03/light-pre-pass-renderer.html, 2008.

[Engel 08a] W. Engel. "Designing a Renderer for Multiple Lights: The Light Pre-Pass Renderer." In *ShaderX7*, edited by Wolfgang Engel, pp. 655–66. Boston: Charles River Media, 2008.

[Engel 09] W. Engel. "The Light Pre-Pass Renderer Mach III." To appear in proceedings of ACM SIGGRAPH09, 2009.

[IBM 08] "Cell Broadband Engine Programming Handbook Version 1.11." Techncial Report, IBM Corporation, 2008. Available at https://www-01.ibm.com/chips/techlib/techlib.nsf.

[IBM 08a] "Synergistic Processing Unit Instruction Set Architecture." Technical Report, IBM Corporation, 2008. Available at https://www-01.ibm.com/chips/techlib/techlib.nsf/techdocs.

[IBM 09] "The Cell Project at IBM." *IBM*. Available at http://researchweb.watson.ibm.com/cell/home.html, 2009.

[Möller 08] T. Akenine-Möller, E. Haines, and N. Hoffman. "Real-Time Rendering." Third edition. Natick, MA: A K Peters, 2008.

[Perthuis 06] C. Perthuis. "Introduction to the Graphics Pipeline of the PS3." Presented at Eurographics, Vienna, Austria, September 4–8, 2006.

[Seiler 08] L. Seiler, D. Carmean, E. Sprangle, T. Forsyth, M. Abrash, P. Dubey, S. Junkins, A. Lake, J. Sugerman, R. Cavin, R. Espasa, E. Grochowski, T. Juni, and P. Hanrahan. "Larabee: A Many Core X86 Architecture for Visual Computing." *ACM Transactions on Graphics* 27:3 (2008).

[Shippy 09] D. Shippy and M. Phipps. *The Race for a New Games Machine: Creating the Chips inside the New Xbox360 & the Playstation 3.* New York: Citadel Press, 2009.

[Swoboda 09] M. Swoboda, "Deferred Lighting and Post Processing on PLAYSTATION3." Presented at Game Developers Conference, San Francisco, March 23–27 2009. Available at http://www.technology.scee.net/files/presentations/gdc2009/DeferredLightingandPostProcessingonPS3.ppt.

[Swoboda 09a] M. Swoboda. Correspondance with author, 2009.

[Valient 07] M. Valient, "Deferred Rendering in Killzone 2." Develop Conference, Brighton, July 2007. Available at http://www.dimension3.sk/mambo/Download-document/Deferred-Rendering-In-Killzone.php.

[Wilson 09] P. Wilson, "Light Pre-Pass Renderer: Using the CIE Luv Color Space." In *ShaderX7*, edited by Wolfgang Engel, pp. 667–77. Boston: Charles River Media, 2008.

Porting Code between Direct3D9 and OpenGL 2.0

Wojciech Sterna

3.1 Introduction

Nowadays portability is an important issue. Windows and Mac OS are both very popular, and Linux, with its increasing ease of use, is also getting noted. Of course computers are only the tip of the iceberg. For game development, consoles are much more important. Many consoles often means many *application programming interfaces* (API), which for the most part do not differ much and work in similar ways. However, some subtle differences always exist, and the programmer's job is to handle them.

The goal of this article is to show major differences between Direct3D9 (D3D) and OpenGL 2.0 (OGL) since these, and their variants, are the most widely used APIs in game development. We will talk about some general issues and resource management. This brief discussion is to give a solid foundation to those who want to port code between D3D9 and OGL.

3.2 General Issues

3.2.1 Object-Oriented API vs. C-styled API

The main difference between D3D and OGL that may be noticed at first glance is architecture. D3D represents an object-oriented approach whereas OGL is just a set of independent functions. However, this architectural difference surprisingly does not make porting code much harder.

Let us consider a common operation of changing render states (blending, stenciling, and so on). In OGL we simply call a proper function that changes

```
// OGL's way.
glBlendFunc(GL_SRC_ALPHA, GL_ONE_MINUS_SRC_ALPHA);

// D3D9's way.
device->SetRenderState(D3DRS_SRCBLEND, D3DBLEND_SRCALPHA);
device->SetRenderState(D3DRS_DESTBLEND, D3DBLEND_INVSRCALPHA);
```

Listing 3.1. Comparison of changing blending state in D3D9 and OGL.

a particular state, and in D3D9 we actually do the same, but we do it through
IDirect3DDevice9 object. This object contains a two-argument function called
SetRenderState: the first argument is the render state we are changing, and the
second is the new value. Listing 3.1 shows a simple comparison between D3D and
OGL in changing blending state.

The difference is very subtle and this is actually how it looks in the case of all
other render states.

One thing that needs to be pointed out is that in D3D9 and OGL, some render
states are merged in one or are separated in two or more function calls. We see
in Listing 3.1 that changing blending function involves one render call in OGL
and two distinct render calls in D3D. This is one example but there are more of
them (especially among stencil-control functions). This needs to be taken into
consideration when writing a wrapper of both APIs.

3.2.2   Avoid Unnecessary Functions Calls

To improve efficiency on the CPU side, it is advisable not to call the same function with the same value over and over again. For instance, there is a function
SetVertexShader in D3D that changes the active vertex shader. If many objects
(with many draw calls) are to be rendered using the same vertex shader, it is
pointless to call **SetVertexShader** before every draw call (what is actually a common practice when we are grouping functions for convenience), not to mention
very expensive!

To solve this problem, a wrapper around frequently used functions should be
written. Such wrapper should simply store currently held values (i.e., bounded
shaders, textures, etc.) and allow for changing them only if a new value is to
be set. Depending on the application's CPU overhead, this may be a crucial
performance factor.

3.2.3   Lost Device

One of the most annoying of D3D9's problems is the problem of lost device. When
the application is running in full-screen mode and gets minimized, all resources

stored in the GPU's memory are lost and need to be recreated. This problem does not concern in OGL (yet some subtle exceptions can occur: see Section 3.3.1 for details).

In D3D9, at the time of creating a particular resource, a programmer can choose a memory pool in which to place a resource. Resources can be stored in GPU memory, system memory, or in both GPU and system memory. This last combination is called *managed*. When a resource is created in that way (managed), a programmer does not have to take care of restoring the resource since its data is backed up by system memory and will be automatically copied to the GPU by D3D after the device is reset. However, some resources, like off-screen render targets, cannot be stored in system memory and need to be recreated manually by a programmer when a device is lost.

The application connected with this chapter, available at http://www.akpeters. com/gpupro, handles lost devices.

3.2.4   Memory Pools

As mentioned in the previous section, D3D9 lets a programmer specify the memory pool where a resource is to be created. We shall now briefly discuss them all.

Default pool. The default is for the resource to be created directly in GPU memory with no system memory copy. A bit paradoxically, this pool is best for resources that are never updated directly via the CPU and for those that are updated very frequently (at least once per frame). All render targets and depth-stencil surfaces must be created in this pool since they are modified strictly on the GPU. Also, dynamic vertex buffers and dynamic textures that change data very frequently via the CPU should be created in this pool.

Managed pool. Use of the managed pool creates a resource in both GPU and system memory. When modifying the data on the CPU, D3D operates strictly on system copy and makes a fast "mem-copy" to the GPU's memory. If the resource is modified on the CPU only once per frame, then managed resources are as fast as default ones. Difference in speed can usually be noticed only if a resource is modified more than once per frame.

System pool. The system pool creates a resource only in system memory. As for OGL, a programmer does not have so many options and all resources are created directly in GPU memory with no system copy. This is equivalent to D3D's default memory pool. However, as mentioned in the previous section, these resources don't have to be recreated when a device is lost.

3.2.5   Unit-Cube Constraints

Unit-cube constraints are one of the most important differences between D3D and OGL. Clip-space's x- and y-coordinates are in the $[-1, 1]$ range in both D3D and OGL. However, the z-coordinate is in the range $[-1, 1]$ in OGL but in the range $[0, 1]$ in D3D. Because of this, one should not use the same projection matrix in both APIs. Let us see what the consequences would be of applying a D3D-like perspective projection matrix in an OGL-based application.

A traditional D3D's perspective projection matrix for a left-handed coordinate system is shown in Equation (3.1):

$$\text{D3DXMatrixPerspectiveLH} = \begin{bmatrix} \frac{2*n}{w} & 0 & 0 & 0 \\ 0 & \frac{2*n}{h} & 0 & 0 \\ 0 & 0 & \frac{f}{f-n} & 1 \\ 0 & 0 & \frac{n*f}{n-f} & 0 \end{bmatrix} \tag{3.1}$$

We are interested only in the z coordinate. The final formulas for z' and w' (since they are needed for normalized device coordinates) in clip-space are

$$z' = \frac{z*f}{f-n} - \frac{n*f}{f-n},$$
$$w' = z.$$

The value of z in NDC (normalized device coordinates) is

$$z'' = \frac{z'}{w'} = \frac{f}{f-n} - \frac{n*f}{z*(f-n)}. \tag{3.2}$$

Let us now assume that $n = 3$ and $f = 10$, and plug these values into z'':

$$z'' = \frac{10}{7} - \frac{30}{z*7}.$$

This leads to

$$z = 3 \quad \Rightarrow \quad z'' = \frac{10}{7} - \frac{30}{3*7} = 0,$$
$$z = 10 \quad \Rightarrow \quad z'' = \frac{10}{7} - \frac{30}{10*7} = 1.$$

So in fact Equation (3.2) maps all z-values between near and far planes to the $[0, 1]$ range, required for D3D.

Now we shall see what would happen if we were to apply Equation (3.2) to OGL's rendering pipeline. Let's again assume $n = 3$ and $f = 10$. The resulting far plane remains the same (since it equals 1 in NDC for both D3D and OGL), but the near plane is shifted a bit. Let us see what z we end up with after equating (3.2) to -1:

$$\frac{10}{7} - \frac{30}{z * 7} = -1 \quad \Rightarrow \quad z = \frac{30}{17}.$$

This result means that if we apply `D3DXMatrixPerspectiveLH` to OGL and pass 3 as the near plane, we will eventually come up with the near plane at distance $\frac{30}{17}$. In fact, as f approaches infinity, the near clipping plane approaches $\frac{n}{2}$. This can be easily checked by simply computing the limit of Equation (3.2) with respect to f, equating it to -1, and finding z as a function of n.

To sum up: theoretically, D3D's projection matrix should not be used as a projection matrix in OGL and vice-versa.

3.3 Resources Management

3.3.1 Textures

Note that in this section we will cover only two-dimensional textures, skipping volume and cube textures discussion. These are handled very similarly to two-dimensional textures in both APIs.

In D3D9 a two-dimensional texture is represented by a `IDirect3DTexture9` interface. Pointer to texture object can be obtained by using `IDirect3DDevice9::CreateTexture` method. It is also possible to use a helper D3DX library to load textures from file or memory (`D3DXLoadTextureFromFile`), which calls `CreateTexture` behind the scenes. During the creation we can also make D3D create a full mipmap chain.

Textures in D3D do not not store any information about filtering and addressing modes. If, for instance, bilinear texture filtering is to be used with a texture, it is specified via so-called *samplers*. A sampler defines what texture is to be used. It also defines additional parameters like filtering and addressing (as was just mentioned). Sampler parameters can be changed with the `IDirect3DDevice9::SetSamplerState` function. A texture can be assigned to a sampler with `IDirect3DDevice9::SetTexture`. Note that in shaders we actually refer not to textures, but to samplers. This is convenient since every sampler has its own index.

In OGL, texture is represented by an unsigned integer value. Texture is created with the `glGenTextures` function and released with `glDeleteTextures`. Data can be assigned to a texture via the `glTexImage2D` function. Unlike D3D, in OGL filtering and addressing modes are defined directly in textures. All texture parameters can be changed with the `glTexParameter` function.

Of course, we must somehow bind used textures to particular *indices* so they can be distinguished in shaders. In D3D we use samplers, which by definition have indices. If we want to assign such an index to OGL's texture, before binding texture (what is done via `glBindTexture`), we must call `glActiveTexture` and pass constant `GL_TEXTUREn`, where `n` is a sampler's index (just like D3D's sampler index).

In Section 3.2.3 it was stated that OGL's resources do not need to be recreated when a device is lost. In general this is true, but there are some exceptions. OGL offers at least three ways to generate mipmaps: One is to use the `gluBuild2DMipmaps` function, which simply iterates over a few `glTexImage2D` calls (does not work with non-rectangular textures). Another is to call `glTex Parameter` with parameter `GL_GENERATE_MIPMAP` set to `GL_TRUE`. The third and newest way is to call the `glGenerateMipmap` function. There are problems with the last solution. If the application loses its device, the mipmaps will not be regenerated automatically and a programmer has to do it. Furthermore, some GPUs have issues with that function. The most recommended way to generate mipmaps in OGL is the second option.

3.3.2   Off-Screen Surfaces and Framebuffers

After including the `EXT_framebuffer_object` extension in OGL's core, the ease of use of render-to-texture functionality has improved dramatically. Moreover, the framebuffer object model is also similar to D3D's, so porting code between these two APIs is more intuitive. We will now introduce a terminology used in D3D and OGL regarding off-screen surfaces/framebuffers.

In D3D9 off-screen surfaces divide into two distinct groups: *render targets* and *depth-stencil surfaces*.

Render target. The *render target* is an off-screen surface, represented by `IDirect3D Surface9`, that can be rendered to. It may be created via `IDirect3DDevice9:: CreateRenderTarget`. If it is created that way it cannot be used as a texture, yet it can use multisampling. The other way to create a render target is to create a texture (via `IDirect3DDevice9::CreateTexture`, for instance) with a usage flag `D3DUSAGE_RENDERTARGET`. After that, this texture can be accessed for surface (one surface for one mipmap of texture). Later on such a surface can be used as a render target via the `IDirect3DDevice9::SetRenderTarget` function.

Depth-stencil surface. The *depth-stencil surface* is an off-screen surface, represented by `IDirect3DSurface9`, that is used as depth-stencil buffer. It is most frequently created via `IDirect3DDevice9::CreateDepthStencilSurface`. However, the depth-stencil surface can also be created by first creating a texture with

D3DUSAGE_DEPTHSTENCIL usage. This allows one to use the depth-stencil buffer as texture, which allows, for instance, one to implement hardware shadow mapping.

In OGL 2.0, as opposed to D3D, render targets and depth-stencil surfaces are not treated separately. The main character here is a *framebuffer* object. A framebuffer object is an off-screen buffer that can have attached multiple texture objects and render-buffer objects. In particular, such a framebuffer could consist of one texture (serving as a render target) and one render-buffer (serving as a depth-stencil buffer). Only one framebuffer object may be created by the application, and we may only change objects attached to it. This gets us closer to D3D's model and is an even faster solution since switching framebuffers takes more time than attaching objects to the framebuffer.

Texture object. A *texture object* is just...texture! We create a texture object, set its attributes, and initialize it through glTexImage (with null data pointer). After that, a texture can be attached to the framebuffer object via glFramebuffer Texture. This generalization allows one to use textures both as render targets and ordinary textures during rendering.

Render-buffer object. A *render-buffer object* is simply a two-dimensional array of pixels that can be rendered to but that cannot be used as a texture. It is actually equivalent to D3D's surface concept. Render-buffer is a great candidate for a depth-stencil buffer (if it is not used, for instance, for hardware shadow mapping, where it should be a texture).

Keep in mind that OGL's off-screen framebuffer requires that all textures and render-buffers bound to it must be of the same size. So if a 512×512 render target is to be used, and if it should have an associated depth-stencil surface, then it must be of size 512×512. In turn, D3D requires that a depth-stencil surface's width and height be equal to or greater than the width and height of a render target.

3.3.3 Vertex Declarations

Vertex declaration, in terms of OGL and D3D, is very interesting because there is nothing like vertex declaration in OGL. There are no other functions like glGenerateVertexDeclaration or glBindVertexDeclaration. At least, not explicitly.

Vertex declaration is an object that defines what kind of data from the vertex buffer will be sent to the GPU. In D3D9, vertex declaration is represented by an IDirect3DVertexDeclaration9 interface. We simply declare an array of D3DVERTEXELEMENT9-type elements, fill it, and pass, along with a pointer to IDirect3DVertexDeclaration9, and to the IDirect3DDevice9::CreateVertex Declaration method.

On the other hand, in OGL vertex declaration is set implicitly through a single `glVertexAttribPointer` function[1] (note that attributes must be first associated with the shader via `glBindAttribLocation`). One thing that must be remembered is that in OGL, setting the vertex declaration must be done after a particular vertex buffer is bound. Please look at the source code of sample application to better understand the differences.

3.3.4   Vertex and Index Buffers

Vertex and index buffers are yet another resource that is easily ported between D3D9 and OGL.

In D3D9, vertex and index buffers are represented by the `IDirect3DVertexBuffer9` and `IDirect3DIndexBuffer9` interfaces, respectively. They can be created via the `IDirect3DDevice9::CreateVertexBuffer` or `IDirect3DDevice9::CreateIndexBuffer` functions, respectively. These functions take a few parameters, among which we can find one responsible for choosing a memory pool. Another important parameter is the buffer's usage. Specifying this parameter can help D3D to use the best possible place to put the buffer. For instance, `D3DUSAGE_DYNAMIC` can be used to mark a buffer as dynamic.

To modify a vertex or index buffer's data, a `IDiredt3D***Buffer9::Lock` method should be called. With this method a pointer to the buffer's data can be obtained. When we are finished with updating the buffer's data, it should be unlocked with `IDiredt3D***Buffer9::Unlock` method.

In OGL, both types of buffers are represented with unsigned integer value. To create a buffer, the `glGenBuffers` function should be called (just as in the case of other `glGen***` OGL functions). However, it is not a complete initialization step. To actually reserve GPU memory for buffer we must first bind it with `glBindBuffer` and then call `glBufferData` to actually reserve the memory. Both of these functions expect as a first parameter a constant, which points to the type of buffer we are dealing with. In the case of vertex and index buffers it can be either `GL_ARRAY_BUFFER` or `GL_ELEMENT_ARRAY_BUFFER` for vertex and index buffer, respectively. One of the parameters of `glBufferData` is the buffer's memory size; another indicates an initial data. A third parameter is similar to D3D's usage parameter, which can be used to mark buffer, for instance, as static or dynamic. One thing that is important to note is that with `glBufferData` we can actually update the buffer's data (second parameter: init data). However, it is very inefficient to do so for dynamic buffers, since this function, every time

---

[1]Vertex declaration can also be set through the set of functions: `glVertexPointer`, `glColorPointer`, `glNormalPointer`, `glTexCoordPointer`. However, these have been marked as deprecated in the new OGL standard and shall be removed from the specification in the future.

```
mapBufferData(vertices);
{
    vertices[0].position = Vec4(...);
    vertices[0].color = Vec4(...);

    ...

}
unmapBufferData();
```

Listing 3.2. First way of updating mapped data.

it is called, reserves a new memory buffer. To actually update the buffer's data, **glBufferSubData** can be used. It can, be there's an even better way.

To update the buffer's data it is usually best to directly map and then fill it. This is the best solution not only because it is the fastest, but also because it makes us even closer to D3D's data update model. To map a buffer we need to call **glMapBuffer**, get a pointer to buffer's data, fill the data, and unmap the buffer with **glUnmapBuffer**. The procedure looks exactly as in D3D. In these terms, OGL programmers usualy use **glBufferData** to only reserve memory, passing as init data a null pointer, and filling the buffer with data strictly through mapping functions.

There are two ways in which a buffer can be updated via mapping/locking functions. The first way is shown in Listing 3.2; the second is shown in Listing 3.3.

First of all, it is important to note that during the static buffer's lock, the GPU must wait until the CPU finishes updating data. In these terms the most efficient way to update data is the second, where we are using temporary data and do a fast copy to GPU's memory. However, this concerns only OGL and D3D's default memory pool. With D3D's managed pool, both ways are nearly identical (the first is even better). It is so because managed resource has a local copy and D3D operates on this copy and in fact, when the buffer is being unlocked, does

```
{
    tempVertices[0].position = Vec4(...);
    tempVertices[0].color = Vec4(...);

    ...

}

mapBufferData(vertices);
    memCopy(vertices, tempVertices);
unmapBufferData();
```

Listing 3.3. Second way of updating mapped data.

a fast copy to GPU memory behind the programmer's back. So with a managed pool there is no need to use any temporary data.

A slightly different situation takes place when using dynamic buffers. In such cases only the second way should be used. Besides, during the lock call, GPU may continue rendering old data while CPU is updating buffer with new data. This prevents GPU from stall. More information about updating dynamic buffers can be found in [Microsoft 09].

3.3.5   Shaders

In D3D9, shaders can be written in low-level assembly language or *high level shader language* (HLSL), which is compiled down to assembly. Vertex and pixel shaders are two distinct objects and are handled separately.

In OGL situation is similar: one can write shaders in low-level *OpenGL assembly language* (ARB) or high-level *OpenGL shading language* (GLSL). However, in GLSL, vertex and pixel (fragment) shaders are treated as one object. A programmer writes separately vertex and fragment shader code, but after compilation (in program) these two shaders have to be linked together and used as one shader object. This introduces a potential problem in porting since it often happens that few vertex shaders are used in combination with one pixel shader, or vice versa. With GLSL, every needed pair has to be prepared.

The most universal shader language is *Cg*. Its syntax is identical to HLSL. Cg is in fact some kind of abstract shader language. It (more precisely, Cg runtime) allows us to compile a shader to any profile we wish—D3D/OGL assembly or GLSL. Thankfully, the same shader can be written for both D3D and OGL. Only at compilation time must we specify which profile we wish to compile to. This way we can easily generate two shaders: one for D3D and one for OGL. However, some subtle differences between D3D and OGL may force us to write a slightly different Cg shader for each API. For instance, input vertex shader semantics can be different. D3D usually uses semantics like `POSITION` or `COLOR`, whereas OGL uses semantics in the form of `ATTRIBn` (this is true when using `glVertexAttribPointer`; when using `glVertexPointer` and other functions alike, semantics are identical to those from D3D9).

3.4   Notes on Debugging

To keep the application away from bugs, debugging tools are needed. There are many tools available for both APIs. Some are good for one purpose, some for another.

D3D9 allows the programmer to run in two modes: retail or debug with built-in debugging support. When debug mode is turned on, D3D reports (through the

Visual Studio output window, for instance) every illegal operation, error codes— even redundant functions calls. Another very important tool for the D3D programmer is PIX. This application allows one to view many rendering statistics, view functions log call, and even see a full history of every rendered pixel.

OGL programmers unfortunately don't have so much luck as there is no built-in debug mode. However, there are at least two nice tools very useful for every OGL programmer: `gDEBugger` and `GLIntercept`. The former is an excellent tool that offers functionality similar to PIX, including offering many charts and statistics. The latter is great for quickly finding any OGL runtime errors and for logging functions calls. It is even possible to see graphically what textures are bound to particular samplers.

All of these tools are a must for every D3D/OGL programmer. When they are properly used, they can drastically reduce the time spent finding bugs.

3.5 A Word on Sample Application

There are not many listings in this article because there is no sense in showing too many of them. Instead, a source code of sample application should be examined.

The source code available at http://www.akpeters.com/gpupro shows implementation of a cross-renderer that supports D3D9 and OGL. One can easily see how all subtle differences between these two APIs are handled in real application.

The renderer that is used by sample application is a foundation of BlossomEngine. This engine has been written specifically for an amateur project game (currently under development): *Greedy Car Thieves* [GCT 10], a remake of *Grand Theft Auto 2*.

A very nice source of information on porting code and writing a cross-renderer is the Ogre 3D engine. It is a free open-source project with neatly written and commented code.

3.6 Conclusion

After the release of OGL 2.0 specification, ease of porting code between it and D3D9 has increased dramatically. Fortunately, OGL 2.0 is supported by a wide veriety of GPUs, so in most cases it is not necessary to write additional code paths that, for instance, would use something different than framebuffer object for render-to-texture. Both APIs are nearly identical in use, and this "nearly" was discussed in this article.

Bibliography

[Microsoft 09] Microsoft Corporation. "DirectX SDK." http://msdn.microsoft .com/en-us/directx/default.aspx, 2009.

[GCT 10] "Greedy Car Thieves." http://www.gct-game.net.

4

VIII

Practical Thread Rendering
for DirectX 9

David Pangerl

4.1 Abstract

This article describes a practical and efficient solution for multi-core processor DirectX 9 rendering. The solution significantly accelerates the rendering of complex scenes on multi-core processors by using double buffered command buffers and dedicated rendering thread to execute the command buffers. Its main advantages over similar implementations are the following:

- It is extremely easy to add into any DirectX 9 application.

- It supports all DirectX functions.

- It supports dynamic buffers.

- It supports D3DX functions (e.g., font rendering).

- It supports miscellaneous functions (e.g., win pix).

The implementation requires the developer only to replace the main device class `IDirect3DDevice9` with the one supplied with this solution (`TDxDevice`).

4.2 Introduction

DirectX 9 is implemented so that all functions are DLL function calls. As such they can not be in-lined and thus require some additional instruction to execute. Additionally, they internally tend to frequently synchronize with hardware and can suffer unpredicted time delays (specific to the application rendering pipeline,

DirectX release and device driver version). On the other hand, the DirectX design itself requires issuing multiple functions for rendering a single primitive (set render state, render target, source streams, vertex shader, pixel shader, textures, and, finally, render), even further worsening the situation. In the end, all this function calls and inherent synchronization constitutes in a significant overhead that our solution eliminates.

In the last decade the processor industry has changed the road from developing faster processor into developing multi-core processors.

Our solution takes advantage of the parallelism offered by multi-core processors by creating a dedicate thread for rendering and transferring all the DirectX work to that thread.

4.3   Solution

The solution itself is very plain and simple; all DirectX functions calls are efficiently queued into the command buffer (together with the copy of all function volatile data), and executed on a dedicated rendering thread.

Functions that require immediate return (e.g., CreateDevice) are buffered into the immediate buffer, synchronized with rendering thread, and executed immediately so that the result can be returned.

The trick is to store the function and function parameters directly into our command buffer. In order to do that we make a virtual class with the `Execute` function that we template into a class which can save parameters. In the main buffer class we use `placement new` to create that template directly into the command buffer in specific offset (see Listing 4.1).

4.3.1   Why is it Faster?

The usual game cycle is divided into two steps: an *update* followed by a *render*. In the update step, all system and game objects are updated and then visualized in the render step. Due to the nature of game objects, the update step is usually internally split into several worker threads to optimize execution. However, the rendering step can not be split since DirectX itself does not support that. Consequently, all rendering commands are executed from a single thread.

This is what we do much faster! In fact, more than 100 times faster. We replace the DirectX 9 device with our own, which buffers all the commands but does so really quickly. We used template functions that are in-lined, producing a very fast buffering. Our buffering functions take in average 17 instructions when parameters are not copied and in average 129 instruction when parameters are copied. Just for comparison; an average DirectX function takes 15,231 instructions.

```
class TExecute {
public:
   virtual void                   Execute() const=0;
};

template <typename TR, typename T0>
class TBufferedFunction1 : public TExecute {
protected:
   typedef TR                     (*TFunction)(T0);
   int                            size;
   TFunction                      Function;
   T0                             Param0;
public:
   TBufferedFunction1(TFunction funct, T0 param0)
   {
      size     = sizeof( *this );
      Function = funct;
      Param0   = param0;
   }
public:
   void                           Execute() const {Function( Param0 );}
};

class TBufferFunction {
protected:
   int                            offset;
   char                           *aBuffer;
public:
   TBufferFunction()
   {
      offset=0;
      aBuffer=0;
   }
public:
   template <typename TR, typename T0>
   void                           Buffer(TR (*funct)(T0), T0 param0)
   {
      typedef TBufferedFunction1<TR,T0>T;
      new( &aBuffer[ offset ] ) T ( funct , param0 );
      offset+=sizeof( T );
   }
};
```

Listing 4.1. The solution.

Once rendering is done (signaled with the `IDirect3DDevice9::Present` function), we check if previous rendering has already finished; we do not want to buffer more than one frame ahead (since DirectX already buffers multiple frames ahead). We then synchronize, exchange buffers, and go to the next cycle (see Table 4.1).

Function	Calls	DX cycles	Out cycles	x times faster
SetRenderState	956678	49	16	3.0
SetVertexShaderConstantF	718149	7910	223	35.4
DrawIndexedPrimitive	624299	894	17	52.1
SetSamplerState	359649	66	16	4.1
SetTexture	334216	72	18	4.1
SetStreamSource	328894	113	17	6.6
SetVertexDeclaration	328846	84	16	5.3
SetPixelShader	261353	141	15	9.1
SetVertexShader	261339	250	21	11.7
SetIndices	134897	133	16	8.4
SetPixelShaderConstantF	120313	118	53	2.2
DrawPrimitive	98162	923	16	57.1
UnlockVertexBuffer	98162	88	15	5.8
LockVertexBuffer	98161	234963	23	10056.2
SetRenderTarget	37398	482	20	24.4
SetDepthStencilSurface	28407	254	17	15.0
Write (write text)	22871	15436	263	58.8
EndScene	22656	160	16	10.1
BeginScene	22656	151	16	9.4
WriteUni (write unicode text)	19542	85354	154	553.0
Clear	16540	1106	33	33.1
LockRect	1438	17743	57	308.9
UnlockRect	1438	13117	16	845.4
SetViewport	1438	992	19	51.5
SetPixelShaderConstantI	1438	180	69	2.6

Table 4.1. Comparison of the most used DirectX 9 functions.

4.3.2   Command Buffer

The command buffer is actually a memory buffer that stores functions and their parameters. We chose to use double buffering since it is a simple synchronization technique that effectively avoids data races by synchronizing threads on one point only.

The command buffer is implemented with the use of templates, which enables easy usage and high optimization level (all buffering code is in-lined).

4.3.3   Immediate Commands

Immediate commands are actually a bit slower than direct DirectX calls since they require synchronization with rendering thread. Such implementation is required since DirectX 9 requires all function calls to be issued from one thread (the thread that actually created the `IDirect3DDevice9`).

However, the use of these commands is reserved mainly for application startup when all objects are created. It does not influence the main application performance.

It is important to note that a DirectX 9 device can be created in a multi-threaded way, but the implementation is much slower than the one presented in this article.

Here is a list of all immediate functions:

- `CreateDevice`

- `GetAvailableTextureMem`

- `EvictManagedResources`

- `GetDirect3D`

- `GetDeviceCaps`

- `CreateAdditionalSwapChain`

- `Reset`

- `CreateTexture`

- `CreateVolumeTexture`

- `CreateCubeTexture`

- `CreateVertexBuffer`

- `CreateIndexBuffer`

- `CreateRenderTarget`

- `CreateDepthStencilSurface`

- `GetRenderTargetData`

- `GetFrontBufferData`

- `CreateOffscreenPlainSurface`

- `GetRenderTarget`

- `GetDepthStencilSurface`

- `CreateVertexDeclaration`

- `CreateVertexShader`

- `CreatePixelShader`

4.4   Conclusion

The solution described in this article can provide a very easy way to optimize your application. Our test applications showed the optimization up to 200%. However, in a real-time game we achieved only a 15% optimization since the rendering thread was already CPU-bound.

4.5   Future Work

The main focus of our further research will be to separate rendering into several threads (e.g., main scene render, shadows, user interface). The idea is to create sub-command buffers that will able to split the rendering step into several threads.

IX Game Postmortems

The section "Game Postmortems" is a new section that looks back on the graphics programming challenges of popular games. It covers the games *Call of Juarez: Bound in Blood, Just Cause 2, Miner Wars*, and *Spore*.

The first article in the section, "Stylized Rendering in *Spore*," covers the scriptable PostFX pipeline used in the game. Shalin Shodhan and Andrew Willmott show how they scripted the pipeline and certain effects like filters for oil paint, watercolor, eight-bit, film noir, and others.

The postmortem of *Call of Juarez: Bound in Blood*, by Pawel Rohleder and Maciej Jamrozik, covers the lighting and shadowing techniques, PostFX, screen-space ambient occlusion (SSAO), motion-blur, tone mapping, edge anti-aliasing, and the rendering of natural phenomena: water, rain, volumetric fog, and light shafts.

In "Making it Large, Beautiful, Fast, and Consistent: Lessons Learned Developing *Just Cause 2*," Emil Persson covers lighting and soft shadowing techniques, character shadows, soft particles, SSAO, challenges with floating-point precision of position calculations, cloud rendering, particle trimming, constant buffer usage, gamma correction, and many other topics.

In the last section in the article, Marek Rosa covers destructible volumetric terrain in the massively multiplayer online game *Miner Wars*. He is using a voxel map to represent terrain but the engine does not draw voxels directly; instead it polygonizes them to triangles prior to rendering or detecting collision. The standard marching cubes algorithm is used for polygonization.

—Matthias Wloka

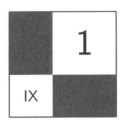

Stylized Rendering in *Spore*

Shalin Shodhan and Andrew Willmott

As screen effects and deferred shading become standard fare in game engines, a good compositing tool becomes a key part of the rendering pipeline. In the game *Spore*, we used a scriptable filter chain system to process frames at runtime. A filter chain is essentially just a series of parameterized image processing shaders applied in order. Every frame in our game is processed and composited using this system. In addition to the standard art-directed look of *Spore*, we created a set of specialized filters to generate dramatically different visual styles for the game. Figure 1.1 shows a *Spore* rendered as an oil painting. These were so compelling that we shipped them with *Spore* as player-enabled cheats. In this article we would like to breakdown some of the visual styles we generated and share details about the design and implementation of our Filter Chain system.

1.1 Filter Chain System

GPU implementations of image processing techniques like blur, edge detection etc. are widely available. Our goal was to build a system with a palette of such filters that artists could use to author visual styles. Figure 1.2 shows how this system is placed in the rendering pipeline.

1.1.1 Design Considerations

Rapid iteration and scripting. Rapid iteration is key for artists working in accordance with art direction. So our scripts are hot-loadable in development builds. This means that an artist can tweak a parameter or change the script and see the updated results while the game is running. The scripting itself is very simple. In fact there are only two types of commands in the script! Listing 1.1 shows a simple bloom filter chain.

Figure 1.1. An airplane made in *Spore* rendered as an oil painting.

Filters. Each filter corresponds to a single shader applied to a screen aligned quad. It can take up to four textures and up to 16 constant float parameters as input. It is scripted using the following command:

<filterName>   <inTex>   <outTex> [<param1> ...]

The `filterName` corresponds to a pre-defined set of filters like blur, compress, etc., while `inTex` and `outTex` are source and destination textures for the filter.

A number of filter specific constant parameters can be specified.

Textures. Each filter chain can declare its own set of temporary textures to store intermediate results using the following command:

texture <name> -ratio <integer>

Then <name> can be used as <inTex> or <outTex> for a filter. The ratio parameter lets you control the texture size as a fraction of game resolution. Artist generated textures can be accessed by their resource IDs and game-generated or reserved render targets can be referenced by keywords; for example, the frame-buffer is `dest` and the unfiltered scene is `source`.

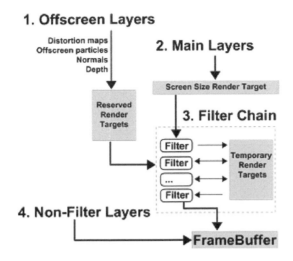

Figure 1.2. Filter Chain system overview.

Integration with effects. An easy win for us was to add this system as a component of our industrial strength effects system, Swarm. This way filter chains were well integrated into the rendering engine. We got scripting and hot-loading for free and our artists, being well-versed in Swarm, could easily get started with filter chains.

Figure 1.3 shows how the cell game's filter chain uses multiple input textures generated by other stages of the rendering pipeline and forms the final composite.

```
# Basic bloom
   filterChain
      texture blur1a -ratio 4
      texture blur2a -ratio 4

      compress source blur1a -bias -.25 -scale 1

      blur blur1a blur2a   -scaleX 2
      blur blur2a blur1a   -scaleY 2
      blur blur1a blur2a   -scaleX -2
      blur blur2a blur1a   -scaleY -2

      add source dest -texture blur1a -sourceMul .75 -addMul 1
   end
```

Listing 1.1. A simple bloom effect as a filter chain.

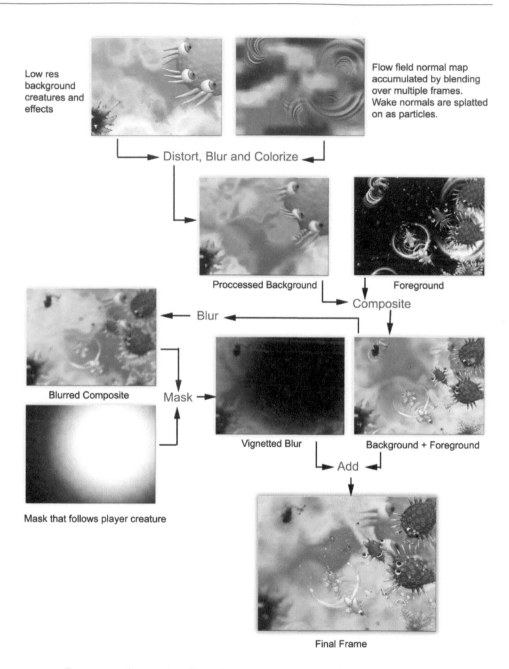

Low res background creatures and effects

Flow field normal map accumulated by blending over multiple frames. Wake normals are splatted on as particles.

Distort, Blur and Colorize

Proccessed Background

Foreground

Composite

Blur

Blurred Composite

Mask

Vignetted Blur

Background + Foreground

Mask that follows player creature

Add

Final Frame

Figure 1.3. A complex filter chain for the cell game's fluid environment.

1.1.2   Implementation

The filter chain system we shipped with *Spore*, by and large, adheres to the design presented above. Some significant additions are given in this section.

Dynamic parameters. Spore's dynamic environment needs call for frame varying parameters. We added global parameters that update per frame and can be accessed by any filter. For example, we use camera height and time of day in doing atmospheric filters for planets as shown in Figure 1.4. In other cases the game needs to smoothly interpolate between two different sets of parameter values for a given filter. For example., whenever the weather system starts to rain, the global colorize filter's color transitions to an overcast gray. We added parameters that support game-controlled interpolation. Finally, we added faders that can smoothly change the strength of a filter.

Custom filters. An important addition to the system is a *custom filter* that can specify its shader as a parameter. This means that a programmer can add a new image technique pretty easily by just adding a new shader to an existing

Figure 1.4. A time-of-day driven colorize filter. This colorized-compressed output is then blurred and added to the scene as bloom.

Size	Count	Memory (KB)	Usage
1024 × 768	3	9216	One full screen buffer held the unfiltered scene. Two full screen and two half screen buffers were available for distortion maps, off screen particles etc. The remaining textures were used as intermediate buffers between filters.
512 × 384	5	3840	
256 × 192	1	192	
128 × 96	2	96	

Table 1.1. Worst-case texture memory usage at 1024 × 768, 13MB.

build. Also, a programmer can optimize artist generated filter chains, by collapsing multiple filters into a single custom filter that achieves the same visual result.

1.1.3　Performance

Filter chains are fairly pixel shader heavy and choked our min spec low end Pixel Shader 2.0 cards. We wrote low, mid and high quality versions of all our filter chains to adapt based on target hardware. Custom filters are a great tool for collapsing multiple filters into a single pass and saving on fill rate.

Buffer size and texture memory usage. We heavily tuned texture sizes for scratch buffers, iterating rapidly with the `ratio` parameter for the `texture` command in filter chain script. After collecting data about texture usage for various filters we preallocated all our render targets. Since only one filter chain was allowed at a time, these textures could be reused. We tried to improve reuse by atlasing but ran into problems with texture addressing and filtering at boundaries for the atlased render targets (see Table 1.1).

1.2　Fun with Filters

Here are a number of experimental rendering styles available in *Spore* as cheats.

1.2.1　Oil Paint Filter

For an oil paint filter (see Listing 1.2), a brush stroke normal map is rendered first. This is used to distort the incoming scene. Then the same normal map is used to light the brush strokes in image space with three lights. Brush strokes can be driven by a ribbon particle effect to make the filter dynamic and more temporally coherent (see Figure 1.5).

The constants in Listing 1.2 control properties of the effect. Larger values of `kDistortionScale` make the effect more impressionistic. The `kNormalScales` values control how detailed the brush strokes look; `kBrighten` is a global adjustment. Light directions and colors can also be used to vary the look.

Figure 1.5. Oil paint filter.

```
# Oil Paint Effect
# kDistortionScale 0.01, kBrighten 2.0
# kNormalScales (1.5, 2.5, 1.6)

# Get the normal map and bring normals into [-1,1] range
half4 pNormalMap = tex2D( normalMap, fragIn.uv0 );
half3 nMapNormal = 2 * pNormalMap.rgb - half3( 1, 1, 1 );

# Distort the UVs using normals (Dependent Texture Read!)
half4 pIn = tex2D(sceneTex,
                  saturate(uv - nMapNormal.xy * kDistortionScale) );

# Generate the image space lit scene
half3 fakeTangN = nMapNormal.rbg * kNormalScales;
fakeTangN = normalize(fakeTangN);

# Do this for 3 lights and sum, choose different directions
# and colors for the lights
half NDotL = saturate(dot(kLightDir, fakeTangN));
half3 normalMappingComponent = NDotL * kLightColor;

# Combine distorted scene with lit scene
OUT.color.rgb =   pIn.rgb * normalMappingComponent * kBrighten;
```

Listing 1.2. Pixel shader snippet for oil paint effect.

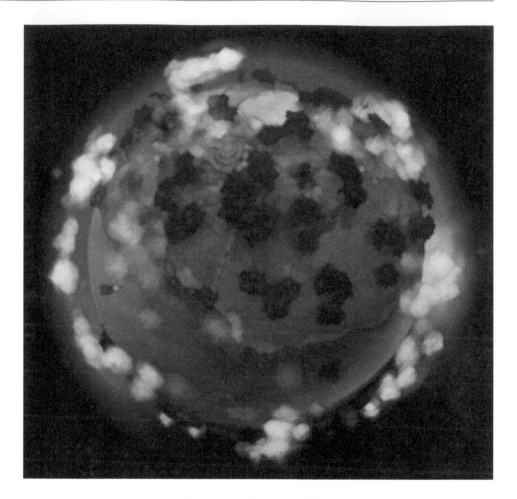

Figure 1.6. Watercolor filter.

1.2.2   Watercolor Filter

For a watercolor filter (see Figure 1.6), a simple Sobel edge version of the incoming scene is multiplied with the original scene. The result is then smoothed using four passes of a smoothing filter that finds the brightest value per channel from four surrounding taps. The edge detection based outlines add some definition that are lost in the smoothing. The offset values and scales in Listing 1.3 let you vary the size of the paint daubs.

```
# Water Color Smoothing
# kScaleX = 0.5, kScaleY = 0.5
# offsetX1 = 1.5 * kScaleX   offsetY1 = 1.5 * kScaleX
# offsetX2 = 0.5 * kScaleX   offsetY2 = 0.5 * kScaleY

# Get the taps
tap0 = tex2D(sceneTex, uv + float2(-offsetX1,-offsetY1));
tap1 = tex2D(sceneTex, uv + float2(-offsetX2,-offsetY2));


tap2 = tex2D(sceneTex, uv + float2(offsetX2, offsetY2));
tap3 = tex2D(sceneTex, uv + float2(offsetX1, offsetY1));

# Find highest value for each channel from all four taps
ret0 = step(tap1, tap0);
ret1 = step(tap3, tap2);
tapwin1 = tap0* ret0 + tap1 * (1.0 - ret0);
tapwin2 = tap2* ret1 + tap3 * (1.0 - ret1);
ret = step(tapwin2, tapwin1);
OUT.color.rgb = tapwin1 * ret + (1.0 -ret) * tapwin2;
```

Listing 1.3. Pixel shader snippet for a smoothing filter to do watercolor.

1.2.3 8-Bit Filter

To create an 8-bit filter (see Listing 1.4), use the round function in the pixel shader and draw to a low res buffer $1/4^{th}$ the size of game resolution with point sampling. This is a really simple effect that makes the game look like an old 8-bit game (see Figure 1.7).

```
# 8 Bit Filter
# kNumBits: values between 8 and 20 look good
half4 source = tex2D(sourceTex, fragIn.uv0 );
OUT.color.rgb = round(source.rgb * kNumBits) / kNumBits;
```

Listing 1.4. Pixel shader snippet for an 8-bit filter.

1.2.4 Film Noir Filter

In creating a film noir filter, first, the incoming scene is converted to black and white. It is then scaled and biased. Some noise is added, A rain particle effect is a nice finishing touch (see Figure 1.8). In Listing 1.5 kNoiseTile can be used to adjust the graininess. kBias and kScale serve as parameters of a linear contrast stretch.

Figure 1.7. An 8-bit filter.

Figure 1.8. Film noir filter.

```
# Film Noir filter
# kNoiseTile is 4.0
# kBias is 0.15, kScale is 1.5
# kNoiseScale is 0.12
pIn = tex2D(sourceTex, uv);
pNoise = tex2D(noiseTex, uv * kNoiseTile) ;

# Standard desaturation
converter = half3(0.23, 0.66, 0.11);
bwColor = dot(pIn.rgb, converter);

# Scale and bias
stretched = saturate(bwColor - kBias) * kScale;

# Add
OUT.color.rgb = stretched  + pNoise * kNoiseScale;
```

Listing 1.5. Pixel shader snippet for film noir filter.

1.2.5 Old Film Filter

For an old film filter (see Figure 1.9), a simple sepia colorize is combined with a sharpen filter. Scratches and vignetting can be done with particle effects (see Listing 1.6).

```
# Old Film Filter
# offsetX and offsetY are 2 pixels. With such wide taps, we
# get that weird sharpness that old photos have.
# kNoiseTile is 5.0, kNoiseScale is 0.18
# kSepiaRGB is (0.8, 0.5, 0.3)

# Get the scene and noise textures
float4 sourceColor = tex2D(sourceTex, uv);
float4 noiseColor = tex2D(noiseTex, uv * kNoiseTile);

# sharpen filter
tap0 = tex2D(sceneTex, uv + float2(0, -offsetY));
tap1 = tex2D(sceneTex, uv + float2(0, offsetY));
tap2 = tex2D(sceneTex, uv + float2(-offsetX, 0));
tap3 = tex2D(sceneTex, uv + float2(offsetX, 0));
sourceColor = 5 * sourceColor - (tap0 + tap1 + tap2 + tap3 );

# Sepia colorize
float4 converter = float4(0.23, 0.66, 0.11, 0);
float bwColor = dot(sourceColor, converter);
float3 sepia = kSepiaRGB * bwColor;

# Add noise
OUT.color = sepia * kTintScale + noiseColor * kNoiseScale;
```

Listing 1.6. Pixel shader snippet for old film filter.

Figure 1.9. Old film filter.

1.3   Cheats

A list of *Spore* cheats to do stylized rendering can be found at http://www.spore.com/comm/tutorials.

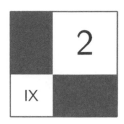

2

## IX

Rendering Techniques in
Call of Juarez: Bound in Blood

Pawel Rohleder and Maciej Jamrozik

2.1 Introduction

Call of Juarez: Bound in Blood (CoJ:BiB) [Techland 09] is a prequel to the *Call of Juarez* game [Techland 07], the 2007 Wild West action shooter developed by Techland. It is published by Ubisoft, developed by Techland and was released on PLAYSTATION3, Xbox360, and PC in the summer of 2009. In general, the game depicts the wildest West ever through the story of Ray and Thomas McCall, two deadly gunslingers who are in a quest for the legendary gold of Juarez (see Figure 2.1).

CoJ:BiB was an 18-month-long FPP shooter game oriented on breath-taking scenarios and cutting-edge graphics technology to provide amazing quality and level of realism during the whole game time. This article demonstrates various rendering techniques used in CoJ:BiB game powered by ChromeEngine 4. We present the advanced lighting and shadowing techniques adopted to complex, open-space virtual environments. We go through the post-processing effects, like screen-space ambient occlusion (SSAO), motion-blur, tone mapping, and edge anti-aliasing used for improving the final image quality. We also show the rendering methods of natural phenomena effects, like photo-realistic looking sky and clouds, water rendering, rain effect, volumetric for and light shafts.

2.2 Deferred Shading

The term *deferred shading* [Hargreaves 04] describes the technique which uses intermediate buffers (called *g-buffer*) storage with screen-space, per pixel information such as diffuse color, normal vector, or depth value. A g-buffer is a collection

Figure 2.1. *Call of Juarez: Bound in Blood* in action.

of screen-sized render targets (MRT), which can be generated in a single pass with the modern graphics hardware (significantly reducing the rendering load). The g-buffer is used then as an input to the shading algorithm (for example a lighting equation) without the necessity of browsing the original geometry (all information required for the calculations at this stage, like position of the pixel in three-dimensional world space, can be extracted from the g-buffer). In this way the algorithm operates on visible pixels only which greatly reduces the lighting computation complexity.

The main advantages of the deferred shading approach are the simplification of the rendering pipeline, ease of managing complex shader resources and calculations, and finally simple and robust management of complex lighting resources (like dynamic lighting). This technique is used with great success in modern post-processing rendering effects like SSAO, depth of field, motion blur, and anti-aliasing.

Deferred shading allows us to use many point light sources, especially in indoor scenes (like building interiors, caves, dungeons, etc.). We extend the dynamic lighting utilization for ambient occlusion approximation by negative light sources for blacking out darker, occluded areas (negative lights and ambient lights; see Figure 2.2). Additionally, inspired by the ability of rendering any form of geometry as a light sources, we have used different-shaped primitives for simple multi-bounce global illumination approximation (lights up ambient factor).

Figure 2.2. Interior scene with dynamic lights and ambient occlusion.

2.3 Single Frame of CoJ:BiB, The Black Magic

At the very beginning of each frame rendering we generate ambient texture for the hemispheric ambient light calculations. The texture has the size of 32 × 32 and consists of procedural generated ambient factors and the assembly of predefined ambient textures. The final texture is used later on to obtain surface ambient factor according to the dot product between surface normal and the sky direction vector.

Next, we generate dynamic clouds mask by blending two artist-controlled masks (i.e., Perlin noise textures). We take control on clouds animation by changing texture coordinates of source textures and the covering factors. The clouds mask is stored in the small texture (/4), which is used later on for clouds shadowing calculations. Then we render the final clouds phenomenon by utilizing the clouds mask and the plane mesh, which is being elevated using volumetric texture, and store the final result in a small (/4) A8R8G8B8 texture.

Now comes the time for the scene-solid geometry rendering into the MRT buffer (configured as shown in Table 2.1). Color buffer contains albedo color surface and the specular shininess mask, which is arbitrary specular factor vector sampled from the texture (this method is cheaper than raising to a power for specular calculations). Normals are stored in camera(view) space and the alpha channel

Buffer	R8G8B8 (24-bit)	A8 (8-bit)
Color	color albedo RGB	specular shininess mask
Normal	XYZ in view space	subsurface scattering mask
Depth*	ARGB (32-bit coded value)	

Table 2.1. MRT configuration in CoJ:BiB (*PC only).

holds the subsurface scattering mask, which is used for thin surface (like leaves and canvas) lighting. Additionally, on PC platform we store depth information into A8R8G8B8 for performance issues. After that we resolve depth buffer into R32F format texture and generate coarse small depth buffer (/4) for further calculations.

Subsequently, we utilize small (/4) render target to perform so called ambient lights rendering pass which affects ambient lighting only. Ambient lights are simple mesh primitives (or their segments), like cylinders, pyramids, cones, boxes, and spheres rendered with depth test disabled and with MIN/MAX blending functions (they can overlap on each other). This way we can approximate a simple one-bounce global illumination pass, which lights up ambient light using primitive's color factor. Next, we utilize depth information and Perlin noise texture to render volumetric fog represented by simple mesh in world space (volumetric fog information is being stored in another small (/4) render target).

Afterwards, we take care of the coarse deferred shadows rendering. We render sun shadows with normal bias without any smoothing, and that is stored in an R channel of coarse (/4) A8R8G8B8 render target. The next two channels contain cloud shadows and SSAO factor. SSAO is approximated by handling nearby pixels in screen-space as a spherical occluders which block the surrounding light. Our solution takes 24 samples per pixel (on each platform) and transforms them back into the world space using a depth buffer. At the final stage we blur the whole shadow buffer into, /16 which is used later for particles shading.

Then the sky dome mesh is rendered, along with depth-based fog calculations and stencil utilization, which is followed by the most complex and time consuming process—the sun lighting pass.

Full screen sun lighting pass is being rendered into HDR format (RGBA16F for PC and RGB10A2F for Xbox360) and utilizes stencil buffer for masking out sky pixels (we don't want to calculate sun light for sky dome). In this pass we calculate smooth and stable shadows from the sun with smooth transition between all shadow map cascades. We use four cascades and texture mapping coordinates to determine sampling weights for each cascade. We perform normal bias (different per each cascade) to overcome flickering sun blind effect on shadowed areas. We also apply shadow from clouds and SSAO performing bilateral up sampling

Figure 2.3. Volumetric ground fog, light shafts, and sun rendering.

[Tomasi 98] from the coarse /4 buffer. Additionally, sun lighting pass performs ambient lighting using ambient texture and surface normal in camera space. Finally, we calculate specular lighting and subsurface scattering mask which approximate two-sided lighting on thin surfaces.

After sun lighting phase we apply dynamic lighting by rendering light meshes (spheres, hemispheres, boxes), which is a typical solution for a deferred shading approach. Similar to the previous step, we use stencil test to light everything except the sky pixels. We also use dynamic branching in the pixel shader for performance reasons (see Figure 2.3). To avoid issues with dynamic lights rendering when the camera is inside the light mesh, we push and squeeze the mesh by the camera plane, which means we are always outside of it. That means that we have one DIP per light, and we can use instancing to speed up the lighting process. At this stage we also render objects that emit light or use cube-mapped materials.

Next we draw a full-screen quad with depth-based fog determination which is followed by the sun mesh rendering pass. After the sun, which is being rendered with maximum illumination intensity, we add clouds and volumetric fog with depth blending.

At this stage we handle (optionally) precipitation effect rendering (see Figure 2.4). Depth of field effect is applied to obtain drenching rainfall effect. Based

Figure 2.4. Rain effects in CoJ:BiB.

on the fact that the sun is covered by the clouds layer during the heavy rain, we place virtual sun at its zenith and utilize sun shadows to determine which pixels may by affected by the rain (i.e., roof may block the rain). Lastly, we render a cylindrical mesh around the player with thousands of droplets falling from the sky (figure below presents the achieved results).

Next we do the standard forward rendering pass for the transparent geometry, which is the water surfaces, glass surfaces, and particles (explosions, smoke, etc.). At this moment the scene rendering pass has been finished. Now it is time for tone mapping by calculating the average luminance in the process of reducing HDR buffer into 1×1 texture, which at the end is combined with the previous frame average luminance (ping pong buffer), which models inertia between adjacent levels of luminance.

As part of the tone-mapping process, we also apply color flattening, auto-exposure, glowing, blurring, depth-of-field, edge anti-aliasing, desaturation, sepia, and any other filters we can think of. At the final stage of frame rendering we transform each pixel from gamma space into the normal color space and apply artist-controlled color curves as well as predefined color sets to obtain the ultimate image with appropriate color saturation on different hardware (LCD, CRT, etc.; see Figure 2.5).

Figure 2.5. Tone-mapped scene with transition between shadowed and lit areas.

2.4　What Else Do We Have?

2.4.1　Terrain

ChromeEngine4 utilizes heightmap-based geometry enhanced with geomipmapping and polygon reduction algorithms to create massive, realistic environments. Apart from this, we have tools for procedural vegetation and meshes spreading, which allows the covering of terrain with standard and artists' created grass and bushes or rocks on mountains slopes. Additionally, our flexible road system gives the ability to create paths, roads, streams, or rivers fitted to terrain very efficiently.

2.4.2　Geometry

In CoJ:BiB we focused on highly optimized geometry rendering pipeline for open space environments (90% of game scenes are outdoors). We have dedicated a system for effective handling of a large amount of static objects with portals, occluders, and level-of-detail optimization mechanisms. The tiny objects system is responsible for drawing all detailed geometry around the player (small rocks, bushes, grass, and debris) which gives player feeling of very rich environment. We also utilize decal system which allows the artists to add extra world detail anywhere they want.

Figure 2.6. Wild West scenery at sunset.

2.4.3   Materials

Artists can easily create and manage materials via material editor tool where they can take advantage of all modern per-pixel lighting techniques including normal mapping, virtual displacement mapping, environment mapping, or parametrized Phong lighting. Advanced users can access GPU shaders directly to modify all visual aspects of rendered objects (see Figure 2.6). The material system is fully integrated with a post-processing manager, which is also manageable via external scripts (meaning the artists can control each element of the frame-rendering process).

2.5   Conclusion

This article presents various rendering techniques used in *Call of Juarez: Bound in Blood* first-person shooter game. We go through a very detailed description of single-frame rendering based on the deferred shading method. At the end, we included additional information about various systems that are the integral tool-kit enclosed in ChromeEngine4.

2.6 Acknowledgments

Special thanks to Matthias Wloka and Wolfgang Engel for their guidance and review of this article. We also thank Bartosz Bień from Techland for his invaluable notes and suggestions.

Bibliography

[Techland 07] TECHLAND, *Call of Juarez*. Available at http://www.coj-game .com/, September 2009.

[Techland 09] TECHLAND, *Call of Juarez: Bound in Blood*. Available at http:// www.callofjuarez.com, September 2009.

[Hargreaves 04] S. HARGREAVES. "Deferred Shading." Presented at the Game Developer's Conference, San Jose, CA, March 24–26 2004. Available at http://www.talula.demon.co.uk/DeferredShading.pdf, September 2009;

[Tomasi 98] C. TOMASI and R. MANDUCHI. "Bilateral Filtering for Gray and Color Images." *Proccedings of the Sixth International Conference on Computer Vision* (1998):839–846.

Making it Large, Beautiful, Fast, and Consistent: Lessons Learned Developing *Just Cause 2*

Emil Persson

3.1 Introduction

Just Cause 2 is a sandbox game developed by Avalanche Studios for PC, Xbox 360 and PLAYSTATION 3. Its main visual traits are an enormous landscape with huge draw distance, an over-the top visual style, varied environments from forests to cities, different climate zones from desert to jungle, and a continuous day cycle. Developing *Just Cause 2* turned out to be a challenge in many ways. We had three different platforms with wildly varying abilities and performance characteristics. We also found that the platforms sometimes behaved differently even when running equivalent code.

This article covers some of the more interesting graphical techniques that give the game its distinctive look as well as how we dealt with performance issues and the efforts we made to keep the visual appearance consistent across platforms.

3.2 Making it Large and Beautiful

3.2.1 Dynamic Lights

The original *Just Cause* had some support for dynamic lights, but was limited to a few lights active at any given time for performance reasons. For *Just Cause 2*, we wanted to improve that. Instead of solving the problem by moving to a deferred renderer we came up with a technique for rendering a large number of dynamic lights with forward rendering without multi-passing or otherwise increasing the number of draw calls.

X		Y	Z	$1 / R^2$
R		G	B	—

Table 3.1. Light constants.

Light indexing. The fundamental problem with rendering multiple lights without multi-passing is how to feed the information about the lights to the shader, particularly when there are a large number of them. One solution is to provide that information in screen-space, such as in the *light-indexed deferred rendering technique* [Trebilco 09]. However, it is quite prone to artifacts to do so since chances are that several lights line up and occupy the same area in screen-space: e.g., looking down a line of street lamps, or just about any area where there are many semi-large lights around. Instead, we found that doing it in world space has much fewer overlaps. Furthermore, the overlap is not view-dependent, which means that we can design things to keep overlap within the technique's limitations.

We provide the light information to the shader through a 128×128 light index texture in RGBA8 format. This texture is mapped in the XZ plane around the camera position and is point-sampled. Each texel is mapped over a 4m × 4m area and holds four indices to the lights that affect that square. This means we cover an area of 512m × 512m where dynamic lights are active. The active lights are stored in a separate list, either in shader constants or as one-dimensional textures depending on the platform. Although with 8-bit channels one could index up to 256 lights, we limited the system to 64 simultaneous lights in order to fit the light information into shader constants. Each light takes two constant registers holding the position, reciprocal squared radius, and color (see Table 3.1).

Additionally, there is an extra "disabled" light slot with all these set to zero. This brings the total register count to 130. When one-dimensional textures are used, the disabled light is instead encoded in the border color. The position and reciprocal squared radius is stored in RGBA16F format and the color in RGBA8. In order to preserve precision, the position is stored in a local space relative the center of the texture.

The light index texture is generated on the CPU from the global list of lights. First its location is placed such that the texture area is fully utilized and as little space as possible ends up behind the camera. Among the lights that are enabled and fall within the area of the index texture, the most relevant lights are selected based on priority, approximate size on the screen, and other factors. Each light is inserted into available channels of the texels it covers. If the texel is covered by more than four lights we need to drop lights. If at insertion time a texel is full, we check whether the incoming light should replace any of the existing lights, based on maximum attenuation factor in the tile to reduce the visual error of dropped lights. These errors show up as lighting discontinuities around tile

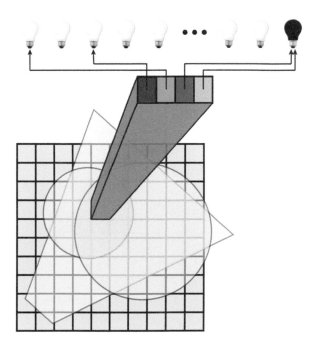

Figure 3.1. Light indexing in axis-aligned world space. Texture is placed such that as much of its area as possible is within the view frustum. The illustrated 4m × 4m area is intersected by two lights that are indexed by R and G channels. The unused slots reference the disabled light.

borders. Generally these errors are small, but they can be very obvious when they move around. To avoid that problem, we snap the index texture to texel-sized coordinates. In practice, dropped lights are quite rare, and where they occur it is usually hard to detect, even if you know what to look for. See Figure 3.1.

Lighting model. For performance reasons the lighting model for the dynamic lights is quite simple. It consists of diffuse lighting, specular lighting, and the attenuation factor. The specular lighting is used primarily for characters. The PC version of *Just Cause 2* also offers specular for the dynamic lights on a wider range of materials.

An important aspect of the lighting equation is that lights need to be range limited and fall to zero at the light radius. The traditional attenuation equation as used in the past by fixed function lighting was thus not an option, besides that it is very expensive. Initially we implemented probably the cheapest useful attenuation possible:

```
atten = saturate(1 - lightpos.w * dot(lVec, lVec));
```

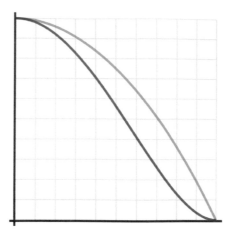

Figure 3.2. The new attenuation function (blue) compared to the old (green).

The w component of `lightpos` holds the reciprocal squared radius (see Table 3.1), which makes this equation fall to zero at the light radius. This amounts to a three component vector and a scalar instruction per light. Other than speed, the advantage of this equation compared to more realistic variants is that it preserves a lot of the energy quite far out in the light sphere, which means you can keep your lights smaller. The disadvantage is that it creates a quite blobby light, which often looks unrealistic. We also found that when applied to vertex lighting, it often became very obvious that lighting was done per vertex. After frequent artist nagging we looked for a better attenuation curve without compromising performance. We found that this simple modification tremendously improved the visual quality without sacrificing much speed or reducing the high energy attribute too much:

```
atten *= atten;
```

This creates an attenuation curve that is roughly a reversed s-curve (see Figure 3.2).

Optimizations. One of the first and most obvious optimizations we did was to add dynamic branching to avoid doing any lighting computations for the majority of the pixels where no dynamic light is needed. We found performance to be best when nesting two branches. So we either evaluate zero, two, or four lights. With this optimization we found that this much more flexible system generally performed at the same level as the old lighting system; sometimes a bit slower and sometimes a bit faster. Unfortunately, one of the consoles is rather lacking in the dynamic branching performance. The branching coherency is excellent though,

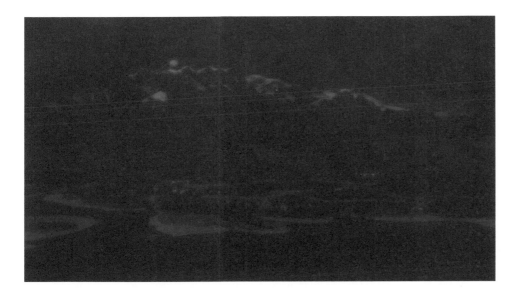

Figure 3.3. Distant lights in action.

so we do see a decent performance improvement where there are no lights. But there is a constant overhead of having the branching code in the shader in the first place, which makes the worst case performance drop noticeably. So we need other tools as well to maintain good performance on all platforms.

Many objects are limited in size such that they are normally not affected by more than four lights in the first place. We implemented a system to look up the best lights for such objects from the bounding box and instead pass the lights in a small array of constants and used different shaders for different light counts. For certain materials, such as for instance foliage, we found that it was good enough to use vertex lighting. For platforms that use lights in constants we also changed the index texture format to use integers instead of normalized values, which saved a few instructions.

Distant lights. Since the light index texture is 128×128 and each texel is $4m \times 4m$ the dynamic lights system covers a $512m \times 512m$ area. Given the size of our world, it is desirable to give lights beyond that which have a visual impact as well. We added a distant lights system that added a lot of life to night scenes (see Figure 3.3). We simply rendered all lights as point sprites. In DirectX 10, where point sprites are deprecated, we emulate them using two triangles.

In addition to the visual improvement, it really helped gameplay at night to have roads, settlements, and various interesting spots in the world light up and made player navigation easier and more interesting.

3.2.2   The Shadowing System

For shadows we use *cascaded shadow mapping* [Engel 06, Zhang 09]. We use three buffers in an atlas. The areas covered by the individual maps are adjusted dynamically depending on several factors. The most important factor is the height above the ground of the player. When the player is on or close to the ground the buffers are pulled in for better quality of the shadows at the expense of shorter range. When the player is flying far up in the air, the range becomes more important and the buffers are expanded. While all buffers are expanded, we usually keep the inner buffer fairly small even when flying high. This is to maintain a sharp shadow of the main character himself as he is skydiving or hang gliding. In the game, the shadow buffer parameters are handled automatically using logic that has been carefully tuned together with artists to provide the best use of the available buffers for most situations. In cut scenes the shadows are fully controlled by artists.

Each shadow map focuses on a point a distance in front of the player. A well-known problem with this is that as the camera view changes and shadow maps move around, ugly flickering artifacts occur along shadow edges. We solved this by aligning the shadow maps at the texel, taking out any frame-to-frame sub-texel offset. This solved the problem when looking around, but not when the player is traveling vertically and the shadow map ranges change. This was solved by using a threshold for applying a new range. If the new range differs by less than 7% from the current range, we simply don't change it. The 7% is a magic number derived from plain ocular inspection. There will still be a slight snap as you cross the threshold and ranges are adjusted, but having that happen once in a while is much more acceptable and discreet, unlike the really distracting large-scale flickering that was happening in every frame if one was up in the air.

By placing the three buffers into an atlas we only need to select the tile and sample the buffer once. The downside of this technique is that there is a noticeable seam where the switch to the next tile occurs, a phenomenon which can be observed in many recent games. One solution is to sample the next buffer as well and do a fade as one gets close to the edge. This eliminates the problem, but at the expense of requiring two samples. Although we support this technique in the engine, instead we most frequently dither, which allows us to sample only once. A pseudo-random number is derived from the screen position of the pixel and added to the fade value, which causes different pixels to swap to the next buffer at different times. It can look something like this:

```
float2 rc = { 0.782934f, -0.627817f };
float rnd = frac(dot(In.Position.xy, rc));
...
fade = saturate(fade + rnd);
```

Figure 3.4. Soft shadows. Notice the sharp shadow at the base of the tree that gets progressively softer. Notice also that the foliage casts a very soft shadow.

The constants are chosen by entering a couple of random numbers, testing them in the game, repeating several times, and selecting the numbers that look best. The visual quality can differ greatly depending on the selected numbers.

Soft shadows. For the PC version of *Just Cause 2*, we offer a soft shadows option for those with powerful GPUs. While not physically accurate in any way, the algorithm does produce real soft shadows, rather than merely constant-radius blurred shadows as are used in many games (see Figure 3.4). In the first step, the algorithm (See Listing 3.1) searches the neighborhood in the shadow map for occluders. Samples that would cast a shadow counts as occluders The average depth difference to the center sample among occluders is then used as a sampling radius in a second pass and multiple standard PCF samples are taken within this radius and averaged. In order to hide artifacts of a limited number of samples, the sampling pattern is rotated with a pseudo-random angle generated from the screen position.

```
// Setup rotation matrix
float3 rot0 = float3(rot.xy, shadow_coord.x);
float3 rot1 = float3(float2(-1, 1) * rot.yx, shadow_coord.y);

float z = shadow_coord.z * BlurFactor;

// Find average occluder distances.
// Only shadowing samples are taken into account.
[unroll] for (int i = 0; i < SHADOW_SAMPLES; i++)
{
    coord.x = dot(rot0, offsets[i]);
    coord.y = dot(rot1, offsets[i]);

    float depth = ShadowMap.Sample(ShadowDepthFilter, coord).r;

    de.x = saturate(z - depth * BlurFactor);
    de.y = (de.x > 0.0);
    dd += de;
}

// Compute blur radius
float radius = dd.x / dd.y + BlurBias;
rot0.xy *= radius;
rot1.xy *= radius;

// Sample shadow with radius
[unroll] for (int k = 0; k < SHADOW_SAMPLES; k++)
{
    coord.x = dot(rot0, offsets[k]);
    coord.y = dot(rot1, offsets[k]);

    shadow += ShadowMap.SampleCmpLevelZero(
        ShadowComparisonFilter, coord, shadow_coord.z).r;
}
```

Listing 3.1. Soft shadows shader stub.

3.2.3   Character Shadows

Characters can be quite problematic for a shadow mapping solution, in particular if you ever need to view characters up close. In *Just Cause 2* the main character is close to the camera at all times, and even more so in many cut scenes. To get proper shadow rendering on facial details you need very high resolution shadow maps, or you need to tighten up the inner shadow buffer very close around the face—in which case you probably need another shadow buffer just to maintain the same shadow quality elsewhere in the scene. We experimented with a separate character shadow buffer, but ultimately abandoned the idea due to additional memory requirement and implementation issues on some platforms. The

Figure 3.5. Linear interpolated depth (left); linear interpolated light bleed values (right).

separate character shadow buffer did not boost quality of character rendering as much as we wanted. Instead we settled for a *light bleed mapping technique* [Tatarchuk 05]. This is a basic extension of standard shadow mapping, but instead of an abrupt step it uses a soft falloff from light to shadow. Instead of the exponential falloff proposed by Tatarchuk we opted for a linear falloff, primarily because it was cheaper and sufficiently good. Unfortunately it does not work very well to just fetch one linear interpolated depth sample from the shadow map and use that in the light bleed computation. Instead we have to sample the four closest depth values, do the light bleed computation on the different samples, and then filter the result. Otherwise the result is very blocky and nasty artifacts show up on borders between shadow and light (see Figure 3.5).

On DX10.1 it is possible to use `Gather()` to get all samples in a single fetch. On the Xbox 360 where we already had to do four texture fetches due to lack of native PCF filtering, it came down to a few extra ALU operations.

3.2.4 Soft Particles

Soft particles vastly improve the quality of particle systems as it eliminates those nasty sharp edges where particles cut into the underlying geometry. Unfortunately, soft particles are also a good deal more expensive than regular particles. So the consoles use them only on snow smoke where the quality of plain particles was just not acceptable. On the PC version we made it a user option to turn it on for all kinds of particles.

The standard way to do soft particles is to fade away particles with the difference in depth between the stored depth value and the rasterized depth. This can be done either in linear space or with raw depth values, the latter being cheaper while the former is commonly viewed as "correct." However, for *Just Cause 2* using a linear distance difference did not cut it. The reason is that the view distance is huge and the particles vary wildly in scale. A burning car may look best if the fade is a decimeter or so, whereas clouds passing over mountains may need 50m or so. It is, of course, possible to tweak the fade range per particle system or use a reasonable heuristic based on the size of its bounding box. But it turns out that a reasonable fade close up does not necessarily look good at a distance. As you get farther away, and the particle system gets smaller on the screen, the fading range becomes smaller too, and its appearance ultimately approach that of the plain old depth buffer cut (see Figure 3.6).

We came up with a simple formula for the fade that worked well in pretty much every situation:

```
fade = saturate(poly_depth / sampled_depth * k - k);
```

This formula is perhaps more voodoo than science, but it is cheap, works well regardless of the scale of the particle system, and has a built-in adjustment of the fading distance as one moves away from the particle effect. This reason this works is because we use a reversed depth buffer, so Z at the far plane is 0.0 and 1.0 at the near plane. As objects get closer to the camera a smaller linear distance is needed to get the same ratio in Z values. The constant k is selected subjectively. For particle effects we used 8.0, for snow smoke 4.0, and for clouds we used 2.0.

Figure 3.6. Linear fade of the cloud looks fine when viewed from ground level (left). The exact same fade looks very poor from the sky (right).

3.2.5   Ambient Occlusion

For ambient occlusion (AO) we use three different techniques: artist-generated AO, occlusion volumes, and SSAO [Kajalin 09]. The artist-generated ambient occlusion is for static models and consists of an AO channel in the material property texture. In addition, artists sometimes place ambient occlusion geometry at key spots. For dynamic objects we use occlusion volumes to cast an occlusion shadow on the underlying geometry, primarily the ground under characters and vehicles. SSAO is a user option for the PC version of *Just Cause 2*.

AO volumes. The idea behind this technique is that when objects approach other objects they occlude each other; e.g., a vehicle occludes the road beneath it. An approximate occlusion volume is placed at key locations on dynamic objects; e.g., a box under cars and an ellipsoid under each wheel and under the feet of characters. We support boxes and ellipsoids, but theoretically any convex shape could be used. The fragment shader samples the depth buffer and transforms the depth value into the local space of the occlusion volume; an occlusion value is computed based on the local position. Given that we use a forward renderer, the effect is applied after lighting, which is not entirely correct but works well enough for us.

SSAO. At the time of writing we use a fairly standard technique for SSAO, but more advanced options are currently being considered. Our technique is offered as a quality option for high-end GPUs on the PC and the focus is quality over performance. Since SSAO entered the project at a late stage in the project we did not want to make any radical changes to the engine, so we had to work with what we had around. Given that we have a forward renderer, we do not have scene normals available but instead generate them from the depth buffer.

Generating normals from the depth buffer is trickier than it may first seem. It is in fact impossible to make it robust in all cases; e.g., consider the case of a pixel-sized triangle generating a single depth value, whereas at least three depth values are needed to compute the normal. Using a few heuristics, one can usually generate "good enough" normals that eliminate the vast majority of the artifacts. The basic idea is to avoid crossing polygon edges when computing the normal. Depth buffer values are often considered nonlinear because of their distribution of precision across the depth range; however, they are linear in screen-space. This means that stepping the depth buffer we expect the pixel to pixel delta to be constant as long as the values belong to the same triangle. So horizontally we sample the two closest neighbors in both the left and right directions. Then we select the direction that has the smallest difference in delta between the three samples from center and to the left or right. The same is done vertically as well, giving us two tangent vectors, which crossed also gives us the normal. See Listing 3.2.

```
// Center sample
float center = Depth.Sample(Filter, In.TexCoord.xy).r;

// Horizontal and vertical neighbors
float x0 = Depth.Sample(Filter, In.TexCoord.xy, int2(-1,  0)).r;
float x1 = Depth.Sample(Filter, In.TexCoord.xy, int2( 1,  0)).r;
float y0 = Depth.Sample(Filter, In.TexCoord.xy, int2( 0,  1)).r;
float y1 = Depth.Sample(Filter, In.TexCoord.xy, int2( 0, -1)).r;

// Sample another step as well for edge detection
float ex0 = Depth.Sample(Filter, In.TexCoord, int2(-2,  0)).r;
float ex1 = Depth.Sample(Filter, In.TexCoord, int2( 2,  0)).r;
float ey0 = Depth.Sample(Filter, In.TexCoord, int2( 0,  2)).r;
float ey1 = Depth.Sample(Filter, In.TexCoord, int2( 0, -2)).r;

// Linear depths
float lin_depth = LinearizeDepth(center, DepthParams.xy);
float lin_depth_x0 = LinearizeDepth(x0, DepthParams.xy);
float lin_depth_x1 = LinearizeDepth(x1, DepthParams.xy);
float lin_depth_y0 = LinearizeDepth(y0, DepthParams.xy);
float lin_depth_y1 = LinearizeDepth(y1, DepthParams.xy);

// Local position (WorldPos - EyePosition)
float3 pos = In.Dir * lin_depth;
float3 pos_x0 = In.DirX0 * lin_depth_x0;
float3 pos_x1 = In.DirX1 * lin_depth_x1;
float3 pos_y0 = In.DirY0 * lin_depth_y0;
float3 pos_y1 = In.DirY1 * lin_depth_y1;

// Compute depth differences in screespace X and Y
float dx0 = 2.0f * x0 - center - ex0;
float dx1 = 2.0f * x1 - center - ex1;
float dy0 = 2.0f * y0 - center - ey0;
float dy1 = 2.0f * y1 - center - ey1;

// Select the direction that has the straightest
// slope and compute the tangent vectors
float3 tanX, tanY;
if (abs(dx0) < abs(dx1))
    tanX = pos - pos_x0;
else
    tanX = pos_x1 - pos;

if (abs(dy0) < abs(dy1))
    tanY = pos - pos_y0;
else
    tanY = pos_y1 - pos;

tanX = normalize(tanX);
tanY = normalize(tanY);
float3 normal = normalize(cross(tanX, tanY));
```

Listing 3.2. Deriving tangent space from depth buffer.

We found this technique to be virtually artifact-free without anti-aliasing. With multisampling enabled, some artifacts occurred. We use a resolved depth buffer for all effects that require depth input. To avoid artifacts elsewhere we resolve depth using the most distant value of the samples rather than the average. Unfortunately this breaks the pixel-to-pixel linearity for edge pixels, creating a few artifacts. It would have been desirable to use a specific sample instead, although that was not entirely artifact-free either. To be completely artifact free we would probably have to use a DirectX 10.1 sample frequency pixel shader, although that would have been massively more expensive.

We sample the depth buffer using Poisson distributed samples in a hemisphere. The computed tangent space is merged into the transformation matrix to make the inner loop of the shader as tight as possible.

3.2.6 The Jitter Bug: Dealing with Floating-Point Precision

Normally, 32-bit floats have sufficient precision for pretty much anything in graphics. But what about a game world that is over a thousand square kilometers, and yet game play takes place on a human scale? As it turns out, it can turn problematic in some cases. Close to the origin there are no problems, but as you approach the edges of the map, floating-point precision problems arise. Our coordinate system is in meters, ranging from -16,384 to 16,384 in x and z. Unfortunately, the lowest precision case where the magnitude of either the x- or z-coordinate (or both) is greater than 8,192 is true for 75% of the map, so it is essentially a universal issue. IEEE-754 has 23 mantissa bits, so the range (8192, 16384) has a precision of $8192 / 2^{23} = 1/1024$, which essentially gives us millimeter precision. That may not sound all that bad until you realize that all rounding errors from every floating-point operation add up, and millimeters turn into centimeters or even decimeters. For an overview of all the subtle ways floating-point can create problems, see [Ericson 07].

In practice what we observed was jittering on many levels. Instead of having trees swaying gently in the wind they would jump around in a jerky manner. Individual grass vertices would snap at different times causing very odd looking behavior. Shadow map texels would not line up very well with the scene geometry, and at the slightest move of the camera, the shadow could jump a decimeter in any random direction. We found jittering occurring both at vertex level and in animation. These phenomena were collectively referred to as the "jitter bug," a pun that still amuses us.

The key to maintaining floating-point precision is to avoid adding or subtracting numbers that vary greatly in magnitude. If you add two numbers together, where one is larger than the other by a factor of two, the smaller number will essentially see its least significant bit thrown away. If they differ by four times, two bits are lost, and so on. Computing $0.05 + 5000 - 5000$ will not result in 0.05 but in 0.0498, whereas $0.05 + 0.05 - 0.05$ comes back as 0.05 just fine. Multiplication and division generally behaves well regardless of scale of the operands though, $0.05 \times 5000.0/5000.0$ computes equally precise as $0.05 \times 0.05/0.05$.

In a traditional vertex pipeline, the input vertex goes through a world matrix, then a view matrix, and finally a projection matrix. Depending on what data we needed in the shader, we often did exactly the above. Sometimes view and projection were merged into a single matrix, but it was very common to first transform into world space because we needed that value in the shader. We then fed that result into a view-projection matrix. The view matrix generally consists of a rotation, scale, and translation. With a small object you could get values in the scale, and rotation part could return values of up to about 1.0. This then is added to the translation part, which could contain values in the 10,000+ range, thus stripping valuable bits out of the scale and rotation part. The view matrix has the same problem because it must bring a large world space position that down to the local space of the camera.

New transformation pipeline. To solve this problem, we rewrote the way we transformed vertices, then computed the transformation matrices to eliminate large translations. The model-view-projection matrix chain can be split into these submatrices:

$$[\text{Scale}][\text{Rotation}][\text{Translation}] \times [\text{Translation}][\text{Rotation}] \times [\text{Projection}]$$

This can be rewritten like this by merging the translation parts of the model and view matrices:

$$[\text{Scale}][\text{Rotation}] \times [\text{Translation}][\text{Translation}] \times [\text{Rotation}] \times [\text{Projection}]$$

The translation part of the model matrix is the world position of the model and the translation of the view matrix minus the eye position. So the translation matrix in the middle is just `world_pos - eye_pos`, or the position of the model relative to the camera if you will, which is much more manageable. If a world position in the shader is necessary, a world matrix will be provided. But instead of multiplying that through another matrix, we compute a merged model-view-projection matrix using the technique explained above, and transform the input vertex instead. This eliminates all vertex-level jittering. On the downside, more computations are necessary. Instead of using per-frame static view, projection, and view-projection matrices, we now have to compute the merged model-view-projection matrix per instance. It also results in having to set more shader constants.

Other floating-point precision issues. Similar solutions were applied to animation levels jittering and jittering in vertex skinning. We also had floating-point problems in the time dimension as well for systems that depend on any monotonically increasing value. One example is the water animation. For this reason we reset the water animation as soon as there was no visible water patch on the screen.

There were also precision issues with the depth buffer. We needed to have the near plane fairly close, but the far plane is very distant, which results in z-fighting in the distance. This was mostly solved by reversing the depth buffer and switching to **GREATER** depth test. This, together with a floating-point depth buffer, eliminated most of the problems. The floating-point buffer helps since its non-linear nature basically cancels the non-linear nature of the depth buffer value distribution. However, reversing the depth buffer helped significantly, even with a standard fixed-point depth buffer, because by reversing the depth buffer, the floating-point computations during transformations lost less precision. As a result, more precisely rasterized depth values are created.

3.3 Making it Consistent

3.3.1 Same-Same, but Different

Not all games studios spend significant time making the experience consistent across platforms. The result is that many games look very different depending on the machine, even when they are running essentially equivalent rendering code. At Avalanche Studios we have artists with very sensitive eyes who will cry blood at the slightest visual deviation from their carefully tweaked assets, so we have spent valuable time making sure our rendering code produces the same output on all platforms.

Cross-platform consistency. The sources of visual deviation vary. Many sources such as different output chips, different blending implementations, different handling of sRGB, different precision, etc. are hardware-related. But there are also software-related differences. Early in the development of *Just Cause 2*, each platform had its own implementation of many core rendering blocks. Much of this was a legacy from the organic growth of the original *Just Cause* code base. It became clear early on that having three different implementations of everything was a maintenance nightmare. A fix made on one platform was not always integrated to the other, features would be left unimplemented on a platform or two, and soon enough the different platforms were doing completely different things. In addition, this was hardly optimal from a productivity point of view.

Low-level API. The first thing we had to do to deal with these problems was to make a platform independent interface and use a single implementation of most stuff common to all platforms. Each platform has its own native graphics application programming interface (API): DirectX 10 for PC, DirectX 9 for our editor

```
union BlendState {
    uint32 Index;
    struct {
        int BlendEnable : 1;
        int SrcBlend    : 4;
        int DstBlend    : 4;
        // etc.
        ...
    };
};
```

Listing 3.3. Blend state.

and tools, a fancier version of DirectX 9 for Xbox360 and libgcm for PLAYSTA-TION 3. We designed a low-level graphics API that would sit on top of each platform's native graphics API. We wanted to keep the API as thin and simple as possible so that the compiler would be able to inline functions and execute the native API's code directly and as often as possible. For this reason much of the API became somewhat similar in style to LibGCM simply because it collapses many render states together that were hard to separate. One of the key elements of this design is that it is stateless; this is very important for being able to do multithreaded rendering using command buffers. Instead a context parameter is sent to each call. The context is just a pointer to a structure that is implementation dependent and hidden behind the API. The task of minimizing redundant state changes is placed on higher level code. For various practical reasons though, some states are sometimes mirrored in the context.

When we designed the API, we had not yet made the switch to DirectX 10 for the PC; otherwise it would have made sense to design it more like the state objects in DirectX 10 since they pack an even greater number of inseparable states together. However, since the PC is the most powerful platform it was decided to keep most of the original design to be friendly to the consoles. The DirectX 10 implementation had to be a good deal more stateful than the others. The other platforms, while having different style and capabilities, are similar enough that mapping the same API to each is relatively straightforward, with few performance concerns. With DirectX 10 being fundamentally different in many ways, mapping was not as easy. DX9 style render states had to be translated to DX10 state objects dynamically. In order to keep the overhead of this to a minimum, we packed states into a bit-field identifying the entire state of a certain state class; e.g., for blend states (see Listing 3.3).

Setting a render state simply boils down to updating the corresponding bits in the union. In the draw call the index value is compared to the previous index. Depending on the state class checked, this amounts to just a 32-bit or 64-bit integer comparison. If any of the states changed, the index value is used to look up and set the corresponding state object. The sampler state is bigger though, and there are 16. Fortunately, they are changed relatively rarely. So a special dirty bit was added to skip the entire check of them for most draw calls.

Shader constant management. Another major challenge was with handling shader constants. DirectX 9 hardware has a fixed set of constant registers whereas DirectX 10 has constant buffers. When used correctly, constant buffers can improve performance by reducing traffic between the CPU and GPU. When used incorrectly, the traffic can balloon up to massive amounts and reduce performance significantly. The latter is the common case for any naïve port where a single 256 register constant buffer is used, including our initial DirectX 10 implementation. Before optimization we typically uploaded 10–30MB of constant data every frame. This naturally turned the PCIe bus into the bottleneck. After optimization we typically uploaded 0.2–0.5MB constants per frame and observed substantially improved performance.

Coming up with a common interface for constants was not as straightforward as it initially seemed. It had to be fast on all platforms, safe and maintainable. The latter points cannot be emphasized enough. Littering the shader code with lots of `#ifdefs` or mixing `register()` and `packoffset()` declarations opens up for all kinds of nasty mismatches between platforms, which can create hard to track bugs or worse go undetected into the final product.

Our final solution is a hybrid between the register and constant buffer philosophies. On the shader side we have a few macros that set up constant buffers for us. It can look like this:

```
CB(0, PerFrameConsts , 0,  64);
CB(1, MaterialConsts , 64, 16);
CB(2, InstanceConsts , 80, 24);
```

After the expansion of the CB macro we get this on DirectX10:

```
cbuffer cb0 : register(b0) {
    float4 PerFrameConsts[64];
}
cbuffer cb1 : register(b1) {
    float4 MaterialConsts[16];
}
cbuffer cb2 : register(b2) {
    float4 InstanceConsts[24];
]
```

On other platforms we got this:

```
float4 PerFrameConsts[64] : register(c0);
```

```
float4 MaterialConsts[16]  :  register(c64);
float4 InstanceConsts[24]  :  register(c80);
```

Declaring shader variables are then done as static assignments from the provided arrays:

```
static float3 Offset   = InstanceConsts[0].xyz;
static float  Radius   = InstanceConsts[0].w;
static float3 Position = InstanceConsts[1].xyz;
static float4 Color    = InstanceConsts[2];
```

In the rendering code the constant buffer layout is specified with corresponding calls:

```
SetVertexConstantBufferSize(ctx, CB_0, 0,  64);
SetVertexConstantBufferSize(ctx, CB_1, 64, 16);
SetVertexConstantBufferSize(ctx, CB_2, 80, 24);
```

On DirectX 10 this selects the best fit constant buffer from a pool of pre-created buffers of various sizes. On the other platforms, it merely stores the offsets and sizes. Constants are then set by calls such as this:

```
SetVertexConstants(ctx, CB_2, 2, &Color, 1);
```

One great benefit of using this method is that we get a direct 1:1 mapping between the shader and rendering code on all platforms. We also eliminate the chance of any register mismatch in individual constants between platforms. If it is broken anywhere it is broken on all platforms. We can also place an **ASSERT()** in the **SetConstants()** calls to detect if we are writing outside any buffer, which helps catch errors.

For performance reasons it is not possible to do a partial constant buffer update in DirectX 10. So the **SetConstants()** calls store the constants into an array of **float4**, which essentially mirrors what would be in the constant registers on the other platforms. The actual constant buffer is later updated with the values in the array. An advantage of doing it this way is that any constant that was not updated after constant buffers changed will get the old value from the array. This way the DX10 path can maintain 100% compatibility with the other platforms even across constant buffer switches.

Most of our constant updates go through the above path, but we also support a more direct constant buffer interface for DirectX 10, where we can set a user supplied constant buffer to a slot instead of selecting one from the pool. This constant buffer can then be locked and filled manually where this provides a performance advantage. In some cases we also use pre-created **IMMUTABLE** constant buffers to eliminate the update all together.

3.3.2 Gamma

One of the decisions we made relatively early in development was to use linear lighting. The reasoning was simple: quality is better and transforming back and forth between gamma space and linear space comes for free on all our target hardware. Unfortunately, it turned out that hardware does not treat sRGB the same way. In hindsight, if we had known about what problems were ahead, we might have stuck to doing lighting in gamma space for this hardware generation.

The sRGB blending problem. In an unfortunate oversight, IHV's DirectX 9 level chips were designed to do render target sRGB transformation directly after the fragment shader. This works fine as long as blending is turned off. When blending is enabled, however, it occurs in sRGB space rather than linear space. The impact of this depends on the blending mode. For regular alpha translucency blend it is not much of a problem. For instance, if the incoming fragment is 0.3 and the render target has 0.7 in sRGB space and incoming alpha is 0.5 you get this:

$$(0.3^{1/2.2} \times (1 - 0.5) + 0.7^{1/2.2} \times 0.5)^{2.2} = 0.477$$

The result is not very far from the ideal linear result of 0.5. The story is quite different for additive blending. If the incoming fragment is 0.3 and the render target has 0.3 in sRGB space you get this:

$$(0.3^{1/2.2} + 0.3^{1/2.2})^{2.2} = 1.378$$

For alpha translucency blend, the non-linearities more or less cancel each other. For additive blending the error is instead amplified and you can get values as far off as in the example above. You do not expect $0.22 + 0.22$ to saturate to full white.

Fortunately, the DirectX 10 specification is clear about blending happening in linear space, so for PC games targeting DirectX 10 there is consistent blending across hardware vendors. Unfortunately, there will be problems if one of the consoles has the problem, which was certainly an issue for *Just Cause 2*. For our online hunting title *theHunter* (PC only), this is also an issue because it uses DirectX 9, and all shader model 3 cards from this IHV are affected.

Dealing with this issue was troublesome. The blender is a small piece of fixed function hardware with relatively few configurations and a minimal set of inputs. Also, one of the inputs—the destination color—is inaccessible from the fragment shader, which makes it impossible to correctly compensate for the error there. After a number of code and shader tweaks and careful side-by-side comparisons, we came up with a reasonable compromise that satisfied the artists. The first thing we did was move the multiplication of source color by alpha, from the blender into the shader, which at least made that part of the equation equal across platforms.

It also freed up one blender input. This turned out to be useful for additive particles where we could now apply the classic *soft add* blend mode. Soft add is like regular additive blending, except that the source color is multiplied with INV_DSTCOLOR instead of ONE. As the destination buffer gets brighter, the incoming values are dampened, which means more things can be added together before it saturates to full white. Meanwhile, it behaves much like a regular add when the destination is dark. Using this technique on additive particles helped control the tendency of incorrect adds to shoot through the roof too quickly, and it made the particles look more consistent across platforms.

Since our particles systems had been tuned by artist on the incorrect blending platform, we had to adjust the correctly behaving blends to mimic the incorrect behavior. While these adjustments were not exact, we did a number of tweaks through ocular inspection of our common effects. We ended up squaring the alpha and multiplying by 2.35 in the fragment shader for additive particles. While there are still visible differences in some effects, most looked similar enough to be acceptable. For alpha translucency we ended up raising alpha to the power of 1.18. This roughly compensated for the small difference mentioned earlier. A similar problem in our sun halo was dealt with by simply changing a constant to bring the intensity to the same range.

Other gamma issues. While one console had a problem with blending, we found that the other console was not very accurate when sampling sRGB textures. A simple piece-wise linear function was used, which was obvious when viewing a gradient. As a result, the rendering on this particular console was more prone to banding and other artifacts. In addition, we also had to add a compensation curve in one of our post-effects shaders to reduce the differences. Furthermore, the output to the monitor was not entirely correct. Given identical values in the front-buffer, different results were sent over the HDMI cable on the different platforms. Fortunately, we could solve this problem by loading a custom gamma compensation curve that eliminated the differences.

Lessons learned. One of our mistakes was letting artists tune particle effects on a single platform for a considerable amount of time. With thousands of effects, compensations on the artists' side to even out differences was not an option. Had this problem been caught earlier, there might have been a better solution.

Another blunder was not immediately fixing the sRGB code for our DirectX 9 path when first implementing linear lighting. Instead, there was a quick fix in the shaders. Rather than using the more correct power of 2.2, we used a power of 2.0, which was close enough for a programmer's eye and of course substantially faster. At this point DirectX 9 was only used internally for our tools so this did not seem important. Later when it work on *theHunter* started, it was decided to use DirectX 9, artists carefully tweaked lighting and assets for this code. When the code was later fixed to use actual sRGB texture sampling and sRGB writes, artists complained that it did not look the same anymore. Given the substantial performance gain we observed, it was not an option to leave the old shader compensation code. Instead, artists had to go over all the settings again and tweak for the new shader environment.

3.4 Making it Fast

3.4.1 Cloud Rendering Optimization

Clouds are an important component of the game world. The clouds in *Just Cause 2* consist of a layer of cirrus clouds with a cumulus cloud layer below it. The cirrus clouds are implemented as planar textured surfaces and a single draw call is used to render all cirrus clouds. Each cloud chooses its texture from an atlas of all cirrus cloud types. The cumulus clouds are implemented as view-aligned surfaces. As with the cirrus clouds, everything is rendered with a single draw call and individual cloud images are selected from a texture atlas.

When the player travels near the ground, clouds generally do not cause a performance issue. However, *Just Cause 2* is not a game where the player necessarily stays close to the ground: a player may very well decide to take a plane in the clouds. In fact, it is required to be far up in the sky to complete some missions. Cirrus clouds are usually not problematic, but cumulus clouds could easily take four to five milliseconds when the player is in the sky, and we got many layers of overdraw covering much of the screen. The clouds are rendered with a trivial fragment shader, so there were not many optimization opportunities there. Instead, the bottleneck was in the ROPs. Modern GPUs are increasingly getting more powerful in terms of ALU and texturing power, but ROP power has been lagging. So while the consoles were suffering from this problem, PC GPUs were not doing much better and the ROPs were in fact an even bigger bottleneck, relatively speaking.

The clouds were originally rendered as simple quads. However, we noted that many of the cloud textures contained a substantial amount of empty space where alpha was zero. So a lot of the rendered fragments did not contribute to the final results. To cut down on the fill requirements we decided to trim the clouds. We stuck to four vertices per cloud in order to not increase memory requirements, but depending on which atlas tile was used, an optimized quad was selected that closely enclosed the cloud (see Figure 3.7). The result of this optimization surpassed

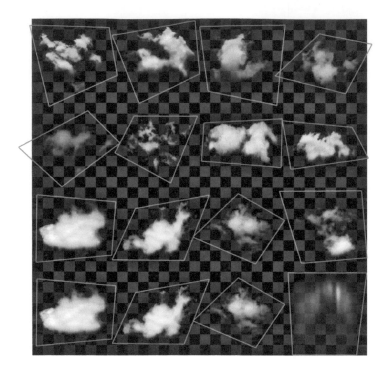

Figure 3.7. Cloud atlas with optimized quads.

our expectations, as the rendering time was now down to around two to three milliseconds at no visual loss.

To reduce flickering while players fly through clouds, the clouds were faded away as they come closer to the camera. Consequently, some of the most expensive clouds also contributed the least to the final result as they were close to the camera and covered substantial screen-space but were essentially faded away. Instead of just checking the vertex alpha to be greater than zero, we used a small but positive alpha threshold to allow us to reject the worst offenders. With a very conservative threshold we could still shave off a substantial amount of the remaining rendering time and landed at about 1.5 milliseconds, or nearly three times faster the speed of original implementation.

3.4.2   Particle Trimming

Given the success of our cloud optimizations, we decided to apply the same trimming technique to our particle systems. There are many objects that can blow up in *Just Cause 2*, and when an enemy grenade lands at your feet you do not want a low frame-rate added to your problems.

But there was just one problem: whereas the cloud atlas consists of 16 different clouds, the particle systems are composed of dozens of different textures, containing everything from a single particle image to 64 atlas tiles each. For the clouds we had tweaked the quad vertices manually by exposing some variables in the in-game debug menu. This was good enough for a small set of textures and a task that had to be done only once. But now we faced a task that was an order of magnitude greater. After first attempting to go along the manual tweaking route, we quickly discovered not only that this was inefficient, but also that four vertices were not enough since the optimal quad would often cut into particles in neighboring atlas tiles. Furthermore, with more vertices it was not as clear, just from looking at a particle texture, which polygon would be the most optimal.

In order to deal with this problem we came up with an algorithm for automating the process, and a tool was written that, given an input texture and an alpha threshold value, computed the smallest enclosing convex polygon of the desired number of vertices. At the core of the algorithm was a convex hull. Edge pixels of the particle are detected and the convex hull was updated iteratively. In the end we had a convex hull, typically consisting of a few dozen vertices. All permutations of the hull edges were then checked, and the one resulting in the smallest area while fully enclosing the particle was selected. This step was done using a brute force traversal over all permutations of the edges. This was usually not a problem, but the running time can quickly shoot through the roof if the number of vertices gets large. For this reason the hull is initially reduced to at most 50 edges by eliminating edges one by one, in each step removing the edge that results in the smallest expansion of the hull. With this tool, the task that previously took one programmer a day was now done instantly and more accurately, leaving us to cut and paste the result. The tool is open source and available online [Persson 09].

3.4.3 Memory Optimizations

Getting the most out of the available memory is very important, in particular on the consoles. One of the most important things we did to keep memory consumption in control was to allocate budgets for various subsystems. When the budget was exceeded the requested resources were replaced with dummy resources; e.g., a texture going over the budget was replaced with a green texture. When there were too many textures used in a particular location, green textures showed up in the game, giving visual feedback to level designers that they needed to rework the area to keep memory consumption in check.

Just Cause 2 needed a number of render targets. In addition to the back buffer, there is the multi-sampled color and depth buffer, as well as a non-multi-sampled depth buffer that the GUI requires, a shadow buffer, a reflection buffer, two half- and quarter-resolution temporaries for the post-effects, non-multi-sampled

resolved back buffer, depth buffer, and a velocity buffer. In order to reduce the
memory footprint of all this, we first did the obvious optimization—namely, reducing the shadow buffer precision from 24-bit to 16-bit. At 1024×3072, our
shadow buffer required 12MB of memory. Changing this to 16-bit buffers got the
cost down to 6MB. As it turned out, we did not need any more precision than
that. The shadow bias value we used was a good deal greater than the contribution of the lower 8-bits. We did encounter a problem in that one of the consoles
did not support 16-bit depth buffers natively. This was solved with an additional
conversion pass using raw memory reads and writes to convert from a swizzled
32-bit depth buffer to the swizzled 16-bit format.

For the post-effects we used two copies of the temporary render targets because
we were ping ponging between the render targets for some filters. On one console,
however, we realized that this was not necessary due to its special memory architecture: in practice it was already ping ponging between EDRAM and the video
memory, so we removed the redundant copy there. We also realized that several
of the render targets had no overlap in time. For instance, the time from we rendered to the shadow buffer to the time we last used its content never overlapped
with the life time of the post-effect temporaries. On the consoles where we had
direct control over video memory, we took advantage of this fact to reuse some of
the memory of render targets by placing other temporally non-overlapping render
targets on top of it. The shadow buffer, which is the largest texture, gobbled up
several of the smaller render targets. By carefully shuffling render targets around
we were able to save about 5MB of render target space.

Another memory optimization we did was to replace 32-bit floats in vertex
buffers with 16-bit fixed points together with a scale value for unpacking. One
problem with this was that positions generally are three values, but there are no
SHORT3N attribute types: only 2N or 4N. Instead of wasting space for a fourth
value, we found that we could use a SHORT4N value but set the stride of the vertex
to cut those last two bytes out of the vertex. For instance, if only POSITION is
used, we would declare it as SHORT4N but use six bytes as our stride, as opposed
to eight bytes. This trick worked on all platforms.

One of the more obvious ways to reduce memory consumption was to use compressed textures, which we did for nearly everything. A less obvious trick is to pack
several textures into one compressed texture. Many materials are fairly uniformly
colored, so you can get a long way by using just a luminance texture together with
vertex colors. An artist can optionally place three different luminance textures
into the channels of a DXT1 texture, which works well for generic textures with
little uniquely identifiable detail, such as plain concrete. This essentially gives us
textures at as low as 1.33bpp. For the texture fetch we configure the sampler to do
the swizzle automatically so we can use the same shader for channel textures and
regular full color textures at no extra cost. This is supported by most hardware,

but unfortunately on the PC there is no such functionality in DirectX (OpenGL has the `GL_EXT_texture_` swizzle extension though), so we had to use a few ALU operations to sort out the swizzle.

3.5 Conclusion and Future Work

This article has presented a number of techniques we implemented in the Avalanche Engine for *Just Cause 2*. Various issues we encountered have been discussed as well as the solutions we came up with. We have also covered miscellaneous optimizations and memory savings.

At the time of this writing *Just Cause 2* is in beta stage and we are in bug stomping mode. Whether any significant new features will go into *Just Cause 2* before the release is anyone's guess, but looking forward we have a number of ideas of where to go next. With DirectX 11 around the corner there are many interesting we would like to use. The compute shader is something that would come to great use for our post effects, both as an optimization for existing post effect and an enabler for future techniques. Using the tessellator for our terrain seems like an obvious improvement, although we have concluded that it would be non-trivial. There are a number of other code driven systems that could use it with relatively small amount of effort, such as grass and water waves.

We still have not tapped the consoles on all the available power either. We do multi-thread our rendering on the consoles, and have good utilization of the available CPU cores (including SPUs), but there is still work to be done on threading all our systems. On the PC we utilize the available cores pretty well for general tasks, but we still do not multi-thread rendering. This is something we would like to do with DirectX 11 and its deferred contexts.

Over the years, deferred shading has come up numerous times. Still we stuck to forward rendering until the end. Chances are we will opt for some kind of deferred approach in future projects though. The main motivation would be to improve performance and flexibility for dynamic lights.

3.6 Acknowledgments

I would like to thank my fellow colleagues at Avalanche for the support in writing this article and for all their hard work in bringing the Avalanche Engine to world class quality as well as their performance and the intellectually stimulating environment they have created here at Avalanche Studios. Without the bright minds of all the people here, none of this would have been possible.

Our thoughts also go out to all former Avalanche employees that could not stay with us to the conclusion of this project. Thanks for the great work you did during your time with us. All of our continued friendship is deeply appreciated. Keep up the good work where you are now!

Special thanks to Viktor Blomberg for his endless flow of bright ideas; may the magic shader constants be with you! Alvar Jansson for all the Gothenburgian puns; work would not be half as fun without them! Christian Nilsendahl for the friendly leadership. Christian Murray for keeping a keen eye on performance and slapping us all once in a while when we submitted substandard code. John Fuller for proof reading. Christofer Sundberg for his ability to turn the very depths of hell into something ultimately positive. Ingela Hellqvist and Linda Bäcklund for all the candy.

Bibliography

[Trebilco 09] amian Trebilco. "Light-Indexed Deferred Rendering." In *ShaderX7*, edited by Wolfgang Engel. pp. 243–256. Boston: Charles River Media, 2008.

[Engel 06] olfgang Engel. "Cascaded Shadow Maps." In *ShaderX7*, edited by Wolfgang Engel. pp. 197–206. Boston: Charles River Media, 2008.

[Zhang 09] an Zhang, Alexander Zaprjagaev, and Allan Bentham. "Practical Cascaded Shadow Maps." In *ShaderX7*, edited by Wolfgang Engel. pp. 305–329. Boston: Charles River Media, 2008.

[Tatarchuk 05] atalya Tatarchuk. "Advances in Real-Time Skin Rendering." Available at http://developer.amd.com/media/gpu_assets/D3DTutorial05_Real-Time_Skin_Rendering.pdf, 2009.

[Kajalin 09] ladimir Kajalin. "Screen-Space Ambient Occlusion." In *ShaderX7*, edited by Wolfgang Engel. pp. 413–424. Boston: Charles River Media, 2008.

[Ericson 07] hrister Ericson. *"Physics for Games Programmers: Numerical Robustness (for Geometric Calculations)."* Available at http://realtimecollisiondetection.net, 2009.

[Persson 09] mil Persson. "Particle Trimmer." Available at http://www.humus.name, 2009.

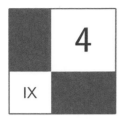

Destructible Volumetric Terrain

Marek Rosa

4.1 Introduction

Most modern video games utilize non-destructible environments. The exceptions almost always focus on destructible terrain features, such as buildings or forests, but the terrain itself remains static.

We are developing a game whose main focus is destructible terrain in all directions: *Miner Wars* [Miner 09]. *Miner Wars* is a six-degree of freedom underground and space shooter with fully destructible environments, which combines a single player story and MMO game.

Because the core feature of *Miner Wars* is instant destruction of terrain, the engine cannot depend on pre-computed data. Every terrain change computes in real time, consuming as little memory as possible and without visible delays. The environment thus depends on volume information—not only surfaces—thus, we prefer a voxel representation for the terrain.

All images in this article (e.g., Figures 4.1 and 4.2) are from the actual game and do not employ any offline rendering or post-processing.

4.1.1 Challenges

This article presents our solutions to the following challenges: how to convert custom three-dimensional models to voxel representations (see Section 4.2), how to minimize the memory requirements of using large voxel maps (see Section 4.3), how to quickly convert voxels to triangles (see Section 4.4), how to seamlessly texture-map these free-form surfaces (see Section 4.5), how to reduce repeated texture patterns (see Section 4.6), how to perform tangent space calculations in a pixel shader (see Section 4.7), how to utilize multi-material voxel maps (see Section 4.8), how to apply level-of-detail simplifications (see Section 4.9), and, finally, how best to employ ambient light (see Section 4.10).

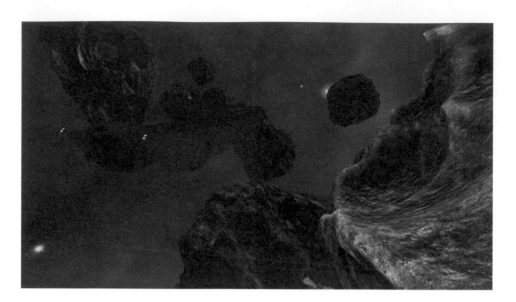

Figure 4.1. Volumetric terrain depicting an asteroid belt.

4.1.2   Engine Structure

As mentioned earlier, the building blocks of our engine are voxels. A voxel, in our implementation, is a three-dimensional pixel with a real size in meters. Each holds information about its density—empty, full, or in between—and its material type, used for texturing, destruction resistance, and game logic.

We define a voxel map as a set of voxels (e.g., $256 \times 512 \times 256$). Each voxel map contains both data cells, which hold voxels, and render cells containing static vertex buffers and triangle indices.

Miner Wars' engine does not draw voxels directly; instead, it polygonizes them, converting them to triangles prior to rendering or detecting collisions. We use the standard marching cubes algorithm ["Marching" 09] for polygonization.

4.2   Converting Custom 3D Models into Voxel Representations

When starting game development on *Miner Wars*, we soon realized that our needs would not be met by existing voxel modeling tools. We therefore created terrain, such as asteroids, using a standard modeling tool, such as Autodesk's 3ds Max, and then exported the terrain as a voxel representation.

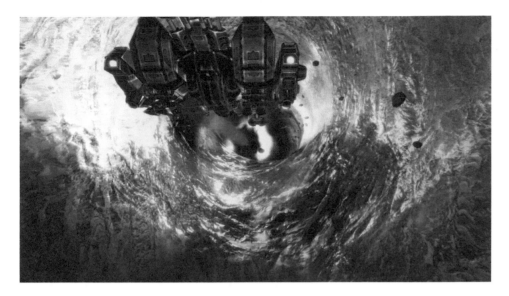

Figure 4.2. A mining ship digs a tunnel with explosives. The tunnel's surface is bump-mapped ice.

Converting a three-dimensional model to voxels requires the engine to determine how much matter each voxel contains, using the following algorithm: first, the engine loads the exported three dimensional model into memory, reading only the vertex coordinates and triangle indices and ignoring any additional data.

Next the engine rescales the model so as to fill a voxel map as much as possible without having any part of the model extend beyond the confines of the map. Imagine every voxel contains a set of grid points (see Figure 4.3). While the figure shows $4 \times 4 \times 4$ grid points per voxel, our implementation actually uses $8 \times 8 \times 8$ grid points.

After rescaling the model, our engine casts a ray from every bottom grid point along the positive Y-direction and checks for intersections with all triangles of the model. After hitting the closest triangle, the engine marks all grid points below the intersection as empty and then continues intersection testing. When the engine detects the next triangle, it marks all grid points between it and the previous intersection as full. Our engine toggles this logic after every hit—from empty to full and vice versa.

Finally, the engine stops the calculation when reaching a top grid point. In this manner, the number of grid points that are inside versus outside the model determines each voxel's density.

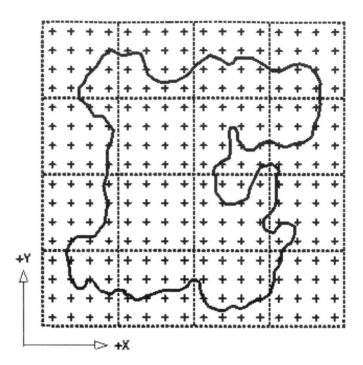

Figure 4.3. A voxel map with dashed lines representing voxel boundaries. This illustration depicts 4×4 voxels; crosses represent grid points inside voxels; and solid lines represent a three-dimensional model.

Using the surface normal of a boundary triangle to determine whether the encountered boundary is the beginning or the end of a solid part of the model is inadvisable: a model with inaccurate normals or inaccurate geometry (e.g., overlapping or intersecting triangles) tends to produce unreasonable results. The results of our algorithm are fine-grained enough that a model of a sphere converted to voxel representation maintains its shape if larger than $32 \times 32 \times 32$ voxels.

To optimize performance, the engine does not test rays against every triangle. Instead, it projects triangles onto the XZ-plane and stores references in a hash table, where XZ voxel coordinates are the key. Then, only triangles in the relevant column are tested.

4.3   Memory Requirements for Large Voxel Maps

Experiments showed us that voxels representing an area of 15 meters allow fine detail of terrain yet a still low number of voxels. Thanks to that, asteroids in our game can be as large as 7,680 meters, assuming voxel maps are built from $512 \times 512 \times 512$ voxels.

Even so, such a large voxel map consumes 128 MB just to store density values. Multiply that figure by 20, and you quickly hit the end of 32-bit memory space. Because of this, we decided to compress voxels in memory. At this point, it's worth mention that we did not choose octrees for voxel storage in this release, though we are considering it for a future release.

Every voxel map stores these data in memory: voxel densities, voxel materials, and voxel triangles.

Voxel densities. The voxel map is divided into data cells. Each data cell contains a set of $8 \times 8 \times 8$ voxels. Data cells are allocated only if voxels in the data cell are not completely full. References to data cells are contained in a hash table. The advantage of this approach is that it is easy to determine if the area bounded by a data cell is full or empty. This, in turn, speeds polygonization.

A drawback of this approach is that if a voxel map reaches $1024 \times 1024 \times 1024$ and a large part of the voxel map is empty, too many data cells need to be allocated. This makes octrees a likely solution.

Voxel materials. To compactly store voxel materials in memory, we could have chosen RLE compression for columns of voxel materials. This method benefits from a good compression ratio but suffers from slow read access, because each read first requires decompression.

Our actual implementation, however, relies on reducing the granularity of voxel materials. This approach stores one material for several adjacent voxels. For example, one material data value may describe $2 \times 2 \times 2$ voxels.

Voxel triangles. Voxel triangles are used to compute game physics (e.g., a projectile hitting the terrain, collision detection, etc.). Triangles are stored in a FIFO cache and recalculated after every change in the environment.

4.4 Polygonization from Voxels to Triangles

Voxels must be polygonized to triangles during level initialization and after every change in the terrain, such as an explosion. The second situation, terrain change, must be handled in real time, without visible time delays and only on affected areas. For this reason, we came up with idea of render cells. Each render cell holds a set of $8 \times 8 \times 8$ data cells, thus covering an area of $64 \times 64 \times 64$ voxels, and it contains static vertex buffers and triangle indices. Because render cells don't contain dynamic vertex buffers, they are allocated and recreated after every change.

Render cells are stored in FIFO cache and accessed by render cell coordinate. When a cell is changed, it is invalidated in the cache.

Experiments with different video cards and render cell sizes showed us that the dimensions we chose are appropriate. To leverage modern multi-core processor architecture, we optimized calculation of data cells in parallel threads.

4.5   Seamless Texture-Mapping for Free-Form Surfaces

Projecting two-dimensional texture onto a free-form surface is a problem because a texture image is represented in two dimensions, whereas a free-form surface has three-dimensional curves and holes.

To render diffuse, specular, and other types of free-form texture, the simplest approach is to project the surface's triangles along one axis (X, Y, or Z) representing the triangle's most significant direction as determined by normal vector. This is a fast approach, but viewers will notice seams where triangles with different orientations meet.

Our solution to this dilemma is tri-planar texture mapping calculated by the pixel shader. We project the texture along the X-, Y-, and Z- axes and then blend texture colors according to tri-planar weight (as demonstrated in Listing 1). So, for example, a pixel predominantly facing the Y direction will receive most of its texture color from this direction. We speed texture coordinate calculation when projecting on the XZ-plane by using the XZ-values of vertex coordinates and ignoring Y.

Next, we calculate texture coordinates from vertex world coordinates. It is assumed that repeated textures are used (WRAP), thus texture coordinates can be outside the <0..1> range. Another benefit is that it is easy to create custom texture scaling.

Tri-planar weights are calculated per pixel; therefore they are based on an interpolated normal vector (see Listing 4.1).

In our implementation, we store only vertex position, vertex normal, and ambient value in the vertex buffer. This approach to tri-planar texture mapping is reasonably fast, and it produces no visible seams and no texture stretching.

```
float3 GetTriplanarWeights(float3 normal)
{
    float3 axisWeights;
    axisWeights = (abs(normal.xyz) - 0.2) * 7;
    axisWeights = pow(axisWeights, 3.0);
    axisWeights /= (axisWeights.x +
                    axisWeights.y + axisWeights.z).xxx;
    return axisWeights;
}
```

Listing 4.1. Calculating tri-planar blending weights.

4.6 Reducing Repeated Texture Patterns

Repeating texture patterns can be easily observed, especially on distant terrain.

As shown in Listing 4.2, We reduce texture monotony by changing the texture scale factor as a function of the texture's distance from the camera. As you will recall, our engine calculates texture coordinates from world coordinates and then scales them.

Surfaces close to the camera are rendered with small texture scale, while distant surfaces use a large texture scale. Of course, hard switching between these is undesirable, so in the pixel shader, every texture is calculated for both close and far surfaces. The final texture color is then interpolated according to the distance from pixel to camera.

The result of this approach is high detail texturing on near surfaces without repeated patterns on distant surfaces.

Another positive side effect is that, if integrated with bump mapping, distant surfaces display artificial curvature from normal map texture. No real geometry is involved (see Figure 4.4).

```
const float VoxelTextureDistanceNear = 10;
const float VoxelTextureDistanceFar = 100;

const float VoxelTextureScaleNear = 10;
const float VoxelTextureScaleFar = 100;

float distanceForTextures =
    saturate((distanceToCamera - VoxelTextureDistanceNear) /
             (VoxelTextureDistanceFar - VoxelTextureDistanceNear));

float2 uvForAxisXNear = wordPosition.zy / VoxelTextureScaleNear;
float2 uvForAxisYNear = wordPosition.xz / VoxelTextureScaleNear;
float2 uvForAxisZNear = wordPosition.xy / VoxelTextureScaleNear;
float2 uvForAxisXNear = wordPosition.zy / VoxelTextureScaleFar;
float2 uvForAxisYNear = wordPosition.xz / VoxelTextureScaleFar;
float2 uvForAxisZNear = wordPosition.xy / VoxelTextureScaleFar;

float4 diffuseTextureNear = GetTexture(uvForAxisXNear, uvForAxisYNear,
                                       uvForAxisZNear);

float4 diffuseTextureFar = GetTexture(uvForAxisXFar, uvForAxisYFar,
                                      uvForAxisZFar);

float4 finalTexture = lerp(diffuseTextureNear, diffuseTextureFar,
                           distanceForTextures);
```

Listing 4.2. Calculating texture coordinates for near and distant surfaces and then blending by distance. Scale and distance constants were chosen empirically.

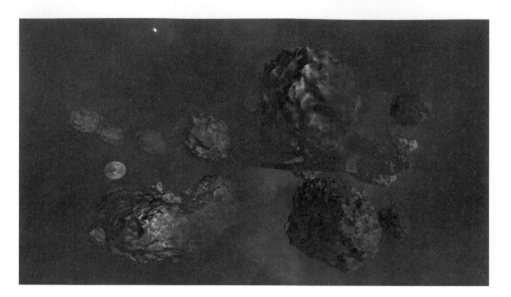

Figure 4.4. Distant asteroids appear more realistic and texture monotony is reduced.

4.7   Tangent Space Calculation in the Pixel Shader

Rendering a bump-mapped surface requires that the normal vector obtained from
the normal map be transformed to world space. This is usually done using tangent
space transformations. However, as calculating tangent space may be difficult on
a free-form surface, we have chosen to employ a trick similar to that used in
tri-planar texturing, whereby we project the pixel along three axes and retrieve
normal vectors from the normal map, just as we do for regular texture.

Next we fix the orientation of retrieved normal vectors, as they may point in a
direction opposite the surface (see *sign* multiplication in Listing 4.3), and, finally,
we calculate final normal vector using blending weight.

This procedure is best explained by source code:

Although this solution is only an approximation, it works very well in all
circumstances, even when triangles with different orientation meet. It is well
suited for natural textures, such as rocks, ice, moss, etc. Using this method, there
is no need to store tangent and binormal vectors in a vertex buffer or to transform
the normal vector to tangent space, which involves matrix multiplication.

4.8   Multi-material Voxel Maps

Every voxel has a specified material. For the purposes of this chapter, think of it
as a texture. Transitions between different voxel materials always occur on voxel

```
// 'normal' is pixel's original normal vector (interpolated by
vertex shader)

// Normal for axis X
float3 normalForAxisX = tex2D(TextureNormalMap, uvForAxisX).zyx;
normalForAxisX.x *= sign(normal.x);

// Normal for axis Y
float3 normalForAxisY = tex2D(TextureNormalMap, uvForAxisY).xzy;
normalForAxisY.y *= sign(normal.y);

// Normal for axis Z
float3 normalForAxisZ = tex2D(TextureNormalMap, uvForAxisZ).yxz;
normalForAxisZ.z *= sign(normal.z);

// Blend normals using triplanar weights
float3 finalNormal =
   normalForAxisX * triplanarWeights.x +
   normalForAxisY * triplanarWeights.y +
   normalForAxisZ * triplanarWeights.z;
```

Listing 4.3. Calculating and blending normal vectors by projecting pixels along three axes and fixing orientation (HLSL).

triangles. Every triangle vertex has only one material, determined by the material of the voxel to which it is nearest. Some triangles have only one material; others have two or three.

Triangles are divided into single-material and multi-material categories. Single-material calculations, as described earlier, are the easiest to handle, though multi-material triangles add much-needed realism (see Figure 4.5).

Multi-material triangles are rendered using additive alpha-blending in multiple passes. Each multi-material triangle is stored in a vertex buffer as many times as there are different materials on it, up to three. Vertex alpha is used for rendering only involved material.

To render a multi-material triangle, we process black color only on the first pass, so that additive alpha blending can then be used. On passes two, three, and four, we switch textures and then render the triangle. This pass is additive. Vertex alpha is interpolated across the triangle, thus only areas with actual texture are rendered.

The need for alpha-blending is a disadvantage of this solution, but blending in the pixel shader is not possible for us because voxel textures are repeated, ruling out a simple texture atlas. In addition, calculating repeated texture coordinates in the pixel shader creates visible seams at texture borders, and since we are targeting DirectX 9.1, we cannot use texture arrays from DirectX 10.0.

Figure 4.5. Multi-material terrain on an asteroid.

4.8.1   Multiple Dynamic Lights

Because multi-material rendering depends on alpha-blending, it is not possible to render dynamic lights in further passes. In addition, deriving texture and normal vector is a complicated task, and we do not want to do it for every dynamic light.

Our solution is based on adding dynamic lights to final color in a loop, so that diffuse/specular textures and normal vectors are reused. Iterating zero to eight lights in the pixel shader is possible on today's hardware.

4.9   Level of Detail

Level of detail (LOD) allows drawing large terrains without stressing the hardware. In our game, the average asteroid is built from around 300,000 triangles. If there are more asteroids on the screen, the game's frame rate quickly drops, making large terrains impossible in the absence of LOD (see Figure 4.6).

LOD works on the render cell level (remember one render cell contains $64 \times 64 \times 64$ voxels), rendering each cell in either normal or low detail, based on distance to camera.

A low detail render cell is calculated in almost same way as a normal detail render cell, but instead of using all of its $64 \times 64 \times 64$ voxels, we use only averaged values of its data cells (remember one render cell has $8 \times 8 \times 8$ data cells, where

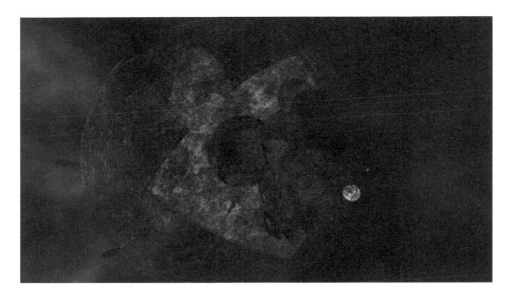

Figure 4.6. Level of detail as a wireframe render.

one data cell has $8 \times 8 \times 8$ voxels). It is almost like having a render cell made of $8 \times 8 \times 8$ voxels. Material values are chosen in a similar manner—the most common material in a data cell is used so that a low detail render cell retains its texture.

Caching a low detail render cell in a FIFO cache works same way as for normal detail. However, a problem arises where cells with different LOD meet: the geometry of low detail and normal detail render cells does not fit together.

Our solution is to compare a given render cell with adjacent cells. If a low detail render cell is adjacent to a normal detail cell, the low detail cell is rendered in low detail and normal detail, as well. The result is that render cells in a specific area around the camera are rendered in both normal and low detail. Close render cells are never rendered with low detail.

Transitions between different LOD levels are almost invisible, and the viewer will hardly notice. In a future release, we plan to alpha-blend different LOD levels, but, because alpha-blending is already used for rendering multi-material voxels, it is impossible right now.

4.10 Ambient Light

Another way of enhancing perception of the terrain is ambient lighting. In the actual release of *Miner Wars*, we stick to three-point lighting, the simplest form of ambient lighting (see ["Three-Point" 09]). The final ambient factor is packed in a vertex buffer.

In future engine development, we plan to do ambient occlusion by casting random rays through voxels. The benefits of this approach are that it is easy to traverse voxels (see [Cohen 94]) and static shadows are generated as byproduct.

4.11   Conclusion

For players who are constantly looking for the next level of realism in their games, volumetric destructible terrain offers a constantly changing environment and consequently richer game play. As a bonus, replayability is enhanced, giving the gamer a greater sense of value—and a higher regard for the game's developer.

During the development of *Miner Wars* and its volumetric destructible terrain, our primary challenges were to maintain a high frame rate during terrain changes and to use memory efficiently.

The solution we chose, voxels, is very well suited for representing terrains, such as those found in *Miner Wars*, though architectural work where crisp edges are needed would benefit from a different approach.

Our implementation runs smoothly in HD 1080p at 60 FPS on an average hardware setup that includes a Core2 Duo 2.5 GHz processor, an NVIDIA GeForce 8800 GTS video card, and 1 GB RAM.

Apart from the obvious graphical advantages of voxel terrain, there are others that the gamer will never see, yet nonetheless appreciate, in terms of overall game play. Voxel traversal, for example, allows intersection testing for ambient occlusion, AI navigation, volume calculations and voxel collision detection. Voxel terrain can be used as another type of geometric primitive, thus omitting triangles from some types of intersection queries (e.g., sphere vs. voxel terrain). It is fast and precise, and we use it for all collision detection, except those involving projectiles and missiles.

For debugging purposes, I recommend creating another simple voxel renderer that will visualize actual voxels and not triangles. In our case, we are rendering voxels as billboards. It is useful especially when importing custom three-dimensional models or when testing collision and detection.

Bibliography

[Miner 09] *Miner Wars*. Available at http://www.MinerWars.com, 2009.

["Three-Point" 09] "Three-Point Lighting." *Wikipedia*. Available at http://en
.wikipedia.org/wiki/Three-point_lighting, 2009.

[Cohen 94] Daniel Cohen. "Voxel Traversal along a 3D Line." In *Graphics Gems IV*, edited by Paul S. Heckbert, pp. 366–69. San Diego: Academic Press, 1994

["Marching" 09] "Marching Cubes." *Wikipedia.* Available at http://en.wikipedia .org/wiki/Marching_cubes, 2009.

Beyond Pixels and Triangles

With the increasing performance and parallelism of graphic processors and the introduction of accelerated general compute systems such as CUDA or the DirectX 11 Compute Shaders, the appeal of transferring complex and CPU hungry tasks to the GPU more compelling than ever. The latest advances in GPU technologies and APIs makes it easier than ever to implement a broad range of algorithms ranging from offline shading, to AI and physics using GPU acceleration. This section will thus cover articles that present techniques that go beyond pixels and triangles and by taking advantage of hardware acceleration. This section includes the following articles:

The first article, "Parallelization Implementation of Universal Visual Computer," is written by Tze-Yui Ho, Ping-Man Lam, and Chi-Sing Leung. This article explores a framework for the generalization of image processing algorithms that can run a wide range of filters using a single set of shaders. The article exposes a few practical examples and compares the performance of such algorithm compared to a CPU based implementation.

The following article, "Accelerating Virtual Texturing Using CUDA," written by Charles-Frederik Hollemeersch, Bart Pieters, Peter Lambert, and Rik Van de Walle, explores a virtual texturing system similar to the one use in *Quake Wars* and *Rage*. The article focuses on how several of the problems related to such an algorithm can by solved on the GPU using CUDA, thereby reducing the CPU requirements for such an implementation.

Next we move on to "Efficient Rendering of Highly Detailed Volumetric Scenes with GigaVoxels" by Cyril Crassin, Fabrice Neyret, Miguel Sainz, and Elmar Eisemann. We examine a new framework for the compression and efficient rendering of large volumetric data sets (or voxels). We see how we can even take advantage of this data structure to efficiently render additional effects such as LODs or depth of field.

Then we follow with "Spatial Binning on the GPU," written by Christopher Oat, Joshua Barczak, and Jeremy Shopf. In this article we explore an algorithm that allows the spatial sorting of a large set of data points. Such an algorithm is crucial for various algorithms such as the simulation of fluids or large particle sets.

Finally, in "Real-Time Interaction between Particles and the Dynamic Mesh on the GPU" by Vlad Alexandrov, we explore how we can implement the interaction between particles and geometry. The article looks at an algorithm that can be used to represent collision geometry in a GPU friendly form that can then be used by a particle simulation to implement real-time particle to geometry interactions.

—Sebastien St-Laurent

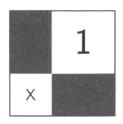

Parallelized Implementation of Universal Visual Computer

Tze-Yui Ho, Ping-Man Lam, and Chi-Sing Leung

1.1 Introduction

Graphics applications and image processing are usually achieved by tailor-made algorithms. For example, the operations used in noise removal may differ significantly from reaction diffusion [Turk 91]. Instead of implementing individual algorithms, it is interesting to implement a single universal visual algorithm applicable to wide range of applications. One of such possible architectures is the *cellular neural network* (CNN) [Chua 98] [Chua and Yang 98b] [Chua and Yang 98a] [K.R. Crounse and Chua 93].

A CNN consists of a number of identical cells, which are arranged in a two-dimensional structure and are only connected to neighboring cells, where each cell has input, current, and next states. Distant cells are influenced by the others through data propagation between neighboring cells. With the CNN approach, different applications, such as visual processing and optimization, are achieved using the same algorithm with a different set of parameters. Although the local connectivity of the cells is well suited for implementation on a GPU, there are two additional issues that we have to address: first, the computational model of GPU is based on four-channel data, but the CNN data is conventionally organized in a one-channel format; second, the data transfer rate between the GPU and main memory is much slower than the transfer rate between the CPU and main memory.

This article presents an efficient GPU implementation for the CNN algorithm. The implementation fully utilizes the four-channel processing power of the GPU and minimizes the data transfers between the main memory and GPU. The article is organized as follows: Section 1.2 reviews the algorithm behind CNN; Section 1.3

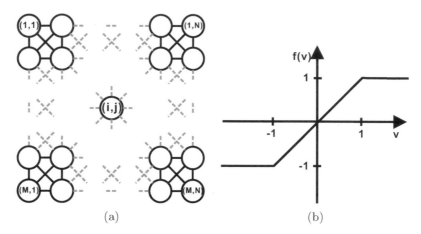

Figure 1.1. (a) Two-dimensional CNN; (b) Piecewise-linear function used in a CNN cell.

describes our implementation; the performance of our approach is reported in Section 1.4; and finally, conclusions are drawn in Section 1.5.

1.2   Background

A two-dimensional CNN consists of a number of connected cells which are arranged in a two-dimensional grid structure as shown in Figure 1.1(a). A cell interacts with its neighboring cells directly whereas distant cells interact with each others indirectly by means of data propagation. For a cell $C(i, j)$ located at the ith row and the jth column in a two-dimensional CNN of size $M \times N$, the set of its neighboring cells are defined as

$$\eta_r(i, j) = \{C(i, j)|\max(|k - i|, |l - j|) \leqslant r\},$$

where $k \in \{1, \cdots, M\}$, $l \in \{1, \cdots, N\}$ and r is a positive integer. The parameter r defines the number of neighboring cells.

Let v_u, v_x, and v_y be the input, current, and next states of a cell, respectively. The dynamic equation of a CNN is given by

$$\frac{\mathrm{d}}{\mathrm{d}t}v_{x,i,j}(t) = -v_{x,i,j}(t) + \sum_{C(k,l)\in\eta_r(i,j)} A(i, j; k, l)v_{y,k,l}(t)$$
$$+ \sum_{C(k,l)\in\eta_r(i,j)} B(i, j; k, l)v_{u,k,l} + I,$$

where I is the input bias, $A(i, j; k, l)$ and $B(i, j; k, l)$ are the coefficients governing the state changes which are usually spatial invariant. We refer to these coefficients

$$A = \begin{bmatrix} -0.03 & -0.08 & -0.12 & -0.08 & -0.03 \\ -0.08 & -0.35 & -0.6 & -0.35 & -0.08 \\ -0.12 & -0.6 & 1.05 & -0.6 & -0.12 \\ -0.08 & -0.35 & -0.6 & -0.35 & -0.08 \\ -0.03 & -0.08 & -0.12 & -0.08 & -0.03 \end{bmatrix}, B = \begin{bmatrix} 0 & 0 & 0.06 & 0 & 0 \\ 0 & 0.35 & 0.75 & 0.35 & 0 \\ 0.06 & 0.75 & 2.12 & 0.75 & 0.06 \\ 0 & 0.35 & 0.75 & 0.35 & 0 \\ 0 & 0 & 0.06 & 0 & 0 \end{bmatrix}, I = 0$$

Figure 1.2. Cloning templates for half-toning.

as "cloning templates." The output $v_{y,i,j}(t)$ is derived from $v_{x,i,j}(t)$ by

$$v_{y,i,j}(t) = f(v_{x,i,j}(t)),$$

where the function $f(v) = \frac{1}{2}(|v + 1| - |v - 1|)$ is a piecewise-linear function as shown in Figure 1.1(b). In a time-discrete CNN [M. Brucoli 95], the time variable t is replaced with nh, where h is the time step, and n is the discrete time index. Hence, the discrete time dynamic equation is given by

$$v_{x,i,j}(n + 1) = v_{x,i,j}(n) + I$$
$$+ h \left(\sum_{C(k,l) \in \eta_r(i,j)} (A(i,j;k,l)v_{y,k,l}(n) + B(i,j;k,l)v_{u,k,l}) \right).$$
$$(1.1)$$

By considering the property of the CNN, we know that the state of a CNN must reach a stable equilibrium. In particular, the state variable $v_{x,i,j}$ converges to a real number and the output variable $v_{y,i,j}$ converges to either 1 or -1.

The templates values (the input bias I and cloning templates $\{A(i,j;k,l),$ $B(i,j;k,l)\}$) controls the functionality of a CNN. Figure 1.2 shows the typical 5×5 cloning templates for halftone. Other applications, such as edge detection, can also be achieved using the same updating equation but with different cloning templates.

1.3   CNN Implementation

1.3.1   Overview

In our implementation, there are two textures for input and one texture for output. The first input texture is the input state texture U which stores the time-invariant data. The other input texture is the current state texture X_{old} which stores the current state $v_{x,i,j}(n)$. The output texture is the next state texture X_{new} which stores the next state $v_{x,i,j}(n + 1)$.

Initially, the current state texture is zero-initialized and the input state texture is uploaded to GPU. Then, the interaction between CNN cells (Equation (1.1))

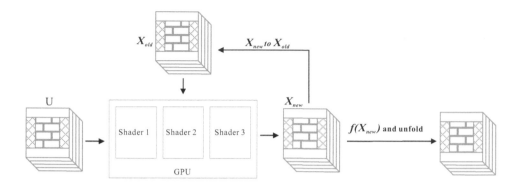

Figure 1.3. Our GPU-based iterating process.

is simulated by a number of shaders. After updating, the next state texture that stores the updated state is obtained and will be considered as the current state in the next iteration. After a number of iterations, we obtained the final result from the next state texture. Figure 1.3 shows the structure of our GPU-based CNN simulator.

1.3.2   Using the Four-Channel Textures

To fully utilize the four-channel processing power of the GPU, the input, current, and next states are partitioned vertically into four segments as shown in Figure 1.4, and are compacted into four-channel textures such that four cells can be performed in a row.

From Equation (1.1), there are time-invariant data, given by

$$u(i,j) = h\Big(\sum_{C(k,l)\in\eta_r(i,j)} B(i,j;k,l)v_{u,k,l} \Big) + I.$$

All values of $[u(i,j)]$ are pre-computed to form a texture. Then they are partitioned vertically into four segments with resolution equal to $M \times \frac{N}{4}$. To simplify

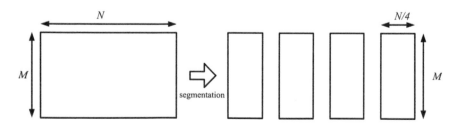

Figure 1.4. The input state texture is divided into four segments.

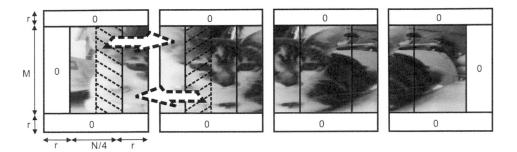

Figure 1.5. To resolve the data access problems at the edge of the texture, they are padded to each segment. The segments are stacked up to form a four-channel texture.

the retrieval of neighboring values near the edge, we pad the edges of each segment as shown in Figure 1.5. Similarly, we create two more four-channel textures, with the same resolution, for the current state and next state textures.

1.3.3 Shader Implementation

We perform Equation (1.1) iteratively using three shaders, namely Shader 1, Shader 2, and Shader 3. Note that the left edge, the central region, and the right edge in the four-channel output state texture are handled by different shaders to avoid the unnecessary memory traffic.

Shader 1 computes the central region of the next state data $[v_{x,i,j}(n+1)]$, while Shader 2 and Shader 3 handle the edge regions. So the three shaders input from (and output to) different regions of the textures. Within an iteration, X_{new} is computed using U and X_{old}. Afterward, we swap the contents of X_{new} and X_{old}. Note that we do not need to explicitly exchange the contents of X_{new} and X_{old}. Instead we do the swapping virtually by swapping their texture IDs.

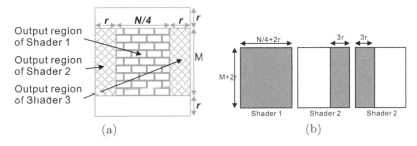

Figure 1.6. (a) Output regions in X_{new}. (b) Input regions in U and X_{old}.

```
void main(
  float2 tc : TEXCOORD0, // cell index
  uniform samplerRECT utex, // time-invariant data
  uniform samplerRECT xtex, // current state data
  uniform float T[9], // cloning template
  out float4 state : COLOR0 // output
){
  // Evaluate the next state using Equation (1.1).
  state = cnn_state( tc, utex, xtex, T );
}

// The implemenation of Equation (1.1)
float4 cnn_state( float2 tc,
  samplerRECT utex, samplerRECT xtex,
  float T[9]
){
  float4 state, curr;
  int i;

  // Retrieve current state.
  curr = f4texRECT(xtex,tc);

  // Evaluate cells in the neighborhood.
  state = 0;
  for( i=0; i<4; i++ )
    state += clamp(f4texRECT(xtex,
      float2(tc.x+i%3-1,tc.y+i/3-1)),-1,1)*T[i];
  for( i=5; i<9; i++ )
    state += clamp(f4texRECT(xtex,
      float2(tc.x+i%3-1,tc.y+i/3-1)),-1,1)*T[i];
  state += T[4]*clamp(curr,-1,1);
  state *= CNN_STEP;

  // Return the next state.
  return state + f4texRECT(utex,tc) -CNN_STEP*curr +curr;
}
```

Listing 1.1. Shader 1, the shader for the central region.

Shader 1 is the core shader for computing the next state data $[v_{x,i,j}(n+1)]$. It outputs data for the central region of X_{new} as shown in Figure 1.6(a). It takes as input the regions of U and X_{old} as illustrated in Figure 1.6(b). The Cg script of Shader 1 is presented in Listing 1.1.

After Shader 1 is executed, the central region of the next state data $[v_{x,i,j}(n+1)]$ it output to X_{new}. Then we proceed to process the edges of X_{new}. Although the next state data of the edges can be obtained from the central region of X_{new}, which has just been computed, copying this data to the edges is not very efficient. This is the case because a FBO cannot be a texture and a frame buffer, simultaneously. In order to obtain the edges of X_{new} by copying, we will need an

```
void cnn_ledge(
  float2 tc : TEXCOORD0,
  uniform samplerRECT utex,
  uniform samplerRECT xtex,
  uniform float T[9],
  out float4 state : COLOR0
){
  // Evaluate the next state using Equation (1.1).
  state = cnn_state( tc, utex, xtex, T );
  // Sizzle to match the output channels.
  state = float4( 0, state.xyz );
}
```

Listing 1.2. Shader 2, the shader for the left edge.

extra intermediate frame buffer which can result in a large amount of data traffic. Therefore, instead of copying, we make use of two additional shaders, Shader 2 and Shader 3, to update the edge regions directly from U and X_{old}.

Shader 2 is designed to update the left edge of X_{new}. Its output region consists of the leftmost r columns of X_{new} as shown in Figure 1.6(a). The output will cover the rightmost $3r$ columns of U and X_{old} as shown in Figure 1.6(b). Shader 2 performs the same four-channel rendering process as Shader 1 does. Then the resulting values are sizzled to match the output channels with their corresponding edges. The Cg script of Shader 2 is presented in Listing 1.2.

Shader 3 is designed to update the right edge of X_{new}. Its output consists of the right edge of X_{new} as shown in Figure 1.6(a). Its input objects are the leftmost $3r$ columns in X_{old} and the leftmost $3r$ columns in U as shown in Figure 1.6(b). The implementations of Shader 2 and Shader 3 are almost the same, the only difference being that the resulting values are sizzled differently. The Cg script of Shader 3 is presented in Listing 1.3. Note that the number of pixels processed in

```
void cnn_redge(
  float2 tc : TEXCOORD0,
  uniform samplerRECT utex,
  uniform samplerRECT xtex,
  uniform float T[9],
  out float4 state : COLOR0
){
  // Evaluate the next state using Equation (1.1).
  state = cnn_state( tc, utex, xtex, T );
  // Sizzle to match the output channels.
  state = float4( state.yzw, 0 );
}
```

Listing 1.3. Shader 3, the shader for the right edge.

CNN Size	CPU	CPU with SSE	Our Method
512x512	82.03	188.32	1828.15
1024x1024	20.85	43.84	566.57
2048x2048	5.31	10.86	150.60
3072x3072	2.36	4.79	84.77

Table 1.1. The performance of the three approaches for the 3×3 cloning templates. The performance is measured in number of iterations per second.

Shader 1 is far greater than that in Shader 2 and Shader 3. Hence the processing time is dominated by Shader 1.

1.4   Results

In our experiment, three CNN simulators were implemented. The first one is our GPU-based simulator, whereas the other two are CPU-based simulators. One of the CPU-based simulators is written in C++ and the other one is written in C++ with the SSE instruction set. All three simulators were tested on a personal computer equipped with a Pentium 4 3.0 GHz CPU, 1GB RAM, and a PX7900 GTX HDH display card. Furthermore, we consider two cloning template sizes, 3×3 (r=1) and 5×5 (r=2). The performance results are tabulated in Tables 1.1 and 1.2. From the tables, our GPU-based simulator can run 21 times faster as compared to the CPU-based simulator written in C++, and around nine times faster as compared to the CPU-based simulator using SSE. In particular, for the 3×3 cloning templates, our GPU-based simulator is able to achieve 1828 iterations per second when the CNN size is 512×512, while the CPU-based simulator can achieve only less than 90 iterations per second. Even with SSE, the CPU-based simulator achieves less than 190 iterations per second.

A CNN-based half-toning algorithm [K.R. Crounse 93] is implemented to test the functionality of our CNN simulator. Figure 1.7 shows the result from half-toning a 512×512 grayscale image using the templates in Figure 1.2. More results can be found in Figures 1.8 and 1.9.

CNN Size	CPU	CPU with SSE	Our Method
512x512	39.51	95.51	831.25
1024x1024	9.92	23.27	237.02
2048x2048	2.50	5.77	63.05
3072x3072	1.11	2.56	28.37

Table 1.2. The performance of the three approaches for the 5×5 cloning templates, measured in number of iterations per second.

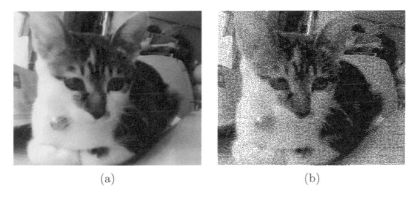

Figure 1.7. A half-toning example: (a) original; (b) half-toned.

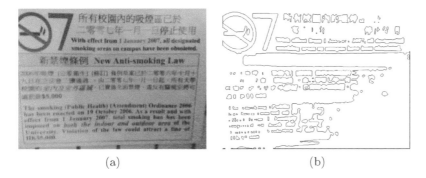

Figure 1.8. An edge extraction example: (a) original; (b) extracted edge.

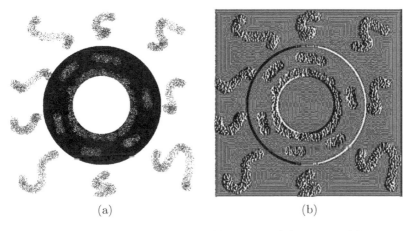

Figure 1.9. A reaction diffusion example: (a) original; (b) reaction diffusion result.

1.5   Conclusion

In this article we demonstrated a simple and cost-effective solution that implements a CNN on the consumer-level, which can run 8-17 times faster than CPU-based simulators. No tailor-made and expensive hardware is needed to achieve such a high performance. There are three main features in our implementation enabling this improvement. Firstly, we organize the CNN data as four-channel textures, and hence, we can process four cells in a row to fully utilize the four-channel computational power of the GPU. Secondly, we swap the content of the state textures virtually by swapping their texture IDs, and this allows us to fully take advantage of the four-channel parallel processing power of the GPU. Lastly, the data traffic is further reduced by using three different shaders to update the edge and central regions.

1.6   Acknowledgments

The work was supported by research grants from Hong Kong Government (Project No. CityU 116508).

Bibliography

[Chua and Yang 98a] L. O. Chua and L. Yang. *Cellular Neural Networks: Applications*, 35. Singapore: World Scientific, 1998.

[Chua and Yang 98b] L. O. Chua and L. Yang. "Cellular Neural Networks: Theory." *IEEE Trans. on Circuits and System* 35:10 (1998), 1257–1268.

[Chua 98] L. O. Chua. *A Paradigm for Complexity*. Singapore: World Scientific, 1998.

[K.R. Crounse and Chua 93] T. Roska K.R. Crounse and L.O. Chua. "Image Halftoning with Cellular Neural Networks." *IEEE Trans. Circuits Syst. Part II* 40:4 (1993), 267–283.

[K.R. Crounse 93] L.O. Chua K.R. Crounse, T. Roska. "Image Halftoning with Cellular Neural Networks." *IEEE Trans. Circuits Syst. Part II* 40:4 (1993), 267–283.

[M. Brucoli 95] G. Grassi M. Brucoli, L. Carnimeo. "Discrete-Time Cellular Neural Networks for Associative Memories with Learning and Forgetting Capabilities." *IEEE Trans. Circuits Syst. Part I* 42:7 (1995), 396–399.

[Turk 91] G. Turk. "Generating Textures on Arbitrary Surfaces using Reaction Diffusion." *ACM SIGGRAPH*, pp. 289–298.

Accelerating Virtual Texturing Using CUDA

Charles-Frederik Hollemeersch, Bart Pieters, Peter Lambert, and Rik Van de Walle

For a long time games have used textures to add surface details and diversity to their virtual worlds. These textures usually consist of a basic set of different surface appearances which are then composed at runtime by shaders to calculate the final surface appearance. Recently there has been an increased interest in *virtual texturing* technologies [Barrett 08, Lefebre et al. 04, Mittring 08]. Virtual texturing allows very large textures (in the order of one gigapixel) to be applied to the game's geometry while still remaining within the limits of today's hardware. This allows far more varied worlds than can be achieved with composing tiling textures at a lower or comparable render cost.

One of the first commercial systems to employ these techniques was id Software's Mega Texturing technology [van Waveren 08] as used in the game *Enemy Territory Quake Wars*. This technology is loosely based on clipmapping [Tanner et al. 98] and shares the same limitation that only a single rectangle in texture space is available at the highest resolution. Hence its use is limited to nearly planar geometries with regular texture coordinates. In their upcoming game *Rage*, these limitations have been addressed by adopting a fully functional virtual texturing system [van Waveren 09].

Extending this technique to arbitrary geometries and texture coordinate mappings adds a substantial overhead to the technique. Besides the streaming, (de)compression and texture updates, the additional cost of determining what parts of the texture are referenced by the rendered frame is introduced. Existing systems usually involve a lot of expensive CPU work and CPU to GPU data transfers.

In this chapter, we want to demonstrate how NVIDIA's compute unified device architecture platform can be used to reduce this CPU work and how it can be used to efficiently stream data between system memory and GPU memory. CUDA provides a straightforward way to address the GPU for general purpose computations, without the need to translate the problem in terms of shaders and textures. Although we implemented our system using CUDA, the theory will be equally applicable to upcoming vendor independent standards such as OpenCL or the DirectX Compute Shaders. The required hardware is getting cheaper and is no longer only available to the high-end market segment, making its use in commercial games attractive.

2.1   Introduction

2.1.1   Virtual Texturing

Virtual texturing is loosely based on the idea of virtual memory. The texture address space is logically divided into chunks called pages, then at runtime only the pages needed by the current view are loaded into fast texture memory. The rest of the texture is stored on disk in a page file and loaded by the game on demand. The set of pages needed by the current frame is referred to as the working set.

A major difference with traditional virtual memory is the presence of mipmaps. Distant portions of the texture should be loaded at a lower resolution. Mipmapping not only helps to reduce the working set: it also provides high quality, alias-free filtering of the texture in the distance. Another difference with traditional virtual memory is that we do not wait for a page to become available

Figure 2.1. The logical page quad tree, and its application onto a three-dimensional surface.

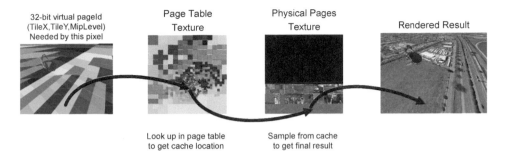

Figure 2.2. Schematic overview of the steps needed to render a virtual texture.

when a page miss occurs. Instead the system uses a lower resolution mipmap of the required page. This helps to ensure a constant frame rate. If the page loading can keep up with the view changes, this lower resolution fall back will generally not be noticeable to the player.

Logically the whole texture can be seen as a quad tree of tiles. At the root it is just a single page containing the lowest mipmap level. Every page then has four child pages on the higher resolution mipmap level. Figure 2.1 shows this page data quad tree structure and how it can be applied to a scene in three-dimensional. Notice how further away geometry references lower resolution mipmapped pages.

As with virtual memory, a page translation table (stored in a texture on the GPU) is then used to translate between virtual page identifiers (pageIds) and the location of the page in physical memory (a big cache texture allocated on the GPU). Figure 2.2 shows how these different data structures work together to get the final textured result.

The final result of rendering with virtual texturing looks like any traditional texture. In particular, there are no limits or requirements on the geometry or texture coordinates. Things like mirrored texture coordinates are transparently handled by the virtual texture system. From an artist's point of view, the system just "works," simply providing very detailed textures all over the world.

2.1.2 GPU Computing and CUDA

GPU computing has evolved a lot in recent years. It is moving away from graphics language based programming (e.g., Cg, HLSL, GLSL, etc.) to specialized parallel computing APIs. One of the first such APIs was NVIDIA's CUDA. CUDA provides a flexible programming model for mapping data parallel applications to the GPU. Currently the CUDA architecture can be accessed trough NVIDIA's proprietary extension to the C language. These extensions allow the programmer to specify the location where code and data needs to be located and executed.

This way, the programmer can transparently interface GPU code from CPU code without manually needing to manage the GPU. In the near future new ways to approach the GPU will become available. Both OpenCL and DirectX compute shaders will provide the programmer with a vendor independent GPU computing API with capabilities similar to C for CUDA. Porting to OpenCL from CUDA is reported to be relatively straightforward [NVIDIA 09].

Although the computing environment runs on the same hardware as the traditional shaders of the graphics pipeline, there are some important differences between these two environments. The first difference is the possibility to do scattered writes. While a graphics shader always generates a limited number of outputs in a set of predefined output registers, GPU computing environments allow arbitrary GPU memory access. This coupled with the ability to synchronize between different threads running on the GPU, allows more flexibility in the code and more effective parallel programming methods to be implemented. In addition to this, recent hardware also supports global atomic operations, making buffer and queue management easier. Finally, CUDA also provides asynchronous versions of its API. This allows the CPU and GPU to work independently of each other without needing unnecessary synchronization between them.

To efficiently use the power of these GPU computing environments it is still necessary to develop sufficiently parallel algorithms that work efficiently with the underlying SIMD hardware implementation. This means that diverging branches still imply a performance loss and that a sufficiently large number of threads has to be provided at once.

2.2   Implementing Virtual Texturing

To understand the rest of this chapter, it is necessary to provide some additional details about our implementation of virtual texturing. The architecture of our virtual texturing system is shown in Figure 2.3. The subsystems shown on the figure are largely independent in the code allowing us to easily test different approaches and acceleration strategies. We now briefly describe the function of the different subsystems and their interactions:

- The *page file* contains the source data for every page in our virtual address space. Mipmaps and pages are generated off line and compressed using a custom DCT (i.e., JPEG like) image compressor. Pages in our system contain a 120×120 pixel payload with a four pixel border on all sides. This ensures artifact free anisotropic filtering, which results in our textures getting sizes of a power of two multiplied by 120.

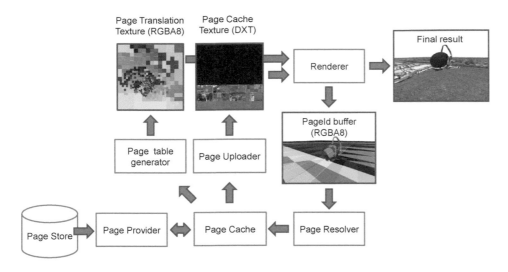

Figure 2.3. Overview of our virtual texturing system.

- The *page provider* provides the rest of our virtual texturing system with decompressed pages from the page file. The file loading and DCT decompression runs in a separate CPU thread and communicates with the main rendering thread via append/consume buffers.

- The main function of the *page cache* is to manage the physical texture. It uses a LRU strategy to decide what pages to replace when new pages are requested. The size of our cache is currently 4096×4096 texels (1024 pages). This is sufficient for rendering at a resolution of 1280×1024 with anisotropic filtering. We currently do not have special handling when the working set exceeds the cache capacity (the cache thrashes constantly). This could easily be handled by dynamically adapting the lod bias, resulting in gradually requesting lower resolution mipmaps till the full working set fits in the cache [van Waveren 09].

- The *page uploader* takes the loaded pages from the provider and efficiently transfers them to the GPU. On the GPU, mipmaps are generated and the results are encoded to the DXT format before being stored in the physical page texture. Because we want to use hardware accelerated trilinear filtering, our system requires the page cache to have mipmaps for its pages. By carefully sampling from the physical texture (see Section 2.3.2), it is sufficient for a single mipmap level to be present in order to support full trilinear filtering. In Section 2.4.2 we will describe these steps in more detail.

- The *page table generator* is responsible for maintaining the page table based on the list of pages present in the cache. Note that even a single page change could require updating large sections of the page table since pages on higher mipmap levels can span large portions of the virtual address space. We will show how we efficiently maintain the page table using the geometry shader in Section 2.4.3.

- The *page resolver* is responsible for determining which pages of the texture are needed by the frame. Our system uses an approach similar to [Barrett 08, van Waveren 08]. This works by rendering the view to a separate buffer containing the pageIds needed by the corresponding pixels. This buffer is then analyzed to extract the list of pageIds required by this frame. In Section 2.4.1 we will describe how this subsystem can be implemented on the GPU. The resulting list of pages (4kb of data) is then transferred to the CPU asynchronously and presented to the page cache.

- The *renderer* finally uses the textures prepared by the other subsystems to render the final texture mapped and filtered result.

2.3   Rendering with Virtual Texturing

In this section we describe how a virtual texture can be sampled and filtered assuming that the cache and translation textures have been correctly initialized. We will also show how to achieve trilinear and anisotropic filtering trough reuse of the existing graphics hardware. The shader we present in this section is mainly written for readability. It also uses the integer instructions available on the most recent generation of hardware. Integer instructions may, however, be slower than using only floating-point operations.

2.3.1   Translating Virtual into Physical Addresses

The translation texture contains for every virtual page the corresponding physical page. By using nearest filtering when sampling this texture, we can simply use the unmodified virtual texture coordinates (in the range [0-1]) to get the information about the required page. To make sure that the correct mipmap level of the page translation texture will be sampled we also scale the derivatives of the texture coordinates accordingly. If we do not factor in this scale, the hardware mipmapping unit would choose the mipmap level to achieve a 1:1 pixel ratio of the translation texture instead of a 1:1 ratio of the virtual texture. Since our virtual texture is larger than the translation table by a factor of the page size, we arrive at the following shader code:

```
float2 virDdX = ddx(i.uv)*PageContentSize;
float2 virDdY = ddy(i.uv)*PageContentSize;
float4 pageInf = tex2D(page_image,i.uv,virDdX,virDdY)*255;
```

The page translation texture then provides us with the following information: the X and Y channel contain the cache tile index, the Z channel the mipmap level of the cache tile, and the W channel the mipmap level of the virtual page. The first three parameters allow us to correctly scale the texture coordinates for sampling from the page cache. The fourth allows us to generate the pageId buffer without much additional work since we immediately know the mipmap level needed for this pixel. We will describe the pageId buffer generation in more detail in Section 2.3.4.

Finally, note that when using trilinear filtering, we need to set an additional mip bias of -0.5 on the page translation texture object. This ensures that the correct miplevels are requested by our system. A downside of this is that the frame's working set also increases since the range of texture data needed at the highest quality increases as a result of this bias. This effect will be even stronger when we use anisotropic filtering since this can require biases of up to the maximum degree of anisotropy.

2.3.2 Sampling the Cache Texture

We now have all the information to sample from the page cache. The page cache texture contains the physical pages, and the first mipmap level of the cache texture contains the page mipmaps generated by our uploading pipeline (see Section 2.4.2). Because we previously requested the lowest (i.e., highest resolution) mipmap level of the virtual texture we need to sample for this pixel. Mipmap levels beyond the second level will not be needed since trilinear filtering only blends between two levels in the mipmap. In theory these lower mipmaps could be sampled under extreme minification (e.g., when we need to sample the 4×4 pixel mipmap level of the whole $16k \times 16k$ texture). When these mipmap levels are needed we simply handle them by clamping to first mipmap level of the 1×1 page level of the virtual texture (i.e., we sample from the 60×60 mipped page where a 4×4 would be required). This could in theory lead to aliasing in this case. However, we never encountered any problems with this approach since it is unlikely to be so far away from the virtual texture that its screen space is less than 60×60 pixels.

We can now easily calculate the offset within this page by first calculating the offset in a [0-1] range and then converting this offset to pixels by scaling. We also add in the bias to account for the four pixel overlap between pages:

```
float2 cacheId = pageInf.xy;
float availableMipLevel = pageInf.z;
float numPagesOnLevel = PagesOnAxis
     * pow(0.5,availableMipLevel);
```

```
float2 offset = frac(i.uv * numPagesOnMipLevel)
        * PageContentSize + BorderSize;
```

To calculate the updated derivatives for trilinear filtering, we first convert the input texture coordinates in the [0-1] range to pixel units on the current mipmap level. We then divide this value by the page cache size in pixels to convert those derivatives into the [0-1] space expected by the hardware when sampling from the page cache:

```
float deltaScale = numPagesOnLevel
        * PageContentSize * (1.0f / CacheSizePixels);
float2 sampDeltaX = ddx(i.uv)*deltaScale;
float2 sampDeltaY = ddy(i.uv)*deltaScale;
```

The final sample from the cache can be implemnted as follows:

```
float2 cachePos = cacheId * PageSize;
float4 final = tex2D(cache_image,
    (cachePos + offset)*(1.0f / CacheSizePixels),
    sampDeltaX,sampDeltaY);
```

2.3.3   Anisotropic Filtering

When working with anisotropic filtering the hardware automatically adds an additional negative bias to the mipmap level calculation. This bias depends on the degree of anisotropy. If the texture minification is near isotropic this bias is zero, if the texture is seen at a highly anisotropic angle this bias is clamped to the maximum level of anisotropy selected. This negative bias could of course lead to aliasing on the main axis of anisotropy. It is exactly this aliasing that is then avoided by doing multiple samples on this axis from the selected mipmap level.

If we want to ensure correct texturing results under anisotropic filtering we have to provide a similar bias to the mipmap level we select from our virtual texture. This bias can be calculated as follows. We refer to the anisotropic texture filtering extension specification [NVIDIA 99] for more details on this formula:

```
float deltaX = length(ddx(i.uv)*TextureSize);
float deltaY = length(ddy(i.uv)*TextureSize);

float deltaMax = max(deltaX, deltaY);
float deltaMin = min(deltaX, deltaY);
float N = min(ceil(deltaMax/deltaMin),MAX_ANISOTROPY);

int level = min(max((int)(log2(deltaMax/N)),0),MaxMipLevel);
```

Note that we cannot simply let the hardware select the mipmap level anymore when sampling from the page translation texture, since the hardware would not take into account the additional anisotropic bias we mentioned above. Trying to enable anisotropic filtering on the page translation texture to work around this would of course sample invalid blended pageIds. Hence, we have to explicitly provide the mipmap level that we request of our virtual texturing system:

```
float4 cache = tex2Dlod(page_image,float4(i.uv,0.0,level));
```

By simply sampling as described in Section2.3.2 and setting the anisotropy on the page cache as follows, we will then get exact anisotropic filtered results.

```
cacheTexture->bind();
glTexParameteri(GL_TEXTURE_2D,
                GL_TEXTURE_MAX_ANISOTROPY_EXT, 4);
```

2.3.4 Generating the PageId Buffer for the Resolver

As mentioned in Section 2.3.1, our translation texture contains the mipmap level of the page in its w channel. Hence by simply sampling from the page translation texture with the correct derivatives we can easily determine the mipmap level needed by this pixel. Once the level is known, the page indexes can easily be calculated based on the textures coordinates as follows:

```
int     levelSize = TextureSize >> mipLevel;
float2 virtualPixelsUv = i.uv * levelSize;
int2    virtualTilesUv = virtualPixelsUv * pixelsToPage;

int4 resultI =  int4(
  (virtualTilesUv.x & 0xFF),
  (virtualTilesUv.y & 0xFF),
  ((virtualTilesUv.x >> 8) << 4) | (virtualTilesUv.y >> 8),
  level
);
```

2.4 GPU-Based Acceleration

Many of the processes introduced in Section 2.2 lend themselves well to parallelization on the GPU. They involve pixel-like operations that can easily be parallelized. Secondly, much of the output data will be needed on the GPU for rendering so it is desirable to try and do the calculations as close to the GPU as possible. In the following sections, we will describe how we mapped some of the virtual texturing processes to the GPU.

2.4.1   Accelerating the Resolver

One of the biggest differences between a traditional texture streaming system and virtual texturing is the need for a resolver. Determining every frame which texture pages are needed for all the visible geometry in the frame is one of the most expensive steps in a virtual texturing system. The resolver usually works by first rendering a lower resolution view with a special shader that outputs the pageId needed by every rendered pixel followed by an analysis phase on the CPU that looks at the pageId's in the framebuffer and requests the new pages from the streaming thread (see Listing 2.1).

Our implementation differs from the previously described approach in several key aspects. First it does not require an extra rendering pass to generate the pageId buffer. This is achieved by outputting to an additional render target when the scene geometry is rendered. In a deferred rendering system this would ideally be during the G-buffer construction phase. In a more traditional rendering approach this could be done when rendering the z-prepass.

The downside of this approach is that our pageId buffer is generated at full resolution. However, rendering the frame geometry again is usually a lot more expensive than the additional shader and ROP cost of rendering the pageId buffer at full resolution. Because we will analyze the pageId buffer on the GPU there is also no need to stream the data to the CPU for the analysis step. So the increased size of the pageId buffer does not put an additional strain on the system bus. In fact, as we will describe below how our system actually reduces the CPU-GPU transfer by only transferring the compact list of required pageIds back to the CPU.

After rendering the frame, the prepared pageId buffer is then mapped in our GPU computing environment. Depending on the hardware capabilities and GPU computing API this might simply mean locking the graphics API's render target memory or doing a copy of the buffer to prepare it for processing by the GPU computing environment. One important note when using OpenGL through the Pixel Buffer Object extension is to use the BGRA pixel format. Data in this format can generally be copied faster because the hardware natively renders to BGRA and thus no byte swapping will be needed during the copy.

Once the buffer has been mapped to the GPU computing environment, a kernel is started that processes every pixel in the image and marks the pageId corresponding to that pixel as used. Instead of analyzing all the pixels in the buffer, we could reduce this cost by only starting a thread every nth pixel. During tests, we noticed no significant performance increase when analyzing the frame at a lower resolution.

After all the pageIds needed by this frame have been identified, a second kernel is started that packs the list of used pages to a single continuous buffer of page IDs. This buffer is then transferred to the CPU. To pack this list, we could use a

```
__global__ void markUsedPagesKernel(
    int *pixelBuffer, int width, int height,
    int frameId, int *outputBuffer)
{
    int2 pixelCoord;
    pixelCoord.x = blockIdx.x * blockDim.x + threadIdx.x;
    pixelCoord.y = blockIdx.y * blockDim.y + threadIdx.y;

    if ( pixelCoord.x >= width || pixelCoord.y >= height ) {
        return;
    }

    int4 pixel;
    pixel = tex2D(renderTexture,pixelCoord.x, pixelCoord.y);

    //Swizzle around (caused by BGRA rendering).
    int tileX = pixel.z;
    int tileY = pixel.y;
    int level = pixel.w;

    // Do some sanity checks on the shader output...
    if ( level > info.numLevels ) {
        return;
    }

    int levelWidth = sizeForMipLevel(level);

    if ( tileX >= levelWidth || tileY >= levelWidth ) {
        return;
    }

    // Calculate the level buffer.
    int *levelData = outputBuffer + offsetForMipLevel(level);

    // Mark this page as touched.
    levelData[tileY * levelWidth + tileX] = frameId;
}
```

Listing 2.1. CUDA kernel that marks the pages used by this frame.

prefix-sum based system [Harris et al. 08], but we instead opted to use a much simpler global atomics based system. This system works by maintaining a single counter that contains the number of pageIds required so far. When a thread encounters a required pageId, it increases the counter through an atomic operation to allocate a slot in the output list. It then continues to write the pageId to the allocated slot. Because the atomic operations are guaranteed to be mutually exclusive, no two threads can reserve the same output slot.

```
__global__ void gatherUsedPagesKernel(
    int *usedPages, int numPages,
    int frameId, unsigned int *outList)
{
    int offset = blockIdx.x * blockDim.x + threadIdx.x;

    // Check in range.
    if (offset > numPages) {
        return;
    }

    // A large portion of threads will return here.
    if ( usedPages[offset] != frameId ) {
        return;
    }

    int level = mipLevelForOffset(offset);
    int levelOfs = offset - offsetForMipLevel(level);
    int size = sizeForMipLevel(level);

    int x = levelOfs & (size-1);
    int y = levelOfs / size;

    // This will wrap around if more than MAX_FRAME_PAGES
    // are requested.
    int outIndex = atomicInc(outList, MAX_FRAME_PAGES);
    outList[outIndex+1] = make_pageId(x,y,level);
}
```

Listing 2.2. Cuda kernel to pack the list of used pages.

Since atomic operations require serialization of the memory accesses, a bottleneck may develop if many threads try to access the same counter. However, only a small number of pages is actually used every frame and hence there is a clear upper limit to the number of calls done on our atomic counter. Secondly, from performance measurements using the CUDA visual profiler, we determined that this step is certainly not the bottleneck. Hence, we decided use the current approach. The code of the packing kernel can be found in Listing 2.2.

The final step of our resolver is then transferring the packed list back to the CPU (see Figure 2.4). To ensure that we do not need to synchronize with the GPU, this transfer is started asynchronously. Because the actual number of pages that was emitted by the packer is not yet known to the CPU when the transfer is started, we instead transfer a single fixed size buffer containing the atomic counter and the maximum number of pages packed per frame. This results in more data transferred than strictly needed. However, it is much faster than starting

Kernel 1: Mark this
frame's used pageIds

Kernel 2: Pack the list
of page IDs for transfer

Asynchronous transfer
to the CPU

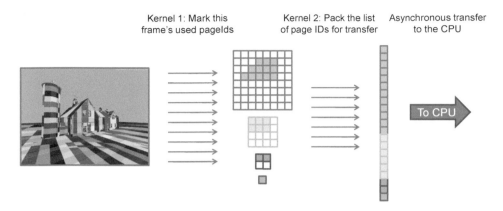

Figure 2.4. The resolver pipeline.

a synchronous GPU-CPU transfer to read back the number of pages emitted followed by an asynchronous copy of the actual page data. Also note that this buffer is only four kilobytes. Thus the overhead of starting a transfer generally overshadows the actual data transfer time.

2.4.2 Asynchronous Uploading and Compression

Another big issue with virtual texturing systems is getting the dynamically loaded data efficiently onto the GPU. For page data that needs no further processing, the Pixel Buffer Object(PBO) OpenGL extension [Biermann et al. 04] offers an efficient transfer path. When properly used, this extension provides high speed asynchronous data transfers between the CPU and GPU. Listing 2.3 shows how the PBO extension can be used to upload DXT compressed pages.

The `glBufferData` call at line two hints to the driver that we will replace the whole buffer. This will allow the driver to optimize our transfer knowing that the old data will not be referenced anymore. (The `WRITE_ONLY` parameter alone is not enough since it still allows us rewrite only certain parts of the buffer.) We will use a similar approach with VBOs in Section 2.4.3 to transfer the list of pages in the cache to the GPU when updating the page table.

PBOs allow only limited flexibility on the upload path and we would like to dynamically generate mipmaps and transcode our data to DXT. Hence, we chose to use CUDA for uploading and processing the page data. CUDA allows high-speed asynchronous copies from system memory to GPU memory. These asynchronous copies require the data to be in page-locked memory which can be allocated trough the CUDA API. To minimize the CPU processing of the uploaded data even further, our loading thread immediately loads and decodes the data to

```
glBindBuffer(GL_PIXEL_UNPACK_BUFFER_ARB, uploadFBO);
glBufferData(GL_PIXEL_UNPACK_BUFFER_ARB, size, 0,
   GL_STREAM_DRAW_ARB);
buff = glMapBuffer(GL_PIXEL_UNPACK_BUFFER_ARB,GL_WRITE_ONLY);
[put some data in buff...]
glUnmapBuffer(GL_PIXEL_UNPACK_BUFFER_ARB);
glBindBuffer(GL_PIXEL_UNPACK_BUFFER_ARB, copyFBO);
glBindTexture(GL_TEXTURE_2D, theTexture);
glCompressedTexSubImage2D(GL_TEXTURE_2D,
   0,xoffsets[idx],yoffsets[idx],
   PAGE_SIZE,PAGE_SIZE,
   GL_COMPRESSED_RGBA_S3TC_DXT5_EXT,
   DXT_PAGE_SIZE,
   (unsigned char *)(idx*DXT_PAGE_SIZE));
```

Listing 2.3. Pseudocode to upload a page using the PBO OpenGL extension.

page locked memory. This way, the CPU does not need to touch the data outside of the page provider thread.

When new pages are made available by the page provider, our main thread simply passes the buffer to CUDA to be uploaded asynchronously. It then calls the necessary kernels to generate the mipmaps and to do the DXT encoding. The DXT encoder immediately writes its results to an OpenGL Pixel Buffer Object. Finally, the buffer is then transferred to the page cache texture using high-speed GPU-GPU memory transfers.

Modern GPU hardware allows overlapping kernel execution with data transfers. We exploit this capability by starting to encode the first few pages while additional pages are still being downloaded. To use this capability, we have to organize our CUDA calls in two "streams." All CUDA calls executed within a single stream are executed sequentially. The GPU will not start executing our encoding kernel before the asynchronous data transfer has finished. However, calls in different streams are not ordered across stream boundaries; thus, by executing our uploading and compression in several streams, parallel uploading and encoding of pages can be achieved.

A second thing to take into consideration is that CUDA kernels only perform optimally if they are given enough work (i.e., threads) to complete in one time. Ideally, several thousands of threads have to be provided to the hardware at once. Because we perform the DXT encoding with a single thread per 4×4 block, we have only 1024 threads available per page (i.e., 32×32 DXT blocks on a 128×128 pixel page). This is too low to efficiently use the full capacity of the graphics hardware. Therefore we first upload several pages before starting the encoding process on a group of pages. Although our demo only loads diffuse textures additional channels of texture data, such as normals and specular colors, should also help to

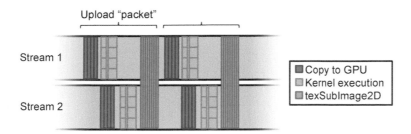

Figure 2.5. Parallel uploading and compression of upload packets using CUDA streams.

increase the thread count to a level that optimally uses the available computing power.

Finally, we would like to have a limit to the number of GPU buffers used for the compression and uploading of the pages. Therefore we split the data into "upload packets." A fixed number of packets is uploaded, compressed and copied to the texture. In this way we only need buffer space for the pages in a single packet. This packeting also helps to reduce the switching overhead between the GPU computing and graphics contexts (i.e., CUDA and OpenGL), which may be an expensive operation depending on the platform.

Figure 2.5 gives an overview of how the pages are grouped in packets and then split over several streams to be uploaded and compressed. After mipmap generation and compression, the streams are again synchronized and the data is transferred to the cache texture using `texSubImage2D`.

We now discuss the actual kernel implementation of the upload system. The first kernel in our system is the mipmap generation. Mipmaps are currently generated by a simple 2×2 average. The memory where the pages were uploaded is first mapped as a two-dimensional texture. Mapping memory as textures does not require and additional memory copy under the latest versions of CUDA. Reading the uploaded data trough a CUDA texture has several advantages compared with just reading them as raw memory. First CUDA textures are cached with optimizations for two-dimensional locality. Although our kernel only reads the input data once, this may still help since the data of neighboring threads can be fetched into the cache together. Secondly, texturing allows automatic unpacking of the data without requiring manual shifting and masking of the RGBA8 data. Finally, CUDA textures like their OpenGL counterparts allow for hardware accelerated filtering. Filtering allows us to do the 2×2 average with a single texture sampling operation.

The second kernel then compresses the uploaded data to the DXT texture compression format. This kernel is currently invoked twice, once for the base level and once for the generated mipmaps. There has been much previous work on achieving real time DXT compression [van Waveren 06]. Although these algo-rithms were developed for CPU use, they are also efficient on GPUs since they do not cause a lot of diverging branches. We again sample the source data through a texture since we require a lot of spatially local samples to encode a 4×4 block.

The most significant disadvantage of our current implementation is that it requires a lot of registers while processing the 16 pixels in a block sequentially. This means that the GPU can schedule less threads at once, preventing it from optimally hiding memory access latencies. Modifying the code to use fast per SIMD-unit shared memory besides registers is not an ideal solution either as this memory is equally limited in size. The best solution would be to move away from having one thread per 4×4 DXT block toward a system that uses one thread per pixel or per channel. These approaches would lead to 16 or 4 threads per DXT block with a significantly reduced per thread register count. This leads to more threads but also more calculations running in parallel with less sequential pro-cessing per block. These modifications will likely result in improved compression times.

2.4.3   Updating the Page Table

As described in Section 2.2, the page table provides the translation between a virtual page identifier and an actual physical page. Since not all requested virtual pages are necessarily available in the cache, the page table contains the best available physical page for every virtual page. It also needs to provide the mipmap level of that physical page so that the texture coordinates within the page can properly be adapted.

This page table can easily be generated on the CPU and then transferred to the GPU. By carefully maintaining the modified regions a small number of texSubImage 2D calls suffice to update the page table.

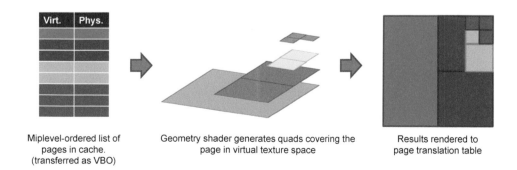

Miplevel-ordered list of   Geometry shader generates quads covering the   Results rendered to
pages in cache.   page in virtual texture space   page translation table
(transferred as VBO)

Figure 2.6. Generating the page translation table using a geometry shader.

```
POINT TRIANGLE_OUT
void geometry_main(AttribArray<vsVertex> inverts) {
    float4 pageId = inverts[0].pageId*255;
    float2 physId = inverts[0].physId;
    int currentLevel = (int)LevelInfo.x;
    float levelScale = LevelInfo.y;

    // Higher miplevels cover larger areas
    // in the translation table.
    float scale = (1<<((int)pageId.w-currentLevel));
    pageId.xy *= scale;

    gs2psVertex vert;
    //Write the physical page address and the number of pages
    //on the miplevel of this virtual page. We write this
    //instead of the miplevel because it saves operations
    //in the pixel shader.
    vert.color = float4(physId.x/255.0,physId.y/255.0,
                    0.0,((int)PagesOnAxis>>pageId.w)/255.0);

    //Generate a quad & range compress to normalized dev coords.
    vert.pos = float4(float2(pageId.x       ,pageId.y      )
            *levelScale*2-1,0.0,1.0);
    emitVertex(vert);
    vert.pos = float4(float2(pageId.x+scale,pageId.y      )
            *levelScale*2-1,0.0,1.0);
    emitVertex(vert);
    vert.pos = float4(float2(pageId.x       ,pageId.y+scale)
            *levelScale*2-1,0.0,1.0);
    emitVertex(vert);
    vert.pos = float4(float2(pageId.x+scale,pageId.y+scale)
            *levelScale*2-1,0.0,1.0);
    emitVertex(vert);
}
```

Listing 2.4. Cg code for the page table geometry shader.

To simplify the system and to guarantee a constant and minimum amount of data transfer between the CPU and the GPU, we chose to implement the page translation texture generation on the GPU as well. We transfer information about pages currently available in the physical cache to the GPU and then use a geometry shader while rendering to the page table texture mipmap levels to generate the page table. In our current implementation this results in a transfer of 12 bytes per page (or 12 kilobyte for the whole translation table).

Figure 2.6 shows how the geometry shader reads the physical page information we transferred and generates a quad of the correct size in virtual texture space to render into the translation texture. By ordering the page table information we send from lowest to highest resolution, we avoid needing a depth buffer when rendering to the page table texture. This ordering only takes a minimal amount of extra work at the CPU side since we simply maintain a linked list per mipmap level without requiring any sorting on the CPU. The code of the geometry shader can be found in Listing 2.4.

2.5 Results

We have now finished presenting the various GPU-based optimizations our virtual texturing implementation provides. In this section we will briefly discuss the performance of our system. These results should give a clear picture of the performance impact of our technique on traditional game rendering architectures. Table 2.1 shows the main performance results for our GPU-based virtual texturing system. These results were measured on an Intel Core 2 Quad CPU, with a NVIDIA GeForce GTX 285 graphics card and 2 gigabyte of RAM. The results are expressed in milliseconds per frame so it should be easy to determine how much the different virtual texturing subsystems will contribute to a game frame. All results where averaged over 100 frames. The page upload time is also averaged after uploading a full upload packet as described in Section 2.4.2. Note that the page uploading and page table updates do not necessarily have to be done every frame. These tasks will only be executed when new pages arrive from the background loading thread. We did not include results for the CPU based steps of our loading thread since we did not do any special optimizations on them. However, they are currently capable of providing pages on time without any visible popping.

From this table we can conclude that we can compress, generate mipmaps and update the cache texture for more than 4,700 pages per second. This is equivalent to about 78 mega pixels per second. Several times more than needed to update small portions of the cache per frame. In frames per second our system performs well over 400Hz with a static camera and around 350Hz when moving around at walking speeds.

Comparing our results with other systems is difficult since not many results from other sources are available. One source [van Waveren 09] quotes 8ms of virtual texturing overhead per frame. Although details are not mentioned, we can conclude that our system should at least perform equally well if not better under similar circumstances.

Subsystem	Frame times
Resolver	1.2ms
Update page table	0.7ms
Upload+Process 1 page	0.21ms

Table 2.1. Performance results of the virtual-texturing subsystems.

2.6 Conclusion

In this chapter we have shown how CUDA and GPU computing in general can benefit virtual texturing and game rendering. From our results we can conclude that GPU-based virtual texturing is a promising game technology that offers high real-time performance. Although it creates extra GPU overhead compared with normal texturing, it also helps to make other areas of the renderer faster. Texture blending, decals, batches and extra geometry to support texture atlases can all be greatly reduced since the frame is rendered with only a few detailed textures. This, coupled with the simplicity of the texturing working all over the game world without any special care by artists, makes it very attractive for deployment in game engines. In the future we hope to investigate more efficient compressions systems and how they can be efficiently mapped to the GPU. This will allow us to keep more texture information in the virtual texture and should allow more advanced lighting models. In addition to this, we also want to investigate how this technique can be expanded to alpha blended textures, leading to a fully transparent virtual texturing system.

2.7 Acknowledgments

The research activities that have been described in this chapter were funded by Ghent University, the Interdisciplinary Institute for Broadband Technology (IBBT), the Institute for the Promotion of Innovation by Science and Technology in Flanders (IWT), the Fund for Scientific Research-Flanders (FWOFlanders), the Belgian Federal Science Policy Office (BFSPO), and the European Union.

Bibliography

[Barrett 08] Sean Barrett. "Sparse Virtual Textures." In *GDC 2008 presentation*, 2008.

[Biermann et al. 04] Ralf Biermann, Derek Cornish, Matt Craighead, Bill Licea-Kane, and Brian Paul. "Pixel Buffer Object."

[Harris et al. 08] Mark Harris, Shubhabrata Sengupta, and John D. Owens. "Parallel Prefix Sum (Scan) with CUDA." *GPU Gems 3*, pp. 851–876.

[Lefebre et al. 04] Sylvain Lefobre, Jérome Darbon, and Fabrice Neyret. "Unified Texture Management for Arbitrary Meshes." *Research Report No. 5210*.

[Mittring 08] Martin Mittring. "Advanced Virtual Texture Topics." *ACM SIGGRAPH 2008 Classes*.

[NVIDIA 99] NVIDIA. *Texture Filter Anisotropic.* Santa Clara: NVIDIA Corporation, 1999.

[NVIDIA 09] NVIDIA. *OpenCL JumpStart Guide.* Santa Clara: NVIDIA Corporation, 2009.

[Tanner et al. 98] Christopher C. Tanner, Christopher J. Migdal, and Michael T. Jones. "The Clipmap: A Virtual Mipmap." *Proceedings of the 25th Annual Conference on Computer Graphics and Interactive Techniques.*

[van Waveren 06] Jan-Paul van Waveren. "Real-Time DXT Compression."

[van Waveren 08] Jan-Paul van Waveren. "Geospatial Texture Streaming from Slow Storage Devices."

[van Waveren 09] Jan-Paul van Waveren. "ID Tech 5 Challenges." *SIGGRAPH 2009: Beyond Programmable Shading Course.*

3

X

Efficient Rendering of Highly Detailed Volumetric Scenes with GigaVoxels

Cyril Crassin, Fabrice Neyret, Miguel Sainz, and Elmar Eisemann

3.1 Introduction

GigaVoxels is a voxel-based rendering pipeline that makes the display of very large volumetric datasets very efficient. It is adapted to memory-bound environments and is designed for the data-parallel architecture of the GPU. It is capable of

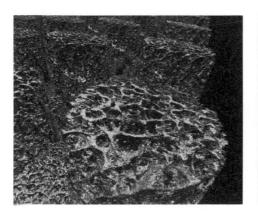

Figure 3.1. Examples of scenes composed, respectively, of 8192^3 and 2048^3 voxels rendered interactively using our engine.

rendering objects at a detail level that matches the screen resolution and interactively adapts to the current point of view. Invisible parts are never even considered for contribution to the final image (see Figure 3.1). As a result, the algorithm obtains interactive to real-time frame rates and demonstrates the use of extreme amounts of voxels in rendering, which is applicable in many different contexts. This is also confirmed by many game developers who seriously consider voxels as a potential standard primitive in video games. We will also show in this chapter that voxels are already powerful primitives that, for some rendering tasks, achieve higher performance than triangle-based representations.

3.2   Voxel Representations

The name *voxel* comes from "volumetric elements" and it represents the generalization in three-dimensional of the pixels. Voxels are axis-aligned cubes that contain some data, usually a density value, or a color value and opacity. Voxels are well-suited for complex or fuzzy data, such as clouds, smoke or foam. They handle semi-transparency gracefully due to their inherent spatial organization, whereas triangles would need costly sorting operations. Further we show that they offer a promising way to unify texture and geometry simplifying filtering simpler and making voxels a good candidate to address aliasing issues that are hard to deal with for triangulated models.

Multi-resolution representations are easily obtainable, making output-sensitive results possible. Basically, you only pay for what you see. This allows us to represent very detailed scenes with gigantic voxel volumes at high frame rates with our GPU-based implementation. Very large terrains or detailed models are particularly interesting targets for voxel representations. The most prominent feature from an implementation standpoint is that the level of detail (LOD) adjustments are automatically handled and no special object testing is needed.

Even though our main focus will be on games, voxels are often used in other contexts, such as scientific visualization or offline rendering by visual effect companies. The latter are particularly drawn to voxels due to the high rendering quality [Kapler 03, Krall and Harrington 05], which we maintain to a large extent in our approach.

Despite their many advantages, the use of voxels has drawbacks and there are reasons why they are less often employed than their triangular counterpart. Triangles have been natively supported on dedicated graphics hardware since the beginning. Real-time, high-quality voxel rendering has only become feasible since the introduction of programmable shaders. But there is a more general problem, which is that detailed representations use gigantic amounts of memory that cannot be stored on the graphics card. Hence, until recently, voxel effects in video games were mostly limited to small volumes for gaseous materials or to the particular scenario of height-field rendering. The development of an entire rendering system, capable of displaying complex voxel data, is all but trivial and has been in the way of more involved usage of volumetric rendering in real-time applications. This chapter will propose an approach to overcome the difficulties related to large volume rendering.

3.3 The GigaVoxels Approach

To address the display of memory-intensive voxel data, we proposed *GigaVoxels* [Crassin et al. 09], a new rendering pipeline for high-performance visualization of large and detailed volumetric objects and scenes. We showed that entire volumetric environments can be displayed in real time without the need to revert to a triangle-based representation. Voxels increase the amount of displayable detail significantly beyond the limits of what can be achieved with polygons at similar frame rates and support transparency effects natively. Our system is entirely GPU-based and achieves real-time performance for scenes consisting of billions of voxels.

In this chapter, we will present a full NVIDIA CUDA implementation of the GigaVoxels engine (see Figure 3.2). CUDA is a general purpose parallel computing language that allows to program directly the data-parallel architecture of NVIDIA GPUs [NVIDIA 09]. Among other things, CUDA enabled us to implement a very efficient cache mechanism managed entirely on the GPU. The CPU workload is

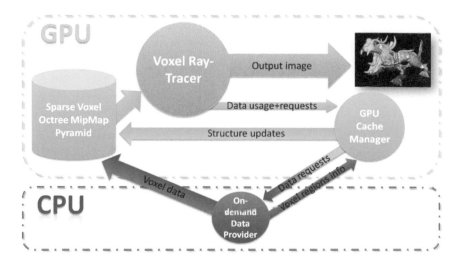

Figure 3.2. Global view of the GigaVoxels rendering engine.

very low and limited to data transfer, with no longer needs to track and manage the memory layout on the CPU.

Our data representation is a sparse voxel hierarchy that allows to efficiently encode and compress constant regions in space (Section 3.4). The rendering is based on a ray casting algorithm (Section 3.5). The rays themselves directly trigger a paging system to request missing data (Section 3.6). This paging system is based on a cache mechanism fully implemented on GPU that maintains newly used data in video memory, while recycling oldest (Section 3.6.2).

While we will first focus on a single volume, we will also show how to manage entire scenes of disjoint volumetric elements (Sections 3.7, 3.8). Finally we explain how to add game effects, such as soft shadows and depth of field approximations (Section 3.9).

3.4   Data Structure

The key to our efficient rendering technique is a hierarchical representation of the voxel data, efficient for both dynamic storage and rendering. It allows us to adapt the volume's internal resolution, to compact empty spaces, and to omit occluded parts according to the current point of view. This greatly reduces the memory consumption and avoids storing the entire information on the GPU.

In practice, the initial volumetric data set is embedded in a space subdivision structure, in form of an octree. To each node of this octree, a voxel volume of small

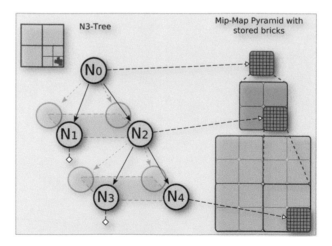

Figure 3.3. Our sparse voxel octree data structure. This structure stores a whole voxel scene or object filtered at multiple resolutions. Bricks are referenced by octree nodes providing a sparse mipmap pyramid of the voxels.

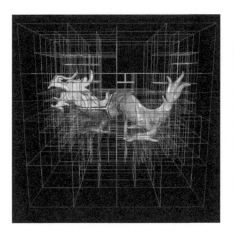 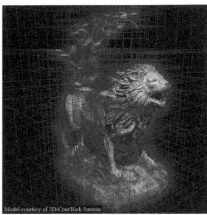

Figure 3.4. Spatial partitioning of the octree structure. A voxelized version of the Stanford XYZRGB-Dragon model rendered at around 50FPS and a 2048^3 voxels lion model modelized directly in voxels using 3D-Coat software and rendered at 20–40FPS with GigaVoxels.

resolution, e.g., 16^3 or 32^3 is associated, which we refer to as *brick*. Each node is associated to a certain spatial extent in the entire volume, and eight children always cover exactly the spatial extent of their parent.

Figure 3.3 summarizes the data structure of our approach and will be of help during the following discussion. Such a structure combines two major advantages: the octree leads to a compact storage (empty space skipping, occlusion culling, local refinement), whereas the bricks are implemented as small three-dimensional textures and, thus, benefit from hardware-based interpolation and cache coherence (see Figure 3.4). Another advantage is the constant size of the node and brick data types. Consequently, it is simple to densely store them in memory pools on the GPU. This facilitates the update mechanisms that are crucial to ensure the presence of the data needed to produce the output image.

An important property of this structure is that it provides information at multiple scales, in order to match the resolution needed for a given point of view. It is built from a precomputed mipmap pyramid, obtained by downsampling the voxel object.

3.4.1 Structure Storage: The Pools

Our data is stored in two GPU memory regions; the *node pool* stores the octree as a pointer-based tree and the bricks are organized into a *brick pool*. These pools are used as caches (see Section 3.6.2), and their size is fixed once at initialization time. In a video game context, they would be chosen depending on available video memory and bandwidth between GPU and CPU.

In order to be modifiable directly from a CUDA kernel, the node pool is implemented in global linear GPU memory. It is accessed from a CUDA kernel as a *linear texture*, in order to take advantage of the texture cache. Instead of storing each node separately, a single entity in the node cache actually regroups eight octree nodes together. The reason will become clear in the next section, but intuitively, these eight elements correspond exactly to the eight subnodes of the same parent node. We call this $2 \times 2 \times 2$ nodes organization a *node tile*.

The brick pool is implemented in a CUDA Array (that is a three-dimensional texture), in order to be able to use three-dimensional addressing, hardware texture interpolation, as well as a three-dimensional coherent cache. To ensure correct interpolation, we store bricks with an additional one voxel border. A current limitation of CUDA Arrays is that the direct modification from a CUDA kernel is not exposed in the current version CUDA 2.2.

3.4.2   Octree Implementation

Figure 3.5 shows the data elements in an octree node. Each node is composed of a data entry, and a subnode (child) pointer. The data can either be a constant value (for empty/homogeneous volume), or a pointer towards a brick (a small texture). As indicated before, each entity in the node pool corresponds to eight subnodes. It is exactly this property that allows us to only rely on a single child pointer. Because all subnodes are stored contiguously in memory, one can address any single one by adding a constant offset to the pointer. Figure 3.6 illustrates a simple example. Note that this organization also allows the structure to be flexible enough to manipulate generalized N^3-trees instead of simple octrees (which is an N^3-tree with $N = 2$), subdividing space into N on each axis. Such structure can provide interesting properties as explained in [Crassin et al. 09].

This structure produces a very compact octree encoding as each node is represented by only two 32-bit integer values. The first integer is used to define the octree structure, the second to associate volume data. With the first, one bit

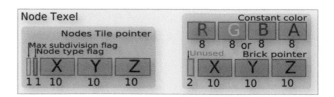

Figure 3.5. Compact octree node encoding into two 32-bit values.

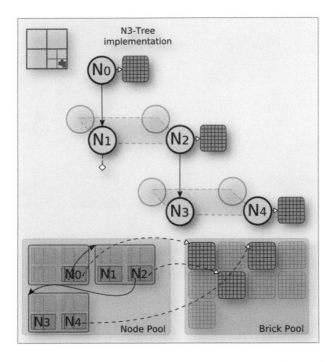

Figure 3.6. Our sparse voxel octree structure encoded in the node pools.

indicates whether a node is *terminal*, which means *refined to a maximum*, i.e., whether the original volume still contains more data and so the node could be subdivided if needed. Another bit is used to indicate the nature of the second integer value; either it represents a constant color or a pointer to a brick encoded on 30 bits. The same amount, 30 bits, is used for the child pointer to the subnodes. The pointers describe the position of the corresponding element with three 10-bit xyz-coordinates and are zero if there is no data to point to.

The potential performance penalty during traversal, due to missing links between neighboring voxels, is highly outweighed by the small memory requirements. In fact, the compactness and coherence allow for a very efficient ray casting (Section 3.5.1). Further, the structure is intended to adapt to the current viewpoint and a smaller memory footprint implies a more efficient and simpler update.

To enhance traversal efficiency during rendering, both parts of a node description (subnode pointer and data, see Figure 3.5) are not interleaved in memory, but stored in two separate arrays. Indeed, since each part of the node description is not used in the same rendering sequence, this allows us to further enhance data access coalescing and texture cache efficiency.

Figure 3.7. Examples of participating medias rendered with GigaVoxels.

3.5   Rendering

Since our rendering engine is designed to deal with semi-transparent voxel data, we need to evaluate the final color that reaches the eye after the compositing of various colored voxels (see Figure 3.7). Intuitively, this means that one has to integrate the voxels color and opacity along the ray. To do so, we evaluate a simple optical model describing the light transfer inside the volume. We use the Emission-Absorption optical model, neglecting scattering and indirect illumination. For a survey on GPU volume rendering, we refer the reader to the book [Hadwiger et al. 06]. In this section, we explain only the rendering component of our system. Currently, we assume that the present data structure contains all necessary data for rendering. Refinement and update mechanisms will be discussed later in Section 3.6.

3.5.1   Hierarchical Volume Ray Casting

The color of each pixel is evaluated by traversing the structure using volume ray casting [Kruger and Westermann 03, Roettger et al. 03, Scharsach 05], executed by a CUDA kernel (see Figure 3.8). We generate one thread per screen pixel, each tracking one ray through the structure in order to evaluate the volume-rendering equation corresponding to the optical model. The ray traversal is front to back. Starting from the near plane[1], we accumulate color C and opacity α, until we leave the volume, or the opacity saturates (meaning that the matter becomes opaque), so that farther elements would be hidden.

---

[1]Alternatively, another proxy surface can be used to initialize the rays, e.g., a bounding box or a mesh surface.

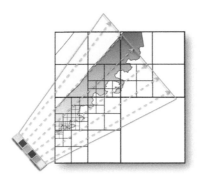

Figure 3.8. Illustration of the volume ray casting process launching one ray per pixel and traversing the hierarchical structure.

3.5.2 Octree and Node Traversal

The octree structure is traversed using a stackless algorithm similar to the kd-restart algorithm presented in [Horn et al. 07] and developed for kd-tree traversal (see Figure 3.9).

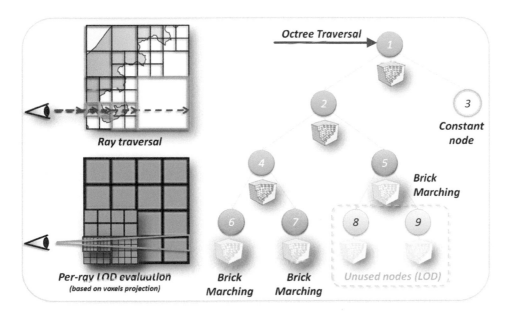

Figure 3.9. Illustration of the structure traversal with bricks marching and LOD computations based on projected voxel size.

This traversal is in fact a series of successive top-down descents in the tree. For each descent, a ray starts from the root node and then proceeds downwards (Section 3.5.4). The descent stops at a node whose resolution is sufficient enough for the current view (Section 3.5.3).

Such a node either contains a constant value or a pointer to a brick. For a constant node, the distance between entry and exit point is used to analytically integrate the constant color along the ray.

For a brick, we rely on a ray marching to accumulate samples and evaluate the volume rendering equation. More details on ray marching can be found in [Engel et al. 01, Scharsach 05, Hadwiger et al. 06]. For each sample read in a brick, we take advantage of hardware trilinear interpolation. The stepping distance between these samples is computed relative to the LOD mechanism described Section 3.5.4. It is possible to include a direct illumination component for opaque objects by storing normals per voxel and by applying a Blinn-Phong model. Once the ray leaves the brick, we use the new ray position as the origin for the next top-down descent in the tree.

3.5.3   Descending in the Octree

The descent is fast because, following [Lefebvre et al. 05], the point's coordinates can be used directly to locate it in the octree as illustrated in Figure 3.10.

Let $x \in [0,1]^3$ be the point's local coordinates in the node's bounding box and c be the pointer to its children. Since subnodes are stored contiguously in the node pool (see Section 3.4.2) a three-dimensional offset is enough to select a child. In practice, we store the children in a way such that the node containing x is at location $int(2x)$, the integer part of $2x$ on each axis: e.g., in one-dimensional for one axis with $x_{axis} \in [0,1]$, there are two possible offset values for the children,

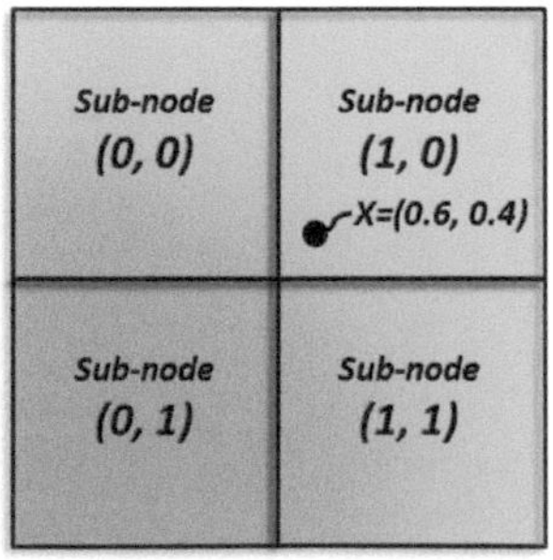

<table>
<tr><td>Sub-node
(0, 0)</td><td>Sub-node
(1, 0)
X=(0.6, 0.4)</td></tr>
<tr><td>Sub-node
(0, 1)</td><td>Sub-node
(1, 1)</td></tr>
</table>

$$
\begin{aligned}
\text{Index}_{2D} &= \text{int}(x * N) \\
&= \text{int}((0.6 * 2, 0.4 * 2)) \\
&= \text{int}((1.2, 0.8)) \\
&= (1, 0)
\end{aligned}
$$

Figure 3.10. Two-dimensional localization into a node tile to find the index of the subnode where x lies.

namely 0 ($x < 0.5$) and 1 ($x >= 0.5$). In general, to descend into the subnode containing x, we can thus use the pointer $c + \text{int}(2x)$. We then update x to $2x - \text{int}(2x)$ and continue the descent[2].

3.5.4 Tracing Cones: LOD and Volume MipMapping

We have seen in the last section how to do an efficient descent in the octree in order to find successive bricks. We will now explain how to choose when to stop such a descent and how to then traverse its associated volume data. In order to find our criterion, we will investigate how data should be integrated in the per-pixel color determination.

One screen pixel is associated to more than just a line in space. It actually corresponds to a cone because a pixel covers an area and not a single point (as illustrated in Figure 3.11). This is typically the source of aliasing that arises when a single ray is used to sample the scene.

Whereas classical rasterization or ray tracing-based rendering relies on multi-sampling to deal with aliasing, we instead launch a single ray per pixel, and deal with the aliasing by filtering the voxel representation. More precisely, while traversing the scene along the ray, we chose our lookups from a prefiltered volume representation. In practice, we rely on a similar technique as usually employed for two-dimensional textures: mipmapping. In fact, our data structure already encodes a sparse mipmap pyramid in order to provide different levels of detail. Each such level can be interpreted as a filtered version of the volume. At each traversal step, we select the volume resolution (and so the depth in the octree), in order to account for the volume hit simultaneously along a cone. The step size

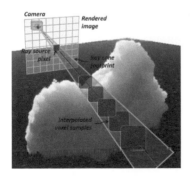
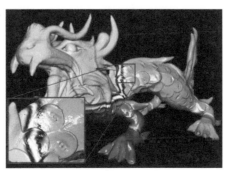

Figure 3.11. Left: illustration of the cone footprint of a ray launched from one pixel using perspective projection. Right: the XYZRGB-dragon rendered with volume mipmapping.

---

[2]Note that this descent can be generalized to N^3-Trees using $c + \text{int}(x * N)$, and updating x with $x * N - \text{int}(x * N)$.

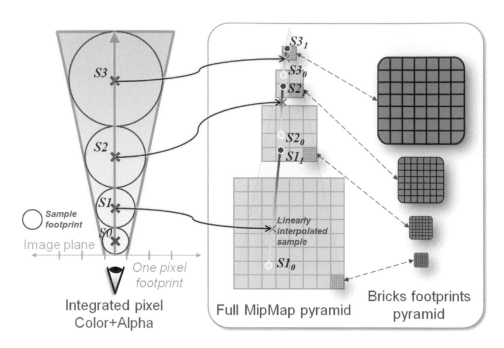

Figure 3.12. Illustration of one ray sampling using quadrilinear interpolation in the voxel mipmap pyramid.

is adapted accordingly in order to reflect the resolution of the corresponding level of detail. This principle is illustrated in Figure 3.12.

More precisely, during top-down traversal, we estimate the voxel size V via $V := \frac{N}{M}$, where N is the current node's side length and M^3 the brick resolution. We estimate its projection size from the viewpoint on the near plane by $V_{\mathrm{proj}} := V \frac{n}{d}$, where d is the node's distance to the near plane n. Based on the field-of-view of the camera, we can then compare this size to the pixel's size P. If $V_{\mathrm{proj}} < P$, the descent can be stopped and we traverse the current node.

This LOD selection allows us to always use the minimal voxel resolution required for a given point of view, minimizing the memory requirement and rendering cost.

Even though this approach is simple, it leads to a rough and discretized approximation of the cone footprint that produces resolution discontinuities especially visible during motion. Smooth transitions between bricks can only be achieved by making the voxels "grow" continuously along the ray. Consequently, we rely on a simultaneous interpolation between two mipmap levels, leading to a quadrilinear filtering. To have access to the lower resolution brick during the marching step,

```
//Brick value access with mipmapping. Templated with the data layer
//(color, normal, etc.) in which data is read.
template<int datalayer>
__device__
float4 getBrickValueMipMap(
        float3 posInPool0, float3 posInPool1, float3 posInPool2,
        float3 posInBrick, float nodeSize, float t,
        float2 minMaxMipMapLevel){
    //Compute mipmap level based on the distance to the view plane t
    //and the node size,
    float mipmaplevel=getMipMapLevel<mode>(t, nodeSize);
    //Clamp mimap level.
    mipmaplevel=clamp(mipmaplevel, minMaxMipMapLevel.x,
                      minMaxMipMapLevel.y);
    //Compute interpolation first level.
    float mipmaplevelI=floorf(mipmaplevel);
    float interp=(mipmaplevel-mipmaplevelI);
    float4 vox, vox0, vox1;
    float3 samplePos0, samplePos1; float3 brickPos0, brickPos1;
    //Select brick addresses.
    if(mipmaplevel<1.0f){
        brickPos0=posInPool0; brickPos1=posInPool1;
        samplePos0= (posInBrick); samplePos1= (posInBrick)*0.5f;
    }else
        brickPos0=posInPool1;    brickPos1=posInPool2;
        samplePos0= (posInBrick)*0.5f; samplePos1= (posInBrick)*0.25f;
    }
    //Get first trilinearly interpolated sample.
    vox0=getBrickValue<datalayer>(brickPos0, samplePos0);
    //Compute interpolation.
    const float interpThreshold=0.0001f;
    if(interp>interpThreshold){
        //Get second trilinearly interpolated sample.
        vox1=getBrickValue<datalayer>(brickPos1, samplePos1);
        //Compute linear interpolation.
        vox=vox0*(1.0f-interp)+vox1*(interp);
    }else
        vox=vox0;

    return vox;
}
```

Listing 3.1. Code of brick sampling function with mipmap quadrilinear interpolation.

we remember the last three visited nodes during the descent. It can be shown that this number is sufficient in practical scenarios. We will show later (in Section 3.9) that this mipmap mechanism can also be used to efficiently implement blur effects.

Listing 3.1 shows a CUDA implementation of the quadrilinear interpolated fetching of samples into a brick.

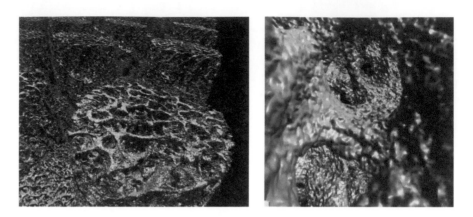

Figure 3.13. Examples of a very large 8192^3 voxel scene composed of medical data and rendered at 20–40FPS using GigaVoxels on an NVIDIA GTX 280 GPU.

3.6   Out-of-Core Data Management

So far we have seen how to efficiently use our data structure for rendering. Now, we will investigate how the GigaVoxels engine deals with arbitrarily large amounts of voxel data (see Figure 3.13).

Our whole data-management scheme is organized around a cache mechanism managing both the octree structure and the bricks (see Figure 3.14). The cache

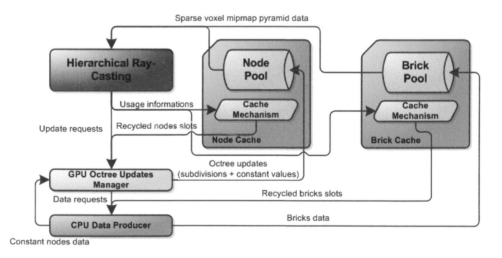

Figure 3.14. General view of the cache mechanism and data updates flows.

is in charge of maintaining the most recently used elements on the GPU, while providing room for new elements by recycling the oldest ones. This results in a fully scalable solution that can deal with extremely large volumes.

When the point of view changes, some missing data that was previously occluded, or out-of-frustum, might becomes visible. Updates to the structure are requested directly by the voxel ray tracer, on a per-ray basis. In this way, it is possible to only trigger data management based on what is actually needed for the current point of view. Each ray informs accurately about the needed data instead of having to heuristically estimate the need for data. This also leads to minimal CPU intervention, since both LOD and visibility computations are performed per-ray on the GPU.

3.6.1 Global Scheme

During the traversal of the hierarchical volume described in Section 3.5.1, rays visit several nodes in the structure. For some rays, the data needed to get the right volume resolution (according to the LOD mechanism described Section 3.5.4) might be missing. Nodes might need to be subdivided, implying the need for new data, or nodes could be present at the right depth, but might miss the according volume data. In both cases, a ray will *ask* for missing data by issuing an *update request*. This request will not be processed immediately, but instead be added to a batch of requests. Structure updates are then executed incrementally, from top to bottom, subdividing nodes one level at a time. This scheme ensures that unnecessary nodes (not accessed by rays because of occlusions for instance) will never be created nor filled with data. With this strategy, we avoid excessive data refinement and we reduce data requests, resulting in a higher frame rate.

The rendering process is organized into passes (see Figure 3.15). Each pass interleaves a ray casting phase, producing an image, a batch of requests, and an update phase. The update phase fulfills update requests by uploading new data to the GPU and updating the structure providing the rays with the necessary data for the next ray casting pass.

To provide a control over image quality during updates, multiple passes can be issued per frame. In this case, rays will stop whenever data is missing and traversal is continued from this point in the following pass in a stop-and-go manner. The number of passes authorized per frame depends on the application context. For games, it is acceptable that some frames show less details, to favor high frame rates which can be achieved by producing an image even when data is missing. For this rays can rely on some coarser data that is actually present in upper levels in the tree. For instance, for offline rendering, physical simulations, or movie productions, it is important that each frame is accurately computed. Hence the stop-and-go solution is most appropriate.

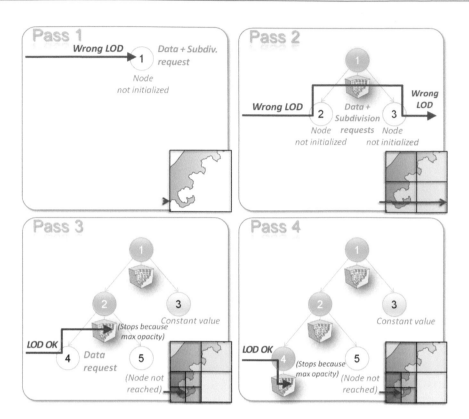

Figure 3.15. Illustration of ray-guided multi-pass update sequence for one ray. In pass (1), the ray hits a node not initialized and requests data and subdivision (since needed LOD is not reached). At the end of the pass, a brick is loaded for the node and it gets subdivided. In pass (2), the ray goes down, traverses newly created nodes and uses the higher level brick in order to produce an image. Data is requested for both nodes and LOD is still not reached. The first node gets a brick and the second, a constant value. In pass (3), the ray traverses the first new node and requests data for it. Subdivision is not requested since correct LOD is reached. The second new node is not touched because, due to opacity, the ray stops in the middle of the upper brick. Starting from pass (4) the ray got all data it needs and no more update is necessary.

The progressive top-down refinement scheme we use (first low, then high details) is very useful to ensure real-time responsiveness even in the case of fast movements and small time budgets per frames. The disadvantage of this strategy is that for fast movements, this can potentially lead to a data upload at the wrong resolution because even more precision might be needed. In practice, this is not objectionable. The lower resolution data is always eight times cheaper to load

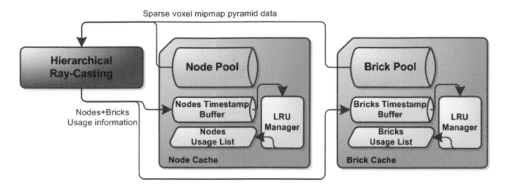

Figure 3.16. Global view of node pool and brick pool cache mechanisms with their GPU LRU management.

than the full resolution (the eight child nodes cover the same spatial extent as their parent) and more than a level is rarely jumped for reasonable motions.

In the following, we will first explain how our cache mechanism is implemented and then describe the ray based update mechanism.

3.6.2 GPU Cache Mechanism

The cache mechanism basically relies on a *least recently used* (LRU) scheme in order to allocate slots for new nodes or bricks, by recycling slots occupied by those elements that have not been used for a long time (see Figure 3.16).

In practice, both memory pools, node pool, and brick pool are managed as caches. In order to maintain these caches, rays provide information about the nodes and bricks that were traversed during the ray casting process. Both caches are implemented in the same way, except that for the brick pool the cache elements are bricks and for the node pool the smallest managed entity is the node tile, grouping $2 \times 2 \times 2$ nodes (Section 3.4.1).

It is important to note that in this context, because of the cache mechanism, the structure updates (described Section 3.6.3) are performed lazily and only when necessary. At a given point in time, the octree leafs don't necessarily correspond to the nodes used during the rendering. For instance, it might be that the current tree encodes a very fine representation, but due to a distant point of view, the used data might solely be taken from higher node levels. The unused nodes, though currently unimportant, might need to be reactivated, hence, it makes sense to try to keep them in memory as long as no other data is needed. But if new data is needed, these are the first elements to be overwritten. In the following, we will explain how to establish such a mechanism.

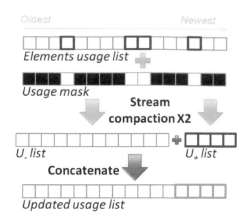

Figure 3.17. Illustration of the sorting procedure for the *element usage lists* based on stream compaction. The *usage list* is separated into a list of nodes used in the current pass and a list of nodes not used. The list of used nodes is then concatenated at the end of the list of unused nodes.

Per-ray data usage information. To keep track of the elements used by each ray, we associate a timestamp buffer to each of the managed pools (node pool and brick pool). This timestamp buffer "attaches" a 32-bit integer timestamp to each element (node tile or brick) of the pool.

During the ray traversal of the structure, this timestamp is renewed. Each time a ray uses a node, its associated timestamp set to the time of the current pass. In the same way for bricks, each time a brick is used during the traversal, its associated timestamp is updated.

Due to the parallel computation model of the GPU, many threads may write to the same timestamp buffer element at the same time. But since all rays will write the same value (the time of the current rendering pass), no atomic operations are needed and the approach remains efficient.

LRU management. The previously described timestamps are then used by the LRU mechanism to keep track of the oldest elements which are the candidates that might be overwritten with new data. In order to classify the elements, we maintain for both caches (node and brick) a list of element addresses sorted by usage called the *usage list*, a one-dimensional buffer of 32-bit values that contains as many entries as there are elements in the corresponding pool. Each entry contains the 30-bit address of its corresponding pool element.

In a usage list, the last used elements are kept at the end of the list, whereas the beginning contains those that were not used for a long time. When n new elements need to be inserted, the n elements corresponding to the first n entries of the list are recycled (Figure 3.17).

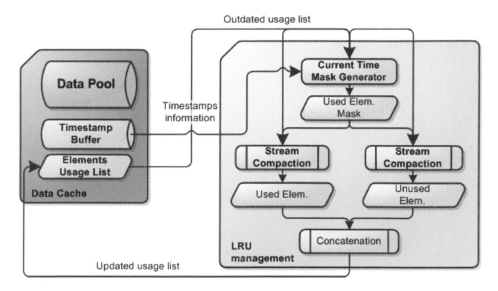

Figure 3.18. Update procedure of the caches usage list.

Maintaining usage list ordering. To maintain a usage list efficiently, we do not need to rely on sorting operations. Instead, we make use of two order-maintaining stream-compaction steps. This procedure is illustrated in Figures 3.18 and 3.17.

We first generate a *usage mask*. In practice, we use one of the remaining bits in the usage-list entry as a flag. This mask indicates, for each element of the usage list, if it was used in the current rendering pass. For this, we launch a kernel with one thread per usage-list element, and verify the corresponding timestamp. If the element was used in the current frame, its timestamp will match the current time step. The usage list then undergoes two stream compaction[3] steps to separate the used $\mathbf{U}_+$ from the unused elements $\mathbf{U}_-$ based on the usage mask. Because the stream compaction algorithm preserves the initial element order, the list of the unused elements will still have the oldest elements at the beginning and the most recently used in the end. Therefore, when concatenating $\mathbf{U}_+$ to the end of the $\mathbf{U}_-$, we obtain an updated and accurately sorted usage list.

LRU invalidation procedure. Update procedures will retrieve entries from the front of the usage list and, hence, retrieve information about where to overwrite older data. Unfortunately, this overwriting can introduce problems because elements in the data structure with pointers to this location will still assume that the old content is located at that address.

---

[3] We rely on the CUDA *Thrust* library to implement all stream compaction operations involved in the data management system.

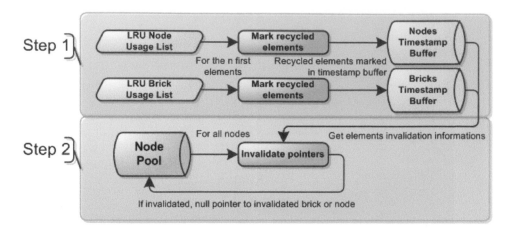

Figure 3.19. Two step pointers invalidation procedure.

In other words, each time cache elements are deleted in order to make room for new data, an *invalidation procedure* has to be executed to remove all the references to the data being recycled. More specifically, this means that when a *node tile* is deleted, all pointers in the octree that still reference this element, have to be invalidated (meaning *set to NULL*). The same care has to be applied when bricks are removed and all nodes pointing to such a brick should have their pointer invalidated.

This cleanup procedure is not straightforward because nodes and bricks could be referenced by more than just a single parent, as is needed in the case of recursive definitions, as well as instancing (Section 3.7).

Our solution to invalidate pointers reliably is to use a two step procedure illustrated in Figure 3.19 before overwriting elements. First, for both the node cache and the brick cache, we perform a kernel launch with one thread for each of the n recycled elements in the usage list (the n first elements). These threads set the timestamp buffer value of the according elements to a special value (in practice, we reserve zero for this purpose) using a memory scattering operation.

The second step then consists in testing every node in the *nodepool*. If it points to an element (a node or a brick) that was flagged with a zero timestamp its corresponding pointer is nulled. These steps are done in parallel for all nodes in the node pool using a kernel launch.

Once all pointers are invalidated, the elements to be recycled can be overwritten with new content, uploaded by the CPU. The usage list will automatically update itself in the next frame when the new elements are used.

3.6.3   Structure Update Requests Management

We have just seen how to decide about the importance of data elements by sorting them according to usage using an LRU scheme. Further, we discussed how to invalidate elements in order to enable overwriting. Now, we will discuss how the actual update mechanism is triggered and controlled (see Figure 3.20). First, we will talk about how we make it possible to use per-ray requests to determine which information should be uploaded to the GPU. We then discuss how to analyze these requests and trigger the CPU-side update.

3.6.4   Per-ray Requests

To enable per-ray node subdivisions and data load requests, we rely on a special *request buffer*. Its size is chosen to match exactly the number of nodes in the node pool, and it is arranged in the same way, so that there is a one-to-one correspondence between each node and the request buffer entry. Both can be accessed with the same address. Hence, we can store one request slot per node. In practice, this request slot is a 32-bit value. Two bits encode the type of the request. The first bit can indicate the need for a subdivision, the second for a data fetch. The other 30 bits store the node address. This latter information may seem redundant, as it could easily be derived from the address of the request slot, but it will facilitate the subsequent steps. We make the distinction between subdivision and data requests in order to avoid having to transfer all data after a subdivision. This could be wasteful because some child nodes might be invisible.

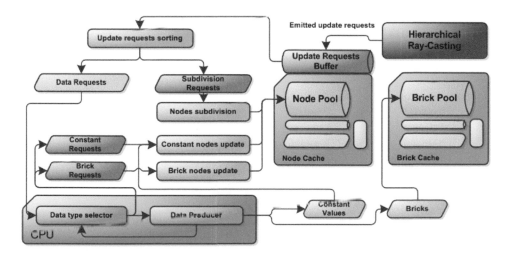

Figure 3.20. General structure updates flow with per-ray requests collection, request type sorting, data type retrieval through CPU producer and structure updates.

Request buffer elements are zeroed at the beginning of each render pass. During ray casting, each time a ray requests an update for a node, it fills the corresponding request buffer entry. While many rays with different needs (subdivision/ data request/both) might ask for an update in parallel, and so access the same request slot concurrently, we want to avoid expensive atomic operations in global memory.

The first observation is that the 30 bits containing the node's address will always be the same, since it is always the slot address itself. So concurrent write will not be a problem for this part. A potential issue could only arise from the first two bits that encode the updates.

The different conflicts that can potentially appear are the following:

1. If the node is terminal, meaning that it cannot be refined, only data requests can be made. Whether a node is terminal is indicated by a flag (see Section 3.4.2).

2. If the node has data, obviously no ray would ask for data. Any update request is thus a subdivision request.

3. If the node has no data but children, it indicates that an update implies a data request.

4. If the node does not have data and no children, both kind of requests could be made.

Only the last case could lead to potential conflicts between rays. Two types of nodes fall into this category: uninitialized nodes (right after a subdivision), and nodes whose brick data was deleted (recycled in the cache). For both cases we force to always demand data. This allows us to detect constant and terminal nodes for which a refinement operation is impossible.

However, in theory, when rays ask for a *subdivision and data* or *data only*, only one of the two might prevail. Therefore a conflict is possible but we do not consider this situation as a problem. If only a data request flag is kept, instead of both, then the data is loaded, but no subdivision is performed. Data-only rays are satisfied, but not the subdivision rays. Fortunately, the latter will be in the next pass because, now that data is present, subsequent requests for this node can only be subdivision requests. This scheme does introduce a one-pass delay for the subdivision in the case a conflict actually occurs, but the treatment is much simpler and more efficient than other solutions.

3.6.5 Requests Type Sorting

After the ray traversal, the request buffer is filled. Now, we want to collect the needed update operations. For this, the request buffer is reduced on the GPU using a stream compaction algorithm keeping only non-zero elements (as illustrated Figure 3.21).

The resulting *compacted request list* is then split into a *data request list* and a *subdivision request list*, using two more stream reduction steps. Both lists contain the addresses in the node pool of those nodes that require to load data and to subdivide nodes, respectively.

Data requests are applied before dealing with subdivisions in order to ensure that, in case of both data and subdivision request (see previous section), a constant or terminal node will not be subdivided.

The length of these lists is an indicator for the memory that is needed to update the structure according to the requests. Whereas the subdivision requests can be treated on the GPU, data requests support from the CPU. Only the CPU is able to determine the constantness of a region, and to load new data from a mass storages (usually the hard disk).

In the following, we will discuss how both data and subdivision requests are handled.

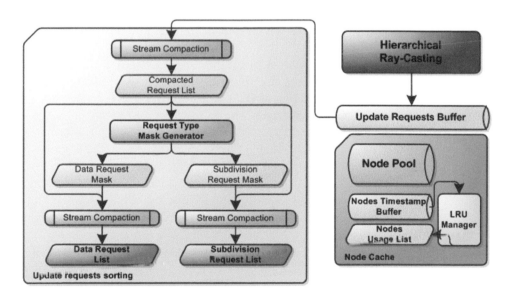

Figure 3.21. Request collection and sorting flow from the request buffer to the data request list and subdivision request list.

3.6.6   Dealing with Data Requests

Data requests correspond to missing data. This information has to be loaded or produced on the CPU side. Thus, the data request list needs to be sent to the CPU.

One important observation is that the CPU needs two kinds of information in order to update the data: *what* to load and *where* to store it. For the moment, let's concentrate on the question of what to load. What we need is information about the spatial extent of the node addressed in the data request. Only this localization information allows us to fetch the corresponding data from the disk. Unfortunately there is no relationship between the address of a node, which is contained in the data requests and the spatial extent it represents. In fact, due to the cache mechanism, the organization of the nodes in the node pool can be arbitrary and it has nothing to do with the actual scene.

To be able to provide the information about the spatial organization, we add another two arrays to our GPU memory:

First, to each node, we associate a code, which we call *localization code* that encodes the node's position in the octree and is stored in three times 10 bits, grouped in a single 32-bit integer. Each 10-bits represent one axis. Bit by bit, this series encodes a sequence of space subdivisions, so basically a descent in the octree. More precisely, the nth bit of the first 10-bit value represents the child taken on the X axis at level n. Each bit represents the choice (left or right child) along this axis. This is similar to the descent in the octree from top-to-bottom, described in Section 3.5.3.

Second, each node will also store a *localization depth value* in form of an 8-bit integer. It encodes how deep in the tree the node is located. A localization depth of n means that only the first n bits of the localization code are needed to reach the node in the tree. Consequently, these two values describe exactly one node in an octree subdivision structure. This allows us to derive exactly what information needs to be loaded or produced on the CPU side.

In practice it is actually possible to reduce both array sizes by a factor of eight by storing these values per node tile (group of eight nodes) instead of per single node. This is possible because the CPU will also have access to the node's address. Due to the fact that nodes in a tile are grouped together in memory, the node address allows us to complete its localization code. We can derive the final bit that misses from the node's localization code with respect to the tile's localization code from the last bit of the node's address.

Of course, the values in these two arrays need to be updated or created when nodes are spawned. This is the case when a subdivision is applied and we will detail this simple process in Section 3.6.8, when explaining how to treat subdivision requests.

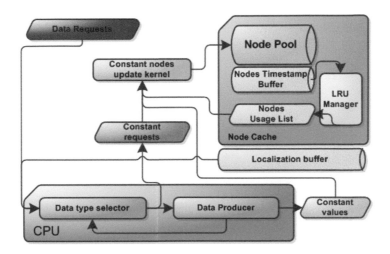

Figure 3.22. Constant nodes update execution flow. Constant information is provided by the CPU data producer.

3.6.7 Separating Constant from Brick Nodes

Now, that we have seen how the CPU determines what data needs to be loaded, let us look at the actual update process. On the CPU side, each request is passed to a data provider managing an on-disk data representation of the volume. The data provider determines, for each element of the data request list, whether the corresponding voxel region is constant or requires a brick. Accordingly, the data-request list is split into a list of nodes requiring a constant value L_c and a list of nodes requiring bricks L_b. Both types are handled independently.

Updating constant nodes. Constant nodes are simple to treat because the necessary data field to store the value is already present in the node pool (see Figure 3.5). To make the update efficient, nodes in the octree structure are updated in parallel using a single kernel launch on all entries of L_c and getting data from a list of all corresponding constant values (see Figure 3.22).

Updating brick nodes. More work is needed for the brick nodes in L_b. Bricks are provided one by one by the CPU data provider (see Figure 3.23). Each new brick emplacement in the brick pool is provided via the cache mechanism, recycling the oldest bricks slots (Section 3.6.2).

We have seen how the GPU-side cache maintains a usage list of all bricks. Its first entries contain the addresses of those elements that should be overwritten first. To determine where to upload the n new bricks, the CPU simply reads back

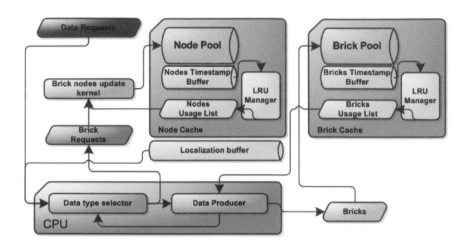

Figure 3.23. Brick update execution flow. Bricks data is provided by the CPU data producer.

the n first entries of the usage list. Bricks are then uploaded to these addresses in the brick pool.

The next step is to invalidate all pointers that refer to the overwritten elements. We have seen this mechanism in Section 3.6.2. The final step is to update the nodes themselves. Their pointers must be corrected to reference the new bricks. This is done in parallel by launching an update kernel with a thread for each element in $\mathbf{L}_b$. The new brick pointers are read from the n first elements of the bricks' usage list.

To gain some performance, we do not perform these last steps right away because other invalid pointers might arise from the subdivision requests. So we only use a single correction step to invalidate brick pointers, as well as child pointers, once the subdivisions were applied. We will discuss these next.

3.6.8   Dealing with Subdivision Requests

Contrary to data requests, subdivision requests do not require any CPU intervention and can be addressed directly on the GPU. In principle, the update mechanism is somewhat similar to the solution for bricks. If n subdivision requests occurred, we start a kernel with n threads. Thread i fetches the ith subdivision request and the ith entry of the node usage list. The subdivision request contains the address of the node to subdivide. Consequently, we update its pointer to the address fetched from the node usage list, at which location we will store our new node.

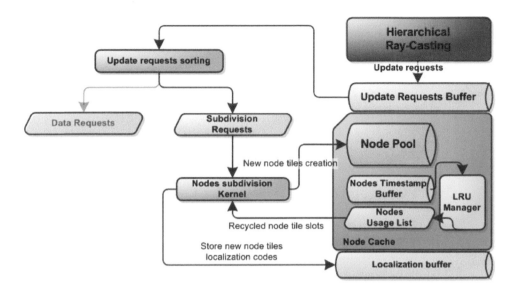

Figure 3.24. Subdivision requests execution on the GPU.

Finally, all pointers to the overwritten elements need to be invalidated. We do this in parallel with the brick pointer invalidation of overwritten elements, as described in Section 3.6.2. The final element to talk about is the localization code and localization depth of node tiles. These values were needed by the CPU to be able to associate to each node a corresponding region in space and, hence, the corresponding data to be uploaded. In order to initialize these values for the child node tile, we proceed as follows. We use the address of the node N that needs a subdivision. N's address can be truncated in order to find the address of the node tile $\mathbf{N}$ that contains N. This address allows us to retrieve N's localization code and localization depth. The new tile depth is obtained by incrementing the old depth by one. The new localization code can be found, based on the same principle we used to reduce the memory requirements of the localization code by a factor of eight in the last section. In other words, we make use of N's address itself to discover which child of $\mathbf{N}$ N corresponds to. Accordingly, this position indicates the missing bit in the localization code for the new node tile (see Figure 3.24).

3.6.9 Implementation Summary

Figure 3.25 presents a summary of all permanent GPU memory regions used by our data management mechanism. Presented memory occupancies correspond to the ones used in most of our example scenes and gives an idea of the relative sizes

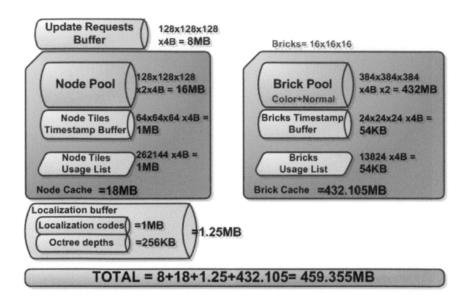

Figure 3.25. Summary of the memory requirement of every GPU memory regions used for a typical usage case.

of the memory regions. Unsurprisingly, the brick pool appears to be the largest buffer of our implementation. The node pool may seem oversized compared to the brick pool, but it allows us to better cache the subdivision structure which leads to a performance increase. Finally, all regions used by the data management algorithm are relatively small.

3.7 Octree-Based Synthesis

Our pointer-based octree structure allows us to produce many interesting scenarios.

A first feature is the ability to implement instancing of interior branches, as well as recursions. We can reuse subtrees by making nodes share common subnodes. This can be very advantageous if a model has repetitive structures and can significantly reduce the necessary memory consumption. This kind of octree instancing is illustrated Figure 3.26.

The node pointers further allow us to create recursions in the graph. This is particularly interesting in the context of fractal-like representations. The self-similarity is naturally handled and the resulting volumes are virtually of an infinite resolution. Figure 3.27 shows an example of a Sierpinski sponge fractal. It is implemented using the generalization of our octree, an N^3-tree node with $N = 3$ (see Section 3.4.2).

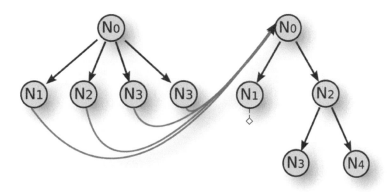

Figure 3.26. Example graph of an octree using instancing.

Figure 3.27. Example of a Sierpinski sponge fractal fully implemented with recursivity in the octree. This example is running at around 70FPS. The bottom graph shows the only recursively linked node used in this case.

3.8   Voxel Object Instancing

Our ray-tracing framework is compatible with several voxel entities present in the scene. In such scenario, when different objects are mixed, multiple GigaVoxels octrees are handled in the node pool and managed by the cache mechanism.

For each object, a bounding volume is drawn. A fragment shader outputs ray origins on the bounding volume, as well as the direction of the corresponding view rays. These rays are used to initialize the ray casting process. Scaling, rotation and LODs are automatically handled and allow us to represent scenes with many complex objects at high frame rates. Figure 3.28 shows an example of such a scene.

Figure 3.28. Examples of free instancing of GigaVoxels objects in space.

3.9 MipMap-Based Blur Effects

Throughout this chapter we have shown that our hierarchical structure is the key element to enable the treatment of the large data volumes. We further pointed out in Section 3.5.4 that the way we traverse this structure can be related to an approximative cone tracing. Cone tracing has many interesting applications and even though our solution is approximate, it enables us to benefit from these possibilities.

First we will explain how to integrate shadow computations in our application. Then we will illustrate how the same algorithms can be used to produce approximate soft shadows. Finally we will show how a similar scheme can be used in the context of depth of field rendering. Interestingly, even though this process is very challenging for triangular models, volume rendering benefits from the out-of-focus effect; the stronger the lens blur, the more performance is gained.

3.9.1 Soft Shadows

Shadows are an important cue that help us to evaluate scene configurations and spatial relations. Further, it is a key element to make images look realistic. So far, this point has not been addressed in our current pipeline. Here, we will explain how our rendering engine can be used to obtain convincing shadow effects for gigantic volumetric models (see Figure 3.29).

Before tackling soft shadows, let us take a look at the case of a point light source. Given a surface point P in our volumetric scene, or volumetric model, we want to determine how much light reaches P. This basically remounts to shooting a ray from P towards the light source. If the opacity value of the ray saturates on

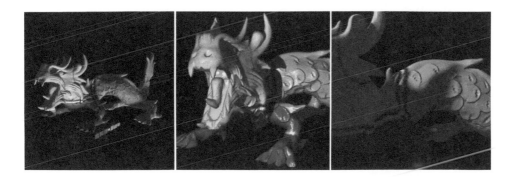

Figure 3.29. Example of soft shadows rendered by launching secondary rays and using the volume mipmapping mechanism to approximate integration over the light source surface. Interestingly, the blurrier the shadows, the cheaper it is to compute.

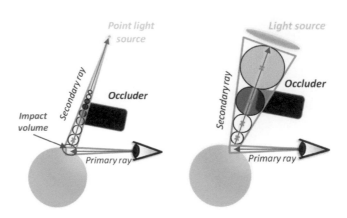

Figure 3.30. Illustration of shadow computation for a point light source, taking impact volume into account (left). Soft shadows computation for a surface light source (right).

the way to the light, the P lies in shadow. If the ray traversed semi-transparent materials without saturating, the accumulated opacity value gives us the intensity of the soft shadow. It should be pointed out that this traversal can be used to also accumulate colors to naturally handle colored shadows.

In practice, we do not really have an impact *point*. Rather, due to our traversal inspired by cone tracing, we obtain an *impact volume* at the intersection between the cone and the object. To take this into account, we should not shoot a simple ray, but again an entire cone. This *light cone*'s apex will lie on the light source itself and its radius is defined by the size of the impact volume (see Figure 3.30).

To sample the light cone, we perform a similar traversal as for the view. Only this time, the resolution is defined by the light cone instead of the pixel cone radius. During this traversal we accumulate the opacity values. Once the value saturates, the ray traversal can be stopped.

To approximate soft shadows, we compute a shadow value at the impact volume V. If V were a point, a cone instead of a simple shadow ray would need to be tested for intersection. This cone would be defined by the light source and the impact point. Consequently, a possible approximation for an impact volume V is to define a cone that contains not only the light, but also V (see Figure 3.30). Again, we accumulate the volume values. The resulting value reflects how much the light is occluded.

This very coarse approximation is extremely efficient, delivers acceptable shadows and is fully compatible with the cache mechanism presented in Section 3.6.

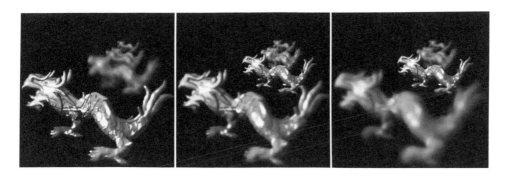

Figure 3.31. Example of depth of field rendering with GigaVoxels thanks to the volume mipmapping. Once again, the blurrier the objects, the cheaper it is to render.

3.9.2 Depth of Field

Another very important element for realistic images is the depth-of-field lens blur, present in any camera, as well as our own optical system. It results from the fact that the aperture of a real pinhole camera is actually finite. Consequently, unlike standard openGL/DirectX rendering, each image point reflects a set of rays, passing through the aperture and lens. The lens can only focus this set of rays on a single point for elements situated on the focal plane. As illustrated in Figure 3.31 this set of rays can again be grouped in some form of double cone, the *lens cone*. This lens cone defines the resolution that should be used during the traversal in order to approximate this integral over the camera lens.

Paradoxically, the more blur is introduced, the faster the rendering becomes, and the less memory is necessary to represent the scene. This is very different for triangle-based solutions, where depth of field, and even approximations, are extremely costly processes. In games, depth of field is usually performed as a

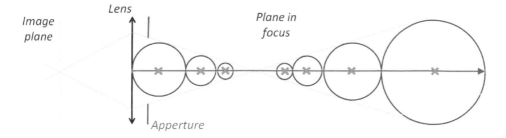

Figure 3.32. Illustration of the cone tracing used to approximate depth of field effect with a single ray.

post-process by filtering the resulting image with spatially varying kernels. One problem of such a filtering process is the lack of hidden geometry. In our volumetric representation, *hidden* geometry is integrated as much as it is necessary to produce the final image (see Figure 3.32). The algorithm does not need to be adapted to consider the different reasons for why volume information is needed. Disocclusion due to depth of field, transparency and shadows are all handled in the same manner. In fact, any kind of secondary ray is supported, showing the versatility of our framework.

3.10   Conclusion

In this chapter, we have seen how to efficiently deal with the main problem of voxel representations: huge memory consumption. The data sets we work with exceed the memory of current GPUs by large amounts. Our efficient strategies to adapt the volume resolution according to the point of view enable us to completely overcome the memory limitation by transferring data only when necessary and applying updates to the structure solely where needed.

The presented approach underlines that voxels have many interesting properties. We showed how to reduce aliasing, represent transparent materials, and allow recursive or instanced scene definitions. Furthermore, our algorithm inherently implements several acceleration methods that usually have to be addressed with particular routines and strategies: Frustum culling, visibility testing, LOD selection, temporal coherence, and refinement strategies. They are all integrated in the same framework: our per-ray queries. Consequently, the code to treat complex geometry becomes much simpler and easier to maintain, which is important for practical implementations.

Our GigaVoxels approach can, in some scenarios, be more efficient than their triangular mesh counterpart. We showed how to produce approximate shadow and depth of field effects that appear more convincing than many standard approaches applied for computer games based on image filtering techniques. Interestingly, in contrast to these triangle-based solutions, effects like depth of field or approximate soft shadows decrease the computational workload when compared to a pinhole image or hard shadows. Thus resulting in more realism for less computational power.

All these advantages hint at a more extensive future use of volumetric representations in real-time applications, such as games. Our GigaVoxel engine is an efficient solution in this context and we believe it will open up the road to many interesting special effects, of which we have currently only scratched the surface.

Bibliography

[Crassin et al. 09] Cyril Crassin, Fabrice Neyret, Sylvain Lefebvre, and Elmar Eisemann. "GigaVoxels : Ray-Guided Streaming for Efficient and Detailed Voxel Rendering." In *ACM SIGGRAPH Symposium on Interactive 3D Graphics and Games (I3D)*. ACM, 2009. Available online (http://artis.imag.fr/Publications/2009/CNLE09).

[Engel et al. 01] Klaus Engel, Martin Kraus, and Thomas Ertl. "High-Quality Pre-integrated Volume Rendering Using Hardware-Accelerated Pixel Shading." In *ACM SIGGRAPH/EUROGRAPHICS Workshop on Graphics hardware (HWWS)*, pp. 9–16, 2001.

[Hadwiger et al. 06] Markus Hadwiger, Joe M. Kniss, Christof Rezk-salama, Daniel Weiskopf, and Klaus Engel. *Real-Time Volume Graphics*, 2006.

[Horn et al. 07] Daniel Reiter Horn, Jeremy Sugerman, Mike Houston, and Pat Hanrahan. "Interactive k-d Tree GPU Raytracing." In *ACM Siggraph Symposium on Interactive 3D Graphics and Games (I3D)*, 2007.

[Kapler 03] Alan Kapler. "Avalanche! Snowy FX for XXX." *SIGGRAPH Sketch* (2003): 1.

[Krall and Harrington 05] Joshua Krall and Cody Harrington. "Modeling and Rendering of Clouds on 'Stealth.'" *SIGGRAPH Sketch* (2005).

[Kruger and Westermann 03] J. Kruger and R. Westermann. "Acceleration Techniques for GPU-based Volume Rendering." In *VIS '03: Proceedings of the 14th IEEE Visualization 2003 (VIS'03)*. Washington, DC: IEEE Computer Society, 2003.

[Lefebvre et al. 05] Sylvain Lefebvre, Samuel Hornus, and Fabrice Neyret. *GPU Gems 2: Programming Techniques for High-Performance Graphics and General-Purpose Computation*, Chapter Octree Textures on the GPU, pp. 595–613. Boston: Addison Wesley, 2005. Available online (http://www-evasion.imag.fr/Publications/2005/LHN05a).

[NVIDIA 09] NVIDIA. *CUDA Programming Guide 2.2*, 2009.

[Roettger et al. 03] Stefan Roettger, Stefan Guthe, Daniel Weiskopf, Thomas Ertl, and Wolfgang Strasser. "Smart Hardware-Accelerated Volume Rendering." In *VISSYM '03: Proceedings of the Symposium on Data Visualisation 2003*. Eurographics Association, 2003.

[Scharsach 05] Henning Scharsach. "Advanced GPU Raycasting." In *Central European Seminar on Computer Graphics*, pp. 69–76, 2005.

4

Spatial Binning on the GPU
Christopher Oat, Joshua Barczak, and Jeremy Shopf

4.1 Introduction

Many applications require that an array of unsorted point data be sorted into spatial bins prior to being processed. For example, particle system simulations using the *discrete element method* (DEM) [Bell et al. 05, Harada 07] require a nearest-neighbor search to apply particle-to-particle repulsive forces. It is important to use a spatial data structure to accelerate nearest-neighbor searches, as a brute-force search on n elements will require an expensive $O(n)$ search per element. By partitioning the particles into spatial bins, the search can be limited to nearby particles, which dramatically reduces its computational cost.

In a GPU-based simulation, constructing these data structures on the GPU is necessary to maintain high performance. If these data structures are to be built by the CPU, particle positions must be transferred out of graphics memory into system memory, and the resulting data structure must be transferred in the opposite direction. In addition to consuming precious bus bandwidth, these kinds of hybrid GPU/CPU approaches require synchronization between GPU and CPU, which reduces utilization by introducing stalls.

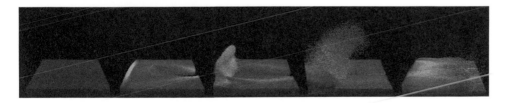

Figure 4.1. Five still frames taken from a particle system in which more than 500,000 particles are simulated entirely on the GPU. Particles are shaded to indicate their velocity. The particles react to a user-applied force that pushes them towards a collision plane.

In this work, we present a new technique for sorting point data into spatial bins using graphics hardware. Our method operates by repeatedly scattering point primitives into successive slices of a texture array. Dual-depth testing [Everitt 01] is used to ensure that all elements are binned sequentially (and, as a side effect, causes them to be binned in sorted order). Unlike previous techniques, we can use geometry shaders to eliminate previously binned elements from the working set, which provides significantly better performance scaling. Our technique can be implemented using any Direct3D 10 capable consumer hardware, without need for GPU compute APIs thus, making it applicable to a wide range of graphics chips.

We begin by describing our data structure and how we construct and query it. Then, we outline three applications of our method in particle simulation, artificial intelligence, and bucket sort. We provide a performance comparison of our approach against a popular method for sorting data into a grid on the GPU and show that our method is more efficient. Finally, we provide our conclusions.

4.2   Binning

Sorting data into bins on the GPU is challenging for a number of reasons. Many consumer grade graphics chips do not support APIs that allow generalized atomic writes, so updating a linked list or placing a data element at the end of an array is nontrivial. The construction must be made as efficient as possible because real-time, dynamic applications will have to reconstruct this data structure on every update (i.e., once every frame in a game). Querying the data structure must also be fast, since nearest-neighbor searches, one of our primary applications, will require multiple queries to gather all the binned elements near a particular point. We begin by describing the data structure itself, then describe how the data structure is queried, and finally explain how the data structure is updated.

Our binning algorithm makes use of a two-dimensional depth texture array and a single two-dimensional color buffer to construct a data structure for storing items in bins (see Figure 4.2). The color buffer is used to record the number of items in each bin (*bin load*). The depth texture array contains application-dependent key values that identify the binned items. A given two-dimensional texel address in this array serves as a bin. A single bin is a set of texels which share the same two-dimensional coordinates in successive texture array slices. Our binning algorithm guarantees that items are stored in bins, starting at the first slice of the array, in ascending order based on their key values. This fact may be useful for certain applications. For example, it can be exploited to perform a restricted form of bucket sort, as described later. Sorted bins also allow applications to employ binary search when looking for a particular item in a particular bin. For

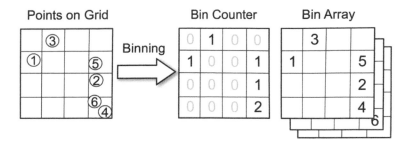

Figure 4.2. Illustration of our binning data structure. Points are mapped to texel locations on a grid. The bin counter keeps track of the number of points in each grid cell. Point IDs are stored in sorted order in successive slices of the bin array.

applications that do not need any particular ordering, simply binning the item IDs is sufficient.

4.2.1   Queries

Fetching items from a particular bin is very straightforward: the load on a particular bin is determined by reading the corresponding texel from the bin counter, and the ith element in the bin is read by fetching from slice i in the depth texture array. Applications can use bin load and dynamic flow control to ensure that only occupied slots in a particular bin are fetched.

4.2.2   Building the Data Structure

To build our bin structure, we perform a series of rendering passes in which point primitives are used to represent each item to be binned. We refer to the data that is to be placed into bins as the *working set*. As items are placed into bins, they are removed from the working set. A given bin can only receive one item per iteration, so the update process may require multiple passes before the working set is eliminated. In the limit, the algorithm requires a number of rendering passes equal to the bin capacity.

We begin by clearing the bin counters to 0 to indicate that the bins are all empty. All of the slices of the bin array are cleared to 1.0. During each pass, the vertex shader determines which bin a particular item belongs in, and computes a corresponding pixel position for the point primitive. This effectively scatters the points into their corresponding bins. The point's depth value is set by mapping the key value onto [0,1). The rendering state is set such that the GPU's depth unit will pass fragments that are *less than* the depth value stored in the depth buffer.

For each binning iteration, the corresponding slice of the bin array is used as a depth buffer. In all iterations after the first, the slice used in the previous iteration is bound as a texture for input, and the vertex shader rejects the item it is processing if its depth value is *greater than or equal to* the value stored in the previous slice. Points can be marked as "rejected" by setting their depth value to some value outside of the valid depth range (for example, a rejected vertex could have its depth value set to -1.0). The depth unit remains configured to *less than*.

Much like depth peeling, we are effectively implementing a dual-depth buffer that causes the point with the lowest value that is greater than the previously binned value to pass. Performing the *greater than or equal to* test in the vertex shader rather than the pixel shader allows us to avoid inserting clip/kill instructions into our pixel shader and allows the GPU to use its early-Z culling hardware. This dual-depth test causes the first iteration to store the lowest keyed item in each bin, the second iteration to store the second lowest, etc. To compute the bin counts, the pixel shader simply writes the iteration number into the bin count texture (1 in the first pass, 2 in the second, and so on), causing it to be updated whenever an element is binned.

Predicated iteration. For situations in which the maximum bin load is low, it is possible that all the points will have been placed in bins before the binning algorithm has finished iterating. For example, if the maximum bin load is two, then the binning algorithm can be terminated after two iterations. One way to detect that the working set has been eliminated is by using GPU queries to test whether any points pass the Z test (indicating that the working set is non-empty). Unfortunately, this kind of query would result in a CPU/GPU synchronization that would negatively impact performance.

The predicated rendering functionality provided by Direct3D 10 can be used to control the execution of the binning algorithm without introducing synchronization stalls. The draw calls for each iteration are predicated on the condition that the previous iteration resulted in items being scattered into bins. If no items are binned during a particular iteration, then we know that the working set has been eliminated and binning can safely terminate. Using cascaded predicated draw calls (each draw is predicated on the previous one) will result in the remaining draw calls being skipped. Thus the GPU takes full responsibility for terminating the algorithm.

Stream reduction. Using predicated iteration provides a performance gain by eliminating redundant rendering passes after all items have been binned. However, each pass still operates on the full data set, resulting in wasted processing for the items that have already been binned. This wasted work can be avoided by reducing the size of the point stream after each binning iteration, so the GPU only processes items that are still in the working set. This is easily implemented using geometry shaders.

To implement stream reduction, the point primitives are passed to a geometry shader that discards those points that have been flagged to indicate they failed the second-depth test, as described earlier. Points that pass the test are streamed into a buffer, which is used as input in subsequent iterations. This happens concurrently with rasterization and fixed-function depth testing. The Direct3D 10 call DrawAuto() can be used to submit the reduced working sets without querying how many items are in the working set, thus avoiding another source of CPU/GPU synchronization. Using this technique, points will be removed from the working set on the next iteration, after they have been binned. Note that no points can be removed from the working set during the first iteration, so stream output and second-depth testing should not be applied to it.

4.2.3 Handling Overflow

An overflow condition occurs when the iteration count reaches or exceeds the bin array depth before the working set is eliminated (i.e., before all items have been binned). This can occur if too many items fall into a given bin. In practice, overflow often can be prevented by using a large enough number of bins (thus dividing the data set among many bins) or by simply increasing the bin capacity to accommodate the worst-case bin load.

Testing for overflow requires an additional iteration with a query to find the number of items that remain in the working set (recall that items are not removed from the working set until after they are binned). If any points pass the Z test during this final iteration, then overflow has occurred and must be dealt with accordingly. Depending on the application, it may be possible to stop iterating once the algorithm has reached the last bin array slice, process those items that have been binned, then continue to bin the remainder by wrapping around and rendering into the first slice of the bin array. Other applications may need to allocate a larger bin structure and simply try again.

4.2.4 Item Distribution

If the items that are to be binned are not uniformly distributed into the bins, then bin space may be wasted. Nonuniform bin distribution can also increase the likelihood of overflow and reduce binning performance. In order to make the best use of the bin space and reduce the chances of overflow, it can be advantageous to anticipate the probable distribution of items into bins. If the item distribution can be anticipated or approximated, then a special hashing function can be constructed that maps items to bins uniformly. Determining a good hashing function is highly application dependent and depends entirely on the type of items you are trying to bin. In the next section we cover a few different binning applications.

4.3   Applications

Many applications require spatial binning. In this section we describe GPU implementations of three applications that benefit from spatial binning. Particle systems have been used in many games and films for many different kinds of effects. We first describe a GPU particle simulation that uses binning for accelerating particle-to-particle interaction. Next we describe a method for path planning that uses spatial binning to detect and avoid local collisions with other agents. Finally we show how to implement a restricted version of bucket sort using our binning algorithm.

4.3.1   Particle Systems

The DEM is used to simulate the behavior of particle systems both on the CPU [Bell et al. 05] as well as the GPU [Harada 07]. We use binning to construct a spatial data structure to facilitate nearest-neighbor searches when computing particle collision forces. Using a spatial hashing function $\mathbf{R}^3$ is implicitly subdivided into an infinite uniform grid, which is used to map particle positions to bin addresses. Each particle searches its bin and neighboring bins for other particles. Setting the grid cell size to be approximately the diameter of a particle allows us to limit our search to immediate neighbors while effectively limiting the maximum load on any particular bin. Particle-to-particle collisions are modeled using the spring and damping forces given by equations below [Harada 07]:

$$\mathbf{f}_{ij}^{\mathrm{spring}} = -k_s \left(d - |\mathbf{r}_{ij}| \right) \frac{\mathbf{r}_{ij}}{|\mathbf{r}_{ij}|}$$

$$\mathbf{f}_{ij}^{\mathrm{damp}} = \eta \left(v_j - \mathbf{v}_i \right).$$

Collisions occur (and forces are computed) when the distance between two particles is less than the particle diameter d.

If $\mathbf{x}_i$ and $\mathbf{x}_j$ are the positions of particles i and j with $\mathbf{v}_i$ and $\mathbf{v}_j$ denoting their velocities, then the relative position of particle j to particle i is

$$r_{ij} = x_j - x_i.$$

The force imparted on particle i when colliding with particle j is computed as follows:

$$\mathbf{f}_{ij} = \mathbf{f}_{ij}^{\mathrm{spring}} + \mathbf{f}_{ij}^{\mathrm{damp}}$$

Here, k_s is the spring coefficient and η is the damping coefficient. The total repulsive force, $\mathbf{f}_i$, on particle i due to collision from particles in its neighborhood, N (particles in i's bin and its immediate neighboring bins), is computed as

$$\mathbf{f}_i = \sum_{k \in N} \mathbf{f}_{ik}$$

Figure 4.1 shows still frames from our GPU-based particle system with more than 500,000 particles. Every frame, the particles are binned into a $128 \times 128 \times 128$ grid that is used to compute particle collisions.

4.3.2 Agent Avoidance

We also use our binning algorithm to conduct neighborhood searches for autonomous agents in a path-planning simulation (Figure 4.3). In this application, the simulation domain is of a known fixed size, so a uniform grid is appropriate. During path planning, each agent must conduct a search over the agents in its local neighborhood in order to alter its path to avoid collisions.

Each agent evaluates a number of fixed directions relative to the direction in which it wishes to move. Each direction is evaluated to determine the time to

Figure 4.3. Path finding with local avoidance is implemented on the GPU using binning. Agents move from goal to goal while avoiding local obstacles and each other.

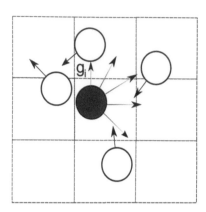

Figure 4.4. Each agent evaluates a fixed number of potential movement directions based on the positions and velocities of agents in its current and adjacent bins.

collision with nearby agents (Figure 4.4). Each direction is given a fitness function based on the angle relative to the desired direction and the time to collision. Time to collision is determined by evaluating a swept circle-circle collision test, in which the radius of each circle is equal to the radius of the bounding circle of the associated agent. The updated velocity (given by $\mathbf{v}_i$ below) is then calculated based on the direction with the highest fitness, $\mathbf{d}_i$, and the minimum time to collision in that direction:

$$\text{fitness}\,(d) = w_i t\,(\mathbf{d}) + (\mathbf{g}_i \cdot \mathbf{d}) \cdot \frac{1}{2} + \frac{1}{2},$$

$$\mathbf{d}_i = \arg\max_{\mathbf{p}_i \in V} \text{fitness}\,(\mathbf{p}_i)\,,$$

$$\mathbf{v}_i = \mathbf{d}_i \min\left(s_a, s_a t \frac{(\mathbf{d}_i)}{\nabla ft}\right),$$

w_i is a per-agent factor affecting the preference to move in the global direction or avoid nearby agents, $t\,(\mathbf{x})$ returns the minimum time-to-collision with all agents in direction $\mathbf{x}$, V is the set of discrete directions to evaluate, $\mathbf{g}_i$ is the preferred movement direction determined by a separate global path planner, s_a is the speed of agent a, ∇ft is time-delta since the last simulation frame, and $\mathbf{v}_i$ is the final velocity of agent i. This local avoidance method was previously described in [Shopf et al. 08].

4.3.3   Bucket Sort

Our binning algorithm can be used to implement a restricted version of bucket sort. Because we cannot support duplicate entries in the working set (they would fail the dual-depth test and be removed during the reduction phase), this kind of bucket sort implementation is limited to random arrays of unique values. It is also required that a loose upper and lower bound on the input values be known. If the input's distribution is known, this distribution may be used to partition the input domain such that the expected bin load is the same for all bins. If the distribution is not known, then the loose bounds are used to partition the input domain uniformly.

The binning algorithm is executed using the input data as the working set. When the binning algorithm terminates, a final gathering pass is executed to collect the results. The gather pass takes a vertex buffer containing a single point for each bin. The bins are in ascending order in the vertex buffer such that the bin associated with the lowest partition of the input domain is first in the array. In the geometry shader, the associated bin's contents are fetched and are streamed out in ascending order. Because binning ensures that the data within a bin is in ascending order, no sorting need be performed in the geometry shader. The result of the gathering pass is an output buffer containing the input data sorted in ascending order.

4.4   Results

We evaluated our binning technique using synthetic tests that bin random sets of points based on their spatial locations. For each experiment, we used a fixed bin count and averaged the time required to bin 100 randomly generated point sets of a given size. We repeated this process for many different point set sizes and a few different grid sizes. To map a three-dimensional grid onto a two-dimensional texture, a flat three-dimensional texture is used [Harris et al. 03]. These experiments were conducted on a 3 GHz CPU with 2 GB of RAM, and an ATI Radeon HD 4870 graphics card. We did not check for overflow during our experiments, but instead were careful to allocate enough bin capacity such that overflow was statistically unlikely to occur.

4.4.1   Binning Performance

We first examine the effect of our stream reduction and predication optimizations. The results are illustrated in Figure 4.5. In our experiments, we found that predication is an effective optimization, but also that stream reduction tends to be much more effective. We also found that adding predication to stream reduction does not significantly change performance. This result is to be expected since the predication merely skips draw calls which, because of stream reduction, would do no work to begin with.

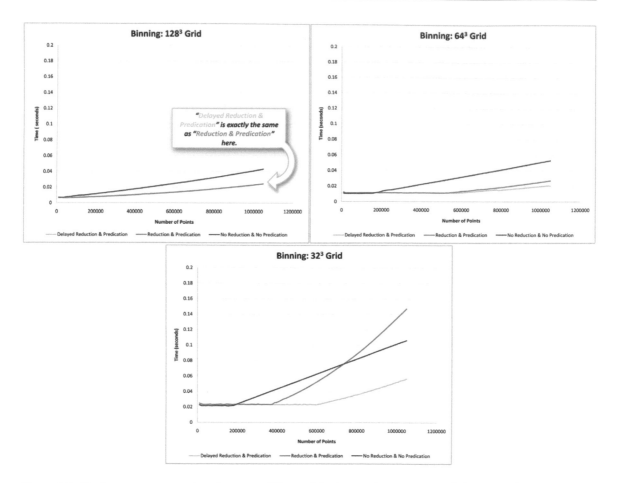

Figure 4.5. Performance comparison between different binning optimizations on different uniform grid sizes. Delayed reduction has no effect on performance for the $128 \times 128 \times 128$ grid (top) because our heuristic chooses to not delay in this case.

While we found stream reduction to be generally effective, an interesting counterexample is visible in the $32 \times 32 \times 32$ grid results in Figure 4.5. In this case, the number of bins is small, which implies that the average object count per bin (*bin load*) grows very quickly. As the bin load increases, fewer items are successfully binned during each pass, and the stream reduction gradually becomes less and less effective at eliminating work. Eventually, the extra bandwidth needs to repeatedly stream the active particles in and out of memory begins to outweigh the performance gained by removing items from the working set. In contrast, the naive binning algorithm does not need to repeatedly stream out its working set.

We found that this effect can be mitigated by simply delaying the start of stream reduction for a few iterations. With this modification, stream reduction is delayed until its eventual use will result in a large number of items being removed from the stream all at once, instead of removing them gradually and cycling the rest in and out of memory. This results in a significant performance improvement, compared to reducing on each iteration. This modification should not be applied blindly, as it may be harmful when the bin loads are low. We discuss a heuristic for choosing the number of iterations to be performed before reducing the working set in the next paragraph.

The question of whether and how to delay stream reduction must be decided on a case-by-case basis, but we can provide some general guidelines. Intuition suggests (and our results indicate) that stream reduction is most effective when the average bin load is low, and when the fraction of occupied bins (*bin spread*) is high. A high spread causes more items to be removed from the working set in each pass, and a low load ensures that the removed items represent a larger percentage of the total. In high-load, low-spread situations (many particles going into a few bins), stream reduction is at a serious disadvantage, and a delay is most likely to be helpful. Delays may also be beneficial in high-load, high-spread situations (many particles going into many bins).

In our experiments, we obtained the best results by delaying stream reduction until the number of iterations exceeds the expected bin load (which, for a uniform distribution, is equal to the particle count divided by the bin count). We use delayed stream reduction in this fashion for all subsequent experiments.

4.4.2 Comparison to Stencil Routing

We also compared our binning technique to the stencil routing implementation described in [Harada 07]. The results of these experiments are shown in Figure 4.6. In addition to the conventional stencil routing algorithm, we also tested an augmented version that uses our predicated iteration optimization to cull redundant rendering passes, as described earlier. This simple modification provides a significant performance improvement to the stencil routing algorithm, and provides more rigorous competition for our proposed technique. For these experiments, we used delayed stream reduction, as described above, using a delay count equal to the average bin load.

On the far left side of each plot, CPU performance is the bottleneck, and predicated stencil routing is extremely competitive. The stencil routing algorithm incurs significantly less driver overhead, because it does not need to switch render targets as often and does not need to ping-pong between Z-buffers and stream output targets. In the limit, however, we find that our binning technique with stream reduction soundly defeats both variants of stencil routing.

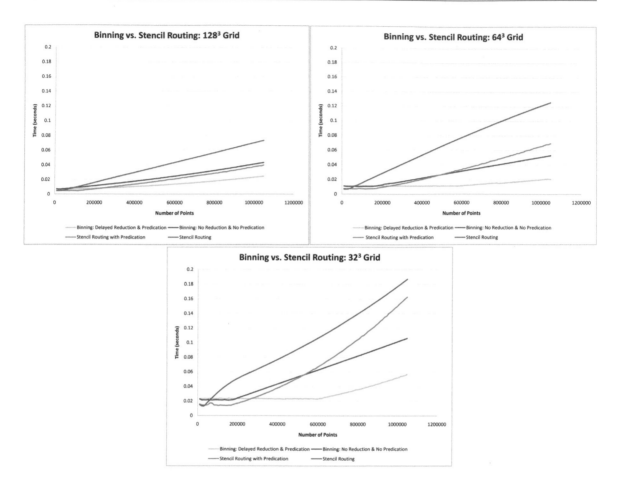

Figure 4.6. Comparison between binning and stencil routing on different uniform grid sizes.

4.5   Conclusion

We have presented a new method for sorting point data into spatial bins using graphics hardware with a standard graphics API. Our technique does not require special Compute Shaders or support for atomic operations and is more efficient than stencil routing because it reduces the working set as it iterates and stops iterating once it is done. We have shown how binning can be implemented without introducing CPU/GPU synchronization and we have outlined several applications that benefit from this technique.

4.6 Acknowledgments

The author's would like to thank the members of AMD's Game Computing Applications Group (where this work was originally produced) for their thoughtful discussion and encouragement.

Bibliography

[Amada et al. 04] T. Amada, M. Imura, Y. M. Yoshinhiro Yasimuro, and K. Chihara. "Particle-Based Fluid Simulation on GPU." *ACM Workshop on General-Purpose Computing on Graphics Processors* (2004), 154–59.

[Bell et al. 05] N. Bell, Y. Yu, and P. J. Mucha. "Particle-Based Simulation of Granular Materials." *SCA '05: Proceedings of the 2005 ACM SIGGRAPH/Eurographics Symposium on Computer Animation* (2005), 77–86.

[Everitt 01] C. Everitt. "Interactive Order-Independent Transparency." NVIDIA. White Paper, 2001.

[Harada et al. 07a] T. Harada, S. Koshizuka, and Y. Kawaguchi. "Sliced Data Structure for Particle-Based Simulations on GPUs." *GRAPHITE '07: Proceedings of the 5th International Confer- ence on Computer Graphics and Interactive Techniques in Australia and Southeast Asia* (2007), 55–62.

[Harada et al. 07b] T. Harada, S. Koshizuka, and Y. Kawaguchi. "Smoothed Particle Hydrodynamics on GPUs." *Proceedings of Computer Graphics International* (2007), 63–70.

[Harada 07] T. Harada. "Real-Time Rigid Body Simulation on GPUs." In *GPU Gems 3* edited by Hubert Nguyen, pp. 611–32. Boston: Addison-Wesley, 2008.

[Harris et al. 03] M. J. Harris, W. V. Baxter, T. Scheuermann, and A. Lastra. "Simulation of Cloud Dynamics on Graphics Hardware." *HWWS '03: Proceedings of the ACM SIGGRAPH/EUROGRAPHICS Conference on Graphics Hardware* (2003), 92–101.

[Mammen 89] A. Mammen. "Transparency and Antialiasing Algorithms Implemented with the Virtual Pixel Maps Technique." *IEEE Computer Graphics Applications* 9:4 (1989), 43–55.

[Purcell et al. 03] T. J. Purcell, C. Donner, M. Cammarano, H. W. Jensen, and P. Hanrahan. "Photon Mapping on Programmable Graphics Hardware." *Proceedings of the ACM SIGGRAPH/EUROGRAPHICS Conference on Graphics Hardware* (2003), 41–50.

[Shopf et al. 08] J. Shopf, J. Barczak, C. Oat, and N. Tatarchuk. "March of the Froblins: Simulation and Rendering Massive Crowds of Intelligent and Detailed Creatures on GPU." *SIGGRAPH '08: ACM SIGGRAPH* (2008), 52–101.

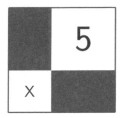

Real-Time Interaction between Particles and the Dynamic Mesh on the GPU

Vlad Alexandrov

5.1 Introduction

DirectX 10-capable hardware significantly eases the implementation of non- rasterization tasks. For instance, it is now possible and convenient to advance a particle system entirely on GPU. Sometimes it becomes desirable to see this system interact with the environment, which may include dynamic meshes. This requires the mesh geometry to be represented in a way that allows efficient access by shader programs advancing the particle system. One of the ways to achieve this representation is voxeliztion: the rendering of the mesh slices into a volume texture [K. Crane 07]. Such an approach tends to consume a significant amount of the card's fill rate, especially when high precision is required. This article describes an alternative to voxelization: spatial partitioning of the mesh triangles. The triangles are partitioned into a set of cuboid cells and can be later accessed by the shader using a simple constant time lookup procedure. The presented approach imposes no limitation on the number of triangles that be assigned to a single cell. Thus, complete coverage of a dynamic object is achieved with maximum possible precision.

5.2 Process Overview

The partitioning method will be presented in context of a water particle system, which interacts with a skeleton animated mesh.

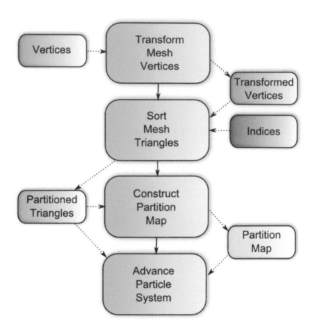

Figure 5.1. Process overview.

The process is depicted in Figure 5.1. We start with transforming the mesh's vertices using **Stream Out**. The vertices are skinned and transformed into the partitioning volume space. This helps us prevent unnecessary transformations in subsequent draw calls. Next, we partition the mesh triangles by rearranging their locations according to cell placement. This operation is similar to sorting and results in a continuous triangle buffer. The cells without triangles are not represented in the buffer; thus a map is required for efficient access. This map is built in the third step. After it is ready, the particle system gets advanced using the buffer and the map in order to account for interaction with the dynamic mesh.

5.3   Sorting the Triangles

The mesh is partitioned into cuboid cells using a set of **Stream Out** draw calls. In order to avoid the necessity of moving all the vertex data while partitioning the mesh, the process is done on index level. The indices of the mesh and the partitioning information are organized into a structure T (Figure 5.2), which conveniently fits into a **R16G16B16A16_UINT** value. To accelerate the process while maintaining a reasonable amount of draw calls, a binary partitioning scheme is used. Following are the steps that lead to partitioning of the triangles along the x-axis:

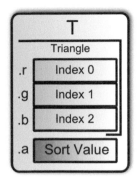

Figure 5.2. Structure T components.

1. Set a single partitioning plane perpendicular to the x-axis in the middle of the volume.

2. Invoke a draw call allowing only the triangles that are at least partially located in the negative subspace to be output. The Sort Value(.a) in the T structure receives zero to its *highest meaningful bit* (HMB). The HMB location is determined by the number of cells being partitioned into.

3. Invoke a draw call targeted into the same output buffer, this time allowing only positive subspace triangles in. The HMB of .a is set to one for these triangles.

4. Swap input/output buffers.

5. Set two partitioning planes located at 0.25*Width and 0.75*Width along the x-axis.

6. Invoke a draw call allowing only the triangles that are located in the two negative subspaces. Use the Sort Value from the previous output in order to determine which plane to test against. Shift the value in .a right, filling the HMB with zero.

7. Similar to the previous step, invoke a draw call allowing only the triangles in the two positive subspaces. Shift the value in .a right, filling the HMB with one.

8. Set four partition planes at 0.125*Width, 0.375*Width, 0.625*Width, and 0.875*Width.

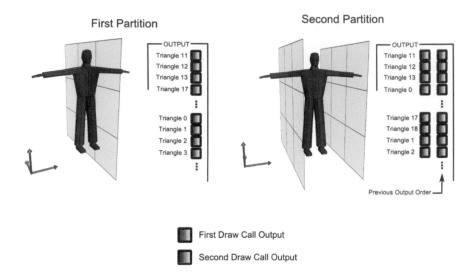

Figure 5.3. Sorting mesh triangles.

The first two partitions are depicted in Figure 5.3. After we have sorted the triangles along the x-axis, we proceed with y- and z-axes starting with one plane again, but continuing to shift the .a value of T, filling its HMB with appropriate values. Note that starting with step 6, we need to use DrawAuto for draw calls, as the triangles that happen to appear in both subspaces are duplicated. We thus lose the trace of the number of vertices in the output buffer after the first pair of draw calls. Furthermore, the actual number of triangles may increase after each iteration. This implies that the output buffers should be considerably larger than the triangle count of a mesh.

```
VSOut main_vs( VSIn i )
{
    VSOut o;

    // The first partition plane is located at X=0.
    o.orient_idx.x = asuint( i.pos.x * orient );
    o.orient_idx.y = i.vidx;

    return o;
}
```

Listing 5.1. First partitioning step.

```
[maxvertexcount(1)]
void main_gs(    triangle GSIn ia[3],
                 inout PointStream< GSOut > os )
{

    uint orient1 = ia[0].orient_idx.x;
    uint orient2 = ia[1].orient_idx.x;
    uint orient3 = ia[2].orient_idx.x;

    // At least one non-negative value means
    // the triangle is inside a proper subspace.
    if( !(orient1 & orient2  & orient3 & 0x80000000) )
    {
        GSOut o;

        uint id1 = ia[0].orient_idx.y;
        uint id2 = ia[1].orient_idx.y;
        uint id3 = ia[2].orient_idx.y;

        // Pack the output values.
        o.T.x = id1 + (id2 << 16);

        // The subspaceID constant is preshifted and
        // consists of zero bits except for the HMB.
        o.T.y = id3 + subspaceID;

        os.Append( o );
    }
}
```

Listing 5.2. Geometry shader.

Because the first partitioning step does not yet have the T structures ready, it uses a different shader set. The vertex shader tests if the vertex is located in the proper subspace (see Listing 5.1).

Even though the whole product `i.pos.x * orient` is written in the output, we are only interested in its sign bit, which is the most significant bit according to IEEE 754 standard. A geometry shader is used to sum up vertex shader results and perform the necessary geometry reduction (see Listing 5.2).

One thing to note about the shader is the number of the output components, which is two. Unfortunately, D3D10 does not allow to output 16-bit components using **Stream Out**; thus we need to pack four components into two 32-bit values.

The rest of partitioning draw calls use T structures as both input and output. This allows to move much more work into the vertex shader, as the T structure allows to access all triangle information there (see Listing 5.3).

```
VSOut main_vs( VSIn i, uniform int compIdx )
{
    // Shift is a constant containing the number of
    // completed partitioning operations.
    float plane = IndexToCoord.Load( i.T.a >> shift )
                        * dimension;

    uint3 orients;

    // Multiply by 2 to account for 2*float3
    // data per vertex(pos+normal).
    uint4 idxes_adj = i.T * 2;

    [unroll]
    for( int ii = 0; ii < 3; ii ++ )
    {
        float3 pos = VertexBuffer.Load( idxes_adj[ii] );
        orients[ii] = asuint( (pos[compIdx] - plane)
                                    * orient);
    }

    VSOut o;
    o.outside_idxes.x = orients.x & orients.y &
                        orients.z & 0x80000000;
    o.outside_idxes.yz = packIndices( uint4(idxes.xyz,
                                (T.a >> 1)
                                + instanceID ) );

    return o;
}
```

Listing 5.3. Rest of the draw call.

Geometry shader tests if `o.outside_idxes.x` is zero to determine if the triangle in .yz is to be let through.

After these steps are complete, we have a buffer with triangles sorted according to the .a component of the T structure. The component holds cuboid cell index composed of cell's integer coordinates, albeit with reversed bit order. Note that the reversed order is due to the fact that we partitioned the triangles according to larger subdivisions first. One would argue that we should have started with smaller subdivisions, thus achieving more convenient triangle order. This would simplify addressing of the buffer during the particle processing stage; however, some of the triangles may stretch through several subspaces, which requires appropriate duplicates to be made before finer grain partitioning takes place.

5.4 Building the Buffer Map

The buffer with ordered triangles we generated in the previous section is impossible to address efficiently in raw form. We need to construct a map, which will help us translate cuboid coordinates into displacement within the ordered triangle buffer. The method used to construct the map may vary according to the nature of the computing power we are willing to sacrifice. Map construction can sacrifice either fill rate or draw call count. Both methods rely on rendering into a buffer, which can be bound as a render target under D3D10. The format of the buffer should be either R16_UNORM or R32_FLOAT, depending on the blending capabilities of the device (R16_UNORM is not blendable on some DX10 GPUs). Using a buffer as a render target puts a limit on the number of cuboid cells that we may divide our mesh into. Under D3D10, this limit is guaranteed to be no less than 8192 cells. However, by adding some complexity to the algorithm, mapping to a two-dimensional texture can be implemented. On the other hand, practical considerations suggest that 4096 cells ($16 \times 16 \times 16$) are enough to partition the triangles to achieve sufficiently effective access.

Let us first describe the fill rate intensive method. We'll put the total number of T items in N and examine the T entry of the ordered buffer with the Sort Value of i.

We can construct the map by drawing N lines covering the pixels [i, N-1] (Figure 5.4). The output of the pixel shader should be set to 1.f (1.f/65535 in case of R16_UNORM), and blending mode set to ONE ONE. As result, each pixel

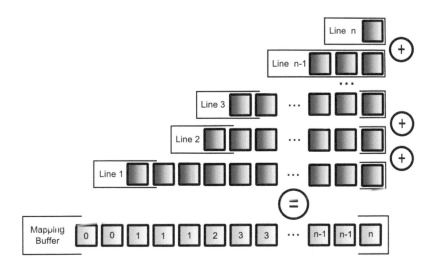

Figure 5.4. Fill rate intensive map construction.

of the buffer will contain the sum of the number of T structures in all preceding pixels, each of which represents a single cuboid cell. The expansion of each T entry (which is essentially a vertex) into a line segment can be implemented using a geometry shader.

As we can see, this method requires just one `DrawAuto call`. However, the number of pixels drawn can be estimated as $N * M/2$, where M is the number of triangles in the ordered buffer, and N is the number of subdivided cells. For instance, let us say we partition a mesh into 4096 cuboid cells while having 700 triangles in the mesh. After partitioning process had been completed, the number of triangles increased to 1024. If `R16_UNORM buffer` is used as a map, we can expect to consume as much as 4MB of fill rate.

Let us thus examine an alternative approach. In order for it to work, we need two similar buffers, which are used to implement a ping pong scheme. Here is a sequence of actions that leads towards its completion (`i` starts from one):

1. For step i of the process:

   - divide the buffer map into 2^i parts.

   - output 1.0f(or 1.f/65535) pixels for all T that fall into odd parts according to their `Sort Value` with blend mode set to `ONE ONE`. The position of the output is located at starts of the respective parts.

2. If $i < 1$, switch input/output buffer maps.

3. If $i > 1$, sum current output values and the values from the previous step i-1.

Steps 1..3 are repeated until the whole buffer is covered. Figure 5.5 depicts the first several steps of the process.

As we can see, the number of draw calls required for this method is equal to $2 * \log_2 N$, where N is the number of cuboid cells. On the other hand, the fill rate load is considerably lower:

- Each step **1** draws the number of pixels, which is approximately equal to $M/2$, where M is the number of mesh triangles.

- The sum of all steps 3 yields a number of output pixels that is equal to the sum of the geometric series: $4 + .. + 2^{n-1}, n = 1..log_2N$

This sum is equal to $4 * (2^{\log_2 N - 1} - 1) = 2 * N - 4$. Thus, total pixels drawn can be estimated as $\log_2 N * M/2 + 2 * N - 4$. Assuming we have 4096 cells and 1024 triangles in the ordered buffer, the number of pixels drawn is equal to $12 * 512 + 8188 = 14332$.

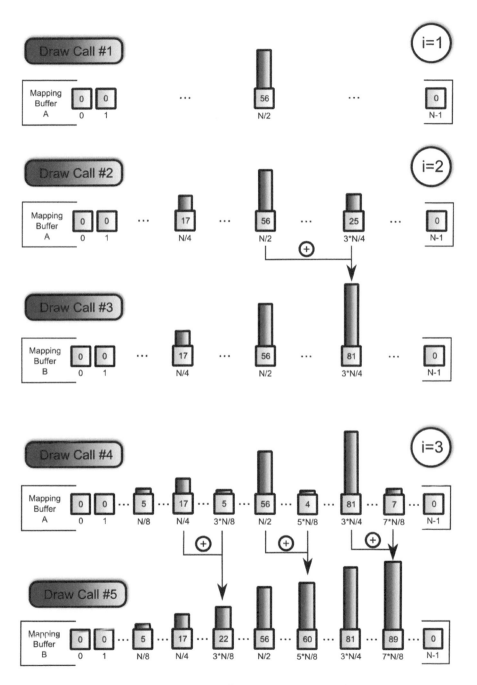

Figure 5.5. Fill rate effective map construction.

For both methods, the complexity of involved shaders is very low: the toughest shader allocates only two registers and executes in 15 instructions. Hence, the first method is fill rate limited and the second one is likely to be CPU-bound.

The buffer map also allows us to determine the number of triangles in the cell. We simply subtract the current displacement from the adjacent one. One may notice that this makes it impossible to find out the number of the triangles in the last cell. We address this issue by displacing the input/output coordinate by one to the left during the construction stage, and adding a final draw call which counts all the triangles in the last cell.

5.5   Addressing the Buffer

Let us assume we have a particle P located at Px, Py, Pz. The partitioned volume is defined by the corner Sx, Sy, Sz and dimensions W,H,D.

For P to be located inside the volume, the following expressions must be true:

$$0 <= Px - Sx <= W,$$
$$0 <= Py - Sy <= H,$$
$$0 <= Pz - Sz <= D.$$

These expressions can be reordered and vectorized for more efficient shader execution. Let us say we have a **float3** constant S defining the volume corner, and **float3** constant E defining the corner $Sx+W$, $Sy+H$, $Sz+D$. The absence of P in the partitioned volume can be determined by the following code:

```
float3 inPos = min( E - P, 0 );
float3 inNeg = min( P - S, 0 );
return asuint( dot( inPos, 1 ) + dot( inNeg, 1 ) );
```

This check may be used early in the shader in order to efficiently branch out all the particles that are not located in the volume.

Once we have determined that we are inside the volume, we need to find out which cuboid cell our particle is in. Let us say that volume dimensions are stored in **float3** constant **VolumeDims**:

```
float3 diff = P - S;
uint3 cellCoord = diff * VolumeDims;
```

We must then transform **cellCoord** into a buffer map index. This can be achieved using the following code:

```
uint buffCoord = cellCoord.z
                 + ( cellCoord.y << CellBitsTransform.x )
                 + ( cellCoord.x << CellBitsTransform.y );
```

```
uint reverseBits ( uint val )
{
    uint v1 = val & 0xff00;
    uint v2 = val << 16;
    val = v1 | v2;

    v1 = val & 0x0f0f00;
    v2 = val >> 8 & 0xf0f0;
    val = v1 | v2;

    v1 = val & 0x33330;
    v2 = val >> 4 & 0xcccc;
    val = v1 | v2;

    v1 = val & 0x15554;
    v2 = val >> 2 & 0xaaaa;
    val = (v1 | v2) >> CellBitsTransform.z
                    & CellBitsTransform.w;

    return val;
}
```

Listing 5.4. Bit reversing.

This code relies on the fact that we sorted the particles first along the x-axis, then along y, and lastly along z. The CellBitsTransform is a uint4 constant that holds width and height dimensions of the volume in terms of partitioning depth in .xy. That is, if we divided along the x-axis four times (giving us 16 cuboid cells along x), and did the same along the y-axis, we put four into the constant's .x component and eight into .y.

Next we have to reverse the bit order, as our buffer map was constructed using the .a value of structure T, which contains cuboid cell coordinates bits in reversed order. This may be done either with the help of additional reversal buffer or with bitwise operations. The following function does fast 16-bit reversal using 32-bit registers (see Listing 5.4).

The .z component of CellBitsTransform structure contains the number of excess zero bits that will be present at the start after the reversing procedure. The .w component contains the appropriate mask (reversing operations produce some junk in unused higher bits).

Now that the bits are reversed, we read two adjacent map buffer values. Remember that the coordinates are displaced by one during the map construction in order to create extra space for total triangle count in the last value:

```
// .Load(-1) returns 0
uint indexesStart = BufferMap.Load( bufferCoord - 1 );
uint indexesEnd   = BufferMap.Load( bufferCoord );
```

```
// scan through triangles, see if we intersect one
for( uint i = indexesStart; i < indexesEnd; i ++ )
{
   uint3 idxes_x2 = Indexes.Load( i ) * 2;

   float3 verts[3];
   [unroll]
   for( uint ii = 0; ii < 3; ii++ )
   {
       verts[ii] = Vertices.Load( idxes_x2[ii] )
                   + obstacleVolumePos;
   }

   float3 AB = verts[1] - verts[0];
   float3 AC = verts[2] - verts[0];

   float3 triNorm = cross( AB, AC );

   float3 vec1 = pos      - verts[0];
   float3 vec2 = nextPos  - verts[0];

   float d1 = dot( vec1, triNorm );
   float d2 = dot( vec2, triNorm );

   // IEEE 754 specifies float sign bit to be the MSB.
   // If d1 and d2 have different signs, then
   // the triangle plane was intersected.
   if( (asuint(d1) ^ asuint(d2)) & 0x80000000 )
   {
       float3 OA = verts[0] - pos;
       float3 OB = verts[1] - pos;
       float3 OC = verts[2] - pos;

       // Normals of pyramid's sides.
       float3 N1 = cross( OA, OB );
       float3 N2 = cross( OB, OC );
       float3 N3 = cross( OC, OA );

       uint3 d = asuint( float3( dot( N1, moveVec ),
                                 dot( N2, moveVec ),
                                 dot( N3, moveVec ) ) );

       // If all the sign bits indicate negative,
       // then moveVec goes through the pyramid OABC
       if( d.x & d.y & d.z & 0x80000000 )
       {
           CollisionProcedure( triNorm, pos );
       }
   }
}
```

Listing 5.5. Intersecting triangles.

We now know the displacements in the sorted buffer that mark the start and the end of the cuboid our particle is in. We can now scan through the triangles present there. In the following code, `pos` holds particle position, `nextPos` holds the position of the particle in the next frame in case its movement is unobstructed, and `moveVec` is equal to `nextPos - pos`. The intersection code does not actually look for intersection point; it merely finds out if the intersection takes place. This can be achieved by checking two conditions:

1. `pos` and `nextPos` should lie on opposite sides of the triangle plane.

2. `moveVec` should go inside the pyramid with apex `pos` and base being the current triangle.

In our simulation, the intersection point is ignored and reflection from the current position is performed (see Listing 5.5).

5.6   Performance

The demo available at http://www.akpeters.com/gpupro was tested on a NVIDIA GeForce 8800 GTX card in performance mode (see readme.txt). The particle system consisted of varying number of particles, which averaged to 65,000. Around 20,000 of them are estimated to be tested for collision every frame. An approximation mesh of 1,500 triangles was used for colliding. Partitioning depth was set to four along each axis, which results in 4096 cuboid cells. NVIDIA PerfHUD Frame Profiler tool was used to measure the GPU timings. The partitioning process took 48 draw calls to complete. The combined GPU execution time was approximately 0.8 milliseconds. Advancing the particle system took the GPU around 2.2 milliseconds to complete. The scene was rendered with 90–110 frames per second, depending on the mesh transformation state. With the particle system rendering turned off, partitioning and advancing alone gave a FPS in the range of 160–240.

5.7   Conclusion

An alternative approach for the volumetric representation of a dynamic mesh was described. The benefits of the method are low fill rate consumption and maximum coverage precision (see Figure 5.6). Furthermore, the approach maps nicely to D3D10 API, preventing the need to use multiple APIs to achieve physical interaction between dynamic mesh and particle systems computed entirely on the GPU.

Figure 5.6. Water of Life versus Alan Smithee.

Bibliography

[K. Crane 07] S. Tariq K. Crane, I. Llamas. "Real-Time Simulation and Render-
    ing of 3D Fluids." *GPU Gems 3*, pp. 633–676.

Section Editors

Wessam Bahnassi began his professional career about nine years ago when he started the development of the real-time 3D engine DirectSkeleton and its pipeline tools for In|Framez. He led the development team for several games and real-time demos based on the same engine in addition to his many contributions and publications in graphics and programming in general. Wessam has been a Microsoft Most Valuable Professional (MVP) for DirectX technologies for four years. Currently, he works at Electronics Arts Montreal doing console and PC graphics and game programming for some of EA's great titles.

Kristof Beets is Business Development Manager for POWERVR Graphics at Imagination Technologies, which includes leading the in-house demo development team and supporting ongoing business opportunities. Previously, he created the POWERVR Insider ecosystem and worked on SDKs and tools for both PC and mobile products and has published articles in ShaderX2, X5, X6, and X7. He has spoken at various industry events including SIGGRAPH, GDC, and Eurographics.

Carsten Dachsbacher is an assistant professor at the Visualization Research Center (VISUS) of the University of Stuttgart. Prior to joining VISUS he was a post-doctoral fellow at REVES/INRIA Sophia-Antipolis, France. He received a PhD from the University of Erlangen, Germany. His research includes real-time computer graphics, interactive global illumination, and GPU techniques. He has published several articles at various conferences, including SIGGRAPH and Eurographics. Carsten has been a tutorial speaker at Eurographics, the Game Developers Conference, and SIGGRAPH.

Wolfgang Engel is the CTO and co-founder of Confetti Special Effects, Inc.. Before that he worked for more than four years in Rockstar's core technology group as the lead graphics programmer. He is the editor and founder of the ShaderX and

GPU Pro books and the author of several other books; he loves to talk about graphics programming at all major conferences world-wide. He is also an MVP DirectX since July 2006 and active in several advisory boards in the industry.

Sam Martin is presently the lead programmer at Geomerics where he works on Enlighten. There he fell in love with lighting as he nurtured their real time radiosity SDK from its conception. In a previous relationship with computational geometry he developed the navigation system behind Lionhead's *Black & White 2*. There was also a fling with Lionhead's early core tech team, and he doesn't forget the good old times he had with Intrepid and Kuju London.

Christopher Oat is a senior graphics programmer at Rockstar Games, where he works on real-time graphics techniques for Rockstar's well known titles. Previously he was the demo team lead in AMD's Game Computing Applications Group, where he developed state-of-the art demos for the latest graphics platforms. Christopher has published his work in various books and journals and has presented his work at graphics and game developer conferences worldwide. Many of the projects that Christopher has worked on can be found at http://www.chrisoat.com.

Sebastien St-Laurent holds a degree in Computer Engineering from Sherbrooke University in Quebec (Canada) where he graduated at the top of his class in 1999. Since then, he has worked at many video game companies including Z-Axis, Microsoft, and Neversoft. His interest, focus, and passion has always been computer graphics. Sebastien St-Laurent is also the author of *Shaders for Game Programmers and Artists* and *The COMPLETE Effect and HLSL Guide*.

Natasha Tatarchuk is a graphics architect at Bungie where she's working on state-of-the-art next-gen game graphics algorithms. Previously she was a graphics software architect and a project lead in the game computing application group at AMD Graphics Products Group (office of the CTO), where she pushed parallel computing boundaries, investigating innovative real-time graphics techniques. Additionally, she had been the lead of ATI's demo team, creating innovative interactive renderings, and the lead for the tools group at ATI Research.

Contributors

Vlad Alexandrov is currently involved in game engine development at Skyfallen Entertainment, Russia. He spends a lot of his spare time playing around with GPU computing and different rendering techniques.

Kristof Beets is business development manager for POWERVR Graphics at Imagination Technologies, which includes leading the in-house demo development team and supporting ongoing business opportunities. Previously, he created the POWERVR Insider ecosystem and worked on SDKs and tools for both PC and mobile products and has published articles in *ShaderX2*, *X5*, *X6*, and *X7*. He has spoken at various industry events including SIGGRAPH, GDC, and Eurographics.

Andrea Bizzotto received his BA and MS degrees in computer engineering from the University of Padova, Italy. After completing college, he joined Imagination Technologies as a graduate development engineer, where he developed a range of 3D demos for Imagination's POWERVR Insider ecosystem. His research interests include 3D graphics, computer vision, image processing, algorithm theory, and software design.

Tamy Boubekeur is an associate professor in computer science at Telecom Paris-Tech (formally ENST Paris), the telecommunication graduate school of the Paris Institute of Technology (France). He is a faculty member of LTCI, the CNRS laboratory for information processing and communication. His areas of research include 3D computer graphics, geometric modeling, real-time rendering, and interaction. More info at www.telecom-paristech.fr/~boubek.

Ken Catterall graduated from the University of Toronto in 2005 as a specialist in software engineering, where he developed an interest in computer graphics.

Subsequently he has been working at Imagination Technologies as a business development engineer. Ken has been developing and supporting some of Imagination's key graphics demos, as well as publishing articles in *ShaderX6* and *ShaderX7*.

Matthäus G. Chajdas is a starting PhD student at TU München. He recently graduated from the University of Erlangen, having worked on virtual texture mapping and automatic texturing methods, the latter in cooperation with REVES/INRIA. He is mainly interested in improving the quality of real-time graphics through novel rendering algorithms and simplified content generation.

Péter Dancsik received his MS in technical informatics in 2009 from the Budapest University of Technology and Economics. During his graduate work he researched real-time ray tracing on the GPU. His interests include real-time rendering and GPU programming.

Jürgen Döllner is a professor at the Hasso-Plattner-Institut of the University of Potsdam, where he directs the computer graphics and visualization division. He has studied mathematics and computer science and received a PhD in computer science. He researches and teaches real-time computer graphics, spatial visualization, software visualization, and spatial data infrastructures.

Adrian Egli received his MSc (Diplom) degree in computer science at ETH Zurich. Since 2004 he has been working for the OpenSceneGraph community and on web-based real-time rendering software at AS Software GmbH. He is also involved in various projects at the Computer Graphics and Vision Group of University Basel. His personal homepage can be found at www.3dhelp.ch.

Thomas Engelhardt received his MS in computer science from the University of Erlangen-Nuremberg and is now a PhD student in computer graphics at VISUS (Institute for Visualization), University of Stuttgart, Germany. His research interests focus on efficient GPU techniques and rendering algorithms for interactive global illumination.

Holger Gruen is working within the European developer relations team of AMD's graphics products division. He has worked on real-time 3D technology for games and simulations for over 15 years. His job at AMD is to support game developers in getting the most out of AMD's GPUs.

Thorsten Grosch is a junior professor of computational visualistics at the University of Magdeburg, Germany. Prior to this appointment he worked as a post-doctoral fellow at MPI Informatik in Saarbruecken. Thorsten received his PhD at the University of Koblenz-Landau; his main research interest is in the area of real-time global illumination.

Benjamin Hathaway is an experienced graphics programmer who has programmed everything from the Spectrum to the mighty PS3. He began his career as a frustrated artist who was unable to draw objects that rotated and who set about writing something that could... he has never looked back since. With over 14 years of industry experience, Benjamin has worked for the likes of Bits Studios (engine/lead Xbox programmer), Criterion (RenderWare core graphics engineer), Criterion Games (post processing: *Burnout Paradise*), Electronic Arts (Core Tech), and Rockstar. He can currently be found at Black Rock Studio, specializing in low-level optimization, post-processing, and generally achieving parity between the PS3 and Xbox 360 (*Pure* and *Split/Second*).

Graham Hemingway is a PhD student (who really hopes to graduate one day soon) at Vanderbilt University in Nashville, Tennessee. His research interests include CAD model visualization, formal methods for developing safety-critical embedded systems, and large-scale heterogeneous distributed simulation.

Pedro Hermosilla is an MS student at Universitat Politècnica de Catalunya in Barcelona. He worked at McNeel during 2008 and now works with the Moving Graphics Group. He is interested in real-time rendering, non-photorealistic rendering, and illumination techniques.

Tze-Yui Ho received his BSc (Hon) and MPhil degrees in mathematics from Hong Kong University of Science and Technology in 2002 and in electronics from City University of Hong Kong in 2007. He is currently working toward a PhD at the City University of Hong Kong. His research interest is three-dimensional graphics. He has seven years of GPU programming experience.

Charles Hollemeersch received his BS and MS degrees from the Ghent University, Belgium, in 2004. From 2004 to 2006 he worked with Splash Damage, UK, where he was a graphics programmer in the computer game industry. In 2007 he returned to Belgium and joined BARCO n.v., where he worked on safety-critical avionics software. At the end of 2007 he joined the multimedia lab of the Department of Electronics and Information Systems of Ghent University-IBBT (Belgium) as a researcher. His research interests include GPU parallelization and optimization, computer graphics, and video processing.

Mengcheng Huang is currently a PhD candidate in computer graphics at the Institute of Software, Chinese Academy of Sciences. His research interests include real-time rendering, GPGPU, interactive user interface and Internet-based computer vision.

David Illes is a PhD student at the Budapest University of Technology and Economics. His research interests include distributed fluid simulation, GPU-related algorithms, and tools development for computer animated productions. He has been working as a freelancer software developer for several animation studios, including Next Limit Technologies, Axis Animation, Digic Pictures, and GYAR Post Production.

Henry Kang received the BS in computer science from Yonsei University, Korea, in 1994 and his MS and PhD degrees in computer science from the Korea Advanced Institute of Science and Technology (KAIST) in 1996 and 2002, respectively. He is currently an associate professor of computer science at the University of Missouri-St. Louis, USA. His research interests include nonphotorealistic rendering and animation, illustrative visualization, image and video processing, image-based modeling and rendering, and facial expression animation.

Hyunwoo Ki is a graphics engineer at INNOACE Co., Ltd. He is named in the Marquis *Who's Who in the World* (2010 edition). He received an MS in media engineering at Soongsil University and contributed to *ShaderX7* and *Game Programming Gems 8*. He is interested in real-time lighting and shadowing for next-generation graphics engines.

Denis Kravtsov graduated from Saint-Petersburg State Polytechnic University. He worked on the multiplatform title *TimeShift* at Saber Interactive. Denis is currently a PhD student at the National Centre for Computer Animation, Bournemouth University.

Kaori Kubota is a graphics programmer in the technical development department at KOEI in Japan. She began shader programming six years ago and has written various shaders for KOEI's games. Recently she has been involved with a shader development system.

Jan Eric Kyprianidis graduated in mathematics from the University of Hamburg, Germany, in 2005. Until 2007 he was a senior software engineer at Adobe Systems. He is currently a research scientist with the computer graphics group of the Hasso-Plattner-Institut at the University of Potsdam, Germany. His research interests include non-photorealistic rendering and digital image processing.

Ping Man Lam received his BEng and PhD degrees in electronics from the City University of Hong Kong in 2002 and 2007, respectively. His research interest is in computer graphics.

Chi Sing Leung is currently an associate professor in the Department of Electronic Engineering, City University of Hong Kong. His research interests include data mining and computer graphics. He received the 2005 IEEE Transactions on Multimedia Prize Paper award.

Hung-Chien Liao is a graduate of Full Sail University. He is very interested in graphics programming, which he considers a puzzle to a beautiful world. Currently, he is working at Tencent Boston as a senior engine programmer.

Hugh Malan works as a graphics developer for Realtime Worlds in Scotland; his past projects include *Crackdown*, the *Realworldz* demo for 3Dlabs, and *DeepUV* for Right Hemisphere.

Stephen McAuley is a graphics programmer at Bizarre Creations, where he has worked on titles such as *Project Gotham Racing 4*, *The Club*, and *Boom Boom Rocket*. He graduated with a first-class honors degree in mathematics from Queens' College, University of Cambridge, in 2005 and undertook Part III of the Mathematical Tripos before starting work in the games industry. He enjoys participating in the demo scene, which originally sparked his interest in real-time computer graphics.

Christopher Oat is a senior graphics programmer at Rockstar Games, where he works on real-time graphics techniques for Rockstar's well known titles. Previously he was the demo team lead in AMD's Game Computing Applications Group, where he developed state-of-the art demos for the latest graphics platforms. Christopher has published his work in various books and journals and has presented his work at graphics and game developer conferences worldwide. Many of the projects that Christopher has worked on can be found at http://www.chrisoat.com.

Emil Persson is developing rendering technology at Avalanche Studios and has been deeply involved in *Just Cause 2*. Formerly Emil was an ISV Engineer at ATI / AMD, where he assisted the world's top game developers with optimizations, implementing rendering techniques, and taking full advantage of the latest hardware, as well as writing technical papers and developing SDK samples. Emil is running a website at http://www.humus.name, where he blogs about graphics technology and posts demo applications.

Pawel Rohleder claims he's been interested in computer graphics and the game industry since he was born. He is very keen on figuring out how all things (algorithms) work and then trying to improve them. He started programming games professionally in 2002. Since 2006 he has been working at Techland as a 3D graphics programmer and research coordinator. He is also a PhD student in computer graphics at Wroclaw University of Technology.

Marek Rosa is the founder of Keen Software House Ltd. and game director on Miner Wars video game, where he implemented voxel engine VRAGE, which completely utilized fully deformable environment. Throughout his 12-year career he has worked as a programmer and team leader for Telco and financial institutions.

Andrew Senior graduated from Teesside University in 2007, where he received a BS in Visualization. After graduation he started working for Imagination Technologies, where he develops 3D graphical demos for Imagination's POWERVR Insider ecosystem.

Shalin Shodan joined Maxis in 2005 to work on *Spore*, armed with a fancy Masters degree in Entertainment Technology from Carnegie Mellon University. In 2009 he joined Pixar Animation Studios since he needed more time to render his frames. He still loves GPUs dearly and is very excited to be a part of the *GPU Pro* book!

Wojtek Sterna has been interested in computer graphics since 2004. He started with OpenGL, but quickly got interested in Direct3D. Since he couldn't decide which API was more convenient, he ended up using both. Currently Wojtek is working as a graphics/engine and gameplay programmer on amateur-project game *Greedy Car Thieves* (http://gct-game.net), a net remake of *Grand Theft Auto 2*, running in full 3D with eye-catching graphics. He is also an undergraduate student in computer science at Wroclaw University of Technology.

László Szécsi is an assistant professor at the Budapest University of Technology and Economics. He is lecturing on computer graphics, game development, GPU programming, and object-oriented programming. His research interests include interactive global illumination rendering and procedural geometry modeling.

Steven Tovey is a graphics coder in the Core Technologies Team at Bizarre Creations, where he is currently chained to a PS3 working on *Blur* (and another couple of unannounced titles). Prior to joining the Bizarre crew, he enjoyed stints at both Juice Games and Slitherine Software, where he worked on a bunch of different stuff, some of which glimpsed the light of day. He regrettably holds a first class honors degree in computer games technology, which basically means he's stuck doing this forever.

Pere-Pau Vázquez is an associate professor at the Universitat Politècnica de Catalunya in Barcelona. His research interests are illustrative visualization, GPU-accelerated rendering, and the applications of information theory to computer graphics.

Chris Wyman is an assistant professor in the Computer Science Department at the University of Iowa. His research interests focus on interactive global illumination techniques, specular materials, and participating media.

Xiao Yi is currently a PhD student in the Department of Electronic Engineering, City University of Hong Kong. His research focuses on computer graphics.

Fan Zhang received his PhD in computer science from the Chinese University of Hong Kong in 2007. Since then he has started his career in the gaming industry as a rendering programmer. His research mainly focuses on novel real-time rendering techniques.

Chong Zhao received his BS in Computer Science and MS in Math from JiLin University, China, and the Math Institute of Chinese Academy of Science, China, respectively. Now he is pursing his PhD in the Department of Computer Science in the Chinese University of Hong Kong, Hong Kong. His research interests include computer graphics, computer aided geometry modeling, multiresolution analysis theory, and application.

T - #1003 - 101024 - C740 - 235/191/40 - PB - 9781568814728 - Gloss Lamination